Database Processing

Fundamentals, Design, and Implementation

David M. Kroenke
University of Washington

PEARSON

Prentice
Hall

Upper Saddle River, New Jersey 07458

Library of Congress Cataloging-in-Publication Data
Kroenke, David.
    Database processing: fundamentals, design, and implementation / David M.
Kroenke.—10th ed.
        p. cm.
    Includes bibliographical references and index.
    ISBN 0-13-167267-3 (alk. paper)
        1. Database management. I. Title.

QA76.9.D3K7365 2005
005.7'4—dc22   2004061616

VP/Editorial Director: Jeff Shelstad
AVP/Executive Editor: Bob Horan
Project Manager: Lori Cerreto
Senior Media Project Manager: Nancy Welcher
AVP/Executive Marketing Manager: Debbie Clare
Marketing Assistant: Joanna Sabella
Managing Editor: John Roberts
Production Editor: Suzanne Grappi
Permissions Supervisor: Charles Morris
Manufacturing Buyer: Diane Peirano
Design Director: Maria Lange
Art Director: Pat Smythe
Interior Designer: Karen Quigley
Cover Designer: Karen Quigley
Line Art: BookMasters, Inc.
Manager, Print Production: Christy Mahon
Composition: Integra Software Services
Full-Service Project Management: Jennifer Welsch/BookMasters, Inc.
Printer/Binder: Courier/Kendalville
Typeface: 10/12 Simoncini Garamond

Credits and acknowledgments borrowed from other sources and reproduced, with
permission, in this textbook appear on appropriate page within text.

Microsoft® and Windows® are registered trademarks of the Microsoft Corporation in
the U.S.A. and other countries. Screen shots and icons reprinted with permission from the
Microsoft Corporation. This book is not sponsored or endorsed by or affiliated with the
Microsoft Corporation.

Pearson Education LTD.   Pearson Education Australia PTY, Limited
Pearson Education Singapore, Pte. Ltd   Pearson Education North Asia Ltd
Pearson Education, Canada, Ltd   Pearson Educación de Mexico, S.A. de C.V.
Pearson Education–Japan   Pearson Education Malaysia, Pte. Ltd

10 9 8 7 6 5 4 3 2
ISBN 0-13-167267-3

BRIEF CONTENTS

CONTENTS

Part 5: Database Access Standards 409

Part 6: Conclusion 531

While preparing the tenth edition of this text, I decided to make major changes to the text's organization and content. The basic structure of the first nine editions was designed for a teaching environment that no longer exists. Unlike the early years of database processing, today students have ready access to data modeling and DBMS products. Furthermore, today's students are too impatient to start a class with lengthy conceptual discussions on data modeling and database design. They want to do something, see a result, and obtain feedback. Also, in the current economy, students need to reassure themselves that they are learning marketable skills.

SQL

Given these changes in the classroom environment, the first change I made was to move SQL forward, all the way up to Chapter 2. Actually, I moved just the presentation of SQL SELECT statements to Chapter 2, leaving the discussion of SQL DDL and other DML statements for Chapters 7 and 8.

By presenting SQL SELECT statements in Chapter 2, students learn early in the class how to query data and obtain results, seeing firsthand some of the ways that database technology will be useful to them.

The text assumes that students will work through the SQL statements and examples with a DBMS product. This is practical today, because every student has access to Microsoft Access. The text can be purchased with versions of SQL Server and Oracle as well. Alternatively, MySQL is available to students as a free download. Thus, students can actively use a DBMS product by the end of the first week of class.

> **B T W**
>
> The presentation and discussion of SQL is spread over three chapters so that students can learn about this important topic in small bites. SQL SELECT statements are taught in Chapter 2. SQL DDL and SQL DML statements are presented in Chapter 7. Correlated subqueries and EXISTS/NOT EXISTS statements are described in Chapter 8. Each topic appears in the context of accomplishing practical tasks. Correlated subqueries, for example, are used to verify functional dependency assumptions, a necessary task for database redesign.
>
> This box illustrates another new feature of this edition: BTW boxes are used to separate comments from the text discussion. Sometimes they present ancillary material; other times they reinforce important concepts.

A Spiral Approach to Database Design

Today, databases arise from three sources: (1) from the integration of existing data from spreadsheets, data files, and database extracts; (2) from the development of new information systems projects, and (3) from the need to redesign an existing database to adapt to changing requirements. As I thought about these three sources, I realized that they present instructors with a significant pedagogical opportunity. Rather than teach database design just once from data models, why not teach database design three times, once for each of these sources? This idea turned out to be even more successful than I expected.

Design Iteration 1: Databases from Existing Data

Considering the design of databases from existing data, I asked myself, if someone were to email me a set of tables and say, "Create a database from them," how would I proceed? I would examine the tables in light of normalization criteria and then determine whether the new database was for query only or whether it was for query and update. Depending on the answer, I would denormalize the data, joining them together, or I would normalize the data, pulling them apart. All of which is important for students to know and understand.

Therefore, the first iteration of database design gives instructors a rich opportunity to teach normalization, not as a set of theoretical concepts, but rather as a useful toolkit for making design decisions for databases created from existing data. Additionally, as I've learned from recent data mining consulting experiences, the construction of databases from existing data is an increasingly common task that is often assigned to junior staff members. Learning how to apply normalization to the design of databases from existing data not only provides an interesting way of teaching normalization, it is also common and useful!

Furthermore, large organizations are increasingly licensing standardized software from vendors such as SAP, Oracle, and Siebel. Such software already has a database design. But with every organization running the same software, many are learning that they can only gain a competitive advantage if they make better use of the data in those predesigned databases. Hence, students who know how to extract data and create read-only databases for reporting and data mining have obtained marketable skills in the world of ERP and other packaged software solutions.

Design Iteration 2: Data Modeling and Database Design

The second source of databases is from new systems development. Although not as common as in the past, many databases are still created from scratch. Thus, students still need to learn data modeling, and they still need to learn how to transform data models into database designs.

Semantic Object Modeling Moved to Appendix

I lost the battle for the semantic object model (SOM). The entity-relationship (E-R) model had too much market momentum for SOM to overcome it. Also, a new data modeling technique requires the support of a major player like Microsoft or Oracle, and we were never able to obtain that support. And, I have to admit the possibility that SOM was not significantly better than the E-R model. Hard for me to believe, but maybe so. In any case, SOM is presented in Appendix E, but the E-R data model is used everywhere else in the text. With that decision, the next was which version of E-R to use.

IDEF1X Has Been Replaced by the Crow's Foot Model

The ninth edition of this text used IDEF1X extensively, but since then, I've concluded that IDEF1X is not worth the trouble it causes. The essence of E-R modeling is more easily taught using the crow's foot version of the E-R model, and I have used it throughout.

IDEF1X is explained, however, in Appendix B in case your students will graduate into an environment where it is used. At one point, I thought IDEF1X might be worth teaching because it is a national standard, but Jack Becker at the University of North Texas put the nail in the coffin when he said, "So was Ada."

This text teaches and uses the simple, plain vanilla, crow's foot version of the E-R model.

B T W

In my opinion, the best E-R data modeling tool for teaching is ERwin from Computer Associates. A free version of ERwin with a 60-day license can be obtained from *www.ca.com*. Search for the "All Fusion ERwin download."

I prefer ERwin over Visio for two reasons. One, Visio is a general-purpose graphics program that has a data modeling template. Accordingly, most of the error messages and help text is generalized, confusing, and unhelpful. ERwin is built specifically for data modeling. Unlike Visio, you cannot use it to design your kitchen or garden, but you can build comprehensive data models with it.

Second, Visio is more of a table modeling than a data modeling tool. In particular, it is not possible to represent an N:M strong entity relationship in Visio. Instead, the intersection table must be constructed and modeled. This confounds data modeling with database design in just the way that I am attempting to teach my students to avoid.

This does not mean that you must use ERwin to use this book. You can use Visio or any other E-R data modeling product. But, if you're looking for a tool to use, I recommend ERwin.

I have no association, in any way, with Computer Associates. I do not own their stock, I do not consult for their engineers, I do not teach their seminars. I just like their product.

Database Design from E-R Data Models

As discussed in Chapter 6, designing a database from data models consists of three tasks: representing entities and attributes with tables and columns; representing maximum cardinality by creating and placing foreign keys; and representing minimum cardinality via constraints, triggers, and application logic.

The first two tasks are straightforward. However, designs for minimum cardinality are more difficult. Required parents are easily enforced using NOT NULL foreign keys and referential integrity constraints. Required children are more problematic. I have simplified the discussion of this topic from the ninth edition, however, by limiting the use of referential integrity actions and by supplementing those actions with design documentation. See the discussion around Figure 6-27.

Although the design for required children is complicated, it is important for students to learn. It also provides a reason for students to learn about triggers as well. In any case, the discussion of these topics is much simpler than it was in prior editions because of the use of the crow's foot model and the use of ancillary design documentation.

Design Iteration 3: Database Redesign

Database redesign is both common and difficult. As stated in Chapter 8, information systems cause organizational change. New information systems give users new behaviors, and as users behave in new ways, they require changes in their information systems.

Database redesign, the third iteration of database design, is by nature complex. Depending on your students, you may wish to skip it, and you can do so without loss of continuity.

Database redesign is presented after the discussion of SQL DDL and DML in Chapter 7 because it requires the use of advanced SQL. It also provides a practical reason to teach correlated subqueries and EXISTS/NOT EXISTS statements.

 ## Business Intelligence: Reporting and Data Mining

Another new feature of this text is a new chapter (Chapter 15) on business intelligence (BI) systems. The chapter includes a discussion on data management for data warehouses and data marts. It also describes reporting and data mining applications, including OLAP.

Chapter 15 presents two applications that should be particularly interesting to students. The first is RFM analysis, a reporting application frequently used by mail order and e-commerce companies. The complete RFM analysis is accomplished in Chapter 15 through the use of standard SQL-92 statements. Additionally, this chapter includes a market-basket analysis that is also performed using SQL correlated subqueries. This chapter can be assigned at any point after Chapter 8 and could be used as a motivator to illustrate the practical applications of SQL midcourse.

 ## Active Use of a DBMS Product

As stated earlier, this edition assumes that the students will actively use a DBMS product. The question is, which one? Realistically, most of us have four alternatives to consider: Microsoft Access, Oracle, Microsoft SQL Server, or MySQL. You can use any of those products with this text, and tutorials for each of them are presented in Appendix A and Chapters 10, 11, and 14, respectively.

Given the limitations of class time, I have found it necessary to pick and use just one of these products. I usually devote a portion of a lecture to discussing the characteristics of each, but I have found it best to limit student work to one of them.

Using Access

The primary advantage of Access is accessibility. Most students already have a copy, and if not, copies are easily obtained. Many students will have used Access in their introductory or other classes. Appendix A is a tutorial on Access for students who have not used it but who wish to use it with this book.

However, Access has several disadvantages. First, as explained in Chapter 1, Access is a combination application generator and DBMS. Access confuses students because it confounds database processing with application development. Also, Access hides SQL behind its query processor and makes SQL appear as an afterthought rather than a foundation. Furthermore, as discussed in Chapter 2, Access does not correctly process some of the basic, SQL-92 standard statements. Finally, Access does not support triggers. You can simulate triggers by trapping Windows events, but that technique is nonstandard and it miscommunicates the nature of trigger processing.

Using Oracle, SQL Server, or MySQL

Which of these products to use depends on your local situation. Oracle, a superb enterprise-class DBMS product, is difficult to install. However, if you have local staff to support your students, it can be an excellent choice. Oracle's SQL*Plus is a handy tool for learning SQL, triggers, and stored procedures, as shown in Chapter 10. In my experience, students require considerable support to install Oracle on their own computers, and you may be better off to use Oracle from a central server.

SQL Server, although probably not as robust as Oracle, is easy to install on Windows machines, and it provides the capabilities of an enterprise-class DBMS product. It can be driven from Visual Studio .NET, but I use the Enterprise Manager and Query Analyzer. SQL Server can be used to learn SQL, triggers, and stored procedures, as shown in Chapter 11.

By the time you read this, Microsoft may have released SQL Server 2005, and it promises to have many new and important features. It also appears to be far more complicated than the current version of SQL Server, so be prepared to make adjustments. T-SQL is still supported and the knowledge students learn with SQL Server 2000 will be applicable to the 2005 version.

MySQL is an open-source DBMS product that is receiving increased attention and market share. The capabilities of MySQL are continually being upgraded, and you can now write stored procedures. However, MySQL does not support triggers, which I view as a significant limitation. Still, it's an excellent product and fun to use. See Chapter 14 for its use with Java Server Pages.

B T W

If the DBMS you use is not driven by local circumstances and you do have a choice, I recommend using SQL Server. It has all of the features of an enterprise-class DBMS product, and it is easy to install and use. You can order this text with a shrink-wrapped version of SQL Server and a 90-day license. You also can order the text with a shrink-wrapped version of Oracle.

Overview of the Chapters in the Tenth Edition

Chapter 1 sets the stage by introducing database processing, describing basic components of database systems, and summarizing the history of database processing. Chapter 2 presents SQL SELECT statements. It also includes sections on how to submit SQL statements to Access, Oracle, and SQL Server. If the students are using Access for the first time, they will also need to study Appendix A at this point.

The next four chapters, Chapters 3 through 6, present the first two iterations of database design. Chapter 3 presents the principles of normalization using Boyce-Codd normal form. It describes the problems of multivalued dependencies and explains how to eliminate them. This foundation in normalization is applied in Chapter 4 to the design of databases from existing data.

Chapters 5 and 6 describe the design of new databases. Chapter 5 presents the E-R data model. Traditional E-R symbols are explained, but the majority of the chapter uses the crow's foot notation. Chapter 5 provides a taxonomy of entity types, including strong, ID-dependent, weak but not ID-dependent, subtype, and recursive. The chapter concludes with a simple modeling example for a university database.

Chapter 6 describes the transformation of data models into database designs by converting entities and attributes to tables and columns, by representing maximum cardinality by creating and placing foreign keys, and by representing minimum cardinality via DBMS constraints, triggers, and application code. The primary section of this chapter parallels the entity taxonomy in Chapter 5.

Chapter 7 presents SQL DDL and DML. SQL DDL is used to implement the design of an example introduced in Chapter 6. INSERT, UPDATE, and DELETE statements are discussed, as are SQL views. Additionally, the principles of embedding SQL in program code are presented, and triggers and stored procedures are explained.

Database redesign, the third iteration of database design, is described in Chapter 8. This chapter presents SQL correlated subqueries and EXISTS/NOT EXISTS statements and uses those statements in the redesign process. Reverse engineering is described, and basic redesign patterns are illustrated and discussed.

Chapters 9, 10, and 11 consider the management of multiuser organizational databases. Chapter 9 describes database administration tasks, including concurrency, security, and backup and recovery. Chapters 10 and 11 then describe Oracle and SQL Server, respectively. These chapters show how to use these products to create database structures and process SQL statements. They also explain concurrency, security, and backup and recovery with each product. The discussion in Chapters 10 and 11 parallels the order of discussion in Chapter 9.

Chapters 12, 13, and 14 address standards for accessing databases. Chapter 12 presents ODBC, OLE DB, ADO, and ASP. It illustrates the use of these technologies for the publication of both SQL Server and Oracle databases via Active Server Pages. Chapter 13 describes the integration of XML and database technology. The chapter begins with a primer on XML and then shows how to use the FOR XML SQL statement in SQL Server. The chapter concludes with a Visual Basic .NET application that uses ADO.NET to create a dataset from the tables in an Oracle database.

Chapter 14 presents data access standards for the open source/Java world. It describes JDBC and discusses and illustrates Java Server Pages. It concludes with a survey of MySQL.

Chapter 15 concludes the text with a discussion of business intelligence systems, data warehouses, and data marts. It illustrates the use of SQL for RFM reporting analysis and for market-basket analysis.

 # Supplements: *www.prenhall.com/kroenke*

This text is accompanied by a wide variety of supplements. Please visit the text's Web site at ***www.prenhall.com/kroenke*** to access the instructor and student supplements described below. The Instructor Resources are also available on CD-ROM. Please see your Prentice Hall representative for more details. All supplements were written by David Auer of Western Washington University.

For Students

- An *Interactive Study Guide* with multiple-choice, true/false, and essay questions. Students receive automatic feedback to their answers. Responses to the essay questions and results from the multiple-choice and true/false questions can be emailed to the instructor after a student finishes a quiz.
- *PowerPoint Presentation Slides* highlight key terms and concepts.
- All of the *Sample Databases* used in this text are available in Access, SQL Server, and Oracle format.
- *Glossary*

For Instructors

- The *Instructor's Resource Manual* provides sample course syllabi, teaching suggestions, and answers to end-of-chapter review, project, and case questions.
- The *Test Item File* and *TestGen* include an extensive set of test questions in multiple-choice, true/false, fill-in-the-blank, short-answer, and essay format. The difficulty level and where the topic is covered in the text are noted for each question. The Test Item File is available in Microsoft Word and in TestGen. TestGen is a comprehensive suite of tools for testing and assessment. It enables instructors to easily create and distribute tests for their courses, either by printing and distributing them

through traditional methods or by online delivery via a LAN. TestGen features Screen Wizards to assist you as you move through the program, and the software is backed with full technical support.

■ *PowerPoint Presentation Slides* feature lecture notes that highlight key terms and concepts. Instructors can customize the presentation by adding their own slides or editing the existing ones.

■ The *Image Library* is a collection of the text art organized by chapter. This includes all figures, tables, and screenshots (as permission allows) to enhance class lectures and PowerPoint presentations.

Materials for Your Online Course

Prentice Hall supports our adopters using online courses by providing files ready for upload into both WebCT and BlackBoard course management systems for our testing, quizzing, and other supplements. Please contact your local PH representative or ***mis_service@prenhall.com*** for further information on your particular course.

Acknowledgments

I am grateful for the support of many people in the development of this tenth edition. David Auer at Western Washington University has provided invaluable assistance, not only in creating the Instructor's Manual, Test Item File, and PowerPoint slides, but also by helping me shape the organization of this edition and by providing a detailed and insightful review of the manuscript. I would also like to thank Rick Mathieu at James Madison University for interesting and insightful discussions on the database course.

Professor Doug MacLachlan from the Marketing Department at the University of Washington was most helpful to me in understanding the goals, objectives, and technology of data mining, particularly as it pertains to marketing. I would also like to thank Chris Wilkins for his help in testing my Java code. Don Nilson of the Microsoft Corporation helped me understand the importance of XML to database processing.

In addition, I wish to thank the reviewers of this edition:

Richard Chrisman, *Northeast Community College*
Richard Clemens, *West Virginia Wesleyan College*
Thomas A. Easton, *Thomas College*
Robert Hofkin, *Goldey-Beacom College*
Douglas M. Kline, *University of North Carolina at Wilmington*
James Marlatt, *University of Colorado at Boulder*
Michael L. Monroe, *Virginia Western Community College*
Tina Ostrander, *Highline Community College*
Daria Santerre, *Norwalk Community College*
Jack Warner, *University of Oklahoma*
Daniel Zhu, *Iowa State University*

Finally, I wish to thank my editor, Bob Horan, for his advice and assistance through three editions, so far(!), of this text. I also thank Lori Cerreto for keeping this project on track. Most importantly, I wish to thank my wife Lynda for her love and support through so many of these writing projects!

David Kroenke
Seattle, Washington

David M. Kroenke

Work Experience

David M. Kroenke has more than 35 years experience in the computer industry. He began as a computer programmer for the U.S. Air Force, working both in Los Angeles and at the Pentagon, where he developed one of the world's first DBMS products while part of a team that created a computer simulation of World War III. That simulation served a key role for strategic weapons studies during a 10-year period of the Cold War.

From 1973 to 1978, Kroenke taught in the College of Business at Colorado State University. In 1977, he published the first edition of *Database Processing,* a text that is currently published in its tenth edition. In 1978, he left Colorado State and joined Boeing Computer Services, where he managed the team that designed database management components of the IPAD project. After that, he joined with Steve Mitchell to form Mitchell Publishing and worked as an editor and author, developing texts, videos, and other educational products and seminars. Mitchell Publishing was acquired by Random House in 1986. During these years he also worked as an independent consultant, primarily as a database disaster repairman helping companies recover from failed database projects.

In 1982, Kroenke was one of the founding directors of the Microrim Corporation. From 1984 to 1987, he served as the Vice President of Product Marketing and Development and managed the team that created and marketed the DBMS product R:base 5000 as well as other related products.

For the next five years, Kroenke worked independently while he developed a new data modeling language called the *semantic object model.* He licensed this technology to the Wall Data Corporation in 1992 and then served as the Chief Technologist for Wall Data's SALSA line of products. He was awarded three software patents on this technology.

Since 1998, Kroenke has continued consulting and writing. His current interests concern the practical applications of data mining techniques

on large organizational databases. An avid sailor, he wrote *Know Your Boat: The Guide to Everything That Makes Your Boat Work,* which was published by McGraw-Hill in 2002.

Consulting

Kroenke has consulted with numerous organizations during his career. In 1978, he worked for Fred Brooks, consulting with IBM on a project that became the DBMS product DB2. In 1989, he consulted for the Microsoft Corporation on a project that became Microsoft Access. In the 1990s, he worked with Computer Sciences Corporation and with General Research Corporation for the development of technology and products that were used to model all of the U.S. Army's logistical data as part of the CALS project. Additionally, he has consulted for Boeing Computer Services, the United States Air Force Academy, Logicon Corporation, and other smaller organizations.

Publications

- *Database Processing,* Prentice Hall, ten editions, 1977–present
- *Database Concepts,* Prentice Hall, two editions, 2004
- *Know Your Boat: The Guide to Everything that Makes Your Boat Work,* McGraw-Hill, 2002
- *Management Information Systems,* Mitchell Publishing/Random House, three editions, 1987–1992
- *Business Computer Systems,* Mitchell Publishing/Random House, five editions, 1981–1990
- *Managing Information for Microcomputers,* co-author with Donald Nilson, Microrim Corporation, 1984
- *Database Processing for Microcomputers,* co-author with Donald Nilson, Science Research Associates, 1985
- *Database: A Professional's Primer,* Science Research Associates, 1978

Teaching

Kroenke taught in the College of Business at Colorado State University from 1973 to 1978. He also has taught part-time in the Software Engineering program at Seattle University. From 1990 to 1991, he served as the Hanson Professor of Management Science at the University of Washington. He currently teaches at the University of Washington. During his career, he has been a frequent speaker at conferences and seminars for computer educators. In 1991, the International Association of Information Systems named him Computer Educator of the Year.

Education

B.S., Economics, United States Air Force Academy, 1968
M.S., Quantitative Business Analysis, University of Southern California, 1971
PhD, Engineering, Colorado State University, 1977

Personal

Kroenke is married, lives in Seattle, and has two grown children and two grandchildren. He enjoys skiing, sailing, and building small boats. His wife tells him he enjoys gardening as well.

Getting Started

The two chapters in Part 1 provide an introduction to database processing. In Chapter 1, we consider the characteristics of databases and describe important database applications. Chapter 1 also describes the various database components and provides a survey of the knowledge you need to learn from this text. The chapter also summarizes the history of database processing.

You will start working with a database in Chapter 2 and use that database to learn how to use SQL, a database-processing language, to query database data. You will learn how to query both single and multiple tables, and you will use SQL to investigate a practical example—looking for patterns in stock market data. Together, these two chapters will give you a sense of what databases are and how they are processed.

Introduction

This chapter introduces database processing. We will first consider the nature and characteristics of databases and then survey a number of important and interesting database applications. Next, we will describe the components of a database system and then, in general terms, describe how databases are designed. After that, we will survey the knowledge that you need to work with databases as an application developer or as a database administrator. Finally, we conclude this introduction with a brief history of database processing.

This chapter assumes a minimal knowledge of database use. It assumes that you have used a product such as Microsoft Access to enter data into a form, to produce a report, and possibly to execute a query. If you have not done these things, you should obtain a copy of Access and work through the tutorial in Appendix A.

The Characteristics of Databases

The purpose of a database is to help people keep track of things. It does this by storing data in tables, where each table has rows and columns like those in a spreadsheet. A database usually has multiple tables, and each table contains data about a different type of thing. For example, Figure 1-1 shows a database with three tables: the STUDENT table has data about students, the GRADE table has data about grades, and the CLASS table has data about classes.

Each row of a table has data about a particular instance. For example, each row of the STUDENT table has data about one of four students: Cooke, Lau, Harris, and Greene. Similarly, each row of the CLASS table has data about a particular class. The columns of the table store characteristics about each of these instances. The first column of STUDENT stores StudentNumber, the second column stores StudentName, and so forth.

Although, in theory, you could switch the rows and columns by putting instances in the columns and characteristics in the rows, this is never done. Every database in this text, and 99.999999 percent of all databases throughout the world, store instances in rows and characteristics in columns, just as shown in Figure 1-1.

A Note on Conventions

In this text, table names appear in capital letters. This convention will help you to distinguish table names in explanations. However, you are not required to set table names in capital letters. Access and similar programs will allow you to write a table name as STUDENT, student, Student, stuDent, or in some other way.

Additionally, in this text column names begin with a capital letter. Again, this is just a convention. You could write the column name Term as term, teRm, TERM, or in any other way. To ease readability, we will sometimes create compound column names in which the first letter of each element of the compound word is capitalized. Thus, in Figure 1-1, the STUDENT table has columns StudentNumber, StudentName, and EmailAddress. Again, this capitalization is just a convenient convention. However, following these or other consistent conventions will make interpretation of database structures easier. For example, you will always know that STUDENT is the name of a table and that Student is the name of a column of a table.

A Database Has Data and Relationships

The database in Figure 1-1 shows data not only about students, classes, and grades, it also shows relationships among the rows in those tables. For example, StudentNumber

The Key Database Characteristic: Related Tables

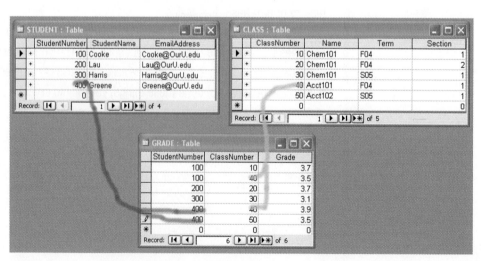

Figure 1-2

Need for Relationships

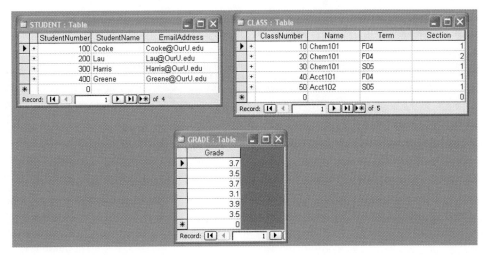

400, who is Greene, earned a Grade of 3.9 in ClassNumber 40, which is Acct101. He also earned a Grade of 3.5 in ClassNumber 50, which is Acct102.

Figure 1-1 illustrates an important characteristic of database processing: Databases store not only rows of data, but also relationships among the rows of data. To see why this is important, examine Figure 1-2. In this figure, the database contains all of the basic data, but the relationship data are missing. In this format, the GRADE data are useless. It is like the joke about the sports commentator who announced: "Now for tonight's baseball scores: 2–3, 7–2, 1–0, and 4–5." The scores are useless without knowing the teams that earned them. Thus, a database contains both data and the relationships among the data.

Databases Create Information

In your previous classes, you learned the difference between data and information. Data are recorded facts or figures. Information is knowledge derived from data. Or, using another common definition, information is data presented in a meaningful context.

Databases record facts and figures; they record data. They do so, however, in a way that enables them to produce information. The data in Figure 1-1 can be manipulated to produce a student's GPA, the average GPA for a class, the average number of students in a class, and so forth. In Chapter 2, you will be introduced to a language called Structured Query Language, or SQL, that you can use to produce information from database data.

To summarize, databases store data in tables, and they represent the relationships among the rows of those tables. They do so in a way that facilitates the production of information.

Database Examples

Today, database technology is part of almost every information system. This fact is not surprising when we consider that every information system needs to store data and the relationships among those data. Still, the vast array of applications that use this technology is staggering.

Single-User Database Applications

Consider, for example, the applications listed in Figure 1-3. The first application is used by a single salesperson to keep track of the customers she has called and the

Figure 1-3		**Example Database Uses**		

Application	Example Users	Number of Users	Typical Size	Remarks
Sales contact manager	Salesperson	1	2,000 rows	Products such as **GoldMine** and Act! are database centric.
Patient appointment (doctor, dentist)	Medical office	15 to 50	100,000 rows	Vertical market software vendors incorporate databases into their software products.
Customer Resource Management (CRM)	Sales, marketing, or customer service departments	500	10 million rows	Major vendors such as Siebel and PeopleSoft build applications around the database.
Enterprise Resource Processing (ERP)	An entire organization	5,000	10 million+ rows	SAP uses a database as a central repository for ERP data.
E-commerce site	Internet users	Possibly millions	1 billion+ rows	Drugstore.com has a database that grows at the rate of 20 million rows per day!
Digital dashboard	Senior managers	500	100,000 rows	Extractions, summaries, and consolidations of operational databases.
Data mining	Business analysts	25	100,000 to millions+	Data are extracted, reformatted, cleaned, and filtered for use by statistical data mining tools.

contacts that she's had with them. Most salespeople do not build their own contact manager applications; instead, they license products such as GoldMine (see ***www.frontrange.com/goldmine***) or ACT! (see ***www.act.com***).

Multiuser Database Applications

The next applications in Figure 1-3 are those that involve more than one user. The patient-scheduling application, for example, may have 15 to 50 users. These users will be appointment clerks, office administrators, nurses, dentists, doctors, and so forth. A database like this one may have as many as 100,000 rows of data in perhaps 5 or 10 different tables.

When more than one user employs a database application, there is always the chance that one user's work may interfere with another's. Two appointment clerks, for example, might assign the same appointment to two different patients. Special concurrency-control mechanisms are used to coordinate activity against the database to prevent such conflict. You will learn about these mechanisms in Chapter 9.

The third row of Figure 1-3 shows an even larger database application. Customer Resource Management (CRM) is an information system that manages customer contacts from initial solicitation through acceptance, purchase, continuing purchase, support, and so forth. CRM systems are used by salespeople, sales managers, customer service and support staff, and other personnel. A CRM database in a larger company might have 500 users and 10 million or more rows in perhaps 50 or more tables. According to Microsoft, in 2004 Verizon had a SQL Server customer database that contained more than 15 terabytes of data. If that data were published in books, a bookshelf 450 miles long would be required to hold them.

Enterprise Resource Planning (ERP) is an information system that touches every department in a manufacturing company. It includes sales, inventory, production planning, purchasing, and other business functions. SAP is the leading vendor of ERP applications, and a key element of their product is a database that integrates data from these various business functions. An ERP system may have 5,000 or more users and perhaps 100 million rows in several hundred tables.

E-Commerce Database Applications

E-commerce is another important database application. Databases are a key component of e-commerce order entry, billing, shipping, and customer support. Surprisingly, however, the largest databases at an e-commerce site are not order-processing databases. The largest databases are those that track customer browser behavior. Most of the prominent e-commerce companies, such as Amazon.com (*www.amazon.com*) and Drugstore.com (*www.drugstore.com*) keep track of the Web pages and the Web page components that they send to their customers. They also track customer clicks, additions to shopping carts, order purchases, abandoned shopping carts, and so forth.

E-commerce companies use Web activity databases to determine which Web page items are popular and successful and which are not. They also can conduct experiments to determine if a purple background generates more orders than a blue one, and so forth. Such Web usage databases are huge. For example, Drugstore.com adds 20 million rows to its Web log database each day!

Reporting and Data Mining Database Applications

Two other example applications in Figure 1-3 are digital dashboards and data mining applications. These applications use the data generated by order processing and other operational systems to produce information to help manage the enterprise. Such applications do not generate new data, instead they summarize existing data to provide insights to management. Digital dashboards and other reporting systems assess past and current performance. Data mining applications predict future performance. We will consider such applications in Chapter 15. The bottom line is that database technology is used in almost every information system and involves databases ranging in size from a few thousand rows to many millions of rows.

B T W

Do not assume that just because a database is small that its structure is simple. For example, consider parts distribution for a company that sells $1 million in parts per year and parts distribution for a company that sells $100 million in parts per year. Despite the difference in sales, the companies have similar databases. Both have the same kinds of data, about the same number of tables of data, and the same level of complexity in data relationships. Only the amount of data varies from one to the other. Thus, although a database for a small business may be small, it is not necessarily simple.

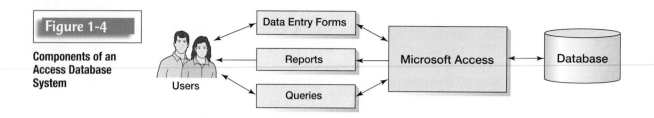

Figure 1-4

Components of an
Access Database
System

Components of a Database System

Figure 1-4 shows the structure of a typical Access database system. Users interact with the application through data entry forms like the one shown in Figure 1-5. They also request reports and perform queries against the database data. Access then processes the forms, produces the reports, and runs the queries.

Microsoft Access is a low-end product intended for individuals and small workgroups. As such, Microsoft has done all that it can to hide the underlying database technology from the user. Although hiding the technology is an effective strategy for beginners working on small databases, it won't work for database professionals who work with applications such as most of those described in Figure 1-3. For larger, more complex databases, it is necessary to understand the technology and components that Microsoft hides.

Applications, SQL, and the DBMS

Figure 1-6 is the same as Figure 1-5 except that the Access cover has been pulled off. As shown in the figure, databases have three components: applications, SQL, and the DBMS. **Applications** are computer programs that users interact with directly. Applications accept data from users, process it according to application-specific requirements, and use SQL to transfer data to and from the database. In the case of Access, applications create and process forms, reports, and queries. Other applications do far more, as you will learn.

SQL, or **Structured Query Language**, is an internationally recognized standard language that is understood by all commercial database management system products.

Figure 1-5

An Example Data
Entry Form

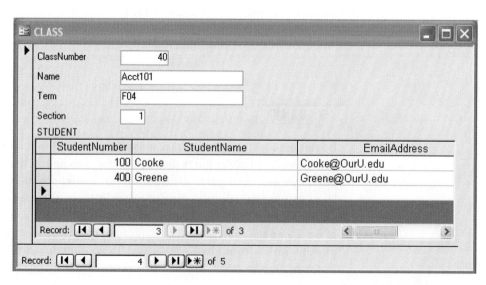

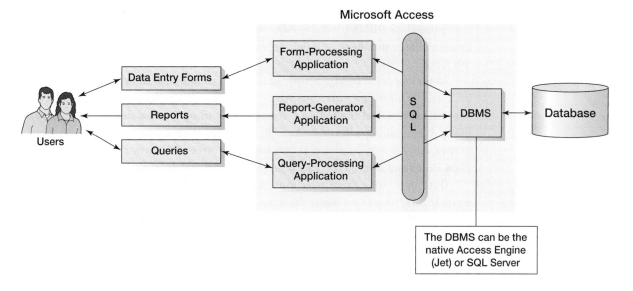

Figure 1-6   Under the Cover of an Access Application

To give you a taste of SQL, here is a sample SQL statement for processing the STUDENT table in Figure 1-1:

SELECT   **StudentName, EmailAddress**

FROM   **STUDENT**

WHERE   **StudentNumber > 200;**

This SQL statement will obtain the name and e-mail address of all students having a StudentNumber greater than 200. For the data in Figure 1-1, this statement will produce the StudentName and EmailAddress for students Harris and Greene.

As shown in Figure 1-6, the Access form, report, and query applications create SQL statements and pass them to the DBMS for processing. The **DBMS**, or **database management system**, creates, processes, and administers the database. A DBMS is a large and complicated product and few organizations write their own DBMS program. Instead, DBMS products are licensed from vendors such as Microsoft, Oracle, and IBM.

What Is Microsoft Access?

Before continuing, we need to clear up a common misconception: Microsoft Access is *not* just a DBMS. Rather, it is a DBMS *plus* an application generator. Access contains a DBMS engine that creates, processes, and administers the database. It also contains form, report, and query components that are the Access application generator.

Internally, the application components hidden under the Access cover use SQL to call the DBMS that is also hidden under that cover. At Microsoft, the DBMS engine within Access is called Jet. You seldom hear about Jet because Microsoft does not sell Jet as a separate product.

> **B T W**
>
> With Microsoft Access 2000 and later versions, you can replace Jet with Microsoft's enterprise-class DBMS product—SQL Server. You would do this if you wanted to process a large database or if you needed the advanced functions and features of SQL Server.
>
> To replace Jet with SQL Server, you need a computer that has both products installed. If your computer has Access 2003, select *File New Project using new data* and then select the option *Create a project using a new database*. If you are using Access 2000, select *File New/Project (New Database)* and then *Create a project using a new database*. If you are using Access XP, select *File New Project (New Database)* and then *Create a project using a new database*.
>
> Once you make these selections, Access will use SQL Server rather than Jet as its DBMS. Jet will no longer be used. Also note that you can attach your project to a SQL Server database on another computer if you have processing rights on that computer.

Components of an Enterprise-class Database System

Figure 1-7 shows the components of an enterprise-class database system. Here, the applications and the DBMS are not under the same cover as they are in Access. Instead, the applications are separate from each other and separate from the DBMS.

Database Applications

As exemplified by the list in Figure 1-3, dozens of different types of database applications are available. Figure 1-7 shows SAP applications that connect to the database over a corporate network. Such applications are sometimes called client/server applications because the application program is a client that connects to a database server. Client/server applications often are written in Visual Basic, C++, or Java.

A second category of applications in Figure 1-7 is e-commerce and other applications that run on a Web server. Users connect to such applications via Web browsers such as Internet Explorer and Netscape Navigator. Common Web servers include Microsoft's Internet Information Server (IIS) and Apache. Common languages for Web server applications are PHP, Java, and the Microsoft .NET languages such as C# and

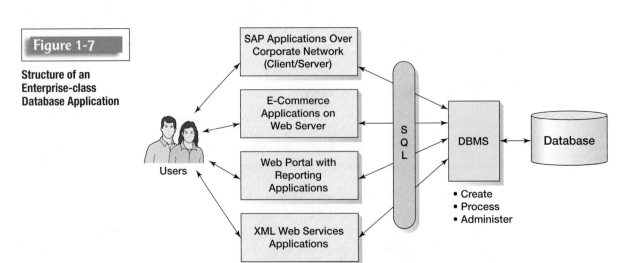

Figure 1-7

Structure of an Enterprise-class Database Application

VB.NET. We will discuss some of the technology for such applications in Chapters 12, 13, and 14.

A third category of applications is reporting applications that publish the results of database queries on a corporate portal or other Web site. Such reporting applications are often created using third-party report generation and digital dashboard products from vendors such as Cognos and MicroStrategy. We will describe these applications in Chapter 15.

The last category of applications is XML Web services. These applications are at the leading edge of database processing. They use a combination of the XML markup language and other standards to enable program-to-program communication. In this way, the code that comprises an application is distributed over several different computers. Web services can be written in Java or any of the .NET languages. We will discuss this important new class of applications in Chapter 13.

All of these database applications get and put database data by sending SQL statements to the DBMS. These applications may create forms and reports, or they may send their results to other programs. They also may implement application logic that goes beyond simple form and report processing. For example, an order entry application uses application logic to deal with out-of-stock items and backorders.

The DBMS

As stated earlier, the DBMS manages the database. It processes SQL statements and provides other features and functions for creating, processing, and administering the database. Figure 1-8 presents the four most prominent DBMS products. The products are shown in order of increasing power, features, and difficulty of use. Access (really Jet) is the easiest to use and the least powerful. SQL Server has far more power; it can process larger databases, faster, and it includes features for multiuser control, backup and recovery, and other administrative functions.

DB2 is a DBMS product from IBM. Most people would agree that it has faster performance than SQL Server, that it can handle larger databases, and that it is also more difficult to use. Finally, the fastest and most capable DBMS is Oracle from the Oracle Corporation. Oracle can be configured to offer very high performance on exceedingly large databases that operate 24/7, year after year. Oracle is also far more difficult to use and administer than SQL Server.

The Database

The last component in Figure 1-7 is the database. A **database** is a self-describing collection of integrated tables. Integrated tables are tables that store both data and the relationships among the data. The tables in Figure 1-1 are *integrated* because they store not just student, class, and grade data, but also data about the relationships among the rows of data.

A database is *self-describing* because it contains a description of itself. Thus, databases contain not only tables of user data, but also tables of data that describe that user

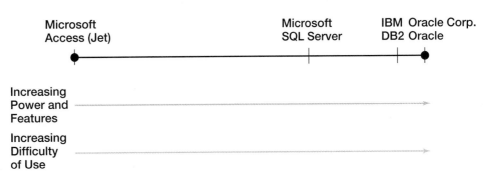

Figure 1-8

Common Professional View of DBMS Products

Figure 1-9

Typical Metadata Tables

USER_TABLES Table

TableName	NumberColumns	PrimaryKey
STUDENT	3	StudentNumber
CLASS	4	ClassNumber
GRADE	3	(StudentNumber, ClassNumber)

USER_COLUMNS Table

ColumnName	TableName	DataType	Length (bytes)
StudentNumber	STUDENT	Integer	4
StudentName	STUDENT	Text	50
EmailAddress	STUDENT	Text	50
ClassNumber	CLASS	Integer	4
Name	CLASS	Text	50
Term	CLASS	Text	5
Section	CLASS	SmallInteger	2
StudentNumber	GRADE	Integer	4
ClassNumber	GRADE	Integer	4
Grade	GRADE	Decimal	(3, 2)

data. Such descriptive data is called **metadata** because it is data about data. The form and format of metadata varies from DBMS to DBMS. Figure 1-9 shows generic metadata tables that describe the tables and columns for the database in Figure 1-1.

You can examine metadata to determine if particular tables, columns, indexes, or other structures exist in a database. For example, the following statement queries the SQL Server metadata table SYSOBJECTS to determine if a user table (Type = 'U') named CLASS exists in the database. If it does, the table is dropped (removed) from the database.

If Exists

    (SELECT   *

    FROM   **SYSOBJECTS**

    WHERE   **[Name] = 'CLASS'**

       AND   **Type = 'U')**

  DROP TABLE CLASS

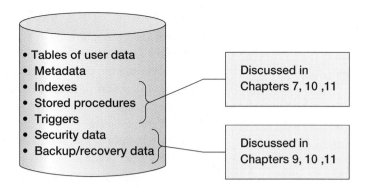

Figure 1-10

Database Contents

Do not be concerned with the syntax of this statement. You will learn what it means and how to write such statements yourself as we proceed. For now, just understand that this is one way that database administrators use metadata.

> **B T W**
>
> Because metadata is stored in tables, you can use SQL to query it as just illustrated. Thus, by learning how to write SQL to query user tables, you will also learn how to write SQL to query metadata. To do that, you just apply the SQL statements to metadata tables rather than user tables.

In addition to user tables and metadata, databases contain other elements, as shown in Figure 1-10. These other components will be described in detail in subsequent chapters. For now, however, understand that indexes are structures that speed the sorting and searching of database data. Triggers and stored procedures are programs that are stored within the database. Triggers are used to maintain database accuracy and consistency and to enforce data constraints. Stored procedures are used for database administration tasks and are sometimes part of database applications. You will learn more about these different elements in Chapters 7, 10, and 11.

Security data defines users, groups, and allowed permissions for users and groups. The particulars depend on the DBMS product in use. Finally, backup and recovery data are used to save database data to backup devices as well as to recover the database after failure. You will learn more about security and backup and recovery data in Chapters 9, 10, and 11.

Database Design

Database design is both difficult and important. Determining the proper structure of tables, the proper relationships among tables, the appropriate data constraints, and other structural components is challenging, and sometimes even daunting. Consequently, the world is full of poorly designed databases. Such databases do not perform well. They may require application developers to write overly complex and contrived SQL to get wanted data, they may be difficult to adapt to new and changing requirements, or they fail in some other way.

Figure 1-11

**Three Types of
Database Design**

- From Existing Data (Chapters 3 and 4)
    Analyze spreadsheets and other data tables
    Extract data from other databases
    Design using normalization principles
- New Systems Development (Chapters 5 and 6)
    Create data model from application requirements
    Transform data model into database design
- Database Redesign (Chapter 8)
    Migrate databases to newer databases
    Integrate two or more databases
    Reverse engineer and design new databases using
    normalization principles and data model transformation

Note: Chapter 7 discusses database implementation using SQL. You need that knowledge
before you can understand database redesign.

Because database design is both difficult and important, we will devote most of the first half of this text to the topic. As shown in Figure 1-11, there are three types of database design.

Database Design from Existing Data

The first type of database design involves databases that are constructed from existing data, as shown in Figure 1-12. In some cases, a development team is given a set of spreadsheets or a set of text files with tables of data. The team is required to design a database and import the data from those spreadsheets and tables into a new database.

Figure 1-12

**Databases Originating
from Existing Data**

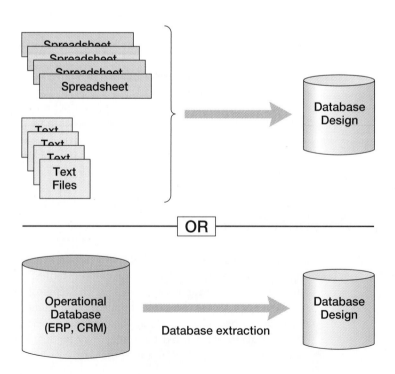

Figure 1-13			Data Import: One or Two Tables?

EmpNum	EmpName	DeptNum	DeptName
100	Jones	10	Accounting
150	Lau	20	Marketing
200	McCauley	10	Accounting
300	Griffin	10	Accounting

(a) One-Table Design

OR?

DeptNum	DeptName
10	Accounting
20	Marketing

EmpNum	EmpName	DeptNum
100	Jones	10
150	Lau	20
200	McCauley	10
300	Griffin	10

(b) Two-Table Design

Alternatively, databases can be created from extracts of other databases. This alternative is especially common in reporting and data mining applications. For example, data from an operational database, such as a CRM or ERP database, may be copied into a new database that will be used only for studies and analysis. As you will learn in Chapter 15, such databases are used in facilities called **data marts**. The data mart databases often are exported to other analytical tools, such as SAS's Enterprise Miner, SPSS's Clementine, or Insightful Corporation's I-Miner.

When creating a database from existing data, database developers must determine the appropriate structure for the new database. A common issue is how the multiple files or tables in the new database should be related. However, even the import of a single table can pose design questions. Figure 1-13 shows two different ways of importing a simple table of employees and their departments. Should this data be stored as one table or two?

Decisions such as this are not arbitrary. Database professionals use a set of principles, collectively called **normalization**, or **normal forms**, to guide and assess database designs. You will learn those principles and their role in database design in Chapter 3.

Database Design from New Systems Development

A second way that databases are designed is from the development of new information systems. As shown in Figure 1-14, requirements for a new system, such as desired data entry forms and reports, user requirements statements, use cases, and other requirements, are analyzed to create the database design.

In all but the simplest system development projects, the step from user requirements to database design is too big. Accordingly, the development team proceeds in two steps. First, the team creates a **data model** from the requirements

Figure 1-14   Databases Originating from New Systems Development

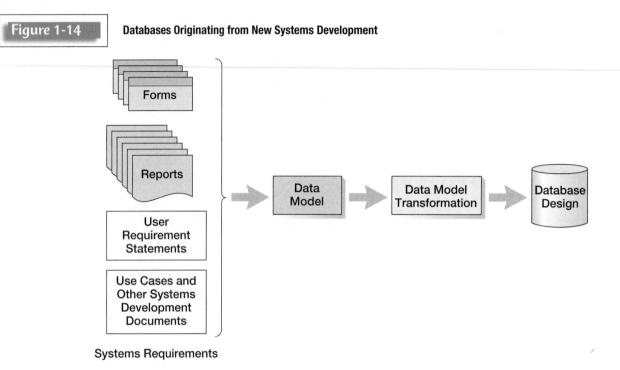

Systems Requirements

statements and then transforms that data model into a database design. You can think of a data model as a blueprint that is used as a design aid on the way to a database design.

In Chapter 4, you will learn about the most popular data modeling technique—**entity-relationship data modeling**. You also will see how to use the entity-relationship model to represent a variety of common form and report patterns. Then, in Chapter 5, you will learn how to transform entity-relationship data models into database designs.

Database Design from Redesign

Database redesign is the third way that databases are designed. As shown in Figure 1-15, there are two common types of database redesign. In the first, a database is adapted to new or changing requirements. This process sometimes is called **database migration**. In the migration process, tables may be created, modified, or removed; relationships may be altered; data constraints may be changed; and so forth.

The second type of database redesign involves the integration of two or more databases. This type of redesign is common when adapting or removing legacy systems. It is also common for enterprise application integration, when two or more previously separate information systems are adapted to work with each other.

Database redesign is complicated. There is no getting around that fact. If this is your first exposure to database design, your instructor may skip this topic. If this is the case, after you have gained more experience, you should reread this material. In spite of its difficulty, database redesign is important.

To understand database redesign, you need to know SQL statements for defining database structures and more advanced SQL statements for querying and updating a database. Consequently, we will not address database redesign until after Chapter 7, which presents advanced SQL.

Figure 1-15

Databases Originating from Database Redesign

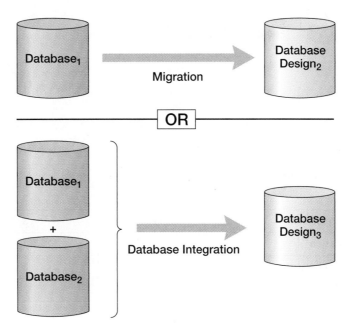

What You Need to Learn

In your career, you may work with database technology as either a user or as a database administrator. As a **user** you may be a *knowledge worker* who prepares reports, mines data, and does other types of data analysis or you may be a programmer who writes applications that process the database. Alternatively, you might be a **database adminis-trator** who designs, constructs, and manages the database itself. Users are primarily concerned with constructing SQL statements to get and put the data they want. Database administrators are primarily concerned with the management of the database. The domains for each of these roles are shown in Figure 1-16.

Both users and database administrators need all of the knowledge in this text. However, the emphasis on each topic differs for the two groups. Figure 1-17 shows my opinion as to the relative importance of each topic to each group. Discuss this table with your instructor. He or she may have knowledge about your local job market that affects the relative importance of these topics.

Figure 1-16

Working Domains of Knowledge Workers, Programmers, and Database Administrators

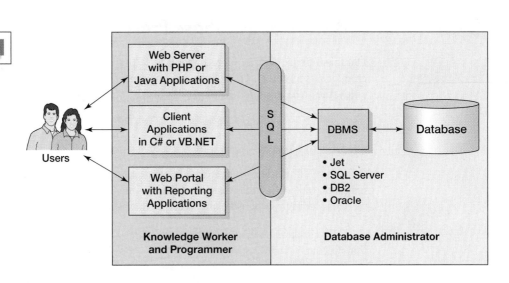

Figure 1-17   Priorities of What You Need to Know

Topic	Chapter	Importance to Knowledge Worker and Programmer	Importance to Database Administrator
Basic SQL	Chapter 2	1	1
Design via normalization	Chapter 3	2	1
Data modeling	Chapter 5	1	1
Data model transformation	Chapter 6	2	1
DDL SQL	Chapter 7	2	1
Constraint enforcement	Chapter 7	3	1
Database redesign	Chapter 8	3	2, but 1 for senior DBA
Database administration	Chapter 9	2	1
SQL Server, Oracle specifics	Chapter 10, 11	3	1
Database application technology	Chapters 12, 13, 14, and 15	1	3

1 = Very important; 2 = Important; 3 = Less important   Warning: Opinions vary, ask your instructor for his or hers.

B T W

The most exciting and interesting jobs in technology are always those on the leading edge. If you live in the United States and are concerned about outsourcing, a recent study by the Rand Corporation[1] indicates that the most secure jobs in the United States involve the adaptation of new technology to solve business problems in innovative ways.

Right now, the leading edge involves the integration of XML, Web services, and database processing. You will need all of the fundamentals presented in this book, especially the material in Chapter 13, to work in this exciting new area. If I were starting out in database processing today, I would make learning about the integration of XML and database technology a top priority.

 ## A Brief History of Database Processing

Database processing emerged around 1970 and has been continuously evolving and changing since then. This continual change has made it a fascinating and thoroughly enjoyable field in which to work. Figure 1-18 summarizes the major eras of database processing.

The Early Years

Prior to 1970, all data were stored in separate files, most of which were kept on reels of magnetic tape. Magnetic disks and drums (magnetic cylinders that are no longer used) were exceedingly expensive and very small. Today's 1.44 megabyte floppy disk has more

[1]Karoly, Lynn A., and Constantijn W. A. Panis. *The 21st Century at Work*. Santa Monica, CA: The Rand Corporation, 2004.

Figure 1-18	Database History

Era	Years	Important Products	Remarks
Predatabase	Before 1970	File managers	All data were stored in separate files. Data integration was very difficult. File storage space was expensive and limited.
Early database	1970–1980	ADABAS, System2000, Total, IDMS, IMS	First products to provide related tables. CODASYL DBTG and hierarchical data models (DL/I) were prevalent.
Emergence of relational model	1978–1985	DB2, Oracle	Early relational DBMS products had substantial inertia to overcome. In time, the advantages weighed out.
Microcomputer DBMS products	1982–1992	dBase-II, R:base, Paradox, Access	Amazing! A database on a micro. All micro DBMS products were eliminated by Microsoft Access in the early 1990s.
Object-oriented DBMS	1985–2000	Oracle ODBMS and others	Never caught on. Required relational database to be converted. Too much work for perceived benefit.
Web databases	1995–present	IIS/ASP, Apache/PHP, and Java	Stateless characteristic of HTTP was a problem at first. Early applications were simple one-stage transactions. Later, more complex logic developed.
XML and Web services	1998–present	XML, SOAP, WSDL, UDDI, and other standards	XML provides tremendous benefits to web based applications. Very important today. May replace relational databases during your career. See Chapter 13.

capacity than many disks of that era. Memory was expensive as well. In 1969, we were processing payroll on a computer that had 32,000 bytes of memory! (The computer on which I write this history has 2 gigabytes of memory.)

Integrated processing was an important but very difficult problem. An insurance company, for example, wanted to relate customer account data to customer claim data. Accounts were stored on one magnetic tape, and claims were stored on another. To process claims, the data on the two tapes had to be integrated somehow.

The need for data integration drove the development of the first database technology. By 1973, several commercial DBMS products had emerged. These products were in use by the mid-1970s. The first edition of this text, copyrighted 1977, featured the DBMS products ADABAS, System2000, Total, IDMS, and IMS. Of those five, only ADABAS and IMS are still in use, and neither of them has substantial market share today.

Those early DBMS products varied in the way that they structured data relationships. One method, called **Data Language/I**, or **DL/I**, used hierarchies or trees (see Appendix D) to represent relationships. IMS, which was developed and licensed by IBM, was based on this model. IMS had success at many organizations, particularly among large manufacturers, and is still in limited use today.

Another technique for structuring data relationships used data structures called *networks*. The CODASYL Committee (the group that developed the programming language COBOL) sponsored a subcommittee called the Database Task Group (DBTG). This subcommittee developed a standard data model that came to bear its name—the **CODASYL DBTG** model. It was an unnecessarily complicated model (everyone's favorite idea made it into the committee's design), but several successful DBMS products were developed using it. The most successful was IDMS, and its vendor, the Cullinane Corporation, was the first software company to be listed on the New York Stock Exchange. To my knowledge, no IDMS database is in use today.

The Emergence and Dominance of the Relational Model

In 1970, a then little-known IBM engineer named E. F. Codd published a paper in the *Communications of the ACM*[2] in which he applied the concepts of a branch of mathematics called relational algebra to the problem of "shared data banks," as databases were then known. Codd's work was at first viewed as too theoretical for practical implementation. Practitioners argued that it was too slow and required so much storage that it would never be useful in the commercial world.

The 1977 edition of this text featured a chapter on the relational model (which Codd himself reviewed). Many years later, Wayne Ratliff stated that he had the idea for creating the dBase series of products for personal computers while reading that very chapter.[3]

B T W

Today, there are as many opportunities for innovation as there were for Wayne Ratliff in 1977. Perhaps you can read Chapter 13 and develop an innovative product that integrates XML and DBMS processing in a new way. Just as in 1977, no product has a lock on the future; opportunity awaits you!

The relational model, relational algebra, and later, SQL made sense. They were not needlessly complicated; rather, they seemed to boil down the data integration problem to a few essential ideas. Over time, Codd convinced IBM management to develop relational-model DBMS products. The result was IBM's DB2 and its variants, which are still very popular today.

Meanwhile, other companies were considering the relational model as well, and by 1980 several more relational DBMS products had been released. The most prominent and important of those was Oracle Corporation's Oracle. Oracle achieved success for many reasons, one of which was that it would run on just about any computer and just about any operating system. (Some users complained, "Yes, and equally badly on all of them." Another, when asked "Should we sell it to communist Russia?" responded, "Only as long as they have to take the documentation with it.")

However, in addition to being able to run on many different types of machines, Oracle had, and continues to have, an elegant and efficient internal design. You will

---

[2]Codd, E. F. "A Relational Model of Data for Large Shared Databanks," *Communications of the ACM*, June 1970, pp. 377–387.
[3]Ratliff, C. Wayne. "dStory: How I Really Developed dBASE," *Data Based Advisor*, March 1991, p. 94.

learn aspects of that design in the concurrency-control section in Chapter 10. That excellent design, together with hard-driving and successful sales and marketing, has pushed Oracle to the top of the DBMS market.

Meanwhile, Gordon Moore and others were hard at work at Intel. By the early 1980s, personal computers were prevalent, and DBMS products were developed for them. Developers of microcomputer DBMS products saw the advantages of the relational model and developed their products around it. dBase was the most successful of the early products, but another product, R:base, was the first to implement true relational algebra and other operations on the PC. Later, another relational DBMS product named Paradox was developed for personal computers. Eventually, it was acquired by Borland.

Alas, it all came to an end when Microsoft entered the picture. Microsoft released Access in 1991 and priced it at $99. No other PC DBMS vendor could survive at that price point. Access killed R:base and Paradox, and then Microsoft bought a dBase "work-alike" product called FoxPro and used it to eliminate dBase. Although Microsoft continues to sell FoxPro under the name Visual FoxPro, Microsoft Access is the only major survivor of that bloodbath of PC DBMS products.

Post-Relational Developments

In the mid-1980s, object-oriented programming (OOP) emerged, and its advantages over traditional structured programming were quickly recognized. By 1990, some vendors had developed object-oriented DBMS products (OODBMS or ODBMS). These products were designed to make it easy to store the data encapsulated in OOP objects. Several special-purpose OODBMS were developed, and Oracle added OOP constructs to Oracle to enable the creation of a hybrid called an *object-relational DBMS*.

OODBMS never caught on, and today that category of DBMS products is fading away. There were two reasons for their lack of acceptance. First, using an OODBMS required that the relational data be converted from relational format to object-oriented format. By the time OODBMS emerged, billions upon billions of bytes of data were stored in relational format in organizational databases. No company was willing to undergo the expensive travail of converting those databases to be able to use the new OODBMS.

Second, object-oriented databases had no substantial advantage over relational databases for most commercial database processing. As you will see in the next chapter, SQL is not object oriented. But it works, and thousands of developers have created programs that use it. Without a demonstrable advantage over relational databases, no organization was willing to take on the task of converting their data to OODBMS format.

Meanwhile, the Internet took off. By the mid-1990s, it was clear that the Internet was one of the most important phenomena in history. It changed, forever, the ways that customers and businesses relate to each other. Early Web sites were nothing more than online brochures, but within a few years dynamic Web sites that involved querying and processing databases began to appear.

However, one substantial problem existed. HTTP is a stateless protocol; a server receives a request from a user, processes the request, and then forgets about the user and the request. Many database interactions are multistage. A customer views products, adds one or more to a shopping cart, views more products, adds more to the shopping cart, and eventually checks out. A stateless protocol cannot be used for such applications.

Over time, capabilities emerged to overcome this problem. Web application developers learned to add SQL statements to their Web applications, and soon thousands of databases were being processed over the Web. You will learn more about such processing in Chapter 12.

The last row in Figure 1-18 brings us to the present. In the late 1990s, XML was defined to overcome the problems that occur when HTML is used to exchange business documents. The design of the XML family of standards not only solved the problems of

HTML, it also meant that XML documents were superior for exchanging views of database data. In 2002, Bill Gates said that "XML is the lingua-franca of the Internet Age." As you will learn in Chapter 13, however, two key problems that remain are (1) getting data from a database and putting it into an XML document and (2) taking data from an XML document and putting it into a databases. In fact, this is where future application programmers can enter the picture.

XML database processing was given a further boost with the definition of XML Web service standards such as SOAP (not an acronym), WSDL (Web Services Description Language), UDDI (Universal Description, Discovery, and Integration), and others. Using Web services, it is possible to expose nuggets of database processing to other programs that use the Internet infrastructure. This means, for example, that in a supply chain management application, a vendor can expose portions of its inventory application to its suppliers. Further, it can do so in a standardized way.

XML Web services bring us to the edge of the IT volcano, where the magma of new technology is just now oozing out of the ground. What happens next will be, in part, up to you.

⑨ SUMMARY

The purpose of a database is to help people keep track of things. Databases store data in tables in which each table has data about a different type of thing. Instances of the thing are stored in the rows of tables, and the characteristics of those instances are stored in columns. In this text, table names are written in all capital letters; column names are written in initial capital letters. Databases store data and the relationships among the data. Databases store data, but they are structured so that information can be created from that data.

Figure 1-3 lists many important examples of database applications. Databases can be processed by a single user or by many users. Those that support many users require special concurrency-control mechanisms to ensure that one user's work does not conflict with a second user's work.

Some databases involve just a few users and thousands of rows of data in a few tables. At the other end of the spectrum, some large databases, such as those that support ERP applications, support thousands of users and include many millions of rows in several hundred different tables.

Some database applications support e-commerce activities. Some of the largest databases are those that track users' responses to Web pages and Web page components. These databases are used to analyze customers' responses to different Web-based marketing programs.

Digital dashboards, data mining applications, and other reporting applications use database data that is generated by transaction processing systems to help manage the enterprise. Digital dashboards and reporting systems assess past and current performance. Data mining applications predict future performance.

Microsoft Access is a low-end product that hides much of the database technology that you need to learn. Under its cover, Access has applications components, SQL, and a DBMS. Access applications components construct and process forms, reports, and queries. They get and put data by submitting SQL statements to the DBMS. SQL is an internationally recognized language for processing databases.

A DBMS is a large and complicated program that creates, processes, and administers a database. DBMS products are licensed from software vendors.

Microsoft Access is not a DBMS but rather is an application generator plus a DBMS. The application generator consists of applications components that create and process forms, reports, and queries. The default Access DBMS product is called Jet, which is not licensed as a separate product. SQL Server can be substituted for Jet to support larger databases.

Enterprise database systems do not combine applications and the DBMS as Access does. Instead, applications are programs separate from each other and from the DBMS. Figure 1-7 shows four categories of database applications: client/server applications, Web applications, reporting applications, and XML Web services applications.

The four most popular DBMS products, in order of power, features, and difficulty of use, are Access (really Jet), SQL Server, DB2, and Oracle. Jet and SQL Server are licensed by Microsoft, DB2 is licensed by IBM, and Oracle is licensed by the Oracle Corporation.

A database is a self-describing collection of integrated tables. Such tables store data and the relationships among the data. A database is self-describing because it contains a description of itself. Metadata is data about data. Databases contain metadata that describes the structure of the database. Most DBMS products carry metadata in the form of tables. As shown in Figure 1-10, databases also contain indexes, triggers, stored procedures, security features, and backup and recovery data. You will learn more about each of these topics in this text.

Database design is both difficult and important. Most of the first half of this text concerns database design. Databases arise in three ways: from existing data, from new systems development, and from database redesign. Normalization is used to guide the design of databases from existing data. Data models are used to create a blueprint from system requirements. The blueprint is later transformed into a database design. Most data models are created using the entity-relationship model. Database redesign occurs when an existing database is adapted to support new or changed requirements or when two or more databases are integrated.

With regards to database processing, you can have one of two roles: user or database administrator. You may be a *user* of a database/DBMS as a knowledge worker or as an application programmer. Alternatively, you might be a *database administrator* who designs, constructs, and manages the database itself. The domains of each role are shown in Figure 1-16, and the priorities as to what you need to know for each role are shown in Figure 1-17.

The history of database processing is summarized in Figure 1-18. In the early years, prior to 1970, database processing did not exist, and all data was stored in separated files. The need for integrated processing drove the development of early DBMS products. The CODASYL DBTG and DL/I data models were prevalent. Of the DBMS products used at that time, only ADABAS and IMS are still in use.

The relational model rose to prominence in the 1980s. At first, the relational model was judged to be impractical, but over time relational products such as DB2 and Oracle achieved success. During this time, DBMS products were developed for personal computers as well. dBase, R:base, and Paradox were all PC DBMS products that were eventually consumed by the success of Microsoft Access.

Object-oriented DBMS products were developed in the 1990s but never achieved commercial success. More recently, Web-based databases have been developed to support e-commerce. Features and functions have been implemented to overcome the stateless nature of HTTP. XML and XML Web services databases are at the leading edge of database processing.

◉ REVIEW QUESTIONS

1.1   Give an example of two related tables other than one in this book. Use the STUDENT and GRADE tables in Figure 1-1 as an example pattern for your tables. Name the tables and columns using the conventions in this book.

1.2   Explain how the two tables you provided in question 1.1 are related.

1.3   Show your two tables from question 1.1 without the columns that represent the relationships. Explain how the value of your two tables is diminished without the relationships.

1.4   Define the terms data and information. Explain how the two terms differ.

1.5   Give an example of information that could be determined using the two tables you provided in your answer to question 1.1.

1.6   Give examples of a single-user database application and a multiuser database application other than ones shown in Figure 1-3.

1.7   What problem can occur when a database is processed by more than one user?

1.8   Give an example of a database application that has hundreds of users and a very large and complicated database. Use an example other than one in Figure 1-3.

1.9   What are the largest databases used by e-commerce companies such as Amazon.com?

1.10   How do the e-commerce companies use these databases?

1.11   How do digital dashboard and data mining applications differ from transaction processing applications?

1.12   Explain why a small database is not necessarily simpler than a large one.

1.13   Explain the components in Figure 1-5.

1.14   Why does Microsoft Access hide important database technology?

1.15   Describe the components shown in Figure 1-6.

1.16   What is SQL and why is it important?

1.17   What does DBMS stand for?

1.18   What is the function of the DBMS?

1.19   Name three vendors of DBMS products.

1.20   Is Microsoft Access a DBMS? Why or why not?

1.21   What is the function of the application generator in Access?

1.22   What is the name of the DBMS engine within Access? Why do we rarely hear about that engine?

1.23   Why would someone choose to replace the native Access DBMS engine with SQL Server?

1.24   Name the components of an enterprise-class database system.

1.25   Name and describe the four categories of database applications.

1.26   How do database applications get and put database data?

1.27   Name the four DBMS products described in this chapter.

1.28   Explain how the products in your answer to question 1.27 compare in terms of power, features, and ease of use.

1.29   Define the term database.

1.30   Why is a database considered to be self-describing?

1.31   What is metadata? How does this term pertain to a database?

1.32   What advantage is there in storing metadata in tables?

1.33   List the components of a database other than user tables and metadata.

1.34   List several consequences of a poorly designed database.

1.35   Explain two ways that a database can be designed from existing data.

1.36   What is a data mart?

1.37   Describe the general process of designing a database for a new information system.

1.38   Explain two ways that databases can be redesigned.

1.39   What does the term database migration mean?

1.40   Summarize the various ways that you might work with database technology.

1.41   What job functions does a knowledge worker perform?

1.42   What job functions does a database administrator perform?

1.43   Explain the meaning of the domains in Figure 1-16.

1.44   What need drove the development of the first database technology?

1.45   What are Data Language/I and CODASYL DBTG?

1.46   Who was E. F. Codd?

1.47   What were the early objections to the relational model?

1.48   Name two early relational DBMS products.

1.49   What are some of the reasons for Oracle's success?

1.50   Name three early personal computer DBMS products.

1.51   What happened to the products in your answer to question 1.50?

1.52   What was the purpose of OODBMS products?

1.53   Describe two reasons that OODBMS products were not successful.

1.54   What characteristic of HTTP was a problem for database processing applications?

1.55   What comment did Bill Gates make regarding XML?

1.56   What two key problems exist for processing database data using XML?

⊚ PROJECT QUESTIONS

To perform the following projects you will need a computer that has Microsoft Access installed. If you have no experience working with Access, read Appendix A before you proceed.

1.57   Create a new database named Project One and create the following two tables in that database:

DEPARTMENT (DepartmentName, OfficeNumber, Phone) and

EMPLOYEE (EmployeeName, Email, DepartmentName)

Assume that all columns have text data and set the length of the text field to an appropriate value.

1.58   Add at least two rows to the DEPARTMENT table and at least five rows to the EMPLOYEE table. Ensure that all rows in the EMPLOYEE table have a valid value for DepartmentName.

1.59   Using the Access form wizard, create a form that has all of the data from both tables. When asked how you want to view your data, select *by DEPARTMENT*. Choose the default options for other questions that the wizard asks. Open your form and page through your departments.

1.60   Using the Access report wizard, create a report that has all of the data from both tables. When asked how you want to view your data, select *by DEPARTMENT*. Choose the default options for other questions that the wizard asks. Print your report.

1.61   Explain, to the level of detail in this chapter, what is going on under Access' cover in questions 1.59 and 1.60. What subcomponent created the form and report? Where is the data stored? What role do you think SQL is playing?

1.62   If you doubt that Access is really using SQL, open your form in design mode (click the design icon at the top of the Access window when your form is open). Right-click on the upper-left-hand corner of your subform (the area where EMPLOYEE data is displayed). Click Properties, and then select the Data tab. Click the button with the three periods next to the RecordSource property, which displays a dialog box asking if you want to display the Query Builder. Click the Yes button. In the SQL Statement: Query Builder window that opens, right click in the gray area of the top pane and select SQL View. The SQL that Access is using to populate your subform will appear. Now close all open Windows and select No every time Access asks if you want to save your changes. Write "I saw the SQL" for your answer to this question.

    If you do not doubt that Access is using SQL, then just write "I believe Access uses SQL" for your answer to this question and start on your accounting homework.

Introduction to Structured Query Language

This chapter introduces **Structured Query Language (SQL)**. SQL statements are divided into two categories: **data manipulation language (DML)** statements, which are used for querying and modifying data, and **data definition language (DDL)** statements, which are used for creating tables, relationships, and other structures. This chapter considers only DML statements for querying data. The remaining DML statements for inserting, modifying, and deleting data are discussed in Chapter 7. That chapter also presents SQL DDL statements.

SQL Background

SQL was developed by the IBM Corporation in the late 1970s and was endorsed as a national standard by the American National Standards Institute (ANSI) in 1992. The version presented here is based on that standard, which is sometimes referred to as SQL-92. A later version, SQL3, incorporates some object-oriented concepts. This later version has received little attention from commercial DBMS vendors and is unimportant for practical database processing. We will not consider it in this text.

SQL is not a complete programming language like Java or C#. Instead, it is called a **data sublanguage** because it has only those statements needed for creating and processing database data and metadata. You can use SQL statements in many different ways. You can submit them directly to the DBMS for processing. You can embed SQL statements into client/server application programs. You can embed them into Web pages, and you can use them in reporting and data extraction programs. You also can execute SQL statements directly from Visual Studio .NET and other development tools.

SQL is ubiquitous, and SQL programming is a critical skill. Today, all DBMS products process SQL. As explained in Chapter 1, if you have used Microsoft Access, you have used SQL, even if you didn't know it. Every time you process a form, create a report, or run a query, Access generates SQL and sends it to Jet, Access' internal DBMS engine. To do more than elementary database processing, you need to uncover the SQL hidden by Access. Further, once you know SQL, you will find it easier to write a query statement in SQL rather than fight with the graphical forms, buttons, and other paraphernalia that you must use to create queries with Access.

Enterprise-class DBMSs such as Oracle, DB2, SQL Server, and MySQL[1] require that you know SQL. With these products, all data manipulation is expressed using SQL.

Cape Codd Outdoor Sports

Cape Codd Outdoor Sports is a fictitious company based on a real outdoor retail equipment vendor. Cape Codd sells recreational outdoor equipment in 15 retail stores across the United States and Canada. It also sells merchandise over the Internet from a Web storefront application and via mail order. All retail sales are recorded in a sales database managed by Oracle, as shown in Figure 2-1.

The Retail Sales Data Extraction

Cape Codd's marketing department wants to perform an analysis of in-store sales. Accordingly, marketing analysts ask the IS department to extract retail sales data from the operational database. To perform the marketing study, they do not need all of the order data. They want just the tables and columns shown in Figure 2-2.

Three tables are desired: RETAIL_ORDER, ORDER_ITEM, and SKU_DATA. The RETAIL_ORDER table has data about each order, the ORDER_ITEM table has data about each item in an order, and the SKU_DATA table has data about each **SKU,** or **stock keeping unit.** You can think of a SKU as an identifier for a particular item that Cape Codd sells.

RETAIL_ORDER Data

As shown in Figure 2-2, RETAIL_ORDER has columns for OrderNumber, StoreNumber, StoreZip (the zip code of the store selling the order), OrderMonth, OrderYear, and OrderTotal. This extract only includes data for retail store sales. All

---

[1]MySQL is an open-source DBMS product that you can download from www.mysql.com. It is common in the Linux environment and is introduced in some detail in Chapter 14, beginning on page 499.

Cape Codd Retail Sales Extraction

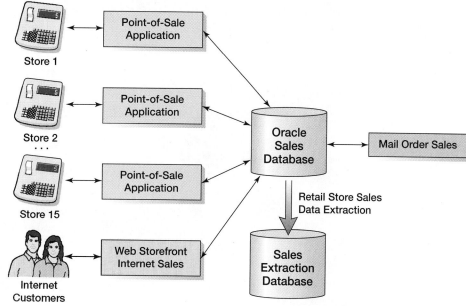

other types of sales (and returns and other sales-related transactions) are removed during the extraction process.

The data extraction process selects only a few columns of the operational data. The Point of Sale (POS) and other applications process far more data than shown here. They also keep that data in a different format. For example, the raw order data in the Oracle database stores OrderDate in the date format MM/DD/YYYY (e.g., 10/22/2004 for October 22, 2004). The extraction program converts OrderDate into the values of OrderMonth and OrderYear that marketing wants. Such filtering and data transformation are typical of a data extraction process.

Figure 2-2

Retail Sales Extracted Data Format

Table	Column	Date Type
RETAIL_ORDER	OrderNumber	Integer
	StoreNumber	Integer
	StoreZip	Character (9)
	OrderMonth	Character (12)
	OrderYear	Integer
	OrderTotal	Currency
ORDER_ITEM	OrderNumber	Integer
	SKU	Integer
	Quantity	Integer
	Price	Currency
	ExtendedPrice	Currency
SKU_DATA	SKU	Integer
	SKU_Description	Character (35)
	Department	Character (30)
	Buyer	Character (30)

Figure 2-3

**Sample Data from
Retail Sales Extract**

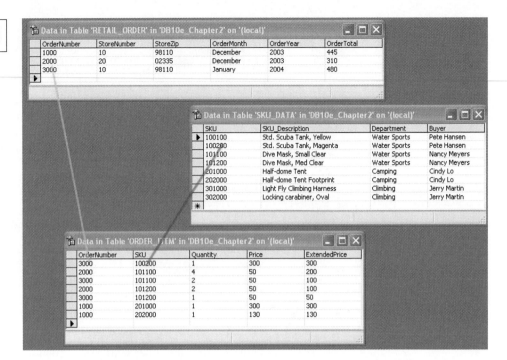

Figure 2-3 shows example extracted RETAIL_ORDER data. The first row has data extracted from OrderNumber 1000, the second has data from OrderNumber 2000, and so forth.

ORDER_ITEM Data

The ORDER_ITEM table stores an extract of the items purchased in each order. There is one row in the table for each SKU in an order. To understand this table, think about a sales receipt you get from a retail store. That receipt has data for one order. It includes basic order data such as the date and order total, and it has one line for each item you purchase. The rows in the ORDER_ITEM table correspond to the lines on such an order receipt.

OrderNumber relates to OrderNumber in the RETAIL_ORDER table. SKU is the number of the stock keeping unit and relates to SKU in the SKU_DATA table (discussed in the next section). Quantity is the number of items of that SKU purchased in that order. Price is the price of each item, and ExtendedPrice is equal to Quantity * Price. ORDER_ITEM data are shown in the bottom part of Figure 2-3. The first row relates to order 3000 and to SKU 100200. One item, 100200, was purchased for 300, and the ExtendedPrice is 300. The second row relates to order 2000; in that row, 4 items 101100 were purchased for 50, and the ExtendedPrice is 4 * 50, or 200. This structure is typical for items in orders; you will see it again in Chapters 5 and 6, where you will create a data model of a complete order and then design the database for that data model.

B T W

You would expect the total of ExtendedPrice for all rows for a given order to equal OrderTotal in the RETAIL_ORDER table. They do not. For order 3000, for example, the sum of the ExtendedPrice is 300 + 100 + 50, or 450. However, the OrderTotal for order 3000 is 480. The difference occurs because OrderTotal includes tax, shipping, and other charges that do not appear in the data extract.

SKU_DATA Table

The SKU_DATA table has columns SKU, SKU_Description, Department, and Buyer. SKU is an integer value that identifies a particular product that Cape Codd sells. SKU_Description contains a brief text description of each item. Department and Buyer identify the department and individual who is responsible for purchasing the product. As with the other tables, these columns are a subset of the SKU data stored in the operational database.

Data Extracts Are Common

Before we continue, realize that the data extraction process described here is not just an academic exercise. To the contrary, such extract processes are realistic, common, and important. Right now, hundreds of businesses worldwide are creating extract databases just like the one created by Cape Codd.

In the next sections of this chapter, you will learn how to write SQL statements to process the extracted data. This knowledge is exceedingly valuable and practical. Again, right now, as you read this paragraph, hundreds of people are writing SQL to create information from extracted data. The SQL you will learn in this chapter will be an essential asset to you as a knowledge worker, application programmer, or database administrator. Invest the time to learn SQL; the investment will pay great dividends later in your career.

The SQL SELECT/FROM/WHERE Framework

This section introduces the fundamental statement framework for SQL query statements. After we discuss this basic structure, you will learn how to submit SQL statements to Access, SQL Server, and Oracle. If you choose, you can then follow along with the text and process additional SQL statements as they are explained in the rest of this chapter.

Reading Specified Columns from a Single Table

We begin very simply. Suppose we want to obtain just the values of the Department and Buyer columns of the SKU_DATA table. A SQL statement to read that data is the following:

```
SELECT      Department, Buyer
FROM        SKU_DATA;
```

When the DBMS processes this statement for the data in Figure 2-3, the result will be:

Department	Buyer
Water Sports	Pete Hansen
Water Sports	Pete Hansen
Water Sports	Nancy Meyers
Water Sports	Nancy Meyers
Camping	Cindy Lo
Camping	Cindy Lo
Climbing	Jerry Martin
Climbing	Jerry Martin

SQL statements transform tables. They start with a table, process that table in some way, and then place the results in a table structure. Even if the result of the processing is just a single number, that number is considered to be a table with one row and one column. As you'll learn at the end of this chapter, some SQL statements process multiple tables. Regardless of the number of input tables, though, the result of every SQL statement is a single, output table.

Also, notice that SQL statements terminate with a semicolon. This semicolon is required by the SQL-92 standard. Although some DBMS products will allow you to omit the semicolon, some will not, so develop the habit of terminating SQL statements with a semicolon.

The order of the column names in the SELECT phrase determines the order of the columns in the results table. Thus, if we switch Buyer and Department in the SELECT phrase, they will be switched in the output table as well. Hence, the SQL statement:

SELECT   **Buyer, Department**

FROM   **SKU_DATA;**

will produce the following table:

Buyer	Department
Pete Hansen	Water Sports
Pete Hansen	Water Sports
Nancy Meyers	Water Sports
Nancy Meyers	Water Sports
Cindy Lo	Camping
Cindy Lo	Camping
Jerry Martin	Climbing
Jerry Martin	Climbing

Notice that some rows are duplicated in these results. The data in the first and second row, for example, is identical. We can eliminate duplicates by using the DISTINCT keyword as follows:

SELECT   **DISTINCT Buyer, Department**

FROM   **SKU_DATA;**

The result of this statement is:

Buyer	Department
Cindy Lo	Camping
Jerry Martin	Climbing
Nancy Meyers	Water Sports
Pete Hansen	Water Sports

All of the duplicate rows have been removed.

B T W

The reason that SQL does not automatically eliminate duplicate rows is that it can be very time consuming to do so. To determine if any rows are duplicates, every row must be compared with every other row. If there are 100,000 rows in a table, that checking will take a long time. Hence, by default, duplicates are not removed. It is always possible to force their removal using the DISTINCT keyword, however.

Suppose that we want to view all of the columns of the SKU_DATA table. To do so, we can name each column in the SELECT statement as follows:

SELECT   **SKU, SKU_Description, Department, Buyer**

FROM   **SKU_DATA;**

The result will be a table with all rows and all four of the columns in SKU_Data. However, SQL provides a shorthand notation for querying all of the columns of a table. The shorthand is to use an asterisk:

SELECT   *

FROM   **SKU_DATA;**

The result is:

SKU	SKU_Description	Department	Buyer
100100	Std. Scuba Tank, Yellow	Water Sports	Pete Hansen
100200	Std. Scuba Tank, Magenta	Water Sports	Pete Hansen
101100	Dive Mask, Small Clear	Water Sports	Nancy Meyers
101200	Dive Mask, Med Clear	Water Sports	Nancy Meyers
201000	Half-dome Tent	Camping	Cindy Lo
202000	Half-dome Tent Footprint	Camping	Cindy Lo
301000	Light Fly Climbing Harness	Climbing	Jerry Martin
302000	Locking carabiner, Oval	Climbing	Jerry Martin

which contains all rows and all of the columns in the SKU_DATA table.

Reading Specified Rows from a Single Table

Suppose we want all of the columns of the SKU_DATA table, but we want only the rows for the Water Sports department. We can obtain that result by using the WHERE clause as follows:

SELECT   *

FROM   **SKU_DATA**

WHERE   **Department = 'Water Sports';**

The result of this SQL statement is:

SKU	SKU_Description	Department	Buyer
100100	Std. Scuba Tank, Yellow	Water Sports	Pete Hansen
100200	Std. Scuba Tank, Magenta	Water Sports	Pete Hansen
101100	Dive Mask, Small Clear	Water Sports	Nancy Meyers
101200	Dive Mask, Med Clear	Water Sports	Nancy Meyers

In a WHERE clause, if the column contains text or date data, the comparison values must be enclosed in single quotation marks (' '). If the column contains numeric data, however, the comparison values need not be in quotes. Thus, to find all of the SKU rows with a value greater than 200,000, we would code:

```
SELECT        *
FROM          SKU_DATA
WHERE         SKU > 200000;
```

The result is:

SKU	SKU_Description	Department	Buyer
201000	Half-dome Tent	Camping	Cindy Lo
202000	Half-dome Tent Footprint	Camping	Cindy Lo
301000	Light Fly Climbing Harness	Climbing	Jerry Martin
302000	Locking carabiner, Oval	Climbing	Jerry Martin

As stated, the comparison value for a numeric column is not enclosed in quotes. Notice, too, that no comma is provided in the numeric value.

Reading Specified Columns and Specified Rows from a Single Table

So far, we have selected certain columns and all rows and we have selected all columns and certain rows. We can combine these operations to select certain columns and certain rows by naming the columns we want and using the WHERE clause. For example, to obtain the SKU_Description and Department of all products in the Climbing department, we specify:

```
SELECT        SKU_Description, Department
FROM          SKU_DATA
WHERE         Department = 'Climbing';
```

The result is:

SKU_Description	Department
Light Fly Climbing Harness	Climbing
Locking carabiner, Oval	Climbing

SQL does not require that the column used in the WHERE clause also appear in the SELECT column list. Thus, we can specify:

```
SELECT        SKU_Description, Buyer
FROM          SKU_DATA
WHERE         Department = 'Climbing';
```

where the qualifying column, Department, does not appear in the SELECT column list. The result is:

SKU_Description	Buyer
Light Fly Climbing Harness	Jerry Martin
Locking carabiner, Oval	Jerry Martin

> **B T W**
>
> Standard practice is to write SQL statements with SELECT, FROM, and WHERE on separate lines. This practice is just a coding convention, however; SQL parsers do not require it. You could code the last SQL statement as SELECT SKU_Description, Buyer FROM SKU_DATA WHERE Department = 'Climbing';, all on one line, and all DBMS products would process it. The standard multiline coding convention makes SQL easier to read, however. You are encouraged to write your SQL according to it.

Submitting SQL Statements to the DBMS

Before continuing the explanation of SQL, it will be useful for you to learn how to submit SQL statements to a DBMS. That way, you can work along with the text by keying and running SQL statements as you read the discussion.

> **B T W**
>
> You can learn SQL without running the queries in a DBMS. If for some reason you do not have Access, SQL Server, or Oracle, do not despair. You can learn SQL without them. Chances are your instructor, like most of us in practice today, learned SQL without a DBMS. It is just that SQL statements are easier to understand and remember if you can run the SQL while you read.

The particular means by which you submit SQL statements depends on the DBMS. Here we will describe the process for Access, SQL Server, and Oracle.

Submitting SQL to Access

Before you can execute SQL statements, you need a computer that has Access installed, and you need an Access database that contains the tables and sample data in Figure 2-3. Access is part of many versions of Microsoft Office, so it should not be too difficult to find a computer that has it.

Some menu choices vary slightly among the different versions of Access. The discussion here is based on Access 2003. If you have a different version of Access, the commands may be slightly different. This should not pose a significant problem, however.

To obtain the database, tables, and data in Figure 2-3, you can proceed in one of two ways. First, you can download the Access database named Chapter_2.mdb from this text's Web site at *www.prenhall.com/kroenke*. Alternatively, you can create your own database and then add the tables and data in Figure 2-3 using the process explained in Appendix A. You will need to do one or the other before you can proceed.

To process a SQL statement in Access, open the database and create a new Query window by clicking the Queries tab on the left-hand side of the Access window. Then click New along the top of the database window as shown in Figure 2-4. Click OK to select Design View and then click Close on the Show Table dialog box. (Because we are entering our own SQL, we need not specify a table in this window.) Next, select View on the Access menu and then click SQL View as shown in Figure 2-5.

Figure 2-4

**Creating a New Query
in Access**

Figure 2-5

**Selecting SQL View
in Access**

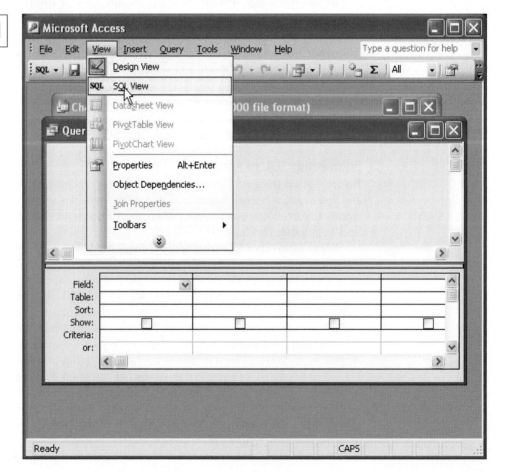

Figure 2-6

Running SQL Code in Access

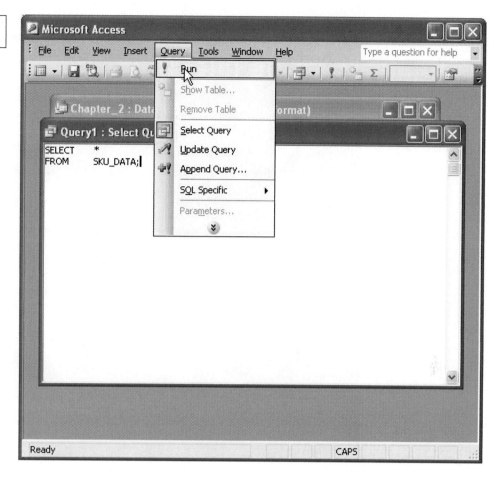

Next, enter a SQL statement into the blank window that appears. In Figure 2-6, the following SQL statement has been entered:

SELECT   *

FROM   **SKU_DATA;**

After keying in the SQL statement, click Query on the Access menu and click Run as shown in Figure 2-6. The results will appear as shown in Figure 2-7.

If you wish to change your query statement or enter a new one, select View from the Access menu and then select SQL View as before. At this point, you can change your SQL statement or key a new one. You also can save the statement by selecting File/Save while the query window is active.

B T W

Microsoft Access is a DBMS product for beginners. It does not correctly process all of the SQL statements in this chapter. The SQL statements shown here are standard SQL that you need to know. Rather than reduce our discussion to just those statements that Access can process, we will show all important SQL statements and mark any that Access cannot process as {Fails in Access}. It is frustrating that Access is unable to process certain SQL statements. If it bothers you, write to Microsoft and tell them to fix the Access SQL parser.

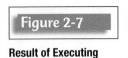

Figure 2-7

Result of Executing the Query in Access

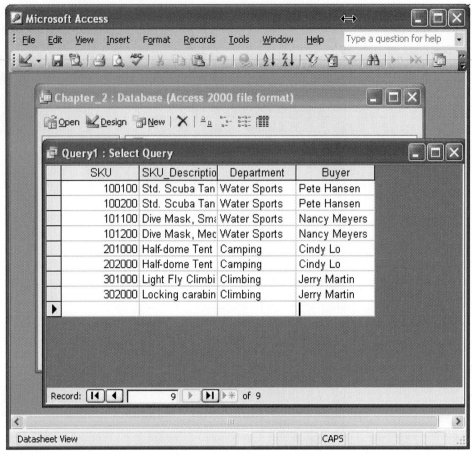

Submitting SQL to SQL Server

Before you can enter SQL statements to SQL Server, you need access to a computer that has SQL Server installed and that has a database with the tables and data shown in Figure 2-3. Your instructor may have installed SQL Server in your computer lab and entered the data for you. If so, follow his or her instructions for accessing that database.

Alternatively, if you purchased the version of this text that is shrink-wrapped with the SQL Server Trial Version, you can install that trial version on any Windows computer and then create the tables and data in Figure 2-3. You will need to read the introductory discussion to SQL Server in Chapter 11, starting on page 372. Also, the text's Web site has files and instructions that will help you create the Cape Codd extract database in SQL Server.

The easiest way to practice SQL with SQL Server is to enter SQL statements into the Query Analyzer window as explained in Chapter 11. Figure 2-8 shows the execution of the SQL statement:

SELECT   *

FROM   **SKU_DATA;**

in the SQL Server Query Analyzer.

Submitting SQL to Oracle

Before you can enter SQL statements to Oracle, you need access to a computer that has Oracle installed and that has a database with the tables and data shown in Figure 2-3.

Figure 2-8

Executing SQL Using the SQL Server Query Analyzer

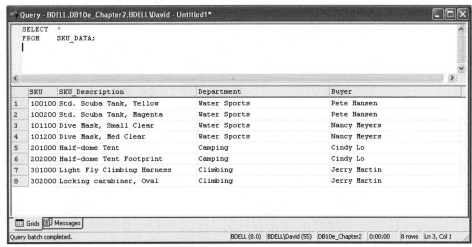

Your instructor may have installed Oracle on a computer in the lab and entered the data for you. If so, follow his or her instructions for accessing that database. Alternatively, if you purchased the version of this text that is shrink-wrapped with Personal Oracle, you can install that trial version on any Windows computer and then create the tables and data in Figure 2-3. Follow the instructions in the introduction to Oracle in Chapter 10, starting on page 326. Also, the text's Web site has files and instructions that will help you create the Cape Codd extract database in Oracle.

The easiest way to practice SQL with Oracle is to enter SQL statements into the Oracle tool SQL Plus as explained in Chapter 10. Figure 2-9 shows the execution of the SQL statement:

SELECT   SKU, DEPARTMENT, BUYER

FROM   SKU_DATA;

in SQL Plus.

You can also enter statements into Oracle using a graphical Windows tool, which is illustrated on pages 340–342. Doing so, however, takes you away from the classic Oracle that *real* database administrators use. If you're going to work with Oracle, at least use SQL Plus for a while.

Figure 2-9

Executing SQL Using Oracle's SQL Plus

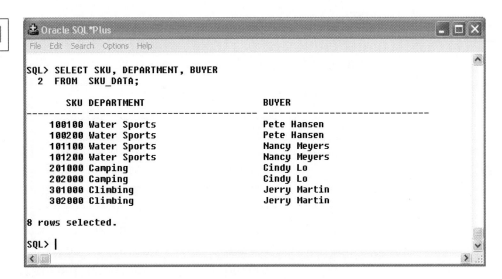

Continuation of SQL for Querying a Single Table

This section presents more SQL statements for processing a single table. As we proceed, you will begin to see how powerful SQL can be for querying databases and for creating information from existing data. For illustration, the output shown here was generated using SQL Server; output from other DBMS products will be similar.

Sorting the Results

The order of the rows produced by a SQL statement is arbitrary and determined by programs in the bowels of each DBMS. The example result in Figure 2-3 was produced by Access, and it determined the order shown. Oracle, SQL Server, DB2, and other DBMS products will produce different orders. Note also that for the ORDER_ITEM table, the rows for order 3000 are mixed throughout the results.

If you want the DBMS to display the rows in a particular order, you can use the ORDER BY phrase. For example, the SQL statement:

SELECT   *

FROM   **ORDER_ITEM**

ORDER BY   **OrderNumber;**

will result in the following:

OrderNumber	SKU	Quantity	Price	ExtendedPrice
1000	201000	1	300.0000	300.0000
1000	202000	1	130.0000	130.0000
2000	101100	4	50.0000	200.0000
2000	101200	2	50.0000	100.0000
3000	101200	1	50.0000	50.0000
3000	101100	2	50.0000	100.0000
3000	100200	1	300.0000	300.0000

We can sort by two columns by adding a second column name. For example, to sort first by OrderNumber and then by Price within OrderNumber, code the following:

SELECT   *

FROM   **ORDER_ITEM**

ORDER BY   **OrderNumber, Price;**

The result is:

OrderNumber	SKU	Quantity	Price	ExtendedPrice
1000	202000	1	130.0000	130.0000
1000	201000	1	300.0000	300.0000
2000	101100	4	50.0000	200.0000
2000	101200	2	50.0000	100.0000
3000	101200	1	50.0000	50.0000
3000	101100	2	50.0000	100.0000
3000	100200	1	300.0000	300.0000

If we want to sort the data by Price and then by OrderNumber, we would reverse the order of those columns in the ORDER BY clause as follows:

SELECT   *

FROM   **ORDER_ITEM**

ORDER BY   **Price, OrderNumber;**

Note to Access users: Unlike the SQL Server output shown here, Access displays dollar signs in the output of currency data.

By default, rows are sorted in ascending order. To sort in descending order, add the keyword DESC after the column name. Thus, to sort first by Price in descending order and then by OrderNumber in ascending order, we can specify:

SELECT   *

FROM   **ORDER_ITEM**

ORDER BY   **Price DESC, OrderNumber ASC;**

The result is:

OrderNumber	SKU	Quantity	Price	ExtendedPrice
1000	201000	1	300.0000	300.0000
3000	100200	1	300.0000	300.0000
1000	202000	1	130.0000	130.0000
2000	101100	4	50.0000	200.0000
2000	101200	2	50.0000	100.0000
3000	101200	1	50.0000	50.0000
3000	101100	2	50.0000	100.0000

Because the default order is ascending, it is unnecessary to specify ASC in the last SQL statement. Thus, the following SQL statement is equivalent:

SELECT   *

FROM   **ORDER_ITEM**

ORDER BY   **Price DESC, OrderNumber;**

WHERE Clause Options

SQL includes a number of WHERE clause options that greatly expand SQL's power and utility. In this section, we consider three options: compound clauses, ranges, and wildcards.

Compound WHERE Clauses

SQL WHERE clauses can include multiple conditions by using the AND, OR, IN, and NOT IN operators. For example, to find all of the rows in SKU_DATA that have a Department named Water Sports and a Buyer named Nancy Meyers, we can code:

SELECT   *

FROM   **SKU_DATA**

WHERE   **Department = 'Water Sports'**

    AND   **Buyer = 'Nancy Meyers';**

The result is:

SKU	SKU_Description	Department	Buyer
101100	Dive Mask, Small Clear	Water Sports	Nancy Meyers
101200	Dive Mask, Med Clear	Water Sports	Nancy Meyers

Similarly, to find all of the rows of SKU_DATA for either the Camping or Climbing departments, we can code:

SELECT   *

FROM   **SKU_DATA**

WHERE   **Department = 'Camping'**

     OR   **Department = 'Climbing';**

The result is:

SKU	SKU_Description	Department	Buyer
201000	Half-dome Tent	Camping	Cindy Lo
202000	Half-dome Tent Footprint	Camping	Cindy Lo
301000	Light Fly Climbing Harness	Climbing	Jerry Martin
302000	Locking carabiner, Oval	Climbing	Jerry Martin

Three or more AND and OR conditions can be combined, but in such cases the IN and NOT IN operators are easier to use. For example, suppose we want to obtain all of the rows in SKU_DATA for buyers Nancy Meyers, Cindy Lo, and Jerry Martin. We could construct a WHERE clause with two ANDs, but an easier way to do this is to use the IN keyword as follows:

SELECT   *

FROM   **SKU_DATA**

WHERE   **Buyer IN ('Nancy Meyers', 'Cindy Lo', 'Jerry Martin');**

In this format, a set of values is enclosed in parentheses. A row is selected if Buyer is equal to any one of the values provided. The result is:

SKU	SKU_Description	Department	Buyer
101100	Dive Mask, Small Clear	Water Sports	Nancy Meyers
101200	Dive Mask, Med Clear	Water Sports	Nancy Meyers
201000	Half-dome Tent	Camping	Cindy Lo
202000	Half-dome Tent Footprint	Camping	Cindy Lo
301000	Light Fly Climbing Harness	Climbing	Jerry Martin
302000	Locking carabiner, Oval	Climbing	Jerry Martin

Similarly, if we want to find rows of SKU_DATA for which the buyer is someone other than Nancy Meyers, Cindy Lo, or Jerry Martin, we would code:

SELECT   *

FROM   **SKU_DATA**

WHERE   **Buyer NOT IN ('Nancy Meyers', 'Cindy Lo', 'Jerry Martin');**

The result is:

SKU	SKU_Description	Department	Buyer
100100	Std. Scuba Tank, Yellow	Water Sports	Pete Hansen
100200	Std. Scuba Tank, Magenta	Water Sports	Pete Hansen

Observe an important difference between IN and NOT IN. A row qualifies for an IN condition if the column is equal to *any* of the values in the parentheses. However, a row qualifies for a NOT IN condition if it is not equal to *all* of the items in the parentheses.

Ranges in WHERE Clauses

SQL WHERE clauses can specify ranges of data values by using the BETWEEN keyword. For example, the following SQL statement:

SELECT   *

FROM   ORDER_ITEM

WHERE   ExtendedPrice BETWEEN 100 AND 200;

will produce the following:

OrderNumber	SKU	Quantity	Price	ExtendedPrice
2000	101100	4	50.0000	200.0000
3000	101100	2	50.0000	100.0000
2000	101200	2	50.0000	100.0000
1000	202000	1	130.0000	130.0000

Notice that both the ends of the range, 100 and 200, are included in the resulting table. The preceding SQL statement is equivalent to:

SELECT   *

FROM   ORDER_ITEM

WHERE   ExtendedPrice > = 100

    AND   ExtendedPrice < = 200;

Note, too, that the ORDER BY keyword can be combined with any WHERE clause:

SELECT   *

FROM   ORDER_ITEM

WHERE   ExtendedPrice BETWEEN 100 AND 200

ORDER BY   OrderNumber DESC;

which will produce the following result:

OrderNumber	SKU	Quantity	Price	ExtendedPrice
3000	101100	2	50.0000	100.0000
2000	101200	2	50.0000	100.0000
2000	101100	4	50.0000	200.0000
1000	202000	1	130.0000	130.0000

Wildcards in WHERE Clauses

The keyword LIKE can be used in WHERE clauses to specify matches on portions of column values. For example, suppose we want to find the rows in the SKU_DATA table for all buyers whose first name is Pete. To find such rows, we use the keyword LIKE with the wildcard character % as follows:

SELECT   *

FROM   SKU_DATA

WHERE   Buyer LIKE 'Pete%';

The percent symbol (%) is a wildcard that stands for any sequence of characters. When used with LIKE, the string 'Pete%' means any sequence of characters that start with the letters *Pete*. The result of this query is:

SKU	SKU_Description	Department	Buyer
100100	Std. Scuba Tank, Yellow	Water Sports	Pete Hansen
100200	Std. Scuba Tank, Magenta	Water Sports	Pete Hansen

> The wildcard % and underscore (_) characters are specified in the SQL-92 standard. They are accepted by all DBMS products *except Microsoft Access*. For Access, use the asterisk (*) instead of the % and a ? instead of the underscore. This difference exists because the designers of Access chose to follow the Microsoft DOS wildcards rather than the SQL-92 wildcards.

Suppose we want to find the rows in SKU_DATA for which the SKU_Description includes the word *Tent* somewhere in the description. Because the word *Tent* could be at the front, the end, or in the middle, we need to place a wildcard on both ends of the LIKE phrase as follows:

SELECT   *

FROM   SKU_DATA

WHERE   SKU_Description LIKE '%Tent%';

The result is:

SKU	SKU_Description	Department	Buyer
201000	Half-dome Tent	Camping	Cindy Lo
202000	Half-dome Tent Footprint	Camping	Cindy Lo

This query will find rows in which the word *Tent* occurs in any place in the SKU_Description.

Sometimes we need to search for a particular value in a particular location in the column. For example, assume SKU values are coded such that a 2 in the third position from the right has some particular significance, maybe it means that the product is a variation of another product. For whatever reason, assume that we need to find all

SKUs that have a 2 in the third column from the right. Suppose we try the following SQL statement:

```
SELECT      *

FROM        SKU_DATA

WHERE       SKU LIKE '%2%';
```

The result is:

SKU	SKU_Description	Department	Buyer
100200	Std. Scuba Tank, Magenta	Water Sports	Pete Hansen
101200	Dive Mask, Med Clear	Water Sports	Nancy Meyers
201000	Half-dome Tent	Camping	Cindy Lo
202000	Half-dome Tent Footprint	Camping	Cindy Lo
302000	Locking carabiner, Oval	Climbing	Jerry Martin

This is *not* what we wanted. We mistakenly retrieved all rows that had a 2 in any position in the value of SKU.

To find such products correctly, we cannot use SKU LIKE '%2%'. Instead, we must use an underscore (_) to represent a single, unspecified character. The following SQL statement will find all SKU_DATA rows with a value of 2 in the third position:

```
SELECT      *

FROM        SKU_DATA

WHERE       SKU LIKE '%2_ _';
```

Observe that there are two underscores; one for the first position on the right and another for the second position on the right. The result is:

SKU	SKU_Description	Department	Buyer
100200	Std. Scuba Tank, Magenta	Water Sports	Pete Hansen
101200	Dive Mask, Med Clear	Water Sports	Nancy Meyers

which is the result we want.

Performing Calculations in SQL Queries

It is possible to perform certain types of calculations in SQL query statements. One group of calculations involves the use of built-in SQL functions. Another group involves simple arithmetic operations on the columns in the SELECT statement. We will consider each in turn.

Using SQL Built-in Functions

SQL provides five built-in functions for performing arithmetic on table columns: SUM, AVG, MIN, MAX, and COUNT. Some DBMS products extend these standard built-in functions by providing additional functions. Here, we will focus on the five standard functions.

Suppose we want to know the sum of OrderTotal for all of the orders in RETAIL_ORDER. We can obtain that sum as follows:

```
SELECT      SUM (OrderTotal)

FROM        RETAIL_ORDER;
```

The result will be:

```
(No column name)
```
```
1235.0000
```

Recall that the result of a SQL statement is always a table. In this case, the table has one row and one column that contains the sum of OrderTotal.

The OrderTotal sum is not a column in a table, so the DBMS has no column name to provide. The preceding result was produced by SQL Server, and it names the column '(No column name)'. Other DBMS products take other equivalent actions.

This result is ugly. We would prefer to have a meaningful column name, and SQL allows us to assign one using the AS keyword. If we specify:

SELECT   **SUM (OrderTotal) AS OrderSum**

FROM   **RETAIL_ORDER;**

The result will be:

```
OrderSum
```
```
1235.0000
```

which is a more meaningful label. The name *OrderSum* is arbitrary; we are free to pick any name that we think would be meaningful to the user of the result. We could pick OrderTotal_Total, OrderTotalSum, or whatever.

The utility of the built-in functions increases when you use them with a WHERE clause. For example, we can code:

SELECT   **SUM (ExtendedPrice) AS Order3000Sum**

FROM   **ORDER_ITEM**

WHERE   **OrderNumber = 3000;**

The result is:

```
Order3000Sum
```
```
450.0000
```

The built-in functions can be mixed and matched in a single statement. For example, we can code:

SELECT   **SUM (ExtendedPrice) AS OrderItemSum,**

             AVG (ExtendedPrice) AS OrderItemAvg,

             MIN (ExtendedPrice) AS OrderItemMin,

             MAX (ExtendedPrice) AS OrderItemMax

FROM   **ORDER_ITEM;**

The result is:

OrderItemSum	OrderItemAvg	OrderItemMin	OrderItemMax
1180.0000	168.5714	50.0000	300.0000

The function COUNT sounds similar to SUM, but it is different. COUNT counts the number of rows, whereas SUM adds the values in a column. If we code:

SELECT   COUNT(*) AS NumRows

FROM   ORDER_ITEM;

the result will be:

NumRows
7

This result indicates there are seven rows in the table. Notice that we need to provide an asterisk after the COUNT function when we want to count rows. COUNT is the only built-in function that requires an asterisk. Also, COUNT can be used on any type of data, but SUM, AVG, MIN, and MAX can only be used on numeric data.

COUNT can have some surprising results. For example, suppose you want to count the number of departments in the SKU_DATA table. If we code:

SELECT   COUNT (Department) AS DeptCount

FROM   SKU_DATA;

the result will be:

DeptCount
8

which is the number of rows in the SKU_DATA table and not the number of unique values of Department. If we want to count the unique values of Department, we need to use the DISTINCT keyword as follows:

SELECT   COUNT (DISTINCT Department) AS DeptCount

FROM   SKU_DATA;

{Fails in Access}
The result is:

DeptCount
3

Except for grouping (defined later), you cannot combine a table column name with a built-in function. If we code:

SELECT   Department, COUNT(*)

FROM   SKU_DATA;

the result in SQL Server is:

```
Server: Msg 8118, Level 16, State 1, Line 1
Column 'SKU_DATA.Department' is invalid in the select list because it is
not contained in an aggregate function and there is no GROUP BY clause.
```

(This error message is particular to SQL Server. However, you will receive an equivalent message from Access, Oracle, or DB2.)

You should understand one other limitation of built-in functions. You cannot use them in a WHERE clause. Thus, you cannot code:

SELECT   *

FROM   **RETAIL_ORDER**

WHERE   **OrderTotal > AVG (OrderTotal);**

An attempt to code such a statement will also result in an error statement from the DBMS. In Chapter 7, you will learn how to obtain the desired result using a sequence of SQL views.

Arithmetic in SELECT Statements

It is possible to do basic arithmetic in SQL statements. For example, suppose we want to compute the values of extended price, perhaps because we want to verify the accuracy of the data in the ORDER_ITEM table. To compute the extended price, we code:

SELECT   **Quantity * Price AS EP**

FROM   **ORDER_ITEM;**

The result is:

EP
300.0000
200.0000
100.0000
100.0000
50.0000
300.0000
130.0000

If we want to compare this computed value to the stored value of ExtendedPrice, we can code:

SELECT   **Quantity * Price AS EP, ExtendedPrice**

FROM   **ORDER_ITEM;**

The result is:

EP	ExtendedPrice
300.0000	300.0000
200.0000	200.0000
100.0000	100.0000
100.0000	100.0000
50.0000	50.0000
300.0000	300.0000
130.0000	130.0000

Now we can visually compare the two values to ensure that the stored data are correct.

Another use for expressions in SQL statements is to perform string manipulation. Suppose we want to combine the Buyer and Department columns into a single column named Sponsor. If we code the statement:

SELECT   **Buyer + 'in' + Department AS Sponsor**

FROM   **SKU_DATA;**

the result will be:

Sponsor	
Pete Hansen	in Water Sports
Pete Hansen	in Water Sports
Nancy Meyers	in Water Sports
Nancy Meyers	in Water Sports
Cindy Lo	in Camping
Cindy Lo	in Camping
Jerry Martin	in Climbing
Jerry Martin	in Climbing

This result is also ugly. We can eliminate the extra spaces by using more advanced functions. The syntax and use of such functions vary from one DBMS to another, however, and a discussion of the features of each product will take us away from the point of this discussion. To learn more, search on *string functions* in the documentation for your DBMS.

Just to illustrate the possibilities, however, here is a SQL Server statement that strips the tailing blanks off the right-hand side of Buyer and Department:

SELECT   **DISTINCT RTRIM (Buyer) + 'in' + RTRIM (Department) AS Sponsor**

FROM   **SKU_DATA;**

The result is:

Sponsor
Cindy Lo in Camping
Jerry Martin in Climbing
Nancy Meyers in Water Sports
Pete Hansen in Water Sports

This result is more visually pleasing.

Grouping

In SQL, rows can be grouped according to common values using the GROUP BY keyword. For example, if you specify GROUP BY Department in a SELECT statement on the SKU_DATA table, the DBMS will first sort all rows by Department and then combine all of the rows having the same value into a group for that department. As many groups will be formed as there are unique values of Department.

For example, the SQL statement:

SELECT   **Department, COUNT(*) AS Dept_SKU_Count**

FROM   **SKU_DATA**

GROUP BY   **Department;**

produces the following result:

Department	Dept_SKU_Count
Camping	2
Climbing	2
Water Sports	4

To obtain this result, the DBMS first sorts the rows according to Department and then counts the number of rows having the same value of Department.

Another example using GROUP BY is:

SELECT   **SKU, AVG (ExtendedPrice) AS AvgEP**

FROM   **ORDER_ITEM**

GROUP BY   **SKU;**

The result for this statement is:

SKU	AvgEP
100200	300.0000
101100	150.0000
101200	75.0000
201000	300.0000
202000	130.0000

Here the rows have been sorted and grouped by SKU and the average ExtendedPrice for each group of SKU items has been calculated.

More than one column can be included in a GROUP BY expression. For example, the SQL statement:

SELECT   **Department, Buyer, COUNT(*) AS Dept_Buyer_SKU_Count**

FROM   **SKU_DATA**

GROUP BY   **Department, Buyer;**

groups rows according to the value of Department first, then according to Buyer, and then counts the number of rows for each combination of Department and Buyer. The result is:

Department	Buyer	Dept_Buyer_SKU_Count
Camping	Cindy Lo	2
Climbing	Jerry Martin	2
Water Sports	Nancy Meyers	2
Water Sports	Pete Hansen	2

When using GROUP BY, only the column or columns in the GROUP BY expression and the SQL built-in functions can be used in the SELECT expression. The following expressions will result in an error:

SELECT	**SKU, Department, COUNT(*) AS Dept_SKU_Count**
FROM	**SKU_DATA**
GROUP BY	**Department;**

Statements like this one are invalid because there are many values of SKU for each Department group. The DBMS has no place to put those multiple values in the result. If you do not understand the problem, try to process this statement by hand. It cannot be done.

Of course, WHERE and ORDER BY clauses can also be used with SELECT statements, as shown here:

SELECT	**Department, COUNT(*) AS Dept_SKU_Count**
FROM	**SKU_DATA**
WHERE	**SKU <> 302000**
GROUP BY	**Department**
ORDER BY	**Dept_SKU_Count;**

{Fails in Access.}
The result is:

Department	Dept_SKU_Count
Climbing	1
Camping	2
Water Sports	4

Notice that one of the rows of the Climbing department has been removed from the count because it did not meet the WHERE condition. Without the ORDER BY clause, the rows would be presented in arbitrary order of Department. With it, the order is as shown.

In general, place WHERE before GROUP BY. Some DBMS products do not require that placement, but others do. To be safe, always put WHERE before GROUP BY.

SQL provides one more GROUP BY feature that extends its functionality even further. The HAVING operator restricts the groups that are presented in the result.

We can restrict the previous query to display only groups having more than one row by coding:

SELECT	**Department, COUNT(*) AS Dept_SKU_Count**
FROM	**SKU_DATA**
WHERE	**SKU <> 302000**
GROUP BY	**Department**
HAVING	**COUNT (*) > 1**
ORDER BY	**Dept_SKU_Count;**

{Fails in Access}
The result is:

Department	Dept_SKU_Count
Camping	2
Water Sports	4

Comparing this result with the previous one, the row for Climbing (which has a count of 1) has been eliminated.

B T W

Any SQL built-in function can be used in the HAVING clause. For example, the following is valid SQL:

SELECT	COUNT(*) AS SKU_Count, SUM(Price) AS TotalRev, SKU
FROM	ORDER_ITEM
GROUP BY	SKU
HAVING	SUM (Price) = 100;

Run this query to see the results.

Be aware that there is an ambiguity in statements that include both WHERE and HAVING clauses. The results vary depending on whether the WHERE condition is applied before or after the HAVING. To eliminate this ambiguity, WHERE is *always* applied before HAVING.

Looking for Patterns in NASDAQ Trading

Before we continue our discussion of SQL, consider an example problem that will illustrate the power of the SQL just described.

Suppose that a friend tells you that she suspects the stock market tends to go up on certain days of the week and down on others. She asks you to investigate past trading data to determine if this is true. Specifically, she wants to trade an index fund called the NASDAQ 100, which is a stock fund of the 100 top companies traded on the NASDAQ exchange. She gives you a table of data of past years of NASDAQ 100 trading data for analysis. Assume she gives you the data in the form of a table named NDX in a relational database. (You can find this table on this text's Web site at *www.prenhall.com/kroenke*.)

Investigating the Characteristics of the Data

Suppose you first decide to investigate the general characteristics of the data. You begin by seeing what columns are present in the table by issuing the query:

SELECT   *

FROM   NDX;

The first five rows of that query are as follows:

TClose	PriorClose	ChangeClose	Volume	TMonth	TDayOfMonth	TYear	TDayOfWeek	TQuarter
1520.46	1530.65	-10.1900...	24827600.0	January	9	2004	Friday	1
1530...	1514.26	16.39000...	26839500.0	January	8	2004	Thursday	1
1514.26	1501.26	13.0	22942800.0	January	7	2004	Wednesday	1
1501.26	1496.58	4.680000...	22732200.0	January	6	2004	Tuesday	1
1496...	1463.57	33.00999...	23629100.0	January	5	2004	Monday	1

Assume that you learn that the first column has the value of the fund at the close of a trading day, the second column has the value of the fund at the close of the prior trading day, and the third row has the difference between the current day's close and the prior day's close. Volume is the number of shares traded, and the rest of the data concerns the trading date.

Next, you decide to investigate the change of the stock price by issuing the query:

SELECT   AVG (ChangeClose) AS AverageChange,

              MAX (ChangeClose) AS MaxGain,

              MIN (ChangeClose) AS MaxLoss

FROM   NDX;

The result is:

AverageChange	MaxGain	MaxLoss
0.28116702819958445	399.59999999999991	-401.02999999999992

B T W

DBMS products have many functions for formatting query results to reduce the number of decimal points displayed, to add currency characters such as $ or £, or to make other formatting changes. However, these functions are DBMS-dependent. Search the documentation of your DBMS for the term *formatting results* to learn more about such functions.

Just out of curiosity, you decide to determine which days had the maximum and minimum change. To avoid having to key in the long string of decimal places that would be required to make an equal comparison, you use a greater than and less than comparison with values that are close:

SELECT   ChangeClose, TMonth, TDayOfMonth, TYear

FROM   NDX

WHERE   ChangeClose > 398

   OR   ChangeClose < -400;

The result is:

ChangeClose	TMonth	TDayOfMonth	TYear
-401.02999999999992	January	3	1994
399.59999999999991	January	3	2001

This result is surprising! Is there some reason that both the greatest loss and the greatest gain both occurred on January 3? You begin to wonder if your friend might have a promising idea.

Searching for Patterns in Trading by Day of Week

You want to determine if there is a difference in the average trade by day of week. Accordingly, you create the SQL statement:

SELECT   TDayOfWeek, AVG (ChangeClose) AS AvgChange

FROM   NDX

GROUP BY   TDayOfWeek;

The result is:

TDayOfWeek	AvgChange
Monday	-1.0357792946529938
Tuesday	-0.7144067796608546
Friday	0.1460217391304174
Wednesday	0.7779405520170057
Thursday	2.1741297297297497

Indeed, there does seem to be a difference according to the day of the week. The NASDAQ 100 appears to go down on Monday and Tuesday and then go up on the other three days of the week. Thursday, in particular, seems to be a good day to trade long.

But, you begin to wonder, is this pattern true for each year? To answer that question, you code:

SELECT   TDayOfWeek, TYear, AVG (ChangeClose) AS AvgChange

FROM   NDX

GROUP BY   TDayOfWeek, TYear

ORDER BY   TDayOfWeek, TYear DESC;

Because there are 20 years of data, this query results in 100 rows. To ease your analysis, you decide to restrict the number of rows to the most recent five years:

SELECT   TDayOfWeek, TYear, AVG (ChangeClose) AS AvgChange

FROM   NDX

WHERE   TYear > '1999'

GROUP BY   TDayOfWeek, TYear

ORDER BY   TDayOfWeek, TYear DESC;

Partial results from this query are as follows:

TDayOfWeek	TYear	AvgChange
Friday	2004	-7.2700000000000955
Friday	2003	-2.4849999999999635
Friday	2002	-2.1941999999999688
Friday	2001	-19.594399999999979
Friday	2000	8.8980392156862962
Monday	2004	33.009999999999991
Monday	2003	3.7741666666666802
Monday	2002	-2.6022916666666447
Monday	2001	-3.7527083333332976
Monday	2000	-19.899574468085014
Thursday	2004	16.3900000000001
Thursday	2003	5.7070000000000229
Thursday	2002	-3.779799999999975
Thursday	2001	9.3144000000000329
Thursday	2000	24.766274509803957
Tuesday	2004	4.6800000000000637
Tuesday	2003	4.4130769230769431
Tuesday	2002	-7.858823529411759
Tuesday	2001	-8.8845999999999723
Tuesday	2000	-3.5062745098038532
Wednesday	2004	13.0
Wednesday	2003	-1.6959615384615176

Alas, it does not appear that day of week is a very good predictor of gain or loss. At least not for this fund over this period of time.

We could continue this discussion to further analyze this data, but by now you should understand how useful SQL can be for processing a table. Suggested additional exercises are included in the SQL problems at the end of this chapter.

Now we will conclude this chapter by describing SQL for querying two or more tables.

Querying Two or More Tables with SQL

Suppose that you want to know the revenue generated by SKUs managed by the Water Sports department. We can compute revenue as the sum of ExtendedPrice, but we have a problem. ExtendedPrice is stored in the ORDER_ITEM table, and Department is stored in the SKU_DATA table. We need to process data in two tables, and all of the SQL presented so far operates on a single table at a time.

SQL provides two different techniques for querying data from multiple tables: subqueries and joins. Although both work with multiple tables, they are used for slightly different purposes, as you will learn.

Querying Multiple Tables with Subqueries

How can we obtain the sum of ExtendedPrice for items managed by the Water Sports department? If we somehow knew the SKU values for those items, we could use a WHERE clause with the IN keyword.

For the data in Figure 2-3, the SKU values for items in Water Sports are 100100, 100200, 101100, and 101200. Knowing those values, we can obtain the sum of their ExtendedPrice with the following SQL statement:

SELECT	SUM (ExtendedPrice) AS Revenue
FROM	ORDER_ITEM
WHERE	SKU IN (100100, 100200, 101100, 101200);

The result is:

Revenue
750.0000

But in general, we do not know the necessary SKU values ahead of time. We do have a way to obtain them, however, using SQL on the SKU_DATA table. To obtain the SKU values for the Water Sports department, we just code:

SELECT	SKU
FROM	SKU_DATA
WHERE	Department = 'Water Sports';

The result of this SQL statement is:

SKU
100100
100200
101100
101200

which is the desired list of SKU values.

Now we need only combine the last two SQL statements to obtain the result we want. We replace the list of values in the first SQL statement with the second SQL expression as follows:

SELECT	SUM (ExtendedPrice) AS Revenue	
FROM	ORDER_ITEM	
WHERE	SKU IN	
	(SELECT	SKU
	FROM	SKU_DATA
	WHERE	Department = 'Water Sports');

The result is:

Revenue
750.0000

which is the same result as before.

The second SELECT statement, the one enclosed in parentheses, is called a **subquery.** We can use multiple subqueries to process three or even more tables. For example, suppose we want to know the name of the buyers who manage any product purchased in January 2004. First, note that Buyer is stored in the SKU_DATA table and OrderMonth and OrderYear are stored in the RETAIL_ORDER table.

We can use a SQL statement with two subqueries to obtain the desired data as follows:

```
SELECT      Buyer
FROM        SKU_DATA
WHERE       SKU IN
            (SELECT      SKU
             FROM        ORDER_ITEM
             WHERE       OrderNumber IN
                         (SELECT      OrderNumber
                          FROM        RETAIL_ORDER
                          WHERE       OrderMonth = 'January'
                          AND         OrderYear = 2004));
```

The result of this statement is:

Buyer
Pete Hansen
Nancy Meyers
Nancy Meyers

To understand this statement, work from the bottom up. The bottom SELECT obtains the list of OrderNumbers of orders sold in January 2004. The middle SQL statement obtains the SKU values for items sold in orders in January 2004. Finally, the top-level SELECT obtains Buyer for all of the SKUs found in the middle SELECT.

Any of the SQL that you have learned earlier in this chapter can be applied to a table generated by a subquery, regardless of how complicated the SQL looks. For example, we can apply DISTINCT on the results to eliminate duplicate rows. Or, we can apply GROUP BY and ORDER BY as follows:

```
SELECT      Buyer, COUNT (*) AS NumberSold
FROM        SKU_DATA
WHERE       SKU IN
            (SELECT      SKU
             FROM        ORDER_ITEM
             WHERE       OrderNumber IN
                         (SELECT      OrderNumber
                          FROM        RETAIL_ORDER
                          WHERE       OrderMonth = 'January'
                          AND         OrderYear = 2004))
GROUP BY    Buyer
ORDER BY NumberSold DESC;
```

{Fails in Access}

The result is:

Buyer	NumberSold
Nancy Meyers	2
Pete Hansen	1

Subqueries are very powerful, but they do have a serious limitation. The selected data can only come from the top-level table. We cannot use a subquery to obtain data that arise from more than one table. To do so, we must use a join instead.

Querying Multiple Tables with Joins

The join operator is used to combine two or more tables by concatenating (sticking together) the rows of one table with the rows of another table. Consider the two tables in Figure 2-10. The STUDENT table has three columns about students, and the PROJECT_GRADE table has three columns about grades students have earned in a class.

We can concatenate the rows of one table with the rows of the second table with the following SQL statement:

SELECT   *

FROM   **STUDENT, PROJECT_GRADE;**

This statement will just stick every row of one table together with every row of the second table. For the data in Figure 2-10, the result is:

Figure 2-10

**STUDENT and
PROJECT_GRADE Data**

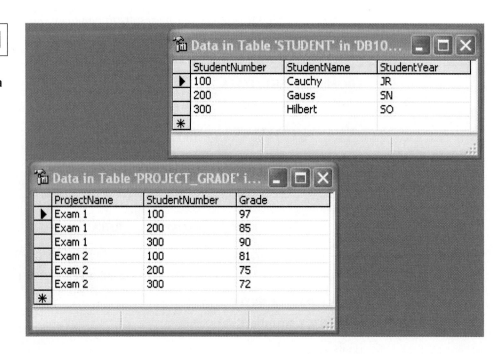

StudentNumber	StudentName	StudentYear	ProjectName	StudentNumber	Grade
100	Cauchy	JR	Exam 1	100	97
100	Cauchy	JR	Exam 1	200	85
100	Cauchy	JR	Exam 1	300	90
100	Cauchy	JR	Exam 2	100	81
100	Cauchy	JR	Exam 2	200	75
100	Cauchy	JR	Exam 2	300	72
200	Gauss	SN	Exam 1	100	97
200	Gauss	SN	Exam 1	200	85
200	Gauss	SN	Exam 1	300	90
200	Gauss	SN	Exam 2	100	81
200	Gauss	SN	Exam 2	200	75
200	Gauss	SN	Exam 2	300	72
300	Hilbert	SO	Exam 1	100	97
300	Hilbert	SO	Exam 1	200	85
300	Hilbert	SO	Exam 1	300	90
300	Hilbert	SO	Exam 2	100	81
300	Hilbert	SO	Exam 2	200	75
300	Hilbert	SO	Exam 2	300	72

Because there are three rows of students and six rows of exams, there are 3 times 6, or 18, rows in this table. Notice that student Cauchy has been combined with all six rows in PROJECT_GRADE, student Gauss has been combined with all six rows, and student Hilbert has been combined with all six rows.

Now, if you are one of these three students, you have an objection to this table. You have been associated not only with your own grades, but also with the grades of the other two students. This is illogical; what we need to do is to select only those rows for which the StudentNumber of STUDENT matches the StudentNumber in PROJECT_GRADE. This is easy to do, we just apply a WHERE clause to the SQL statement:

SELECT   *

FROM   **STUDENT, PROJECT_GRADE**

WHERE   **STUDENT.StudentNumber = PROJECT_GRADE.StudentNumber;**

The result is:

StudentNumber	StudentName	StudentYear	ProjectName	StudentNumber	Grade
100	Cauchy	JR	Exam 1	100	97
200	Gauss	SN	Exam 1	200	85
300	Hilbert	SO	Exam 1	300	90
100	Cauchy	JR	Exam 2	100	81
200	Gauss	SN	Exam 2	200	75
300	Hilbert	SO	Exam 2	300	72

If you compare this result with the data in Figure 2-10, you will see that only the appropriate grades are associated with each student. You also can tell that this has been done by noticing that in each row the value of StudentNumber from STUDENT (the first column) equals the value of StudentNumber from PROJECT_GRADE (the next to last column). This was not true for the prior result.

B T W

The syntax STUDENT.StudentNumber simply means the StudentNumber from the STUDENT table. Similarly, PROJECT_GRADE.StudentNumber refers to the StudentNumber in the PROJECT_GRADE table. You can always qualify a column name with the name of its table like this. We have not done so previously because we were working with only one table, but the SQL shown previously would have worked just as well with syntax like SKU_DATA.Buyer rather than just Buyer or ORDER_ITEM.Price instead of Price.

The table that is formed by concatenating two tables is called a **join.** The process of creating such a table is called **joining the two tables.** When the tables are joined using an equal condition (like the one on StudentNumber), this join is called an **equijoin.** When people say *join,* 99.99999 percent of the time they mean an equijoin.

We can use a join to obtain data from two or more tables. For example, using the data in Figure 2-3, suppose we want to show the name of the Buyer and the ExtendedPrice of the sales of all items managed by that Buyer. The following SQL will obtain that result:

SELECT   **Buyer, ExtendedPrice**

FROM   **SKU_DATA, ORDER_ITEM**

WHERE   **SKU_DATA.SKU = ORDER_ITEM.SKU;**

The result is:

Buyer	ExtendedPrice
Pete Hansen	300.0000
Nancy Meyers	200.0000
Nancy Meyers	100.0000
Nancy Meyers	100.0000
Nancy Meyers	50.0000
Cindy Lo	300.0000
Cindy Lo	130.0000

Again, the result of every SQL statement is just a single table, so we can apply any of the SQL you learned for a single table to this result. For example, we can use GROUP BY and ORDER BY as follows:

SELECT   **Buyer, SUM(ExtendedPrice) AS BuyerRevenue**

FROM   **SKU_DATA, ORDER_ITEM**

WHERE   **SKU_DATA.SKU = ORDER_ITEM.SKU**

GROUP BY   **Buyer**

ORDER BY   **BuyerRevenue DESC;**

{Fails in Access}

The result is:

Buyer	BuyerRevenue
Nancy Meyers	450.0000
Cindy Lo	430.0000
Pete Hansen	300.0000

We can extend this syntax to join three or more tables. For example, suppose we want to obtain the Buyer and the ExtendedPrice and OrderMonth for all purchases of items managed by each buyer. To retrieve that data, we need to join all three tables together as follows:

SELECT	**Buyer, ExtendedPrice, OrderMonth**
FROM	**SKU_DATA, ORDER_ITEM, RETAIL_ORDER**
WHERE	**SKU_DATA.SKU = ORDER_ITEM.SKU**
AND	**ORDER_ITEM.OrderNumber = RETAIL_ORDER.OrderNumber;**

The result is:

Buyer	ExtendedPrice	OrderMonth
Pete Hansen	300.0000	January
Nancy Meyers	200.0000	December
Nancy Meyers	100.0000	January
Nancy Meyers	100.0000	December
Nancy Meyers	50.0000	January
Cindy Lo	300.0000	December
Cindy Lo	130.0000	December

which we could improve with ORDER BY and perhaps grouping as well.

Joins also can be written using another syntax, and there is a bit more for you to learn about joins when values are missing, but this chapter is long enough. We will finish the discussion of joins in Chapter 7. If you just cannot wait, turn to pages 234–239 for the rest of the join story.

Comparing Subqueries and Joins

Subqueries and joins both process multiple tables, but they differ slightly. As mentioned earlier, a subquery can only be used to retrieve data from the top table. A join can be used to obtain data from any number of tables. Thus, a join can do everything a sub-query can do, and more. So why learn subqueries? For one, if you just need data from a single table, you might use a subquery because it is easier to write and understand. This is especially true when processing multiple tables.

In Chapter 8, however, you will learn about a type of subquery called a **correlated subquery.** A correlated subquery can do work that is not possible with joins. Thus, it is important for you to learn about both joins and subqueries, even though right now it appears that joins are uniformly superior. If you're curious, ambitious, and courageous, read the discussion of correlated subqueries on pages 267–269.

⊚ SUMMARY

Wow! That was a full chapter!

There are two kinds of SQL statements: DML and DDL statements. DML statements include statements for querying data and for inserting, updating, and deleting data. This chapter addresses only DML query statements.

SQL was developed by IBM and has been endorsed by the ANSI SQL-92 standard. SQL is a data sublanguage that can be embedded in full programming languages or submitted directly to the DBMS. Knowing SQL is critical for knowledge workers, application programmers, and database administrators.

All DBMS products process SQL. Access hides SQL, but SQL Server, Oracle, DB2, and MySQL require that you use it.

The examples in this chapter are based on three tables extracted from the operational database at Cape Codd Sports. Such database extracts are common and important. Sample data for the three tables is shown in Figure 2-3.

The basic structure of a SQL query statement is SELECT/FROM/WHERE. The columns to be selected are listed after SELECT, the table(s) to process is listed after FROM, and any restrictions on data values are listed after WHERE. In a WHERE clause, character and date data values must be enclosed in single quotes. Numeric data need not be enclosed in quotes. You can submit SQL statements directly to Access, SQL Server, and Oracle, as described in this chapter.

This chapter explained the use of the following keywords: ORDER BY, DESC, ASC, AND, OR, IN, NOT IN, BETWEEN, LIKE, % (* for Access), _ (? for Access), SUM, AVG, MIN, MAX, COUNT, AS, GROUP BY, and HAVING. You should know how to mix and match these features to obtain the results you want. By default, WHERE is applied before HAVING.

You can query multiple tables using subqueries and joins. Subqueries are nested queries that use the keywords IN and NOT IN. A SQL SELECT expression is placed inside parentheses. Using a subquery, you can display data from the top table only. A join is created by specifying multiple table names in the FROM phrase. A WHERE clause is used to obtain an equijoin. In most cases, equijoins are the most sensible option. Joins can display data from multiple tables. In Chapter 8, you will learn another type of subquery that can perform work that is not possible with joins.

⊚ REVIEW QUESTIONS

2.1   What does SQL stand for?

2.2   What does DML stand for? What are DML statements?

2.3   What does DDL stand for? What are DDL statements?

2.4   Summarize the background of SQL.

2.5   What is SQL-92? How does it relate to the SQL statements in this chapter?

2.6   Why is SQL described as a data sublanguage?

2.7   Describe three ways that SQL can be used.

2.8   Explain how Access uses SQL.

2.9   Explain how enterprise-class DBMS products use SQL.

2.10 What does SKU stand for? What is a SKU?

2.11 Summarize how data were altered and filtered in creating the Cape Codd data extraction.

2.12 Explain, in general terms, the relationships among the RETAIL_ORDER, ORDER_ITEM, and SKU_DATA tables.

Use the following table for questions 2.13 through 2.40:

INVENTORY (SKU, Description, QuantityOnHand, QuantityOnOrder,
Warehouse)

Assume that Description and Buyer have character data and that all other columns have
numeric data. If you have a copy of Access, run your queries against the INVENTORY
table included in the database Chapter_2.mdb, which you can download from the text's
Web site at ***www.prenhall.com/kroenke***.

2.13 Write a SQL statement to display SKU and Description.

2.14 Write a SQL statement to display Description and SKU.

2.15 Write a SQL statement to display Warehouse.

2.16 Write a SQL statement to display Warehouse with no duplications.

2.17 Write a SQL statement to display all of the columns without using *.

2.18 Write a SQL statement to display all of the columns using *.

2.19 Write a SQL statement to display all data on products having a QuantityOnHand
greater than 0.

2.20 Write a SQL statement to display the SKU and Description on products having
QuantityOnHand equal to 0.

2.21 Write a SQL statement to display the SKU, Description, and Warehouse on products having QuantityOnHand equal to 0. Sort the results in ascending order by
Warehouse.

2.22 Write a SQL statement to display the SKU, Description, and Warehouse on products having QuantityOnHand equal to 0. Sort the results in descending order by
Warehouse and ascending order of QuantityOnHand.

2.23 Write a SQL statement to display SKU and Description for all products that have
a QuantityOnHand equal to 0 and a QuantityOnOrder greater than 0.

2.24 Write a SQL statement to display SKU and Description for all products that have
a QuantityOnHand equal to 0 or QuantityOnOrder equal to 0.

2.25 Write a SQL statement to display the SKU and Description of all items stored in
the Seattle, Chicago, or New Jersey warehouse. Do not use IN.

2.26 Write a SQL statement to display the SKU and Description of all items stored in
the Seattle, Chicago, or New Jersey warehouse. Use IN.

2.27 Write a SQL statement to display the SKU and Description of all items not stored
in the Seattle, Chicago, or New Jersey warehouse. Do not use NOT IN.

2.28 Write a SQL statement to display the SKU and Description of all items not stored
in the Seattle, Chicago, or New Jersey warehouse. Use NOT IN.

2.29 Write a SQL statement to display the SKU, Description, and QuantityOnHand for
all products having a QuantityOnHand greater than 1 and less than 10. Use
BETWEEN.

2.30 Write a SQL statement to show SKU and Description for all products having a
description starting with 'Half-dome'.

2.31 Write a SQL statement to show SKU and Description for all products having a
description that includes the word 'Foot'.

2.32 Write a SQL statement to show SKU and Warehouse for all products having a 'w'
in the third position from the left in Warehouse.

2.33 Write a SQL expression that uses all of the built-in functions on the
QuantityOnHand column. Include meaningful column names in the result.

2.34 Explain the difference between COUNT and SUM.

2.35 Write a SQL expression to produce a single column called ItemLocation that combines the Description, the phrase "is located in," and Warehouse for all products
that have a QuantityOnHand greater than 0. Do not be concerned with removing
trailing blanks.

2.36 Write a SQL expression to display the Warehouse and a count of
QuantityOnHand, grouped by Warehouse. Name the count TotalItemsOnHand
and display the results in descending order of TotalItemsOnHand.

2.37 Write a SQL expression to display the Warehouse and a count of QuantityOnHand, grouped by Warehouse. Omit all items that have a count greater than 2. Name the count TotalItemsOnHand and display the results in descending order of TotalItemsOnHand.

2.38 Write a SQL expression to display the Warehouse and a count of QuantityOnHand grouped by Warehouse. Omit all items that have a count greater than 2. Show only groups having fewer than 2 item counts. Name the count TotalItemsOnHand and display the results in descending order of TotalItemsOnHand.

2.39 In your answer to question 2.38, was the WHERE or HAVING applied first? Why?

2.40 Write a SQL expression to display the Warehouse, the sum of QuantityOnOrder and sum of QuantityOnHand, grouped by Warehouse and QuantityOnOrder. Omit all items that have a count greater than 2. Name the count of QuantityOnOrder as TotalItemsOnOrder and the count of QuantityOnHand as TotalItemsOnHand.

Use the following two tables in your answers to questions 2.41 through 2.47:

INVENTORY (SKU, Description, QuantityOnHand, QuantityOnOrder, Warehouse)

WAREHOUSE (Warehouse, Manager, SquareFeet)

2.41 Write a SQL statement to show the SKU and Description of all items stored in a warehouse managed by 'Smith'. Use a subquery.

2.42 Write a SQL statement to show the SKU and Description of all items stored in a warehouse managed by 'Smith'. Use a join.

2.43 Write a SQL statement to show the Warehouse and average QuantityOnHand of all items stored in a warehouse managed by 'Smith'. Use a subquery.

2.44 Write a SQL statement to show the Warehouse and average QuantityOnHand of all items stored in a warehouse managed by 'Smith'. Use a join.

2.45 Write a SQL statement to show the Warehouse, Manager, and QuantityOnHand of all items stored in a warehouse managed by 'Smith'. Use a join.

2.46 Explain why you cannot use a subquery in your answer to question 2.45.

2.47 Explain how subqueries and joins differ.

PROJECT QUESTIONS

The following questions refer to the NDX data table on page 53. You can obtain a copy of this data in the Access database, Chapter_2.mdb, which is located on the text's Web site at *www.prenhall/kroenke.*

2.48 Write SQL queries to produce the following results:
  a. The ChangeClose on Fridays.
  b. The minimum, maximum, and average ChangeClose on Fridays.
  c. The average ChangeClose grouped by TYear. Show TYear.
  d. The average ChangeClose grouped by TYear and TMonth. Show TYear and TMonth.
  e. The average ChangeClose grouped by TYear, TQuarter, TMonth shown in descending order of the average (you will have to give a name to the average in order to sort by it). Show TYear, TQuarter, and TMonth. Note that months appear in alphabetical and not calendar order. Explain what you need to do to obtain months in calendar order.

    f. The difference between the maximum ChangeClose and the minimum ChangeClose grouped by TYear, TQuarter, TMonth shown in descending order of the difference (you will have to give a name to the difference in order to sort by it). Show TYear, TQuarter, and TMonth.

    g. The average ChangeClose grouped by TYear shown in descending order of the average (you will have to give a name to the average in order to sort by it). Show only groups for which the average is positive.

    h. Display a single field with the date in the form day/month/year. Do not be concerned with trailing blanks.

2.49 It is possible that volume (the number of shares traded) has some correlation with the direction of the stock market. Use the SQL you have learned in this chapter to investigate this possibility. Develop at least five different SQL statements in your investigation.

MARCIA'S DRY CLEANING

Marcia's Dry Cleaning is an upscale dry cleaner in a well-to-do suburban neighborhood. Marcia makes her business stand out from the competition by providing superior customer service. She wants to keep track of each of her customers and their orders. Ultimately, she wants to notify them that their clothes are ready via e-mail. To provide this service, she has developed an initial database with several tables. Three of those tables are the following:

    CUSTOMER (Phone, FirstName, LastName, Email)

    INVOICE (Number, DateIn, DateOut, TotalAmt, Phone)

    INVOICE_ITEM (Number, Item, Quantity, UnitPrice)

Code SQL statements to produce the following information:

A Show all data in each of the tables.

B List the Phone and LastName of all customers.

C List the Phone and LastName for all customers with a FirstName of 'Nikki'.

D List the Phone, DateIn, and DateOut of all orders in excess of 100.

E List the Phone and FirstName of all customers whose first name starts with 'B'.

F List the Phone and FirstName of all customers whose last name includes the characters 'cat'.

G List the Phone, FirstName, and LastName for all customers whose second and third numbers of their phone number are 23.

H Determine the maximum and minimum TotalAmts.

I Determine the average TotalAmt.

J Count the number of customers.

K Group customers by LastName and then by FirstName.

L Count the number of customers having each combination of LastName and FirstName.

M Show the FirstName and LastName of all customers who have had an order with TotalAmt greater than 100. Use a subquery. Present the results sorted by LastName in ascending order and then FirstName in descending order.

N Show the FirstName and LastName of all customers who have had an order with TotalAmt greater than 100. Use a join. Present results sorted by LastName in ascending order and then FirstName in descending order.

O Show the FirstName and LastName, of all customers who have had an order with an Item named 'Dress Shirt'. Use a subquery. Present results sorted by LastName in ascending order and then FirstName in descending order.

P   Show the FirstName and LastName of all customers who have had an order with an Item named 'Dress Shirt'. Use a join. Present results sorted by LastName in ascending order and then FirstName in descending order.

Q   Show the FirstName, LastName, and TotalAmt of all customers who have had an order with an Item named 'Dress Shirt'. Use a join with a subquery. Present results sorted by LastName in ascending order and then FirstName in descending order.

┤M├ MORGAN IMPORTING

Morgan Importing purchases antiques and home furnishings in Asia and ships those items to a warehouse facility in Los Angeles. Mr. Morgan uses a database to keep a list of items purchased, shipments, and shipment items. His database includes the following tables:

SHIPMENT (Number, Shipper, DepartureDate, ArrivalDate, InsuredValue)

SHIPMENT_ITEM (Number, Item, Quantity, Value)

ITEM_PURCHASE (Item, Store, Quantity, City, Date, LocalCurrencyAmt, ExchangeRate)

Code SQL statements to produce the following information:

A   Show all data in each of the tables.

B   List the Number and Shipper of all shipments.

C   List the Number and Shipper for all shipments that have an insured value greater than 10000.

D   List the Number and Shipper of all shippers whose name starts with 'AB'.

E   Assume DepartureDate and ArrivalDate are in the format MM/DD/YY. List the Number, Shipper, and ArrivalDate of all shipments that departed in December.

F   Assume DepartureDate and ArrivalDate are in the format MM/DD/YY. List the Number, Shipper, and ArrivalDate of all shipments that departed on the tenth day of any month.

G   Determine the maximum and minimum InsuredValue.

H   Determine the average InsuredValue.

I   Count the number of shipments.

J   Show Item, Store, and a calculated column named StdCurrencyAmount that is equal to LocalCurrencyAmt times the ExchangeRate for all rows of ITEM_PURCHASE.

K   Group item purchases by City and Store.

L   Count the number of purchases having each combination of City and Store.

M   Show the Shipper and DepartureDate of all shipments that have an item with a value of 1000 or more. Use a subquery. Present results sorted by Shipper in ascending order and then DepartureDate in descending order.

N   Show the Shipper and DepartureDate of all shipments that have an item with a value of 1000 or more. Use a join. Present results sorted by Shipper in ascending order and then DepartureDate in descending order.

O   Show the Shipper and DepartureDate of all shipments that have an item that was purchased in Singapore. Use a subquery. Present results sorted by Shipper in ascending order and then DepartureDate in descending order.

P   Show the Shipper and DepartureDate of all shipments that have an item that was purchased in Singapore. Use a join. Present results sorted by Shipper in ascending order and then DepartureDate in descending order.

Q   Show the Shipper, DepartureDate of shipment, and Value for items that were purchased in Singapore. Use a combination of a join and a subquery. Present results sorted by Shipper in ascending order and then DepartureDate in descending order.

Database Design

The four chapters in Part 2 discuss database design principles and techniques. Chapters 3 and 4 describe the design of databases that arise from existing data sources, such as spreadsheets, text files, and database extracts. We begin in Chapter 3 by defining the relational model and discussing normalization, a process that transforms relations with modification problems. Then, in Chapter 4, we use normalization principles to guide the design of databases from existing data.

Chapters 5 and 6 examine the design of databases that arise from the development of new information systems. Chapter 5 describes the entity-relationship data model, a tool used to create plans for constructing database designs. As you will learn, such data models are developed by analysis of forms, reports, and other information systems requirements. Chapter 6 concludes this part by describing techniques for transforming entity-relationship data models into relational database designs.

The Relational Model and Normalization

As stated in Chapter 1, databases arise from three sources: from existing data, from the development of new information systems, and from the redesign of existing databases. In this chapter and the next, we consider the design of databases from existing data such as spreadsheets or extracts of existing databases.

The premise of Chapters 3 and 4 is that you have received one or more tables of data from some source that are to be stored in a new database. The question is: Should this data be stored as is, or should it be transformed in some way before it is stored? For example, consider the two tables in the top part of Figure 3-1. These are the SKU_DATA and ORDER_ITEM tables used in the database in Chapter 2.

You can design the new database to store this data as two separate tables, or you can join the tables together and design the database with just one table. Each alternative has advantages and disadvantages. When you make the decision to use one design, you obtain certain advantages at the expense of certain costs. The purpose of this chapter is to help you understand those advantages and costs.

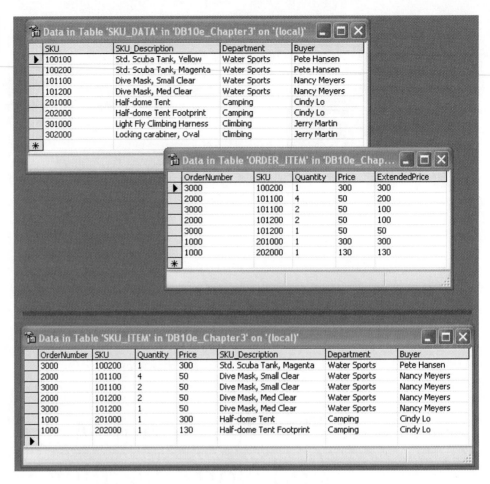

Figure 3-1

How Many Tables?

Such questions do not seem difficult, and you may be wondering why we need two chapters to answer them. In truth, even a single table can have surprising complexity. Consider, for example, the table in Figure 3-2, which shows sample data extracted from a corporate database. This simple table has three columns: the buyer's name, the SKU of the products that the buyer purchases, and the names of the buyer's college major(s). Buyers manage more than one SKU, and they can have multiple college majors.

To understand why this is an odd table, suppose that Nancy Meyers is assigned a new SKU, say 101300. What addition should we make to this table? Clearly, we need to add a row for the new SKU, but if we add just one row, say the row ('Nancy Meyers', 101300, 'Art'), it will appear that she manages product 101300 as an Art major, but not as an Info Systems major. To avoid such an illogical state, we need to add two rows: ('Nancy Meyers', 101300, 'Art') and ('Nancy Meyers', 101300, 'Info Systems').

Figure 3-2

PRODUCT_BUYER,
a Strange Table

BuyerName	SKU_Managed	CollegeMajor
Nancy Meyers	101100	Art
Nancy Meyers	101100	Info Systems
Nancy Meyers	101200	Art
Nancy Meyers	101200	Info Systems
Pete Hansen	100100	Business
Pete Hansen	100200	Business

This is a strange requirement. Why should we have to add two rows of data simply to record the fact that a new SKU has been assigned to a buyer? Further, if we assign the product to Pete Hansen instead, we would only have to add one row, but if we assigned the product to a buyer who had four majors, we would have to add four new rows.

The more one thinks about the table in Figure 3-2, the more strange it becomes. What changes should we make if SKU 101100 is assigned to Pete Hansen? What changes should we make if SKU 100100 is assigned to Nancy Meyers? What should we do if all the SKU values in Figure 3-2 are deleted? Later in this chapter, you will learn that these problems arise because this table has a problem called a *multivalued dependency*. Even better, you will learn how to remove that problem.

Tables can have many different patterns; some patterns are susceptible to serious problems and other patterns are not. Before we can address this question, however, you need to learn basic terms.

Relational Model Terminology

Figure 3-3 lists the most important terms used by the relational model. By the time you finish Chapters 3 and 4, you should be able to define each of these terms and explain how each pertains to the design of relational databases. Use this list of terms as a check on your comprehension.

We begin with the definition of the term *relation*.

Relation

So far, we have used the terms *table* and *relation* interchangeably. In fact, a relation is a special case of a table. This means that all relations are tables, but not all tables are relations. Codd defined the characteristics of a relation in his 1970 paper that laid the foundation for the relational model.[1] Those characteristics are summarized in Figure 3-4.

Figure 3-3

Important Relational Model Terms

- Relation
- Functional dependency
- Determinant
- Candidate key
- Composite key
- Primary key
- Surrogate key
- Foreign key
- Referential integrity constraint
- Normal form
- Multivalued dependency

---

[1]Codd, E. F. "A Relational Model of Data for Large Shared Databanks," *Communications of the ACM*, June 1970, pp. 377–387.

Figure 3-4

Characteristics of
Relations

- Rows contain data about an entity
- Columns contain data about attributes of the entities
- All entries in a column are of the same kind
- Each column has a unique name
- Cells of the table hold a single value
- The order of the columns in unimportant
- The order of the rows is unimportant
- No two rows may be indentical

B T W

In Figure 3-4 and in this discussion, we use the term *entity* to mean an instance of some identifiable thing. A customer, a salesperson, an order, a part, and a lease are all examples of what we mean by an entity. When we introduce the entity-relationship model in Chapter 5, we will make the definition of entity more precise. For now, just think of an entity as some identifiable thing that users want to track.

Characteristics of Relations

First, for a table to be a relation, the rows of the table must store data about an entity and the columns of the table must store data about the characteristics of those entities. Further, in a relation, all of the values in a column are of the same kind. If, for example, the second column of the first row of a relation has FirstName, then the second column of every row in the relation has FirstName. Also, the names of the columns are unique; no two columns in the same relation may have the same name.

B T W

Columns in different relations may have the same name. In Chapter 2, for example, two relations had a column named SKU. When there is risk of confusion, we precede the column name with the relation name followed by a period. Thus, the name of the SKU column in the SKU_DATA relation is SKU_DATA.SKU, and column C1 of relation R1 is named R1.C1. Because relation names are unique within a database, and because column names are unique within a relation, the combination of relation name and column name uniquely identifies every column in the database.

Each cell of a relation has only a single value or item; multiple entries are not allowed. The table in Figure 3-5(a) is not a relation because the Phone values of employees Caruthers and Bandalone store multiple phone numbers.

In a relation, the order of the rows and the order of the columns are immaterial. No information can be carried by the ordering of rows or columns. The table in Figure 3-5(b) is not a relation because the entries for employees Caruthers and Caldera require a particular row arrangement. If the rows in this table were rearranged, we would not know which employee has the indicated Fax and Home numbers.

Finally, according to the last characteristic in Figure 3-4, for a table to be a relation, no two rows can be identical. As you learned in Chapter 2, some SQL statements do produce tables with duplicate rows. In such cases, you can use the DISTINCT

Figure 3-5

Tables That Are Not Relations

(a) Table with Multiple Entries per Cell

EmployeeNumber	FirstName	LastName	Department	Email	Phone
100	Jerry	Johnson	Accounting	JJ@somewhere.com	236-0000
200	Mary	Abernathy	Finance	MA@somewhere.com	444-8898
300	Liz	Smathers	Finance	LS@somewhere.com	777-0098
400	Tom	Caruthers	Accounting	TC@somewhere.com	236-0000, 236-0991, 236-0991
500	Tom	Jackson	Production	TJ@somewhere.com	444-9980
600	Eleanore	Caldera	Legal	EC@somewhere.com	767-0900
700	Richard	Bandalone	Legal	RB@somewhere.com	767-0900, 767-0011

(b) Table with Required Row Order

EmployeeNumber	FirstName	LastName	Department	Email	Phone
100	Jerry	Johnson	Accounting	JJ@somewhere.com	236-9987
200	Mary	Abernathy	Finance	MA@somewhere.com	444-8898
300	Liz	Smathers	Finance	LS@somewhere.com	777-0098
400	Tom	Caruthers	Accounting	TC@somewhere.com	236-9987
				Fax:	236-9987
				Home:	555-7171
500	Tom	Jackson	Production	TJ@somewhere.com	444-9980
600	Eleanore	Caldera	Legal	EC@somewhere.com	767-0900
				Fax:	236-9987
				Home:	555-7171
700	Richard	Bandalone	Legal	RB@somewhere.com	767-0900

keyword to force uniqueness. Such row duplication only occurs as a result of SQL manipulation. Tables that you design to be stored in the database should never contain duplicate rows.

B T W

Do not fall into a common trap. Even though every cell of a relation must have a single value, this does not mean that all values must have the same length. The table in Figure 3-6 is a relation even though the length of the Comment column varies from row to row. It is a relation because, even though the comments have different lengths, there is only *one* comment per cell.

Figure 3-6   **Relation with Variable-length Column**

EmployeeNumber	FirstName	LastName	Department	Email	Phone	Comment
100	Jerry	Johnson	Accounting	JJ@somewhere.com	236-9987	Joined the Accounting Department in March after completing his MBA at night. Will sit for CPA exam this fall.
200	Mary	Abernathy	Finance	MA@somewhere.com	444-8898	
300	Liz	Smathers	Finance	LS@somewhere.com	777-0098	
400	Tom	Caruthers	Accounting	TC@somewhere.com	236-9987	
500	Tom	Jackson	Production	TJ@somewhere.com	444-9980	
600	Eleanore	Caldera	Legal	EC@somewhere.com	767-0900	
700	Richard	Bandalone	Legal	RB@somewhere.com	767-0900	Is a full time consultant to legal on a retainer basis.

Alternative Terminology

As defined by Codd, the columns of a relation are called **attributes,** and the rows of a relation are called **tuples** (rhymes with "couples"). Most practitioners, however, do not use these academic-sounding terms and use the terms *column* and *row*, instead. Also, even though a table is not necessarily a relation, most practitioners mean *relation* when they say *table.* Thus, in most conversations, the terms *relation* and *table* are synonymous. In fact, for the rest of this book, *table* and *relation* will be used synonymously.

Table	Column	Row
Relation	Attribute	Tuple
File	Field	Record

Figure 3-7

**Three Sets of
Equivalent Terms**

Additionally, a third set of terminology also is used. Some practitioners use the terms *file*, *field*, and *record* for the terms *table, column,* and *row.* These terms arose from traditional data processing and are common in connection with legacy systems. Sometimes, people mix and match these terms. You might hear someone say, for example, that a relation has a certain column and contains 47 records. These three sets of terms are summarized in Figure 3-7.

Functional Dependency

Functional dependencies are the heart of the database design process, and it is vital for you to understand them. We first explain the concept in general terms and then examine two examples.

We begin with a short excursion into the world of algebra. Suppose you are buying boxes of cookies and someone tells you that each box costs $5.00. With this fact, you can compute the cost of several boxes with the formula:

$$CookieCost = NumberOfBoxes \times \$5$$

A more general way to express the relationship between CookieCost and NumberOfBoxes is to say that CookieCost *depends upon* NumberOfBoxes. Such a statement tells us the character of the relationship between CookieCost and NumberOfBoxes, even though it doesn't give us the formula. More formally, we can say that CookieCost is **functionally dependent** on NumberOfBoxes. Such a statement can be written as:

NumberOfBoxes → CookieCost

This expression can be read as "NumberOfBoxes *determines* CookieCost." The variable on the left, here NumberOfBoxes, is called the **determinant.**

Using another formula, we can compute the extended price of a part order by multiplying the quantity of the item times its unit price, or:

$$ExtendedPrice = Quantity \times UnitPrice$$

In this case, we say that ExtendedPrice is functionally dependent on Quantity and UnitPrice, or:

(Quantity, UnitPrice) → ExtendedPrice

Here, the determinant is the composite (Quantity, UnitPrice).

Functional Dependencies That Are Not Equations

In general, a functional dependency exists when the value of one or more attributes determines the value of another attribute. Many functional dependencies exist that do not involve equations. Consider an example. Suppose you know that a sack contains either red, blue, or yellow objects. Further, suppose you know that the red objects weigh 5 pounds, the blue objects weigh 3 pounds, and the yellow objects weigh 7 pounds. If a friend looks into the sack, sees an object, and tells you the color of the object, you can tell her the weight of the object. We can formalize this as:

ObjectColor → Weight

Thus, we can say that Weight is functionally dependent on ObjectColor and that ObjectColor determines Weight. The relationship here does not involve an equation, but the functional dependency holds. Given a value for ObjectColor, you can determine the object's weight. If we also know that the red objects are balls, the blue objects are cubes, and the yellow objects are cubes, we can also say:

ObjectColor → Shape

Thus, ObjectColor determines Shape. We can put these two together to state:

ObjectColor → (Weight, Shape)

Thus, ObjectColor determines Weight and Shape.
  Another way to represent these facts is to put them into a table:

Object Color	Weight	Shape
Red	5	Ball
Blue	3	Cube
Yellow	7	Cube

This table meets all of the conditions listed in Figure 3-4 and is a relation. You may be thinking that we performed a trick or sleight of hand to arrive at this relation, but in truth, the only reason for having relations is to store instances of functional dependencies. If there were a formula by which we could take ObjectColor and somehow compute Weight and Shape, then we would not need the table. We would just make the computation. Similarly, if there were a formula by which we could take EmployeeNumber and compute EmployeeName and HireDate, then we would not need an EMPLOYEE relation. However, because there is no such formula, we must store the combinations of EmployeeNumber, EmployeeName, and HireDate in the rows of a relation.

Composite Functional Dependencies

The determinant of a functional dependency can consist of more than one attribute. For example, a grade in a class is determined by both the student and the class, or (StudentName, ClassName) → Grade. In this case, the determinant is called a **composite determinant.**

  Notice that both the student and the class are needed to determine the grade. In general, if (A, B) → C, then neither A nor B will determine C by itself. On the other hand, if A → (B, C), then it is true that A → B and A → C. Work through examples of your own for both of these cases so that you understand why this is true.

Finding Functional Dependencies

To fix the idea of functional dependency in your mind, consider what functional dependencies exist in the SKU_DATA and ORDER_ITEM tables in Figure 3-1.

Functional Dependencies in the SKU_DATA Table

To find functional dependencies in a table, we must ask, Does any column determine the value of another column? For example, consider the values of the SKU_DATA table in Figure 3-1:

SKU	SKU_Description	Department	Buyer
100100	Std. Scuba Tank, Yellow	Water Sports	Pete Hansen
100200	Std. Scuba Tank, Magenta	Water Sports	Pete Hansen
101100	Dive Mask, Small Clear	Water Sports	Nancy Meyers
101200	Dive Mask, Med Clear	Water Sports	Nancy Meyers
201000	Half-dome Tent	Camping	Cindy Lo
202000	Half-dome Tent Footprint	Camping	Cindy Lo
301000	Light Fly Climbing Harness	Climbing	Jerry Martin
302000	Locking carabiner, Oval	Climbing	Jerry Martin

Consider the last two columns. If we know the value of Department, can we determine a unique value of Buyer? No, we cannot, because a Department may have more than one Buyer. In this sample data, 'Water Sports' is associated with Pete Hansen and Nancy Meyers. Therefore, Department does not functionally determine Buyer.

What about the reverse? Does Buyer determine Department? In every row, for a given value of Buyer, do we find the same value of Department? Every time Jerry Martin appears, for example, is he paired with the same department? The answer is yes. Further, every time Cindy Lo appears, she is paired with the same department. The same is true for the other buyers. Therefore, assuming that these data are representative, Buyer does determine Department, and we can write:

Buyer → Department

Does Buyer determine any other column? If we know the value of Buyer, do we know the value of SKU? No, we do not, because a given buyer has many SKUs assigned to him or her. Does Buyer determine SKU_Description? No, because a given value of Buyer occurs with many values of SKU_Description.

B T W

As stated, for the Buyer → Department functional dependency, a Buyer is paired with one and only one value of Department. Notice that a buyer can appear more than once in the table, but if so, that buyer is always paired with the same department. This is true for all functional dependencies. If A→ B, then each value of A will be paired with one and only one value of B. A particular value of A may appear more than once in the relation, but if so, it is always paired with the same value of B. Note, too, that the reverse is not necessarily true. If A→ B, then a value of B may be paired with many values of A.

What about the other columns? It turns out that if we know the value of SKU, we also know the values of all of the other columns. In other words:

SKU → SKU_Description

because a given value of SKU will have just one value of SKU_Description.

SKU → Department

because a given value of SKU will have just one value of Department.

SKU → Buyer

because a given value of SKU will have just one value of Buyer.
We can write these three statements as:

SKU → (SKU_Description, Department, Buyer)

For the same reasons, SKU_Description determines all of the other columns, and we can write:

SKU_Description → (SKU, Department, Buyer)

In summary, the functional dependencies in the SKU_DATA table are:

SKU → (SKU_Description, Department, Buyer)

SKU_Description → (SKU, Department, Buyer)

Buyer → Department

B T W

You cannot always determine functional dependencies from sample data. You may not have any sample data, or you may have just a few rows that are not representative of all of the data conditions. In such cases, you must ask the users who are experts in the application that creates the data. For the SKU_DATA table, you would ask questions such as, "Is a Buyer always associated with the same Department?" and "Can a Department have more than one Buyer?" In most cases, answers to such questions are more reliable than sample data. When in doubt, trust the users.

Functional Dependencies in the ORDER_ITEM Table

Now consider the ORDER_ITEM table in Figure 3-1. For convenience, here is a copy of the data in that table:

OrderNumber	SKU	Quantity	Price	ExtendedPrice
3000	100200	1	300	300
2000	101100	4	50	200
3000	101100	2	50	100
2000	101200	2	50	100
3000	101200	1	50	50
1000	201000	1	300	300
1000	202000	1	130	130

What are the functional dependencies in this table? Start on the left. Does OrderNumber determine another column? It does not determine SKU because several SKUs are associated with a given order. For the same reasons, it does not determine Quantity, Price, or ExtendedPrice. What about SKU? SKU does not determine OrderNumber because several OrderNumbers are associated with a given SKU. It does not determine Quantity or ExtendedPrice for the same reason.

What about SKU and Price? From this data, it appears that

SKU → Price

but that might not be true in general. In fact, we know that prices can change after an order has been processed. Further, an order might have special pricing due to a sale or promotion. To keep an accurate record of what the customer actually paid, we need to associate a particular SKU price with a particular order. Thus:

(OrderNumber, SKU) → Price

Considering the other columns, Quantity, Price, or ExtendedPrice do not determine anything else. You can decide this by looking at the sample data. You can re-enforce this conclusion by thinking about the nature of sales. Would a Quantity of 2 ever determine an OrderNumber or a SKU? This makes no sense. At the grocery store, if I tell you I bought two of something, you have no reason to conclude that my OrderNumber was 1010022203466 or that I bought carrots. Quantity does not determine OrderNumber or SKU.

Similarly, if I tell you that the price of an item was $3.99, there is no logical way to conclude what my OrderNumber was or that I bought a jar of green olives. Thus, Price does not determine OrderNumber or SKU. Similar comments pertain to ExtendedPrice. It turns out that no single column is a determinant in the ORDER_ITEM table.

What about pairs of columns? We already know that (OrderNumber, SKU) → Price. Examining the data, (OrderNumber, SKU) determines the other two columns as well. Thus:

(OrderNumber, SKU) → (Quantity, Price, ExtendedPrice)

This functional dependency makes sense. It means that given a particular order and a particular item on that order, there is only one quantity, one price, and one extended price.

Notice, too, that because ExtendedPrice is computed from the formula ExtendedPrice = Quantity * Price, then:

(Quantity, Price) → ExtendedPrice

In summary, the functional dependencies in ORDER_ITEM are:

(OrderNumber, SKU) → (Quantity, Price, ExtendedPrice)

(Quantity, Price) → ExtendedPrice

No single skill is more important for designing databases than the ability to identify functional dependencies. Make sure you understand the material in this section. Work problems 3.52 and 3.53 and the Marcia's Dry Cleaning and Morgan Importing projects at the end of the chapter. Ask your instructor for help if necessary. You must understand functional dependencies and be able to work with them.

When Are Determinant Values Unique?

In the previous section, you may have noticed an irregularity. Sometimes the determinants of a functional dependency are unique in a relation, and sometimes they are not. Consider the SKU_DATA relation, with determinants SKU, SKU_Description, and Buyer In SKU_DATA, the values of both SKU and SKU_Description are unique in the table. For example, the SKU value 100100 appears just once. Similarly, the SKU_Description value 'Half-dome Tent' occurs just once. From this, it is tempting to conclude that values of determinants are always unique in a relation. However, this is *not* true.

For example, Buyer is a determinant, but it is not unique in SKU_DATA. The buyer 'Cindy Lo' appears in two different rows. In fact, for this sample data, all of the buyers occur in two different rows.

In truth, a determinant is unique in a relation only if it determines every other column in the relation. For the SKU_DATA relation, SKU determines all of the other columns. Similarly, SKU_Description determines all of the other columns. Hence, they both are unique. Buyer, however, only determines the Department column. It does not determine SKU or SKU_Description.

The determinants in ORDER_ITEM are (OrderNumber, SKU) and (Quantity, Price). Because (OrderNumber, SKU) determines all of the other columns, it will be unique in the relation. The composite (Quantity and Price) only determines ExtendedPrice. Therefore, it will not be unique in the relation.

This fact means that you cannot find the determinants of all functional dependencies simply by looking for unique values. Some of the determinants will be unique, but some will not. Instead, to determine if column A determines column B, look at the data and ask, "Every time that a value of column A appears is it matched with the same value of Column B?" If so, it can be a determinant of B. Again, however, sample data can be incomplete, so the best strategies are to think about the nature of the business activity from which the data arise and to ask the users.

Keys

The relational model has more keys than a locksmith. There are candidate keys, composite keys, primary keys, surrogate keys, and foreign keys. In this section, we will define each of these types of key. Because key definitions rely on the concept of functional dependency, make sure you understand that concept before reading on.

In general, a **key** is a combination of one or more columns that is used to identify particular rows in a relation. Keys that have two columns or more are called **composite keys.**

Candidate Key

A **candidate key** is a determinant that determines all of the other columns in a relation. The SKU_DATA relation has two candidate keys: SKU and SKU_Description. Buyer is a determinant, but it is not a candidate key because it only determines Department.

The ORDER_ITEM table has just one candidate key: (OrderNumber, SKU). The other determinant in this table, (Quantity, Price), is not a candidate key because it determines only ExtendedPrice.

Candidate keys identify a unique row in a relation. Given the value of a candidate key, we can find one and only one row in the relation that has that value. For example, given the SKU value of 100100, we can find one and only one row in SKU_DATA. Similarly, given the OrderNumber and SKU values (2000, 101100), we can find one and only one row in ORDER_ITEM.

Primary Key

When designing a database, one of the candidate keys is selected to be the **primary key.** This term is used because this key will be defined to the DBMS, and the DBMS will use it as its primary means for finding rows in a table. A table has only one primary key. The primary key can have one column or it can be a composite.

In this text, to clarify discussions, we will sometimes indicate table structure by showing the name of a table followed by the names of the table's columns enclosed in parentheses. When we do this, we will underline the column(s) that comprise the primary key. For example, we can show the structure of SKU_DATA and ORDER_ITEM as follows:

SKU_DATA (<u>SKU</u>, SKU_Description, Department, Buyer)

ORDER_ITEM (<u>OrderNumber</u>, <u>SKU</u>, Quantity, Price, ExtendedPrice)

This notation indicates that SKU is the primary key of SKU_DATA and that (OrderNumber, SKU) is the primary key of ORDER_ITEM.

B T W

What do you do if a table has no candidate keys? In that case, define the primary key as the collection of all of the columns in the table. Because there are no duplicate rows in a stored relation, the combination of all of the columns of the table will always be unique. Again, while tables generated by SQL manipulation may have duplicate rows, the tables that you design to be stored should never be constructed to have duplication. Thus, the combination of all columns is always a candidate key.

Surrogate Key

A **surrogate key** is an artificial column that is added to a table to serve as the primary key. The DBMS assigns a unique value to a surrogate key when the row is created. The assigned value never changes.

Surrogate keys are used when the primary key is large and unwieldy. For example, consider the relation RENTAL_PROPERTY:

RENTAL_PROPERTY (<u>Street</u>, <u>City</u>, <u>State/Province</u>, <u>Zip/PostalCode</u>, <u>Country</u>, Rental_Rate)

The primary key of this table is (Street, City, State/Province, Zip/PostalCode). As you will learn in Chapter 6, for good performance, a primary key should be short and, if possible, numeric. The primary key of RENTAL_PROPERTY is neither.

In this case, the designers of the database would likely create a surrogate key. The structure of the table would then be:

RENTAL_PROPERTY (<u>PropertyID</u>, Street, City, State/Province, Zip/PostalCode, Country, Rental_Rate)

The DBMS will assign a numeric value to PropertyID when a row is created. Using that key will result in better performance than using the original key. Note that surrogate key values are artificial and have no meaning to the users. In fact, surrogate key values are normally hidden in forms and reports.

Foreign Key

A **foreign key** is a column or composite of columns that is the primary key of a table other than the one in which it appears. The term arises because it is a key of a table *foreign* to the one in which it appears. In the following two tables, DEPARTMENT.DepartmentName is the primary key of DEPARTMENT, and

EMPLOYEE.DepartmentName is a foreign key. In this text, we will show foreign keys in italics:

DEPARTMENT (<u>DepartmentName</u>, BudgetCode, ManagerName)

EMPLOYEE   (<u>EmployeeNumber</u>, EmployeeName, *DepartmentName*)

Foreign keys express relationships between rows of tables. In this example, the foreign key EMPLOYEE.DepartmentName stores the relationship between an employee and his or her department.

Consider the SKU_DATA and ORDER_ITEM tables. SKU_DATA.SKU is the primary key of SKU_DATA, and ORDER_ITEM.SKU is a foreign key.

SKU_DATA (<u>SKU</u>, SKU_Description, Department, Buyer)

ORDER_ITEM (<u>OrderNumber</u>, *<u>SKU</u>*, Quantity, Price, ExtendedPrice)

Notice that ORDER_ITEM.SKU is both a foreign key and also part of the primary key of ORDER_ITEM. This condition sometimes occurs, but it is not required. In the example above, EMPLOYEE.DepartmentName is a foreign key, but is not part of the EMPLOYEE primary key. You will see some uses for foreign keys later in this chapter and the next, and you will study them at length in Chapter 6.

In most cases, we need to ensure that the values of a foreign key match a valid value of a primary key. For the SKU_DATA and ORDER_ITEM tables, we need to ensure that all of the values of ORDER_ITEM.SKU match a value of SKU_DATA.SKU. To accomplish this, we create a **referential integrity constraint,** which is statement that limits the values of the foreign key. In this case, we create the constraint:

ORDER_ITEM.SKU must exist in SKU_DATA.SKU

This constraint stipulates that every value of SKU in ORDER_ITEM must match a value of SKU in SKU_DATA.

Normal Forms

All relations are not equal. Some are easy to process, and others are problematical. Relations are categorized into **normal forms,** according to kinds of the problems that they have. Knowledge of these normal forms will help you create appropriate database designs. To understand normal forms, we need first to define modification anomalies.

Modification Anomalies

Consider the EQUIPMENT_REPAIR relation in Figure 3-8, which stores data about manufacturing equipment and equipment repairs. Suppose we delete the data for repair number 2100. When we delete this row (the second one in Figure 3-8), we remove not only data about the repair, but also data about the machine itself. We will no longer

ItemNumber	Type	AcquisitionCost	RepairNumber	RepairDate	RepairAmount
100	Drill Press	3500	2000	5/5/04	375
200	Lathe	4750	2100	5/7/04	255
100	Drill Press	3500	2200	5/19/04	178
300	Mill	27300	2300	5/19/04	1785
100	Drill Press	3500	2400	5/11/04	0
100	Drill Press	3500	2600	6/1/04	275

Figure 3-8

The EQUIPMENT_REPAIR Table

Figure 3-9

ItemNumber	Type	AcquisitionCost	RepairNumber	RepairDate	RepairAmount
100	Drill Press	3500	2000	5/5/04	375
200	Lathe	4750	2100	5/7/04	255
100	Drill Press	3500	2200	5/19/04	178
300	Mill	27300	2300	5/19/04	1785
100	Drill Press	3500	2400	5/11/04	0
100	Drill Press	5500	2500	6/1/04	275

The EQUIPMENT_
REPAIR Table after
Incorrect Update

know, for example, that the machine was a Lathe and that its AcquisitionPrice was 4750. When we delete one row, the structure of this table forces us to lose facts about two different things, a machine and a repair, This condition is called a **deletion anomaly.**

Now suppose we want to enter the first repair for a piece of equipment. To enter repair data, we need to know not just RepairNumber, RepairDate, and RepairAmount, we also need to know ItemNumber, Type, and AcquisitionCost. If we work in the repair department, this is a problem because we are unlikely to know the value of AcquisitionPrice. The structure of this table forces us to enter facts about two entities when we just want to enter facts about one. This condition is called an **insertion anomaly.**

Finally, suppose we want to change existing data. If we alter a value of RepairNumber, RepairDate, or RepairAmount, there is no problem. But, if we alter a value of ItemNumber, Type, or AcquisitionCost, we may create a data inconsistency. To see why, suppose we update the last row of the table in Figure 3-8, using the data (100, 'Drill Press, 5500, 2500, '6/1/04', 275).

Figure 3-9 shows the table after this erroneous update. The drill press has two different AcquisitionCosts. Clearly, this is an error. Equipment cannot be acquired at two different costs. If there were, say, 10,000 rows in the table, however, it might be very difficult to detect this error. This condition is called an **update anomaly.**

B T W

Notice that the EQUIPMENT_REPAIR table in Figures 3-8 and 3-9 duplicates data. For example, the AcquisitionCost of the same item of equipment appears several times. Any table that duplicates data is susceptible to update anomalies like the one in Figure 3-9. A table that has such inconsistencies is said to have data integrity problems.

As you will learn in Chapter 4, to improve query speed we sometimes design a table to have duplicated data. Be aware, however, that any time we design a table this way, we open the door to data integrity problems.

A Short History of Normal Forms

When Codd defined the relational model, he noticed that some tables had modification anomalies. In his second paper,[2] he defined first, second, and third normal forms, which are usually denoted 1NF, 2NF, and 3NF. He defined any table that meets the conditions to be a relation (Figure 3-4) to be in 1NF, and he noted that some tables in 1NF had modification anomalies. He found that he could remove some of those anomalies by applying certain conditions. A relation that met those conditions was said to be in 2NF. He also observed, however, that relations in 2NF could also have anomalies, and so he defined 3NF, which is a set of conditions that removes even more anomalies. As time went by, other researchers found still other ways that anomalies can occur, and **Boyce-Codd Normal Form (BCNF)** was defined.

---

[2]Codd, E. F. and A. L. Dean. "Proceedings of 1971 ACM-SIGFIDET Workshop on Data Description," *Access and Control*, San Diego, California, November 11–12, 1971 ACM 1971.

| Figure 3-10 | Summary of Normalization Theory |

Source of Anomaly	Normal Forms	Design Principles
Functional dependencies	1NF, 2NF, 3NF, BCNF	BCNF: Design tables so that every determinant is a candidate key
Multivalued dependencies	4NF	4NF: Move each multivalued dependency to a table of its own
Data constraints and oddities	5NF, DK/NF	DK/NF: Make every constraint a logical consequence of candidate keys and domains

These normal forms are defined so that a relation in BCNF is in 3NF, a relation in 3NF is in 2NF, and a relation in 2NF is in 1NF. Thus, if you put a relation into BCNF, it is automatically in the lesser normal forms.

Normal forms 2NF through BCNF concern anomalies that arise from functional dependencies. Other sources of anomalies were found later, and they led to the definition of fourth and fifth normal forms (4NF and 5NF). So it went, with researchers chipping away at modification anomalies, each one improving on the prior normal form.

In 1982, Fagin published a paper that took a different tack.[3] Instead of looking for just another normal form, Fagin asked, "What conditions need to exist for a relation to have no anomalies?" In that paper, he defined **domain key normal from,** which is abbreviated **DK/NF.** Fagin ended the search for normal forms by showing that a relation in DK/NF has no modification anomalies, and further, that a relation that has no modification anomalies is in DK/NF.

Normalization Categories

As shown in Figure 3-10, normalization theory can be divided into three major categories. Some anomalies arise from functional dependencies, some arise from multivalued dependencies, and some arise from data constraints and odd conditions.

BCNF, 3NF, and 2NF, are all concerned with anomalies that are caused by functional dependencies. A relation that is in BCNF has no modification anomalies from functional dependencies. It is also automatically in 2NF and 3NF. Consequently, we will not consider 2NF or 3NF further. See Date[4] if you want to learn their definitions. Instead, we will focus on transforming relations into BCNF.

As shown in the second row of Figure 3-10, some anomalies arise because of another kind of dependency called a multivalued dependency. Those anomalies can be eliminated by placing each multivalued dependency in a relation of its own, a condition known as 4NF. You will see how to do that in the last section of this chapter.

The third source of anomalies is esoteric. These problems involve specific, rare, and even strange data constraints. Accordingly, we will not discuss them in this text.

---

[3]Fagin, R. "A Normal Form for Relational Databases that Is Based on Domains and Keys," *ACM Transactions on Database Systems,* September 1981, pp. 387–414.
[4]Date, C. J. *Database Systems,* 8th ed. Addison-Wesley, 2003.

Eliminating Anomalies from Functional Dependencies

Most modification anomalies occur because of problems with functional dependencies. You can eliminate such problems if you design (or redesign) your tables so that every determinant is a candidate key. This condition, which is the definition of BCNF, will eliminate all anomalies due to functional dependencies.

The general strategy is summarized in Figure 3-11. Identify every functional dependency in the relation. Identify candidate keys. If there are determinants that are not candidate keys, then the relation is not in BCNF, and it has modification anomalies. To put the relation into BCNF, follow the procedure in step 3. To fix that procedure in your mind, we will illustrate it with five different examples.

Example 1

Consider the SKU_DATA table:

SKU_DATA (SKU, SKU_Description, Department, Buyer)

As discussed earlier, this table has three functional dependencies:

SKU → (SKU_Description, Department, Buyer)

SKU_Description → (SKU, Department, Buyer)

Buyer → Department

SKU and SKU_Description determine all of the columns in the table, so they are candidate keys. Buyer is a determinant, but it does not determine all of the other columns, and hence is not a candidate key. Hence, SKU_DATA has a determinant that is not a candidate key and is therefore not in BCNF. It will have modification anomalies.

To remove such anomalies, in step 3A we move the columns of functional dependency whose determinant is not a candidate key into a new table. In this case, we place Buyer and Department into a new table:

BUYER (Buyer, Department)

Figure 3-11   **Process for Putting a Relation into BCNF**

1. Identify every functional dependency
2. Identify every candidate key
3. If there is a functional dependency that has a determinant that is not a candidate key:
   A. Move the columns of that functional dependency to a new relation
   B. Make the determinant of that functional dependency the primary key of the new relation
   C. Leave a copy of the determinant as a foreign key in the original relation
   D. Create a referential integrity constraint between the original relation and the new relation
4. Repeat step 3 until every determinant of every relation is a candidate key

(Note: In step 3, if there is more than one such functional dependency, start with the one with the most columns.)

Note: In step 3, if there is more than one such functional dependency, start with the one with the most columns.

Next, in step 3B, we make the primary key of the new table the determinant of the functional dependency. In this case, Buyer becomes the primary key:

BUYER (<u>Buyer</u>, Department)

Next, following step 3C, we leave a copy of the determinant as a foreign key in the original relation. Thus, SKU_DATA becomes:

SKU_DATA_2 (<u>SKU</u>, SKU_Description, *Buyer*)

The resulting tables are thus:

SKU_DATA_2 (<u>SKU</u>, SKU_Description, *Buyer*)

BUYER (<u>Buyer</u>, Department)

where SKU_DATA_2.Buyer is a foreign key to the BUYER table.

Both of these tables are now in BCNF and will have no anomalies due to functional dependencies. For the data in these tables to be consistent, however, we also need to define the referential integrity constraint in step 3D:

SKU_DATA_2.Buyer must exist in BUYER.Buyer

This statement means that every value in the Buyer column of SKU_DATA_2 must also exist as a value in the Buyer column of BUYER. Sample data for the resulting tables are shown in Figure 3-12.

Example 2

Now consider the EQUIPMENT_REPAIR relation in Figure 3-8. The structure of the table is:

EQUIPMENT_REPAIR (ItemNumber, Type, AcquisitionCost, RepairNumber, RepairDate, RepairAmount)

Examining the data in Figure 3-8, the functional dependencies are:

ItemNumber → (Type, AcquisitionCost)

RepairNumber → (ItemNumber, Type, AcquisitionCost, RepairDate, RepairAmount)

Figure 3-12

Sample Data for SKU_DATA_2 and BUYER Relations

SKU_DATA_2 Relation

SKU	SKU_Description	Buyer
100100	Std. Scuba Tank, Yellow	Pete Hansen
100200	Std. Scuba Tank, Magenta	Pete Hansen
101100	Dive Mask, Small Clear	Nancy Meyers
101200	Dive Mask, Med Clear	Nancy Meyers
201000	Half-dome Tent	Cindy Lo
202000	Half-dome Tent Footprint	Cindy Lo
301000	Light Fly Climbing Harness	Jerry Martin
302000	Locking carabiner, Oval	Jerry Martin

BUYER Relation

Buyer	Department
Cindy Lo	Camping
Jerry Martin	Climbing
Nancy Meyers	Water Sports
Pete Hansen	Water Sports

Both ItemNumber and RepairNumber are determinants, but only ItemNumber is a candidate key. Accordingly, EQUIPMENT_REPAIR is not in BCNF and is subject to modification anomalies. Following the procedure in Figure 3-11, we place the columns of the problematic functional dependency into a separate table as follows:

ITEM (ItemNumber, Type, AcquisitionCost)

and remove all but ItemNumber from EQUIPMENT_REPAIR to create:

REPAIR (*ItemNumber*, RepairNumber, RepairDate, RepairAmount)

We also need to create the referential integrity constraint:

REPAIR.ItemNumber must exist in ITEM.ItemNumber

Data for these two new relations are shown in Figure 3-13.

B T W

There is another, more intuitive way to think about normalization. Remember Ms. Gazernenplatz, your eighth grade English teacher? She said that every paragraph should have a single theme. If you write a paragraph that has two themes, you should break it up into two paragraphs, each with a single theme.

The problem with the EQUIPMENT_REPAIR relation is that it has two themes: one about repairs and a second about items. We eliminated modification anomalies by breaking that single table with two themes into two tables, each with a single theme. Sometimes, it is helpful to look at a table and ask, "How many themes does it have?" If it has more than one, then redefine the table so that it has a single theme.

Example 3

Consider now the ORDER_ITEM relation with structure:

ORDER_ITEM (OrderNumber, SKU, Quantity, Price, ExtendedPrice)

with functional dependencies:

(OrderNumber, SKU) → (Quantity, Price, ExtendedPrice)

(Quantity, Price) → ExtendedPrice

Figure 3-13

Sample Data for the REPAIR and ITEM Relations

REPAIR Relation

ItemNumber	RepairNumber	RepairDate	RepairAmount
100	2000	5/5/04	375
200	2100	5/7/04	255
100	2200	5/19/04	178
300	2300	5/19/04	1785
100	2400	5/11/04	0
100	2600	6/1/04	275

ITEM Relation

ItemNumber	Type	AcquisitionCost
100	Drill Press	3500
200	Lathe	4750
300	Mill	27300

This table is not in BCNF because the determinant (Quantity, Price) is not a candidate key. We can follow the same normalization practice as illustrated in examples 1 and 2, but in this case, because the second functional dependency arises from the formula ExtendedPrice = Quantity * Price, we reach a silly result.

To see why, follow the procedure in Figure 3-11 to create tables such that every determinant is a candidate key. This means that we move the columns Quantity, Price, and ExtendedPrice to tables of their own as follows:

EXTENDED_PRICE (<u>Quantity</u>, <u>Price</u>, ExtendedPrice)

ORDER_ITEM (<u>OrderNumber</u>, <u>SKU</u>, *Quantity, Price*)

Notice that we left both Quantity and Price in the original relation as a composite foreign key. These two tables are in BCNF, but the values in the EXTENDED_PRICE table are ridiculous. They are just the results of multiplying Quantity by Price. We need not create a table to store these results, instead, any time we need to know ExtendedPrice, we just compute it. In fact, we can define this formula to the DBMS and let the DBMS compute the value of ExtendedPrice when necessary. You will see how to do this with Oracle and SQL Server in Chapters 10 and 11, respectively.

Using the formula, we can remove ExtendedPrice from the table. The resulting table is in BCNF:

ORDER_ITEM (<u>OrderNumber</u>, <u>SKU</u>, Quantity, Price)

Note that Quantity and Price are no longer foreign keys.

Example 4

Consider the following table that stores data about student activities:

STUDENT_ACTIVITY (SID, Name, Club, Cost, AmtPaid)

where SID is a student identifier, Name is student name, Club is the name of a club, Cost is the cost of joining a club, and AmtPaid is the amount the student has paid to that club. Figure 3-14 shows sample data for this table.

SID is a unique student identifier, so we know that SID → Name. However, does SID → Club? It does if a student belongs to just one club, but it does not if a student belongs to more than one club. Looking at the data, student 200 belongs to two different clubs, so SID does not determine Club. SID does not determine Cost or AmtPaid, either.

Now consider the Name column. Does Name determine SID? Is, for example, the value 'Jones' always paired with the same value of SID? No, there are two students named 'Jones', and they have different SID values. Name does not determine any other column in this table, either. Considering the next column, Club, we know that many students can belong to a club. Therefore, Club does not determine SID or Name. Does Club determine Cost? Is the value 'Scuba', for example, always paired with the same value of Cost? From this data, it appears so, and using just this sample data, we can conclude that Club determines Cost.

Figure 3-14

Sample Data for the
STUDENT_ACTIVITY
Relation

SID	Name	Club	Cost	AmtPaid
100	Jones	Scuba	400	0
200	Chau	Scuba	400	400
200	Chau	Skiing	550	550
300	Garrett	Climbing	150	150
400	Jones	Skiing	550	550

However, this data is just a sample. Logically, it is possible for students to pay different costs, perhaps because they select different levels of club membership. If that were the case, then we would say (SID, Club) → Cost. To find out, we need to check with the users. Here, assume that all students pay the same cost for a given club. The last column is AmtPaid, and it does not determine anything.

So far, we have two functional dependencies:

SID → Name

Club → Cost

Are there other functional dependencies with composite determinants? No single column determines AmtPaid, so consider possible composite determinants for it. The amount paid is dependent on both the student and the club the student has joined. Therefore, it is determined by the combination of the determinants Student and Club. Thus, we can say

(SID, Club) → AmtPaid

So far we have three determinants: SID, Club, and (SID, Club). Are any of these candidate keys? Do any of these determinants identify a unique row? From the data, it appears that (SID, Club) identifies a unique row and is a candidate key. Again, in real situations, we would need to check this assumption out with the users.

STUDENT_ACTIVITY is not in BCNF because columns SID and Club are both determinants, but neither is a candidate key. SID and Club are only part of the candidate key (SID, Club).

B T W

Both SID and Club are *part of* the candidate key (SID, Club). This, however, is not good enough. A determinant must have all of the same columns to be the same as a candidate key. You can remember this fact with the anonymous ditty: "I swear to construct my tables so that all nonkey columns are dependent on the key, the whole key, and nothing but the key, so help me Codd."

To normalize this table, we need to construct tables so that every determinant is a candidate key. We can do this by creating a separate table for each functional dependency as we did before. The result is:

STUDENT (SID, Name)

CLUB (Club, Cost)

PAYMENT (_SID_, _Club_, Cost)

with referential integrity constraints:

PAYMENT.SID must exist in STUDENT.SID

and

PAYMENT.Club must exist in CLUB.Club

These tables are in BCNF and will have no anomalies from functional dependencies. The sample data for the normalized tables are shown in Figure 3-15.

Figure 3-15

Sample Data for
STUDENT, PAYMENT,
and CLUB Relations

STUDENT Relation

SID	Name
100	Jones
200	Chau
300	Garrett
400	Jones

CLUB Relation

Club	Cost
Climbing	150
Scuba	400
Skiing	550

PAYMENT Relation

SID	Club	AmtPaid
100	Scuba	0
100	Skiing	550
200	Scuba	400
300	Climbing	150
400	Skiing	550

Example 5

Now consider a normalization process that requires two iterations of step 3 in the procedure in Figure 3-11. To do this, extend the SKU_DATA relation by adding the budget code of each department as follows:

SKU_DATA_3 (SKU, SKU_Description, Department, Dept_BudgetCode, Buyer)

Sample data for this relation are shown in Figure 3-16.

SKU_DATA_3 has the following functional dependencies:

SKU → (SKU_Description, Department, Dept_BudgetCode, Buyer)

SKU_Description → (SKU, Department, Dept_BudgetCode, Buyer)

Buyer → (Department, Dept_BudgetCode)

Department → Dept_BudgetCode

Of the four determinants, both SKU and SKU_Description are candidate keys, but neither Department nor Buyer is a candidate key. Therefore, this relation is not in BCNF.

To normalize this table, we must transform this table into two or more tables that are in BCNF. In this case, there are two problematic functional dependencies, and according to the note at the end of the procedure in Figure 3-11, we take the one with the largest number of columns first. In this case, we take the columns of

Figure 3-16

Sample Data for the
SKU_DATA_3 Relation

SKU	SKU_Description	Department	Dept_BudgetCode	Buyer
100100	Std. Scuba Tank, Yellow	Water Sports	BC-100	Pete Hansen
100200	Std. Scuba Tank, Magenta	Water Sports	BC-100	Pete Hansen
101100	Dive Mask, Small Clear	Water Sports	BC-100	Nancy Meyers
101200	Dive Mask, Med Clear	Water Sports	BC-100	Nancy Meyers
201000	Half-dome Tent	Camping	BC-200	Cindy Lo
202000	Half-dome Tent Footprint	Camping	BC-200	Cindy Lo
301000	Light Fly Climbing Harness	Climbing	BC-300	Jerry Martin
302000	Locking carabiner, Oval	Climbing	BC-300	Jerry Martin

Buyer → (Department, Dept_BudgetCode)

and place them in a table of their own.

Next, we make the determinant the primary key of the new table, remove all columns except Buyer from SKU_DATA_3, and make Buyer a foreign key of the new version of SKU_DATA_3. The results are:

BUYER (<u>Buyer</u>, Department, Dept_BudgetCode)

SKU_DATA_4 (<u>SKU</u>, SKU_Description, *Buyer*)

We also create the referential integrity constraint:

SKU_DATA_4.Buyer must exist in BUYER.Buyer

The functional dependencies from SKU_DATA_4 are:

SKU → (SKU_Description, Buyer)

SKU_Description → (SKU, Buyer)

and the functional dependencies from BUYER are:

Buyer → (Department, Dept_BudgetCode)

Department → Dept_BudgetCode

BUYER is not in BCNF because Department is a determinant that is not a candidate key. In this case, we must move (Department, Dept_BudgetCode) into a table of its own. Following the procedure in Figure 3-11, we now have:

BUYER_2 (<u>Buyer</u>, *Department*)

DEPARTMENT (<u>Department</u>, Dept_BudgetCode)

and

SKU_DATA_4 (<u>SKU</u>, SKU_Description, *Buyer*)

with referential integrity constraints:

SKU_DATA_4.Buyer must exist in BUYER_2.Buyer

and

BUYER_2.Department must exist in DEPARTMENT.Department

The functional dependencies from all three of these tables are:

Buyer → Department

Department → Dept_BudgetCode

SKU → (SKU_Description, Buyer)

SKU_Description → SKU, Buyer

Figure 3-17

Sample Data for
BUYER_2,
DEPARTMENT, and
SKU_DATA_4 Relations

BUYER_2 Relation

Buyer	Department
Cindy Lo	Camping
Jerry Martin	Climbing
Nancy Meyers	Water Sports
Pete Hansen	Water Sports

DEPARTMENT Relation

Department	Dept_BudgetCode
Camping	BC-200
Climbing	BC-300
Water Sports	BC-100

SKU_DATA_4 Relation

SKU	SKU_Description	Buyer
100100	Std. Scuba Tank, Yellow	Pete Hansen
100200	Std. Scuba Tank, Magenta	Pete Hansen
101100	Dive Mask, Small Clear	Nancy Meyers
101200	Dive Mask, Med Clear	Nancy Meyers
201000	Half-dome Tent	Cindy Lo
202000	Half-dome Tent Footprint	Cindy Lo
301000	Light Fly Climbing Harness	Jerry Martin
302000	Locking carabiner, Oval	Jerry Martin

At last, every determinant is a candidate key and all three of the tables are in BCNF. The results of these operations are shown in Figure 3-17.

Eliminating Anomalies from Multivalued Dependencies

All of the anomalies in the last section were due to functional dependencies. Anomalies can arise from another kind of dependency, **multivalued dependency,** as well. A multivalued dependency occurs when a determinant is matched with a particular *set* of values. Examples of multivalued dependencies are:

Employee $\rightarrow\rightarrow$ Degree

Employee $\rightarrow\rightarrow$ Sibling

PartKit $\rightarrow\rightarrow$ Part

Such expressions are read as "Employee multidetermines Degree" and "Employee multidetermines Sibling" and "Part_Kit multidetermines Part." Note that multideterminants are shown with a double arrow rather than a single arrow.

In each case, the determinant is associated with a set of values. Example data for each of these multidependencies are shown in Figure 3-18. Employee Jones, for example, has degrees AA and BS. Employee Greene has degrees BS, MS, and PhD. Employee Chau has just one degree, BS. Similarly, Employee Jones has siblings (brothers and sisters) Fred, Sally, and Frank. Employee Greene has sibling Nikki, and Employee Chau has siblings Jonathan and Eileen. Finally PartKit Bike Repair has parts Wrench, Screwdriver, and Tube Fix. Other kits have parts as shown in Figure 3-18.

Unlike functional dependencies, the determinant of a multivalued dependency can never be the primary key. In all three of the tables in Figure 3-18, the primary key consists of the composite of the two columns in each table. The primary key of the EMPLOYEE_DEGREE table is the composite (Employee, Degree).

Multivalued dependencies pose no problem as long as they exist in tables of their own. None of the tables in Figure 3-18 have modification anomalies. However, if A$\rightarrow\rightarrow$B, then

Figure 3-18

Three Examples
of Multivalued
Dependencies

Employee →→ Degree

Employee	Degree
Jones	BS
Jones	AA
Greene	PhD
Greene	MS
Greene	BS
Chau	BS

Employee →→ Sibling

Employee	Sibling
Jones	Fred
Jones	Sally
Jones	Frank
Greene	Nikki
Chau	Jonathan
Chau	Eileen

PartKit →→ Part

PartKit	Part
Bike Repair	Wrench
Bike Repair	Screwdriver
Bike Repair	Tube Fix
Vice	Vice Jaw
Vice	Handle
Vice	Extension Screw
First Aid	Bandaids
First Aid	Aspirin
First Aid	Elastic Band
First Aid	Ibprofin

any relation that contains A, B, and one or more additional columns will have modification anomalies.

For example, consider the situation if we combine the employee data in Figure 3-18 into a single table with three columns (Employee, Degree, Sibling) as shown in Figure 3-19.

Now, what actions need to be taken if student Jones earns an MBA? We must add two rows to the table. If we do not, if we only add the row ('Jones', 'MBA', 'Fred'), it will

Figure 3-19

Relation with Two
Multivalued
Dependencies

Employee	Degree	Sibling
Jones	AA	Fred
Jones	BS	Fred
Jones	AA	Sally
Jones	BS	Sally
Jones	AA	Frank
Jones	BS	Frank
Greene	BS	Nikki
Greene	MS	Nikki
Greene	PhD	Nikki
Chau	BS	Jonathan
Chau	BS	Eileen

Figure 3-20

Relation with a
Functional Dependency
and a Multivalued
Dependency

PartKit	Part	Price
Bike Repair	Wrench	14.95
Bike Repair	Screwdriver	14.95
Bike Repair	Tube Fix	14.95
Vice	Vice Jaw	125.00
Vice	Handle	125.00
Vice	Extension Screw	125.00
First Aid	Bandaids	24.95
First Aid	Aspirin	24.95
First Aid	Elastic Band	24.95
First Aid	Ibprofin	24.95

appear as if Jones is an MBA with her brother, but not with her sister. On the other hand, suppose Greene earns an MBA? Then we need only add one row ('Greene', 'MBA', 'Nikki'). But, if Chau earns an MBA, we need to add two rows. These are insertion anomalies. There are equivalent modification and deletion anomalies as well.

In Figure 3-19, we combined two multivalued dependencies into a single table and obtained modification anomalies. Unfortunately, we will also get anomalies if we combine a multivalued dependency with any other column, even if that other column has no multivalued dependency.

Figure 3-20 shows what happens when we combine the multivalued dependency PartKit →→ Part with the functional dependency PartKit → Price. For the data to be consistent, we must repeat the value of price for as many rows as each kit has parts. For this example, we must add three rows for the Bike Repair kit and four rows for First Aid kit. The result is duplicated data that can cause data integrity problems.

Now you also know the problem with the relation in Figure 3-2. Anomalies exist in that table because BuyerName →→ SKU_Managed and BuyerName →→ CollegeMajor. Fortunately, it is easy to deal with multivalued dependencies: Put them into a table of their own. None of the tables in Figure 3-18 have modification anomalies, because each table consists of only the columns in a single, multivalued dependency. Thus, to fix the table in Figure 3-2, we must move BuyerName and SKU_Managed into one table and BuyerName and CollegeMajor into a second table:

PRODUCT_BUYER_SKU (BuyerName, SKU_Managed)

PRODUCT_BUYER_MAJOR (BuyerName, CollegeMajor)

The results are shown in Figure 3-21.

If we want to maintain strict equivalence between these tables, we would also add the referential integrity constraint:

**PRODUCT_BUYER_SKU.BuyerName must be identical to
PRODUCT_BUYER_MAJOR.BuyerName**

Figure 3-21

Placing Two of
the Multivalued
Dependencies
in Figure 3-2 into
Separate Relations

BUYER_SKU Table

BuyerName	SKU_Managed
Nancy Meyers	101100
Nancy Meyers	101200
Pete Hansen	100100
Pete Hansen	100200

BUYER_MAJOR Table

BuyerName	CollegeMajor
Nancy Meyers	Art
Nancy Meyers	Info Systems
Pete Hansen	Business

This referential integrity constraint may not be necessary, depending on the requirements of the application.

Notice that when you put multivalued dependencies into a table of their own, they disappear. The result is just a table with two columns, and the primary key (and sole candidate key) is the composite of those two columns. When multivalued dependencies have been isolated in this way, the table is said to be in **fourth normal form,** or **4NF.**

The hardest part of multivalued dependencies is finding them. Once you know they exist in a table, just move them into a table of their own. Whenever you encounter tables with odd anomalies, especially anomalies that require you to insert, modify, or delete different numbers of rows to maintain integrity, check for multivalued dependencies.

B T W

You will sometimes hear people use the term *normalize* in phrases like, "that table has been normalized" or "check to see if those tables are normalized." Unfortunately, not everyone means the same thing with these words. Some people do not know about BCNF, and they will use it to mean tables in 3NF, which is a lesser form of normalization, one that allows for anomalies from functional dependencies that BCNF does not allow. Others use it to mean tables that are both BCNF and 4NF. Others may mean something else. The best choice is to use the term *normalize* to mean tables that are in both BCNF and 4NF.

⊚ SUMMARY

Databases arise from three sources: from existing data, from new systems development, and from the redesign of existing databases. This chapter and the next are concerned with databases that arise from existing data. Even though a table is a simple concept, certain tables can lead to surprisingly difficult processing problems. This chapter uses the concept of normalization to understand and possibly solve those problems. Figure 3-3 lists terms you should be familiar with.

A relation is a special case of a table; all relations are tables, but not all tables are relations. Relations are tables that have the properties listed in Figure 3-4. Three sets of terms are used to describe relation structure: (relation, attribute, tuple); (table, column, row); and (file, field, and record). Sometimes these terms are mixed and matched. In practice, the terms *table* and *relation* are commonly used synonymously, and we will do so for the balance of this text.

In a functional dependency, the value of one attribute, or attributes, determines the value of another. In the functional dependency $A \rightarrow B$, attribute A is called the determinant. Some functional dependencies arise from equations, but many others do not. The purpose of a database is, in fact, to store instances of functional dependencies that do not arise from equations. Determinants that have more than one attribute are called composite determinants. If $A \rightarrow (B, C)$, then $A \rightarrow B$ and $A \rightarrow C$. However, if $(A, B) \rightarrow C$, then, in general, neither $A \rightarrow C$ nor $B \rightarrow C$.

If $A \rightarrow B$, the values of A may or may not be unique in a relation. However, every time a given value of A appears, it will be paired with the same value of B. A determinant is unique in a relation only if it determines every other attribute of the relation. You cannot always rely on determining functional dependencies from sample data. The best idea is to verify your conclusions with the users of the data.

A key is a combination of one or more columns used to identify one or more rows. A composite key is a key with two or more attributes. A determinant that determines every other attribute is called a candidate key. A relation may have more than one candidate key. One of them is selected to be used by the DBMS for finding rows and is called the primary key. A surrogate key is an artificial attribute used as a primary key. The value of a surrogate key is supplied by the DBMS and has no meaning to the user. A foreign key is a key in one table that references the primary key of a second table. A referential integrity constraint is a limitation on data values of a foreign key that ensures that every value of the foreign key has a match to a value of a primary key.

The three kinds of modification anomalies are insert, update, and delete. Codd and others defined normal forms for describing different table structures that lead to anomalies. Some anomalies arise from functional dependencies. Three forms, 2NF, 3NF, and BCNF, are used to treat such anomalies. In this text, we are only concerned with the best of these forms, BCNF. If a relation is in BCNF, then no anomalies from functional dependencies can occur. A relation is in BCNF if every determinant is a candidate key.

Some anomalies arise from multivalued dependencies. A multidetermines B, or $A \rightarrow\rightarrow B$, if A determines a set of values. If A multidetermines B, then any relation that contains A, B, and one or more other columns will have modification anomalies. Anomalies due to multivalued dependencies can be eliminated by placing the multivalued dependency in a table of its own.

REVIEW QUESTIONS

3.1   Name three sources for databases.

3.2   What is the basic premise of this and the next chapter?

3.3   Explain what is wrong with the table in Figure 3-2.

3.4   Define each of the terms listed in Figure 3-3.

3.5   Describe the characteristics of a table that make it a relation.

3.6   Give an example of two tables that are not relations.

3.7   Suppose that two columns in two different tables have the same column name. What convention is used to give each a unique name?

3.8   Must all the values in the same column of a relation have the same length?

3.9   Explain the three different sets of terms used to describe tables, columns, and rows.

3.10 Explain the difference between functional dependencies that arise from equations and those that do not.

3.11 Intuitively, what does the functional dependency PartNumber → PartWeight mean?

3.12 Explain the following statement: "The only reason for having relations is to store instances of functional dependencies."

3.13 What does the expression (FirstName, LastName) → Phone mean?

3.14 What is a composite determinant?

3.15 If (A, B) → C , then can we also say that A → C?

3.16 If A → (B, C), then can we also say that A → B?

3.17 For the SKU_DATA table in Figure 3-1, explain why Buyer determines Department, but Department does not determine Buyer.

3.18 For the SKU_DATA table in Figure 3-1, explain why SKU_Description → (SKU, Department, Buyer).

3.19 If it is true that PartNumber → PartWeight, does that mean that PartNumber will be unique in a relation?

3.20 Under what conditions will a determinant be unique in a relation?

3.21 What is the best test for determining whether a determinant is unique?

3.22 What is a composite key?

3.23 Explain the difference between a candidate key and a primary key.

3.24 What is a surrogate key?

3.25 Where does the value of a surrogate key come from?

3.26 When would you use a surrogate key?

3.27 What is a foreign key?

3.28 The term domestic key is not used. If it were used, however, what do you think it would mean?

3.29 What is a normal form?

3.30 Illustrate deletion, modification, and insertion anomalies on the STUDENT_ ACTIVITY relation in Figure 3-14.

3.31 Explain why duplicated data leads to data integrity problems.

3.32 What relations are in 1NF?

3.33 Which normal forms are concerned with functional dependencies?

3.34 If a relation is in BCNF, what can we say about it with regard to 2NF and 3NF?

3.35 What conditions are required for a relation to be in BCNF?

3.36 What normal form is concerned with multivalued dependencies?

3.37 What is the premise of Fagin's work on DK/NF?

3.38 Summarize the three categories of normalization theory.

3.39 In general, how can you transform a relation not in BCNF into ones that are in BCNF?

3.40 What is a referential integrity constraint?

3.41 Explain the role of referential integrity constraints in normalization.

3.42 Why is an un-normalized relation like a paragraph with multiple themes?

3.43 In example 3, why is the EXTENDED_PRICE relation silly?

3.44 In example 4, under what conditions is (SID, Club) $\rightarrow$ Cost more accurate than Club $\rightarrow$ Cost?

3.45 If a determinant is part of a candidate key, is that good enough for BCNF?

3.46 In example 5, why are the following two tables not correct?

DEPARTMENT (<u>Department</u>, Dept_BudgetCode, Buyer)

SKU_DATA_4 (<u>SKU</u>, SKU_Description, *Department*)

3.47 How does a multivalued dependency differ from a functional dependency?

3.48 Consider the relation:

PERSON (Name, Sibling, Shoe_Size)

Assume Name $\rightarrow\rightarrow$ Sibling and Name $\rightarrow$ Shoe_Size. Describe deletion, modification, and insertion anomalies for this relation.

3.49 Place the PERSON relation into 4NF.

3.50 Consider the relation:

PERSON_2 (Name, Sibling, Shoe_Size, Hobby)

Assume Name $\rightarrow\rightarrow$ Sibling, Name $\rightarrow$ Shoe_Size, and Name $\rightarrow\rightarrow$ Hobby. Describe deletion, modification, and insertion anomalies for this relation.

3.51 Place the PERSON_2 relation into 4NF.

PROJECT QUESTIONS

3.52 Consider the table:

STAFF_MEETING (EmployeeName, ProjectName, Date)

The rows of this table record the fact that an employee from a particular project attended a meeting on a given date. Assume that a project meets at most once per day. Also, assume that only one employee represents a given project, but that employees can be assigned to multiple projects.

a. State the functional dependencies.

b. Transform this table into one or more tables in BCNF. State the primary keys, candidate keys, foreign keys, and referential integrity constraints.

c. Is your design in part b an improvement over the original table? What advantages and disadvantages does it have?

3.53 Consider the table:

STUDENT (Number, Name, Dorm, RoomType, DormCost, Club, ClubCost, Sibling, Nickname)

Assume that students pay different dorm costs, depending on the type of room they have, but that all members of a club pay the same cost. Assume that students can have multiple nicknames.

a. State any multivalued dependencies.

b. State the functional dependencies.

c. Transform this table into two or more tables such that each table is in BCNF and in 4NF. State the primary keys, candidate keys, foreign keys, and referential integrity constraints.

MARCIA'S DRY CLEANING

A Assume that Marcia keeps a table of data about her customers. Consider just the following part of that table:

CUSTOMER (Phone, FirstName, LastName)

Explain the conditions under which each of the following are true:

1 **Phone → (FirstName, LastName)**

2 **(Phone, FirstName) → LastName**

3 **(Phone, LastName) → FirstName**

4 **(LastName, FirstName) → Phone**

5 **Phone →→ LastName**

6 **Phone →→ FirstName**

7 **Phone →→ (FirstName, LastName)**

Is condition 7 the same as conditions 5 and 6? Why or why not?

B Consider the tables:

CUSTOMER (Phone, FirstName, LastName)

ORDER (OrderNumber, DateIn, DateOut, *Phone*)

State an appropriate referential integrity constraint.

C   Consider the tables:

CUSTOMER (Phone, <u>FirstName</u>, <u>LastName</u>)

ORDER (<u>OrderNumber</u>, DateIn, DateOut, *FirstName, LastName*)

What does the following referential integrity constraint mean?

ORDER. (FirstName, LastName) must be in CUSTOMER (FirstName, LastName)

Is this constraint the same as:

ORDER. (FirstName) must be in CUSTOMER (FirstName)

and

ORDER. (LastName) must be in CUSTOMER (LastName)

Explain why or why not.

D   Do you prefer the design in B or the design in C? Explain your reasoning.

E   Transform the following table into two or more tables in BCNF and 4NF. Indicate the primary keys, candidate keys, foreign keys, and referential integrity constraints. Make and state assumptions as necessary.

ORDER (CustomerNumber, FirstName, LastName, Phone, OrderNumber, DateIn, DateOut, ItemType, Quantity, ItemPrice, ExtendedPrice, SpecialInstructions)

F   Explain how your answer to question E changes depending on whether you assume CustomerNumber → (FirstName, LastName) or CustomerNumber →→ (FirstName, LastName).

MORGAN IMPORTING

A   Morgan keeps a table of data about the stores from which he purchases. The stores are located in different countries and have different specialties. Consider the following relation:

STORE (Name, City, Country, Owner, Specialty)

Explain the conditions under which the following are true:

1   **Name → City**

2   **City → Name**

3   **City → Country**

4   **(Name, Country) → (City, Owner)**

5   **(City, Specialty) → Name**

6 **Owner** $\rightarrow\rightarrow$ **Name**

7 **Name** $\rightarrow\rightarrow$ **Specialty**

B With regard to the relation in part A:
   1 Specify which of the dependencies in part A seem most appropriate for a small import–export business.
   2 Given your assumptions in B.1, transform the STORE table into a set of tables that are in both 4NF and BCNF. Indicate the primary keys, candidate keys, foreign keys, and referential integrity constraints.

C Consider the relation:

SHIPMENT (ShipmentNumber, VendorName, VendorContact, VendorFax, DepartureDate, ArrivalDate, CountryOfOrigin, Destination, ShipmentCost, InsuranceValue, Insurer)

   1 Write a functional dependency that expresses the fact that the cost of a shipment between two cities is always the same.
   2 Write a functional dependency that expresses the fact the insurance value is always the same for a given vendor.
   3 Write a functional dependency that expresses the fact the insurance value is always the same for a given vendor and country of origin.
   4 Describe two possible multivalued dependencies in SHIPMENT.
   5 State what you believe are reasonable functional dependencies for the SHIPMENT relation for a small import–export business.
   6 State what you believe are reasonable multivalued dependencies for the SHIPMENT relation.
   7 Using your assumptions in 5 and 6, transform SHIPMENT into a set of tables in BCNF and 4NF. Indicate the primary keys, candidate keys, foreign keys, and referential integrity constraints.

Database Design Using Normalization

Chapter 3 defined the relational model, described modification anomalies, and discussed normalization using BCNF and 4NF. In this chapter, we apply those concepts to the design of databases that are created from existing data.

The premise of this chapter is that you have received, from some source, one or more tables of data that are to be stored in a new database. The question is, should that data be stored as is, or should it be transformed in some way before it is stored? Normalization theory plays an important role, as you will see.

Assess Table Structure

When someone gives you a set of tables and asks you to construct a database to store them, your first step should be to assess the tables' structure and content. General guidelines for assessing a table's structure are summarized in Figure 4-1.

Begin by counting the number of rows in each table using COUNT(*). Then, to determine the number and type of the table's columns, use SELECT *. If your table has thousands or millions of rows, however, a full query will take considerable time. One way to limit the results of this query is to use the TOP keyword. For example, to obtain all columns for the first 10 rows of the SKU_DATA table, you would code:

```
SELECT      TOP 10 *

FROM        SKU_DATA;
```

This query will show you all columns and data for 10 rows. If you want the top 50 rows, just use TOP 50 instead of TOP 10, and so on.

As shown in Figure 4-1, you should examine the data and determine the functional dependencies, multivalued dependencies, candidate keys, and each table's primary key. Also, look for possible foreign keys. Again, you can base your conclusions on sample data, but that data may not have all of the possible data cases. Therefore, verify your assumptions and conclusions with the users.

With regard to foreign keys, it is risky to assume that referential integrity constraints have been enforced on the data. Instead, check it yourself. For example, suppose you receive data for the following two tables:

SKU_DATA (SKU, SKU_Description, Department, Buyer)

and

BUYER (BuyerName, Department)

After investigation, you learn that SKU is the primary key of SKU_DATA, and that BuyerName is the primary key of BUYER. You also think that SKU_DATA.Buyer is likely a foreign key to BUYER.BuyerName. The question is whether the following referential integrity constraint holds:

SKU_DATA.Buyer must exist in BUYER.BuyerName

You can use SQL to determine whether this is true. The following query will return any values of the foreign key that violate the constraint:

```
SELECT      Buyer
FROM        SKU_DATA
WHERE       Buyer NOT IN

            (SELECT     Buyer

            FROM        SKU_DATA, BUYER

            WHERE       SKU_DATA.Buyer = BUYER.BuyerName);
```

The subquery finds all values of Buyer for which there is a match between SKU_DATA.Buyer and BUYER.BuyerName. If there is any value of Buyer that is not in this subquery, then that value will be displayed in the top query. All such values violate the referential integrity constraint.

After you have assessed the input tables, your next steps depend on whether you are creating an updatable database or a read-only database. We will consider updatable databases first.

Figure 4-1

Guidelines for
Assessing Table
Structure

- Count rows and examine columns
- Examine data values and interview users to determine:
  - Multivalued dependencies
  - Functional dependencies
  - Candidate keys
  - Primary keys
  - Foreign keys
- Assess validity of assumed referential integrity constraints

Designing Updatable Databases

If you are constructing an updatable database, then you need to be concerned about modification anomalies and inconsistent data. Consequently, you must carefully consider normalization principles. Before we begin, let's first review the advantages and disadvantages of normalization.

Advantages and Disadvantages of Normalization

Figure 4-2 summarizes the advantages and disadvantages of normalization. On the positive side, normalization eliminates modification anomalies and reduces data duplication. Reduced data duplication eliminates the possibility of data integrity problems due to inconsistent data values. It also saves file space.

B T W

Why do we say *reduce* data duplication rather than *eliminate* data duplication? The answer is that we cannot eliminate all duplicated data because we must duplicate data in foreign keys. We cannot eliminate Buyer, for example, from the SKU_DATA table, because we would then not be able to relate BUYER and SKU_DATA rows. Values of Buyer are thus duplicated in the BUYER and SKU_DATA tables.

This observation leads to a second question: If we only *reduce* data duplication, how can we claim to *eliminate* inconsistent data values? Data duplication in foreign keys will not cause inconsistencies because referential integrity constraints prohibit them. As long as we enforce such constraints, the duplicate foreign key values will cause no inconsistencies.

Figure 4-2

Advantages and
Disadvantages of
Normalization

- Advantages
  - Eliminate modification anomalies
  - Reduce duplicated data
    - Eliminate data integrity problems
    - Save file space
- Disadvantages
  - More complicated SQL required for multitable subqueries and joins
  - Extra work for DBMS can mean slower applications

Figure 4-3

The **EQUIPMENT_REPAIR**
Table

ItemNumber	Type	AcquisitionCost	RepairNumber	RepairDate	RepairAmount
100	Drill Press	3500	2000	5/5/04	375
200	Lathe	4750	2100	5/7/04	255
100	Drill Press	3500	2200	5/19/04	178
300	Mill	27300	2300	5/19/04	1785
100	Drill Press	3500	2400	5/11/04	0
100	Drill Press	3500	2600	6/1/04	275

On the negative side, normalization requires application programmers to write more complex SQL. To recover the original data, they must write subqueries and joins to connect data stored in separate tables. Also, with normalized data, the DBMS must read two or more tables, and this can mean slower application processing.

Functional Dependencies

As you learned in Chapter 3, we can eliminate anomalies due to functional dependencies by placing all tables in BCNF. Most of the time, the problems of modification anomalies are so great that you should put your tables into BCNF. There are exceptions, however, as you will see.

Normalizing with SQL

As discussed in Chapter 3, a table is in BCNF if all determinants are candidate keys. If any determinant is not a candidate key, we must break the table into two or more tables. Consider an example. Suppose you are given the EQUIPMENT_REPAIR table in Figure 4-3 (the same table shown in Figure 3-8). In Chapter 3, we found that ItemNumber is a determinant, but not a candidate key. Consequently, we created the ITEM and REPAIR tables shown in Figure 4-4. In these tables, ItemNumber is a determinant and a candidate key of ITEM, and RepairNumber is a determinant and primary key of REPAIR; thus both tables are in BCNF.

Now, as a practical matter, how do we transform the data in the format in Figure 4-3 to that in Figure 4-4? To answer that question, we need to use the SQL INSERT command. You will learn the particulars of this command in Chapter 7. For now, we will jump ahead and use one version of it to illustrate the practical side of normalization.

First, we need to create the structure for the two new tables in Figure 4-4. If you are using Microsoft Access, you can follow the procedure in Appendix A to create the tables. Later, in Chapter 7, you will learn how to create tables using SQL, a process that works for all DBMS products.

Figure 4-4

Sample Data for the
ITEM and **REPAIR**
Relations

ITEM Relation

ItemNumber	Type	AcquisitionCost
100	Drill Press	3500
200	Lathe	4750
300	Mill	27300

REPAIR Relation

ItemNumber	RepairNumber	RepairDate	RepairAmount
100	2000	5/5/04	375
200	2100	5/7/04	255
100	2200	5/19/04	178
300	2300	5/19/04	1785
100	2400	5/11/04	0
100	2600	6/1/04	275

Once the tables are created, you can fill them using the SQL INSERT command. To fill the ITEM table, we use:

INSERT INTO ITEM

> **SELECT**   **DISTINCT ItemNumber, Type, AcquisitionCost**
>
> **FROM**   **EQUIPMENT_REPAIR;**

Notice that we must use the DISTINCT keyword because the combination (ItemNumber, Type, AcquisitionCost) is not unique in the EQUIPMENT_REPAIR table. Once we have created the rows in ITEM, we can then use the following INSERT command to fill the rows of REPAIR:

INSERT INTO REPAIR

> **SELECT**   **ItemNumber, RepairNumber, RepairDate, RepairAmount**
>
> **FROM**   **EQUIPMENT_REPAIR;**

As you can see, the SQL statements for normalizing tables are relatively simple. After this transformation, we should probably remove the EQUIPMENT_REPAIR table. For now, you can do this using the graphical tools in Access, SQL Server, or Oracle. In Chapter 7, you will learn how to remove tables using the SQL DROP command. You will also learn how to create the referential integrity constraint that ItemNumber in REPAIR exist in ItemNumber in ITEM.

If you want to practice this exercise, download the Access database Chapter_4.mdb from the text's Web site at **www.prenhall.com/kroenke**. This database has the EQUIP-MENT_REPAIR table with data. Create the new tables (see Appendix A) and then do the normalization by executing the INSERT statements illustrated.

This process can be extended to any number of tables. We will consider richer examples of it in Chapter 7. For now, however, you should have the gist of the process.

Choosing Not to Use BCNF

Although in most cases the tables in an updatable database should be placed in BCNF, in some situations BCNF is just too pure. The classic example of unneeded normalization involves zip and similar postal codes. Consider the following table for customers in the United States:

CUSTOMER (<u>Number</u>, Name, Street, City, State, Zip)

The functional dependencies of this table are:

Number → (Name, Street, City, State, Zip)

and

Zip → (City, State)

This table in not in BCNF because Zip is a determinant that is not a candidate key. We can normalize this table as follows:

CUSTOMER_2 (<u>Number</u>, Name, Street, *Zip*)

ZIP_CODE (<u>Zip</u>, City, State)

with constraint:

CUSTOMER_2.Zip must exist in ZIP_CODE.Zip

The tables CUSTOMER_2 and ZIP_CODE are in BCNF, but consider these tables in light of the advantages and disadvantages of normalization listed in Figure 4-2. Normalization eliminates modification anomalies, but how often does zip code data change? How often does the post office change the city and state assigned to a zip code value? Almost never. The consequences on every business and person would be too severe. So, even though the design allows anomalies to occur, in practice, they will not occur because the data never change. Consider the second advantage: Normalization reduces data duplication and hence improves data integrity. In fact, data integrity problems can happen in the single-table example if someone enters the wrong value for City, State, or Zip. In that case, the database will have inconsistent Zip values. But, normal business processes will cause zip code errors to be noticed, and they will be corrected without problem.

Now consider the disadvantages of normalization. Two separate tables require application programs to write more complex SQL. They also require the DBMS to process two tables, which may make the applications slow. Weighing the advantages and disadvantages, most practitioners would say that the normalized data are just too pure. Zip code data would therefore be left in the original table.

In summary, when you design an updatable database from existing tables, examine every table to determine if it is in BCNF. If a table is not in BCNF, then the table is susceptible to modification anomalies and inconsistent data. In almost all cases, transform the table into tables that are in BCNF. However, if the data are never modified and if data inconsistencies will be easily corrected via the normal operation of business activity, then you may choose not to place the table into BCNF.

Multivalued Dependencies

Unlike functional dependencies, the anomalies from multivalued dependencies are so serious that multivalued dependencies should always be eliminated. Unlike BCNF, there is no gray area. Just place the columns of a multivalued dependency in tables of their own.

As shown in the last section, normalization is not difficult. It does mean that application programmers will have to write subqueries and joins to re-create the original data. Writing subqueries and joins, however, is *nothing* compared with the complexity of code that must be written to handle the anomalies due to multivalued dependencies.

Some experts might object to such a hard and fast rule, but it is justifiable. Although there may be a few rare, obscure, and weird cases in which multivalued dependencies are not problematical, such cases are not worth remembering. Until you have years of database design experience, always eliminate multivalued dependencies from any updatable table.

 # Designing Read-Only Databases

In the course of your career, you will likely be given tables of data and asked to create a read-only database. In fact, this task is commonly assigned to beginners.

Read-only databases are used for querying, reporting, and data mining applications, as you will learn in Chapter 15. Because such databases are never updated, the design guidelines and design priorities are different than those for updatable databases.

For several reasons, normalization is seldom an advantage for a read-only database. For one, if a database is never updated, then no modification anomalies can occur. Hence, considering Figure 4-2, the only reason to normalize a read-only database is to reduce data duplication. However, with no update activity, there is no risk of data integrity problems, so the only remaining reason to avoid duplicated data is to save file space.

Today, however, file space is exceedingly cheap, nearly free. So unless the database is enormous, the cost of storage is minimal. It is true that the DBMS will take longer to find and process data in large tables, so data might be normalized to speed up processing. But even that advantage is not clear-cut. If data are normalized, then data from two or more tables may need to be read, and the time required for the join may overwhelm the time savings of searching in small tables. In almost all cases, normalization of the tables in a read-only database is a bad idea.

Denormalization

Often the data for a read-only database are extracted from operational databases. Because such databases are updatable, they are probably normalized. Hence, you will likely receive the extracted data in normalized form. In fact, if you have a choice, ask for normalized data. For one, normalized data are smaller in size and can be transmitted to you more quickly. Also, if the data are normalized, it will be easier for you to reformat the data for your particular needs.

According to the last section, you probably do not want to leave the data in normalized form for a read-only database. If that is the case, you will need to **denormalize,** or join, the data prior to storage.

Consider the example in Figure 4-5. This is a copy of the normalized student/club/payment data in Figure 3-15. Suppose that you are creating a read-only database that will be used to report amounts due for student club payments. If you store the data in this three-table form, every time someone needs to compare AmtPaid with Cost, he or she must join the three tables together. To do this, that person will need to know how to write a three-table join, and the DBMS will need to perform the join every time the report is prepared.

You can reduce the complexity of the SQL required to read these data and also reduce DBMS processing by joining the tables once and storing the joined result as a single table. The following SQL statement will join the three tables together and store them in a new table named PAYMENT_DATA:

INSERT   INTO PAYMENT_DATA

       SELECT   STUDENT.SID, Name, CLUB.Club, Cost, AmtPaid

       FROM   STUDENT, PAYMENT, CLUB

       WHERE   STUDENT.SID = PAYMENT.SID

       AND   PAYMENT.Club = CLUB.Club;

Figure 4-5

Sample Data for the STUDENT, CLUB, and Relations

STUDENT Relation

SID	Name
100	Jones
200	Chau
300	Garrett
400	Jones

CLUB Relation

Club	Cost
Climbing	150
Scuba	400
Skiing	550

PAYMENT Relation

SID	Club	AmtPaid
100	Scuba	0
100	Skiing	550
200	Scuba	400
300	Climbing	150
400	Skiing	550

Figure 4-6

SID	Name	Club	Cost	AmtPaid
100	Jones	Scuba	400	0
200	Chau	Scuba	400	400
200	Chau	Skiing	550	550
300	Garrett	Climbing	150	150
400	Jones	Skiing	550	550

Denormalized PAYMENT_DATA Relation

As shown in Figure 4-6, the result of this join is the same as the original STUDENT_PAYMENT table.

As you can see, denormalization is simple. Just join the data together and store the joined result as a table. By doing this when you place the data into the read-only database, you save the application programmers from having to code joins for each application, and you also save the DBMS from having to perform joins and subqueries every time the users run a query or create a report.

Customized Duplicated Tables

Because there is no danger of data integrity problems in a read-only database, and because the cost of storage today is miniscule, read-only databases are often designed with many copies of the same data, each copy customized for a particular application.

For example, suppose a company has a large PRODUCT table with the columns listed in Figure 4-7. The columns in this table are used by different business processes. Some are used for purchasing, some are used for sales analysis, some are used for displaying parts on a Web site, some are used for marketing, and some are used for inventory control.

The values of some of these columns, such as those for the picture images, are large. If the DBMS is required to read all of these data for every query, processing is likely to be slow. Accordingly, the organization might create several customized versions of this table for use by different applications. In an updatable database, so much duplicated data would risk severe data integrity problems, but for a read-only database there is no such risk.

Figure 4-7

Columns in the PRODUCT Table

- SKU (Primary Key)
- PartNumber (Candidate key)
- SKU_Description (Candidate key)
- VendorNumber
- VendorName
- VendorContact_1
- VendorContact_2
- VendorStreet
- VendorCity
- VendorState
- VendorZip
- QuantitySoldPastYear
- QuantitySoldPastQuarter
- QuantitySoldPastMonth
- DetailPicture
- ThumbNailPicture
- MarketingShortDescription
- MarketingLongDescription
- PartColor
- UnitsCode
- BinNumber
- ProductionKeyCode

Suppose for this example that the organization designs the following tables:

PRODUCT_PURCHASING (<u>SKU</u>, SKU_Description, VendorNumber, VendorName, VendorContact_1, VendorContact_2, VendorStreet, VendorCity, VendorState, VendorZip)

PRODUCT_USAGE (<u>SKU</u>, SKU_Description, QuantitySoldPastYear, QuantitySoldPastQuarter, QuantitySoldPastMonth)

PRODUCT_WEB (<u>SKU</u>, DetailPicture, ThumbnailPicture, MarketingShortDescription, MarketingLongDescription, PartColor)

PRODUCT_INVENTORY (<u>SKU</u>, PartNumber, SKU_Description, UnitsCode, BinNumber, ProductionKeyCode)

You can create these tables using the graphical design facilities of Access or another DBMS. Once the tables are created, they can be filled using INSERT commands similar to those already discussed. The only tricks are to watch for duplicated data and to use DISTINCT where necessary. See Review Question 4.10.

Common Design Problems

Although normalization and denormalization are the primary considerations when designing databases from existing data, there are four additional practical problems to consider. See Figure 4-8.

The Multivalue, Multicolumn Problem

The table in Figure 4-7 illustrates the first common problem. Notice the columns VendorContact_1 and VendorContact_2. These columns store the names of two contacts at the part vendor. If the company wanted to store the names of three or four contacts using this strategy, it would add columns VendorContact_3, VendorContact_4, and so forth. Consider another example for an employee parking application. Suppose the EMPLOYEE_AUTO table includes basic employee data plus columns for license numbers for up to three cars. The following is the typical table structure:

EMPLOYEE (<u>EmpNumber</u>, Name, Email, Auto1_LicenseNumber, Auto2_LicenseNumber, Auto3_LicenseNumber)

Other examples of this strategy are to store employees' children's names in columns such as Child_1, Child_2, Child_3, and so forth, for as many children as the designer of the table thinks appropriate. Or, to store a picture of a house in a real estate application in columns labeled Picture_1, Picture_2, Picture_3, and so forth.

Storing multiple values in this way is convenient, but it has two serious disadvantages. The more obvious one is that the number of possible items is fixed. What if there are three contacts at a particular vendor? Where do I put the third name if only columns VendorContact_1 and VendorContact_2 are available? Or, if

Figure 4-8

Practical Problems in Designing Database from Existing Data

- Multivalue, Multicolumn Problem
- Inconsistent Values
- Missing Values
- General-Purpose Remarks Column

there are only three columns for child names, where do I put the name of the fourth child? And so forth.

The second disadvantage occurs when querying the data. Suppose I want to know the names of employees who have a child named Gretchen. If there are three child name columns, I must write:

SELECT   *

FROM   **EMPLOYEE**

WHERE   **Child_1 = 'Gretchen'**

    OR   **Child_2 = 'Gretchen'**

    OR   **Child_3 = 'Gretchen';**

Of course, if there are seven child names . . . well, you get the picture.

These problems can be eliminated by using a second table to store the multivalued attribute. For the employee/child case, the tables are:

EMPLOYEE   (<u>EmpNumber</u>, EmpName, Email, ... other data)

CHILD   (<u>ChildName</u>, *EmpNumber*, ... other data)

Using this second structure, employees can have an unlimited number of children, and storage space will be saved for employees who have no children at all. Additionally, to find all of the employees who have a child named Gretchen, we can code:

SELECT   *

FROM   **EMPLOYEE**

WHERE   **EmpNumber IN**

        (SELECT   **EmpNumber**

        FROM   **CHILD**

        WHERE   **ChildName = 'Gretchen');**

This second query is easier to write and understand and will work regardless of the number of children that an employee has.

The alternate design does require the DBMS to process two tables, and if the tables are large and performance is a concern, one can argue that the original design is better. In such cases, storing multi-values in multiple columns may be preferred. Another, less valid objection to the two-table design is as follows: "We only need space for three cars because university policy restricts each employee to registering no more than three cars." The problem with this statement is that databases often outlive policies. Next year that policy may change, and if it does, the database will need to be redesigned. As you will learn in Chapter 8, database redesign is tricky, complex, and expensive. It is better to avoid the need for a database redesign.

B T W

A few years ago, people argued that only three phone number columns are needed per person: Home, Office, and Fax. Later they said, "Well, OK, maybe we need four: Home, Office, Fax, and Mobile." Today, who would want to guess the maximum number of phone numbers a person might have? Rather than guess, just store Phone in a separate table; such a design will allow each person to have from none to an unlimited number of phone numbers.

You are likely to encounter the multivalue, multicolumn problem when creating databases from nondatabase data. It is particularly common in spreadsheet and text data files. Fortunately, the preferred two-table design is easy to create, and the SQL for moving the data to the new design is easy to write.

B T W

The multivalue, multicolumn problem is just another form of a multivalued dependency. For the parking application, for example, rather than store multiple rows in EMPLOYEE for each auto, multiple named columns are created in the table. The underlying problem is the same, however.

Inconsistent Values

Inconsistent values are a serious problem when creating databases from existing data. It occurs because different users or different data sources may use slightly different forms of the same data value. These slight differences may be hard to detect and will create inconsistent and erroneous information.

One of the hardest such problems occurs when different users have coded the same entries differently. One user may have coded a SKU_Description as Corn, Large Can; another may have coded the same item as Can, Corn, Large; and another may have coded the entry as Large Can Corn. Those three entries all refer to the same SKU, but they will be exceedingly difficult to reconcile. These examples are not contrived; such problems frequently occur, especially when combining data from different database, spreadsheet, and file sources.

A related, but simpler, problem occurs when entries are misspelled. One user may enter Coffee, another may enter Coffeee. They will appear as two separate products.

Inconsistent data values are particularly problematic for primary and foreign key columns. Relationships will be missing or wrong when foreign key data is coded inconsistently or misspelled.

Two techniques can be used to find such problems. One is the same as the check for referential integrity shown on page 102. This check will find values for which there is no match and will find misspellings and other inconsistencies.

Another technique is to use GROUP BY on the suspected column. For example, if we suspect that there are inconsistent values on SKU_Description in the SKU_DATA table, we can code:

```
SELECT        SKU_Description, Count(*) as NameCount

FROM          SKU_DATA

GROUP BY      SKU_Description;
```

The result of this query for the SKU_DATA values we have been using is shown in Figure 4-9. In this case, there are no inconsistent values, but if there were, they would stand out. If the list resulting from the select is too long, groups can be selected that have just one or two elements using HAVING. Neither check is foolproof. Sometimes, you just have to read the data.

When working with such data, it is important to develop an error reporting and tracking system to ensure that inconsistencies that users do find are recorded and fixed. Users grow exceedingly impatient with data errors that persist after they have been reported.

Figure 4-9

Using GROUP BY to
Find Inconsistent
Values

SKU_Description	NameCount
Dive Mask, Med Clear	2
Dive Mask, Small Clear	2
Half-dome Tent	2
Half-dome Tent Footprint	2
Light Fly Climbing Harness	2
Locking carabiner, Oval	2
Std. Scuba Tank, Magenta	2
Std. Scuba Tank, Yellow	2

Missing Values

Missing values are a third problem that occurs when creating databases from existing data. A missing value, or **null value,** is a value that has never been provided. It is not the same as a blank value, because a blank value is a value that is known to be blank. A null value is not known to be anything.

The problem with null values is ambiguity. A null value can indicate one of three conditions: The value is inappropriate; the value is appropriate but unknown; or the value is appropriate and known, but no one has entered it into the database. Unfortunately, we cannot tell from a null value which of these conditions is true.

Consider, for example, a null value for the column DateOfLastChildbirth in a PATIENT table. If a row represents a male patient, then the null occurs because the value is inappropriate; a male cannot give birth. Alternatively, if the patient is a female, but the patient has never been asked for the data, then the value is appropriate, but unknown. Finally, the null value could also mean that a date value is appropriate and known, but no one has recorded it into the database.

You can use the SQL term IS NULL to check for null values. For example, to find the number of null values of Quantity in the ORDER_ITEM table, you can code:

SELECT   **COUNT (*) as QuantityNullCount**

FROM   **ORDER_ITEM**

WHERE   **Quantity IS NULL;**

You can also use SELECT * to find the data of any row that has a null value.

When creating a database from existing data, if you try to define a column that has null values as the primary key, the DBMS will generate an error message. You will have to remove the nulls before creating the primary key. Also, you can tell the DBMS that a given column is not allowed to have null values, and when you import the data, if any row has a null value in that column, the DBMS will generate an error message. The particulars depend on the DBMS in use. See Chapter 10 for Oracle and Chapter 11 for SQL Server. You should form the habit of checking for null values in all foreign keys. Any row with a null foreign key will not participate in the relationship. That may or may not be appropriate; you will need to ask the users to find out. Also, null values can be problematic when joining tables together. You will learn how to deal with this problem in Chapter 7.

The General-Purpose Remarks Column

The general-purpose remarks column problem is common, serious, and very difficult to solve. Columns with names such as Remarks, Comments, and Notes often contain important data that are stored in an inconsistent, verbal, and verbose manner. Learn to be wary of columns with any such names.

To see why, consider customer data for a company that sells expensive items such as airplanes, rare cars, boats, or paintings. In a typical setting, someone has used a spreadsheet to track customer data. That person used a spreadsheet not because it was the best tool for such a problem, but rather because he or she had a spreadsheet program and knew how to use it.

The typical spreadsheet has columns like Name, E-mail, Phone, Address, and so forth. It almost always includes a column entitled Remarks, Comments, Notes, or something similar. The problem is that needed data are usually buried in such columns and nearly impossible to dig out. Suppose you want to create a database for a customer contact application for an airplane broker. Assume your design contains the two tables:

CONTACT   (<u>**ID**</u>, **Name, Address, other data . . . ,** *PlaneModel*)

and

AIRPLANE_MODEL (<u>Model</u>, Type, Description, other airplane data)

where CONTACT.PlaneModel is a foreign key to AIRPLANE_MODEL.Model. You want to use this relationship to determine who owns, has owned, or is interested in buying a particular model of airplane.

In the typical situation, the data for the foreign key has been recorded in the Remarks column. If you read the Remarks data, you will find entries like: 'Wants to buy a Piper Seneca II', 'Owner of a Piper Seneca II', and 'Possible buyer for a turbo Seneca'. All three of these rows should have a value of PlaneModel equal to 'Piper Seneca II', but you will pull your hair out making that determination.

Another problem with general-purpose remarks columns is that they are used inconsistently and contain multiple data items. One user may have used it to store the name of the spouse of the contact, another may have used it to store airplane models as just described, and a third may have used it to store the date the customer was last contacted. Or, the same user may have used it for all three purposes at different times!

The best solution in this case is to identify all of the different purposes of the remarks column, create new columns for each of those purposes, and then extract the data and store it into the new columns as appropriate. However, this solution can seldom be automated.

In practice, all solutions require patience and hours of labor. Learn to be wary of such columns, and don't take such jobs on a fixed-price basis!

⊚ SUMMARY

When constructing a database from existing data, the first step is to asses the structure and content of the input tables. Count the number of rows and use SELECT TOP 10 * to learn the columns in the data. Then, examine the data and determine functional dependencies, multivalued dependencies, candidate keys, each table's primary key, and foreign keys. Check out the validity of possible referential integrity constraints.

Design principles differ depending on whether an updatable or read-only database is being constructed. If the former, then modification anomalies and inconsistent data are concerns. The advantages of normalization are elimination of modification anomalies, reduced data duplication, and the elimination of data inconsistencies. The disadvantages are that more complex SQL will be required and application performance may be slower.

For updatable databases, most of the time the problems of modification anomalies are so great that all tables should be placed in BCNF. SQL for normalization is easy to write. In some cases, if the data will be updated infrequently and if inconsistencies are readily corrected by business processes, then BCNF may be too pure and the tables should be left un-normalized. The problems of multivalued dependencies are so great that they should always be removed.

Read-only databases are created for reporting, querying, and data mining applications. Creating such a database is a task commonly assigned to beginners. When designing read-only databases, normalization is less desired. If input data is normalized, it frequently needs to be denormalized by joining it together and storing the joined result. Also, sometimes many copies of the same data are stored in tables customized for particular applications.

Four common problems occur when creating databases from existing data. The multivalue, multicolumn design sets a fixed number of repeating values and stores each in a column of its own. Such a design limits the number of items allowed and results in awkward SQL query statements. A better design results from putting multiple values in a table of their own.

Inconsistent values result when data arise from different users and applications. Inconsistent foreign key values create incorrect relationships. Data inconsistencies can be detected using SQL statements, as illustrated in this chapter. A null value is not the same as a blank. A null value is not known to be anything. Null values are a problem because they are ambiguous. They can mean that a value is inappropriate; unknown; or known, but not yet been entered into the database.

The general-purpose remarks column is a column that is used for different purposes. It collects data items in an inconsistent and verbose manner. Such columns are especially problematic if they contain data needed for a foreign key. Even if they do not, they often contain data for several different columns. Automated solutions are not possible, and the correction requires patience and labor.

◉ REVIEW QUESTIONS

4.1   Summarize the premise of this chapter.

4.2   When you receive a set of tables, what steps should you take to assess their structure and content?

4.3   Show SQL statements to count the number of rows and to list the top 15 rows of the RETAIL_ORDER table.

4.4   Suppose you receive the following two tables:

DEPARTMENT (DepartmentName, BudgetCode)

EMPLOYEE (EmpNumber, Name, Email, DepartmentName)

and you conclude that EMPLOYEE.DepartmentName is a foreign key to DEPARTMENT.DepartmentName. Show SQL for determining whether the following referential integrity constraint has been enforced:

**EMPLOYEE.DepartmentName must exist in
DEPARTMENT.DepartmentName**

4.5   Summarize how database design principles differ with regards to the design of updatable databases and the design of read-only databases.

4.6   Describe two advantages of normalized tables.

4.7   Why do we say that data duplication is only reduced? Why is it not eliminated?

4.8   If data duplication is only reduced, how can we say that the possibility of data inconsistencies has been eliminated?

4.9   Describe two disadvantages of normalized tables.

4.10   Suppose you are given the table:

EMPLOYEE_DEPARTMENT (EmpNumber, Name, Email, DepartmentName, BudgetCode)

and you wish to transform this table into the two tables:

EMPLOYEE (EmpNumber, Name, Email, DepartmentName)

and

DEPARTMENT (DepartmentName, BudgetCode)

Show SQL statements for filling the EMPLOYEE and DEPARTMENT tables with data from EMPLOYEE_DEPARTMENT.

4.11   Summarize the reasons explained in this chapter for not placing zip code values into BCNF.

4.12   Describe a situation, other than the one for zip codes, in which one would choose not to place tables into BCNF. Justify your decision not to use BCNF.

4.13   According to this text, under what situations should you choose not to remove multivalued dependencies from a relation?

4.14   Compare the difficulty of writing subqueries and joins with the difficulty of dealing with anomalies caused by multivalued dependencies.

4.15   Describe three uses for a read-only database.

4.16   How does the fact that a read-only database is never updated influence the reasons for normalization?

4.17   For read-only databases, how persuasive is the argument that normalization reduces file space?

4.18   What is denormalization?

4.19   Suppose you are given the DEPARTMENT and EMPLOYEE tables in question 4.10 and asked to denormalize them into the EMPLOYEE_DEPARTMENT relation. Show the design of the EMPLOYEE_DEPARTMENT relation. Show a SQL statement to fill this table with data.

4.20   Summarize the reasons for creating customized duplicated tables.

4.21   Why are customized duplicated tables not used for updatable databases?

4.22   List four common design problems when creating databases from existing data.

4.23   Give an example of a multivalue, multicolumn table other than one discussed in this chapter.

4.24   Explain the problems in your example in question 4.23.

4.25   Show how to represent the relation in your answer to question 4.23 with two tables.

4.26   Show how the tables in your answer to question 4.25 solve the problems you identified in question 4.22.

4.27   Explain the following statement: "The multivalue, multicolumn problem is just another form of multivalued dependency." Show how this is so.

4.28   Explain ways in which inconsistent values arise.

4.29   Why are inconsistent values in foreign keys particularly troublesome?

4.30   Describe two ways to identify inconsistent values. Are these techniques certain to find all inconsistent values? What other step can be taken?

4.31 What is a null value?

4.32 How does a null value differ from a blank value?

4.33 What are three interpretations of null values? Use an example in your answer.

4.34 Show SQL for determining the number of null values in the column Name of the table EMPLOYEE.

4.35 Describe the general-purpose remarks column problem.

4.36 Give an example in which the general-purpose remarks column makes it difficult to obtain values for a foreign key.

4.37 Give an example in which the general-purpose remarks column causes difficulties when multiple values are stored in the same column. How is this problem solved?

4.38 Why should one be wary of general-purpose remarks columns?

PROJECT QUESTIONS

The Elliot Bay Sports Club owns and operates three sports club facilities in Houston, Texas. Each facility has a large selection of modern exercise equipment, weight rooms, and rooms for yoga and other exercise classes. Elliot Bay offers three-month and one-year memberships. Members can use the facilities at any of the three club locations.

Elliot Bay maintains a roster of personal trainers who operate as independent consultants. Approved trainers can schedule appointments with clients at Elliot Bay facilities, as long as their client is a member of the club. Trainers also teach yoga, Pilates, and other classes. Answer the following questions, assuming you have been provided the following three tables of data (PT stands for personal trainer):

PT_SESSION (Trainer, Phone, Email, Fee, ClientName, ClientPhone, ClientEmail, Date, Time)

CLUB_MEMBERSHIP (ClientNumber, ClientName, ClientPhone, ClientEmail, MembershipType, EndingDate, Street, City, State, Zip)

CLASS (ClassName, Trainer, StartDate, EndDate, Time, DayOfWeek, Cost)

4.39 Identify possible multivalued dependencies in these tables.

4.40 Identify possible functional dependencies in these tables.

4.41 Classify each table according to whether it is in BCNF or in 4NF. State your assumptions.

4.42 Modify each of these tables so that every table is in BCNF and 4NF. Use the assumptions you made in your answer to question 4.41.

4.43 Using these tables and your assumptions, recommend a design for an updatable database.

4.44 Add a table to your answer to question 4.43 that would allow Elliot Bay to assign members to particular classes. Include an AmtPaid column in your new table.

4.45 Recommend a design for a read-only database that would support the following needs:

a. Enable trainers to ensure that their clients are members of the club.

b. Enable the club to assess the popularity of various trainers.

c. Enable the trainers to determine if they are assisting the same client.

d. Enable class instructors to determine if the attendees to their classes have paid.

MARCIA'S DRY CLEANING

Marcia is in the process of creating databases to support the operation and management of her business. For the past year, she and her staff have been using a cash register system that collects the following data:

SALE (<u>InvoiceNumber</u>, DateIn, DateOut, Total, Phone, FirstName, LastName)

Unfortunately, during rush times, not all of the data are entered, and there are many null values in Phone, FirstName, and LastName. In some cases all three are null, in other cases one or two are null. InvoiceNumber, DateIn, and Total are never null. DateOut has a few null values. Also, occasionally during a rush, phone number and name data have been entered incorrectly.

To help create her database, Marcia purchased a mailing list from a local business bureau. The mailing list includes the following data:

HOUSEHOLD (<u>Phone</u>, <u>FirstName</u>, <u>LastName</u>, Street, City, State, Zip, Apartment)

In some cases, a phone number has multiple names. The primary key is thus the composite (Phone, FirstName, LastName). There are no null values in Phone, FirstName, and LastName, but there are some null values in the address data.

There are many names in SALE that are not in HOUSEHOLD, and there are many names in HOUSEHOLD that are not in SALE.

A Design an updatable database for storing customer and sales data. Explain how to deal with the problems of missing data. Explain how to deal with the problems of incorrect phone and name data.

B Design a read-only database for storing customer and sales data. Explain how to deal with the problems of missing data. Explain how to deal with the problems of incorrect phone and name data.

MORGAN IMPORTING

Phillip Morgan makes periodic buying trips to various countries. During the trips, he keeps notes about the items he purchases and basic data about their shipments. He hired a college student as an intern, and she transformed his notes into the spreadsheets in Figure 4-10. This is just sample data. Phillip has purchased hundreds of items over the years, and they have been shipped in dozens of different shipments.

Phillip wants to enter the information age, thus he has decided to develop a database of his inventory. He wants to keep track of the items he has purchased, their shipments, and eventually customers and sales. To get started, he has asked you to create a database for the data in Figure 4-10.

A Follow the procedure shown in Figure 4-1 to assess these data. List multivalued dependencies, functional dependencies, candidate keys, primary keys, and foreign keys. State your assumptions.

B List questions you would ask Phillip to verify your assumptions.

C Create tables as necessary to eliminate multivalued dependencies, if any.

D The relationship between shipment and item data could be inferred by matching values in the From cells to values in the City cells. Describe two problems with that strategy.

E Describe a change to this spreadsheet that does express the shipment/item relationship.

Figure 4-10   Spreadsheets from Morgan Importing

	A	B	C	D	E	F	G	H	I
1	ShipmentNum	Shipper	Phone	Contact	From	Departure	Arrival	Contents	InsuredValue
2	49100300	Wordwide	800-123-4567	Jose	Philippines	5/5/2004	6/17/1994	QE dining set, large bureau, porcelain lamps	$27,500
3	488955	Intenational	800-123-8898	Marilyn	Singapore	6/2/2004		Miscellaneous linen, large masks, 14 setting Willow design china	$7,500
4	84899440	Wordwide	800-123-4567	Jose	Peru	7/3/2004	7/28/2004	Woven goods, antique leather chairs	
5	399400	Intenational	800-123-8898	Marilyn	Singaporee	8/5/2004	9/11/2004	Large bureau, brass lamps, willow design serving dishes	$18,000
6									
7									
8									
9		Item	Date	City	Store	Salesperson	Price		
10		Willow Serving Dishes	7/15/2004	Singapore	Jade Antiques	Swee Lai	$4,500		
11		Large bureau	7/17/2004	Singapore	Eastern Sales	Jeremey	$9,500		
12		Brass lamps	7/20/2004	Singapore	Jade Antiques	Mr. James	$1,200		
13		QE Dining Set	4/7/2004	Manila	E. Treasures	Gracielle	$14,300		

F Assume that Phillip wishes to create an updatable database from these data. Design tables you think are appropriate. State all referential integrity constraints.

G Assume that Phillip wishes to create a read-only database from these data. Design tables you think are appropriate. State all referential integrity constraints.

H Do these data have the multivalue, multicolumn problem? If so, how will you deal with it?

I Do these data have the inconsistent data problem? If so, how will you deal with it?

J Do these data have a null value data problem? If so, how will you deal with it?

K Do these data have the general-purpose remarks problem? If so, how will you deal with it?

Data Modeling with the Entity-Relationship Model

In this chapter and the next, we consider the design of databases that arise from the development of new information systems. As you will learn, such databases are designed by analyzing requirements and creating a data model, or blueprint, of a database that will meet those requirements. The data model is then transformed into a database design.

This chapter addresses the creation of data models using the entity-relationship data model, the most popular modeling technique. This chapter consists of three major sections. First, we explain the major elements of the entity-relationship model and briefly describe several variations on that model. Next, we examine a number of patterns in forms, reports, and data models that you will encounter when data modeling. We then illustrate the data modeling process using the example of a small database at a university. Before starting, however, you need to understand the purpose of a data model.

The Purpose of a Data Model

A **data model** is a plan, or blueprint, for a database design. By analogy, consider the construction of your dorm or apartment building. The contractor did not just buy some lumber, call for the concrete trucks, and start work. Instead, an architect constructed plans and blueprints for that building long before construction began. If, during the planning stage, it was determined that a room was too small or too large, the blueprint could be changed simply by redrawing the lines. If, however, the need for change occurs after the building is constructed, the walls, electrical system, plumbing, and so on will need to be rebuilt, at great expense and loss of time. It is easier, simpler, and faster to change the plan than it is to change a constructed building.

The same argument applies to data models and databases. Changing a relationship during the data modeling stage is just a matter of changing the diagram and related documentation. Changing a relationship after the database and applications have been constructed, however, is much more difficult. Data must be migrated to the new structure, SQL statements will need to be changed, forms and reports will need to be altered, and so forth.

 # The Entity-Relationship Model

Dozens of different tools and techniques for constructing data models have been defined over the years. They include the hierarchical data model, the network data model, the ANSI/SPARC data model, the entity-relationship data model, the semantic object model, and many others. Of these, the entity-relationship data model has emerged as the standard data model, and we will consider only that data model in this chapter.

The **entity-relationship (E-R) model** was first published by Peter Chen in 1976.[1] In this paper, Chen set out the basic elements of the model. Subtypes (discussed later) were added to the E-R model to create the **extended E-R model,**[2] and today it is the extended E-R model that most people mean when they use the term *E-R model*. In this text, we will use the extended E-R model.

Entities

An **entity** is something that users want to track. It is something that is readily identified in the users' work environment. Example entities are EMPLOYEE Mary Lai, CUSTOMER 12345, SALES-ORDER 1000, SALESPERSON Wally Smith, and PRODUCT A4200. Entities of a given type are grouped into an **entity class.** Thus, the EMPLOYEE entity class is the collection of all EMPLOYEE entities. In this text, entity classes are shown in capital letters.

It is important to understand the differences between an entity class and an entity instance. An entity class is a collection of entities and is described by the structure of the entities in that class. An **entity instance** of an entity class is the occurrence of a particular entity, such as CUSTOMER 12345. An entity class usually has many instances of an entity. For example, the entity class CUSTOMER has many instances—one for each customer represented in the database. The CUSTOMER entity class and two of its instances are shown in Figure 5-1.

---

[1]Chen, Peter P. "The Entity-Relationship Model—Towards a Unified View of Data." *ACM Transactions on Database Systems,* January 1976, pp. 9–36.
[2]Teorey, T. J., D. Yang, and J. P. Fry. "A Logical Design Methodology for Relational Databases Using the Extended Entity-Relationship Model," *ACM Computing Surveys,* June 1986, pp. 197–222.

Figure 5-1

CUSTOMER Entity and
Two Entity Instances

CUSTOMER Entity

CustomerNumber
CustomerName
Street
City
State
Zip
ContactName
Email

Two CUSTOMER Instances

1234	99890
Ajax Manufacturing	Jones Brothers
123 Elm Street	434 10th Street
Memphis	Boston
TN	MA
32455	01234
P_Schwartz	Fritz Billingsley
P_S@Ajax.com	Fritz@JB.com

Attributes

Entities have **attributes** that describe their characteristics. Examples of attributes are EmployeeNumber, EmployeeName, Phone, and Email. In this text, attributes are written in both uppercase and lowercase letters. The E-R model assumes that all instances of a given entity class have the same attributes.

Figure 5-2 shows two different ways of displaying the attributes of an entity. Figure 5-2(a) shows attributes in ellipses that are connected to the entity. This style was used in the original E-R model, prior to the advent of data modeling software products. Figure 5-2(b) shows the rectangle style that is commonly used by data modeling software products today.

Figure 5-2 Variations on Entity Diagram Attribute Displays

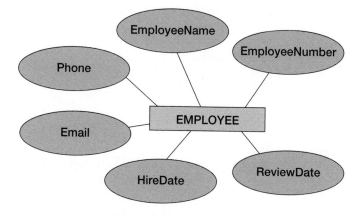

(a) Attributes in Ellipses

(b) Attributes in Rectangle

Identifiers

Entity instances have **identifiers,** which are attributes that name, or identify, entity instances. For example, EMPLOYEE instances can be identified by EmployeeNumber, SocialSecurityNumber, or EmployeeName. EMPLOYEE instances are not likely to be identified by attributes such as Salary or HireDate because these attributes are not normally used in a naming role. Similarly, customers can be identified by CustomerNumber or CustomerName, and sales orders can be identified by OrderNumber.

The identifier of an entity instance consists of one or more of the entity's attributes. Identifiers that consist of two or more attributes are called **composite identifiers.** Examples are (AreaCode, LocalNumber), (ProjectName, TaskName), and (FirstName, LastName, DateOfHire).

B T W

Notice the correspondence of identifiers and keys. The term *identifier* is used in a data model, and the term *key* is used in a database design. Thus, entities have identifiers, and tables (or relations) have keys. Identifiers serve the same role for entities that keys serve for tables.

Entities are portrayed in three levels of detail in a data model. Sometimes the entity and all of its attributes are displayed. In such cases, the identifier of the attribute is shown at the top of the entity and a horizontal line is drawn after the identifier, as shown in Figure 5-3(a). In a large data model, so much detail can make the data model diagrams unwieldy. In those cases, the entity diagram is abbreviated by showing just the identifier, as in Figure 5-3(b), or by showing just the name of the entity in a rectangle, as shown in Figure 5-3(c).

All three techniques are used in practice; the more abbreviated form in Figure 5-3(c) is used to show the big picture and overall entity relationships. The more detailed view in Figure 5-3(a) is frequently used during database design. Most data modeling software products have the ability to show all three displays.

Relationships

Entities can be associated with one another in **relationships.** The E-R model contains both relationship classes and relationship instances.[3] **Relationship classes** are associations among entity classes, and **relationship instances** are associations among entity instances.

Figure 5-3

Variations on Level of Entity Attribute Display

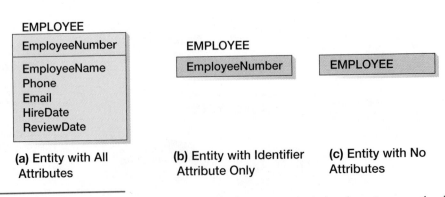

(a) Entity with All Attributes   **(b) Entity with Identifier Attribute Only**   **(c) Entity with No Attributes**

---

[3]For brevity, we sometimes drop the word *instance* when the context makes it clear that an instance rather than an entity class is involved.

In the original E-R model, relationships could have attributes. Today, that feature is no longer used.

Relationships are given names that describe the nature of the relationship. In Figure 5-4, the Qualification relationship shows which employees have which skills. The Assignment relationship shows which combinations of clients, architects, and projects have been created. To avoid unnecessary complexity, in this chapter, we will show the names of relationships only if there is a chance of ambiguity.

B T W

Your instructor may believe that it is important to always show the name of a relationship. If so, be aware that you can name a relationship from the perspective of either of the entities or both. For example, you can name the relationship between DEPARTMENT and EMPLOYEE as Department Consists Of; or you can name it as Employee Works In; or you can name it both ways, using a slash between the two names, Department Consists Of/Employee Works In. Relationship names are a necessity when there are two different relationships between the same two entities.

A relationship class can involve two or more entity classes. The number of entity classes in the relationship is the **degree** of the relationship. In Figure 5-4(a), the Qualification relationship is of degree two because it involves two entity classes: EMPLOYEE and SKILL. The Assignment relationship in Figure 5-4(b) is of degree three because it involves three entity classes: CLIENT, ARCHITECT, and PROJECT. Relationships of degree two are referred to as **binary relationships.** Similarly, relationships of degree three are called **ternary relationships.**

When transforming a data model into a relational design, relationships of all degrees are treated as combinations of binary relationships. The relationship in Figure 5-4(b), for example, is decomposed into three binary relationships, as you will learn in the next chapter. Most of the time, this strategy is not a problem. However, some nonbinary relationships need additional work, as you will learn in Chapter 6, pages 190–192. All data modeling software products require you to express relationships as binary relationships.

Figure 5-4

Binary Versus Ternary Relationships

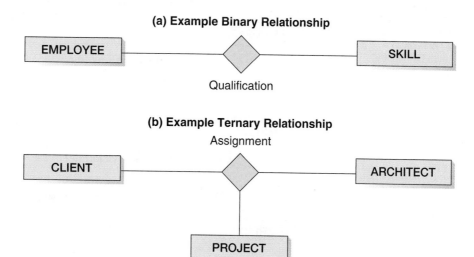

At this point, you may be wondering, "What's the difference between an entity and a table?" So far, they seem like different terms for the same thing. *The principle difference between an entity and a table is you can express a relationship between entities without using foreign keys.* In the E-R model, you can specify a relationship just by drawing a line connecting two entities. Because you are doing logical data modeling and not physical database design, you need not worry about primary and foreign keys, referential integrity constraints, and the like. Most data modeling products will allow you to consider such details if you choose to, but they do not require it.

This characteristic makes entities easier to work with than tables, especially early in a project when entities and relationships are fluid and uncertain. You can show relationships between entities before you even know what the identifiers are. For example, you can say that a DEPARTMENT relates to many EMPLOYEEs before you know any of the attributes of either EMPLOYEE or DEPARTMENT. This characteristic enables you to work from the general to the specific. First identify the entities, then think about relationships, and finally, determine the attributes.

In the entity-relationship model, relationships are classified by their **cardinality,** a word that means "count." The **maximum cardinality** is the maximum number of entity instances that can participate in a relationship instance. The **minimum cardinality** is the minimum number of entity instances that must participate in a relationship instance.

Maximum Cardinality

In Figure 5-5, the maximum cardinality is shown inside the diamond that represents the relationship. The three parts of this figure show the three basic maximum cardinalities in the E-R model. Figure 5-5(a) shows a one-to-one (abbreviated 1:1) relationship.

Figure 5-5

Three Types of Maximum Cardinality

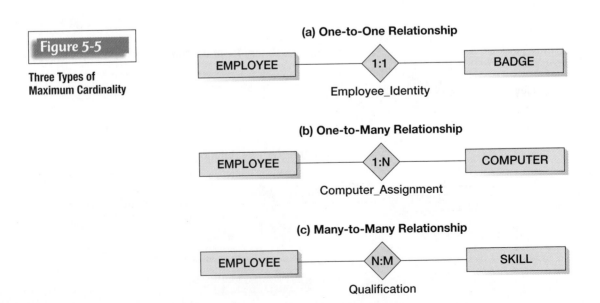

(a) One-to-One Relationship

EMPLOYEE — 1:1 — BADGE

Employee_Identity

(b) One-to-Many Relationship

EMPLOYEE — 1:N — COMPUTER

Computer_Assignment

(c) Many-to-Many Relationship

EMPLOYEE — N:M — SKILL

Qualification

In a 1:1 relationship, an entity instance of one type is related to at most one entity instance of the other type. The Employee_Identity relationship in Figure 5-5(a) associates one EMPLOYEE instance with one BADGE instance. According to this diagram, no employee has more than one badge, and no badge is assigned to more than one employee.

The Computer_Assignment relationship in Figure 5-5(b) illustrates a one-to-many, or 1:N, relationship. Here, a single instance of EMPLOYEE can be associated with many instances of COMPUTER, but a COMPUTER instance is associated with just one instance of EMPLOYEE. According to this diagram, an employee can be associated with several computers, but a computer is assigned to just one employee.

The positions of the 1 and the N are significant. The 1 is close to the line connecting EMPLOYEE, which means that the 1 refers to the EMPLOYEE side of the relationship. The N is close to the line connecting COMPUTER, which means that the N refers to the COMPUTER side of the relationship. If the 1 and the N were reversed and the relationship were written N:1, an EMPLOYEE would have one COMPUTER, and a COMPUTER would be assigned to many EMPLOYEEs.

When discussing one-to-many relationships, the terms **parent** and **child** are sometimes used. The *parent* is the entity on the one side of the relationship, and the *child* is the entity on the many side of the relationship. Thus, in a 1:N relationship between DEPARTMENT and EMPLOYEE, DEPARTMENT is the parent and EMPLOYEE is the child.

Figure 5-5(c) shows a many-to-many, or N:M, relationship. According to the Qualification relationships, an EMPLOYEE instance can be associated with many SKILL instances, and a SKILL instance can be associated with many EMPLOYEE instances. This relationship documents that fact that an employee may have many skills, and a skill may be held by many employees.

Sometimes students wonder why we do not write many-to-many relationships as N:N or M:M. The reason is that cardinality in one direction may be different than the cardinality in the other direction. In other words, in an N:M relationship, N need not equal M. An EMPLOYEE can have five skills, for example, but one of those skills can have three employees. Writing the relationship as N:M highlights the possibility that the cardinalities may be different.

B T W

Relationships like those in Figure 5-5 are sometimes called HAS-A relationships. This term is used because each entity instance has a relationship to a second entity instance. An employee has a badge, and a badge has an employee. If the maximum cardinality is greater than one, then each entity has a set of other entities. An employee has a set of skills, for example, and a skill has a set of employees who have that skill.

Sometimes the maximum cardinality is an exact number. For example, for a sports team, the number of players on the roster is limited to some fixed number, say, 15. In that case, the maximum cardinality between TEAM and PLAYER would be set to 15 rather than to the more general N.

Minimum Cardinality

The minimum cardinality is the number of entity instances that must participate in a relationship. Generally, minimums are stated as either zero or one. If zero, then participation in the relationship is optional, if one, then at least one entity instance must

Figure 5-6

Minimum Cardinality
Examples

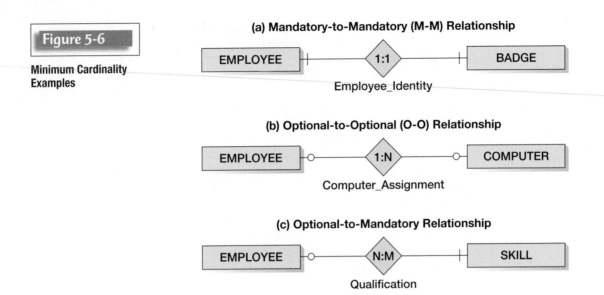

(a) Mandatory-to-Mandatory (M-M) Relationship

EMPLOYEE — ⟨1:1⟩ — BADGE

Employee_Identity

(b) Optional-to-Optional (O-O) Relationship

EMPLOYEE —o ⟨1:N⟩ o— COMPUTER

Computer_Assignment

(c) Optional-to-Mandatory Relationship

EMPLOYEE —o ⟨N:M⟩ — SKILL

Qualification

participate in the relationship. In E-R diagrams, an optional relationship is represented by a small circle on the relationship line; a mandatory relationship is represented by a hash mark or line across the relationship line.

To better understand these terms, consider Figure 5-6. In the Employee_Identity relationship in Figure 5-6(a), the hash marks indicate that an EMPLOYEE is required to have a BADGE, and a BADGE must be allocated to an EMPLOYEE. Such a relationship is referred to as a mandatory-to-mandatory relationship, or M-M relationship, because entities are required on both sides. The complete specification for the Employee_Identity relationship is that it is a 1:1, M-M relationship.

In Figure 5-6(b), the two small circles indicate that the Computer_Assignment relationship is optional-to-optional, or O-O. This means that an EMPLOYEE need not have a COMPUTER, and a COMPUTER need not be assigned to an EMPLOYEE. The Computer_Assignment relationship is thus a 1:N, O-O relationship.

Finally, in Figure 5-6(c), the combination of a circle and a hash mark indicates an optional-to-mandatory relationship. Here, an EMPLOYEE must be assigned to at least one SKILL, but a SKILL may not necessarily be related to any EMPLOYEE. The complete specification for the Qualification relationship is thus an N:M, M-O relationship. The position of the circle and the hash mark are important. Because the circle is in front of EMPLOYEE, it means that the employee is optional in the relationship.

B T W

Sometimes when interpreting diagrams like Figure 5-6(c), students become confused about which entity is optional and which is required. An easy way to clarify this situation is to imagine that you are standing in the diamond on the relationship line. Imagine looking toward one of the entities. If you see an oval in that direction, then that entity is optional; if you see a hash mark, then that entity is required. Thus, in Figure 5-6(c), if you stand on the diamond and look toward SKILL, you see a hash mark. This means that SKILL is required in the relationship.

A fourth option, O-M, is not shown in Figure 5-6. But, if we exchange the circle and the hash mark in Figure 5-6(c), then Qualification becomes an O-M relationship. In that case, an EMPLOYEE need not have a SKILL, but a SKILL must have at least one EMPLOYEE.

As with maximum cardinalities, in rare cases the minimum cardinality is a specific number. To represent the relationship between PERSON and MARRIAGE, for example, the minimum cardinality would be 2:Optional.

Entity-Relationship Diagrams and Their Versions

The diagrams in Figures 5-5 and 5-6 are sometimes referred to as **entity-relationship diagrams.** The original E-R model specified that such diagrams use diamonds for relationships, rectangles for entities, and connected ellipses for attributes, as shown in Figure 5-2. You may still see examples of such E-R diagrams, and it is important for you to be able to interpret them.

For two reasons, however, this original notation is seldom used today. First, there are a number of different versions of the E-R model, and these versions use different symbols. Second, data modeling software products use different techniques. For example, Computer Associate's product ERwin uses one set of symbols, and Microsoft Visio uses a second set.

Variations of the E-R Model

At least three different versions of the E-R model are in use today. One of them, called **Information Engineering,** or **IE,** was developed by James Martin in 1990. This model uses crow's feet to show the many side of a relationship, and it is sometimes called the **crow's foot model.** It is easy to understand, and we will use it throughout this text.

In 1993, the National Institute of Standards and Technology announced another version of the E-R model as a national standard. This version is called **IDEF1X,** or **Integrated Definition 1, Extended.**[4] This standard incorporates the basic ideas of the E-R model, but uses different graphical symbols. Although this model is a national standard, it is difficult to understand and use. As a national standard, however, it is used in government, and thus it may become important to you. Therefore, the fundamentals of the IDEF1X model are described in Appendix B.

Meanwhile, to add further complication, a new object-oriented development methodology called the **Unified Modeling Language (UML)** adopted the E-R model, but introduced its own symbols while putting an object-oriented programming spin on the model. UML notation is summarized in Appendix C.

E-R Variations in Data Modeling Products

In addition to differences due to different versions of the E-R model, there also are differences due to software products. For example, two products that both implement the crow's foot model may do so in different ways. The result is a mess. When creating a data model diagram, you need to know not just the version of the E-R model you are using, but also the idiosyncrasies of the data modeling product you use.

Consider Figure 5-7, which shows three versions of a one-to-many, optional-to-mandatory relationship. Figure 5-7(a) shows the original E-R model version. Figure 5-7(b) shows the crow's foot model as interpreted by ERwin. Here, a crow's foot symbol is used

---

[4]*Integrated Definition for Information Modeling (IDEFIX).* Federal Information Processing Standards Publication 184, 1993.

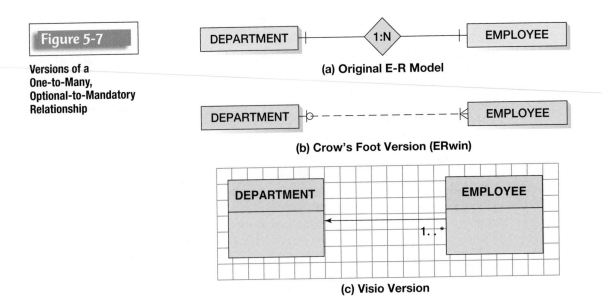

Figure 5-7

Versions of a
One-to-Many,
Optional-to-Mandatory
Relationship

(a) Original E-R Model

(b) Crow's Foot Version (ERwin)

(c) Visio Version

to show the many side of the relationship, and various combinations of an oval, hash mark, and crow's foot are used as follows:

ERwin Symbol Use	Meaning
Oval with hash mark	0 or 1 entities are allowed
Hash mark alone	Exactly 1 entity is allowed
Hash mark with crow's foot	1 or more entities are allowed
Oval, hash mark, and crow's foot	0, 1, or more entities are allowed

Thus, the diagram in Figure 5-7(b) means that a DEPARTMENT has one or more EMPLOYEEs, and an EMPLOYEE belongs to zero or one DEPARTMENTs.

Figure 5-7(c) shows a version of this same relationship drawn using Visio. Here, a line with an arrow shows a one-to-many relationship, but, surprisingly, the arrow points to the one side of that relationship. The notation 1..* means that from one to many EMPLOYEE entities may relate to one DEPARTMENT. The optional DEPARTMENT has no special notation and must be determined in other ways.

Unfortunately, this messy situation is even worse for many-to-many relationships, as shown in Figure 5-8. According to the original E-R model diagram shown in Figure 5-8(a), an EMPLOYEE must have a SKILL, and a SKILL may or may not be held by an EMPLOYEE. The crow's foot version in Figure 5-8(b) shows the N:M maximum cardinalities, but ERwin provides no means to specify the minimum cardinality of a many-to-many relationship. Even worse, Visio will not show a many-to-many relationship at all! Instead, an artificial entity must be created and two one-to-many relationships must be connected to it, as shown in Figure 5-8(c).

Figure 5-8

Versions of a Many-
to-Many, Optional-
to-Mandatory
Relationship

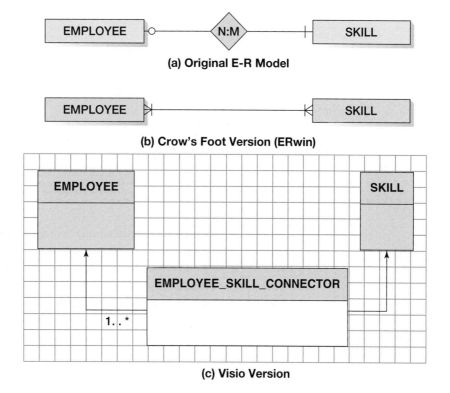

(a) Original E-R Model

(b) Crow's Foot Version (ERwin)

(c) Visio Version

B T W

The team that constructed the data modeling template for Visio did a poor job. The team did not understand that the purpose of a data model is to represent logical structure, not tables. Visio is so table oriented that it forces you to transform the logical model into tables before you can even draw the logical model.

For example, Visio forces you to transform an N:M relationship into two 1:N relationships. As you will learn in the next chapter, during design, we must always change an N:M relationship into two 1:N relationships. However, we ought not to be required to make that transformation during data modeling. We should be able to specify an N:M relationship as a N:M relationship and not worry about the transformation until later. That's why we do data modeling—to work at a higher level of abstraction.

A large data model might have as many as 200 to 300 entities. When validating the logical correctness of the model, reducing complexity is important. Making the data modeler create artificial entities just adds unnecessary complexity and promotes errors. It would be far better just to display the N:M relationship as a logical N:M relationship.

Because of these problems, you might prefer ERwin. Try the free trial version of ERwin at *www.ca.com*. Look for AllFusion ERWin Data Modeler under Trial and Evaluation Software. You can use this product to produce either crow's foot or IDEF1X models.

Making Sense of This Mess

Except for Appendices B and C, for the rest of this text we will use the crow's foot model for E-R diagrams and draw those diagrams using ERwin's notation. You can obtain other products that will produce crow's foot models, and they are easily understood and related to ERwin versions shown here. Be aware that other products may use the oval, hash mark, and crow's foot slightly differently.

Your instructor may have a favorite modeling tool for you to use. If that tool does not support crow's feet, you will have to adapt the data models in this text to your tool. Making these adaptations is a good learning exercise. See, for example, exercises 5.57 and 5.58.

B T W

To reiterate, from now on, all entity-relationship diagrams will use the crow's foot model as drawn using ERwin. With this product, the oval, hash mark, and crow's foot are used together on each end of a relationship line. The oval means zero, the hash mark means one, and the crow's foot means many. An oval with a hash mark is zero or one, a hash mark alone is exactly one, a hash mark with a crow's foot is one or more, and an oval, hash mark, and crow's foot is zero, one, or more.

ID-Dependent Entities

The E-R model includes a special type of entity called an **ID-dependent entity.** An ID-dependent entity is an entity whose identifier includes the identifier of another entity. Consider, for example, an entity for a student apartment. The identifier of such an entity is a composite (ApartmentNumber, BuildingName), where BuildingName is the identifier of the entity BUILDING. ApartmentNumber by itself is insufficient to tell someone where you live. If you say you live in apartment number 5, they must ask you, "In what building?"

Figure 5-9 shows three different ID-dependent entities. In addition to APART-MENT, the entity PRINT is ID-dependent on PAINTING, and the entity EXAM is ID-dependent on PATIENT.

In each of these cases, the ID-dependent entity cannot exist unless the parent (the entity on which it depends) also exists. Thus, the minimum cardinality from the ID-dependent entity to the parent is always one.

Figure 5-9

Example ID-dependent Entities

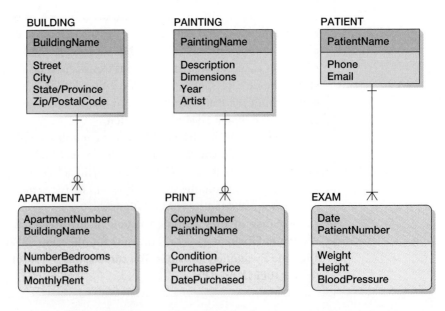

On the other hand, whether the parent is required to have an ID-dependent entity depends on the application requirements. In Figure 5-9, both APARTMENT and PRINT are optional, but EXAM is required. These restrictions arise from the nature of the application and not from any logical requirement.

ID-dependent entities pose restrictions on the processing of the database that is constructed from them. Namely, the row that represents the parent entity must be created before any ID-dependent child row can be created. Further, when a parent row is deleted, all child rows must be deleted as well.

The E-R model uses a special type of relationship called an **identifying relationship** to represent ID-dependent entities. Most data modeling products show an identifying relationship as a solid line and a regular, **nonidentifying relationship** as a dashed line. Again, in an ID-dependent relationship, the parent entity is always required, but the ID-dependent entity may or may not be required.

ID-dependent entities are common. Another example is the entity VERSION in the relationship between PRODUCT and VERSION, where PRODUCT is a software product and VERSION is a release of that software product. The identifier of PRODUCT is ProductName, and the identifier of VERSION is (ProductName, ReleaseNumber). Yet another example is EDITION in the relationship between TEXTBOOK and EDITION. The identifier of TEXTBOOK is Title, and the identifier of EDITION is (Title, EditionNumber).

Weak Entities

The original version of the E-R model included the concept of a **weak entity** and defined a weak entity as any entity whose existence depends on the presence of another entity. A **strong entity** is any entity that is not weak.

All ID-dependent entities are weak. But, according to the original E-R model, some entities that are weak are not ID-dependent. Consider the MODEL and AUTO entities in Figure 5-10. MODEL represents the design of a particular line of cars, and AUTO represents a particular car. Clearly, a car cannot exist without a model; the model is the car's design. Therefore, AUTO is a weak entity. However, the identifier of AUTO is VIN (vehicle identification number—a number that identifies a particular car). VIN does not include the identifier of MODEL, thus AUTO is not ID-dependent.

Figure 5-10

Weak, but not ID-dependent Entity?

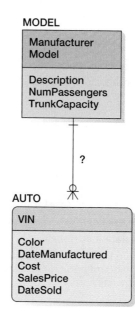

Figure 5-11

Data Model with Weak
Entity Annotation

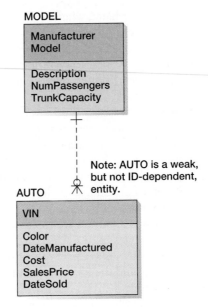

Thus, it is possible for an entity to be weak, but not ID-dependent. With most data modeling tools, however, it is not possible to model such entities. Instead, they must be shown using nonidentifying relationships and a note added to the data model that the entity is weak, as shown in Figure 5-11.

> ### B T W
>
> The fact that an entity has a required relationship to another entity does not make that entity weak. A STUDENT can be required to have an ADVISER, but STUDENT is not existence dependent on an ADVISER. Hence, STUDENT is not a weak entity. For an entity to be weak, its logical existence must require another entity: an EXAM must have a PATIENT, a CAR must have a MODEL, an APPOINTMENT must have a CLIENT. All such entities are weak.

Characteristics of ID-dependent and weak entities are summarized in Figure 5-12.

Subtype Entities

The extended E-R model introduced the concept of subtypes. A **subtype** entity is a special case of another entity called its **supertype.** Students, for example, may be classified as

Figure 5-12   Summary of ID-dependent and Weak Entities

- An ID-dependent entity is an entity whose identifier includes the identifier of another entity.
- Indentifying relationships are used to represent ID-dependent entities.
- A weak entity is an entity whose existence depends on another entity.
- All ID-dependent entities are weak.
- Some entities are weak, but not ID-dependent. Using data modeling tools, they are shown with nonidentifying relationships, with separate documentation indicating they are weak.

Figure 5-13

Example Subtypes

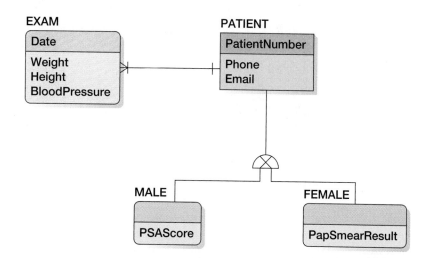

undergraduate or graduate students. In this case, STUDENT is the supertype, and UNDERGRADUATE and GRADUATE are the subtypes. Alternatively, a student could be classified as a freshman, sophomore, junior, or senior. In that case, STUDENT is the supertype, and FRESHMAN, SOPHOMORE, JUNIOR, and SENIOR are the subtypes.

Figure 5-13 shows subtypes for a medical database. The supertype PATIENT has two subtypes: MALE and FEMALE. The supertype contains all attributes common to both types, and the subtypes contain just those attributes that pertain to each subtype. Males have a PSAScore, an exam related to the health of the prostate gland; females have a PapSmearResult, a test related to the health of the uterus. Note that ERwin represents a subtype structure with a dome-shaped symbol.

In some cases, an attribute of the supertype indicates which of the subtypes is appropriate for a given instance. In Figure 5-14, the attribute Sex indicates whether the patient is male or female. An attribute that determines which subtype is appropriate is called a **discriminator.** Using ERwin, the discriminator is shown next to the subtype symbol, as illustrated in Figure 5-14.

Not all supertypes have a discriminator. If not, application code must be written to create the appropriate subtype.

Subtypes can be exclusive or inclusive. If **exclusive,** the supertype relates to at most one subtype. If **inclusive,** the supertype can relate to one or more subtypes. Figure 5-15(a) shows an EMPLOYEE supertype with subtypes MANAGER and DB_ADMIN. The X in the dome means the subtypes are exclusive. Thus, an EMPLOYEE can be either a MANAGER or a DB_ADMIN, but not both.

Figure 5-14

Subtypes with Discriminator Attribute

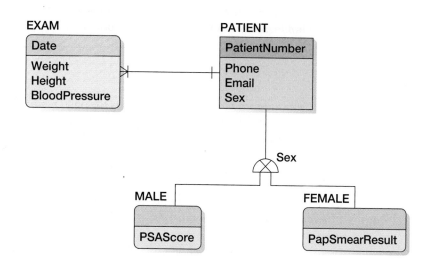

Figure 5-15   Exclusive Versus Inclusive Subtypes

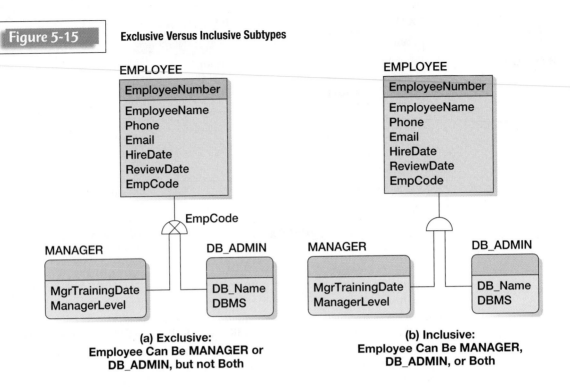

(a) Exclusive:
Employee Can Be MANAGER or
DB_ADMIN, but not Both

(b) Inclusive:
Employee Can Be MANAGER,
DB_ADMIN, or Both

Figure 5-15(b) shows these same subtypes as inclusive (note that there is no X in the dome). Here, an EMPLOYEE can be a MANAGER, a DB_ADMIN, or both. Because a supertype may relate to more than one subtype, inclusive subtypes do not have a discriminator.

B   T   W

Relationships that connect supertypes and subtypes are called IS-A relationships because a subtype *is* the same entity as the supertype. Because this is so, the identifier of a supertype and all of its subtypes must be identical; they all represent different aspects of the same entity. Contrast this term with HAS-A relationships in which an entity has a relationship to another entity, but the identity (and identifier) of the two entities is different.

The most important (some would say the only) reason for creating subtypes in a data model is to avoid value-inappropriate nulls. Females do not receive PSA tests, and males do not receive Pap smears. If PSAScore is an attribute of PATIENT, then that attribute will be required to be null in all PATIENT entities for females. Similarly, if PapSmearResult is an attribute of PATIENT, then it will be required to be null for all males. Such null values can be avoided by creating subtypes.

The elements of the entity-relationship model and their ERwin symbols are summarized in Figure 5-16. The identifier and attributes are shown only in the first example. Note that for 1:1 and 1:N nonidentifying relationships a relationship to a parent entity may be optional. For identifying relationships, the parent is always required.

| Figure 5-16 | ERwin Symbol Summary |

DEPARTMENT DepartmentName BudgetCode OfficeNumber	DEPARTMENT entity; DepartmentName is identifier; BudgetCode and OfficeNumber are attributes.
A B	1:1, nonidentifying relationship. A relates to zero or one B; B relates to exactly one A. Relationship shown using a dashed line.
A B	1:N, nonidentifying relationship. A relates to one or many Bs; B relates to zero or one A. Relationship shown using a dashed line.
A B	Many-to-many, nonidentifying relationship. Minimum cardinality must be shown in notes or annotation. Relationship shown with a solid line.
A B	1:N identifying relationship. A relates to zero, one, or many Bs. B relates to exactly one A. Relationship shown with a solid line. For identifying relationships, the child must always relate to exactly one parent. The parent may relate to zero, one, many, or a combination of these minimum cardinalities.
A C B	A is supertype, C and D are exclusive subtypes. Discriminator not shown. Relationships shown with a solid line.
A C B	A is supertype, C and D are inclusive subtypes. Relationships shown with a solid line.

Patterns in Forms, Reports, and Entity-Relationship Models

A data model is a representation of how users view their world. Unfortunately, you cannot walk up to most computer users and ask questions like, "What is the maximum cardinality between the EMPLOYEE and SKILL entities?" Few users would have any idea of what you mean. Instead, you must infer the data model indirectly from user documents and from users' conversation and behavior.

One of the best ways to infer a data model is to study the users' forms and reports. From such documents, you can learn about entities and their relationships. In fact, the structure of forms and reports determines the structure of the data model, and the structure of the data model determines the structure of forms and reports. This means that you can examine a form or report and determine the entities and relationships that underlie it.

You can also use forms and reports to validate the data model. Rather than showing the data model to the users for feedback, an alternative is to construct a form or report that reflects the structure of the data model and obtain user feedback on that form or report.

For example, if you want to know if an ORDER has one or many SALESPEOPLE, you can show the users a form that has a space for entering just one salesperson's name. If the user asks, "Where do I put the name of the second salesperson?" then you know that orders have at least two and possibly many salespeople. Sometimes, when no appropriate form or report exists, teams create a prototype form or report for the users to evaluate.

All of this means that you must understand how the structure of forms and reports determines the structure of the data model, and the reverse. Fortunately, many forms and reports fall into common patterns. If you learn how to analyze these patterns, you will be well on your way to understanding the logical relationship between forms and reports and the data model. Accordingly, in the next sections we will discuss the most common patterns in detail.

Strong Entity Patterns

Three relationships are possible between two strong entities: 1:1, 1:N, and N:M. When modeling such relationships, you must determine both the maximum and minimum cardinality. The maximum cardinality often can be determined from forms and reports. In most cases, to determine the minimum cardinality, you will have to ask the users.

1:1 Strong Entity Relationships

Figure 5-17 shows a data entry form and a report that indicate a one-to-one relationship between the entities CLUB_MEMBER and LOCKER. The MEMBER_LOCKER form in Figure 5-17(a) shows data for an athletic club member, and it lists just one locker for that member. This form indicates that a CLUB_MEMBER has at most one locker. The report in Figure 5-17(b) shows the lockers in the club and indicates the member who has been allocated that locker. Each locker is assigned to one club member.

The form and report in Figure 5-17 thus suggest that a CLUB_MEMBER has one LOCKER, and a LOCKER is assigned to one CLUB_MEMBER. Hence, the relationship

Figure 5-17

Form and Report Indicating a 1:1 Relationship

(a) Club Membership Data Entry Form

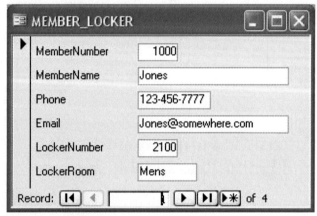

(b) Club Locker Report

CLUB_LOCKERS

LockerRoom	LockerNumber	MemberNumber	MemberName	LockerSize
Mens	2100	1000	Jones	Med
Mens	2115	3000	Wu	Large
Womens	2200	2000	Abernathy	Large
Womens	2217	4000	Lai	Small

Figure 5-18

Data Model for the 1:1
Relationship in
Figure 5-17

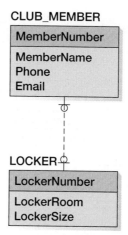

between them is 1:1. To model that relationship, we draw a nonidentifying relationship (meaning the relationship is strong and not ID-dependent) between the two entities, as shown in Figure 5-18. We then set the maximum cardinality to 1:1. You can tell that this is a nonidentifying relationship because the relationship line is dashed. Also, the absence of a crow's foot indicates that the relationship is 1:1.

Regarding minimum cardinality, every club member shown in the form has a locker, and every locker shown in the report is assigned to a club member, so it appears that the relationship is mandatory to mandatory. However, this form and report are just instances; they may not show every possibility. If the club allows social, nonathletic memberships, then not every club member will have a locker. Furthermore, it is unlikely that every locker is occupied; there must be some lockers that are unused and nonallocated. Accordingly, Figure 5-18 shows this relationship as optional to optional, as indicated by the small circles on the relationship lines.

B T W

How do you recognize strong entities? You can use two major tests. First, does the entity have an identifier of its own? If it shares a part of its identifier with another entity, then it is an ID-dependent entity, and is therefore weak. Second, does the entity seem to be logically different from and separate from the other entities? Does it stand alone, or is it part of something else? In this case, CLUB_MEMBER and a LOCKER are two very different, separate things; they are not part of each other or of something else. Hence, they are strong.

Note also that a form or report shows only one side of a relationship. Given entities A and B, a form can show the relationship from A to B, but it cannot show the relationship from B to A at the same time. To learn the cardinality from B to A, you must examine a second form or report, ask the users, or take some other action.

Finally, it is seldom possible to infer minimum cardinality from a form or report. Generally, you must ask the users.

1:N Strong Entity Relationships

Figure 5-19 shows a form that lists the departments within a company. The company has many departments, so the maximum cardinality from COMPANY to DEPARTMENT is N.

What about the opposite direction? To determine if a department relates to one or N companies, we need to examine a form or report that shows the relationship from a

Figure 5-19

Form Indicating a 1:N
Relationship

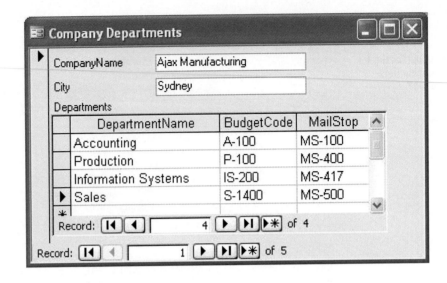

department to a company. However, assume that no such form or report exists. Assume that the users never view company data from the perspective of a department. We cannot ignore the issue because we need to know whether the relationship is 1:N or N:M.

In such a case, we must ask the users or at least make a determination by thinking about the nature of the business setting. Can a department belong to more than one company? Is a department shared among companies? Because this seems unlikely, we can reasonably assume that DEPARTMENT relates to just one COMPANY. Thus, we conclude the relationship is 1:N. Figure 5-20 shows the resulting data model. Note that the many side of the relationship is indicated by the crow's foot next to DEPARTMENT.

Considering minimum cardinality, we do not know if a COMPANY must have a DEPARTMENT or if a DEPARTMENT must have a COMPANY. We will definitely need to ask the users. Figure 5-20 depicts the situation in which a DEPARTMENT must have a COMPANY, but a COMPANY need not have any DEPARTMENTs.

N:M Strong Entity Relationships

Figure 5-21(a) shows a form with data about a supplier and the parts it is prepared to supply. Figure 5-21(b) shows a report that summarizes parts and lists the companies that can supply those parts. In both cases, the relationship is many: A SUPPLIER supplies many PARTs, and a PART is supplied by many SUPPLIERs. Thus, the relationship is N:M.

Figure 5-20

Data Model for the
1:N Relationship
in Figure 5-19

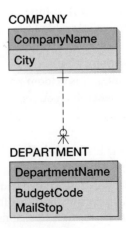

Figure 5-21   Form and Report Indicating an N:M Relationship

(a) SUPPLIERS Form

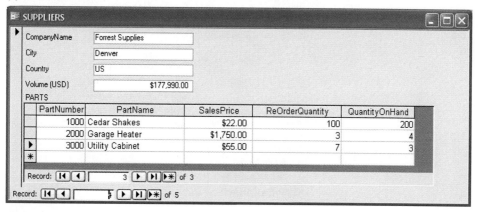

(b) PART Report

PART

Number	PartName	SalesPrice	ROQ	QOH	CompanyName	City	Country
1000	Cedar Shakes	$22.00	100	200			
					Bristol Systems	Machester	England
					ERS Systems	Vancouver	Canada
					Forrest Supplies	Denver	US
2000	Garage Heater	$1,750.00	3	4			
					Bristol Systems	Machester	England
					ERS Systems	Vancouver	Canada
					Kyoto Importers	Kyoto	Japan
					Forrest Supplies	Denver	US
3000	Utility Cabinet	$55.00	7	3			
					Ajax Manufacturing	Sydney	Australia
					Forrest Supplies	Denver	US

Figure 5-22 shows a data model that extends the data model in Figure 5-20 to include this new relationship. A supplier is a company, so we show the supplier entity as a COMPANY.

Because not all companies are suppliers, the relationship from COMPANY to PART must be optional. On the other hand, every part must be supplied from somewhere, so the relationship from PART to SUPPLIER is mandatory.

Figure 5-20 was drawn using ERwin and, as mentioned earlier, ERwin does not allow the data modeler to specify minimum cardinality for N:M relationships. Accordingly, the minimum cardinality is shown as a note next to the relationship.

In summary, the three types of strong entity relationships are 1:1, 1:N, and N:M. You can infer the maximum cardinality in one direction from a form or report. You must examine a second form or report to determine the maximum cardinality in the other direction. If no form or report that shows the relationship is available, you must ask the users. Generally, it is not possible to determine minimum cardinality from forms and reports.

ID-Dependent Relationships

Three principle patterns use ID-dependent entities: multivalued attribute, version/ instance, and association. Because the association pattern is often confused with the N:M strong entity relationships just discussed, we will look at that pattern first.

Adjusted Data Model from Figure 5-20 Showing the N:M Relationship from Figure 5-21

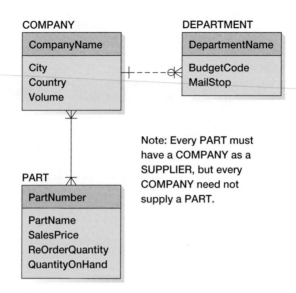

Note: Every PART must have a COMPANY as a SUPPLIER, but every COMPANY need not supply a PART.

The Association Pattern

An association pattern is subtly and confusingly similar to an N:M strong relationship. To see why, examine the report in Figure 5-23 and compare it with the report in Figure 5-21(b). What is the difference? If you look closely, you'll see that the only difference is that the report in Figure 5-23 contains Price, which is the price quotation for a part from a particular supplier. The first line of this report indicates that the part Cedar Shakes is supplied by Bristol Systems for $14.00.

Price is neither an attribute of COMPANY nor is it an attribute of PART. It is an attribute of the combination of a COMPANY with a PART. Figure 5-24 shows the appropriate data model for such a case. Here, a third entity, QUOTATION, has been created to hold the Price attribute. The identifier of QUOTATION is the combination of PartNumber and CompanyName. Note that PartNumber is the identifier of PART, and CompanyName is the identifier of COMPANY. Hence, QUOTATION is ID-dependent on *both* PART and COMPANY.

In Figure 5-24, then, the relationships between PART and QUOTATION and between COMPANY and QUOTATION are both identifying. This fact is shown in Figure 5-24 by the solid, nondashed line that represents these relationships.

Figure 5-23   **Example Report Showing an Association Pattern**

Part Quotations

Number	Name	SalesPrice	ROQ	QOH	Company	City	Price
1000	Cedar Shakes	$22.00	100	200			
					Bristol Systems	Machester	$14.00
					ERS Systems	Vancouver	$12.50
					Forrest Supplies	Denver	$15.50
2000	Garage Heater	$1,750.00	3	4			
					Bristol Systems	Machester	$950.00
					ERS Systems	Vancouver	$875.00
					Kyoto Importers	Kyoto	$1,100.00
					Forrest Supplies	Denver	$915.00
3000	Utility Cabinet	$55.00	7	3			
					Ajax Manufacturing	Sydney	$37.50
					Forrest Supplies	Denver	$42.50

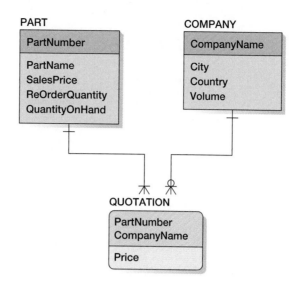

Figure 5-24

Association Pattern for the Report in Figure 5-23

As with all identifying relationships, the parent entities are required. Thus, the minimum cardinality from QUOTATION to PART is one, and the minimum cardinality from QUOTATION to COMPANY also is one. The minimum cardinality in the opposite direction is determined by business requirements. Here, a PART must have a QUOTATION, but a COMPANY need not have a QUOTATION.

B T W

Consider the differences between the data models in Figure 5-22 and Figure 5-24. The only difference between the two is that in the latter, the relationship between COMPANY and PART has an attribute, Price. Remember this example whenever you model an N:M relationship. Is there a missing attribute that pertains to the combination and not just to one of the entities? If so, you are dealing with an association, ID-dependent pattern and not an N:M, strong entity pattern.

Associations can occur among more than two entity types. Figure 5-25, for example, shows a data model for the assignment of a particular client to a particular architect for a particular project. The attribute of the assignment is HoursWorked. This data model shows how the ternary relationship in Figure 5-4(b) can be modeled as a combination of three binary relationships.

The Multivalued Attribute Pattern

In the E-R model as used today,[5] attributes must have a single value. If the CUSTOMER entity has PhoneNumber and Contact attributes, then a customer can have at most one value for phone number and at most one value for contact.

In practice, however, customers can have more than one phone number and one contact. Consider, for example, the data entry form in Figure 5-26. This particular customer has three phone numbers; other customers might have one or two or four, or

---

[5]The original E-R model allowed for multivalued attributes. Over time, that feature has been ignored, and today, most people assume that the E-R model requires single-valued attributes. We will do so in this text.

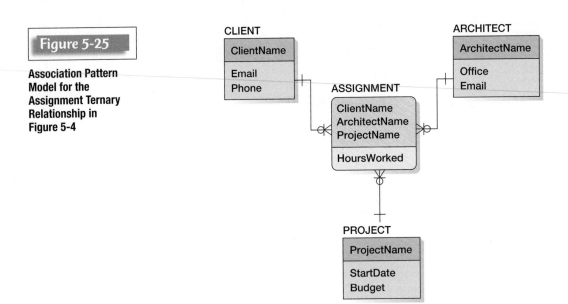

Figure 5-25

Association Pattern
Model for the
Assignment Ternary
Relationship in
Figure 5-4

whatever. We need to create a data model that allows customers to have multiple phones, and placing the attribute PhoneNumber in CUSTOMER will not do it.

Figure 5-27 shows the solution. Instead of including PhoneNumber as an attribute of CUSTOMER, we create an ID-dependent entity, PHONE, that contains the attribute PhoneNumber. The relationship from CUSTOMER to PHONE is 1:N, so a company can have multiple phone numbers. Because PHONE is an ID-dependent entity, its identifier includes both PhoneNumber and CompanyName.

We can extend this strategy for as many multivalued attributes as necessary. The CUSTOMER data entry form in Figure 5-28 has multivalued Phone and multivalued Contact attributes. In this case, we just create a separate ID-dependent entity for each multivalued attribute. The solution is shown in Figure 5-29.

In Figure 5-28, PhoneNumber and Contact are independent. PhoneNumber is the phone number of the company and not necessarily the phone number of a contact. If PhoneNumber is not a general company phone number, but rather the phone

Figure 5-26

Example Data Entry
Form with Multivalued
Attribute

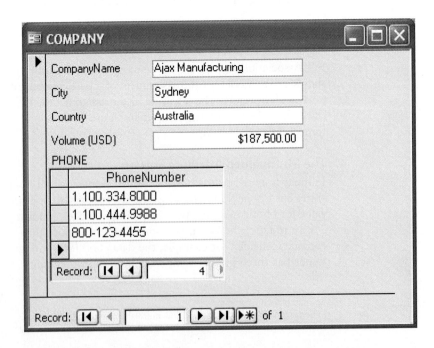

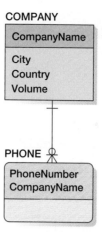

Figure 5-27

Data Model for the
Form in Figure 5-26

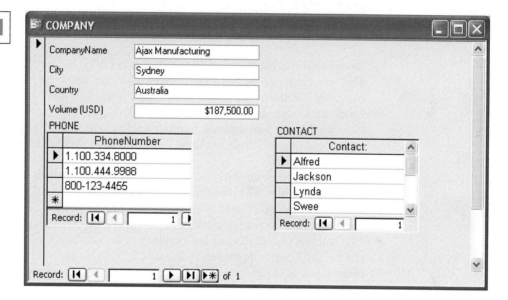

Figure 5-28

Data Entry Form with
Separate Multivalued
Attributes

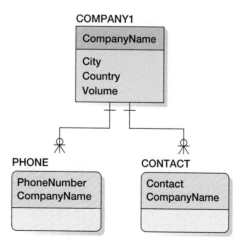

Figure 5-29

Data Model for the
Form in Figure 5-28

number of a particular person at that company, then the data entry form would appear as in Figure 5-30. Here, for example, Alfred has one phone number and Jackson has another.

In this case, the attributes PhoneNumber and Contact belong together. Accordingly, we place them into a single ID-dependent entity, as shown in Figure 5-31.

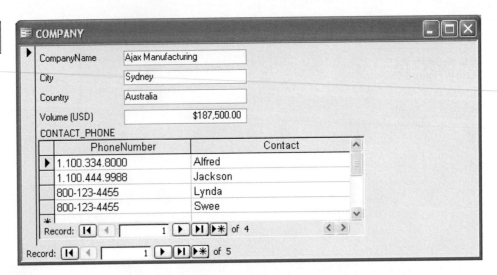

Figure 5-30

Data Entry Form with Composite Multivalued Attribute

Notice that the identifier of PHONE_CONTACT is Contact and CompanyName. This arrangement means that a given Contact name can appear only once per company. Contacts can share phone numbers, however, as shown for employees Lynda and Swee. If the identifier of PHONE_CONTACT was PhoneNumber and CompanyName, then a phone number could occur only once per company, but contacts could have multiple numbers. Work through these examples to ensure that you understand them.

In all of these examples, the child requires a parent, which is always the case for ID-dependent entities. The parent may or may not require a child, depending on the application. A COMPANY may or may not require a PHONE or a CONTACT. You must ask the users to determine whether the ID-dependent entity is required.

Multivalued attributes are common, and you need to be able to model them effectively. Review the models in Figures 5-27, 5-29, and 5-31 and be certain that you understand their differences and what those differences imply.

The Archetype/Instance Pattern

The archetype/instance pattern occurs when one entity represents a manifestation or an instance of another entity. You have already seen one example of archetype/instance in the example of PAINTING and PRINT in Figure 5-9. The

Figure 5-31

Data Model for the Form in Figure 5-30

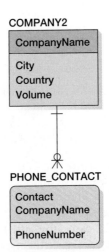

painting is the archetype; the prints made from the painting are the instances of that archetype.

Other examples of archetype/instances are shown in Figure 5-32. One familiar example concerns classes and sections of classes. The class is the archetype, and the sections of the class are instances of that archetype. Other examples involve designs and instances of designs. A yacht manufacturer has various yacht designs, and each yacht is an instance of a particular design archetype. In a housing development, a contractor offers several different house models, and a particular house is an instance of that house model archetype.

As with all ID-dependent entities, the parent entity is required. The child entities (here SECTION, YACHT, and HOUSE) may or may not be required, depending on application requirements.

Logically, the child entity of every archetype/instance pattern is an ID-dependent entity. All three of the examples in Figure 5-32 are accurate representations of the logical structure of the underlying data. However, sometimes users will add additional identifiers to the instance entity and in the process change the ID-dependent entity to a weak entity that is not ID-dependent.

For example, although you can identify a SECTION by class name and section, colleges and universities often will add a unique identifier to SECTION, such as ReferenceNumber. In that case, SECTION is no longer an ID-dependent entity, but it is still existence dependent on CLASS. Hence, in Figure 5-33, SECTION is weak, but not ID-dependent.

A similar change may occur to the YACHT entity. Although the manufacturer of a yacht may refer to it by specifying the hull number of a given design, the local tax authority may refer to it by State and LicenseNumber. If we change the identifier of YACHT from (HullNumber, DesignName) to (LicenseNumber, State), then YACHT is no longer ID-dependent; it becomes a weak, non-ID-dependent entity.

Similarly, although the home builder may think of a home as the third house constructed according to the Cape Codd design, everyone else will refer to it by its address. When we change the identifier of HOUSE from (HouseNumber, ModelName) to (Street, City, State, Zip), then HOUSE becomes a weak, non-ID-dependent entity. All of these changes are shown in Figure 5-33.

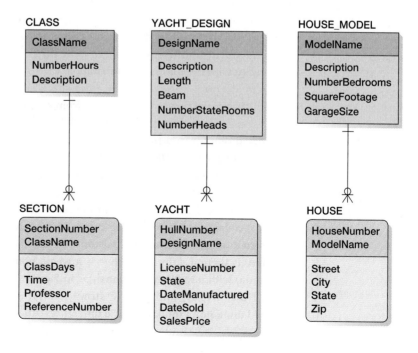

Figure 5-32

Three Archetype/Instance Pattern Examples

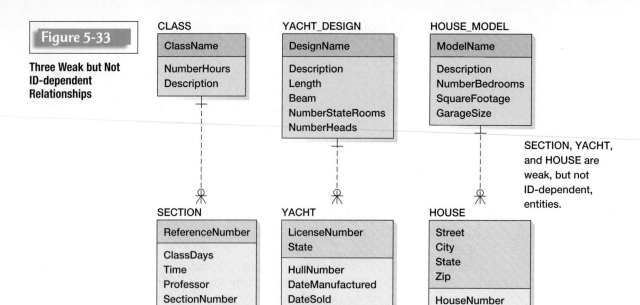

Figure 5-33

Three Weak but Not ID-dependent Relationships

SECTION, YACHT, and HOUSE are weak, but not ID-dependent, entities.

Data modelers continue to debate the importance of weak, non-ID-dependent entities. Everyone agrees that they exist, but not everyone agrees that they are important.

First, understand that existence dependence influences the way we write database applications. For the CLASS/SECTION example in Figure 5-33, we must insert a new CLASS before we can add a SECTION for that class. Additionally, when we delete a CLASS, we must delete all of the SECTIONs for that CLASS as well. This is one reason that some data modelers believe that weak, non-ID-dependent entities are important.

Skeptics say that although weak, non-ID-dependent entities may exist, they are not necessary. They say that we can obtain the same result by calling SECTION strong and making CLASS required. Because CLASS is required, the application will need to insert a CLASS before a SECTION is created and delete dependent SECTIONs when deleting a CLASS. So, according to that viewpoint, there is no practical difference between a weak, non-ID-dependent entity and a strong entity with a required relationship.

Others disagree. Their argument goes something like this: The requirement that a SECTION must have a CLASS comes from a logical necessity. It has to be that way—it comes from the nature of reality. The requirement that a strong entity must have a relationship to another strong entity arises from a business rule. Initially, we say that an ORDER must have a CUSTOMER (both strong entities), and then the application requirements change and we say that we can have cash sales, meaning that an ORDER no longer has to have a CUSTOMER. Business rules change frequently, but logical necessity never changes. We need to model weak, non-ID-dependent entities so that we know the strength of the required parent rule.

And so it goes. You, with the assistance of your instructor, can make up your own mind. Is there a difference between a weak, non-ID-dependent entity and a strong entity with a required relationship? In Figure 5-33, should we call the entities SECTION, YACHT, and HOUSE strong, as long as their relationships are required? I think not; I think there is a difference. Others think differently, however.

Figure 5-34

An Example Sales Order

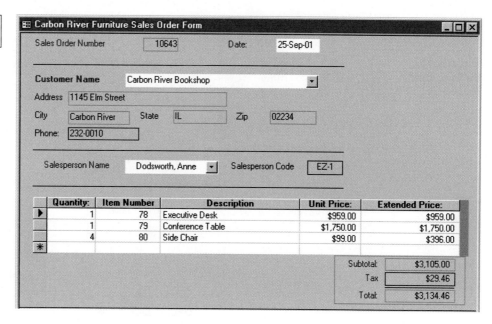

Mixed Identifying and Nonidentifying Patterns

Some patterns involve both identifying and nonidentifying relationships. The classic example is the line-item pattern, but there are other instances of mixed patterns as well. We begin with line items.

The Line-Item Pattern

Figure 5-34 shows a typical sales order, or invoice. Such forms usually have data about the order itself, such as the order number and order date, data about the customer, data about the salesperson, and then data about the items on the order. A data model for a typical SALES_ORDER is shown in Figure 5-35.

In Figure 5-35, CUSTOMER, SALESPERSON, and SALES_ORDER are all strong entities, and they have the nonidentifying relationships you would expect. The relationship from CUSTOMER to SALES_ORDER is 1:N, and the relationship from SALESPERSON to SALES_ORDER also is 1:N. According to this model, a SALES_ORDER must have a CUSTOMER and may or may not have a SALESPERSON. All of this is readily understood.

The interesting relationships concern the line items on the order. Examine the data grid in the form in Figure 5-34. Some of the data values belong to the order itself, but other data values belong to items in general. In particular, Quantity and ExtendedPrice belong to the SALES_ORDER, but ItemNumber, Description, and UnitPrice belong to ITEM. The lines on an order do not have their own identifier. No one ever says, "Give me the data for line 12." Instead, they say, "Give me the data for line 12 of order 12345." Hence, the identifier of a line is a composite of the identifier of a particular line and the identifier of a particular order. Thus, entries for line items are always ID-dependent on the order in which they appear. In Figure 5-35, ORDER_LINE_ITEM is ID-dependent on SALES_ORDER. The identifier of the ORDER_LINE_ITEM entity is (SalesOrderNumber, LineNumber).

Now, and here is the part that is sometimes confusing for students, ORDER_LINE_ITEM is not existence dependent on ITEM. It can exist even if no item has yet been assigned to it. Further, if an ITEM is deleted, we do not want the line item to be deleted with it. The deletion of an ITEM may make the value of ItemNumber and other data invalid, but it should not cause the line item itself to disappear.

On the other hand, consider what happens to a line item when an order is deleted. Unlike with the deletion of an item, which only causes data items to become invalid, the

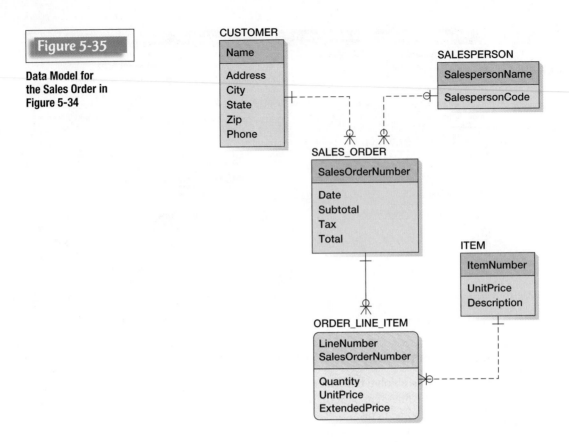

Figure 5-35

Data Model for
the Sales Order in
Figure 5-34

deletion of the order removes the existence of the line item. Logically, a line item cannot exist if its order is deleted. Hence, line items are existence dependent on orders.

Work through each of the relationships in Figure 5-35 and ensure that you understand their type and their maximum and minimum cardinalities. Also understand the implications of this model. For example, do you see why this sales order is unlikely to be used by a company in which salespeople are on commission?

Other Mixed Patterns

Mixed identifying and nonidentifying relationships occur frequently. Learn to look for a mixed pattern when a strong entity has a multivalued composite group and when one of the elements in the composite group is an identifier of a second strong entity.

Consider, for example, baking recipes. Each recipe calls for a certain amount of a specific ingredient, such as flour, sugar, or butter. The ingredient list is a multivalued composite group, but one of the elements of that group, the name of the ingredient, is the identifier of a strong entity. As shown in Figure 5-36, the recipe and the ingredients are strong entities, but the amount and instructions for using each ingredient are ID-dependent on RECIPE.

Or, consider employees' skill proficiencies. The name of the skill and the proficiency level the employee has are a multivalued group, but the skill itself is a strong entity, as shown in Figure 5-37. Dozens of other examples are possible.

Before continuing, compare the models in Figures 5-35 through 5-37 with the association pattern in Figure 5-24. Make sure that you understand the differences and why the model in Figure 5-24 has two identifying relationships and the models in Figures 5-35 through 5-37 have just one.

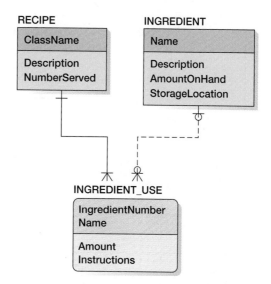

Figure 5-36

Mixed Relationship Pattern for Restaurant Recipe

The For-Use-By Pattern

As stated earlier in this chapter, the major reason for using subtypes in a database design is to avoid value-inappropriate nulls. Some forms suggest the possibility of such nulls when they show blocks of data fields that are grayed out and labeled "For Use by *someone/something* Only." For example, Figure 5-38 shows two grayed-out sections, one for commercial fishers and another for sport fishers. The presence of these grayed-out sections indicates the need for subtype entities.

The data model for this form is shown in Figure 5-39. Observe that each grayed-out section has a subtype. Notice that the subtypes differ not only in their attributes, but that one has a relationship that the other does not have. Sometimes, the only differences between subtypes are differences in the relationships they have.

The nonidentifying relationship from VESSEL to COMMERCIAL_LICENSE is shown as 1:N, mandatory to mandatory. In fact, this form does not have sufficient data for us to conclude that the maximum cardinality from VESSEL to

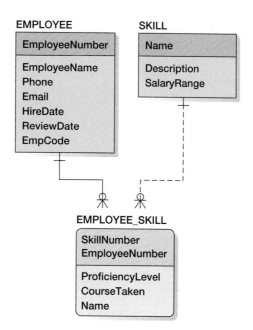

Figure 5-37

Mixed Relationship Pattern for Employee Skills

Figure 5-38

Resident Fishing License 2005 Season State of Washington	License No: 03-1123432

Name:	
Street:	

City:		State:		Zip:	

For use by Commercial Fishers Only		For use by Sport Fishers Only	
Vessel Number:		Number Years at This Address:	
Vessel Name:		Prior Year License Number:	
Vessel Type:			
Tax ID:			

COMMERCIAL_LICENSE is N. This fact was determined by interviewing users and learning that one boat is sometimes used by more than one commercial fisher. The minimum cardinalities indicate a commercial fisher must have a vessel, and that only vessels that are used for licenses are to be stored in this database.

The point of this example is to illustrate how forms often suggest the need for subtypes. Whenever you see a grayed out or otherwise distinguished section of a form with the words "For use by . . . ," think subtype.

Recursive Patterns

A recursive relationship occurs when an entity type has a relationship to itself. The classic examples of recursive relationships occur in manufacturing applications, but there are many other examples as well. As with strong entities, three types of recursive relationships are possible: 1:1, 1:N, and N:M. Let's consider each.

Figure 5-39

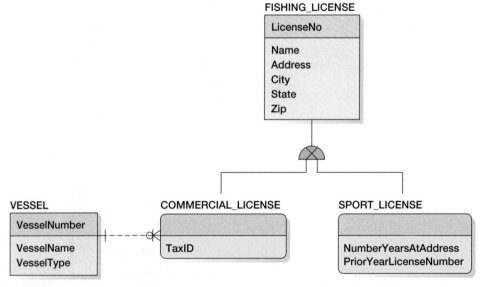

Figure 5-40

Train Model with a 1:1
Recursive Relationship

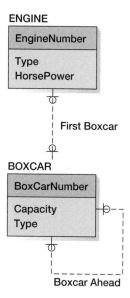

1:1 Recursive Relationships

Suppose you are asked to construct a database for a railroad, and you need to make a model of a freight train. You know that one of the entities is BOXCAR, but how are BOXCARs related? To answer that question, envision a train. Except for the first boxcar, each has one boxcar in front and, except for the last boxcar, each boxcar has one boxcar in back. Thus, the relationship is 1:1 between boxcars, with an optional relationship for the first and last cars.

Figure 5-40 shows a data model in which each BOXCAR has a 1:1 relationship to the BOXCAR ahead. The BOXCAR entity at the head of the train has a 1:1 relationship to ENGINE. (This model assumes a train has just one engine. To model trains with multiple engines, create a second recursive relationship among engines. Construct that relationship just like the Boxcar Ahead relationship.)

Figure 5-41 shows example entity instances that illustrate this data model. Not surprisingly, this set of entity instances looks just like a train.

An alternative model is to use the relationship to represent the BOXCAR behind. Either model works.

Other examples of 1:1 recursive relationships are the succession of U.S. presidents, the succession of deans in a college of business, and the order of passengers on a waiting list.

1:N Recursive Relationships

The classic example of an 1:N recursive relationship occurs in organizational charts, in which an employee has a manager who may, in turn, manage several other employees. Figure 5-42 shows an example managerial chart. Note that the relationship between employees is 1:N. Figure 5-43 shows a data model for the managerial relationship. The crow's foot indicates that a manager may manage more than one employee. The relationship is optional to optional because one manager (the president) has no manager and because some employees manage no one.

Figure 5-41

Sample Entities for the
Model in Figure 5-40

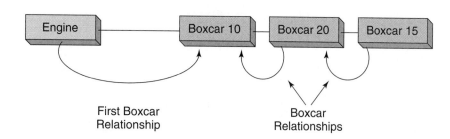

Figure 5-42

**Managerial
Relationships**

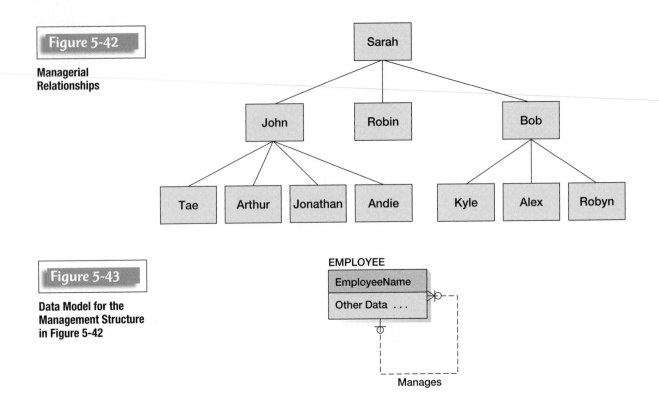

Figure 5-43

**Data Model for the
Management Structure
in Figure 5-42**

Another example of an 1:N recursive relationship concerns maps. For example, a world map has a relationship to many continent maps, each continent map has a relationship to many nation maps, and so forth. A third example concerns biological parents where the relationship from PERSON to PERSON is shown by tracing either mother or father (but not both).

N:M Recursive Relationships

N:M recursive relationships occur frequently in manufacturing applications, where they are used to represent bills of materials. Figure 5-44 shows an example.

The key idea of a bill of materials is that one part is composed of other parts. A child's red wagon, for example, consists of a handle assembly, a body, and a wheel assembly, each of which is a part. The handle assembly, in turn, consists of a handle, a bolt, a washer, and a nut. The wheel assembly consists of wheels, axles, washers, and nuts. The relationship among the parts is N:M because a part can be made up of many parts and because a part (such as washers and nuts) can be used in many parts.

Figure 5-44

**Example Bill of
Materials**

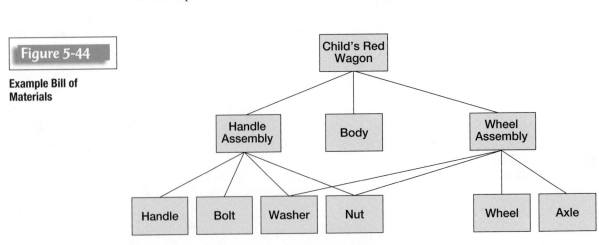

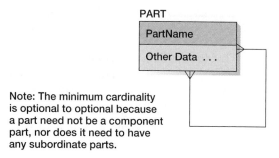

Figure 5-45

An N:M Recursive
Model for the Bill
of Materials in
Figure 5-44

Note: The minimum cardinality
is optional to optional because
a part need not be a component
part, nor does it need to have
any subordinate parts.

The data model for a bill of materials is shown in Figure 5-45. Notice that each part has a N:M relationship to other parts. Because a part need not have any component parts, and because a part need not have any parts that contain it, the minimum cardinality is optional to optional. The minimum cardinality must be shown in a note because of the idiosyncrasy of ERwin regarding N:M relationships.

B T W

What would happen to the data model if the diagram showed how many of each part are used? Suppose, for example, that the wheel assembly requires four washers and the handle assembly requires just one. The data model in Figure 5-45 will not be correct for this circumstance. In fact, adding Quantity to this N:M relationship is analogous to adding Price to the N:M relationship in Figure 5-24. See question 5.67.

N:M recursive relationships can be used to model directed networks, such as the flow of documents through organizational departments or the flow of gas through a pipeline. They also can be used to model the succession of parents, in which both mothers, fathers, and stepparents are included.

If recursive structures seem hard to comprehend, don't fret. They may seem strange at first, but they are not difficult. Work through some data examples to gain confidence. Make up a train and see how the model in Figure 5-40 applies or change the example in Figure 5-42 from employees to departments and see how the model in Figure 5-43 needs to be adjusted. Once you have learned to identify recursive patterns, you'll find it easy to create models for them.

The Data Modeling Process

During the data modeling process, the development team analyzes user requirements and constructs a data model from forms, reports, data sources, and user interviews. The process is always iterative; a model is constructed from one form or report and then supplemented and adjusted as more forms and reports are analyzed. Periodically, users are asked for additional information, such as that needed to assess minimum cardinality. Users also review and validate the data model. During that review, prototypes evidencing data model constructs may need to be constructed, as explained earlier.

To give you an idea of the iterative nature of data modeling, we will consider the development of a simple data model for a university. As you read this example, strive to appreciate how the model evolves as more and more requirements are analyzed.

B T W

The largest data model I have worked on was for the U.S. Army's logistical system. The model contained over 500 different entity types, and it took a team of seven people more than a year to develop, document, and validate. On some occasions, the analysis of a new requirement indicated that the model had been conceived incorrectly, and days of work had to be redone. The most difficult aspect of the project was managing complexity. Knowing which entities related to which; whether an entity had already been defined; and whether a new entity was strong, weak, a supertype, or a subtype required a global understanding of the model. Memory was of poor help because an entity created in July could be a subtype of an entity created hundreds of entities earlier in February. To manage the model, we used many different administrative tools. Keep this example in mind as you read through the development of the Highline University data model.

Suppose the administration at a hypothetical university named Highline University wants to create a database to track colleges, departments, faculty, and students. To do this, a data modeling team has collected a series of reports as part of its requirements determination. In the next sections, we will analyze these reports to produce a data model.

The College Report

The example report in Figure 5-46 is about a college, specifically, the College of Business. This example is one instance of this report; Highline University has similar reports about other colleges, such as the College of Engineering and the College of Social Sciences. The data modeling team needs to gather enough examples to form a representative sample of all the college reports. Here, assume that the report in Figure 5-46 is representative.

Examining the report, we find data specific to the college—such as the name, dean, telephone number, and campus address—and also facts about each department within the college. These data suggest that the data model should have COLLEGE and DEPARTMENT entities with a relationship between them, as shown in Figure 5-47.

The relationship in Figure 5-47 is nonidentifying. This relationship is used because DEPARTMENT is not ID-dependent, and logically, a DEPARTMENT is independent

Figure 5-46

Sample College Report

College of Business Mary B. Jefferson, Dean			
Phone: 232-1187		Campus Address: Business Building, Room 100	
Department	Chairperson	Phone	Total Majors
Accounting	Jackson, Seymour P.	232-1841	318
Finance	HeuTeng, Susan	232-1414	211
Info Systems	Brammer, Nathaniel D.	236-0011	247
Management	Tuttle, Christine A.	236-9988	184
Production	Barnes, Jack T.	236-1184	212

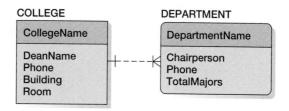

Figure 5-47

Data Model from College Report

of a UNIVERSITY. We cannot tell from the report in Figure 5-46 whether a department can belong to many colleges. To answer this question, we need to ask the users or look at other forms and reports.

Assume we know from the users that a department belongs to just one college, and the relationship is thus 1:N from COLLEGE to DEPARTMENT. The report in Figure 5-46 does not show us the minimum cardinalities. Again, we must ask the users. Assume we learn from the users that a college must have at least one department, and a department must be assigned to exactly one college.

The Department/Professor Report

The Department Report shown in Figure 5-48 contains departmental data along with a list of the professors who are assigned to that department. This report contains data concerning the department's campus address. Because these data do not appear in the DEPARTMENT entity in Figure 5-47, we need to add them, as shown in Figure 5-49(a). This is typical of the data modeling process. That is, entities and relationships are adjusted as additional forms, reports, and other requirements are analyzed.

Figure 5-49(a) shows the relationship between DEPARTMENT and PROFESSOR as N:M, because a professor might have a joint appointment. The data modeling team must further investigate the requirements to determine whether joint appointments are allowed. If not, the relationship can be redefined as a nonidentifying 1:N, as shown in Figure 5-49(b).

Another possibility regarding the N:M relationship is that some attribute about the combination of a professor and a department is missing. If so, then an association pattern is more appropriate. At Highline, suppose the team finds a report that describes the title and employment terms for each professor in each department. Figure 5-49(c) shows an entity for such a report, named APPOINTMENT. As you would expect from the association pattern, APPOINTMENT is ID-dependent on both DEPARTMENT and PROFESSOR.

A chairperson is a professor, so another improvement on the model is to remove the Chairperson data from DEPARTMENT and replace it with a chairperson relationship.

Figure 5-48

Sample Department Report

| Information Systems Department | | |
| College of Business | | |

Chairperson: Brammer, Nathaniel D
Phone: 236-0011
Campus Address: Social Science Building, Room 213

Professor	Office	Phone
Jones, Paul D.	Social Science, 219	232-7713
Parks, Mary B	Social Science, 308	232-5791
Wu, Elizabeth	Social Science, 207	232-9112

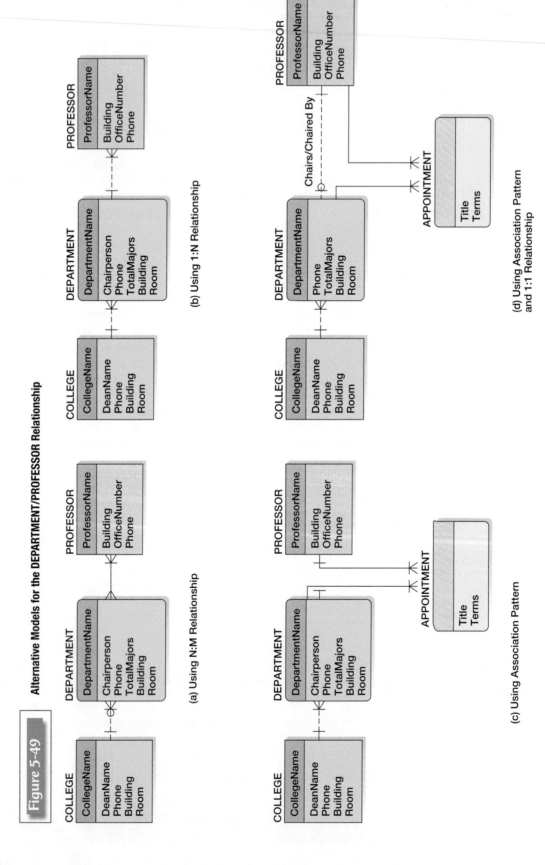

Figure 5-49

Alternative Models for the DEPARTMENT/PROFESSOR Relationship

(a) Using N:M Relationship

(b) Using 1:N Relationship

(c) Using Association Pattern

(d) Using Association Pattern
and 1:1 Relationship

Figure 5-50

Second Department Report

Student Major List Information Systems Department		
Chairperson: Brammer, Nathaniel D Phone: 236-0011		
Major's Name	Student Number	Phone
Jackson, Robin R.	12345	237-8713
Lincoln, Fred J.	48127	237-8713
Madison, Janice A.	37512	237-8713

This has been done in Figure 5-49(d). In the Chairs/Chaired By relationship, the PROFESSOR is the parent entity. A professor can be a chair of zero or one departments, and a department must have exactly one professor as chair.

With the Chairs/Chaired By relationship, the attribute Chairperson is no longer needed in DEPARTMENT, so it is removed. Normally, a chairperson has his or her office in the department office; if this is the case, Phone, Building, and Room in DEPARTMENT duplicate Phone, Building, and OfficeNumber in PROFESSOR. Consequently, it might be possible to remove Phone, Building, and Room from DEPARTMENT. On the other hand, a professor may have a different phone from the official department phone, and the professor may also have an office outside of the department's office. Because of this possibility, we will leave Phone, Building, and Room in DEPARTMENT.

The Department/Major Report

Figure 5-50 shows a report of a department and the students who major in that department. This report indicates the need for a new entity called STUDENT. Because students are not ID-dependent on departments, the relationship between DEPARTMENT and STUDENT is nonidentifying, as shown in Figure 5-51. We cannot determine the

Figure 5-51   **Data Model with STUDENT Entity**

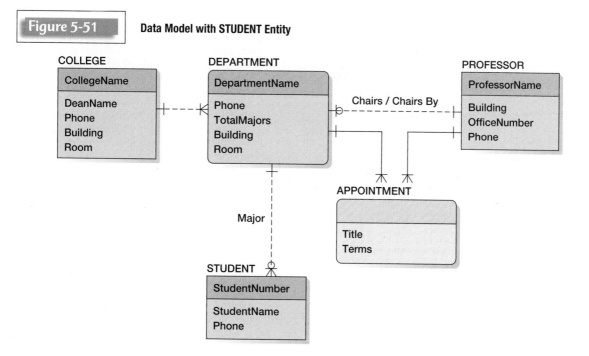

minimum cardinality from Figure 5-50, but assume that interviews with users indicate that a STUDENT must have MAJOR, but no MAJOR need have any students. Also, using the contents of this report as a guide, attributes StudentNumber, StudentName, and Phone are placed in STUDENT.

There are two subtleties in this interpretation of the report in Figure 5-50. First, observe that Major's Name was changed to StudentName when the attribute was placed in STUDENT. This was done because StudentName is more generic. Major's Name has no meaning outside the context of the Major relationship. Additionally, the report heading in Figure 5-50 has an ambiguity. Is the phone number for the department a value of DEPARTMENT.Phone or a value of PROFESSOR.Phone? The team needs to investigate this further with the users. Most likely, it is a value of DEPARTMENT.Phone.

The Student Acceptance Letter

Figure 5-52 shows the acceptance letter that Highline sends to its incoming students. The data items in this letter that need to be represented in the data model are shown in boldface. In addition to data concerning the student, this letter also contains data regarding the student's major department as well as data about the student's adviser.

We can use this letter to add an Advises/Advised By relationship to the data model. However, which entity should be the parent of this relationship? Because an adviser is a professor, it is tempting to make PROFESSOR the parent. However, a professor acts as an adviser within the context of a particular department. Therefore, Figure 5-53 shows APPOINTMENT as the parent of ADVISER. To produce the report in Figure 5-52, the professor's data can be retrieved by accessing the related APPOINTMENT entity and

Figure 5-52

Acceptance Letter

Mr. Fred Parks
123 Elm Street
Los Angeles, CA 98002

Dear **Mr. Parks:**

You have been admitted as a major in the **Accounting** Department at Highline University, starting in the Fall Semester, 2005. The office of the Accounting Department is located in the **Business** Building, Room **210.**

Your adviser is professor **Elizabeth Johnson,** whose telephone number is **232-8740** and whose office is located in the **Business** Building, Room **227.** Please schedule an appointment with your adviser as soon as you arrive on campus.

Congratulations and welcome to Highline University!

Sincerely,

Jan P. Smathers
President

JPS/rkp

Figure 5-53   Data Model with Advises Relationship

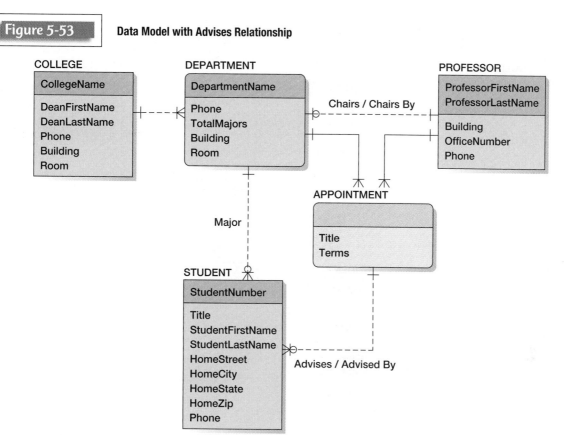

then accessing that entity's PROFESSOR parent. This decision is not cut-and-dried, however. One can make a strong argument that the parent of the relationship should be PROFESSOR.

According to this data model, a student has at most one adviser. Also, a student must have an adviser, but no professor (via APPOINTMENT) need advise any students. These constraints cannot be determined from any of the reports shown and will need to be verified with the users. The acceptance letter uses the title *Mr.* in the salutation. Therefore, a new attribute called Title is added to STUDENT. Observe that this Title is different from the one in APPOINTMENT. This difference will need to be documented in the data model to avoid confusion. The acceptance letter also shows the need to add new home address attributes to STUDENT.

The acceptance letter reveals a problem. The name of the student is Fred Parks, but we have allocated only one attribute, StudentName, in STUDENT. It is difficult to reliably disentangle first and last names from a single attribute, so a better model is to have two attributes: StudentFirstName and StudentLastName. Similarly, note that the adviser in this letter is Elizabeth Johnson. So far, all professor names have been in the format Johnson, Elizabeth. To accommodate both forms of name, ProfessorName in PROFESSOR must be changed to the two attributes ProfessorFirstName and ProfessorLastName. A similar change is necessary for DeanName. These changes are shown in Figure 5-54, which is the final form of this data model.

This section should give you a feel for the nature of a data modeling project. Forms and reports are examined in sequence, and the data model is adjusted as necessary to accommodate the knowledge gained from each new form or report. It is very typical to revise the data model many, many times throughout the data modeling process. See question 5.68 for yet another possible revision.

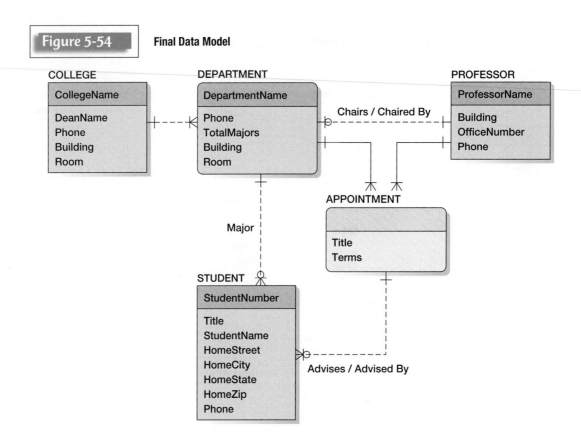

Figure 5-54   Final Data Model

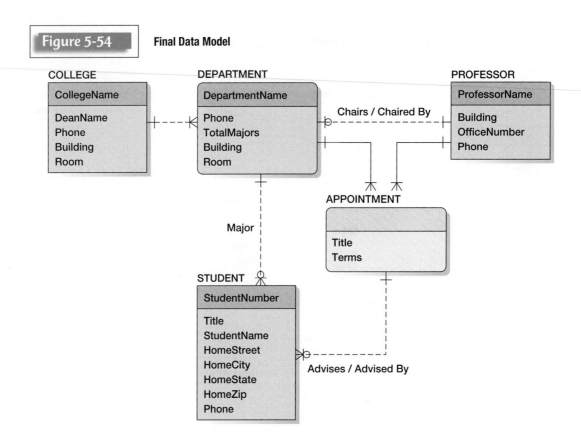

🌀 S U M M A R Y

When databases are developed as part of a new information systems project, the database design is accomplished in two phases. First, a data model is constructed from forms, reports, data sources, and other requirements. The data model is then transformed into a database design. A data model is a blueprint for a database design. Like blueprints for buildings, data models can be altered as necessary, with little effort. Once the database is constructed, however, such alterations are time consuming and very expensive.

The most prominent data model in use today is the entity-relationship, or E-R, data model. It was invented by Peter Chen and extended by others to include subtypes. An entity is something that users want to track. An entity class is a collection of entities of the same type and is described by the structure of the entities in the class. An entity instance is one entity of a given class. Entities have attributes that describe their characteristics. Identifiers are attributes that name entity instances. Composite identifiers consist of two or more attributes.

The E-R model includes relationships, which are associations among entities. Relationship classes are associations among entity classes, and relationship instances are associations among entity instances. Today, relationships are not allowed to have attributes. Relationships can be given names so that they can be identified.

The degree of a relationship is the number of entity types that participate in the relationship. Binary relationships have only two entities types. In practice, relationships of degrees greater than two are decomposed into multiple binary relationships.

The difference between an entity and a table is that you can express an entity relationship without specifying foreign keys. Working with entities reduces complexity and makes it easier to revise the data model as work progresses.

Relationships are classified according to their cardinality. Maximum cardinality is the maximum number of instances that can participate in a relationship instance. Minimum cardinality is the least number of entities that must participate in a relationship.

Relationships commonly have one of three maximum cardinalities: 1:1, 1:N, or N:M. In rare instances, a maximum cardinality might be a specific number, such as 1:15. Relationships commonly have one of four basic minimum cardinalities: optional to optional, mandatory to optional, optional to mandatory, or mandatory to mandatory. In rare cases, the minimum cardinality is a specific number.

Unfortunately, many variations of the E-R model are in use. The original version represented relationships with diamonds. The Information Engineering version uses a line with a crow's foot, the IDEF1X version uses another set of symbols, and UML uses yet another set. To add further complication, many data modeling products have added their own symbols. In this text, we will use the crow's foot model as interpreted by the product ERwin. Other models and techniques are summarized in Appendices B, C, and D.

An ID-dependent entity is an entity whose identifier includes the identifier of another entity. Such entities use an identifying relationship. In such relationships, the parent is always required, but the child (the ID-dependent entity) may or may not be required, depending on application requirements. Identifying relationships are shown with solid lines in E-R diagrams.

A weak entity is an entity whose existence depends on the presence of another entity. All ID-dependent entities are weak. Additionally, some entities are weak, but not ID-dependent. Some people believe such entities are not important; others believe they are.

A subtype entity is a special case of another entity called its supertype. Subtypes may be exclusive or inclusive. Exclusive subtypes sometimes have discriminators, which are attributes that specify a supertype's subtype. The most important (and perhaps only) reason for creating subtypes in a data model is to avoid value-inappropriate nulls.

Relationships among nonsubtype entities are called HAS-A relationships. Relationships among subtypes are called IS-A relationships.

The elements of a data model are constructed by analyzing forms, reports, and data sources. Many forms and reports fall into common patterns. In this text, we discussed the 1:1, 1:N, and N:M strong entity patterns. We also discussed three patterns that use ID-dependent relationships: association, multivalue attribute, and version/instance. Some forms involve mixed identifying and nonidentifying patterns. Line items are the classic example of mixed forms, but there are other examples as well.

The for-use-by pattern indicates the need for subtypes. In some cases, subtypes differ because they have different attributes, but they also can differ because they have different relationships. A recursive relationship occurs when an entity has a relationship to itself. The three types of recursive relationship are 1:1, 1:N, and N:M.

The data modeling process is iterative. Forms and reports are analyzed, and the data model is created, modified, and adjusted as necessary. Sometimes, the analysis of a form or report will require that earlier work be redone. *C'est la vie!*

◉ REVIEW QUESTIONS

5.1 Describe the two phases in designing databases that arise from the development of new information systems.

5.2 In general terms, explain how a data model could be used to design a database for a small video rental store.

5.3 Explain how a data model is like a building blueprint. What is the advantage of making changes during the data modeling stage?

5.4 Who is the author of the entity-relationship data model?

5.5 Define entity. Give an example of an entity (other than one presented in this chapter).

5.6 Explain the difference between an entity class and an entity instance.

5.7 Define attribute. Give an example attribute for the entity in your answer to question 5.5.

5.8 Define identifier. Give an example identifier for the entity in your answer to question 5.5.

5.9 Give an example of a composite identifier.

5.10 Define relationship. Give an example of a relationship (other than one presented in this chapter). Name your relationship.

5.11 Explain the difference between a relationship class and a relationship instance.

5.12 What is the degree of relationship? Give an example of a relationship of degree three (other than one presented in this chapter).

5.13 What is a binary relationship?

5.14 Explain the difference between an entity and a table. Why is this difference important?

5.15 What does cardinality mean?

5.16 Define the terms maximum cardinality and minimum cardinality.

5.17 Give examples of 1:1, 1:N, and N:M relationships (other than those presented in this chapter). Use the traditional diamond notation to diagram your examples.

5.18 Give an example for which the maximum cardinality must be an exact number.

5.19 Give examples of M-M, M-O, O-M, and O-O relationships (other than those presented in this chapter). Use the circle and hash mark notation on the diamond portrayal of relationships.

5.20 Explain, in general terms, how the traditional E-R model, the Information Engineering (crow's foot) version, the IDEF1X version, and the UML version differ. Which version is used primarily in this text?

5.21 Explain how the notations shown in Figure 5-7 differ.

5.22 Explain how the notations shown in Figure 5-8 differ.

5.23 Summarize why the author of this text is frustrated with Microsoft Visio's database template.

5.24 What is an ID-dependent entity? Give an example of an ID-dependent entity (other than one presented in this chapter).

5.25 Explain how to determine the minimum cardinality of both sides of an ID-dependent relationship.

5.26 What rules exist when creating an instance of an ID-dependent entity? What rules exist when deleting the parent of an ID-dependent entity?

5.27 What is an identifying relationship? How is it used?

5.28 Explain why the relationship between PRODUCT and VERSION is an identifying relationship.

5.29 What is a weak entity? How do weak entities relate to ID-dependent entities?

5.30 What distinguishes a weak entity from a strong entity that has a required relationship to another entity?

5.31 Define subtype and supertype. Give an example of a subtype–supertype relationship (other than one presented in this chapter).

5.32 Explain the difference between exclusive subtypes and inclusive subtypes. Give an example of each.

5.33 What is a discriminator?

5.34 Explain the difference between IS-A and HAS-A relationships.

5.35 What is the most important reason for using subtypes in a data model?

5.36 Describe the relationship between the structure of forms and reports and the data model.

5.37 Explain two ways forms and reports are used for data modeling.

5.38 Explain why the form and report in Figure 5-17 indicate that the underlying relationship is 1:1?

5.39 Why is it not possible to infer minimum cardinality from the form and report in Figure 5-17?

5.40   Describe two tests for determining if an entity is strong.

5.41   Why does the form in Figure 5-19 not indicate that the underlying relationship is 1:N? What additional information is required to make that assertion?

5.42   Explain why two forms or reports are usually needed to infer maximum cardinality.

5.43   How can you assess minimum cardinality for the entities in the form in Figure 5-19?

5.44   Explain why the form and report in Figure 5-21 indicate that the underlying relationship is N:M.

5.45   Name three patterns that use ID-dependent relationships.

5.46   Explain how the association pattern differs from the N:M strong entity pattern. What characteristic of the report in Figure 5-23 indicates that an association pattern is needed?

5.47   In general terms, explain how to differentiate an N:M strong entity pattern from an association pattern.

5.48   Explain why two entities are needed to model multivalued attributes.

5.49   How do the forms in Figures 5-28 and 5-30 differ? How does this difference affect the data model?

5.50   Describe, in general terms, the archetype/instance pattern. Why is an ID-dependent relationship needed for this pattern? Use the CLASS/SECTION example in your answer.

5.51   Explain what caused the entities in Figure 5-33 to change from ID-dependent entities.

5.52   Summarize the two sides in the argument about the importance of weak, but not ID-dependent, entities.

5.53   Give an example of the line-item pattern as it could be used to describe the contents of a shipment. Assume that the shipment includes the names and quantities of various items as well as each item's insured value. Place the insurance value per item in an ITEM entity.

5.54   What entity type should come to mind when you see the words "For use by" in a form?

5.55   Give examples of 1:1, 1:N, and N:M recursive relationships (other than those presented in this chapter).

5.56   Explain why the data modeling process must be iterative. Use the Highline University example.

PROJECT QUESTIONS

5.57   This question is for Visio users. Convert the data models in Figures 5-18, 5-22, 5-24, 5-25, 5-32, 5-35, 5-39, and 5-54 into Visio format. Use the Visio arrow notation.

5.58   This question is for Visio users. Convert the data models in Figures 5-18, 5-22, 5-24, 5-25, 5-32, 5-35, 5-39, 5-54 into Visio format. Use the Visio version of the crow's foot model.

Answer the following questions using crow's foot notation.

5.59   Examine the subscription form shown in Figure 5-55. Using the structure of this form, do the following:
a. Create a model with one entity. Specify the identifier and attributes.
b. Create a model with two entities, one for customer and a second for subscription. Specify identifiers, attributes, relationship name, type, and cardinalities.
c. Under what conditions do you prefer the model in A to that in B?
d. Under what conditions do you prefer the model in B to that in A?

Figure 5-55

Subscription Form

Fine
Wood
▲▲▲▲▲Working

To subscribe

☐ 1 year (6 issues) for just $18 — 20% off the newsstand price.
  (Outside the U.S. $21/year—U.S. funds, please)

☐ 2 years (12 issues) for just $34 — save 24%
  (Outside the U.S. $40/2 years—U.S. funds, please)

Name _____

Address_____

City_____ State _____ Zip _____

☐ My payment is enclosed. ☐ Please bill me.

Please start my subscription with ☐ current issue ☐ next issue.

5.60   Consider the traffic citation shown in Figure 5-56. The rounded corners on this form provide graphical hints about the boundaries of the entities represented.

   a. Create a data model with five entities. Use the data items on the form to specify identifiers and attributes for those entities.

   b. Specify relationships among the entities. Name the relationship and give its type and cardinalities. Indicate which cardinalities can be inferred from data on the form and which need to be checked out with systems users.

Figure 5-56

Traffic Citation

WASHINGTON STATE PATROL CORRECTION NOTICE

NAME	*Kroenke* , *David M*
	LAST FIRST
ADDRESS	*5053 88 Ave SE*

CITY *Mecer Island*   STATE *Wa*   ZIP CODE *98040*

DRIVERS LICENSE	STATE ☒	BIRTH DATE	HGT	WGT	EYES
00000	*Wa* F	*2/27/46*	*6*	*165*	*BU*

VEHICLES LICENSE	STATE	COLOR	YEAR	MAKE	TYPE
AAA000	*Wa*		*90*	*Saab*	*900*

VIN

REGISTERED
OWNER

ADDRESS

VIOLATION DATE				DIST	DETACH
MO *11* DAY *7* YEAR *2003*	TIME HOUR: *935*			*2*	*17*

LOCATION
17 MILES *E* OF *Enumckum* ON *SR410*

VIOLATIONS
Writing text while driving

OFFICERS SIGNATURE	*S Scott*	PERSONNEL NUMBER	*850*

☒ This is a warning, no further action is required.

☐ You are released to take this vehicle to a place of repair. Continued operation on the roadway is not authorized.

☐ CORRECT VIOLATION(S) IMMEDIATELY. Return this signed card for proof of compliance within 15/30 days. (if this box checked)

X DRIVERS SIGNATURE

Figure 5-57

E-mail List

	From	Subject	Date ↓	Size
□	WDA2259@sailmail.com	Big Wind	5/13/2002	3 KB
□	WDA2259@sailmail.com	Update	5/12/2002	4 KB
□	WDA2259@sailmail.com	Re: Saturday Am	5/11/2002	4 KB
□	WDA2259@sailmail.com	Re: Weather window!	5/10/2002	4 KB
□	WDA2259@sailmail.com	Re: Howdy!	5/10/2002	3 KB
□	WDA2259@sailmail.com	Still here	5/9/2002	3 KB
□	WDA2259@sailmail.com	Re: Turle Bay	5/8/2002	4 KB
□	WDA2259@sailmail.com	Turle Bay	5/8/2002	4 KB
□	WDA2259@sailmail.com	Re: Hi	5/6/2002	3 KB
□	WDA2259@sailmail.com	Sunday, Santa Maria	5/5/2002	3 KB
□	Ki6yu@aol.com	Cabo, Thurs. Noon	5/2/2002	2 KB
□	WDA2259@sailmail.com	turbo	5/1/2002	3 KB
□	WDA2259@sailmail.com	on our way	4/28/2002	3 KB
□	Tom Cooper	RE: Hola!	4/26/2002	3 KB
□	Tom Cooper	RE: Hola!	4/24/2002	2 KB
□	Tom Cooper	RE: Hola!	4/23/2002	3 KB

5.61   Examine the list of e-mail messages in Figure 5-57. Using the structure and example data items in this list, do the following:

    a. Create a single-entity data model for this list. Specify the identifier and all entities.

    b. Modify your answer to A to include entities SENDER and SUBJECT. Specify the identifiers and attributes of entities and the type and cardinalities of the relationships. Explain which cardinalities can be inferred from Figure 5-57 and which need to be checked out with users.

    c. The e-mail address in the From column in Figure 5-57 is in two different styles. One style has the true e-mail address; the second style (e.g., Tom Cooper) is the name of an entry in the user's e-mail directory. Create two categories of SENDER based on these two styles. Specify identifiers and attributes.

5.62   Examine the list of stock quotes in Figure 5-58. Using the structure and example data items in this list, do the following:

    a. Create a single-entity data model for this list. Specify the identifier and attributes.

    b. Modify your answer to A to include the entities COMPANY and INDEX. Specify the identifier and attributes of the entities and the type and cardinalities

Figure 5-58

Stock Quotes

Symbol	Name	Last	Change	% Chg
$COMPX	Nasdaq Combined Composite Index	1,400.74 ▼	-4.87	-0.35%
$INDU	Dow Jones Industrial Average Index	9,255.10 ▼	-19.80	-0.21%
$INX	S&P 500 INDEX	971.14 ▼	-5.84	-0.60%
ALTR	Altera Corporation	13.45 ▼	-0.450	-3.24%
AMZN	Amazon.com, Inc.	15.62 ▲	+0.680	+4.55%
CSCO	Cisco Systems, Inc.	13.39 ▼	-0.280	-2.05%
DELL	Dell Computer Corporation	24.58 ▼	-0.170	-0.69%
ENGCX	Enterprise Growth C	14.60 ▼	-0.210	-1.42%
INTC	Intel Corporation	18.12 ▼	-0.380	-2.05%
JNJ	Johnson & Johnson	53.29 ▼	-0.290	-0.54%
KO	Coca-Cola Company	56.70 ▼	-0.580	-1.01%
MSFT	Microsoft Corporation	53.96 ▲	+1.040	+1.97%
NKE	NIKE, Inc.	57.34 ▲	+0.580	+1.02%

Figure 5-59

Air Compressor
Specifications

			Air Performance						Approx	Dimensions		
Single Stage												
Set 95 to 150 PSI also available, substitute "E" for "A" in model number, i.e., K15A-30 make K15E-30												
HP	Model	Tank Gal	A @ 125			E @ 150			Ship Weight	L	W	H
			Pump RPM	CFM Disp	DEL'D Air	Pump RPM	CFM Disp	DEL'D Air				
1/2	F12A-17	17	680	3.4	2.2	590	2.9	1.6	135	37	14	25
3/4	F34A-17	17	1080	5.3	3.1	950	4.7	2.3	140	37	14	25
3/4	F34A-30	30	1080	5.3	3.1	950	4.7	2.3	160	38	16	31
1	K1A-30	30	560	6.2	4.0	500	5.7	3.1	190	38	16	34
1 1/2	K15A-30	30	870	9.8	6.2	860	9.7	5.8	205	49	20	34
1 1/2	K15A-60	60	870	9.8	6.2	860	9.7	5.8	315	38	16	34
2	K2A-30	30	1140	13.1	8.0	1060	12.0	7.0	205	49	20	39
2	K2A-60	60	1140	13.1	8.0	1060	12.0	7.0	315	48	20	34
2	GC2A-30	30	480	13.1	9.1	460	12.4	7.9	270	38	16	36
2	GC2A-60	60	480	13.1	9.1	460	12.4	7.9	370	49	20	41
3	GC3A-60	60	770	21.0	14.0	740	19.9	12.3	288	38	16	36
5	GC5A-80	60	770	21.0	14.0	740	19.9	12.3	388	49	20	41
5	GC5A-60	60	1020	27.8	17.8	910	24.6	15.0	410	49	20	41
5	GC5A-80	80	1020	27.8	17.8	910	24.6	15.0	450	62	20	41
5	J5A-80	60	780	28.7	19.0	770	28.6	18.0	570	49	23	43
5	J5A-80	80	780	28.7	19.0	770	28.6	18.0	610	63	23	43

of the relationships. Explain which cardinalities can be inferred from Figure 5-58 and which need to be checked out with users.

c. The list in Figure 5-58 is for a quote on a particular day at a particular time of day. Suppose that the list were changed to show closing daily prices for each of these stocks and that it includes a new column: QuoteDate. Modify your model in B to reflect this change.

d. Change your model in C to include the tracking of a portfolio. Assume the portfolio has an owner name, a phone number, an e-mail address, and a list of stocks held. The list includes the identity of the stock and the number of shares held. Specify all additional entities, their identifiers and attributes, and the type and cardinality of all relationships.

e. Change your answer to question D to keep track of portfolio stock purchases and sales in a portfolio. Specify entities, their identifiers and attributes, and the type and cardinality of all relationships.

5.63 Figure 5-59 shows the specifications for single-stage air compressor products. Note that there are two product categories that are based on Air Performance: The A models are at 125 pounds per square inch of pressure, and the E models are at 150 pounds per square inch of pressure. Using the structure and example data items in this list, do the following:

a. Create a set of exclusive subtypes to represent these compressors. The supertype will have attributes for all single-stage compressors, and the subtypes will have attributes for products having the two different types of Air Performance. Assume that there might be additional products with different types of Air Performance. Specify the entities, identifiers, attributes, relationships, type of category cluster, and possible determinant.

b. Figure 5-60 shows a different model for the compressor data. Explain the entities, their type, the relationship, its type, and its cardinality. How well do you think this model fits the data shown in Figure 5-59?

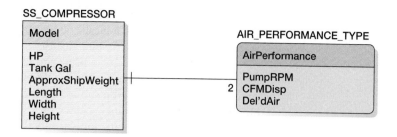

Figure 5-60

Alternative Model for Compressor Data

c. Compare your answer in question A with the model in Figure 5-60. What are the essential differences between the two models? Which do you think is better?

d. Suppose you had the job of explaining the differences in these two models to a highly motivated, intelligent end user. How would you accomplish this?

5.64 Figure 5-61 shows a listing of movie times at theaters in Seattle. Using the data in this figure as an example, do the following:

a. Create a model to represent this report using the entities MOVIE, THEATER, and SHOW_TIME. Assume that theaters may show multiple movies. Although this report is for a particular day, your data model should allow for movie times on different days as well. Specify the identifier of the entities and their attributes.

Figure 5-61

Movie Time Listing

Movie
Men in Black II
Even Tommy Lee Jones at his funniest can't save Will Smith or this goofy alien flick from sequel-itis.

Local Theaters and Showtimes

40 miles from the center of Seattle, WA Change Area
Tue, Jul 9 Wed Thu Fri Sat

Displaying 1 - 32 results, sorted by distance.

AMC Pacific Place 11 (0.5 miles)
600 Pine St, Seattle (206) 652-2404
Showtimes: 11:00 am, 12:00 pm, 12:45 pm, 1:30 pm, 2:30 pm, 3:15 pm, 4:00 pm, 5:00 pm, 5:45 pm, 6:30 pm, 7:30 pm, 8:30 pm, 9:00 pm, 10:00 pm, 10:45 pm

Neptune Theatre (3.9 miles)
1303 NE 45th, Seattle (206) 633-5545
Showtimes: 11:20 am, 1:30 pm, 3:40 pm, 5:50 pm, 8:00 pm, 10:10 pm

Regal Bellevue Galleria 11 (6.2 miles)
500 106th Ave NE, Bellevue (425) 451-7161
Showtimes: 11:00 am, 11:30 am, 1:00 pm, 1:30 pm, 3:00 pm, 3:30 pm, 5:05 pm, 5:35 pm, 7:10 pm, 7:40 pm, 9:20 pm, 9:50 pm

LCE Oak Tree Cinema (6.6 miles)
10006 Aurora Ave N., Seattle (206) 527-1748
Showtimes: 11:45 am, 2:15 pm, 4:45 pm, 7:15 pm, 9:45 pm

LCE Factoria Cinemas 8 (7.8 miles)
3505 Factoria Blvd SE, Bellevue (425) 641-9206
Showtimes: 12:00 pm, 1:00 pm, 2:15 pm, 3:15 pm, 4:30 pm, 5:45 pm, 7:30 pm, 8:15 pm, 9:45 pm, 10:30 pm

Kirkland Parkplace Cinema (8 miles)
404 Parkplace Ctr, Kirkland (425) 827-9000
Showtimes: 12:15 pm, 2:30 pm, 4:45 pm, 7:20 pm, 9:35 pm

Name the relationships and the type and cardinality of all relationships. Explain which cardinalities you can logically deduce from Figure 5-61 and which need to be checked out with users. Assume that distance is an attribute of THEATER.

b. This report was prepared for a user who is located near downtown Seattle. Suppose that it is necessary to produce this same report for these theaters, but for a user located in a Seattle suburb such as Bellevue, Renton, Redmond, or Tacoma. In this case, distance cannot be an attribute of THEATER. Change your answer in A for this situation. Specify the entity identifiers and attributes. Name the relationships and identify the type and cardinality of all relationships.

c. Suppose that you want to make this data model national. Change your answer to B so that it can be used for other metropolitan areas. Change your answer in A for this situation. Specify the entity identifiers and attributes. Name the relationships and identify the type and cardinality of all relationships.

d. Modify your answer to C to include the leading cast members. Assume that the role of a cast member is not to be modeled. Specify the identifier of new entities and their attributes. Name the relationships and identify the type and cardinality of all relationships.

e. Modify your answer to C to include the leading cast members. Assume that the role of a cast member is specified. Specify the identifier of new entities and their attributes. Name the relationships and identify the type and cardinality of all relationships.

5.65 Consider the three reports in Figure 5-62. The data are samples of data that would appear in the reports like these.

Figure 5-62

Cereal Product Reports

Kellogg's®

RICE KRISPIES®

NUTRITION INFORMATION

SERVING SIZE: 1 OZ. (28.4 g, ABOUT 1 CUP)

SERVINGS PER PACKAGE: 13

	CEREAL	WITH ½ CUP VITAMINS A & D SKIM MILK
CALORIES	110	150*
PROTEIN	2 g	6g
CARBOHYDRATE	25 g	31g
FAT	0 g	0g*
CHOLESTEROL	0 mg	0mg*
SODIUM	290 mg	350mg
POTASSIUM	35 mg	240mg

PERCENTAGE OF U.S. RECOMMENDED DAILY ALLOWANCES (U.S. RDA)

PROTEIN	2	10
VITAMIN A	25	30
VITAMIN C	25	25
THIAMIN	35	40
RIBOFLAVIN	35	45
NIACIN	35	35
CALCIUM	**	15
IRON	10	10
VITAMIN D	10	25
VITAMIN B_6	35	35
FOLIC ACID	35	35
PHOSPHORUS	4	15
MAGNESIUM	2	6
ZINC	2	6
COPPER	2	4

*WHOLE MILK SUPPLIES AN ADDITIONAL 30 CALORIES, 4 g FAT, AND 15 mg CHOLESTEROL.
**CONTAINS LESS THAN 2% OF THE U.S. RDA OF THIS NUTRIENT.

INGREDIENTS: RICE, SUGAR, SALT, CORN SYRUP, MALT FLAVORING,

VITAMINS AND IRON: VITAMIN C (SODIUM ASCORBATE AND ASCORBIC ACID), NIACINAMIDE, IRON, VITAMIN B_6 (PYRIDOXINE HYDROCHLORIDE), VITAMIN A (PALMITATE), VITAMIN B_2 (RIBOFLAVIN), VITAMIN B_1 (THIAMIN HYDROCHLORIDE), FOLIC ACID, AND VITAMIN D.
TO KEEP THIS CEREAL FRESH, BHT HAS BEEN ADDED TO THE PACKAGING.

FDA REPORT #6272
Date: 06/30/2003
Issuer: Kellogg's Corporation
Report Title: Product Summary by Ingredient

Corn	Corn Flakes
	Krispix
	Nutrigrain (Corn)
Corn syrup	Rice Krispies
	Frosted Flakes
	Sugar Pops
Malt	Rice Krispies
	Sugar Smacks
Wheat	Sugar Smacks
	Nutrigrain (Wheat)

(a)

SUPPLIERS LIST
Date: 06/30/2003

Ingredient	Supplier	Price
Corn	Wilson	2.80
	J. Perkins	2.72
	Pollack	2.83
	McKay	2.80
Wheat	Adams	1.19
	Kroner	1.19
	Schmidt	1.22
Barley	Wilson	0.85
	Pollack	0.84

(b)

a. Make a list of as many potential entities as these reports suggest.

b. Examine your list to determine whether any entities are synonyms. If so, consolidate your list.

c. Construct a crow's foot model showing relationships among your entities. Name each relationship and specify cardinalities. Indicate which cardinalities you can justify on the basis of these reports and which you will need to check out with the users.

5.66 Consider the CD cover in Figure 5-63.

a. Specify identifiers and attributes for the entities CD, ARTIST, ROLE, and SONG.

b. Construct a crow's foot model showing relationships among these four entities. Name each relationship and specify cardinalities. Indicate which cardinalities you can justify on the basis of the CD cover and which you will need to check out with the users.

c. Consider a CD that does not involve a musical, so there is no need for ROLE. However, the entity SONG_WRITER is needed. Create a crow's foot model for CD, ARTIST, SONG, and SONG_WRITER. Assume that an ARTIST can either be a group or an individual. Assume that some artists record individually and as part of a group.

d. Combine the models you developed in your answers to B and C. Create new entities if necessary, but strive to keep your model as simple as possible. Specify identifiers and attributes of new entities, name new relationships, and indicate their cardinalities.

5.67 Consider the data model in Figure 5-45. How should this model be altered if the users want to keep track of how many of each part are used? Suppose, for example, that the wheel assembly requires four washers and the handle assembly requires just one, and the database must store these quantities. Hint: adding Quantity to this N:M relationship is analogous to adding Price to the N:M relationship in Figure 5-24.

| Figure 5-63 | CD Cover |

West Side Story
Based on a conception of Jerome Robbins

Book by ARTHUR LAURENTS
Music by LEONARD BERNSTEIN
Lyrics by STEPHEN SONDHEIM

Entire Original Production Directed
and Choreographed by JEROME ROBBINS

Originally produced on Broadway by Robert E. Griffith and Harold S. Prince
by arrangement with Roger L. Stevens
Orchestration by Leonard Bernstein with Sid Ramin and Irwin Kostal

HIGHLIGHTS FROM THE COMPLETE RECORDING

Maria . . . . KIRI TE KANAWA
Tony . . . . JOSE CARRERAS
Anita . . . . TATIANA TROYANOS
Riff . . . . KURT OLLMAN
and MARILYN HORNE singing "Somewhere"

Rosalia . . . . Louise Edeiken
Consuela. . . . . Stella Zambalis
Fancisca. . . . . Angelina Reaux
Action . . . . David Livingston
Bernardo . . . Richard Harrell

Diesel . . . . Marty Nelson
Baby John. . . . . Stephen Bogardus
A-rab . . . . Peter Thom
Snowboy . . . . .Todd Lester

1	Jet Song (Riff, Action, Baby John, A-rab, Chorus)	[3'13]
2	Something's Coming (Tony)	[2'33]
3	Maria (Tony)	[2'56]
4	Tonight (Maria, Tony)	[5'27]
5	America (Anita, Rosalia, Chorus)	[4'47]
6	Cool (Riff, Chorus)	[4'37]
7	One Hand, One Heart (Tony, Maria)	[5'38]
8	Tonight (Ensemble) (Entire Cast)	[3'40]
9	I Feel Pretty (Maria, Chorus)	[3'22]
10	Somewhere (A Girl)	[2'34]
11	Gee Officer Krupke (Action, Snowboy, Diesel, A-rab, Baby John, Chorus)	[4'18]
12	A Boy Like That (Anita, Maria)	[2'05]
13	I Have a Love (Maria, Anita)	[3'30]
14	Taunting Scene (Orchestra)	[1'21]
15	Finale (Maria, Tony)	[2'40]

5.68 The data model in Figure 5-54 uses the attribute Room in COLLEGE and DEPARTMENT, but uses OfficeNumber in PROFESSOR. These attributes have the same kind of data, even though they have different names. Examine Figure 5-48 and explain how this situation came to be. Do you think having different names for the same attribute types is rare? Do you think it's problem? Why or why not?

MARCIA'S DRY CLEANING

Suppose that you have been hired by Marcia's Dry Cleaning to create a database application to track customers, orders, and items. Marcia also wants to start a Frequent Cleaner's Club, whereby she will offer a 50 percent discount on every 10th customer order.

A Using your knowledge, create a data model for Marcia's business. Name each entity, describe its type, and indicate all attributes and identifiers. Name each relationship, describe its type, and specify minimum and maximum cardinalities.

B List any item in your answer to A that you believe should be checked out with Marcia and/or her employees.

MORGAN IMPORTING

Suppose that you have been hired by Morgan Importing to create a database application to track stores, purchases, shipments, and shippers. Sometimes several items are purchased from a store on a single visit, but do not assume that all of the items are placed on the same shipment. You want to track each item in a shipment and assign an insurance value to each item.

A Using your knowledge, create a data model for Morgan Importing. Name each entity, describe its type, and indicate all attributes and identifiers. Name each relationship, describe its type, and specify minimum and maximum cardinalities.

B List any item in your answer to A that you believe should be checked out with Phillip Morgan and/or his employees.

Transforming Data Models into Database Designs

This chapter explains the transformation of entity-relationship data models into relational database designs. This transformation consists of three primary tasks: (1) replacing entities and attributes with tables and columns; (2) representing relationships and maximum cardinalities by placing foreign keys; and (3) representing minimum cardinality by defining actions to constrain activities on values of primary and foreign keys. Steps 1 and 2 are relatively easy to understand and accomplish; step 3 may be easy or difficult, depending on the minimum cardinality type.

Create a Table for Each Entity

As shown in Figure 6-1, we begin the database design by creating a table for each entity. In most cases, the table is assigned the same name as the entity. Each attribute of the entity becomes a column of the table. The identifier of the entity becomes the primary key of the table. The example in Figure 6-2 shows the creation of the EMPLOYEE table from the EMPLOYEE entity. In this text, to differentiate entities from tables, we will show entities with shadowed boxes and tables with nonshadowed boxes. This notation will help clarify our discussion, but be aware that it is not standard notation across the industry.

Be certain that you understand the difference between these similar-looking graphics. The shadowed rectangle in Figure 6-2(a) represents a logical structure that has no physical existence. It is a blueprint. The nonshadowed rectangle in Figure 6-2(b) represents a table. It is the same as the following notation that we used in Chapters 3 and 4:

EMPLOYEE (EmployeeNumber, EmployeeName, Phone, Email, HireDate, ReviewDate, EmpCode)

Figure 6-1

Steps for Transforming a Data Model into a Database Design

1. Create a table for each entity:
   — Specify the primary key (consider surrogate keys as appropriate)
   — Specify candidate keys
   — Specify properties for each column:
      • Null status
      • Data type
      • Default value (if any)
      • Specify data constraints (if any)
   — Verify Normalization
2. Create relationships by placing foreign keys
   — Strong (1:1, 1:N, 1:M)
   — ID-dependent (association, multivalue, archetype/instance)
   — Mixed
   — Subtypes
   — Recursive (1:1, 1:N, N:M)
3. Specify logic for enforcing minimum cardinality:
   — M-O
   — O-M
   — M-M

Figure 6-2

Transforming an Entity into a Table

EMPLOYEE

EmployeeNumber
EmployeeName
Phone
Email
HireDate
ReviewDate
EmpCode

(a) EMPLOYEE Entity

EMPLOYEE

🔑 EmployeeNumber
EmployeeName
Phone
Email
HireDate
ReviewDate
EmpCode

(b) EMPLOYEE Table

Note, too, the key symbol next to EmployeeNumber. It documents the fact that EmployeeNumber is the table key, just as the underline does in the notation used in Chapters 3 and 4.

Selecting the Primary Key

The selection of the primary key is important. The DBMS will use the primary key to facilitate searching and sorting of table rows, and some DBMS products use it to organize table storage. DBMS products almost always create indexes and other data structures using the values of the primary key.

The ideal primary key is short, numeric, and fixed. EmployeeNumber in Figure 6-2 meets all of these conditions and is acceptable. Beware of primary keys such as EmployeeName, Email, (AreaCode, PhoneNumber), (Street, City, State, Zip), and other long character columns. In cases like these, when the identifier is not short, numeric, or fixed, consider using another candidate key as the primary key. If there are no candidate keys, or if none of them is any better, consider using a surrogate key.

A **surrogate key** is a DBMS-supplied identifier of each row of a table. Surrogate key values are unique within the table and they never change. They are assigned when the row is created, and they are destroyed when the row is deleted. Surrogate key values are the best possible primary keys because they are designed to be short, numeric, and fixed. Because of these advantages, some organizations have gone so far as to require that surrogates be used for the primary key of every table.

Before endorsing such a policy, however, consider two disadvantages of surrogate keys. First, their values have no meaning to a user. Suppose you want to determine the department to which an employee is assigned. If DepartmentName is a foreign key in EMPLOYEE, then when you retrieve an employee row, you obtain a value such as 'Accounting' or 'Finance'. That value may be all that you need to know about department.

Alternatively, if you define the surrogate key DepartmentSK as the primary key of DEPARTMENT, then DepartmentSK will also be the foreign key in EMPLOYEE. When you retrieve a row of EMPLOYEE, you will get back a number such as 123499788 for the DepartmentSK, a value that has no meaning to you at all. You have to perform a second query on DEPARTMENT to obtain DepartmentName.

The second disadvantage of surrogate keys arises when data are shared among different databases. Suppose, for example, that a company maintains three different SALES databases, one for each of three different product lines. Assume that each of these databases has a table called SALES_ORDER that has a surrogate key called ID. The DBMS assigns values to IDs so that they are unique within a particular database. It does not, however, assign ID values so that they are unique across the three different databases. Thus, it is possible for two different SALES_ORDER rows, in two different databases, to have the same ID value.

This duplication is not a problem until data from the different databases are merged. When that happens, to prevent duplicates, ID values will need to be changed. However, if ID values are changed, then foreign key values may need to be changed as well, and the result is a mess, or at least much work to prevent a mess.

It is, of course, possible to construct a scheme using different starting values for surrogate keys in different databases. Such a policy ensures that each database has its own range of surrogate key values. This requires careful management and procedures, however; and if the starting values are too close to one another, the ranges will overlap and duplicate surrogate key values will result.

Specifying Candidate (Alternate) Keys

The next step in creating a table is to specify candidate keys. Recall from Chapter 3 that candidate keys are alternative identifiers of unique rows in a table. Some products, such as ERwin, use the term **alternate key (AK)** rather than candidate key. Note that the two terms are synonymous.

Figure 6-3(a) shows EMPLOYEE with a primary key of EmployeeNumber and a candidate, or alternate, key of Email. In Figure 6-3(b), CustomerNumber is the primary key of CUSTOMER, and both the composite (Name, City) and Email are candidate keys. In these ERwin diagrams, the symbol AK$n.m$ means the nth alternate key and the mth column of that alternate key. In the EMPLOYEE table, Email is labeled AK1.1 because it is the first alternate key and the first column of that key. CUSTOMER has two alternate keys. The first is a composite of two columns, which are labeled AK1.1 and AK1.2. The nomenclature Name (AK1.1) means that Name is the first column of the first alternate key, and City (AK1.2) means that City is the second column of the first alternate key. In CUSTOMER, Email is marked as AK2.1 because it is the first (and only) column of the second alternate key.

Specify Column Properties

The next step in the creation of a relation is to specify the column properties. Four properties are shown in Figure 6-1: null status, data type, default value, and data constraints.

Null Status

Null status refers to whether the column can have a null value. Typically, null status is specified by using the phrase NULL if nulls are allowed and NOT NULL if not. Thus, NULL

Figure 6-3		
Representing Candidate (Alternate) Keys	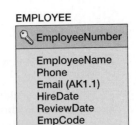	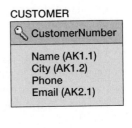

(a)   (b)

Figure 6-4

**Table Display Showing
Null Status**

EMPLOYEE

🔑 EmployeeNumber: NOT NULL

EmployeeName: NOT NULL
Phone: NULL
Email: NULL (AK1.1)
HireDate: NOT NULL
ReviewDate: NULL
EmpCode: NULL

does not mean that the column is always null; it means that null values are allowed. Because of this possible confusion, some people prefer the term NULL ALLOWED rather than NULL. Figure 6-4 shows the null status of each of the columns in the EMPLOYEE table.

B T W

The EMPLOYEE table in Figure 6-4 contains a subtlety. EmployeeNumber, the primary key, is marked NOT NULL, but Email, the alternate key, is marked NULL. It makes sense that EmployeeNumber should not be allowed to be null. If it were, and if more than one row had a null value, then EmployeeNumber would not identify a unique row. Why, however, should Email be allowed to have null values?

The answer is that alternate keys often are used just to ensure uniqueness. Marking Email as a (possibly null) alternate key means that Email need not have a value, but if it has one, that value will be different from all other values of Email in the EMPLOYEE table. This answer is dissatisfying because it means that alternate keys are not truly alternate *primary* keys. Alas, that's the way it is. Just know that primary keys can never be null but that alternate keys can be.

Data Type

The next step is to define the data type for each column. Unfortunately, each DBMS provides a different set of data types. For example, Microsoft Access has a data type called Currency; SQL Server has a data type called Money; and Oracle has no data type for currency. Instead, with Oracle, you use the numeric data type for currency values.

If you know which DBMS you will be using to create the database, you can use that product's data types in your design. Figure 6-5, for example, uses the data types for SQL Server (e.g., datetime is a SQL Server data type). In fact, with many data modeling products, you can specify the DBMS you will use and the data modeling product will supply the appropriate set of data types. This was done using ERwin in Figure 6-5.

If you do not know which DBMS product you will be using, or if you want to preserve independence from a particular DBMS, you can specify the data types in a generic way. Typical generic data types are CHAR (n) for a fixed-length character string of length *n*; VARCHAR (n) for a variable-length character string having a maximum length of *n*; DATE; TIME; MONEY; INTEGER; and DECIMAL. If you work for a larger organization, that company probably has its own generic data standards. If so, you should use those data standards.

Figure 6-5

**Table Display Showing
Data Type**

EMPLOYEE

🔑 EmployeeNumber: int

EmployeeName: char(50)
Phone: char(15)
Email: char(50) (AK1.1)
HireDate: datetime
ReviewDate: datetime
EmpCode: char(18)

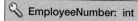

Figure 6-6

**Table Display Showing
Null Status and Data
Type**

EMPLOYEE

🔑 EmployeeNumber: int NOT NULL

EmployeeName: char(50) NOT NULL
Phone: char(15) NULL
Email: char(50) NULL (AK1.1)
HireDate: datetime NOT NULL
ReviewDate: datetime NULL
EmpCode: char(18) NULL

Figure 6-6 shows the table showing both data type and null status. The display becomes crowded, however; and from now on we will show tables with just column names. With most products, you can turn such displays on or off depending on the work you are doing.

Default Value

A **default value** is a value supplied by the DBMS when a new row is created. The value can be a constant, such as the string 'New Hire' for the EmpCode column in EMPLOYEE, or it can be the result of a function, such as the date value of the computer's clock for the HireDate column.

In some cases, default values are computed using more complicated logic. The default value for a price, for example, might be computed by applying a markup to a default cost and then reducing that marked up price by a customer's discount. In such a case, an application component or a trigger (discussed in the next chapter) will be written to supply such a value.

It is possible to use the data modeling tool to record default values, but such values often are shown in separate design documentation. Figure 6-7, for example, shows one way that default values are documented.

Data Constraints

Data constraints are limitations on data values. There are several different types. **Domain constraints** limit column values to a particular set of values. For example, EMPLOYEE.EmpCode could be limited to one of the values ['New Hire', 'Hourly', 'Salary', 'Part Time']. **Range constraints** limit values to a particular interval of values. EMPLOYEE.HireDate, for example, could be limited to dates between January 1, 1990, and December 31, 2010.

An **intrarelation constraint** limits a column's values in comparison with other columns in the same table. The constraint that EMPLOYEE.ReviewDate be at least

Figure 6-7   **Sample Documentation for Default Values**

Table	Column	Default Value
ITEM	ItemNumber	Surrogate key
ITEM	Category	None
ITEM	ItemPrefix	If Category = 'Perishable' then 'P' If Category = 'Imported' then 'I' If Category = 'One-off' then 'O' Otherwise = 'N'
ITEM	ApprovingDept	If ItemPrefix = 'I' then 'SHIPPING/PURCHASING' Otherwise = 'PURCHASING'
ITEM	ShippingMethod	If ItemPrefix = 'P' then 'Next Day' Otherwise = 'Ground'

three months after EMPLOYEE.HireDate is an intrarelation constraint. **Interrelation constraints** limit a column's values in comparison with other columns in other tables. An example for the CUSTOMER table is that CUSTOMER.Name must not be equal to BAD_CUSTOMER.Name, where BAD_CUSTOMER is a table that contains a list of customers with credit and balance problems.

Referential integrity constraints (Chapter 3) are one type of interrelation constraint. Because they are so common, sometimes they are documented only when they are not enforced. For example, to save work, a design team might say that every foreign key is assumed to have a referential integrity constraint to the table that it references and that only exceptions to this rule are documented.

Verify Normalization

The last task in step 1 of Figure 6-1 is to verify table normalization. When data models are developed using forms and reports as guides, they generally result in normalized entities. This occurs because the structures of forms and reports usually reflect how users think about their data. Boundaries of a form, for example, often show the range of a functional dependency. If this is hard to understand, think of a functional dependency as a theme. A well-designed form or report will bracket themes using lines, colors, boxes, or other graphical elements. Those graphical hints will have been used by the data modeling team to develop entities, and the result will be normalized tables.

All of this, however, should be verified. You need to ask whether the resulting tables are in BCNF and whether all multivalued dependencies have been removed. If not, the tables should probably be normalized. On the other hand, as you learned in Chapter 4, sometimes normalization is undesirable. Thus, you should also examine your tables to determine if any normalized ones should be denormalized, as described in Chapter 4.

The result of step 1 is a set of complete, but independent, tables. The next step is to create relationships.

Create Relationships

In general, we create relationships by placing foreign keys into tables. The way in which this is done and the properties of the foreign key columns depend on the type of relationship. In this section, we consider each of the relationships described in Chapter 5: strong entity relationships, ID-dependent relationships, mixed relationships, subtypes, and recursive relationships. We conclude this section with a discussion of special cases of ternary relationships.

Relationships among Strong Entities

As you learned in Chapter 5, strong entity relationships are characterized by their maximum cardinality. The three types of strong entity relationships are 1:1, 1:N, and N:M. Consider each type.

1:1 Strong Entity Relationships

A 1:1 strong entity relationship can be represented in one of two ways. You can place the primary key of the first table in the second, or you can place the primary key of the second table in the first.

Figure 6-8 shows the representation of the 1:1 strong entity relationship between CLUB_MEMBER and LOCKER. In Figure 6-8(a), MemberNumber is placed in LOCKER. In Figure 6-8(b), LockerNumber is placed in CLUB_MEMBER.

Either of these designs will work. If you have a club member's number and want his or her locker, then using the design in Figure 6-8(a), you can query the LOCKER table

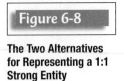

The Two Alternatives for Representing a 1:1 Strong Entity Relationship

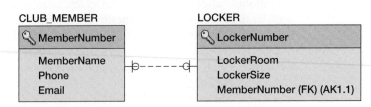

(a) With Foreign Key in LOCKER

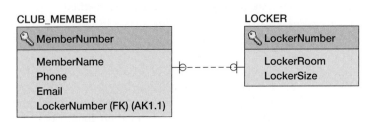

(b) With Foreign Key in CLUB_MEMBER

for the given value of MemberNumber. But, if you have the LockerNumber and want the club member's data, then using the design in Figure 6-8(a), you can query the LOCKER table for the LockerNumber, obtain the MemberNumber, and use that value to query the CLUB_MEMBER table for the rest of the club member's data.

Follow a similar procedure to verify that the design in Figure 6-8(b) works as well. However, one data constraint applies to both designs. Because the relationship is 1:1, a given value of a foreign key can appear only once in the table. For example, in the design in Figure 6-8(a), a given value of MemberNumber can appear just once; each value must be unique in the LOCKER table. If a value of MemberNumber were to appear in two rows, then a member would be assigned to two lockers, and the relationship would not be not 1:1.

To cause the DBMS to enforce uniqueness, we define the foreign key as an alternate key. This technique, though common, is a bit confusing because, logically, MemberNumber is not an alternate key for LOCKER. We are just using the fact that alternate keys are unique to document the uniqueness of the foreign key in a 1:1 relationship. A similar technique is used on the foreign key LockerNumber in Figure 6-8(b).

Although either of the designs in Figure 6-8 will work, a design team may prefer one over the other. If the relationship is either M-O or O-M, then one design will be *greatly* preferred, as you will learn in the section on minimum cardinality design. Also, application requirements may mean that one design is faster than the other.

To summarize, to represent a 1:1 strong entity relationship, place the key of one table in the other table. Enforce the maximum cardinality by making the foreign key an alternate key.

1:N Strong Entity Relationships

A 1:N strong entity relationship is represented by placing the key of the table on the one side into the key of the table on the many side. Recall from Chapter 5 that the term *parent* is used to refer to the table on the one side and the term *child* is used to refer to the table on the many side. Using this terminology, you can summarize the design of 1:N relationships by saying, "Place the key of the parent in the child."

Figure 6-9(a) shows an E-R diagram for the 1:N relationship between COMPANY and DEPARTMENT. The relationship is represented in the design in Figure 6-9(b) by placing the key of the parent (CompanyName) in the child. Because parents have many children (the relationship is 1:N), there is no need to make the foreign key unique.

For 1:N relationships between strong entities, that's all there is to it. Just remember: "Place the key of the parent in the child."

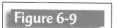

**Representing a 1:N
Strong Relationship**

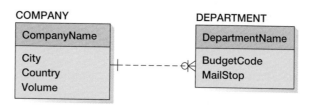

(a) 1:N Strong Entity Relationship

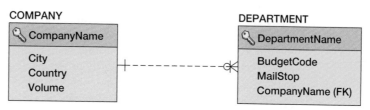

(b) Placing the Key of the Parent in the Child

N:M Strong Relationships

The situation for N:M relationships is more complicated. The problem is that there is no place in either table in a N:M relationship in which to place the foreign key. Consider the example in Figure 6-10(a), which shows a relationship that specifies which companies can supply which parts. A COMPANY may supply many PARTs, and a PART may be supplied by many different COMPANY(ies).

**Representing an N:M
Strong Entity
Relationship**

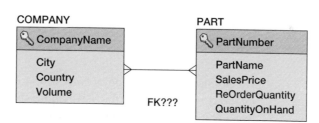

(a) Foreign Key Has No Place in Either Table

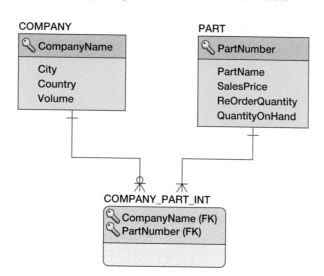

(b) Place Both Foreign Keys in ID-dependent Intersection Table

Suppose we try to represent this relationship by placing the primary key of one table as a foreign key in the second table, as we did for 1:N relationships. Say we place the primary key of PART in COMPANY as follows:

COMPANY (<u>CompanyName</u>, City, Country, Volume, *PartNumber*)

PART (<u>PartNumber</u>, PartName, SalesPrice, ReOrderQuantity, QuantityOnHand)

With this design, a given PartNumber may appear in many rows of COMPANY so that many companies can supply the part. But, how do we show that a company can supply many parts? There is only space to show one part. We do not want to duplicate the entire row for a company just to show a second part; such a strategy would result in unacceptable data duplication and data integrity problems. A similar problem will occur if we try to place the key of COMPANY, CompanyName, into PART.

The solution is to create a third table, called an **intersection table.** Such a table shows the correspondences of a given company and a given part. It has only foreign keys; it contains no user data. For the example in Figure 6-10(a), we create the following intersection table:

COMPANY_PART_INT (<u>*CompanyName*</u>, <u>*PartNumber*</u>)

This table has one row for each company–part combination. Notice that both columns are part of the primary key, and that each column is a foreign key to a different table. Because both columns are keys of other tables, intersection tables are always ID dependent on both of their parent tables.

Thus, in Figure 6-10(b), COMPANY_PART_INT is shown as ID-dependent. Like all ID-dependent tables, the parent tables are required; COMPANY_PART_INT requires both a COMPANY and PART. The parents may or may not require an intersection table row, depending on application requirements. In Figure 6-10(b), a COMPANY need not supply a PART, but a PART must be supplied by at least one COMPANY.

B T W

The problem for the design of N:M strong entity relationships is that they have no direct representation. An N:M relationship must always be decomposed into two 1:N relationships using an intersection table. This is why Visio is unable to represent N:M relationships in a data model. Visio forces you to make the transformation ahead of time, during modeling. As stated in Chapter 5, however, most data modelers consider this requirement to be a nuisance because it adds complexity to data modeling when the whole purpose of data modeling is to reduce complexity to the logical essentials. See the discussion on page 129.

Relationships Using ID-dependent Entities

Figure 6-11 summarizes the four uses for ID-dependent entities. We just described the first use: the representation of N:M strong entity relationships. The remaining three uses were discussed in Chapter 5. Here we will describe the design of relationships for these three uses.

Association Relationships

Recall from Chapter 5 that association relationships are subtly close to N:M strong entity relationships. The only difference between the two types of relationships is that an association relationship has one or more attributes that pertain to the relationship and not to either of the entities. Figure 6-12(a) is a copy of the association relationship created in Figure 5-24. In this example, the association of a company and a part carries an attribute named Price.

Figure 6-11

**Four Uses for
ID-dependent
Entities**

- Representing N:M Relationships
- Association Relationships
- Multivalued Attributes
- Archetype/Instance Relationships

The representation of such a relationship using a table is straightforward. Just create a table that is ID dependent on both of its parents and place the Price attribute in that table. The result for the example in Figure 6-12(a) is the table:

QUOTATION (*CompanyName*, *PartNumber*, Price)

Like all ID-dependent relationships, the parents of an association table are required. The parents may or may not require the rows of the association table, depending on application requirements. In Figure 6-12(b), a COMPANY need not have any QUOTATION rows, but a PART must have at least one QUOTATION row.

Figure 6-12

**Using ID-dependent
Entities for an
Association
Relationship**

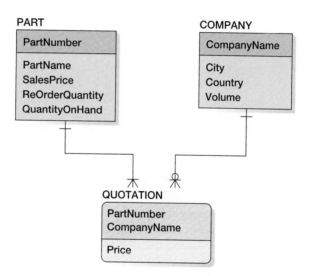

(a) E-R Model from Figure 5-24

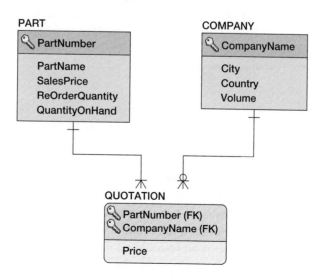

(b) Tables Representing Entities

Association entities sometimes connect more than two entity types. Figure 6-13(a), which is a copy of Figure 5-25, shows an association of CLIENT, ARCHITECT, and PROJECT entities. When there are several participants in the association, the strategy just shown is simply extended. The association table will have the key of each of its parents, as shown in Figure 6-13(b). In this case, the ASSIGNMENT table has three foreign keys and one non-key attribute, HoursWorked.

By the way, in both of these examples, it is only coincidence that the association tables have only one non-key attribute. In general, an association table can have as many non-key attributes as necessary to meet user requirements.

Multivalued Attributes

The third use for ID-dependent entities is to represent multivalued entity attributes. Figure 6-14(a) is a copy of Figure 5-31. Here, COMPANY2 has a multivalued composite, (Contact, PhoneNumber), that is represented by the ID-dependent entity PHONE_CONTACT.

Representing the PHONE_CONTACT entity is straightforward. Just replace it with a table and replace each of its attributes with a column. In this example, the Contact attribute is both a part of the primary key and a foreign key.

Like all ID-dependent tables, PHONE_CONTACT must have a parent row in COMPANY2. On the other hand, a COMPANY2 row may or may not have a required PHONE_CONTACT, depending on application requirements.

Figure 6-13

**Association
Relationship among
Three Entities**

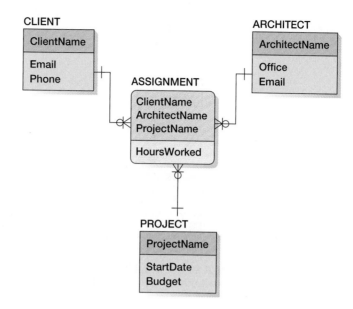

(a) E-R Model from Figure 5-25

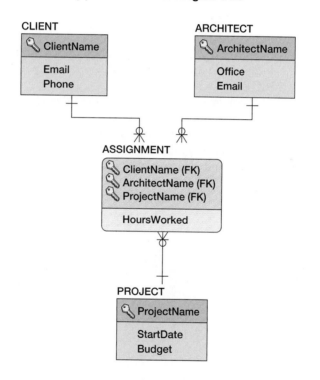

(b) Tables Representing Entities

Archetype/Instance Pattern

The fourth use for ID-dependent entities is the archetype/instance pattern. Figure 6-15(a), which is a copy of Figure 5-32, shows the CLASS/SECTION example from the last chapter, and Figure 6-15(b) shows the relational design.

As noted in the last chapter, however, sometimes the instances of an archetype/instance pattern are given identifiers of their own. In that case, the instance entity becomes a weak, but not ID-dependent, entity. When this occurs, the relationship must be transformed using the rules of a 1:N strong relationship. This just means that the key

Figure 6-14

Using ID-dependent Entities for Multivalued Attributes

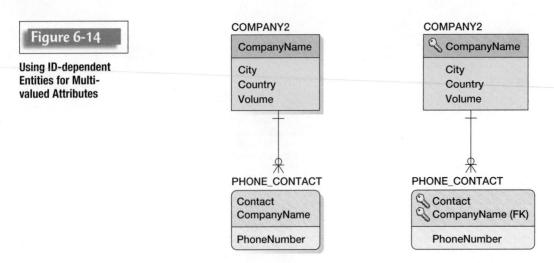

(a) E-R Model with Multivalued Attribute from Figure 5-31

(b) Tables Representing Entities

of the parent should be placed in the child. Figure 6-16(a) shows a copy of Figure 5-33 in which SECTION has been given the identifier ReferenceNumber. In the relational design in Figure 6-16(b), the key of the parent (ClassName) has been placed in SECTION as a foreign key.

Keep in mind, however, that even though SECTION is no longer ID dependent, it is still weak. SECTION requires a CLASS for its existence. This means that a SECTION must always have a CLASS as its parent, and this restriction arises from logical necessity, not just from application requirements. The fact that SECTION is weak should be recorded in design documentation.

Figure 6-15

Standard Archetype/Instance Entity Table Representation

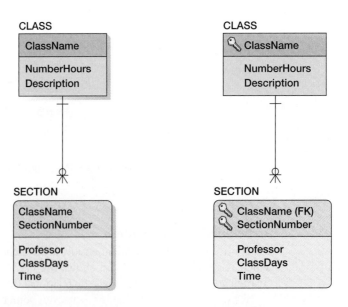

(a) E-R Model with Archetype/ Instance Entities from Figure 5-32

(b) Table Representation of Archetype/Instance Entities

Figure 6-16

Transformation of
Archetype/Instance
by Adding Reference
Number to SECTION

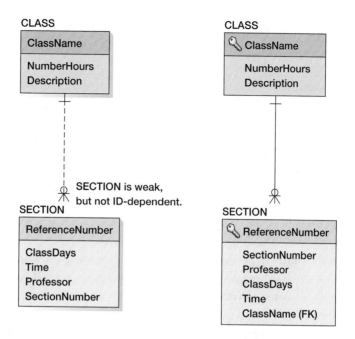

(a) Entity with ReferenceNumber
Attribute from Figure 5-33

(b) Representation of Relationship

B T W

What happens when the identifier of the parent of an ID-dependent entity is replaced with a surrogate key? Consider the example of BUILDING and APARTMENT, in which the identifier of APARTMENT is the composite of an apartment number and a building identifier.

Suppose that the identifier of BUILDING is (Street, City, State/Province, Country). In this case, the identifier of APARTMENT is (Street, City, State/Province, Country, ApartmentNumber). This design can be improved by replacing the long BUILDING identifier with a surrogate key. Suppose that we replace the key of BUILDING with BuildingSK, a surrogate.

Now, with a surrogate key for BUILDING, what is the key of APARTMENT? When we place the key of the parent in the child, we obtain (BuildingSK, ApartmentNumber). But this combination has no meaning to the user. What does an identifier of (10045898, '5C') mean to a user? Nothing. The key became meaningless when Street, City, State/Province, and Country were replaced by BuildingSK in BUILDING.

We can improve the design by using the following principle: When replacing the identifier of the parent of an ID-dependent entity with a surrogate key, replace the identifier of the ID-dependent entity with its own surrogate key. The resulting table will be weak, but not ID dependent.

Mixed Entity Relationships

As you might guess, the design of mixed entity patterns is a combination of strong and ID-dependent designs. Consider the example of employees and skills in Figure 6-17(a), which is a copy of Figure 5-37. Here, the entity EMPLOYEE_SKILL is ID dependent on EMPLOYEE, but has a nonidentifying relationship to SKILL.

Figure 6-17

Representing a Mixed Entity Model

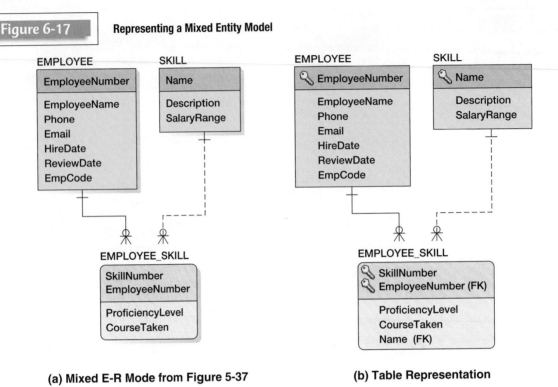

(a) Mixed E-R Mode from Figure 5-37

(b) Table Representation

The design of the E-R model for Figure 6-17(a) is shown in Figure 6-17(b). Notice that EmployeeNumber is both a part of the primary key of EMPLOYEE_SKILL and also a foreign key to EMPLOYEE. The 1:N nonidentifying relationship between SKILL and EMPLOYEE_SKILL is represented by placing the key of SKILL, which is Name, in EMPLOYEE. Note that EMPLOYEE_SKILL.Name is a foreign key but not part of the primary key of EMPLOYEE_SKILL.

A similar strategy is used to model the SALES_ORDER in Figure 6-18(a), which is a copy of Figure 5-35. Here, the ID-dependent table, ORDER_LINE_ITEM, has SalesOrderNumber as part of its primary key and as a foreign key. It has ItemNumber as a foreign key only.

B T W

The design transformation process for all HAS-A relationships can be summarized by the phrase, "Place the key of the parent in the child." For strong entities, a 1:1 relationship can have either entity as the parent, hence the key can go in either table. For 1:N relationships, the key of the parent goes in the child. For N:M relationships, decompose the model into two 1:N relationships by defining an intersection table and place the key of the parent in the child for each.

For identifying relationships, the key of the parent is already in the child, so there is nothing more to do. For mixed relationships, on the identifying side, the key of the parent is already in the child. On the nonidentifying side, place the key of the parent in the child. In short, if you're going to write something on the back of your hand for the exam, write "HAS-A: Place the key of the parent in the child."

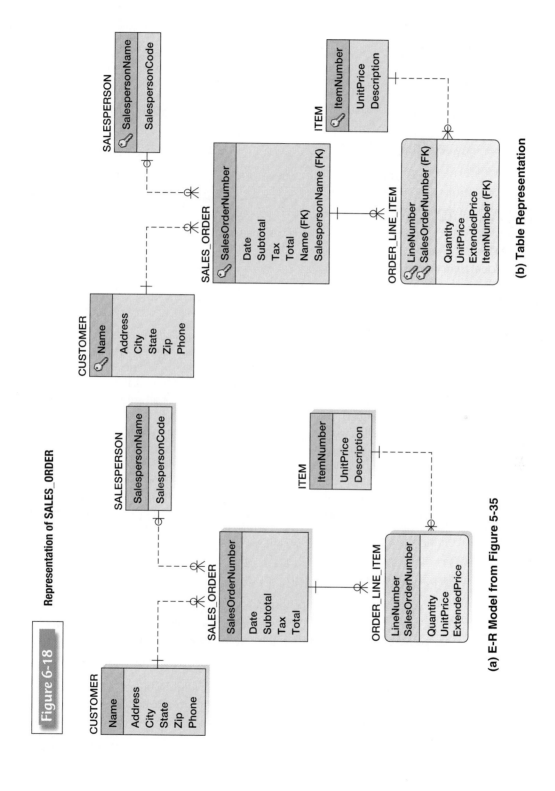

Figure 6-18 Representation of SALES_ORDER

(a) E-R Model from Figure 5-35

(b) Table Representation

Figure 6-19   Representing Subtypes

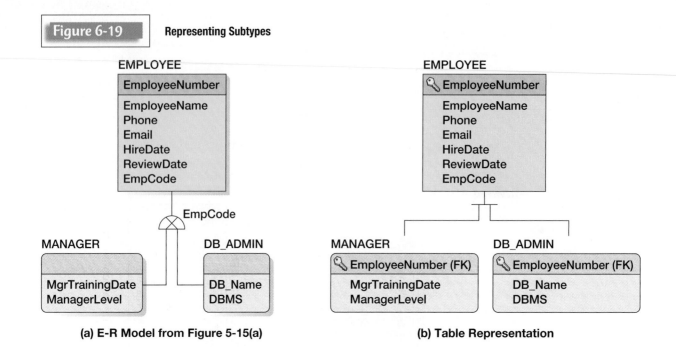

(a) E-R Model from Figure 5-15(a)   (b) Table Representation

Subtype Relationships

Representing subtype relationships is easy. Recall that subtype relationships are also called IS-A relationships because a subtype and its supertype are representations of the same underlying entity. An EMPLOYEE is a MANAGER and a MANAGER is an EMPLOYEE. Because of this equivalence, the keys of all subtype tables are identical to the key of the supertype table.

Figure 6-19(a), which is a copy of Figure 5-15(a), shows an example for two subtypes of EMPLOYEE. Notice that the key of EMPLOYEE is EmployeeNumber and that the key of each of the subtypes also is EmployeeNumber. MANAGER.EmployeeNumber and DB_ADMIN.EmployeeNumber are both primary keys and foreign keys to their supertype.

Discriminator attributes cannot be represented in relational designs. In Figure 6-19, we can do nothing with EmpCode except note in the design documentation that EmpCode determines subtype. Application programs will need to be written to use EnpCode to determine which subtype pertains to a given EMPLOYEE.

Recursive Relationships

The representation of recursive relationships is just an extension of the techniques used for representing strong entities. These techniques may be a bit difficult to comprehend at first because they appear strange, but they involve principles that you have already learned.

1:1 Recursive Relationships

Consider the 1:1 recursive BOXCAR relationship in Figure 6-20(a), which is a copy of Figure 5-40. To represent the relationship, we create a foreign key in BOXCAR that contains the identifier of the boxcar ahead as shown in Figure 6-20(b). Because the relationship is 1:1, we make the foreign key unique by defining it as an alternate (candidate) key. This restriction enforces the fact that a boxcar can have at most one boxcar in front of it.

The notation in Figure 6-20(b) does not have FK in parentheses because ERwin cannot represent the tables that have recursive relationships. The attribute BoxcarNumberAhead was added manually to the diagram in Figure 6-20(b). Notice that both sides of the

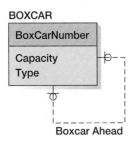

Figure 6-20

Representing 1:1
Recursive
Relationships

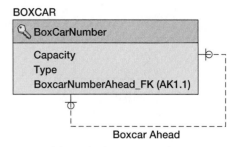

(a) BOXCAR Recursive Relationship
from Figure 5-40

(b) Table Representation

relationship are optional. This occurs because the last car on the train is ahead of no other car, and because the first car on the train has no other car ahead of it. If the data structure were circular, this restriction would not be necessary. For example, if you wanted to represent the sequence of names of the calendar months, and you wanted December to lead to January, then you could have a 1:1 recursive structure with required children.

B T W

If you find the concept of recursive relationships confusing, try this trick. Assume that you have two entities: BOXCAR_AHEAD and BOXCAR_BEHIND, each having the same attributes. Notice that there is a 1:1 relationship between these two entities. Replace each entity with its table. Like all 1:1 strong entity relationships, you can place the key of either table as a foreign key in the other table. For now, place the key of BOXCAR_AHEAD into BOXCAR_BEHIND.

Now realize that BOXCAR_AHEAD only duplicates data that reside in BOXCAR_BEHIND. The data are unnecessary. So, discard BOXCAR_AHEAD and you will have the same design as shown in Figure 6-20(b).

1:N Recursive Relationships

As with all 1:N relationships, 1:N recursive relationships are represented by placing the key of the parent in the child. For the Manages relationship in Figure 6-21(a), which is a copy of Figure 5-43, this means that we place the name of the manager in each employee's row. Thus, in Figure 6-21(b), the EmployeeNameMgr has been added to the EMPLOYEE table.

Notice that both the parent and the child are optional. This is true because the lowest-level employees manage no one and because the highest-level person, the CEO or other most senior person, has no manager. If the data structure were circular, this would not be the case.

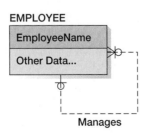

Figure 6-21

Representing 1:N
Recursive
Relationships

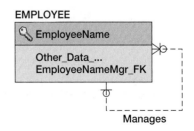

(a) Manages Recursive Relationship
from Figure 5-43

(b) Table Representation

| Figure 6-22 | Representing N:M Recursive Relationships |

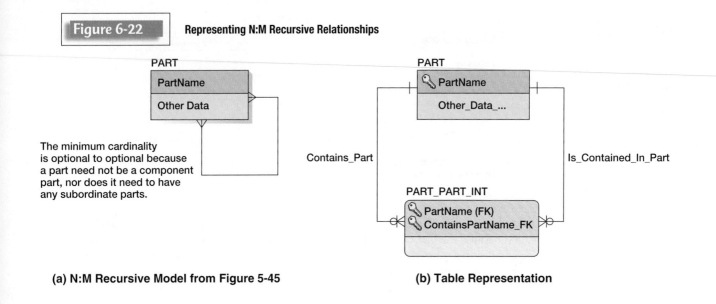

(a) N:M Recursive Model from Figure 5-45   **(b) Table Representation**

N:M Recursive Relationships

The trick for representing N:M recursive relationships is to decompose the N:M relationship into two 1:N relationships. We do this by creating an intersection table, just as we did for N:M relationships between strong entities.

Figure 6-22(a), which is a copy of Figure 5-45, shows an example for a bill-of-materials problem. Each part has potentially many subordinate parts, and each part can be used as a component in potentially many other parts. To represent this relationship, create an intersection table that shows the correspondence of a part/part use. You can model upwards or downwards. If the former, the intersection table will carry the correspondence of a part and where that part is used. If the latter, the intersection table will carry the correspondence of a part and the parts that it contains. Figure 6-22(b) shows the intersection table for modeling downwards in the bill of materials.

Again, if you find this to be confusing, assume that you have two different tables, one called PART and a second called CONTAINED_PART. Create the intersection table between the two tables. Note that CONTAINED_PART duplicates the attributes in PART, and is thus unnecessary. Eliminate the table and you will have the design in Figure 6-22(b).

Representing Ternary and Higher-Order Relationships

As stated in Chapter 5, ternary and higher-order relationships can be represented by multiple binary relationships. Most of the time, such a representation works without problem. However, in some cases, there are constraints that add complexity to the situation. For example, consider the ternary relationship among the entities ORDER, CUSTOMER, and SALESPERSON. Assume that the relationship from CUSTOMER to ORDER is 1:N and that the relationship from SALESPERSON to ORDER also is 1:N. We can represent the three-part relationship among ORDER:CUSTOMER:SALESPERSON as two separate binary relationships, one between ORDER and CUSTOMER and a second between SALESPERSON and CUSTOMER. The design of the tables will be:

CUSTOMER (<u>CustomerNumber</u>, nonkey data attributes)

SALESPERSON (<u>SalespersonNumber</u>, nonkey data attributes)

ORDER (<u>OrderNumber</u>, nonkey data attributes, *CustomerNumber*,
         ***SalespersonNumber*)**

Suppose, however, that the business has a rule that each CUSTOMER can place orders only with a particular SALESPERSON. In this case, the ternary relationship ORDER:CUSTOMER:SALESPERSON is constrained by an additional binary 1:N relationship between SALESPERSON and CUSTOMER. To represent the constraint, we need to add the key of SALESPERSON to CUSTOMER. The three relations will now be:

CUSTOMER (<u>CustomerNumber</u>, nonkey data attributes, *SalespersonNumber*)

SALESPERSON (<u>SalespersonNumber</u>, nonkey data attributes)

ORDER (<u>OrderNumber</u>, nonkey data attributes, *CustomerNumber*, *SalespersonNumber*)

The constraint that a particular CUSTOMER is sold to by a particular SALESPERSON means that only certain combinations of CustomerNumber and SalespersonNumber can exist together in ORDER. Unfortunately, this constraint cannot be expressed in a relational model. It must be documented in the design, however, and enforced by program code. See Figure 6-23.

A constraint that requires one entity to be combined with another entity is called a MUST constraint. Other similar constraints are MUST NOT and MUST COVER. In a MUST NOT constraint, the binary relationship indicates combinations that are not allowed to occur in the ternary relationship. For example, the ternary relationship PRESCRIPTION:DRUG:CUSTOMER can be constrained by a binary relationship in the ALLERGY table that lists the drugs that a customer is not allowed to take. See Figure 6-24.

In a MUST COVER constraint, the binary relationship indicates all combinations that must appear in the ternary relationship. For example, consider the relationship AUTO:REPAIR:TASK. Suppose that a given REPAIR consists of a number of TASKs, all of which must be performed for the REPAIR to be successful. In this case, in the relation AUTO-REPAIR, when a given AUTO has a given REPAIR, then all of the TASKs for that REPAIR must appear as rows in that relation. See Figure 6-25.

Figure 6-23

Ternary Relationship with MUST Constraint

SALESPERSON Table

SalespersonNumber	Other nonkey data
10	
20	
30	

CUSTOMER Table

CustomerNumber	Other nonkey data	SalespersonNumber
1000		10
2000		20
3000		30

— Binary MUST Constraint —

ORDER Table

OrderNumber	Other nonkey data	SalespersonNumber	CustomerNumber
100		10	1000
200		20	2000
300		10	1000
400		30	3000
500			2000

Only 20 is allowed here

Figure 6-24   **Ternary Relationship with MUST NOT Constraint**

DRUG Table

DrugNumber	Other nonkey data
10	
20	
30	
45	
70	
90	

ALLERGY Table

CustomerNumber	DrugNumber	Other nonkey data
1000	10	
1000	20	
2000	20	
2000	45	
3000	30	
3000	45	
3000	70	

Binary MUST NOT Constraint

PRESCRIPTION Table

PrescriptionNumber	Other nonkey data	DrugNumber	CustomerNumber
100		45	1000
200		10	2000
300		70	1000
400		20	3000
500			2000

Neither 20 nor 45 can appear here

None of the three types of binary constraints discussed here can be represented in the relational design. Instead, they are documented in the design and implemented in application code.

Relational Representation of the Highline University Data Model

Figure 6-26 shows the design for the final Highline University data model in Figure 5-54 (page 160). This design is a straightforward application of the principles described in this chapter. In fact, this design was created automatically by ERwin from the data model in Figure 5-54; and it's almost correct!

Review Figure 6-26 to ensure that you understand the representation of every relationship. Observe the note on the side of this figure: DepartmentName should appear as a foreign key twice in the STUDENT table. Once to represent the Major relationship between DEPARTMENT and STUDENT and a second time as part of the composite (DepartmentName, ProfessorFirstName, ProfessorLastName) that is the foreign key for the Adviser relationship between APPOINTMENT and STUDENT.

The omission of the second occurrence of DepartmentName in STUDENT is an error in ERwin; it is unable to show the same attribute in a table more than once. This example illustrates why you need to know database design principles even though tools such as ERwin will create designs for you. Generated designs are not always correct.

Figure 6-25

Ternary Relationship with MUST COVER Constraint

REPAIR Table

RepairNumber	Other nonkey data
10	
20	
30	
40	

TASK Table

TaskNumber	Other nonkey data	*RepairNumber*
1001		10
1002		10
1003		10
2001		20
2002		20
3001		30
4001		40

— Binary MUST COVER Constraint ⌐

AUTO-REPAIR Table

InvoiceNumber	RepairNumber	TaskNumber	Other nonkey data
100	10	1001	
200	10	1002	
300	10	1003	
400	20	2001	
500	20		

2002 must appear here⌐

Figure 6-26

Table Design for Highline University Model in Figure 5-54

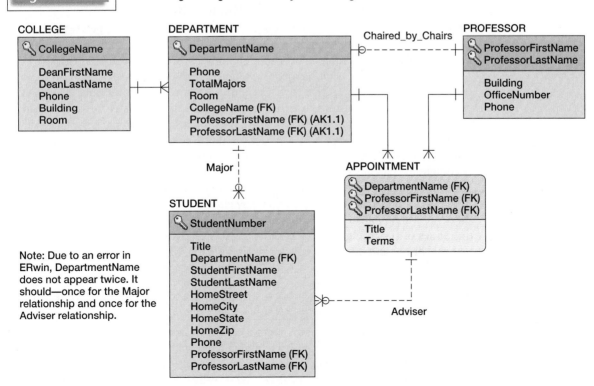

Note: Due to an error in ERwin, DepartmentName does not appear twice. It should—once for the Major relationship and once for the Adviser relationship.

Design for Minimum Cardinality

The third and last step of transforming data models into database designs is to create a plan for enforcing minimum cardinality. Unfortunately, this step can be considerably more complicated than the first two design steps. Relationships that have required children are particularly problematic because we cannot enforce such constraints with database structures. Instead, as you will see, we must design procedures for execution by the DBMS or by applications.

Relationships can have one of four minimum cardinalities: parent optional and child optional (O-O), parent mandatory and child optional (M-O), parent optional and child mandatory (O-M), or parent mandatory and child mandatory (M-M). As far as enforcing minimum cardinality is concerned, no action needs to be taken for O-O relationships, and we need not consider them further. The remaining three relationships pose restrictions on insert, update, and delete activities.

Figure 6-27 summarizes the actions needed to enforce minimum cardinality. Figure 6-27(a) shows needed actions when the parent row is required (M-O and M-M relationships), and Figure 6-27(b) shows needed actions when the child row is required (O-M and M-M relationships). In these figures and the accompanying discussion, the term *action* means **minimum cardinality enforcement action**. We use the shorter term *action* for ease of discussion.

To discuss these rules, we will use the example of a 1:N relationship between DEPARTMENT and EMPLOYEE, where we assume that the primary key and foreign key are both named DepartmentName.

Actions When the Parent Is Required

When the parent is required, we need to ensure that every row of the child table has a valid, non-null value of the foreign key. To accomplish this, we must restrict actions to update or delete the parent's primary key and actions to create or modify the child's foreign key. Consider actions on the parent first.

Actions on the Parent Row When the Parent Is Required

According to Figure 6-27(a), when a new parent is created, nothing needs to be done. No child row can yet be dependent upon the new row. In our example, we can create a new DEPARTMENT and not worry about minimum cardinality enforcement.

However, consider what happens if we attempt to change the value of an existing parent row's primary key. If that row has children, then those children have a foreign key value that matches the current primary key value. If the primary key of the parent changes, then any existing children will become orphans; their foreign key values will no longer match a parent row. To prevent the creation of orphans, either the foreign key values must be changed to match the new value of the parent's primary key or the modification to the parent's primary key must be prohibited.

In our example, if a DEPARTMENT attempts to change its DepartmentName from 'Info Sys' to 'Information Systems', then any child rows that have a foreign key value of 'Info Sys' will no longer match a parent and will be orphans. To prevent orphans, either the values of the foreign key in EMPLOYEE must also be changed to 'Information Systems' or the update to the primary key in DEPARTMENT must be prohibited. The policy of propagating a change from the parent's primary key to the children's foreign key is called **cascading updates.**

Now consider what happens when there is an attempt to delete a parent. If that row has children, and if the deletion is allowed, then the children will become orphans. Hence, when such a delete attempt is made, either the children must be deleted as well or the deletion must be prohibited. Deleting the children along with the parent is called **cascading deletions.** In our example, when an attempt is made to delete a DEPARTMENT, either all related rows in EMPLOYEE must be deleted as well or the deletion must be disallowed.

Figure 6-27

Summary of Actions to
Enforce Minimum
Cardinality

Parent Required	Action on Parent	Action on Child
Insert	None	• Get a parent • Prohibit
Modify key or foreign key	• Change children's foreign key values to match new value (cascade update) • Prohibit	• OK if new foreign key value matches existing parent
Delete	• Delete children (cascade delete) • Prohibit	None

(a) Actions When Parent Is Required

Child Required	Action on Parent	Action on Child
Insert	• Get a child • Prohibit	None
Modify key or foreign key	• Update the foreign key of (at least one) child • Prohibit	• If not last child, OK • If last child, prohibit or find a new replacement
Delete	None	• If not last child, OK • If last child, prohibit or find a new replacement

(b) Actions When Child Is Required

B T W

Generally, cascading deletions are not chosen for relationships between strong entities. The deletion of a DEPARTMENT row should not force the deletion of EMPLOYEE rows. Instead, the deletion should be disallowed. To remove a DEPARTMENT row, the EMPLOYEE rows would be reassigned to a new DEPARTMENT and then the DEPARTMENT row would be deleted.

On the other hand, cascading deletions are almost always chosen for weak child entities. For example, when you delete a COMPANY, you should always delete all of the weak PHONE_NUMBER rows that depend on that COMPANY.

Actions on the Child Row When the Parent Is Required

Now consider actions on the child row. If the parent is required, then when a new child row is created, the new row must have a valid foreign key value. When we create a new EMPLOYEE, for example, if DEPARTMENT is required, then the new EMPLOYEE row must have a valid value for DepartmentName. If not, the insert must be disallowed. Usually there is a default policy for assigning parents to a new row. In our example, when a new row is added to EMPLOYEE, the default policy could be to add the new employee to the department named 'Human Resources'.

With regards to modifications to the foreign key, the new value must match a value of the primary key in the parent. In DEPARTMENT, if we change DepartmentName from 'Accounting' to 'Finance', then there must already be a DEPARTMENT row with the primary key value of 'Finance'. If not, the modification must be prohibited.

B T W

When the parent has a surrogate key, the enforcement actions for update are different between the parent and the child. On the parent side, the surrogate key will never change, and hence update actions can be ignored. On the child side, however, the foreign key can change if the child switches to a new parent. Hence, on the parent side, you can ignore actions when the key is a surrogate. On the child side, however, you must consider update actions even when the parent's key is a surrogate.

If the parent row is required, there are no restrictions on the deletion of the child row. The child can go away without consequence on the parent.

Actions When the Child Is Required

When the child is required, we need to ensure that there is at least one child row for the parent at all times. The last child cannot leave the parent. For example, in the DEPART-MENT/EMPLOYEE relationship, if a DEPARTMENT requires an EMPLOYEE, then the last EMPLOYEE cannot leave the DEPARTMENT. This has ramifications on actions on the child, as shown in Figure 6-27(b).

Enforcing required children is much more difficult than enforcing required parents. To enforce a required parent, we just need to check for a match between primary key and foreign key values. To enforce a required child, we must count the number of children that a parent has. This difference forces us to write code to enforce required children. To begin, consider the required child actions from the perspective of the parent.

Actions on the Parent Row When the Child Is Required

If the child is required, then we cannot create a new parent without also creating a relationship to a child. This means that we must either find an existing child row and change its foreign key to match that of the new parent or we must create a new child row at the same time the parent is created. If neither action can be taken, then the insertion of the new parent must be prohibited. These rules are summarized in the first row of Figure 6-27(b).

If the child is required, then to modify the parent's primary key, either the key of at least one child must also be changed or the update must be disallowed. This restriction never applies to parents with surrogate keys because their values never change.

Finally, if the child is required and the parent is deleted, no action need be taken. Because it is the child that is required, and not the parent, the parent can disappear without any consequence.

Actions on the Child Row When the Child Is Required

As shown in Figure 6-27(b), if the child is required, then no special action needs to be taken when inserting a new child. The child comes into existence without influencing any parent.

However, there are restrictions on updating the foreign key of a required child. In particular, if the child is the last child of its current parent, then the update cannot occur. If it were to occur, the current parent would be childless, and that is not allowed. Thus, a procedure must be written to determine the number of children of the current parent. If that number is two or greater, then the child foreign key value can be changed. Otherwise the update is prohibited.

A similar restriction pertains to the deletion of required children. If the child is the last child to the parent, then the deletion is not allowed. Otherwise, the child can be deleted without restriction.

Implementing Actions for M-O Relationships

Figure 6-28 summarizes the application of the actions in Figure 6-27 for each type of minimum cardinality. As stated earlier, O-O relationships pose no restrictions and need not be considered.

M-O relationships require that the actions in Figure 6-27(a) be enforced. We need to make sure that every child has a parent and that operations on either parent or child rows never create orphans.

Fortunately, these actions are easy to enforce using facilities available in most DBMS products. It turns out that we can enforce these actions with just two limitations. First, we need to define a referential integrity constraint that ensures that every foreign key value has a match in the parent table. Second, we make the foreign key column NOT NULL. With these two restrictions, all of the actions in Figure 6-27(a) will be enforced.

Consider the DEPARTMENT/EMPLOYEE example. If we define the referential integrity constraint:

DepartmentName in EMPLOYEE must exist in DepartmentName in DEPARTMENT

then we know that every value of DepartmentName in EMPLOYEE will match a value in DEPARTMENT. If we then make DepartmentName required, we know that every row in EMPLOYEE will have a valid DEPARTMENT.

Figure 6-28	Relationship Minimum Cardinality	Action to Apply	Remarks
Actions to Apply to Enforce Minimum Cardinality	O-O	Nothing	
	M-O	Parent-required actions (Figure 6-27 (a))	Easily enforced by DBMS; define referential integrity constraint and make foreign key NOT NULL.
	O-M	Child-required actions (Figure 6-27 (b))	Difficult to enforce. Requires use of triggers or other application code.
	M-M	Parent-required actions and child-required actions (Figures 6-27 (a) and 6-27 (b))	Very difficult to enforce. Requires a combination of complex triggers. Triggers can lock each other out. Many problems!

Almost every DBMS product has facilities for defining referential integrity constraints. You will learn how to write SQL statements for that purpose in the next chapter. In those statements, you will have the option of declaring whether updates and deletions are to cascade or are to be prohibited. Once you have defined the constraint and made the foreign key NOT NULL, the DBMS will take care of all of the actions in Figure 6-27(a) for you.

B T W

Recall that in a 1:1 strong entity relationship the key of either table can be placed in the other table. If the minimum cardinality of such a relationship is either M-O or O-M, it is generally best to place the key in the optional table. This placement will make the parent required, which is easier to enforce. With a required parent, all you have to do is define the referential integrity constraint and set the foreign key to NOT NULL. On the other hand, if you place the foreign key so that the child is required, let the work begin! You will have your hands full, as you're about to see.

Implementing Actions for O-M Relationships

Unfortunately, if the child is required, the DBMS does not provide much help. There is no easy mechanism to ensure that appropriate child foreign keys exist nor is there any easy way to ensure that valid relationships stay valid when rows are inserted, updated, or deleted. You're on your own.

In most cases, required children constraints are enforced using triggers, which are modules of code that are invoked by the DBMS when specific events occur. Almost all DBMS products have triggers for insert, update, and delete actions. Triggers are defined for these actions on a particular table. Thus, you can create a trigger on *customer insert* or a trigger on *employee update*, and so forth. You will learn more about triggers in the next chapter.

To see how you would use triggers to enforce required children, consider Figure 6-27(b) again. On the parent side, we need to write a trigger on insert and update on the parent row. These triggers either create the required child or they steal an existing child from another parent. If they are unable to perform one of these actions, they must cancel the insert or update.

On the child side, a child can be inserted without problem. Once a child gets a parent, however, it cannot leave that parent if it is the last or only child. Hence, we need to write update and delete triggers on the child that have the following logic: If the foreign key is null, the row has no parent, and the update or delete can proceed. If the foreign key does have a value, however, check whether the row is the last child. If so, it must either delete the parent, find a substitute child, or disallow the update or delete.

None of these actions will be automatically enforced by the DBMS. Instead, you must write code to enforce these rules. You will see generic examples of such code in the next chapter and real examples for Oracle in Chapter 10 and for SQL Server in Chapter 11.

Implementing Actions for M-M Relationships

It is very difficult to enforce M-M relationships. All of the actions in both Figures 6-27(a) and Figure 6-27(b) must be enforced simultaneously. We have a needy parent and a needy child, and neither will let go of the other.

Consider, for example, the creation of new rows in DEPARTMENT and EMPLOYEE, when those tables have an M-M relationship. On the DEPARTMENT side, we must write an insert department trigger that tries to insert a new EMPLOYEE for the new DEPARTMENT. However, the EMPLOYEE table will have its own insert trigger. When we try to insert the new EMPLOYEE, the DBMS calls the insert employee trigger, which will prevent the insertion of an EMPLOYEE unless it has a DEPARTMENT row. But the new DEPARTMENT row does not yet exist because it is trying to create the new EMPLOYEE row, which does not exist because the new DEPARTMENT row does not yet exist, and round and round we go!

Now consider a deletion in this same M-M relationship. Suppose we want to delete a DEPARTMENT. We cannot delete a DEPARTMENT that has any EMPLOYEE children. So, before deleting the DEPARTMENT, we must first reassign (or delete) all of the employees in that department. However, when we try to reassign the last EMPLOYEE, an EMPLOYEE update trigger will be fired that will not allow the last employee to be reassigned. (The trigger is programmed to ensure that every DEPARTMENT has at least one EMPLOYEE.) We have a stalemate; the last employee cannot get out of the department, and the department cannot be deleted until all employees are gone!

This problem has several solutions, but none are particularly satisfying. In the next chapter, we will show one solution using SQL Views. That solution is complicated and requires careful programming that is difficult to test and fix. The best advice is to avoid M-M relationships if you can. If you cannot avoid them, budget your time with foreknowledge that a difficult task lies ahead.

Designing Special Case M-M Relationships

Not all M-M relationships are as bad as the last section indicates. Although M-M relationships between strong entities generally are as complicated as described, M-M relationships between strong and weak entities are often easier. For example, consider the relationship between COMPANY and PHONE_CONTACT in Figure 6-29. Because PHONE_CONTACT is weak (actually ID dependent), it must have a COMPANY parent. In addition, assume that application requirements indicate that each COMPANY row must have at least one row in PHONE_CONTACT. Hence, the relationship is M-M.

However, transactions are almost always initiated from the side of the strong entity. A data entry form will begin with a COMPANY and then, somewhere in the body of the form, the data from the PHONE_CONTACT table will appear. Hence, all insert, update, and deletion activity on PHONE_CONTACT will come as a result of some action on COMPANY. Given this situation, we can ignore the Action on Child

Figure 6-29

M-M Relationship between COMPANY and PHONE_CONTACT

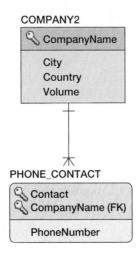

columns in Figures 6-27(a) and 6-27(b); no one will every try to insert, modify, or delete a new PHONE_CONTACT except in the context of inserting, modifying, or deleting a COMPANY.

Because the relationship is M-M, however, we must take all of the actions in the Action on Parent columns of both Figures 6-27(a) and 6-27(b). With regards to inserts on parents, we must always create a child. We can meet this need by writing a COMPANY INSERT trigger that automatically creates a new row of PHONE_CONTACT with null values for Contact and PhoneNumber.

With regard to updates and deletions, all we need to do is to cascade all of the remaining actions in Figures 6-27(a) and 6-27(b). Changes to COMPANY.CompanyName will be propagated to PHONE_CONTACT.CompanyName. The deletion of a COMPANY will automatically delete that company's PHONE_CONTACT rows. This makes sense; if we no longer want data about a company, we certainly no longer want its contact and phone data.

B T W

Because of the difficulty of enforcing M-M relationships, developers look for special circumstances to ease the task. Such circumstances usually exist for relationships between strong and weak entities, as described. For relationships between strong entities, such special circumstances may not exist. In this case, the M-M cardinality is sometimes just ignored. Of course, this cannot be done for applications such as financial management or operations that require careful records management, but, for an application such as airline reservations, where seats are overbooked anyway, it might be better to redefine the relationship as M-O.

Documenting the Minimum Cardinality Design

Because enforcing minimum cardinality can be complicated, and because it often involves the creation of triggers or other procedures, clear documentation is essential. Because the design for the enforcement of required parents is easier than that for required children, we will use different techniques for each.

Documenting Required Parents

Tools such as ERwin and Visio allow you to define referential integrity actions on each table. These definitions are useful for documenting the actions necessary for required parents. According to Figure 6-27(a), three design decisions are necessary for required children: (1) determining whether updates to the parent's primary key should cascade or be prohibited; (2) determining whether deletions of the parent should cascade or be prohibited; and (3) identifying how a parent row is to be selected on the insert of a child.

Figure 6-30 shows the documentation of a required parent relationship between DEPARTMENT and EMPLOYEE. The notation U:C means that updates to the key of DEPARTMENT are to cascade to EMPLOYEE. D:R indicates that deletions of DEPARTMENT are to be restricted, meaning that they will be prohibited if the DEPARTMENT has any EMPLOYEE rows. Finally, the notation I:SD next to EMPLOYEE means that on insert of an EMPLOYEE, a default policy is to be used for finding a DEPARTMENT. (SD stands for *set default*.) That policy will be documented somewhere else in the design documentation. Notations such as U:C are called **referential integrity actions,** or **RI actions.**

Figure 6-30

Example Referential Integrity Actions for an M-O Relationship

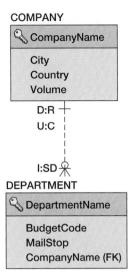

Figure 6-30

Example Referential Integrity Actions for an M-O Relationship

---

B T W

In theory, referential integrity actions can be used to document the actions to be taken to enforce required children as well as required parents. When they are used for both purposes, however, they become confusing and ambiguous. In an M-M relationship, for example, a child may have one set of rules for insert because of its required parent and another set of rules for insert because it is a required child. The insert referential integrity action will be overloaded with these two purposes, and its meaning will be ambiguous, at best. Hence, in this text, we will use referential integrity actions only for documenting required parents. We will use another technique, described next, for documenting required children.

Documenting Required Children

One easy and unambiguous way for defining the actions to enforce a required child is to use Figure 6-27(b) as a boilerplate document. Create a copy of this figure for each relationship that has a required child and fill in the specific actions for insert, update, and delete operations.

For example, consider Figure 6-31, which shows the O-M relationship between HOUSE and INSPECTION. A given house must have at least one inspection, but an inspection need not be related to any house. HOUSE has a surrogate key, HouseSK, and other columns as shown in Figure 6-31.

Because the HOUSE/INSPECTION relationship has a required child, we will fill out the table in Figure 6-27(b). Figure 6-32 shows the result. Here, triggers are described for HOUSE insert and INSPECTION deletion. HOUSE update actions are unneeded because HOUSE has a surrogate key, and INSPECTION update is prohibited because of the surrogate key and also because inspections are never reassigned to a different house.

An Additional Complication

You should be aware of an additional complication that is beyond the scope of this text. A table can participate in many relationships. In fact, there can be multiple relationships between the same two tables. You need to specify a design for the minimum cardinality

Figure 6-31

HOUSE/INSPECTION
O-M Relationship

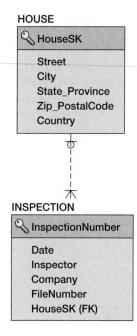

of every relationship. The minimum cardinality of each relationship will vary. Some will be O-M, some will be M-O, and some will be M-M. Some of the relationships will require triggers, which may mean that you have several sets of insert, update, and delete triggers per table. This array of triggers is not only complicated to write and test, the actions of different triggers may interfere with one another during execution.

You will need more experience and knowledge to design, implement, and test such complex arrays of trigger code and DBMS constraints. For now, just be aware that these problems exist.

Summary of Minimum Cardinality Design

Figure 6-33 summarizes the design for relationship minimum cardinality. It shows each type of relationship, the design decisions that need to be made, and the documentation that should be created. Use this figure as a guide.

Figure 6-32

Actions to Enforce the
O-M Relationship
between HOUSE and
INSPECTION

INSPECTION Is Required	Action on HOUSE	Action on INSPECTION
Insert	Trigger to create row in INSPECTION when inserting HOUSE. Disallow HOUSE insert if INSPECTION data are not available.	None.
Modify key or foreign key	Not possible, surrogate key.	Disallow. HOUSE has surrogate key and inspections never change to a different house.
Delete	None.	Trigger to disallow if sole INSPECTION report.

Figure 6-33 Summary of Design for Minimum Cardinality

Relationship Minimum Cardinality	Design Decisions to Be Made	Design Documentation
M-O	• Update cascade or prohibit? • Delete cascade or prohibit? • Policy for obtaining parent on insert of child	Referential integrity (RI) actions plus documentation for policy on obtaining parent for child insert.
O-M	• Policy for obtaining child on insert of parent • Primary key update cascade or prohibit? • Policy for update of child foreign key • Policy for deletion of child	Use Figure 6-27(b) as a boilerplate
M-M	All decisions for M-O and O-M above, plus how to process trigger conflict on insertion of first instance of parent/child and deletion of last instance of parent/child.	For mandatory parent, RI actions plus documentation for policy on obtaining parent for child insert. For mandatory child, use 6-27(b) as a boilerplate. Add documentation on how to process trigger conflict.

The View Ridge Gallery Database

We conclude this chapter with an example design problem. This design will be used throughout the rest of the text, so take the time to understand it. This particular problem was chosen because it has typical relationships and moderate complexity. It has enough challenges to make it interesting, but not so many as to make it overwhelming.

Summary of Requirements

View Ridge Gallery is a small art gallery that sells contemporary European and North American fine art, including lithographs, original paintings, and photographs. All of the lithographs and photos are signed and numbered, and most of the art is priced between $5,000 and $50,000. View Ridge has been in business for 30 years and has one full-time owner, three salespeople, and two workers who make frames, hang art in the gallery, and prepare artwork for shipment. View Ridge holds openings and other gallery events to attract customers to the gallery. Art also is placed on display in local companies and restaurants and in other public places. View Ridge owns all of the art that it sells; it holds no items on a consignment basis.

The requirements for the View Ridge application are summarized in Figure 6-34. First, both the owner and the salespeople want to keep track of their customers' names, addresses, phone numbers, and e-mail addresses. They also want to know which artists have appeal to which customers. The salespeople use this information to determine whom to contact when new art arrives and to personalize verbal and e-mail communications with their customers.

When the gallery purchases new art, data about the artist, the nature of the work, the acquisition date, and the acquisition price are recorded. Also, on occasion, the gallery repurchases art from a customer and resells it, thus a work may appear in the gallery multiple times. When art is repurchased, the artist and work data are not reentered, but the most recent acquisition date and price are recorded. In addition, when art is sold, the purchase date, sales price, and identity of the purchasing customer are stored in the database.

Salespeople want to examine past purchase data so that they can devote more time to the most active buyers. They also sometimes use the purchase records to identify the location of art they have sold in the past.

For marketing purposes, View Ridge wants its database application to provide a list of artists and works that have appeared in the gallery. The owner also would like to be able to determine how fast an artist's work sells and at what sales margin. The database application also should display current inventory on a Web page that customers can access via the Internet.

The View Ridge Data Model

Figure 6-35 shows a data model for the View Ridge database. This model has two strong entities: CUSTOMER and ARTIST. In addition, the entity WORK is ID dependent on ARTIST, and the entity TRANSACTION is ID dependent on WORK. There is also a nonidentifying relationship from CUSTOMER to WORK.

Figure 6-34

Summary of View Ridge Requirements

- Track customers and their artist interests
- Record gallery's purchases
- Record customers' art purchases
- List the artists and works that have appeared in the gallery
- Report how fast an artist's works have sold and at what margin
- Show current inventory in a Web page

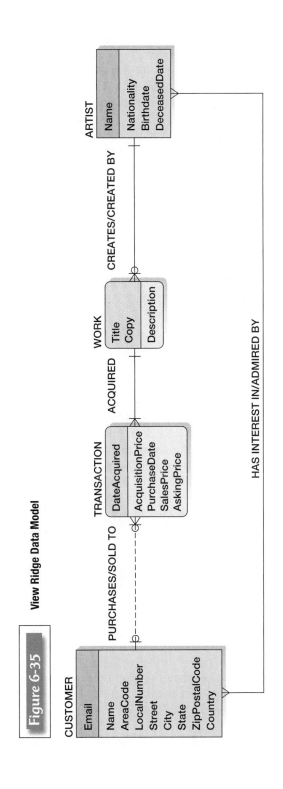

Figure 6-35

View Ridge Data Model

An artist may be recorded in the database even if none of his or her works has appeared in the gallery. This is done to record customer preferences for artists whose works might appear in the future. Thus, an artist may have from zero to many works.

The identifier of WORK is the composite (Title, Copy) because, in the case of lithographs and photos, there may be many copies of a given title. Also, the requirements indicate that a work may appear in the gallery many times, so there is a need for potentially many TRANSACTION entities for each WORK. Each time a work appears in the gallery, the acquisition date and price must be recorded. Thus, each WORK must have at least one TRANSACTION row.

A customer may purchase many works; this is recorded in the 1:N relationship from CUSTOMER to TRANSACTION. Note that this relationship is optional in both directions. Finally, there is a N:M relationship between CUSTOMERs and ARTISTs. This is a N:M strong entity relationship; the team searched in vain for a missing attribute that would indicate an association relationship.

Database Design with Data Keys

A database design for the data model in Figure 6-35 is shown in Figure 6-36. This design uses data keys, and every primary key except ARTIST.Name has problems. The keys for WORK and TRANSACTION are huge, and the key for CUSTOMER is doubtful; many customers may not have an e-mail address. Because of these problems, this design cries out for surrogate keys.

Surrogate Key Database Design

The database design for a surrogate key version of the View Ridge database is shown in Figure 6-37. Notice that the two identifying relationships have been changed to nonidentifying relationships. This was done because once ARTIST has a surrogate key, there is no need to keep ID-dependent keys in WORK and TRANSACTION. Realize that WORK and TRANSACTION are both weak entities even though they are no longer ID dependent.

Notice that ARTIST.Name has been defined as an alternate key. This will ensure that artists are not duplicated in the database. Similarly, (Title, Copy) is defined as an alternate key so that a given work cannot appear more than once.

The foreign key placement is a straightforward application of the techniques described in this chapter. TRANSACTION.CustomerID can have null values; this specification allows the creation of a TRANSACTION row before any customer has purchased the work. All other foreign keys are required.

Minimum Cardinality Enforcement for Required Parents

According to Figure 6-27(a), for each relationship that involves a required parent, we need to decide whether to cascade or prohibit updates to the parent's primary key; whether to cascade or prohibit deletions to the parent; and how to obtain a parent when a new child is created. Each of these decisions is documented in the referential integrity actions in Figure 6-38.

Because all tables have surrogate keys, there is no need for any update cascade behavior on any parent. Some update actions are restricted, but these pertain to the tables as children. The U:R on WORK, for example, indicates that once a work is assigned to an ARTIST, it is never to change to another parent.

Because this database is used to record purchases and sales, View Ridge management never wants to delete any data that are related to a transaction. From time to time, they may remove prior year's data in bulk, but they will do that using bulk data transfer and not as part of any application.

Hence, any CUSTOMER, WORK, or ARTIST row that is related to a TRANSACTION row is never to be deleted. The referential integrity actions in Figure 6-38 document

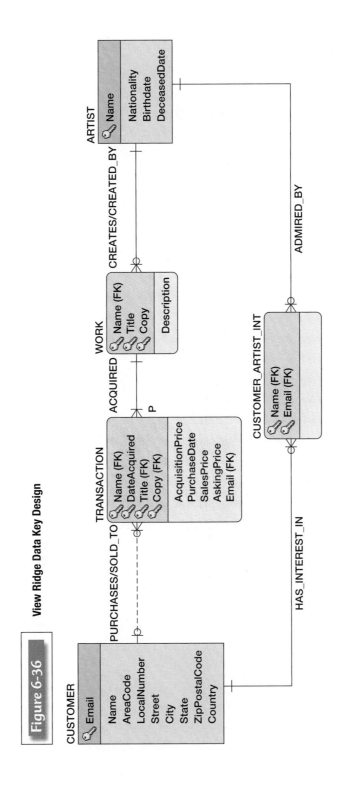

Figure 6-36

View Ridge Data Key Design

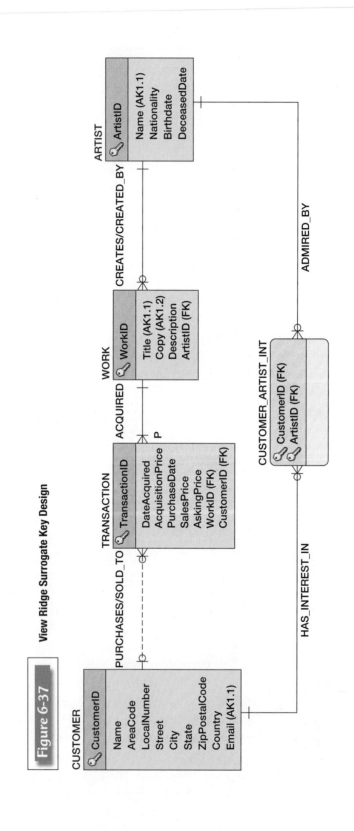

Figure 6-37   View Ridge Surrogate Key Design

Figure 6-38

View Ridge Showing Referential Integrity Actions for M-O Relationships

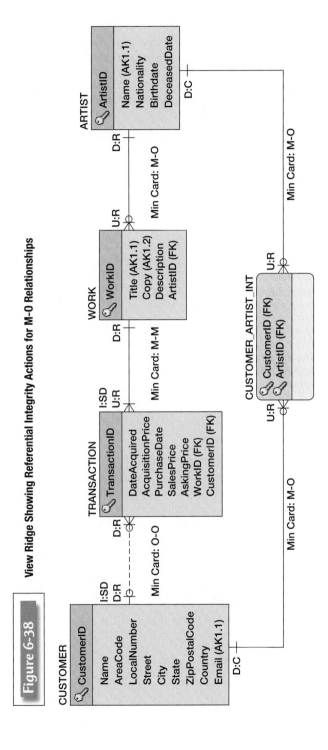

Figure 6-39

Actions to Enforce the
Required Child of the
WORK/TRANSACTION
Relationship

TRANSACTION Is Required	Action on WORK	Action on TRANSACTION
Insert	Trigger to create row in TRANSACTION. TRANSACTION will be given data for DateAcquired and AcquisitionPrice. Other columns will be null.	Will be created by INSERT trigger on WORK.
Modify key or foreign key	Not possible, surrogate key.	Disallow. A TRANSACTION must always refer to the WORK that created it.
Delete	Disallow.	Disallow.

this fact. Note, however, that rows of CUSTOMERs who have never made a purchase and rows of ARTISTs whose works have never been carried in the gallery can be deleted. If either a CUSTOMER or ARTIST is deleted under these circumstances, the deletion will cascade to rows in the intersection table CUSTOMER_ARTIST_INT, as documented in Figure 6-38.

Finally, referential integrity actions for obtaining a parent for WORK and for TRANSACTION are marked I:SD. In both cases, the set default policy will be for the application to provide the ID of the required parent at the time the WORK or TRANSACTION is to be created.

Minimum Cardinality Enforcement for the Required Child

TRANSACTION is the only required child in the database design in Figure 6-38. The actions to enforce that required child are documented in Figure 6-39 (which was created from the a boilerplate in Figure 6-27(b)). According to this document, an INSERT WORK trigger will be written to create the required child. This trigger will be fired whenever a work is first introduced at the gallery. At that time, a new TRANSACTION row will be created to store the values for DateAcquired and AcquisitionPrice.

Changes to the primary key in WORK will not occur because it has a surrogate key. Changes to the foreign key in TRANSACTION will not be allowed because a TRANSACTION never switches to another work. As stated earlier, the gallery has the policy that no transaction or related data will ever be deleted. Consequently, deletions of either WORK or TRANSACTION are not allowed.

We will use this design in many of the following chapters, so be certain that you understand it.

🌀 SUMMARY

Transforming a data model into a database design requires three major tasks: replacing each entity with a table and each attribute with a column; representing relationships and maximum cardinality by placing foreign keys; and representing minimum cardinality by defining actions to constrain activities on values of primary and foreign keys.

During design, each entity is replaced by a table. The attributes of the entity become columns of the table. The identifier of the entity becomes the primary key of the table, and candidate keys in the entity become candidate keys in the table. A good primary key is short, numeric, and fixed. If a good primary key is not available, a surrogate key may be used instead. Some organizations choose to use surrogate keys for all of their tables. An alternate key is the same as a candidate key. The notation AK*n.m* refers to the *n*th alternative key and the *m*th column in that key.

Four properties need to be specified for each table column: null status, data type, default value, and data constraints. A column can be NULL or NOT NULL. Primary keys are always NOT NULL; alternate keys can be NULL. Data types depend on the DBMS to be used. Generic data types include CHAR(n), VARCHAR(n), DATE, TIME, MONEY, INTEGER, and DECIMAL. A default value is a value to be supplied by the DBMS when a new row is created. It can be a simple value or the result of a function. Sometimes triggers are needed to supply values of more complicated expressions.

Data constraints include domain constraints, range constraints, intrarelation constraints, and interrelation constraints. Domain constraints specify a set of values that a column may have; range constraints specify an interval of allowed values; intrarelation constraints involve comparisons among columns in the same table; and interrelation constraints involve comparisons among columns in different tables. A referential integrity constraint is an example of an interrelation constraint.

Once the tables, keys, and columns have been defined, they should be checked against normalization criteria. Usually the tables will already be normalized, but they should be checked in any case. Also, it may be necessary to denormalize some tables.

The second step in database design is to create relationships by placing foreign keys appropriately. For 1:1 strong relationships, the key of either table can go in the other table as a foreign key; for 1:N strong relationships, the key of the parent must go in the child; and for N:M strong relationships, a new table, called an intersection table, is constructed that has the keys of both tables. Intersection tables never have nonkey data.

Four uses for ID-dependent entities are N:M relationships, association relationships, multivalued attributes, and archetype/instance relationships. An association relationship differs from an intersection table because the ID-dependent entity has nonkey data. In all ID-dependent entities, the key of the parent is already in the child. Therefore, no foreign key needs to be created. When an instance entity of the archetype/instance pattern is given a non-ID-dependent identifier, it changes from an ID-dependent entity to a weak entity. The tables that represent such entities must have the key of the parent as a foreign key. They remain weak entities, however. When the parent of an ID-dependent entity is given a surrogate key, the ID-dependent entity is also given a surrogate key. It remains a weak entity, however.

Mixed entities are represented by placing the key of the parent of the nonidentifying relationship into the child. The key of the parent of the identifying relationship will already be in the child. Subtypes are represented by copying the key from the supertype into the subtype(s) as a foreign key. Recursive relationships are represented in the same ways that 1:1, 1:N, and N:M relationships are represented. The only difference is that the foreign key references rows in the table in which it resides.

Ternary relationships are decomposed into binary relationships. However, sometimes binary constraints must be documented. Three such constraints are MUST, MUST NOT, and MUST COVER.

The third step in database design is to create a plan for enforcing minimum cardinality. Figure 6-27 shows the actions that need to be taken to enforce minimum cardinality for required parents and required children. The actions in Figure 6-27(a) must be taken for M-O and M-M relationships; the actions in Figure 6-27(b) must be taken for O-M and M-M relationships.

Enforcing mandatory parents can be done by defining the appropriate referential integrity constraint and by setting the foreign key to null. The designer must specify whether updates to the parent's primary key will cascade or be prohibited, whether deletions to the parent will cascade or be prohibited, and what policy will be used for finding a parent when a new child is created.

Enforcing mandatory children is difficult and requires the use of triggers or application code. The particular actions that need to be taken are shown in Figure 6-27(b). Enforcing M-M relationships can be very difficult. Particular challenges concern the creation of the first parent/child rows and the deletion of the last parent/child rows. The triggers on the two tables interfere with one another. M-M relationships between strong and weak entities are not as problematic as those between strong entities.

In this text, the actions to enforce required parents are documented using referential integrity actions on the table design diagrams. The actions to enforce required children are documented by using Figure 6-27(b) as a boilerplate document. An additional complication is that a table can participate in many relationships. Triggers written to enforce the minimum cardinality on one relationship may interfere with triggers written to enforce the minimum cardinality on another relationship. This problem is beyond the scope of this text, but be aware that it exists. The principles for enforcing minimum cardinality are summarized in Figure 6-33.

A database design for the View Ridge Gallery is shown in Figure 6-38. You should understand this design because it will be used throughout the remainder of this text.

REVIEW QUESTIONS

6.1   Identify the three major tasks for transforming a data model into a database design.
6.2   What is the relationship between entities and tables? Between attributes and columns?
6.3   Why is the choice of the primary key important?
6.4   What are the three characteristics of an ideal primary key?
6.5   What is a surrogate key? What are its advantages?
6.6   When should you use a surrogate key?
6.7   Describe two disadvantages of surrogate keys.
6.8   What is the difference between an alternate key and a candidate key?
6.9   What does the notation LastName (AK2.2) mean?
6.10   Name four column properties.
6.11   Explain why primary keys may never be null, but alternate keys can be null.
6.12   List five generic data types.
6.13   Describe three ways that a default value can be assigned.
6.14   What is a domain constraint? Give an example.
6.15   What is a range constraint? Give an example.
6.16   What is an intrarelation constraint? Give an example.
6.17   What is an interrelation constraint? Give an example.
6.18   What tasks should be accomplished when verifying normalization of a database design?
6.19   Describe two ways to represent a 1:1 strong entity relationship. Give an example other than one in this chapter.
6.20   Describe how to represent a 1:N strong entity relationship. Give an example other than one in this chapter.
6.21   Describe how to represent an N:M strong entity relationship. Give an example other than one in this chapter.
6.22   What is an intersection table? Why is it necessary?
6.23   What is the difference between the table that represents an ID-dependent association entity and an intersection table?

6.24 List four uses for ID-dependent entities.

6.25 Describe how to represent an association entity relationship. Give an example other than one in this chapter.

6.26 Describe how to represent a multivalue attribute entity relationship. Give an example other than one in this chapter.

6.27 Describe how to represent a version/instance entity relationship. Give an example other than one in this chapter.

6.28 What happens when an instance entity is given a non-ID-dependent identifier? How does this change affect relationship design?

6.29 What happens when the parent in an ID-dependent relationship is given a surrogate key? What should the key of the child become?

6.30 Describe how to represent a mixed entity relationship. Give an example other than one in this chapter.

6.31 Describe how to represent a supertype/subtype entity relationship. Give an example other than one in this chapter.

6.32 Describe two ways to represent a 1:1 recursive relationship. Give an example other than one in this chapter.

6.33 Describe how to represent a 1:N recursive relationship. Give an example other than one in this chapter.

6.34 Describe how to represent an N:M recursive relationship. Give an example other than one in this chapter.

6.35 In general, how are ternary relationships represented? Explain how a binary constraint may impact such a relationship.

6.36 Describe a MUST constraint. Give an example other than one in this chapter.

6.37 Describe a MUST NOT constraint. Give an example other than one in this chapter.

6.38 Describe a MUST COVER constraint. Give an example other than one in this chapter.

6.39 Explain in general terms what needs to be done to enforce minimum cardinality.

6.40 Explain the need for each of the actions in Figure 6-27(a).

6.41 Explain the need for each of the actions in Figure 6-27(b).

6.42 State which of the actions in Figure 6-27 must be applied for M-O relationships, O-M relationships, and M-M relationships.

6.43 Explain what must be done for the DBMS to enforce required parents.

6.44 What design decisions must be made to enforce required parents?

6.45 Explain why the DBMS cannot be used to enforce required children.

6.46 What is a trigger? How can triggers be used to enforce required children?

6.47 Explain why the enforcement of M-M relationships is particularly difficult.

6.48 Explain the need for each of the design decisions in Figure 6-33.

6.49 Explain the purpose of each of the referential integrity actions in Figure 6-38.

6.50 Explain the rationale for each of the entries in the table in Figure 6-39.

⊚ PROJECT QUESTIONS

6.51 Answer question 5.59 if you have not already done so. Design a database for your model in question 5.59. Your design should include a specification of tables and attributes as well as primary, candidate, and foreign keys. Also specify how you will enforce minimum cardinality. Document your minimum cardinality enforcement using referential integrity actions for a required parent, if any, and the form in Figure 6-27(b) for a required child, if any.

6.52 Answer question 5.60 if you have not already done so. Design a database for your model. Your design should include a specification of tables and attributes as well as primary, candidate, and foreign keys. Also specify how you will enforce minimum cardinality. Document your minimum cardinality enforcement using referential integrity actions for required parents, if any, and the form in Figure 6-27(b) for required children, if any.

6.53   Answer question 5-61 if you have not already done so. Design a database for your model in question 5-61(c). Your design should include a specification of tables and attributes as well as primary, candidate, and foreign keys. Also specify how you will enforce minimum cardinality. Document your minimum cardinality enforcement using referential integrity actions for required parents, if any, and the form in Figure 6-27(b) for required children, if any.

6.54   Answer question 5-62 if you have not already done so. Design a database for your model in question 5-62(d). Your design should include a specification of tables and attributes as well as primary, candidate, and foreign keys. Also specify how you will enforce minimum cardinality. Document your minimum cardinality enforcement using referential integrity actions for required parents, if any, and the form in Figure 6-27(b) for required children, if any.

6.55   Answer question 5-63 if you have not already done so. Design databases for your model in question 5-63(a) and for the model in Figure 5-60. Your designs should include a specification of tables and attributes as well as primary, candidate, and foreign keys. Also specify how you will enforce minimum cardinality. Document your minimum cardinality enforcement using referential integrity actions for required parents, if any, and the form in Figure 6-27(b) for required children, if any.

6.56   Answer question 5-64 if you have not already done so. Design a database for your model in question 5-64(e). Your design should include a specification of tables and attributes as well as primary, candidate, and foreign keys. Also specify how you will enforce minimum cardinality. Document your minimum cardinality enforcement using referential integrity actions for required parents, if any, and the form in Figure 6-27(b) for required children, if any.

6.57   Answer question 5-65 if you have not already done so. Design a database for your model in question 5-65(c). Your design should include a specification of tables and attributes as well as primary, candidate, and foreign keys. Also specify how you will enforce minimum cardinality. Document your minimum cardinality enforcement using referential integrity actions for required parents, if any, and the form in Figure 6-27(b) for required children, if any.

6.58   Answer question 5-66 if you have not already done so. Design a database for your model in question 5-66(d). Your design should include a specification of tables and attributes as well as primary, candidate, and foreign keys. Also specify how you will enforce minimum cardinality. Document your minimum cardinality enforcement using referential integrity actions for required parents, if any, and the form in Figure 6-27(b) for required children, if any.

MARCIA'S DRY CLEANING

If you have not already done so, complete the Marcia's Dry Cleaning project at the end of Chapter 5. Design a database for the model in your answer. Your design should include a specification of tables and attributes as well as primary, candidate, and foreign keys. Also specify how you will enforce minimum cardinality. Document your minimum cardinality enforcement using referential integrity actions for required parents, if any, and the form in Figure 6-27(b) for required children, if any.

M MORGAN IMPORTING

If you have not already done so, answer the Morgan Importing project at the end of Chapter 5. Design a database for the model in your answer. Your design should include a specification of tables and attributes as well as primary, candidate, and foreign keys. Also specify how you will enforce minimum cardinality. Document your minimum cardinality enforcement using referential integrity actions for required parents, if any, and the form in Figure 6-27(b) for required children, if any.

Database Implementation

Part 3 consists of two chapters. Chapter 7 presents SQL data definition language statements for constructing database components. It also describes the following SQL data manipulation statements: INSERT, UPDATE, and DELETE. You will learn how to construct and use SQL views and how to embed SQL statements into programs. The chapter concludes with a discussion of triggers and stored procedures.

Chapter 8 presents the use of SQL statements to redesign databases. It presents correlated subqueries and EXISTS/NOT EXISTS statements, two advanced SQL statements that are needed for database redesign. Chapter 8 describes reverse engineering, surveys common database redesign problems, and shows how to use SQL to solve those problems.

SQL for Database Construction and Application Processing

In Chapter 2, we introduced SQL and classified SQL statements into two categories: data manipulation language (DML) statements, which are used for querying and modifying data, and data definition language (DDL) statements, which are used for creating tables, relationships, and other structures. Chapter 2 discussed only DML query statements.

This chapter describes and illustrates SQL DDL statements for constructing databases and SQL DML statements for inserting, modifying, and deleting data. We will also describe how to create SQL Views, how to embed SQL statements into application programs, and how to use SQL in triggers and stored procedures.

The knowledge in this chapter is important whether you become a database administrator or an application programmer. Even if you will not construct triggers or stored procedures yourself, it is important that you know what they are, how they work, and how they influence database processing.

SQL DDL, DML, and Joins

Figure 7-1 summarizes the new SQL statements described in this chapter. We begin with SQL DDL statements for managing table structures, including CREATE TABLE, ALTER TABLE, and DROP TABLE. Next, we present the three SQL DML statements: INSERT, UPDATE, and DELETE. Finally, we will add to the knowledge of joins you gained in Chapter 2 by describing a new format and a new type of join.

Managing Table Structure with SQL DDL

The SQL CREATE TABLE statement is used to construct tables, define columns and column constraints, and create relationships. Most DBMS products provide graphical tools for performing these tasks, and you may be wondering why you need to learn SQL to perform the same work. There are four reasons. First, creating tables and relationships with SQL is quicker than with graphical tools. Once you know how to use the SQL CREATE TABLE statement, you will be able to construct tables faster and more easily than by fussing around with buttons and graphical gimmickry. Second, some applications, particularly those for reporting, querying, and data mining, require you to create the same table repeatedly. You can do this efficiently if you create a text file with the necessary SQL CREATE TABLE statements. You then just execute the SQL in the text file when you need to re-create a table. Third, some applications require you to create temporary tables during application work. Chapter 15 (pages 540–542) shows one such application. The only way to create tables from program code is to use SQL. Finally, SQL DDL is standardized and DBMS independent. With the exception of some data types, the same CREATE TABLE statement will work with SQL Server, Oracle, DB2, or MySQL.

B T W

Of course, before you can create any tables, you have to create the database. The SQL-92 standard includes a SQL statement for creating databases, but it is seldom used. Instead, most developers use special commands or graphical tools for creating a database. These techniques are DBMS specific, and we will describe them in context in Chapters 10 (Oracle), 11 (SQL Server), 14 (MySQL), and Appendix A (Access).

Figure 7-1

SQL Statements in this Chapter

- SQL Data Definition Language (DDL)
  - CREATE TABLE
  - ALTER TABLE
  - DROP TABLE
- SQL Data Manipulation Language (DML)
  - INSERT
  - UPDATE
  - DELETE
- Additional join forms
  - Alternative join syntax
  - Outer joins

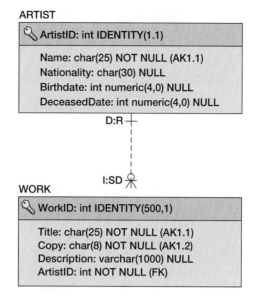

Figure 7-2

ARTIST and WORK
Tables from the View
Ridge Database Design

Creating the ARTIST Table

Figure 7-2 shows two of the tables from the View Ridge design we developed at the end of Chapter 6. This figure shows the data types and null properties for each column. The only new feature is the IDENTITY data type, which is used to specify surrogate keys. In the WORK table, the expression IDENTITY (500, 1) means that WorkID is to be a surrogate key with values starting at 500 and incremented by 1. Thus, the value for the second WORK row will be 501.

B T W

Different DBMS products define surrogate keys in different ways. The IDENTITY keyword shown here works for SQL Server. Oracle, MySQL, and Access use somewhat different techniques for creating surrogate keys. If you are using those products, see the discussion of surrogate keys for Oracle in Chapter 10, MySQL in Chapter 14, or Access in Appendix A.

All of the SQL in this chapter runs on SQL Server. If you are using a different DBMS, you may need to make adjustments. If you have a problem with a SQL statement shown here, consult the chapter or appendix for the DBMS you are using.

Figure 7-3 shows the CREATE TABLE statement for constructing the ARTIST table. The format of CREATE TABLE is the name of the table followed by a list of all column definitions and constraints enclosed in parentheses. SQL has five types of

Figure 7-3

SQL to Create the
Initial Version of the
ARTIST Table

```
CREATE TABLE ARTIST(
     ArtistID              int              NOT NULL IDENTITY (1,  1)
     Name                  char (25)        NOT NULL,
     Nationality           char (30)        NULL,
     Birthdate             numeric  (4, 0)  NULL,
     DeceasedDate          numeric  (4, 0)  NULL,

     CONSTRAINT  ArtistPK  PRIMARY  KEY  (ArtistID) ,
     CONSTRAINT  ArtistAK1  UNIQUE  (Name)

);
```

constraints: PRIMARY KEY, UNIQUE, NULL/NOT NULL, FOREIGN KEY, and CHECK. The purposes of the first three constraints are obvious. FOREIGN KEY is used to define referential integrity constraints; CHECK is used to define data constraints.

In the first section of the CREATE TABLE statement, each column is defined by giving its name, data type, and null status. If you do not specify NULL or NOT NULL, then NULL is assumed. Although SQL-92 defined a large number of data types, each DBMS vendor uses its own, and you must use the data types supported by your DBMS product. Figure 7-4 shows the more common data types for SQL Server and Oracle.

In this database, Birthdate and DeceasedDate are years. BirthYear and DeceasedYear would have been better column names, but that is not how the gallery personnel refer to them. Because the gallery is not interested in the month and day of an artist's birth and death, those columns are defined as Numeric (4,0), which means a four-digit number with zero places to the right of the decimal point.

The last two expressions in the table definition in Figure 7-3 are constraints that define the primary key and a candidate, or alternate, key. As stated in Chapter 6, the primary purpose of an alternate key is to ensure uniqueness of column values. Thus, in SQL, alternate keys are defined using the UNIQUE constraint.

Figure 7-4

SQL Data Types in DBMS Products
(a) Common Data Types in SQL Server
(b) Common Data Types in Oracle

Data Type	Description
Binary	Binary, length 0 to 8,000 bytes.
Char	Character, length 0 to 8,000 bytes.
Datetime	8-byte datetime. Range from January 1, 1753, through December 31, 9999, with an accuracy of three-hundredths of a second.
Image	Variable length binary data. Maximum length 2,147,483,647 bytes.
Integer	4-byte integer. Value range from –2,147,483,648 through 2,147,483,647.
Money	8-byte money. Range from –922,337,203,685,477.5808 through +922,337,203,685,477.5807, with accuracy to a ten-thousandth of a monetary unit.
Numeric	Decimal – can set precision and scale. Range $-10^{38} +1$ through $10^{38} -1$.
Smalldatetime	4-byte datetime. Range from January 1, 1900, through June 6, 2079, with an accuracy of one minute.
Smallint	2-byte integer. Range from –32,768 through 32,767.
Smallmoney	4-byte money. Range from 214,748.3648 through +214,748.3647, with accuracy to a ten-thousandth of a monetary unit.
Text	Variable length text, maximum length 2,147,483,647 characters.
Tinyint	1-byte integer. Range from 0 through 255.
Varchar	Variable-length character, length 0 to 8,000 bytes.

(a)

Data Type	Description
BLOB	Binary large object. Up to 4 gigabytes in length.
CHAR(n)	Fixed length character field of length n. Maximum 2,000 characters.
DATE	7-byte field containing both date and time.
INTEGER	Whole number of length 38.
NUMBER(n,d)	Numeric field of length n, d places to the right of the decimal.
VARCHAR(n) or VARCHAR2(n)	Variable length character field up to n characters long. Maximum value of n = 4,000.

(b)

The format of such constraints is the word CONSTRAINT followed by a constraint name provided by the developer followed by either PRIMARY KEY or UNIQUE and then one or more columns in parentheses. For example, the following statement defines a constraint named *MyExample* that ensures that the combination of first and last name is unique:

CONSTRAINT MyExample UNIQUE (FirstName, LastName),

As stated in Chapter 6, primary key columns must be NOT NULL, but candidate keys can be NULL or NOT NULL.

B T W

SQL originated in the era of punch-card data processing. Punched cards had only uppercase letters, so there was no need to think about case sensitivity. When cards were replaced by regular keyboards, DBMS vendors chose to ignore the difference between uppercase and lowercase letters. Thus, CREATE TABLE, create table, and CReatE taBle are all the same in SQL. NULL, null, and Null are all the same as well.

Notice that the last line of the SQL statement is a closed parenthesis followed by a semicolon. These characters could be placed on the line above, but dropping them to a new line is a style convention that makes it easy to determine the boundaries of CREATE TABLE statements. Also notice that column description constraints are separated by commas but that there is no comma after the last one.

B T W

Many organizations have developed SQL coding standards of their own. Such standards specify not only the format of SQL statements, but also conventions for naming constraints. For example, in the figures in this chapter, we use the suffix PK on the names of all primary key constraints and the suffix FK for all foreign key constraints. Most organizations have standards that are more comprehensive. You should follow your organization's standards, even if you disagree with them. Consistent SQL coding improves organizational efficiency and reduces errors.

Creating the WORK Table and the 1:N ARTIST/WORK Relationship

Figure 7-5 shows SQL statements for creating the ARTIST and WORK tables and their relationship. The only new syntax in this table is the FOREIGN KEY constraint at the end of WORK. Such constraints are used to define referential integrity constraints. The FOREIGN KEY constraint in Figure 7-5 is equivalent to the following referential integrity constraint:

WORK.ArtistID must exist in ARTIST.ArtistID

The foreign key constraint contains a clause that specifies whether updates or deletions are to cascade. The expression DELETE NO ACTION indicates that deletions of rows that have children should be prohibited. The expression DELETE CASCADE would indicate that deletions should cascade. DELETE NO ACTION is the default.

Figure 7-5

SQL to Create the
Relationship
between the ARTIST
and WORK Tables

```
CREATE TABLE ARTIST(
     ArtistID              int                 NOT NULL IDENTITY (1, 1) ,
     Name                  char (25)           NOT NULL,
     Nationality           char (30)           NULL,
     Birthdate             numeric (4, 0)      NULL,
     DeceasedDate          numeric (4, 0)      NULL,

     CONSTRAINT  ArtistPK  PRIMARY  KEY  (ArtistID) ,
     CONSTRAINT  ArtistAK1  UNIQUE  (Name)

);

CREATE TABLE WORK   (
     WorkID                int                 NOT NULL IDENTITY (500,  1) ,
     Title                 char (25)           NOT NULL,
     Copy                  char (8)            NOT NULL,
     Description           varchar (1000)      NULL,
     ArtistID              int                 NOT NULL,

     CONSTRAINT  WorkPK  PRIMARY  KEY  (WorkID) ,
     CONSTRAINT  WorkAK1  UNIQUE  (Title, Copy) ,
     CONSTRAINT  ArtistFK  FOREIGN  KEY (ArtistID) REFERENCES  ARTIST  (ArtistID)
           ON  DELETE  NO  ACTION
           ON  UPDATE  NO  ACTION
);
```

Similarly, the expression UPDATE NO ACTION indicates that updates to the primary key for a table that has children should be prohibited. The expression UPDATE CASCADE would indicate that updates should cascade. UPDATE NO ACTION is the default.

In the present case, the UPDATE NO ACTION is meaningless because the primary key of ARTIST is a surrogate and will never be changed. The UPDATE action would need to be specified for data keys, however. We show the option here so you will know how to code it.

B T W

Note that you must define parent tables before child tables. In this case, you must define ARTIST before WORK. If you try to reverse the order of definition, the DBMS will generate an error message on the FOREIGN KEY constraint because it will not yet know about the ARTIST table.

Similarly, you must delete tables in the opposite order. You must DROP (described later) a child before a parent.

Better SQL parsers would sort all of this out so that statement order would not matter, but, alas, that's not the way it's done! Just remember the following: *Parents are first in and last out.*

Implementing Required Parent Rows

In Chapter 6, you learned that to enforce a required parent constraint, you must define the referential integrity constraint and set the foreign key to NOT NULL. Figure 7-5 does both. WORK.ArtistID is specified as NOT NULL, and the FOREIGN KEY constraint defines the referential integrity constraint. These specifications thus cause the DBMS to enforce the required parent.

If the parent were not required, then we would specify WORK.ArtistID as NULL. In that case, a WORK would not need to have a value for ArtistID, and thus not need a parent. However, the FOREIGN KEY constraint would still ensure that all values of WORK.ArtistID would be present in the ARTIST.ArtistID.

Implementing 1:1 Relationships

SQL for implementing 1:1 relationships is almost identical to that for 1:N relationships as just shown. The only difference is that the foreign key must be declared as unique. For example, if the relationship were 1:1 between ARTIST and WORK, then in Figure 7-5 we would add the constraint:

CONSTRAINT UniqueWork UNIQUE (ArtistID),

The relationship in Figure 7-2 is of course not 1:1, so we will not specify this constraint.

If the parent is required, then the foreign key should be set to NOT NULL. Otherwise, it should be NULL.

Casual Relationships

Sometimes it is appropriate to create a foreign key column but not specify a FOREIGN KEY constraint. In that case, the foreign key value may or may not match a value of the primary key in the parent. If, for example, you define the column DepartmentName in EMPLOYEE but do not specify a FOREIGN KEY constraint, then a row may have a value of DepartmentName that does not match a value of DepartmentName in the DEPARTMENT table.

Such relationships, which we call **casual relationships,** occur frequently in applications that process tables with missing data. For example, you might buy consumer data that includes names of consumers' employers. Assume that you have an EMPLOYER table that does not contain all of the possible companies for which the consumers might work. You want to use the relationship if you happen to have the values, but you do not want to require having those values. In that case, create a casual relationship by placing the key of EMPLOYER in the consumer data table but do not define a FOREIGN KEY constraint.

Figure 7-6 summarizes the techniques for creating relationships using FOREIGN KEY, NULL/NOT NULL, and UNIQUE constraints.

Creating Default Values and Data Constraints with SQL

Figure 7-7 shows an example default value and example data constraints for the View Ridge database. The default value of 'Unknown provenance' is to be given to WORK.Description. The rest of this table shows data constraints.

Figure 7-6

Summary of
Relationship
Definitions Using
CREATE TABLE

Relationship Type	CREATE TABLE Constraints
1:N relationship, parent optional	Specify FOREIGN KEY constraint. Set foreign key NULL.
1:N relationship, parent required	Specify FOREIGN KEY constraint. Set foreign key NOT NULL.
1:1 relationship, parent optional	Specify FOREIGN KEY constraint. Specify foreign key UNIQUE constraint. Set foreign key NULL.
1:1 relationship, parent required	Specify FOREIGN KEY constraint. Specify foreign key UNIQUE constraint. Set foreign key NOT NULL.
Casual relationship	Create a foreign key column, but do not specify FOREIGN KEY constraint. If relationship is 1:1, specify foreign key UNIQUE.

Figure 7-7   Default Values and Data Constraints for View Ridge

Table	Column	Default Value	Constraint
WORK	Description	'Unknown provenance'	
ARTIST	Nationality		IN ('Canadian', 'English', 'French', 'German', 'Mexican', 'Russian', 'Spanish', 'US')
ARTIST	Birthdate		Before DeceasedDate
ARTIST	Birthdate		Four digits: 1 or 2 is first digit, 0 to 9 for remaining three digits
ARTIST	DeceasedDate		Four digits: 1 or 2 is first digit, 0 to 9 for remaining three digits
TRANSACTION	SalesPrice		> 1,000 and <= 200,000
TRANSACTION	PurchaseDate		=> DateAcquired

Artist Nationality is limited to the values in the domain constraint shown; Birthdate is limited by the intrarelation constraint that Birthdate occurs before DeceasedDate. Birthdate and DeceasedDate, which as noted earlier are years, are limited to the domain defined by specifying that the first digit be a 1 or a 2 and the remaining three digits be any decimal numbers. Thus, they can have any value between 1000 and 2999. SalesPrice in the TRANSACTION table is limited by the range constraint, and PurchaseDate is limited by an intrarelation constraint that the PurchaseDate be later than the DateAcquired

Figure 7-7 shows no interrelation constraint. Although the SQL-92 specification defined facilities for creating such constraints, no DBMS vendor has implemented those facilities. Such constraints must be implemented in triggers. An example of this is shown later in the chapter.

Implementing Default Values

Default values are created by specifying the DEFAULT keyword in the column definition just after the NULL/NOT NULL specification. In Figure 7-8, WORK.Description is given the default value of 'Unknown provenance'.

Implementing Data Constraints

The data constraints are created using CHECK CONSTRAINTS. The format is the word CONSTRAINT followed by a developer-provided constraint name followed by the word CHECK and then by the constraint specification in parentheses. Expressions in CHECK constraints are akin to those in the WHERE clause of SQL statements. Thus, the keyword IN is used to provide a list of valid values. NOT IN also can be used for negatively expressed domain constraints (not shown in this example). LIKE is used for the specification of decimal places. Range checks are specified using the less than and greater than symbols (< , >). Because interrelation constraints are unsupported, comparisons can be made only between columns in the same table.

| Figure 7-8 | **SQL to Create the ARTIST and WORK Tables with Data Constraints** |

```
CREATE TABLE ARTIST(
        ArtistID            int             NOT NULL IDENTITY (1, 1),
        Name                char (25)       NOT NULL,
        Nationality         char (30)       NULL,
        Birthdate           numeric (4, 0)  NULL,
        DeceasedDate        numeric (4, 0)  NULL,

        CONSTRAINT  ArtistPK  PRIMARY  KEY  (ArtistID),
        CONSTRAINT  ArtistAK1  UNIQUE  (Name),
        CONSTRAINT  NationalityValues  CHECK
                (Nationality  IN  ('Canadian', 'English', 'French', 'German',
                'Mexican', 'Russian', 'Spanish', 'US')),
        CONSTRAINT  BirthValuesCheck  CHECK  (Birthdate < DeceasedDate),
        CONSTRAINT  ValidBirthYear  CHECK  (Birthdate  LIKE  ' [1 - 2] [0 - 9] [0 - 9] [0 - 9]'),
        CONSTRAINT  ValidDeathYear  CHECK  (DeceasedDate  LIKE  ' [1 - 2] [0 - 9] [0 - 9] [0 - 9]')

);

CREATE TABLE WORK   (
        WorkID              int             NOT NULL IDENTITY (500, 1),
        Title               char (25)       NOT NULL,
        Copy                char (8)        NOT NULL,
        Description         varchar (1000)  NULL DEFAULT 'Unknown provenance',
        ArtistID            int             NOT NULL,

        CONSTRAINT  WorkPK  PRIMARY  KEY  (WorkID),
        CONSTRAINT  WorkAK1  UNIQUE  (Title, Copy),
        CONSTRAINT  ArtistFK  FOREIGN  KEY (ArtistID) REFERENCES  ARTIST (ArtistID)
                ON  DELETE  NO  ACTION
                ON  UPDATE  NO  ACTION
);
```

> **B T W**
>
> **DBMS products are inconsistent in their implementation of CHECK constraints. The LIKE constraint in Figure 7-8, for example, will not work with Oracle. On the other hand, Oracle implements other types of constraints. Unfortunately, you must learn the peculiarities of the DBMS you use to know how best to implement constraints.**

Creating the View Ridge Database

Figure 7-9 shows SQL for creating all of the tables in the View Ridge database documented in Figure 6-37. Read each line and be certain that you understand its function and purpose. Notice that deletions cascade for the relationships between CUSTOMER and CUSTOMER_ARTIST_INT and between ARTIST and CUSTOMER_ARTIST_INT.

The table names WORK and TRANSACTION are enclosed in square brackets ([,]). This was done because the words *work* and *transaction* are reserved words to most DBMS products. Enclosing them in brackets signifies to the SQL parser that these terms have been provided by the developer and are not to be used in the standard way. Ironically, SQL Server can process the word WORK without problem, but Oracle cannot; SQL Server chokes on the word TRANSACTION, but Oracle has no problem with it.

You can find a list of reserved words in the documentation for the DBMS product that you use. Be assured that if you use any keyword from the SQL syntax, such as SELECT, FROM, WHERE, LIKE, ORDER, ASC, DESC for table or column names, you will have problems. Enclose such words in square brackets. Your life will be easier if you can avoid using such terms for tables or columns altogether.

Figure 7-9   **SQL for Creating the View Ridge Tables**

```
CREATE TABLE ARTIST(
        ArtistID            int             NOT NULL IDENTITY (1, 1) ,
        Name                char (25)       NOT NULL,
        Nationality         char (30)       NULL,
        Birthdate           numeric (4, 0)  NULL,
        DeceasedDate        numeric (4, 0)  NULL,

        CONSTRAINT ArtistPK PRIMARY KEY (ArtistID) ,
        CONSTRAINT ArtistAK1 UNIQUE (Name) ,

        CONSTRAINT NationalityValues CHECK
                (Nationality IN ( 'Canadian' , 'English' , 'French' , 'German' ,
                'Mexican' , 'Russian' , 'Spanish' , 'US' ) ) ,
        CONSTRAINT BirthValuesCheck CHECK (Birthdate < DeceasedDate) ,
        CONSTRAINT ValidBirthYear CHECK (Birthdate LIKE ' [1 - 2] [0 - 9] [0 - 9] [0 - 9] ' ) ,
        CONSTRAINT ValidDeathYear CHECK (DeceasedDate LIKE ' [1 - 2] [0 - 9] [0 - 9] [0 - 9] ' )

);

CREATE TABLE [WORK]   (
        WorkID              int             NOT NULL IDENTITY (500, 1) ,
        Title               char (25)       NOT NULL,
        Copy                char (8)        NOT NULL,
        Description         varchar (1000)  NULL DEFAULT 'Unknown provenance' ,
        ArtistID            int             NOT NULL,

        CONSTRAINT WorkPK PRIMARY KEY (WorkID) ,
        CONSTRAINT WorkAK1 UNIQUE (Title, Copy) ,

        CONSTRAINT ArtistFK FOREIGN KEY(ArtistID) REFERENCES ARTIST (ArtistID)
                ON DELETE NO ACTION
                ON UPDATE NO ACTION
);

CREATE TABLE CUSTOMER (

        CustomerID          int             NOT NULL IDENTITY (1000, 1) ,
        Name                char (25)       NOT NULL,
        Street              char (30)       NULL,
        City                char (35)       NULL,
        State               char (2)        NULL,
        ZipPostalCode       char (9)        NULL,
        Country             varchar (50)    NULL,
        AreaCode            char (3)        NULL,
        PhoneNumber         char (8)        NULL,
        Email               char (100)      NULL,

        CONSTRAINT CustomerPK PRIMARY KEY (CustomerID) ,
        CONSTRAINT EmailAK1 UNIQUE (Email)

);

CREATE TABLE [TRANSACTION] (

        TransactionID       int             NOT NULL IDENTITY (100, 1) ,
        DateAquired         datetime        NOT NULL,
        AcquisitionPrice    numeric (8 , 2) NOT NULL,
        PurchaseDate        datetime        NULL,
        SalesPrice          numeric (8 , 2) NULL,
        AskingPrice         numeric (8 , 2) NULL,
        CustomerID          int             NULL,
        WorkID              int             NOT NULL,
```

Figure 7-9	**Continued**

```
        CONSTRAINT          TransactionPK  PRIMARY  KEY  (TransactionID) ,

        CONSTRAINT TransactionWorkFK  FOREIGN  KEY  (WorkID)  REFERENCES  WORK  (W
                ON  UPDATE  NO  ACTION
                ON  DELETE  NO  ACTION,

        CONSTRAINT  TransactionCustomerFK
                FOREIGN  KEY  (CustomerID)  REFERENCES  CUSTOMER  (CustomerID)
                ON  UPDATE  NO  ACTION
                ON  DELETE  NO  ACTION,

        CONSTRAINT          SalesPriceRange  CHECK
                            ( (SalesPrice > 1000)  AND  (SalesPrice  <=200000) ) ,
        CONSTRAINT          ValidTransDate  CHECK  (PurchaseDate  => DateAcquired)
);

CREATE TABLE CUSTOMER_ARTIST_INT (

        ArtistID            int              NOT NULL,
        CustomerID          int              NOT NULL,

        CONSTRAINT  CustomerArtistPK  PRIMARY  KEY  (ArtistID, CustomerID) ,

        CONSTRAINT  Customer_Int_ArtistFK
                FOREIGN  KEY  (ArtistID)  REFERENCES  ARTIST  (ArtistID)
                    ON UPDATE NO ACTION
                    ON DELETE CASCADE,
        CONSTRAINT  Customer_Artist_Int_CustomerFK
        FOREIGN  KEY  (CustomerID)  REFERENCES  CUSTOMER  (CustomerID)
                    ON  UPDATE  NO  ACTION
                    ON  DELETE  CASCADE
);
```

B T W

Every now and then, the DBMS might generate bizarre syntax-error messages. For example, suppose you define a table with the name ORDER. When you submit the statement SELECT * FROM ORDER, you will get very strange messages back from the DBMS.

If you do receive odd messages back from statements that you know are coded correctly, think about reserved words. If a term might be reserved, enclose it in brackets and see what happens when you submit it to the DBMS. No harm is done by enclosing SQL terms in brackets.

If you want to torture your DBMS, you can submit queries like SELECT [Select] FROM [FROM] WHERE [WHERE] < [NOT FIVE];. Most likely, you have better ways to spend your time, however. Without a doubt, the DBMS has better ways to spend its time!

Running the SQL statements in Figure 7-9 with your DBMS will generate all of the tables, relationships, and constraints for the View Ridge database. Figure 7-10 shows the relationships generated in SQL Server.

It is far easier to create these tables and relationships in SQL code than by using graphical tools. It is a nightmare to generate the CHECK constraint using graphical tools. The first problem is to find the proper window for creating the constraint. Once you find that window, you must enter the constraint correctly into the DBMS. For example,

Figure 7-10   SQL Server Relationship Diagram after Running SQL File in Figure 7-9

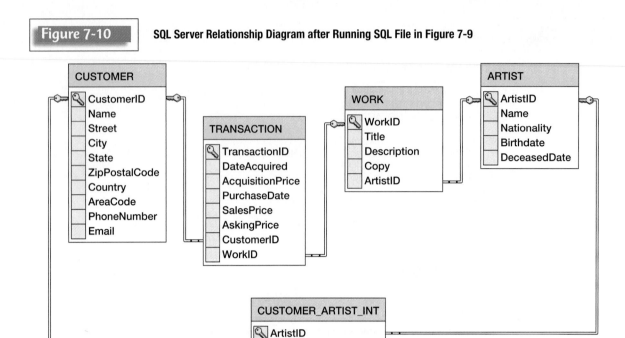

Figure 7-11

Graphical Tool to Define CHECK Constraint

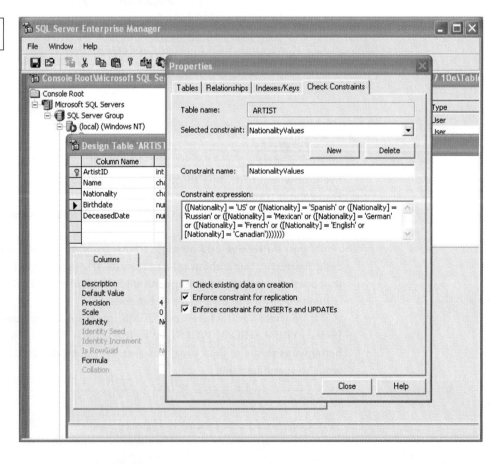

Figure 7-11 shows the coding required by SQL Server for the NationalityValues constraint. As you can see, SQL is much easier than entering the horrible string in Figure 7-11. Furthermore, once you learn SQL DDL, you can use that knowledge with DB2, MySQL, SQL Server, Oracle, or any other DBMS.

ALTER Statement

The ALTER statement is a SQL DDL statement that is used to change the structure of an existing table. It can be used to add, remove, or change columns. It also can be used to add or remove constraints.

Adding and Dropping Columns

The following statement will add a column named MyColumn to the CUSTOMER table:

ALTER TABLE CUSTOMER ADD MyColumn Char(5) NULL;

You can drop an existing column with the statement:

ALTER TABLE CUSTOMER DROP COLUMN MyColumn;

Note the asymmetry in syntax; the keyword COLUMN is used with DROP but not with ADD. You can use ALTER to change column properties as well, as you will see in the next three chapters.

Adding and Dropping Constraints

ALTER can be used to add a constraint as follows:

ALTER TABLE CUSTOMER ADD CONSTRAINT MyConstraint CHECK

    ([Name] NOT IN ('Robert No Pay'));

Notice that Name is enclosed in brackets to avoid confusion with the DBMS keyword *Name*. You can also use ALTER to DROP a constraint:

ALTER TABLE CUSTOMER DROP CONSTRAINT MyConstraint;

B T W

The ALTER statement can be used to add or drop any of the SQL constraints. You can use it to create primary keys and alternate keys, to set null status, to create referential integrity constraints, and to create data constraints. In fact, another SQL coding style uses CREATE TABLE only to declare the table's columns; all constraints are added using ALTER. We do not use that style in this text, but be aware that it does exist and that your employer might require it.

Removing Tables

It is very easy to remove a table in SQL. In fact, it is far too easy. The following statement will drop the TRANSACTION table *and all of its data:*

DROP TABLE [TRANSACTION];

Because this simple statement drops the table and all of its data, be very careful when using it. Do not code this statement on the wrong table!

The DBMS will not drop a table that is the parent in a FOREIGN KEY constraint. It will not do so even if there are no children or even if you have coded DELETE CASCADE. Instead, to drop such a table, you must first either drop the foreign key constraint or drop the child table. Then you can delete the parent table. As mentioned earlier, parent tables must be first in and last out.

The following statements are needed to drop the CUSTOMER table:

DROP TABLE CUSTOMER_ARTIST_INT;

DROP TABLE [TRANSACTION];

DROP TABLE CUSTOMER;

Alternatively, you could drop CUSTOMER with:

ALTER TABLE CUSTOMER_ARTIST_INT

 DROP CONSTRAINT Customer_Artist_Int_CustomerFK;

ALTER TABLE [TRANSACTION]

 DROP CONSTRAINT TransactionCustomerFK;

DROP TABLE CUSTOMER;

 # SQL DML

At this point, you have learned how to query tables using SQL SELECT statements, and you know how to create, alter, and drop tables, columns, and constraints. You do not yet know, however, how to use SQL to insert, modify, and delete data. We consider those statements next.

SQL INSERT Using Column Names

The SQL INSERT command has a number of different options. The standard version is to name the table, name the columns for which you have data, and then list the data in the following format:

INSERT INTO ARTIST ([Name], Nationality, Birthdate, DeceasedDate)

 VALUES ('Tamayo', 'Mexican', 1927, 1998);

Note that both column names and values are enclosed in parentheses. If you are providing data for all of the columns, if that data is in the same order as the columns in the table, and if you have no surrogate keys, then you can omit the column list.

 You need not provide the values in the same order as the columns in the table. If for some reason you want to provide Nationality before Name, you can switch the name of the column and the data value as shown in the following example:

INSERT INTO ARTIST (Nationality, [Name], DeceasedDate, Birthdate)

 VALUES ('Mexican', 'Tamayo',1998, 1927);

If you have partial values, just code the names of the columns for which you have data. For example, if you have only Name and Nationality, code:

INSERT INTO ARTIST ([Name], Nationality) VALUES ('Tamayo', 'Mexican');

You must, of course, have values for all NOT NULL columns.

Bulk INSERT

One of the most often used forms of INSERT uses a SQL SELECT statement to provide values. Suppose you have the names, nationalities, and birth dates of a number of artists in a table named IMPORTED_ARTIST. In this case, you can add those data to the ARTIST table with the following statement:

INSERT INTO ARTIST ([Name], Nationality, Birthdate)

    SELECT [Name], Nationality, Birthdate

    FROM IMPORTED_ARTIST;

Note that the keyword VALUES is not used with this form of insert.

This syntax should seem familiar. We used it for normalization and denormalization examples in Chapters 3 and 4.

SQL UPDATE Command

The SQL UPDATE command changes values of existing rows. The following statement will change the value of City to 'New York City' for the customer whose CustomerID is 1000:

UPDATE	**CUSTOMER**
SET	**City = 'New York City'**
WHERE	**CustomerID = 1000;**

To change the value of both City and State, code the SQL statement:

UPDATE	**CUSTOMER**
SET	**City = 'New York City', State = 'NY'**
WHERE	**CustomerID = 1000;**

The DBMS will enforce all referential integrity constraints when processing UPDATE commands. For the View Ridge database, all keys are surrogate keys, but for tables with data keys, the DBMS will cascade or disallow (NO ACTION) updates according to the specification in the FOREIGN KEY constraint. Also, if there is a FOREIGN KEY constraint, the DBMS will enforce the referential integrity constraint on updates to a foreign key.

Bulk Updates

It is quite easy to make bulk updates with the SQL UPDATE command. It is so easy, in fact, that it is dangerous. The statement:

UPDATE	**CUSTOMER**
SET	**City = 'New York City';**

will change the value of City for every row of the CUSTOMER table. If we had intended to change just the value for customer 1000, we would have an unhappy result—every customer would have the value 'New York City'. You can perform bulk updates using a WHERE clause that finds multiple rows. If, for example, we wanted to change the AreaCode for every customer who lives in Denver, we would code:

UPDATE	**CUSTOMER**
SET	**AreaCode = '303'**
WHERE	**City = 'Denver';**

Updating Using Values from Other Tables

The SQL UPDATE command can set a column equal to the value of a column in a different table. The View Ridge database has no appropriate example for this operation, so suppose instead that we have a table named TAX_TABLE with columns (Tax, City) where Tax is the appropriate tax rate for the City.

Now suppose we have a table named PURCHASE_ORDER that includes the columns TaxRate and City. We can update all rows for purchase orders in the city of Bodega Bay with the following SQL statement:

```
UPDATE       PURCHASE_ORDER

SET          TaxRate =

     (SELECT Tax from TAX_TABLE WHERE TAX_TABLE.City = 'Bodega Bay')

WHERE        PURCHASE_ORDER.City = 'Bodega Bay';
```

More likely, we want to update the value of the tax rate for a purchase order without specifying the city. Say we want to update the TaxRate for purchase order number 1000. In that case, we use the slightly more complex SQL statement:

```
UPDATE       PURCHASE_ORDER

SET          TaxRate =

             (SELECT Tax from TAX_TABLE

             WHERE TAX_TABLE.City = PURCHASE_ORDER.City)

WHERE        PURCHASE_ORDER.Number = 1000;
```

SQL SELECT statements can be combined with UPDATE statements in many different ways. We need to move on to other topics, but try these and other variations of UPDATE on your own.

SQL DELETE Statement

The SQL DELETE statement also is quite easy to use. The following SQL statement will delete the row for a customer with a CustomerID of 1000:

```
DELETE       FROM CUSTOMER

WHERE        CustomerID = 1000;
```

Of course, if you omit the WHERE clause, you will delete every customer row, so be careful with this command as well.

The DBMS will enforce all referential integrity constraints when processing DELETE commands. For example, in the View Ridge database, you will be unable to delete a CUSTOMER row if that row has any TRANSACTION children. Further, if a row with no TRANSACTION children is deleted, any existing CUSTOMER_ARTIST_INT children will be deleted as well. This latter action occurs because of the CASCADE DELETE specification on the relationship between CUSTOMER and CUSTOMER_ARTIST_INT.

New Forms of Join

You learned how to perform joins in Chapter 2. Here we extend that discussion to show a different join syntax and to address ways of processing joins on tables with null values.

> ### B T W
>
> **For the remainder of the text, we will use the sample View Ridge data in Figure 7-12. The surrogate keys are not sequential in this data set because this database has been processed; records for missing surrogate key values have been deleted. You can download this data from the text's Web site at www.prenhall.com/kroenke. If you are loading it into Access or SQL Server, follow the instructions carefully; extra steps will be required to force the example values into the surrogate keys.**

JOIN ON Syntax

In Chapter 2, you learned to code joins using the following syntax:

```
SELECT      *
FROM        ARTIST, WORK
WHERE       ARTIST.ArtistID = WORK.ArtistID;
```

Another way to code this same join is:

```
SELECT      *
FROM        ARTIST JOIN WORK
    ON      ARTIST.ArtistID = WORK.ArtistID;
```

These two joins are equivalent. Some people think that the second format is easier to understand than the first.

You can use this alternate format for joins of three or more tables, as well. If, for example, you want to obtain a list of the names of customers and the names of the artists in which they are interested, code:

```
SELECT      CUSTOMER.Name, ARTIST.Name
FROM        CUSTOMER JOIN CUSTOMER_ARTIST_INT
    ON      CUSTOMER.CustomerID = CUSTOMER_ARTIST_INT.CustomerID
            JOIN ARTIST
                ON CUSTOMER_ARTIST_INT.ArtistID = ARTIST.ArtistID;
```

You can make that statement even simpler by using table aliases:

```
SELECT      C.Name, A.Name
FROM        CUSTOMER AS C JOIN CUSTOMER_ARTIST_INT AS CI
    ON      C.CustomerID = CI.CustomerID
            JOIN ARTIST AS A
                ON CI.ArtistID = A.ArtistID;
```

Figure 7-12

Sample View Ridge Data
(a) Sample ARTIST Data; (b) Sample WORK Data; (c) Sample TRANSACTION Data;
(d) Sample CUSTOMER Data; and (e) Sample CUSTOMER_ARTIST_INT Data

ArtistID	Name	Nationality	Birthdate	DeceasedDate
3	Miro	Spanish	1870	1950
4	Kandinsky	Russian	1854	1900
5	Frings	US	1950	<NULL>
6	Klee	German	1900	<NULL>
8	Moos	US	<NULL>	<NULL>
14	Tobey	US	<NULL>	<NULL>
15	Matisse	French	<NULL>	<NULL>
16	Chagall	French	<NULL>	<NULL>

(a)

TransactionID	DateAcquired	AcquisitionPrice
100	2/27/1974	8750
101	7/17/1989	28900
121	11/17/1989	4500
122	2/27/1999	8000
124	4/7/2001	38700
129	11/21/2001	6750
130	11/21/2001	21500
135	7/17/2002	47000

(c)

CustomerID	Name	Street	City	State	ZipPostalCode
1000	Jeffrey Janes	123 W. Elm St	Renton	WA	98123
1001	David Smith	813 Tumbleweed L	Loveland	CO	80345
1015	Tiffany Twilight	88 - First Avenue	Langley	WA	98114
1033	Fred Smathers	10899 - 88th Ave	Bainbridge Island	WA	98108
1034	Mary Beth Frederic	25 South Lafayette	Denver	CO	80210
1036	Selma Warning	205 Burnaby	Vancouver	BC	V0N 1B4
1037	Susan Wu	105 Locust Ave	Atlanta	GA	23224
1040	Donald G. Gray	55 Bodega Ave	Bodega Bay	CA	92114
1041	Lynda Johnson	117 C Street	Washington	DC	11345
1051	Chris Wilkens	87 Highland Drive	Olympia	WA	98008

(d)

Outer Joins

The join:

SELECT   C.Name, T.SalesPrice

FROM   CUSTOMER C JOIN [TRANSACTION] T

    ON   C.CustomerID = T.CustomerID;

will produce the table in Figure 7-13. This result is correct, but it only shows seven of the ten rows in the CUSTOMER table. What happened to the other three customers?

WorkID	Title	Description	Copy	ArtistID
505	Mystic Fabric	One of the only pr	99/135	14
506	Mi Vida	Very black, but ve	7/100	3
507	Slow Embers	From the artist's c	HC	14
525	Mystic Fabric	Some water dama	105/135	14
530	Northwest by Night	Wonderful, moody	37/50	16

(b)

PurchaseDate	SalesPrice	AskingPrice	CustomerID	WorkID
3/18/1974	18500	20000	1015	505
10/14/1989	46700	47000	1001	505
11/21/2000	9750	10000	1040	525
3/15/2000	17500	17500	1036	525
8/17/2001	73500	75000	1036	506
3/18/2002	14500	15000	1040	507
<NULL>	<NULL>	<NULL>	<NULL>	525
10/2/2002	71500	72500	1015	530

(c continued)

ArtistID	CustomerID
3	1036
5	1015
5	1034
5	1041
5	1051
8	1034
8	1041
14	1001
14	1015
14	1033
14	1034
14	1036
14	1040
14	1041
14	1051
16	1015

(e)

Country	AreaCode	PhoneNumber	Email
USA	206	555-1345	Customer1000@somewhere.com
USA	303	555-5434	Customer1001@somewhere.com
USA	206	555-1000	Customer1015@somewhere.com
USA	206	555-1234	Customer1033@somewhere.com
USA	303	555-1000	Customer1034@somewhere.com
Canada	253	555-1234	Customer1036@somewhere.com
USA	721	555-1234	Customer1037@somewhere.com
USA	705	555-1234	Customer1040@somewhere.com
USA	703	555-1000	<NULL>
USA	206	555-1234	<NULL>

(d continued)

Figure 7-13

Result of Join of
CUSTOMER and
TRANSACTION

Name	SalesPrice
Tiffany Twilight	18500.00
David Smith	46700.00
Donald G. Gray	9750.00
Selma Warning	17500.00
Selma Warning	73500.00
Donald G. Gray	14500.00
Tiffany Twilight	71500.00

Look closely at the data in Figure 7-13 and you will see that the customers that do not appear are customers who never made a purchase at the gallery. The primary key value of these three customers does not match any foreign key value in the TRANSACTION table. Because they have no match, they do not appear in the result of this join.

We can cause all of the rows in CUSTOMER to appear using what is called an **outer join.** The syntax is as follows:

> SELECT   C.Name, T.SalesPrice
>
> FROM   CUSTOMER C LEFT JOIN [TRANSACTION] T
>
> ON   C.CustomerID = T.CustomerID;

The results are shown in Figure 7-14. Notice that the value of SalesPrice is NULL for all customers who have not made purchases.

Outer joins can be either from the left or the right. If the outer join is from the left, then all of the rows on the table on the left (or first table in the join) will be included in the result. If the outer join is on the right, then all rows on the table on the right (or second in the join statement) will be included in the result.

Joins that are not outer joins are called **inner joins.** All of the joins we have presented up to this point have been inner joins, though we did not use that term.

Outer joins can be combined to any level, just as inner joins can. The following SQL statement will obtain a list of every customer and the artists in which they have an interest.

> SELECT   C.[Name] Customer, A.[Name] Artist
>
> FROM   CUSTOMER C LEFT JOIN CUSTOMER_ARTIST_INT CI
>
> ON   C.CustomerID = CI.CustomerID
>
> LEFT JOIN ARTIST A
>
> ON CI.ArtistID = A.ArtistID;

The result is shown in Figure 7-15.

Figure 7-14

Result of LEFT OUTER Join

Name	SalesPrice
Jeffrey Janes	NULL
David Smith	46700.00
Tiffany Twilight	18500.00
Tiffany Twilight	71500.00
Fred Smathers	NULL
Mary Beth Frederickson	NULL
Selma Warning	17500.00
Selma Warning	73500.00
Susan Wu	NULL
Donald G. Gray	9750.00
Donald G. Gray	14500.00
Lynda Johnson	NULL
Chris Wilkens	NULL

Figure 7-15

Result of Nested LEFT OUTER Joins

Customer	Name
Chris Wilkens	Frings
Chris Wilkens	Tobey
David Smith	Tobey
Donald G. Gray	Tobey
Fred Smathers	Tobey
Jeffrey Janes	NULL
Lynda Johnson	Frings
Lynda Johnson	Moos
Lynda Johnson	Tobey
Mary Beth Frederickson	Frings
Mary Beth Frederickson	Moos
Mary Beth Frederickson	Tobey
Selma Warning	Miro
Selma Warning	Tobey
Susan Wu	NULL
Tiffany Twilight	Frings
Tiffany Twilight	Tobey
Tiffany Twilight	Chagall

B T W

It is easy to forget that inner joins will drop nonmatching rows. Some years ago, I had a very large organization as a consulting client. My client had a budgetary-planning application that included a long sequence of complicated SQL statements. One of the joins in that sequence was an inner join that should have been an outer join. As a result, some 3,000 employees dropped out of the budgetary calculations. The mistake was discovered only months later when the actual salary expense exceeded the budget salary expense by a large margin. The mistake was an embarrassment all the way to the Board of Directors.

If we leave either LEFT out of the expression, the null rows will not appear. Also, to check your understanding, code this statement using RIGHT joins and explain the result.

 ## Using SQL Views

A SQL view is a virtual table that is constructed from other tables or views. A view has no data of its own, but obtains data from tables or other views. Views are constructed from SQL SELECT statements; the only limitation on such statements is that they may not contain an ORDER BY clause.[1] The sort order must be provided by the SELECT statement that processes the view.

B T W

Views are a standard and popular SQL-92 construct. Access, however, does not support them. Instead, in Access you can create a *query*, name it, and then save it. You can then process the query in the same ways that we process views in the following discussion.

SQL Server, Oracle, and DB2 all support views, and they are an important structure with many uses. Do not conclude from Access's lack of support that views are unimportant. Read on, and, if possible, use either SQL Server or Oracle to process the statements in this section.

The following statement defines a view named CustomerNameView on the CUSTOMER table:

CREATE VIEW   **CustomerNameView AS**

    SELECT   **[Name] AS CustomerName**

    FROM   **CUSTOMER;**

B T W

Oracle processes the CREATE VIEW statements as written here without difficulty. For SQL Server, however, you must remove the semicolon from the CREATE VIEW statement. I have no idea why SQL Server accepts a semicolon for all other SQL statements but will not accept one for SQL statements that create views. In any case, we will continue to show the semicolon because that is the SQL-92 standard. Be aware, however, that you must remove the semicolon when writing CREATE VIEW statements for SQL Server.

Once the view is created, it can be used in the FROM clause of SELECT statements just like a table. The following obtains a list of customer names in sorted order:

SELECT   *

FROM   **CustomerNameView**

ORDER BY   **CustomerName;**

The result for the sample data in Figure 7-12 is shown in Figure 7-16. Note that the number of columns returned depends on the number of columns in the view, not on the number of columns in the underlying table. In this example, SELECT * produces just one column because the view has just one column.

---

[1]This limitation appears in the SQL-92 standard. Oracle allows views to include ORDER BY, and SQL Server will allow ORDER BY in very limited circumstances.

Figure 7-16

**CustomerNameView
Results**

CustomerName
Chris Wilkens
David Smith
Donald G. Gray
Fred Smathers
Jeffrey Janes
Lynda Johnson
Mary Beth Frederickson
Selma Warning
Susan Wu
Tiffany Twilight

Also notice that the column Name in the CUSTOMER table has been renamed to CustomerName in the view. Because of this, the ORDER BY phrase in the SELECT statement uses CustomerName and not Name. Also, the DBMS uses the label CustomerName when producing results.

Figure 7-17 lists the uses for views. They can hide columns or rows. They also can be used to display the results of computed columns, to hide complicated SQL syntax, and to layer the use of built-in functions to create results that are not possible with a single SQL statement. Additionally, views can provide an alias for table names and thus hide the true table names from applications and users. Views also are used to assign different processing permissions and different triggers to different views of the same table. We will show examples for each of these.

Using Views to Hide Columns and Rows

Views can be used to hide columns to simplify results or to prevent the display of sensitive data. For example, suppose the users at View Ridge want a simplified list of customers that has just names and phone numbers. The following statement defines a view, BasicCustomerData, that will produce that list:

CREATE VIEW BasicCustomerData AS

    SELECT [Name], AreaCode, PhoneNumber

    FROM CUSTOMER;

Figure 7-17

Uses for Views

- Hide columns or rows
- Display results of computations
- Hide complicated SQL syntax
- Layer built-in functions
- Provide level of isolation between table data and users' view of data
- Assign different processing permissions to different views of the same table
- Assign different triggers to different views of the same table

Figure 7-18

BasicCustomerData
Results

Name	AreaCode	PhoneNumber
Jeffrey Janes	206	555-1345
David Smith	303	555-5434
Tiffany Twilight	206	555-1000
Fred Smathers	206	555-1234
Mary Beth Frederickson	303	555-1000
Selma Warning	253	555-1234
Susan Wu	721	555-1234
Donald G. Gray	705	555-1234
Lynda Johnson	703	555-1000
Chris Wilkens	206	555-1234

The results of a SELECT * on this table are shown in Figure 7-18.

If the management of the gallery wants to hide the columns AcquisitionPrice and SalesPrice in TRANSACTION, they can define a view that does not include those columns. One use for such a view is to populate a Web page.

Views also can hide rows by providing a WHERE clause in the view definition. The next SQL statement defines a view of customer name and phone data for all customers with an address in Washington:

CREATE VIEW BasicCustomerData_WA AS

    SELECT Name, AreaCode, PhoneNumber

    FROM CUSTOMER

    WHERE State = 'WA';

Figure 7-19 shows the contents of this view. As desired, only customers who live in Washington are shown in this view. This limitation is not obvious from the results because State is not included in the view. This characteristic is good or bad, depending on the use of the view. It is good if this view is used in a setting in which only Washington customers matter; it is bad if the view miscommunicates that these customers are the only View Ridge customers.

Using Views to Display Results of Computed Columns

Another purpose of views is to show the results of computed columns without requiring the user to enter the computation expression. For example, the following view combines the AreaCode and PhoneNumber columns and formats the result:

CREATE VIEW CustomerPhone AS

    SELECT Name, ('(' + AreaCode + ') ' + PhoneNumber) As Phone

    FROM CUSTOMER;

Figure 7-19

BasicCustomerData_WA
Results

Name	AreaCode	PhoneNumber
Jeffrey Janes	206	555-1345
Tiffany Twilight	206	555-1000
Fred Smathers	206	555-1234
Chris Wilkens	206	555-1234

Figure 7-20

CustomerPhone
Results

Name	Phone
Jeffrey Janes	(206) 555-1345
David Smith	(303) 555-5434
Tiffany Twilight	(206) 555-1000
Fred Smathers	(206) 555-1234
Mary Beth Frederickson	(303) 555-1000
Selma Warning	(253) 555-1234
Susan Wu	(721) 555-1234
Donald G. Gray	(705) 555-1234
Lynda Johnson	(703) 555-1000
Chris Wilkens	(206) 555-1234

When the view user enters:

SELECT   *

FROM   **CustomerPhone;**

the results will be displayed as in Figure 7-20.[2] Placing computations in views has two major advantages. First, it saves users from having to know or remember how to write an expression to get the results they want. Second, it ensures consistent results. If each developer who uses a computation writes his or her own SQL expression, that developer may write it differently and obtain inconsistent results.

Using Views to Hide Complicated SQL Syntax

Another use of views is to hide complicated SQL syntax. Using a view, developers need not enter a complex SQL statement when they want a particular result. Also, such views give the benefits of complicated SQL statements to developers who do not know how to write such statements. This use of views also ensures consistency.

For example, suppose that the View Ridge salespeople want to see which customers are interested in which artists. To display these interests, two joins are necessary: one to join CUSTOMER to CUSTOMER_ARTIST_INT and another to join that result to ARTIST. The following SQL statement defines a view that constructs these joins:

CREATE VIEW CustomerInterests AS

> **SELECT**   **C.Name as Customer, A.Name as Artist**
>
> **FROM**   **CUSTOMER C**
>
> **JOIN**   **CUSTOMER_ARTIST_INT CI**
>
>   **ON C.CustomerID = CI.CustomerID**
>
>   **JOIN ARTIST A**
>
>   **ON CI.ArtistID = A.ArtistID;**

Notice the aliasing of C.Name to Customer and A.Name to Artist. These column aliases are *not* optional; without them, the resulting table has two columns with the name

---

[2]In Oracle, the plus sign (+) must be replaced by double vertical bars (||) for string concatenation.

Name. The DBMS would not be able to distinguish one Name from the other and will generate an error when an attempt is made to create such a view.

This is a complicated SQL statement to write, but once the view is created the result of this statement can be obtained with a simple SELECT statement. For example, the following statement shows the results sorted by Customer:

```
SELECT          *

FROM            CustomerInterests

ORDER BY        Customer;
```

Figure 7-21 displays the result. Clearly, using the view is much simpler than constructing the join syntax. Even developers who know SQL well will appreciate having a simpler view with which to work.

Layering Built-in Functions

Recall from Chapter 2 that you cannot use a computation or a built-in function as part of a WHERE clause. You can, however, construct a view that computes a variable and then write SQL on that view that uses the computed variable in a WHERE clause. To understand this, consider the view definition:

```
CREATE VIEW ArtistWorkNet AS

    SELECT      W.WorkID, Name, Title, Copy, AcquisitionPrice,
                    SalesPrice, (SalesPrice – AcquisitionPrice) AS NetPrice

    FROM        [TRANSACTION] T

    JOIN        WORK W

                ON T.WorkID = W .WorkID

                JOIN ARTIST A

                    ON W.ArtistID = A.ArtistID;
```

This view joins TRANSACTION, WORK, and ARTIST and creates the computed column NetPrice.

Now, we can use NetPrice in a WHERE clause as follows:

```
SELECT      Name, NetPrice

FROM        ArtistWorkNet

WHERE       NetPrice > 10000;
```

Here we are using the result of a computation in a WHERE clause, something that is not allowed in a single SQL statement. Figure 7-22 shows the result.

Such layering can be continued over many levels. We can define another view with another computation on the computation in the first view. For example, consider:

```
CREATE VIEW WorkNet as

    SELECT      Name, Title, Copy, sum(NetPrice)as TotalNet

    FROM        ArtistWorkNet

    GROUP BY    Name, Title, Copy;
```

Figure 7-21

**CustomerInterests
Results**

Customer	Artist
Chris Wilkens	Frings
Chris Wilkens	Tobey
David Smith	Tobey
Donald G. Gray	Tobey
Fred Smathers	Tobey
Lynda Johnson	Tobey
Lynda Johnson	Moos
Lynda Johnson	Frings
Mary Beth Frederickson	Frings
Mary Beth Frederickson	Moos
Mary Beth Frederickson	Tobey
Selma Warning	Tobey
Selma Warning	Miro
Tiffany Twilight	Chagall
Tiffany Twilight	Frings
Tiffany Twilight	Tobey

Now we can use TotalNet in a WHERE clause on the WorkNet view as follows:

SELECT   *

FROM   **WorkNet**

WHERE   **TotalNet < 25000;**

In this SELECT, we are using a view on a view and a built-in function on a computed variable in the WHERE clause. The results are shown in Figure 7-23.

Using Views for Isolation, Multiple Permissions, and Multiple Triggers

Views have three other important uses. For one, they can isolate source data tables from application code. To see how, suppose we define the view:

CREATE VIEW   **CustomerTable1 AS**

    SELECT   *

      FROM   **CUSTOMER;**

Figure 7-22

**Results when Using
NetPrice in a WHERE
Clause**

Name	NetPrice
Tobey	17800.00
Miro	34800.00
Tobey	24500.00

Figure 7-23

Result of Query on WorkNet View

Name	Title	Copy	TotalNet
Chagall	Northwest by Night	37/50	14750.00
Tobey	Mystic Fabric	105/135	7750.00
Tobey	Slow Embers	HC	24500.00

This view assigns the alias CustomerTable1 to the CUSTOMER table. If all application code uses the CustomerTable1 in SQL statements, then the true source of the data is hidden from application programmers.

Such table isolation provides flexibility to the database administration staff. For example, suppose that at some future date the source of customer data is changed to a different table (perhaps one that is imported from a different database) named NEW_CUSTOMER. In this situation, all the database administrator needs to do is redefine CustomerTable1 as follows:

CREATE VIEW   **CustomerTable1 AS**

    SELECT   *

    FROM   **NEW_CUSTOMER;**

All of the application code that uses CustomerTable1 will now run on the new data source without any problem.

Another use for views is to give different sets of processing permissions to the same table. We will discuss security in more detail in Chapters 9 through 11, but for now, understand that it is possible to limit insert, update, delete, and read permissions on tables and views.

For example, an organization might define a view of CUSTOMER called CustomerRead with read only permissions on CUSTOMER and a second view of CUSTOMER called CustomerUpdate with both read and update permissions. Applications that need not update the customer data would work with CustomerRead, whereas those that need to update this data would work with CustomerUpdate.

A last reason for using views is to enable the definition of multiple sets of triggers on the same source data. This technique is commonly used for enforcing O-M and M-M relationships. In this case, one view has a set of triggers that prohibits the deletion of a required child and another view has a set of triggers that deletes a required child as well as the parent. The views are assigned to different applications, depending on the authority of those applications.

Updating Views

Some views can be updated, others cannot. The rules by which this is determined are both complicated and dependent on the DBMS in use. To understand why this is so, consider the following two update requests on views defined in the last section:

UPDATE   **CustomerTable1**

SET   **Email = 'NewEmailAddress@somewhere.com'**

WHERE   **CustomerID = 1000;**

and

UPDATE   **WorkNet**

SET   **TotalNet = 23000**

WHERE   **Artist = 'Tobey';**

Figure 7-24

Guidelines for
Updating Views

> **Updateable Views:**
> • View based on a single table with no computed columns and all
>   non-null columns present in the view
> • View based on any number of tables, with or without computed
>   columns, and INSTEAD OF trigger defined for the view
>
> **Possibly Updateable Views:**
> • Based on a single table, primary key in view, some required
>   columns missing from view, update and delete may be allowed.
>   Insert is not allowed.
> • Based on multiple tables, updates may be allowed on the most
>   subordinate table in the view if rows of that table can be uniquely
>   identified.

The first request can be processed without problem because CustomerTable1 is just an alias for the CUSTOMER table. The second update makes no sense at all. TotalNet is a sum of a computed column. Nowhere in the database is there any such column to be updated.

Figure 7-24 shows general guidelines to determine if a view is updatable. Again, the specifics depend on the DBMS product in use. In general, the DBMS must be able to associate the column(s) to be updated with a particular row in a particular table. A way to approach this question is to ask yourself, "What would I do if I were the DBMS and I were asked to update this view? Would the request make sense, and if so, do I have sufficient data to make the update?" Clearly, if the entire table is present and there are no computed columns, the view is updatable. Also, the DBMS will mark the view as updatable if it has an INSTEAD OF trigger defined for it, as described later.

If any of the required columns are missing, the view clearly cannot be used for inserts. It may be used for updates and deletes, however, as long as the primary key (or, for some DBMS products, a candidate key) is present in the view. Multitable views may be updatable on the most subordinate table. Again, this can only be done if the primary key or candidate key for that table is in the view.

We will revisit this topic for Oracle in Chapter 10 and for SQL Server in Chapter 11.

Embedding SQL in Program Code

SQL statements can be embedded in application programs, triggers, and stored procedures. Before we discuss those subjects, however, we need to explain the placement of SQL statements in program code.

Two problems must be solved. First, some means of assigning the results of SQL statements to program variables must be available. Many different techniques are used. Some involve object-oriented programs, as you will learn in Chapters 12, 13, and 14; others are simpler. For example, in PL/SQL, Oracle's native language, the following statement assigns the count of the number of rows in the CUSTOMER table to the variable named *rowCount*:

```
SELECT      Count(*) into rowcount
FROM        CUSTOMER;
```

A similar statement in SQL Server is:

```
SELECT      @rowcount = Count(*)
FROM        CUSTOMER
```

In either case, the execution of this code will place the number of rows in CUSTOMER into the program variable *rowcount* or *@rowcount*.

The second problem to solve concerns a paradigm mismatch between SQL and application programming languages. SQL is table oriented; SQL SELECT statements start with one or more tables and produce a table as output. Programs, on the other hand, start with one or more variables, manipulate them, and store the result in a variable. Because of this difference, a statement like the following makes no sense:

SELECT   Name into custName

FROM   CUSTOMER;

If there are 100 rows in the CUSTOMER table, there will be 100 values of Name. The program variable custName, however, is expecting to receive just one value.

To avoid this problem, the results of SQL statements are treated as pseudofiles. When a SQL statement returns a set of rows, a **cursor,** or pointer to a particular row is established. The application program can then place the cursor on the first, last, or some other row of the SQL statement output. With the cursor placed, values of columns for that row can be assigned to program variables. When the application is finished with a particular row, it moves the cursor to the next, prior, or some other row, and continues processing.

The typical pattern is as follows:

Open SQL (SELECT * FROM CUSTOMER);

Move cursor to first row;

    While cursor not past end of result {

        Set custName = Name;

        . . . other statements . . .

        Advance cursor to next row;

    };

    . . . continue processing . . .

In this way, the rows of a SQL SELECT are processed one at a time.

You will see many examples of these techniques and others like them in the chapters that follow. For now, try to gain an intuitive understanding of how SQL is embedded in program code.

Using Triggers

A **trigger** is a stored program that is executed by the DBMS whenever a specified event occurs. Triggers for Oracle are written in Java or in a propriety language called **PL/SQL (Programming Language for SQL).** SQL Server triggers are written in a propriety language called **Transact-SQL,** or **T-SQL.** With the advent of the SQL Server 2005 version of SQL Server, they can be written in common language runtime languages such as Visual Basic .NET, C#, and C++. In this chapter, we will discuss triggers in a generic manner without considering the particulars of those languages. We will discuss triggers written in PL/SQL and T-SQL in Chapters 10 and 11, respectively.

A trigger is attached to a table or a view. A table or a view may have many triggers, but a trigger is associated with just one table or view.

A trigger is invoked by an insert, update, or delete request on the table or view to which it is attached. Oracle supports three kinds of triggers: BEFORE, INSTEAD OF, and AFTER. As you would expect, BEFORE triggers are executed before the DBMS processes the insert, update, or delete request. INSTEAD OF triggers are executed in place of any DBMS processing of the insert, update, or delete request. AFTER triggers are executed after the insert, update, or delete request has been processed. Altogether, nine trigger types are possible: BEFORE (Insert, Update, Delete); INSTEAD OF (Insert, Update, Delete); and AFTER (Insert, Update, Delete).

SQL Server supports only INSTEAD OF and AFTER triggers, thus it supports only six trigger types. Other DBMS products support triggers differently. See the documentation of your product to determine which trigger types it supports.

When a trigger is invoked, the DBMS makes the data involved in the requested action available to the trigger code. For an insert, the DBMS will supply the values of columns for the row that is being inserted. For deletions, the DBMS will supply the values of columns for the row that is being deleted. For updates, it will supply both the old and the new values.

The way in which this is done depends on the DBMS product. For now, assume that new values are supplied by prefixing a column name with the expression *new:*. Thus, during an insert on CUSTOMER, the variable new:Name is the value of Name for the row being inserted. For an update, new:Name has the value of Name after the update takes place. Similarly, assume that old values are supplied by prefixing a column name with the expression *old:*. Thus, for a deletion, the variable old:Name has the value of Name for the row being deleted. For an update, old:Name has the value of Name prior to the requested update. (This, in fact, is the strategy used by Oracle. You will see the equivalent SQL Server strategy in Chapter 11.)

Triggers have many uses. In this chapter, we consider the four in Figure 7-25.

Using Triggers to Provide Default Values

Earlier in this chapter, you learned to use the DEFAULT keyword to provide initial column values. DEFAULT works only for simple expressions, however. If the computation of a default value requires complicated logic, then an INSERT trigger must be used instead.

For example, suppose that there is a policy at View Ridge Gallery to set the value of AskingPrice equal either to the AcqusitionPrice or to the AcquisitionPrice plus the average net gain for sales of this art in the past, whichever is greater. The AFTER trigger in Figure 7-26 implements this policy. The code in Figure 7-26 is generic; you will learn how to write such code for Oracle and SQL Server in Chapters 10 and 11, respectively.

After declaring program variables, the trigger reads the TRANSACTION table to find out how many TRANSACTION rows exist for this work. Because this is an AFTER trigger, the new TRANSACTION row for the work will have already been inserted. Thus, the count will be one if this is the first time the work has been in the gallery. If so, the new value of SalesPrice is set to twice the AcquisitionPrice.

If the rowcount is greater than one, then the work has been in the gallery before. To compute the average gain for this work, the trigger uses the ArtistWorkNet described on page 244 to compute Sum(NetPrice) for this work. The sum is placed in the variable sumNetPrice. Notice that the WHERE clause limits the rows to be used in the view to this particular work. The average is then computed by dividing this sum by rowcount minus one.

Figure 7-25

Uses for Triggers

- Provide default values
- Enforce data constraints
- Update views
- Perform referential integrity actions

Figure 7-26

**Default Value
Trigger Code**

```
CREATE TRIGGER TRANSACTION_AskingPriceInitialValue
         AFTER INSERT ON TRANSACTION

DECLARE
         rowcount  as int;
         sumNetPrice  as numeric (10, 2) ;
         avgNetPrice  as numeric (8, 2 ) ;

BEGIN
         /* First find if work has been here before */

         SELECT      Count ( * ) INTO rowcount
         FROM        TRANSACTION T
         WHERE       new:WorkID = T.WorkID ;

         IF rowcount = 1 Then
                 /* This is first time work has been in gallery */

                 new:AskingPrice = 2 * new:AcquisitionPrice;

         ELSE
                 IF rowcount > 1 Then
                         /* Work has been here before */

                         SELECT      Sum(NetPrice) into sumNetPrice
                         FROM        ArtistWorkNet AW
                         WHERE       AW.WorkID = new.WorkID
                         GROUP BY    AW.WorkID ;

                         avgNetPrice = sumNetPrice / (rowcount − 1) ;

                         /* Now choose larger    */
                         IF avgNetPrice > 2 * new:AcquistionPrice Then

                                 new:AskingPrice = avgNetPrice;
                         ELSE
                                 new: AskingPrice = avgNetPrice;

                         END IF ;
                 ELSE
                         /* Error, rowcount cannot be less than 1 −
                         Do something */
                 END IF ;
         END IF ;
END ;
```

You may be wondering, why not use Avg(NetPrice) in the SQL statement? The answer is that the default SQL average function would have counted the new row in the computation of the average. We do not want that row to be included, so we subtract one from rowcount when the average is computed.

Once the value of avgNetPrice has been computed, it is compared with twice the AcquisitionPrice; the larger result is used for the new value of AskingPrice.

Using Triggers to Enforce Data Constraints

A second purpose of triggers is to enforce data constraints. Although SQL CHECK constraints can be used to enforce domain, range, and intrarelation constraints, no DBMS vendor has implemented the SQL-92 features for interrelation CHECK constraints. Consequently, such constraints are implemented in triggers.

Suppose, for example, that the gallery has a special interest in Mexican painters and never discounts the price of their works. Thus, the SalesPrice of a work must always be at least the AskingPrice. To enforce this rule, the gallery database has an insert and update trigger on TRANSACTION that checks to see if the work is by a Mexican painter. If so, the SalesPrice is checked against the AskingPrice. If it is less than the AskingPrice, the SalesPrice is reset to the AskingPrice.

Figure 7-27

Trigger to Enforce
an Interrelation
Data Constraint

```
CREATE TRIGGER TRANSACTION_SalesPriceCheck
           AFTER INSERT, UPDATE ON TRANSACTION

DECLARE

        artistNationality      char ( 30 ) ;

BEGIN
        / * First determine if work is by a Mexican artist * /

        SELECT          Nationality into artistNationality
        FROM            ARTIST A JOIN WORK W
        ON              A.ArtistID = W.ArtistID
        WHERE           W.WorkID = new:WorkID ;

        IF artistNationality  <> 'Mexican' Then Exit Trigger ;

        / * Work is by a Mexican artist; enforce constraint * /

        If new: SalesPrice < new:AskingPrice THEN
        / * Sales Price is too low, reset it * /

                   UPDATE TRANSACTION
                         SET  SalesPrice = new:AskingPrice ;

        / * Note :   the above update will cause a recursive call on this
                     trigger . The recursion will stop the second time
                     through because SalesPrice will be = AskingPrice. * /

        / * Also should send a message to the user saying what's been
             done * /

        END IF ;

END ;
```

Figure 7-27 shows a generic trigger code that implements this rule. This trigger will be fired after any insert or update on a TRANSACTION row. The trigger first checks to determine if the work is by a Mexican artist. If not, the trigger is exited. Otherwise, the SalesPrice is checked against the AskingPrice; if it is less than the AskingPrice, the SalesPrice is set equal to the AskingPrice.

This trigger will be called recursively. The update statement in the trigger will cause an update on TRANSACTION, which will cause the trigger to be called again. The second time, however, the SalesPrice will be equal to the AskingPrice, no more updates will be made, and the recursion will stop.

Updating Views

As stated earlier, the DBMS can update some views and not update others, depending on the way the view is constructed. Applications can sometimes update the views that the DBMS cannot update by applying logic that is particular to a given business setting. In this case, the application-specific logic for updating the view is placed in an INSTEAD OF trigger.

When an INSTEAD OF trigger is declared on a view, the DBMS performs no action other than to call the trigger. Everything else is up to the trigger. If you declare an INSTEAD OF INSERT trigger on view MyView, and if your trigger does nothing other than send an email, then that email becomes the result of an INSERT on the view. INSERT MyView means "Send an email," and nothing more.

More realistically, consider the CustomerInterests view on page 245 (Figure 7-21). This view is the result of two joins across the intersection table between CUSTOMER and ARTIST. Suppose that this view populates a grid on a user form, and further

Figure 7-28

**Trigger for Updating
a View**

```
CREATE TRIGGER CustomerInterest_CustomerName Update
        INSTEAD OF UPDATE ON CustomerInterest

DECLARE

        rowcount          int ;

BEGIN

        SELECT            Count ( * ) into rowcount
        FROM              CUSTOMER
        WHERE             CUSTOMER.NAME = old:Name

        IF      rowcount = 1 Then

        / *  If get here , then only one customer with this name.
             Make the name change.  * /

        UPDATE            CUSTOMER
        SET               CUSTOMER.Name = new:Customer
        WHERE             CUSTOMER.Name = old:Customer;

        ELSE


        / *  Send a message to the user saying cannot update
             because there are too many customers
             with the original name .  * /

        END IF ;

END ;
```

suppose that users want to make customer name corrections, when necessary, on this form. If such changes are not possible, the users will say something like, "But, hey, the name is right there. Why can't I change it?" Little do they know the trials and tribulations the DBMS went through to display those data!

In any case, if the customer name value happens to be unique within the database, the view has sufficient information to update the customer's name. Figure 7-28 shows generic trigger code for such an update. The code just counts the number of customers that have the old value of Name. If only one customer has that value, then the update is made; otherwise, an error message is generated.

Notice that the update activity is on one of the tables that underlie the view. The view, of course, has no real view data. Only actual tables can be updated.

Implementing Referential Integrity Actions

The fourth use of triggers is to implement referential integrity actions. Consider, for example, the 1:N relationship between DEPARTMENT and EMPLOYEE. Assume that the relationship is M-M and that EMPLOYEE.DepartmentName is a foreign key to DEPARTMENT.

To enforce this constraint, we will construct two views, both based on EMPLOYEE. The first view, DeleteEmployee, will delete an EMPLOYEE row only if that row is not the last child in the DEPARTMENT. The second view, DeleteEmployeeDepartment, will delete an EMPLOYEE row; and if that row is the last EMPLOYEE in the DEPARTMENT, it will also delete the DEPARTMENT row.

An organization would make the DeleteEmployee view available to applications that do not have permission to delete a row in DEPARTMENT. The DeleteEmployeeDepartment view would be given to applications that have permission to delete both employees and departments that have no employees.

Figure 7-29

**Trigger to Delete
All but Last Child**

```
CREATE TRIGGER EMPLOYEE_DeleteCheck
        INSTEAD OF DELETION ON DeleteEmployee

DECLARE

        rowcount            int ;

BEGIN
        / * First determine if this is the last employee in the
        department  * /

        SELECT            Count ( * ) into rowcount
        FROM              EMPLOYEE
        WHERE             EMPLOYEE:old:DepartmentName = DEPARTMENT.DepartmentName

        IF       rowcount > 1 Then
                / * Not last employee, allow deletion   * /

                DELETE            EMPLOYEE
                WHERE             EMPLOYEE.EmployeeNumber = old:EmployeeNumber

        ELSE

                / * Send a message to user saying cannot delete last
                employee in a department .  * /

        END IF ;

END ;
```

DeleteEmployee and DeleteEmployeeDepartment views have identical structure. Here is how DeleteEmployee is defined:

CREATE VIEW DeleteEmployee

> **SELECT**   *
>
> **FROM**   **EMPLOYEE;**

A Trigger on DeleteEmployee

The trigger on DeleteEmployee, shown in Figure 7-29, determines if the employee is the last employee in the department. If not, the EMPLOYEE row is deleted; otherwise, nothing is done.

Again, the DBMS does nothing when an INSTEAD OF trigger is declared on the deletion. All activity is up to the trigger. If the employee is the last employee, then this trigger does nothing, which means that no change will be made to the database because the DBMS left all processing tasks to the INSTEAD OF trigger.

A Trigger on DeleteEmployeeDepartment

The trigger on DeleteEmployeeDepartment, shown in Figure 7-30, first checks to determine if the employee is the last employee in the department. If so, the DEPARTMENT is deleted. After that, the employee is deleted. Notice that the row in EMPLOYEE is deleted in either case.

Triggers such as those in Figures 7-29 and 7-30 are used to enforce the referential integrity actions for O-M and M-M relationships, as described at the end of Chapter 6. You will learn how to write them for Oracle in Chapter 10 and for SQL Server in Chapter 11.

Figure 7-30   Trigger to Delete Child and Parent When Necessary

```
CREATE  TRIGGER  EMPLOYEE_DEPARTMENT_DeleteCheck
        INSTEAD  OF  DELETION  ON  DeleteEmployeeDepartment

DECLARE

        rowcount          int ;

BEGIN
        / *  First, delete EMPLOYEE row regardless of whether DEPARTMENT
        will be deleted  * /

        DELETE        EMPLOYEE
        WHERE         EMPLOYEE.EmployeeNumber  =  old:EmployeeNumber ;

        / *    Now determine if this was the last employee in the department
        * /

        SELECT        Count(*)  into  rowcount
        FROM          EMPLOYEE
        WHERE         EMPLOYEE.DepartmentName  =  old:EmployeeNumber ;

        IF      rowcount  =  0  THEN
                /*  No employees, delete DEPARTMENT  */

                DELETE        DEPARTMENT
                WHERE         DEPARTMENT.DepartmentName = old:DepartmentName
        END IF ;

END ;
```

Using Stored Procedures

A *stored procedure* is a program that is stored within the database and compiled when used. In Oracle, stored procedures can be written in PL/SQL or in Java. With SQL Server, stored procedures are written in TRANSACT-SQL. With SQL Server [3] 2005, they can be written in languages such as Visual Basic .NET, C#, and C++.

Stored procedures can receive input parameters and return results. Unlike triggers, which are attached to a given table or view, stored procedures are attached to the database. They can be executed by any process using the database that has permission to use t he procedure. Differences between triggers and stored procedures are summarized in Figure 7-31.

Stored procedures are used for many purposes. Although database administrators use them to perform common administration tasks, their primary use is within database applications. They can be invoked from application programs written in languages such as COBOL, C, Java, C#, or C++. They also can be invoked from Web pages using VBScript or JavaScript. Ad hoc users can run them from products such as SQL*Plus in Oracle or Query Analyzer in SQL Server.

Advantages of Stored Procedures

The advantages of using stored procedures are listed in Figure 7-32. Unlike application code, stored procedures are never distributed to client computers. They always reside in

---

[3] This edition was written before Microsoft had shipped SQL Server 2005. If it has not shipped by the time you read this text, search www.microsoft.com for the term Yukon, the internal code name for SQL Server 2005.

Figure 7-31

Triggers Versus Stored Procedures

- Trigger
  - Module of code that is called by the DBMS when INSERT, UPDATE, or DELETE commands are issued
  - Assigned to a table or view
  - Depending on the DBMS, may have more than one trigger per table or view
  - Triggers may issue INSERT, UPDATE, and DELETE commands and thereby may cause the invocation of other triggers
- Stored Procedure
  - Module of code that is called by a user or database administrator
  - Assigned to a database, but not to a table or a view
  - Can issue INSERT, UPDATE, and DELETE commands
  - Used for repetitive administration tasks or as part of an application

Figure 7-32

Advantages of Stored Procedures

Greater security
Decreased network traffic
SQL can be optimized
Code sharing
    Less work
    Standardized processing
    Specialization among developers

the database and are processed by the DBMS on the database server. Thus, they are more secure than distributed application code, and they also reduce network traffic. Increasingly, stored procedures are the preferred mode of processing application logic over the Internet or corporate intranets. Another advantage of stored procedures is that their SQL statements can be optimized by the DBMS compiler.

When application logic is placed in a stored procedure, many different application programmers can use that code. This sharing results not only in less work, but also in standardized processing. Further, the developers best suited for database work can create the stored procedures while other developers, say those that specialize in Web-tier programming, can do other work. Because of these advantages, it is likely that stored procedures will see increased use in the future.

The Add_WORK Stored Procedure

Figure 7-33 shows a stored procedure that records the acquisition of a work in the View Ridge database. Again, this code is generic, but the code style is close to that used in SQL Server rather than the more Oracle-like style that was used for the trigger examples in the prior section. If you compare the examples in both sections, you can gain a sense of the differences between PL/SQL and T-SQL.

The Add_WORK procedure receives five input parameters and returns none. In a more realistic example, a return parameter would be passed back to the caller to indicate the success or failure of the operation. That discussion takes us away from database concepts, however, and we will omit it here.

This code assumes that the value of ArtistID that is passed to it is a valid ID. To verify this assumption, the first block of statements counts the number of rows that have the given ArtistID value. If the count is zero, then the ArtistID value is invalid, and the procedure writes an error message and returns.

Figure 7-33

Stored Procedure to Record the Acquisition of a WORK

```
CREATE  PROCEDURE  Add_WORK
          (
          @ArtistID  int ,          /* Artist  must  already  exist  in  database  */
          @Title  char (25) ,
          @Copy  char (8) ,
          @Description  varchar (1000) ,
          @AcquisitionPrice  Numeric (6 , 2)
          )

/* Stored  procedure  to  record  the  acquisition  of  a  work .  If  the  work
has  never  been  in  the  gallery  before ,  add  a  new  WORK  row .  Otherwise ,
use  the  existing  WORK  row .  Add  a  new  TRANSACTION  row  for  the  work  and
set  DateAcquired  to  the  system  date .    */

AS

          DECLARE  @rowcount  as  int
          DECLARE  @workID  as  int

/* First  ensure  ArtistID  is  valid    */
          SELECT  @rowcount  =  Count (*)
          FROM  ARTIST  A
          WHERE  A.ArtistID  =  @ArtistID

          IF  @rowcount  =  0
          /* No  such  artist !    */
                    BEGIN
                              Print ' No  artist  with  id  of  '  +  Str (@artistID)
                              Print ' Processing  terminated . '
                              RETURN
                    END

/* Now  see  if  work  is  in  database  */
          SELECT  @rowcount  =  Count (*)
          FROM  WORK  W
          WHERE  W.ArtistID  =  @ArtistID  and
                              W.Title  =  @Title  and
                              W.Copy  =  @Copy

          IF          @rowcount  =  0
                              /* Not  in  database ,  put  it  in  */
                              INSERT  INTO  WORK  (Title,  Copy,  Description,  ArtistID)
                              VALUES  (@Title,  @Copy,  @Description,  @ArtistID)

/* Get  work  surrogate  key  value  */
          SELECT  @workID  =  W.WorkID
          FROM  Work  W
          WHERE  W.ArtistID  =  @ArtistID  and
                    W.Title  =  @Title  and
                    W.Copy  =  @Copy

/* Now  put  TRANSACTION  row  into  database  */
          INSERT  INTO  TRANSACTION  (DateAcquired,  AcquisitionPrice,  WorkID)
                    VALUES  (GetDate ( ),  @AcquisitionPrice,  @workID)

          RETURN
```

Otherwise,[4] the procedure then checks to determine if the work has been in the gallery before. If so, the WORK table will already contain a row for this Artist, Title, and Copy. If no such row exists, the procedure creates a new WORK row. Once that has been done, it then uses a SELECT to obtain a value for WorkID. If the WORK row was just created, this statement is necessary to obtain the new value of WorkID surrogate key. If the work was not created, the SELECT on WorkID is necessary to obtain the WorkID of the existing row.

Once a value of WorkID has been obtained, the new row is inserted into TRANS-ACTION. Notice that the system function GetDate() is used to supply a value for DateAcquired in the new row.

---

[4]This code does not check for more than one row having the given ArtistID because ArtistID is a surrogate key.

This procedure illustrates how SQL is embedded in stored procedures. It is not complete because we need to do something to ensure that either all updates are made to the database or none of them are. You will learn how to do that in Chapter 9. For now, just concentrate on how SQL can be used as part of a database application.

⊚ S U M M A R Y

SQL data definition language (DDL) statements are used to manage the structure of tables. This chapter presented three SQL DDL statements: CREATE TABLE, ALTER TABLE, and DROP TABLE. SQL is preferred over graphical tools for creating tables because it is faster, it can be used to create the same table repeatedly, tables can be created from program code, and it is standardized and DBMS independent.

The IDENTITY (N, M) data type is used to create surrogate key columns, where N is the starting value and M is the increment to be added. The SQL CREATE TABLE statement is used to define the name of the table, its columns, and constraints on columns. There are five types of constraints: PRIMARY KEY, UNIQUE, NULL/NOT NULL, FOREIGN KEY, and CHECK. The purposes of the first three constraints are obvious. FOREIGN KEY is used to create referential integrity constraints; CHECK is used to create data constraints. Figure 7-6 summarizes techniques for creating relationships using SQL constraints.

Simple default values can be assigned using the DEFAULT keyword. Data constraints are defined using CHECK constraints. Domain, range, and intratable constraints can be defined. Although SQL-92 defined facilities for interrelation CHECK constraints, those facilities were not implemented by DBMS vendors. Instead, interrelation constraints are enforced using triggers.

The ALTER statement is used to add and remove columns and constraints. The DROP statement is used to drop tables. In SQL DDL, parents need to be created first and dropped last.

The data manipulation language (DML) SQL statements are INSERT, UPDATE, and DELETE. Each statement can be used on a single row, on a group of rows, or on the entire table. Because of their power, both UPDATE and DELETE need to be used with care.

Some people believe the JOIN ON syntax is an easier form of join. Rows that have no match in the join condition are dropped from the join results. To keep such rows, use a LEFT OUTER or RIGHT OUTER join rather than a regular, or INNER, join.

A SQL view is a virtual table that is constructed from other tables and views. SQL SELECT statements are used to define views. The only restriction is that a view definition may not include an ORDER BY clause.

Views are used to hide columns or rows and to show the results of computed columns. They also can hide complicated SQL syntax, such as that used for joins and GROUP BY queries, and layer computations and built-in functions so that computations can be used in WHERE clauses. Some organizations use views to provide table aliases. Views also can be used to assign different sets of processing permissions to tables and to assign different sets of triggers as well.

The rules for determining whether a view can be updated are both complicated and DBMS specific. Guidelines are shown in Figure 7-24.

SQL can be embedded in program code in triggers, stored procedures, and application code. To do so, there must be a way to associate SQL table columns with program variables. Also, there is a paradigm mismatch between SQL and programs. Most SQL statements return sets of rows; an application expects to work on one row at a time. To resolve this mismatch, the results of SQL statements are processed as pseudofiles using a cursor.

A trigger is a stored program that is executed by the DBMS whenever a specified event occurs on a specified table or view. In Oracle, triggers can be written in Java or in a proprietary Oracle language called PL/SQL. In SQL Server, triggers can be written in a propriety SQL Server language called TRANSACT-SQL, or T-SQL, and soon in languages such as Visual Basic .NET, C#, and C++.

Possible triggers are BEFORE, INSTEAD OF, and AFTER. Each type of trigger can be declared for insert, update, and delete actions, so nine types of triggers are possible. Oracle supports all nine trigger types; SQL Server supports only INSTEAD OF and AFTER triggers.

When a trigger is fired, the DBMS supplies old and new values for the update. New values are provided for inserts and updates, and old values are provided for updates and deletions. How these values are provided to the trigger depends on the DBMS in use.

Triggers have many uses. This chapter discussed four: default values (Figure 7-26), data constraints (Figure 7-27), updating views (Figure 7-28), and enforcing referential integrity (Figures 7-29 and 7-30).

A stored procedure is a program that is stored within the database and compiled when used. Stored procedures can receive input parameters and return results. Unlike triggers, their scope is database-wide; they can be used by any process that has permission to run the stored procedure.

Stored procedures can be called from programs written in standard languages such as Java or C# or in scripting languages such as JavaScript or VBScript. They also can be called from SQL command prompt processors such as Oracle's SQL*Plus or SQL Server's Query Analyzer.

The advantages of using stored procedures are summarized in Figure 7-32. An example stored procedure is shown in Figure 7-33.

REVIEW QUESTIONS

7.1   What does DDL stand for? List the SQL DDL statements.

7.2   What does DML stand for? List the SQL DML statements.

7.3   Explain the meaning of the following expression: IDENTITY (4000, 5).

Use the following three tables in your answers to questions 7.4 to 7.25:

EMPLOYEE (<u>EmpNumber</u>, Name, Email)

PROJECT (<u>ProjectName</u>, Description, StartDate, EndDate)

ASSIGNMENT (<u>*EmpNumber*</u>, <u>*ProjectName*</u>, TotalHoursWorked)

Assume that the relationship from EMPLOYEE to ASSIGNMENT is 1:N, M-O and that the relationship from PROJECT to ASSIGNMENT is 1:N, M-O.

7.4   Write a CREATE TABLE statement for the EMPLOYEE table. Use the SQL Server or Oracle data types shown in Figure 7-4. Assume that Name is required and an alternate key. Email is neither required nor an alternate key.

7.5   Write a CREATE TABLE statement for PROJECT. Assume that only ProjectName is required, and that no column is an alternate key. Use the SQL Server or Oracle data types shown in Figure 7-4.

7.6   Write a CREATE TABLE statement for ASSIGNMENT. Use the EMPLOYEE and PROJECT tables from your answers to questions 7.4 and 7.5. Set the default value of TotalHoursWorked to 3. Cascade updates and deletions from PROJECT to ASSIGNMENT, but cascade only updates from EMPLOYEE.

7.7   Change your answer to question 7.5 to include the constraint that StartDate be prior to EndDate. Also, constrain ProjectNames to the values Red, Blue, or Yellow.

7.8   Change your answer to question 7.6 to make the relationship between EMPLOYEE and ASSIGNMENT a 1:1 relationship.

7.9   Write an ALTER statement to add the column Phone to EMPLOYEE. Assume that Phone is not required.

7.10 Write an ALTER statement to remove the column Email from EMPLOYEE.

7.11 Write an ALTER statement to make Phone an alternate key in EMPLOYEE.

7.12 Write an ALTER statement to drop the constraint that Names be unique in EMPLOYEE.

In your answers to questions 7.13 through 7.25, assume that the EMPLOYEE table has its original format of EmployeeNumber, Name, Email. Assume that the relationship is 1:N from EMPLOYEE to ASSIGNMENT.

7.13 Write an INSERT statement to add the row (12345, 'Jones', 'Jones@MyCorp.com') to EMPLOYEE.

7.14 Write an INSERT statement to add the row (12345, 'Jones@MyCorp.com', 'Jones') to EMPLOYEE.

7.15 Write an INSERT statement to add the row (12345, 'Jones') to EMPLOYEE.

7.16 Assume you have a table named NEW_EMPLOYEE that has the columns Name and EmployeeNumber, in that order. Write an INSERT statement to add all of the rows from the table NEW_EMPLOYEE to EMPLOYEE.

7.17 Write an UPDATE statement to change the name of the employee named 'Jones' to 'Smith'.

7.18 Write an UPDATE statement to change the value of Email of employee 'Jones' to 'Smith@MyCorp.com'.

7.19 Combine your answers to questions 7.16 and 7.17 into one SQL statement.

7.20 Assume that ASSIGNMENT and PROJECT have valid data. Write an UPDATE statement to set the TotalHoursWorked to 15 for every row in ASSIGNMENT having the value 12345 for Employee.

7.21 Assume that you have a table named NEW_EMAIL, which has new values of Email for some employees. NEW_EMAIL has two columns: EmployeeNumber and NewEmail. Write an UPDATE statement to change the values of Email in EMPLOYEE to those in the NEW_EMAIL table.

7.22 Write one DELETE statement that will delete all data for project 'BLUE' and all of its rows in ASSIGNMENT.

7.23 Write a DELETE statement that will delete the row for the employee named 'Smith'. What happens if this employee has rows in ASSIGNMENT?

7.24 Join EMPLOYEE, ASSIGNMENT, and PROJECT using the JOIN ON syntax.

7.25 Join EMPLOYEE and ASSIGNMENT and include all rows of EMPLOYEE in your answer, regardless of whether they have an ASSIGNMENT.

7.26 What is a SQL view? What purposes do views serve?

7.27 What is the limitation on SELECT statements used in SQL views?

7.28 Code a SQL statement to create a view that shows the values of CUSTOMER.State.

7.29 Code a SQL statement to create a view that shows the values of CUSTOMER.State. Remove any duplicates.

7.30 Code a SQL statement to create a view that shows Name, City, and State of CUSTOMER.

7.31 Code a SQL statement to create a view that shows Name, City, and State of CUSTOMER for customers in California.

7.32 Code a SQL statement to create a view that shows CUSTOMER.Name and a computed attribute called Location that combines CUSTOMER.City and CUSTOMER.State in the format 'Chicago, IL'.

7.33 Code a SQL statement to create a view that uses the view you created in your answer to question 7.32, but that shows only customers in California.

7.34 Code a SQL statement to create a view that shows ARTIST.Name, WORK.Title, and WORK.Description.

7.35 Code a SQL statement to create a view that shows CUSTOMER.Name, WORK.Title, and ARTIST.Name for all customer purchases.

7.36 Code a SQL statement to create a view that computes the NetPrice (the difference between SalesPrice and AskingPrice) for each customer purchase.

7.37 Code a SQL statement to create a view that computes the sum of NetPrice for each customer.

7.38 Code a SQL statement to create a view that computes the sum of NetPrice for each combination of customer and artist.

7.39 Describe how views are used to provide an alias for tables. Why is this useful?

7.40 Explain how views can be used to improve data security.

7.41 Explain how views can be used to provide additional trigger functionality.

7.42 Give an example of a view that is clearly updatable.

7.43 Give an example of a view that is clearly not updatable.

7.44 Summarize the general idea for determining whether a view is updatable.

7.45 If a view is missing required items, what action on the view is definitely not allowed?

7.46 Explain the paradigm mismatch between SQL and programming languages.

7.47 How is the mismatch in your answer to question 7.46 corrected?

7.48 What is a trigger?

7.49 What are PL/SQL and T-SQL?

7.50 What is the relationship between a trigger and a table or view?

7.51 Name nine possible trigger types.

7.52 Explain, in general terms, how new and old values are made available to a trigger.

7.53 Describe four uses for triggers.

7.54 Assume that the View Ridge Gallery will allow a row to be deleted from WORK if the work has never been sold. Explain, in general terms, how to use a trigger to accomplish such a deletion.

7.55 What is a stored procedure? How do they differ from triggers?

7.56 Summarize how to invoke a stored procedure.

7.57 Summarize the key advantages of stored procedures.

⊚ PROJECT QUESTIONS

Use the data model in Figure 7-34 and the related database design in Figure 7-35 to answer the following questions.

7.58 Describe the relationships in terms of type (identifying or nonidentifying) and maximum and minimum cardinality.

7.59 Explain the need for each of the foreign keys.

7.60 Referential integrity actions are shown for the COMPUTER/ASSIGNMENT relationship only. Explain why D:C and U:C are necessary.

7.61 Use Figure 6-27(b) as a boilerplate to define triggers for enforcing the required child between EMPLOYEE and ASSIGNMENT. Define the purpose of any necessary triggers. Use the same strategy as illustrated in this chapter for the required EMPLOYEE relationship (pages 252–254).

7.62 Explain the interaction between the trigger in your answer to question 7.61 and the D:C on the COMPUTER/ASSIGNMENT. What do you want to occur? Explain how you can test to find out if it works the way that you want it to.

7.63 Write CREATE TABLE statements for the tables in Figure 7-35. Write CHECK constraints to ensure that Make is Dell, IBM, Compaq, or Other. Also, write constraints to ensure that ProcessorSpeed is between .8 and 5.0 (these are units of Gigahertz).

7.64 Create sample data for this database design. Your data should have at least seven EMPLOYEEs, three computers, and five to seven ASSIGNMENTs. Be sure to

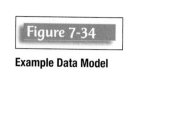

Figure 7-34

Example Data Model

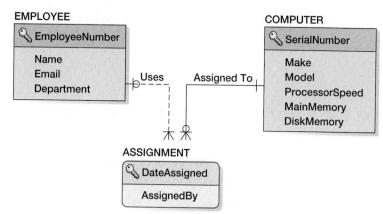

Figure 7-35

Example Database Design

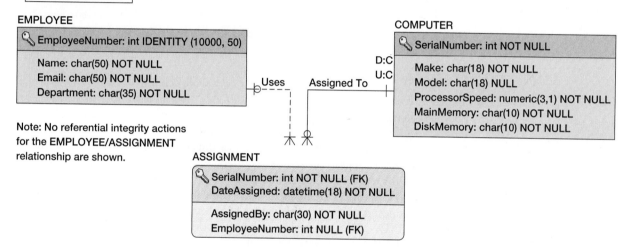

Note: No referential integrity actions for the EMPLOYEE/ASSIGNMENT relationship are shown.

have a least one IBM computer, at least three employees in the Accounting department, and at least two ASSIGNMENTs with a value of 'Jones' for AssignedBy.

7.65 Create an EmployeeView that has EMPLOYEE.Name and EMPLOYEE.Department. Show how to use that view to present employees sorted by name. Show the results of this view for your sample data.

7.66 Create a view AccountingEmployee that uses the EmployeeView but shows just employees in the Accounting department. Show the results of this view for your sample data.

7.67 Create a view of COMPUTER named Computers that displays SerialNumber and Make and Model as one attribute named ComputerType. Place a colon and a space between Model in the format: Dell: 6200 Laptop. Show the results of this view for your sample data.

7.68 Create a view called ComputerMakes that shows the Make and average ProcessorSpeed for all computers. Show the results of this view for your sample data.

7.69 Create a view called ComputerUses that has all of the data of COMPUTER and ASSIGNMENT. Show the results of this view for your sample data.

7.70 Use the ComputerUses view to create another view called ComputerUsesByAssignee that shows all data for COMPUTER and ASSIGNMENT grouped by AssignedBy. Show the results of this view for your sample data.

7.71 Use the view you created called Computers to show computer SerialNumber, ComputerType, and Employee Name. Show the results of this view for your sample data.

7.72   Suppose you want to use a stored procedure to store a new row in COMPUTER. List the minimum list of parameters that need to be in the procedure. Describe, in general terms, the logic of the stored procedure.

⟨M⟩ MARCIA'S DRY CLEANING

Suppose that you have designed a database for Marcia's Dry Cleaning that has the following tables:

CUSTOMER (<u>CustomerSK</u>, Phone, Email, FirstName, LastName)

ORDER (<u>InvoiceNumber</u>, Date, *CustomerSK,* Subtotal, Tax, Total)

ORDER_ITEM (*<u>InvoiceNumber</u>*, <u>ItemNumber</u>, Qty, *Service,* UnitPrice, ExtendedPrice)

SERVICE (<u>Service</u>, Description, UnitPrice)

A   Specify NULL/NOT NULL constraints for each table column.
B   Specify alternate keys, if any.
C   State relationships as implied by foreign keys and specify the maximum and minimum cardinality of each relationship. Justify your choices.
D   Explain how you will enforce the minimum cardinalities in your answer to question C. Use referential integrity actions for required parents, if any. Use Figure 6-27(b) as a boilerplate for required children, if any.
E   Write CREATE TABLE statements for each of the tables using your answers to questions A–D as necessary. Set the first value of CustomerSK to 100 and increment it by 5. Use FOREIGN KEY constraints to create appropriate referential integrity constraints. Set UPDATE and DELETE behavior in accordance with your referential integrity action design. Set the default value of Qty to 1. Write a constraint that SERVICE.Price be between 1.50 and 10.00.
F   Explain how you would enforce the data constraint that ORDER_ITEM.UnitPrice be equal to SERVICE.UnitPrice, where ORDER_ITEM.Service = SERVICE.Service.
G   Write INSERT statements to insert at least three rows into each table.
H   Write an UPDATE statement to change values of SERVICE.Description from Mens Shirt to Mens' Shirts.
I   Write a DELETE statement(s) to delete an ORDER and all of the items on that ORDER.
J   Create a view called OrderSummary that contains ORDER.Date, ORDER_ITEM. Service, and ORDER_ITEM.ExtendedPrice.
K   Create a view called CustomerOrderSummary that contains CUSTOMER.FirstName, CUSTOMER.LastName, CUSTOMER.Phone, ORDER.Date, ORDER.SubTotal, ORDER_ITEM.Service, and ORDER_ITEM.ExtendedPrice.
L   Create a view called CustomerHistory that includes all columns of CustomerOrderSummary and that sums and averages ORDER_ITEM.ExtendedPrice for each customer.
M   Create a view called CustomerCheck that uses CustomerHistory and that shows that any customers for whom the sum of ORDER_ITEM.ExtendedPrice is not equal to ORDER.SubTotal.
N   Explain, in general terms, how you will use triggers to enforce minimum cardinality actions as required by your design. You need not write the triggers, just specify which triggers you need and describe, in general terms, their logic.

MORGAN IMPORTING

Suppose that you have designed a database for Morgan Importing that has the following tables:

> STORE (<u>StoreName</u>, City, Country, Phone, Fax, Email, Contact)

> PURCHASE (<u>PurchaseSK</u>, *StoreName,* Date, Description, Category, PriceUSD)

> SHIPMENT (<u>ShipmentSK</u>, ShipDate, *ShipperName,* ShipperInvoiceNumber, Origin, Destination)

> SHIPMENT_ITEM (*<u>ShipmentSK</u>*, *<u>PurchaseSK</u>*, InsuredValue)

> SHIPPER (<u>ShipperName</u>, Phone, Fax, Email, Contact)

A Do you think STORE should have a surrogate key? If so, create it and make required adjustments in the design. If not, explain why not or make other adjustments to STORE and other tables that you think are appropriate.

B Specify NULL/NOT NULL constraints for each table column.

C Specify alternate keys, if any.

D State relationships as implied by foreign keys and specify the maximum and minimum cardinality of each relationship. Justify your choices.

E Explain how you will enforce the minimum cardinalities in your answer to question D. Use referential integrity actions for required parents, if any. Use Figure 6-27(b) as a boilerplate for required children, if any.

F Write CREATE TABLE statements for each of the tables using your answers to the questions A–E as necessary. Set the first value of PurchaseSK to 500 and increment it by 5. Set the first value of ShipmentSK to 100 and increment it by 1. Use FOREIGN KEY constraints to create appropriate referential integrity constraints. Set UPDATE and DELETE behavior in accordance with your referential integrity action design. Set the default value of InsuredValue to 100. Write a constraint that STORE.Country be limited to seven countries; you can pick the seven countries you want to purchase from.

G Explain how you would enforce the rule that SHIPMENT_ITEM.InsuredValue be at least as great as PURCHASE.PriceUSD.

H Write INSERT statements to insert at least three rows into each table.

I Write an UPDATE statement to change values of STORE.City from New York City to NYC.

J Write a DELETE statement(s) to delete a SHIPMENT and all of the items on that SHIPMENT.

K Create a view called PurchaseSummary that shows only PURCHASE.Date, PURCHASE.Description, and PURCHASE.PriceUSD.

L Create a view called StorePurchaseHistory that shows STORE.StoreName, STORE.Phone, STORE.Contact, PURCHASE.Date, PURCHASE.Description, and PURCHASE.PriceUSD.

M Create a view called StoreHistory that sums the PriceUSD column of StorePurchaseHistory for each store into a column named TotalPurchases.

N Create a view called MajorSources that uses StoreHistory and selects only those stores that have TotalPurchases greater than 100000.

O Explain, in general terms, how you will use triggers to enforce minimum cardinality actions as required by your design. You need not write the triggers, just specify which triggers you need and describe, in general terms, their logic.

Database Redesign

As stated in Chapter 1, databases arise from three sources. They can be created from existing tables and spreadsheets, they can be the result of a new systems development project, or they can be the outcome of database redesign. We have discussed the first two sources in Chapters 2 through 7. In this chapter, we will discuss the last source: database redesign.

We begin with a discussion of the need for database redesign and then we will describe two important SQL statements: correlated subqueries and EXISTS. These statements play an important role when analyzing data prior to redesign. They also can be used for advanced queries and are important in their own right. After that discussion, we will turn to a variety of common database redesign tasks.

The Need for Database Redesign

You may be wondering, "Why do we have to redesign a database? If we build it correctly the first time, why would we ever need to redesign it?" This question has two answers. First, it is not easy to build a database correctly the first time, especially databases that arise from the development of new systems. Even if we obtain all of the users' requirements and build a correct data model, the transformation of that data model into a correct database design is difficult. For large databases, the tasks are daunting and may require several stages of development. During those stages, some aspects of the database will need to be redesigned. Also, inevitably, mistakes will be made that must be corrected.

The second answer to this question is the more important one. Reflect for a moment on the relationship between information systems and the organizations that use them. It is tempting to say that they influence each other; that is, that information systems influence organizations and that organizations influence information systems.

In truth, however, the relationship is much stronger than that. Information systems and organizations do not just influence each other; they *create* each other. When a new information system is installed, the users can behave in new ways. As the users behave in those new ways, they will want changes to the information system to accommodate their new behaviors. As those changes are made, the users will have more new behaviors, they will request more changes to the information system, and so forth in a never-ending cycle.

This circular process means that changes to an information system are not the sad consequence of a poor implementation, but rather are a natural outcome of information system use. Therefore, the need for change to information systems never goes away; it neither can nor should be removed by better requirements definition, better initial design, better implementation, or anything else. Instead, change is part and parcel of information systems use. Thus, we need to plan for it. In the context of database processing, this means we need to know how to perform database redesign.

Additional SQL Statements

Database redesign is not terribly difficult if the database has no data. The serious difficulties arise when we have to change a database that has data and when we want to make changes with minimum impact on existing data. Telling the users that the system now works the way they want but that all of their data were lost while making the change is not acceptable.

Often, we need to know whether certain conditions or assumptions are valid in the data before we can proceed with a change. For example, we may know from user requirements that Department functionally determines BudgetCode, but we may not know whether that functional dependency is correctly represented in all of the data.

Recall from Chapter 2 that if Department determines BudgetCode, every value of Department must be paired with the same value of BudgetCode. If, for example, Accounting has a BudgetCode value of 0005005 in one row, it should have that value in every row in which it appears. Similarly, if Finance has a BudgetCode of 0005007 in one row, it should have that value in all rows in which it appears. Figure 8-1 shows data that violate this assumption. In the last row, the BudgetCode for Accounting is different than for the other rows; it has too many zeroes. Most likely, someone made a keying mistake when entering BudgetCode. Such errors are typical.

Now, before we make a database change, we need to find all such violations and correct them. For the small table shown in Figure 8-1, we can just look at the data, but what if the EMPLOYEE table has 4,000 rows? Two SQL statements are particularly helpful

Table Showing Incorrect Constraint Assumption

EmployeeNumber	Name	Department	BudgetCode
100	Jones	Accounting	0005005
200	Greene	Finance	0005007
300	Abernathy	Finance	0005007
400	Parks	Accounting	0005005
500	Kawai	Production	0005009
600	Lopez	Finance	0005007
700	Greene	Accounting	00050005

in this regard: correlated subqueries and their cousin, EXISTS/NOT EXISTS. We will consider each of these in turn.

Correlated Subqueries

A **correlated subquery** looks very much like the subqueries we discussed in Chapter 2 but in actuality, correlated subqueries are very different. To understand the difference, consider the following subquery, which is like those in Chapter 2:

```
SELECT      A.Name

FROM        ARTIST A

WHERE       A.ArtistID IN

    (SELECT      W.ArtistID

    FROM        WORK W

    WHERE       W.Title = 'Mystic Fabric');
```

The DBMS can process such subqueries from the bottom up. That is, it can first find all of the values of ArtistID in WORK that have the title 'Mystic Fabric' and then process the upper query using that set of values. There is no need to move back and forth between the two SELECT statements. The result of this query is the artist Tobey, as we would expect.

Searching for Multiple Rows with a Given Title

Now, to introduce correlated subqueries, suppose that someone at View Ridge Gallery proposes that the Title column of WORK be an alternate key. If you look at the data in Figure 7-12 (page 236), you can see that there are two copies of the title 'Mystic Fabric', and therefore Title cannot be an alternate key. However, if the WORK table had 10,000 or more rows, this would be difficult to determine. In that case, we need a query that examines the WORK table and displays the Title and Copy of any works that share the same title.

If we were asked to write a program to perform such a query, our logic would be as follows: Take the value of Title from the first row in WORK and examine all of the other rows in the table. If we find a row that has the same title as the one in the first row, we know there are duplicates, so we print the Title and Copy of the first work. We continue searching for duplicate title values until we came to the end of the WORK table.

Then, we take the value of Title in the second row and compare it with all other rows in the WORK table, printing out the Title and Copy of any duplicate works. We proceed in this way until all rows of WORK have been examined.

A Correlated Subquery that Finds Rows with the Same Title

The following correlated subquery performs the action just described:

```
SELECT      W1.Title, W1.Copy
FROM        WORK W1
WHERE       W1.Title IN
               (SELECT    W2.Title
                FROM      WORK W2
                WHERE     W1.Title = W2.Title
                AND       W1.WorkID <> W2.WorkID);
```

The result of this query for the data in Figure 7-12 is:

Mystic Fabric	99/135
Mystic Fabric	105/135

This subquery looks deceptively similar to a regular subquery. To the surprise of many students, this subquery and the one above are drastically different. Their similarity is only superficial.

Before explaining why, first notice the notation in the correlated subquery. The WORK table is used in both the upper and the lower SELECT statements. In the upper statement, it is given the alias W1; in the lower SELECT statement, it is given the alias W2.

In essence, when we use this notation, it is as if we have made two copies of the WORK table. One copy is called W1, and the second copy is called W2. Therefore, in the last two lines of the correlated subquery, values in the W1 copy of WORK are compared with values in the W2 copy.

Difference between Regular and Correlated Subqueries

Now, consider what makes this subquery so different. Unlike a regular subquery, the DBMS cannot run the bottom SELECT by itself, obtain a set of Titles, and then use that set to execute the upper query. The reason for this appears in the last two lines of the query:

```
WHERE     W1.Title = W2.Title
AND       W1.WorkID <> W2.WorkID);
```

In these expressions, W1.Title (from the top SELECT statement) is being compared with W2.Title (from the bottom SELECT statement). The same is true for W1.WorkID and W2.WorkID. Because of this fact, the DBMS cannot process the subquery portion independent of the upper SELECT.

Instead, the DBMS must process this statement as a subquery that is *nested* within the main query. The logic is as follows: Take the first row from W1. Using that row, evaluate the second query. To do that, for each row in W2, compare W1.Title with W2.Title and W1.WorkID with W2.WorkID. If the titles are equal and the values of WorkID are not equal, return the value of W2.Title to the upper query. Do this for every row in W2.

Once all of the rows in W2 have been evaluated for the first row in W1, move to the second row in W1 and evaluate it against all the rows in W2. Continue in this way until all rows of W1 have been compared with all of the rows of W2.

If this is not clear to you, write out two copies of the WORK data from Figure 7-12 on a piece of scratch paper. Label one of them W1 and the second W2 and then work through the logic as described. From this, you will see that correlated subqueries always require nested processing.

A Common Trap

By the way, do not fall into the following common trap:

```
SELECT      W1.Title, w1.Copy

FROM        WORK W1

WHERE       W1.WorkID IN

            (SELECT     W2.WorkID

            FROM        WORK W2

            WHERE       W1.Title = W2.Title

            AND         W1.WorkID <> W2.WorkID);
```

The logic here seems correct, but it is not. No row will ever be displayed by this query, regardless of the underlying data. See if you can see why this is so before continuing.

The bottom query will indeed find all rows that have the same title and different WorkIDs. If one is found, it will produce the W2.WorkID of that row. But that value will then be compared with W1.WorkID. *These two values will always be different because of the condition* W1.WorkID <> W2.WorkID. No rows are returned because the values of the two unequal WorkIDs are used in the IN instead of the values of the two equal Titles.

Using Correlated Subqueries to Check Functional Dependencies

Correlated subqueries can be used to advantage during database redesign. As mentioned, one application of correlated subqueries is to verify functional dependencies. For example, suppose we have EMPLOYEE data like that in Figure 8-1, and we want to know whether the data conform to the functional dependency Department → BudgetCode. If so, every time a given value of Department occurs in the table, that value will be matched with the same value of BudgetCode.

The following correlated subquery will find any rows that violate this assumption:

```
SELECT      E1.Department, E1.BudgetCode

FROM        EMPLOYEE E1

WHERE       E1.Department IN

            (SELECT     E2.Department

            FROM        EMPLOYEE E2

            WHERE       E1.Department = E2.Department

            AND         E1.BudgetCode <> E2.BudgetCode);
```

The results for the data in Figure 8-1 are:

Accounting	0005005
Accounting	0005005
Accounting	00050005

A listing like this can readily be used to find and fix any rows that violate the functional dependency.

EXISTS and NOT EXISTS

EXISTS and NOT EXISTS are another form of correlated subquery. We can write the last correlated subquery in the form of EXISTS, as follows:

SELECT	E1.Department, E1.BudgetCode
FROM	EMPLOYEE E1
WHERE	EXISTS
	(SELECT *
	FROM EMPLOYEE E2
	WHERE E1.Department = E2.Department
	AND E1.BudgetCode <> E2.BudgetCode);

Because EXISTS is a form of a correlated subquery, the processing of the SELECT statements is nested. The first row of E1 is input to the subquery. If the subquery finds any row in E2 for which the department names are the same and the budget codes are different, then the EXISTS is true and the Department and BudgetCode for the first row are selected. Next, the second row of E1 is input to the subquery, the SELECT is processed, and the EXISTS is evaluated. If true, the Department and BudgetCode of the second row are selected. This process is repeated for all of the rows in E1.

Using NOT EXISTS in a Double Negative

The EXISTS keyword will be true if *any* row in the subquery meets the condition. The NOT EXISTS keyword will be true only if *all* rows in the subquery fail the condition. Consequently, the double use of NOT EXISTS can be used to find rows that do not not match a condition. Because of the logic of a double negative, if a row does not (not match any row), then it matches every row. For example, suppose that at View Ridge the users want to know the name of any artist that every customer is interested in. We can proceed as follows. First, produce the set of all customers who are interested in a particular artist. Then, take the complement of that set, which will be the customers who are not interested in that artist. If that complement is empty, then all customers are interested in the given artist.

> **B T W**
>
> The doubly nested NOT EXISTS pattern is famous in one guise or another among SQL practitioners. It is often used as a test of SQL knowledge in job interviews and in bragging sessions, and it can be used to advantage when assessing the desirability of certain database redesign possibilities, as you will see in the last section of this chapter. Therefore, even though this example involves some serious study, it is worth your while to understand it.

The Double NOT EXISTS

The following SQL statement implements the strategy just described:

```
SELECT      A.Name
FROM        ARTIST AS A
WHERE       NOT EXISTS
               (SELECT      C.CustomerID
                FROM        CUSTOMER C
                WHERE       NOT EXISTS
                   (SELECT      CI.CustomerID
                    FROM        CUSTOMER_artist_int CI
                    WHERE       C.CustomerID= CI.CustomerID
                          AND        A.ArtistID = CI.ArtistID));
```

The bottom SELECT finds all of the customers who are interested in a particular artist. As you read this SELECT (the last SELECT in the query), keep in mind that this is a correlated subquery; this SELECT is nested inside the query on CUSTOMER, which is nested inside the query on ARTIST. C.CustomerID is coming from the SELECT on CUSTOMER in the middle, and A.ArtistID is coming from the SELECT on ARTIST at the top.

Now, the NOT EXISTS in the sixth line of the query will find the customers who are not interested in the given artist. If all customers are interested in the given artist, the result of the middle SELECT will be null. If the result of the middle SELECT is null, the NOT EXISTS in the third line of the query will be true and the name of that artist will be produced, just as we want.

Consider what happens for artists who do not qualify in this query. Suppose that every customer except Tiffany Twilight is interested in the artist Miro. (This is not the case for the data in Figure 7-12, but assume that it were true.) Now, for the preceding query, when Miro's row is considered, the bottom SELECT will retrieve every customer except Tiffany Twilight. In this case, because of the NOT EXISTS in the sixth line of the query, the middle SELECT will produce the CustomerID for Tiffany Twilight (because her row is the only one that does not appear in the bottom SELECT). Now, because there is a result from the middle SELECT, the NOT EXISTS in the top SELECT is false and the name Miro will not be included in the output of the query. This is correct because there is a customer who is not interested in Miro.

Again, take some time to study this pattern. It is a famous one, and if you become a database professional, you will certainly see it again in one form or another. In fact, you will not not see it again!

Analyzing the Existing Database

Before we proceed with a discussion of database redesign, reflect for moment on what this task means for a real company whose operations are dependent on the database. Suppose, for example, that you work for a company such as Amazon.com. Further suppose that you have been tasked with an important database redesign assignment, say to change the primary key of the vendor table.

To begin, you may wonder, why would Amazon want to do this? It could be that in the early days, when it only sold books, Amazon used company names for vendors. But, as Amazon began to sell more types of products, company name was no longer sufficient. Perhaps there are too many duplicates, and Amazon may have decided to switch to an Amazon-created VendorID.

Now, what does it mean to switch primary keys? Besides adding the new data to the correct rows, what else does it mean? Clearly, if the old primary key has been used as a foreign key, all of the foreign keys need to be changed as well. So we need to know all of the relationships in which the old primary key was used. But what about views? Do any views use the old primary key? If so, they will need to be changed. What about triggers and stored procedures? Do any of them use the old primary key? Not to mention any application code that may break when the old key is removed.

Now, to create a nightmare, what happens if you get partway through the change process and something fails? Suppose you encounter unexpected data, and you receive errors from the DBMS while trying to add the new primary key. Amazon cannot change its Web site to display "Sorry, our database is broken; come back tomorrow (we hope)!"

This nightmare brings up many topics, most of which relate to systems analysis and design. But with regard to database processing, three principles become clear. First, as the carpenters say, "Measure twice and cut once." Before we attempt any structural changes to a database, we must clearly understand the current structure and contents of the database, and we must know what depends on what. Second, before we make any structural changes to an operational database, we must test those changes on a realistically sized test database that has all of the important test data cases. Finally, if at all possible, we need to create a complete backup of the operational database prior to making any structural changes. If all goes awry, the backup can be used to restore the database while problems are corrected. We will consider each of these important topics next.

Reverse Engineering

Reverse engineering is the process of reading a database schema and producing a data model from that schema. The data model produced is not truly a logical model because entities will be generated for every table, including entities for intersection tables that have no nonkey data and should not appear in a logical model at all. The model generated by reverse engineering is a thing unto itself, a table-relationship diagram that is dressed in entity-relationship clothes. In this text, we will call it the **RE (reverse engineered) data model.**

Figures 8-2(a) and (b) show the RE data model produced by ERwin from a SQL Server version of the View Ridge database, as defined in Chapter 7. Figure 8-2(a) shows what ERwin calls the logical model. If you compare this with the logical model in Figure 7-3, you will see that ERwin came very close to capturing that model. All of the relationship types are correct, and it determined that the minimum cardinality from TRANSACTION to CUSTOMER is zero.

One problem is that it modeled the intersection table as an entity, which it is not, which is typical for RE diagrams. Also, it did not determine that at least one TRANSACTION is required for a WORK. All in all, though, this is reasonable representation of the View Ridge schema. Figure 8-2(b) shows what ERwin calls the physical model. This model is quite accurate. The null/not null specifications are correct, the primary key identities are correct, the alternate key of ARTIST.Name is correct, and all foreign keys are shown correctly. The only problem is that TRANSACTION is not a required child of WORK.

In addition to tables and views, some data modeling products will capture constraints, triggers, and stored procedures from the database. These constructs are not interpreted, but the text of them is imported into the data model. With some products, the relationship of the text to the items it references also is obtained. The redesign of constraints, triggers, and stored procedures is beyond the scope of our discussion here. You should realize that they, too, are part of the database, however, and are subject to redesign.

The RE data model provides a basis to begin the database redesign project. We will use it later in this chapter.

Figure 8-2

Reverse-Engineered Data Model

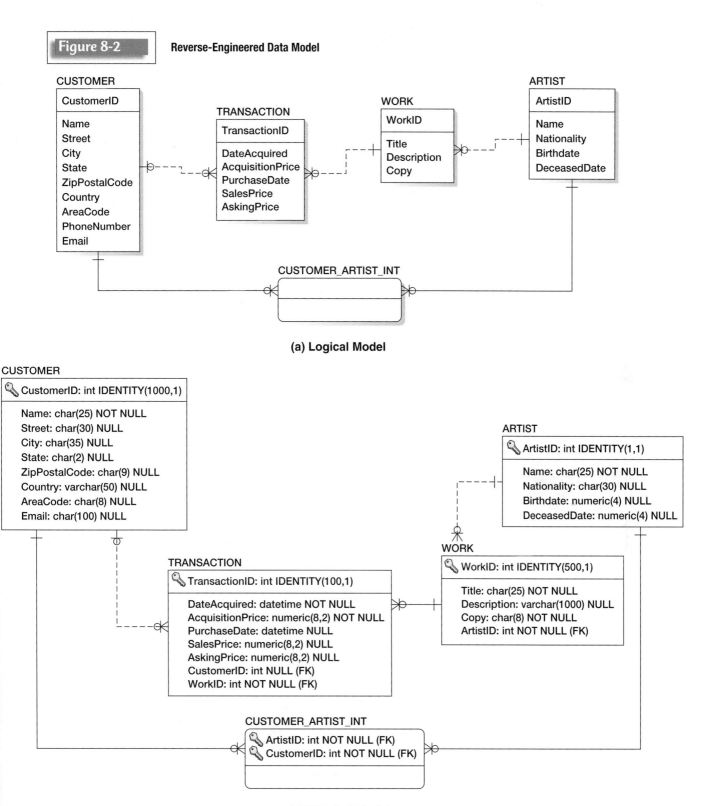

(a) Logical Model

(b) Physical Model

Dependency Graphs

Before making changes to database structures, it is vitally important to understand the dependencies of those structures. What changes will impact what? For example, consider changing the name of a table. Where is the table name used? In which triggers? In which stored procedures? In which relationships? Because of the need to know all of the dependencies, many database redesign projects begin by making a **dependency graph.**

The term *graph* arises from the mathematical topic of graph theory. Dependency graphs are not graphical displays like bar charts, rather they are diagrams that consist of nodes and arcs (or lines) that connect those nodes.

Figure 8-3(a) shows a dependency graph that was constructed by ERwin. It shows that the views BasicCustomerData and BasicCustomerData_WA are dependent on the CUSTOMER table. Figure 8-3(b) shows a similar graph for the tables ARTIST, WORK, TRANSACTION, the view ArtistWorkNet, and views based on it.

Figure 8-3(b) is another typical example of reverse engineering results. It is close, but not quite correct. Consider such results as a good starting point only. In Figure 8-3(b), the problem is that ERwin was unable to interpret the join that creates the ArtistWorkNet view. Therefore, the dependency of ArtistWorkNet on (ARTIST, WORK, TRANSACTION) is not shown.

Figure 8-4 shows a partial dependency graph that was drawn using the results of the RE model, but manually interpreting views and triggers. For simplicity, this graph does not show the views of CUSTOMER, nor does it show CUSTOMER_ARTIST_INT and related structures. Also, the stored procedure Add_Work is not included, nor are the constraints.

Even this partial diagram reveals the complexity of dependencies among database constructs. You can see that it would be wise to tread lightly, for example, when changing

Figure 8-3

Dependence Graph Fragments

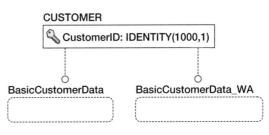

(a) CUSTOMER with Two Views

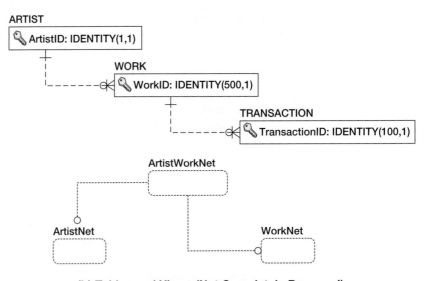

(b) Tables and Views (Not Completely Reversed)

Figure 8-4

**Example Dependency
Graph (Partial)**

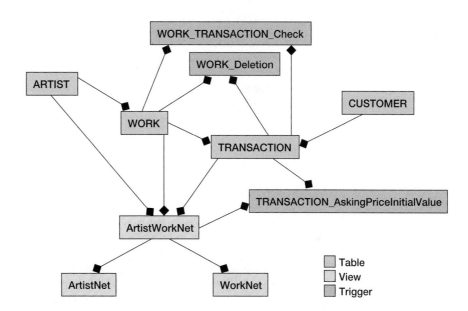

anything in the TRANSACTION table. The consequences of such a change need to be assessed against two relationships, three triggers, and three views. Again, measure twice and cut once!

Database Backup and Test Databases

Because of the potential damage that can be done to a database during redesign, a complete backup of the operational database should be made prior to making any changes. Equally important, it is essential that any proposed changes be thoroughly tested. Not only must structural changes proceed successfully, but all triggers, stored procedures, and applications must also run correctly on the revised database.

Typically, at least three different copies of the database schema are used in the redesign process. One is a small test database that can be used for initial testing. The second is a large test database, which may even be a full copy of the operational database. Sometimes, there are several large test databases. Finally, there is the operational database.

A means must be created to recover all test databases to their original state during the testing process. In that way, the test can be rerun as necessary against the same starting point. Depending on the facilities of the DBMS, backup and recovery or other means are used to restore the database after a test run.

Obviously, for enterprises with very large databases, it is not possible to have a test database that is a copy of the operational database. Instead, smaller test databases need to be created, but those test databases must have all the important data characteristics of the operational database; otherwise, they will not provide a realistic test environment. The construction of such test databases is in itself a difficult and challenging job. In fact, many interesting career opportunities are available for developing test databases and database test suites.

Finally, for organizations that have very large databases, it may not be possible to make a complete copy of the operational database prior to making structural changes. In this case, the database is backed up in pieces, and the changes are made in pieces as well. This task is very difficult and requires great knowledge and expertise. It also requires weeks or months of planning. You may participate as a junior member of a team to make such a change, but you should have years of database experience before you attempt to make structural changes to such large databases. Even then, it is a daunting task.

Changing Table Names and Table Columns

In this section, we will consider alterations to tables and their columns. To accomplish these changes, we will use only SQL-92 statements. Many DBMS products have features to facilitate changing structures other than SQL-92; for example, some products have graphical design tools that simplify this process. But such features are not standardized, and you should not depend on them. The statements shown in this chapter will work with any enterprise-class DBMS product, and most will work with Access as well.

Changing Table Names

At first glance, changing a table name seems like an innocent and easy operation. A review of Figure 8-4, however, shows that the consequences of such a change are greater than you would think. If, for example, we want to change the name of the table WORK to WORK_VERSION2, several tasks are necessary. The constraint that defines the relationship from WORK to TRANSACTION must be altered, ArtistWorkNet view must be redefined, and then WORK_TRANSACTION_Check and WORK_Deletion triggers must be rewritten to use the new name.

Furthermore, there is no SQL-92 command to change the name of the table. Instead, the table needs to be re-created under the new name, and the old table dropped. This requirement, however, suggests a good strategy for making table name changes. First, create the new table with all attendant structures and then drop the old one once everything is working with the new table. If the table to be renamed is too large to be copied, other strategies will have to be used, but they are beyond the scope of this discussion.

This strategy has one serious problem, however. WorkID is a surrogate key. When we create the new table, the DBMS will create new values of WorkID in the new table. The new values will not necessarily match the values in the old table, which means values of the foreign key TRANSACTION.WorkID will be wrong. The easiest way to solve this problem is first to create the new version of the WORK table and not define WorkID as a surrogate key. Then, fill the table with the current values of WORK, including the current values of WorkID. Then, change WorkID to a surrogate key.

First, we create the table by submitting a CREATE TABLE WORK_VERSION2 statement to the DBMS. We make WorkID integer, but not a surrogate key. We also must give new names to the WORK constraints. The prior constraints still exist, and if new names are not used, the DBMS will issue a duplicate constraint error when processing the CREATE TABLE statements. An example of new constraint names is:

CONSTRAINT WorkV2PK PRIMARY KEY (WorkID),

CONSTRAINT WorkV2AK1 UNIQUE (Title, Copy),

CONSTRAINT ArtistV2FK FOREIGN KEY(ArtistID) REFERENCES ARTIST
(ArtistID)

ON DELETE NO ACTION

ON UPDATE NO ACTION

Next, copy the data into the new table with the following SQL statement:

INSERT INTO WORK_VERSION2 (WorkID, Copy, Title, Description, ArtistID)

SELECT WorkID, Copy, Title, Description, ArtistID

FROM WORK;

At this point, alter the WORK_VERSION2 table to make WorkID a surrogate key. In SQL Server, the easiest way to do that is to open the graphical table designer and redefine WorkID as an IDENTITY column (there is no standard SQL for making this change). Set the Identity Seed property to the original value of 500, and SQL Server will set the next new value of WorkID to be the maximum largest value of WorkID plus one. A different strategy is used for surrogate keys with Oracle, as discussed in Chapter 10.

Now all that remains is to define the two triggers. This can be done by copying the text of the old triggers and changing the name WORK to WORK_VERSION2.

At this point, test suites should be run against the database to verify that all changes have been made correctly. After that, stored procedures and applications that use WORK can be changed to run against the new table name.[1] If all is correct, then the foreign key constraint TransactionWorkFK and the table work can be dropped with the following:

ALTER TABLE [TRANSACTION] DROP CONSTRAINT TransactionWorkFK;

DROP TABLE WORK;

The TransactionWorkFK constraint then can be added back to TRANSACTION using the new name for the work table:

ALTER TABLE [TRANSACTION] ADD CONSTRAINT TransactionWorkFK
FOREIGN KEY(WorkID) REFERENCES WORK_VERSION2 (WorkID)

    ON UPDATE NO ACTION

    ON DELETE NO ACTION;

Clearly, there is more to changing a table name than you would think. You now can see why some organizations do not allow programmers or users to employ the true name of a table. Instead, views are described that serve as table aliases, as explained in Chapter 7. If this were done here, only the views that define the aliases would need to be changed when the source table name is changed.

Adding and Dropping Columns

Adding null columns to a table is straightforward. For example, to add the null column DateCreated to WORK, we simply use the ALTER statement as follows:

ALTER TABLE WORK

ADD DateCreated datetime NULL;

If there are other column constraints, such as DEFAULT or UNIQUE, include them with the column definition, just as you would if the column definition were part of a CREATE TABLE statement. However, if you include a DEFAULT constraint, be aware that the default value will be applied to all new rows, but existing rows will have null values.

---

[1]The timing is important. The WORK_VERSION2 table was created from WORK. If triggers, stored procedures, and applications continue to run against WORK while the verification of WORK_VERSION2 is underway, then WORK_VERSION2 will be out of date. Some action will need to be taken to bring it up-to-date before switching the stored procedures and applications over to WORK_VERSION2.

Suppose, for example, that you want to set the default value of DateCreated to 1/1/1900 to signify that the value has not yet been entered. In this case, you would use the ALTER statement:

ALTER TABLE WORK

ADD DateCreated datetime NULL DEFAULT '1/1/1900';

This statement causes DateCreated for new rows in WORK to be set to 1/1/1900 by default. To set existing rows, you would need to execute the following query:

UPDATE WORK

SET   DateCreated ='1/1/1900'

WHERE   DateCreated IS NULL;

Adding NOT NULL Columns

To add a new NOT NULL column, first add the column as NULL. Then, use an UPDATE statement like that just shown to give the column a value in all rows. After the update, the following ALTER TABLE . . . ALTER COLUMN statement can be executed to change DateCreated from NULL to NOT NULL.

ALTER TABLE WORK

ALTER COLUMN DateCreated datetime NOT NULL;

This statement will fail if DateCreated has not been given values in all rows.

Dropping Columns

Dropping nonkey columns is easy. For example, eliminating the DateCreated column from WORK can be done with the following:

ALTER TABLE WORK

DROP COLUMN DateCreated;

To drop a foreign key column, the constraint that defines the foreign key must first be dropped. Making such a change is equivalent to dropping a relationship, and that topic is discussed later in this chapter.

To drop the primary key, the primary key constraint first needs to be dropped. To drop that, however, all foreign keys that use the primary key must first be dropped. Thus, to drop the primary key of WORK and replace it with the composite (Title, Copy, ArtistID), the following steps are necessary:

- Drop the constraint WorkFK from TRANSACTION.
- Drop the constraint WorkPK from WORK.
- Create a new constraint WorkPK using (Title, Copy, ArtistID).
- Create a new constraint WorkFK referencing (Title, Copy, ArtistID) in TRANSACTION.
- Drop column WorkID.

It is important to verify that all changes have been made correctly before dropping WorkID. Once it is dropped, there is no way to recover it except by restoring the WORK table from a backup.

Changing a Column Data Type or Column Constraints

To change a column data type or to change column constraints, the column is redefined using the ALTER TABLE ALTER COLUMN command. However, if the column is being changed from NULL to NOT NULL, then all rows must have a value in that column for the change to succeed. Also, some data type changes may cause data loss. Changing char (50) to Date, for example, will cause loss of any text field that the DBMS cannot successfully transform into a date value. Or, alternatively, the DBMS may simply refuse to make the column change. The results depend on the DBMS product in use.

Generally, converting numeric to char or varchar will succeed. Also, converting date or money or other more specific data types to char or varchar will usually succeed. Converting char or varchar back to date, money, or numeric is risky; and it may or may not be possible.

In the View Ridge schema, if Birthdate had been defined as char(4), then a risky but sensible data type change would be to modify ARTIST.Birthdate to numeric (4,0). This would be a sensible change because all of the values in this column are numeric. Recall the check constraint that was used to define Birthdate (refer to Figure 7-12). The following makes that change and simplifies the CHECK constraint.

ALTER TABLE ARTIST

ALTER COLUMN Birthdate numeric (4,0) NULL;

ALTER TABLE ARTIST

ADD CONSTRAINT NumericBirthYearCheck CHECK

    (Birthdate > 1900 and Birthdate < 2100);

The prior check constraints on Birthdate should now be deleted.

Adding and Dropping Constraints

As already shown, constraints can be added and removed using the ALTER TABLE ADD CONSTRAINT and ALTER TABLE DROP CONSTRAINT statements.

Changing Relationship Cardinalities and Properties

Changing cardinalities is a common database redesign task. Sometimes, the need is to change minimum cardinalities from zero to one or from one to zero. Another common task is to change the maximum cardinality from 1:1 to 1:N or from 1:N to N:M. Another possibility, which is less common, is to decrease maximum cardinality from N:M to 1:N or from 1:N to 1:1. This latter change can only be made with data loss, as you will see.

Changing Minimum Cardinalities

The action to be taken in changing minimum cardinalities depends on whether the change is on the parent side or on the child side of the relationship.

Changing Minimum Cardinalities on the Parent Side

If the change is on the parent side, meaning that the child will or will not be required to have a parent, making the change is a matter of changing whether null values are allowed for the foreign key that represents the relationship. For example, suppose that in the 1:N relationship from DEPARTMENT to EMPLOYEE, the foreign key DepartmentNumber appears in the EMPLOYEE table. Changing whether an employee is required to have a department is simply a matter of changing the null status of DepartmentNumber.

If the change is from a minimum cardinality of zero to one, then the foreign key, which would have been null, must be changed to NOT NULL. Changing a column to NOT NULL can only be done if all the rows in the table have a value. In the case of a foreign key, this means that every record must already be related. If not, all records must be changed so that all have a relationship before the foreign key can be made NOT NULL. In the previous example, every employee must be related to a department before DepartmentNumber can be changed to NOT NULL.

Depending on the DBMS in use, the foreign key constraint that defines the relationship may have to be dropped before the change is made to the foreign key. Then the foreign key constraint can be re-added. The following SQL will work for the preceding example:

ALTER TABLE EMPLOYEE

   DROP CONSTRAINT DepartmentFK;

ALTER TABLE EMPLOYEE

   ALTER COLUMN DepartmentNumber int NOT NULL;

ALTER TABLE EMPLOYEE

   ADD CONSTRAINT DepartmentFK

      FOREIGN KEY (DepartmentNumber)

      REFERENCES DEPARTMENT (DepartmentNumber)

      ON UPDATE CASCADE;

Also, cascade behavior for UPDATE and DELETE must be specified when changing the minimum cardinality from zero to one. In this example, updates are to cascade but deletions will not (recall that the default behavior is NO ACTION).

Changing the minimum cardinality from one to zero is simple. Just change DepartmentNumber from NOT NULL to NULL. You also may want to change the cascade behavior on updates and deletions, if appropriate.

Changing Minimum Cardinalities on the Child Side

As noted in Chapter 6, the only way to enforce minimum cardinality other than zero on the child side of a relationship is to write triggers or application code that enforce the constraint. So, to change the minimum cardinality from zero to one, it is necessary to write the appropriate triggers. Design the trigger behavior using Figure 6-27 and then write the triggers. To change the minimum cardinality from one to zero, just drop the triggers that enforce that constraint.

In the DEPARTMENT EMPLOYEE example, to require each DEPARTMENT to have an EMPLOYEE, triggers would need to be written on INSERT of DEPARTMENT and on UPDATE and DELETE of EMPLOYEE. The trigger code in DEPARTMENT ensures that an EMPLOYEE is assigned to the new DEPARTMENT, and the trigger code in EMPLOYEE ensures that the employee being moved to a new department or the employee being deleted is not the last employee in the relationship to its parent.

This discussion assumes that the required child constraint is enforced by triggers. If the required child constraint is enforced by application programs, then all of those programs also must be changed. Dozens of programs may need to be changed, which is one reason why it is better to enforce such constraints using triggers rather than application code.

Changing Maximum Cardinalities

The only difficulty when increasing cardinalities from 1:1 to 1:N or from 1:N to N:M is preserving existing relationships. This can be done, but it requires a bit of manipulation, as you will see. When reducing cardinalities, relationship data will be lost. In this case, a policy must be created for deciding which relationships to lose.

Changing 1:1 to 1:N

Figure 8-5 shows a 1:1 relationship between EMPLOYEE and PARKING_PERMIT. As you learned in Chapter 6, the foreign key can be placed in either table for a 1:1 relationship. The action to be taken depends on whether EMPLOYEE is to be the parent of the 1:N or whether PARKING_PERMIT is to be the parent.

If EMPLOYEE is to be the parent (employees are to have multiple parking permits), then the only change necessary is to drop the constraint that PARKING_PERMIT. EmployeeNumber be unique. The relationship will then be 1:N.

If PARKING_PERMIT is to be the parent (parking permits are to be allocated to many employees, say for a carpool), then the foreign key and appropriate values must be moved from PARKING_PERMIT to EMPLOYEE. The following SQL will accomplish this:

ALTER TABLE EMPLOYEE

> **ADD COLUMN PermitNumber int null;**

UPDATE EMPLOYEE

> **SET EMPLOYEE.PermitNumber =**
>
> **(SELECT   PP.PermitNumber**
>
> **FROM   PARKING_PERMIT PP**
>
> **WHERE   PP.EmployeeNumber = EMPLOYEE.EmployeeNumber);**

Once the foreign key has been moved over to EMPLOYEE, the EmployeeNumber column of PARKING_PERMIT should be dropped. Next, create a new foreign key constraint to define referential integrity. So that multiple employees can relate to the same parking permit, the new foreign key must not have a UNIQUE constraint.

Changing 1:N to N:M

Suppose that View Ridge Gallery decides that it wants to record multiple purchasers for a given transaction. It may be that some of its art is co-owned between a customer and a bank or a trust account, for example; or perhaps it may want to record the names of both people when a couple purchases art. For whatever reason, this change will require that the 1:N relationship between CUSTOMER and TRANSACTION be changed to an N:M relationship.

Changing a 1:N relationship is surprisingly easy.[2] Just create the new intersection table, fill it with data, and drop the old foreign key column. Figure 8-6 shows the View

Figure 8-5

Example 1:1 Relationship

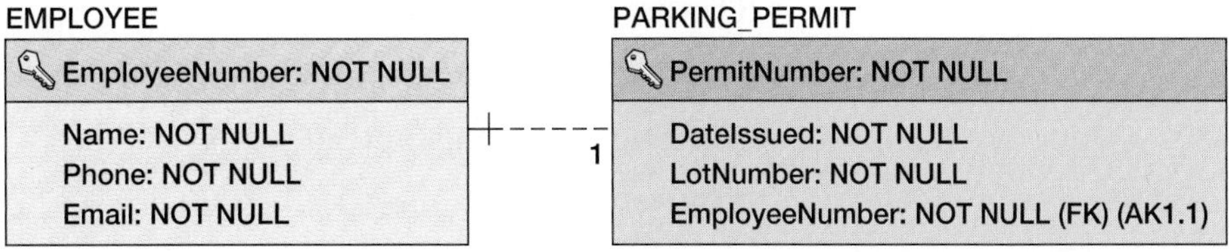

EMPLOYEE

- EmployeeNumber: NOT NULL
- Name: NOT NULL
- Phone: NOT NULL
- Email: NOT NULL

PARKING_PERMIT

- PermitNumber: NOT NULL
- DateIssued: NOT NULL
- LotNumber: NOT NULL
- EmployeeNumber: NOT NULL (FK) (AK1.1)

---

[2]Making the data change is easy. Dealing with the consequences of the data change in views, triggers, stored procedures, and application code will be more difficult. All of these will need to be rewritten to join across a new intersection table. All forms and reports also will need to be changed to portray multiple customers for a transaction; this will mean changing text boxes to grids, for example. All of this work is time consuming, and hence expensive.

Figure 8-6   **View Ridge Database with New N:M Relationship**

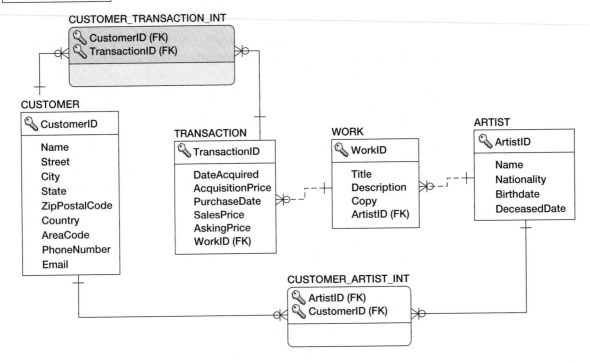

Ridge database design with a new intersection table to support the N:M relationship. We need to create this table and then copy the values of TransactionID and CustomerID from TRANSACTION for rows in which CustomerID is not null. First, create the new intersection table using the following SQL:

```
CREATE TABLE CUSTOMER_TRANSACTION_INT(
    CustomerID         int      NOT NULL,
    TransactionID      int      NOT NULL,
    CONSTRAINT         CustomerTransactionPK
        PRIMARY KEY (CustomerID, TransactionID),
    CONSTRAINT Customer_Transaction_Int_TransactionFK
        FOREIGN KEY (TransactionID) REFERENCES [TRANSACTION]
        (TransactionID),
    CONSTRAINT Customer_Transaction_Int_CustomerFK
        FOREIGN KEY (CustomerID) REFERENCES
        CUSTOMER (CustomerID)
    );
```

Note that there is no cascade behavior for updates because CustomerID is a surrogate key. There is no cascade behavior for deletions because of the business policy never to delete data that involve transactions.

The next task is to fill the table with data from the TRANSACTION table using the following SQL statement:

INSERT INTO CUSTOMER_TRANSACTION_INT (CustomerID, TransactionID)

> **SELECT**   **CustomerID, TransactionID**
>
> **FROM**   **[TRANSACTION]**
>
> **WHERE**   **CustomerID IS NOT NULL;**

Once all of these changes have been made, the CustomerID column of TRANSACTION can be dropped.

Reducing Cardinalities (with Data Loss)

It is easy to make the structural changes to reduce cardinalities. To reduce an N:M relationship to 1:N, we just create a new foreign key in the relation that will be the child and fill it with data from the intersection table. To reduce a 1:N relationship to 1:1, we just make the values of the foreign key of the 1:N relationship unique and then define a unique constraint on the foreign key. In either case, the most difficult problem is deciding which data to lose.

Consider the reduction of N:M to 1:N. Suppose, for example, that the View Ridge Gallery decides to keep just one artist interest for each customer. Thus, the relationship will then be 1:N from ARTIST to CUSTOMER. Accordingly, we add a new foreign key column ArtistID to CUSTOMER and set up a foreign key constraint to ARTIST on that customer. The following SQL will accomplish this:

ALTER TABLE CUSTOMER

> **ADD ArtistID int null;**

ALTER TABLE CUSTOMER

> **ADD CONSTRAINT ArtistInterestFK FOREIGN KEY (ArtistID)**
>
> **REFERENCES ARTIST (ArtistID);**

Updates need not cascade because of the surrogate key, and deletions cannot cascade because the customer may have a valid transaction and ought not to be deleted just because an artist interest goes away.

Now which of a customer's potentially many artist interests should be preserved in the new relationship? The answer depends on the business policy at the gallery. Here, suppose we decide simply to take the first artist interest:

UPDATE   CUSTOMER

SET   ArtistID =

> **(SELECT   Top 1 ArtistID**
>
> **FROM   CUSTOMER_ARTIST_INT CI**
>
> **WHERE   CUSTOMER.CustomerID = CI.CustomerID);**

The phrase Top 1 is used to return the first qualifying row.

All views, triggers, stored procedures, and application code need to be changed to account for the new 1:N relationship. Then the constraints defined on CUSTOMER_ARTIST_INT can be dropped. Finally, the table CUSTOMER_ARTIST_INT can be dropped.

To change a 1:N to a 1:1 relationship, we just need to remove any duplicate values of the foreign key of the relationship and then add a unique constraint on the foreign key. See question 8.51.

Adding and Deleting Tables and Relationships

Adding new tables and relationships is straightforward. Just add the tables and relationships using CREATE TABLE statements with FOREIGN KEY constraints, as shown before. If an existing table has a child relationship to the new table, add a FOREIGN KEY constraint using the existing table.

For example, if a new table, COUNTRY, were added to the View Ridge database with the primary key Name and if CUSTOMER.Country is to be used as a foreign key into the new table, a new FOREIGN KEY constraint would be defined in CUSTOMER:

ALTER TABLE CUSTOMER

   ADD CONSTRAINT CountryFK FOREIGN KEY (Country)

      REFERENCES COUNTRY (Name)

      ON UPDATE CASCADE;

Deleting relationships and tables is just a matter of dropping the foreign key constraints and then dropping the tables. Of course, before this is done, dependency graphs must be constructed and used to determine which views, triggers, stored procedures, and application programs will be affected by the deletions.

As described in Chapter 4, another reason to add new tables and relationships or to compress existing tables into fewer tables is for normalization and denormalization. We will not address that topic further in this chapter, except to say that normalization and denormalization are common tasks during database redesign.

 ## Forward Engineering(?)

You can use a variety of different data modeling products to make database changes on your behalf. To do so, you first reverse engineer the database, make changes to the RE data model, and then invoke the forward-engineering functionality of the data modeling tool.

We will not consider forward engineering here because it hides the SQL that you need to learn. Also, the specifics of the forward-engineering process are product dependent.

Because of the importance of making data model changes correctly, many professionals are skeptical about using an automated process for database redesign. Certainly, it is necessary to test the results thoroughly before using forward engineering on operational data. Some products will show the SQL they are about to execute for review before making the changes to the database.

Database redesign is one area in which automation may not be the best idea. Much depends on the nature of the changes to be made and the quality of the forward-engineering features of the data modeling product. Given the knowledge you have gained in this chapter, you should be able to make most redesign changes by writing your own SQL. There is nothing wrong with that approach!

 # SUMMARY

Database redesign is the third way in which databases can arise. Redesign is necessary both to fix mistakes made during the initial database design and also to adapt the database to changes in system requirements. Such changes are common because information systems and organizations do not just influence each other—they create each other. Thus, new information systems cause changes in systems requirements.

Correlated subqueries and EXISTS/NOT EXISTS are important SQL statements. They can be used to answer advanced queries. They also are useful during database redesign for determining whether specified data conditions exist. For example, they can be used to determine whether possible functional dependencies exist in the data.

A correlated subquery appears deceptively similar to a regular subquery. The difference is that a regular subquery can be processed from the bottom up. In a regular subquery, results from the lowest query can be determined and then used to evaluate the upper-level queries. In contrast, in a correlated subquery, the processing is nested; that is, a row from an upper-level query statement is compared with rows in a lower-level query. The key distinction of a correlated subquery is that the lower-level SELECT statements use columns from upper-level statements. EXISTS and NOT EXISTS are specialized forms of correlated subqueries. With them, the upper-level query produces results, depending on the existence or nonexistence of rows in lower-level queries. An EXISTS condition is true if any row in the subquery meets the specified conditions; a NOT EXISTS condition is true only if all rows in the subquery do not meet the specified condition. NOT EXISTS is useful for queries that involve conditions that must be true for all rows, such as a "customer who has purchased all products." The double use of NOT EXISTS, shown on page 271, is a famous SQL pattern that often is used to test a person's knowledge of SQL.

Before redesigning a database, the existing database needs to be carefully examined to avoid making the database unusable by partially processing a database change. The rule is to measure twice and cut once. Reverse engineering is used to create a data model of the existing database. This is done to better understand the database structure before proceeding with a change. The data model produced, called a reverse engineered (RE) data model, is not a true data model, but is a thing unto itself. Most data modeling tools can perform reverse engineering. The RE data model almost always has missing information; such models should be carefully reviewed.

All of the elements of a database are interrelated. Dependency graphs are used to portray the dependency of one element on another. For example, a change in a table can potentially impact relationships, views, indexes, triggers, stored procedures, and application programs. These impacts need to be known and accounted for before making database changes.

A complete backup must be made to the operational database prior to any database redesign changes. Additionally, such changes must be thoroughly tested, initially on small test databases and later on larger test databases that may even be duplicates of the operational databases. The redesign changes are made only after such extensive testing has been completed.

Database redesign changes can be grouped into different types. One type involves changing table names and table columns. Changing a table name has a surprising number of potential consequences. A dependency graph should be used to understand these consequences before proceeding with the change. Nonkey columns are readily added and deleted. Adding a NOT NULL column must be done in three steps: first, add the column as NULL; then add data to every row; and then alter the column constraint to NOT NULL. To drop a column used as a foreign key, the foreign key constraint must first be dropped.

Column data types and constraints can be changed using the ALTER TABLE ALTER COLUMN statement. Changing the data type to char or varchar from a more specific type, such as date, is usually not a problem. Changing a data type from char or varchar to a more specific type can be a problem. In some cases, data will be lost or the DBMS may refuse the change. Constraints can be added or dropped using the ALTER TABLE ADD/DROP constraint statement. Use of this statement is easier if the developers have provided their own names for all constraints.

Changing minimum cardinalities on the parent side of a relationship is simply a matter of altering the constraint on the foreign key from NULL to NOT NULL or from NOT NULL to NULL. Changing minimum cardinalities on the child side of a relationship can be accomplished only by adding or dropping triggers that enforce the constraint.

Changing maximum cardinality from 1:1 to 1:N is simple if the foreign key resides in the correct table. In that case, just remove the unique constraint on the foreign key column. If the foreign key resides in the wrong table for this change, move the foreign key to the other table and do not place a unique constraint on that table.

Changing a 1:N relationship to an N:M one requires building a new intersection table and moving the primary key and foreign key values to the intersection table. This aspect of the change is relatively simple. It is more difficult to change all of the views, triggers, stored procedures, application programs, and forms and reports to use the new intersection table. Reducing cardinalities is easy, but such changes may result in data loss. Prior to making such reductions, a policy must be determined to decide which data to keep. Changing N:M to 1:N involves creating a foreign key in the parent table and moving one value from the intersection table into that foreign key. Changing 1:N to 1:1 requires first eliminating duplicates in the foreign key and then setting a uniqueness constraint on that key. Adding and deleting relationships can be accomplished by defining new foreign key constraints or by dropping existing foreign key constraints.

Most data modeling tools have the capacity to perform forward engineering, which is the process of applying data model changes to an existing database. If forward engineering is used, the results should be thoroughly tested before using it on an operational database. Some tools will show the SQL that they will execute during the forward-engineering process. Any SQL generated by such tools should be carefully reviewed. All in all, there is nothing wrong with writing database redesign SQL statements by hand rather than using forward engineering.

⊙ REVIEW QUESTIONS

8.1 Explain, one more time, the three ways that databases arise.

8.2 Describe why database redesign is necessary.

8.3 Explain the following statement in your own words: "Information systems and organizations create each other." How does this relate to database redesign?

8.4 Suppose that a table contains two nonkey columns: AdviserName and AdviserPhone. Further suppose that you suspect that AdviserPhone → AdviserName. Explain how to examine the data to determine if this supposition is true.

8.5 Write a subquery, other than one in this chapter, that is not a correlated subquery.

8.6 Explain the following statement: The processing of correlated subqueries is nested, whereas that of regular subqueries is not.

8.7 Write a correlated subquery, other than one in this chapter.

8.8 Explain how the query in your answer to question 8.5 differs from the query in your answer to question 8.7.

8.9 Explain what is wrong with the correlated subquery on page 269.

8.10 Write a correlated subquery to determine whether the data support the supposition in question 8.4.

8.11 Explain the meaning of the keyword EXISTS.

8.12 Answer question 8.10, but use EXISTS.

8.13 Explain how *any* and *all* pertain to EXISTS and NOT EXISTS.

8.14 Explain the processing of the query on page 271.

8.15 Write a query that will display the names of any customers who are interested in all artists.

8.16 Explain how the query in your answer to question 8.15 works.

8.17 Why is it important to analyze the database before implementing database redesign tasks? What can happen if this is not done?

8.18 Explain the process of reverse engineering.

8.19 Why is it important to carefully evaluate the results of reverse engineering?

8.20 What is a dependency graph? What purpose does it serve?

8.21 Explain the dependencies for WORK in the graph in Figure 8-4.

8.22 What sources are used when creating a dependency graph?

8.23 Explain two different types of test databases that should be used when testing database redesign changes.

8.24 Explain the problems that can occur when changing the name of a table.

8.25 Describe the process of changing a table name.

8.26 Considering Figure 8-4, describe the tasks that need to be accomplished to change the name of the table WORK to WORK_VERSION2.

8.27 Explain how views can simplify the process of changing a table name.

8.28 Under what conditions is the following SQL statement valid?

```
INSERT     INTO T1   (A, B)
           SELECT    (C, D) FROM T2;
```

8.29 Show a SQL statement to add an integer column C1 to the table T2. Assume that C1 is NULL.

8.30 Extend your answer to question 8.29 to add C1 when C1 is to be NOT NULL.

8.31 Show a SQL statement to drop the column C1 from table T2.

8.32 Describe the process for dropping primary key C1 and making the new primary key C2.

8.33 Which data type changes are the least risky?

8.34 Which data type changes are the most risky?

8.35 Show a SQL statement to change a column C1 to char(10) NOT NULL. What conditions must exist in the data for this change to be successful?

8.36 Explain how to change the minimum cardinality when a child that was required to have a parent is no longer required to have one.

8.37 Explain how to change the minimum cardinality when a child that was not required to have a parent is now required to have one. What condition must exist in the data for this change to work?

8.38 Explain how to change the minimum cardinality when a parent that was required to have a child is no longer required to have one.

8.39 Explain how to change the minimum cardinality when a parent that was not required to have a child is now required to have one.

8.40 Describe how to change the maximum cardinality from 1:1 to 1:N. Assume that the foreign key is on the side of the new child in the 1:N relationship.

8.41 Describe how to change the maximum cardinality from 1:1 to 1:N. Assume that the foreign key is on the side of the new parent in the 1:N relationship.

8.42 Assume that tables T1 and T2 have a 1:1 relationship. Assume that T2 has the foreign key. Show the SQL statements necessary to move the foreign key to T1. Make up your own names for primary and foreign keys.

8.43 Explain how to transform a 1:N relationship into an N:M relationship.

8.44 Suppose that tables T1 and T2 have a 1:N relationship. Show the SQL statements necessary to fill an intersection T1_T2_INT. Make up your own names for primary and foreign keys.

8.45 Explain how the reduction of maximum cardinalities causes data loss.

8.46 Using the tables in your answer to question 8.44, show the SQL statements necessary to change the relationship back to 1:N. Assume that the first row in the qualifying rows of the intersection table is to provide the foreign key. Use the keys and foreign keys from your answer to question 8.44.

8.47 Using the results of your answer to question 8.46, explain what must be done to convert this relationship to 1:1. Use the keys and foreign keys from your answer to question 8.46.

8.48 In general terms, what must be done to add a new relationship?

8.49 Suppose that tables T1 and T2 have a 1:N relationship, with T2 as the child. Show the SQL statements necessary to remove table T1. Make your own assumptions about the names of keys and foreign keys.

8.50 What are the risks and problems of forward engineering?

⊚ PROJECT QUESTIONS

8.51 Suppose that the table EMPLOYEE has a 1:N relationship to the table PHONE_NUMBER. Further suppose that the primary key of EMPLOYEE is EmployeeID and the columns of PHONE_NUMBER are PHNumber (a surrogate key), AreaCode, LocalNumber, and EmployeeID (a foreign key to EMPLOYEE). Alter this design so that EMPLOYEE has a 1:1 relationship to PHONE_NUMBER. For employees having more than one phone number, keep only the first one.

8.52 Suppose that the table EMPLOYEE has a 1:N relationship to the table PHONE_NUMBER. Further suppose that the key of EMPLOYEE is EmployeeID and the columns of PHONE_NUMBER are PHNumber (a surrogate key), AreaCode, LocalNumber, and EmployeeID (a foreign key to EMPLOYEE). Code all SQL statements necessary to redesign this database so that it has just one table. Explain the difference between the result of question 8.51 and the result of this question.

8.53 Consider the following table:

TASK (EmployeeID, Name, Phone, OfficeNumber, ProjectName, Sponsor, WorkDate, HoursWorked)

with the following possible functional dependencies:

EmployeeID → (Name, Phone, OfficeNumber)

ProjectName → Sponsor

a. Write SQL statements to display the values of any rows that violate these functional dependencies.

b. If no data violate these functional dependencies, can we assume that they are valid? Why or why not?

c. Assume that these functional dependencies are true and that the data have been corrected, as necessary, to reflect them. Code all SQL statements necessary to redesign this table into domain/key normal form. Assume that the table does have data values that must be appropriately transformed to the new design.

MARCIA'S DRY CLEANING

Assume that Marcia has created a database with the tables described at the end of Chapter 7:

> CUSTOMER (<u>CustomerSK</u>, Phone, Email, FirstName, LastName)
>
> ORDER (<u>InvoiceNumber</u>, Date, *CustomerSK*, Subtotal, Tax, Total)
>
> ORDER_ITEM (*<u>InvoiceNumber</u>*, <u>ItemNumber</u>, Qty, *Service*, UnitPrice, ExtendedPrice)
>
> SERVICE (<u>Service</u>, Description, UnitPrice)

Assume that all relationships have been defined, as implied by the foreign keys in this table list.

A Create a dependency graph that shows dependencies among these tables. Explain how you need to extend this graph for views and other database constructs such as triggers and stored procedures.

B Using your dependency graph, describe the tasks necessary to change the name of the ORDER table to CUST_ORDER.

C Write all SQL statements to make the name change described in question B.

D Suppose that Marcia decides to allow multiple customers per order (for customers' spouses, for example). Modify the design of these tables.

E Code SQL statements necessary to redesign the database, as described in your answer to question D.

F Suppose that Marcia considers changing the primary key of CUSTOMER to (FirstName, LastName). Write correlated subqueries to display any data that indicate that this change is not justifiable.

G Suppose that (FirstName, LastName) can be made the primary key of CUSTOMER. Make appropriate changes to the table design with this new primary key.

H Code all SQL statements necessary to implement the changes described in question G.

MORGAN IMPORTING

Assume that Morgan has created a database with the tables described at the end of Chapter 7:

> STORE (<u>StoreSK</u>, StoreName, City, Country, Phone, Fax, Email, Contact)
>
> PURCHASE (<u>PurchaseSK</u>, *StoreSK*, Date, Description, Category, PriceUSD)
>
> SHIPMENT (<u>ShipmentSK</u>, ShipDate, *ShipperName*, ShipperInvoiceNumber, Origin, Destination)
>
> SHIPMENT_ITEM (*<u>ShipmentSK</u>*, *<u>PurchaseSK</u>*, InsuredValue)
>
> SHIPPER (<u>ShipperName</u>, Phone, Fax, Email, Contact)

Assume that all relationships have been defined as implied by the foreign keys in this table list.

A Create a dependency graph that shows dependencies among these tables. Explain how you need to extend this graph for views and other database constructs such as stored procedures.

B Using your dependency graph, describe the tasks necessary to change the name of the SHIPMENT table to MORGAN_SHIPMENT.

C Write all SQL statements to make the name change described in question B.

D Suppose that Morgan decides to allocate some purchases to more than one shipment. Make design changes in accordance with this new fact. You will need to make assumptions about how purchases are divided and allocated to shipments. State your assumptions.

E Code SQL statements to implement your redesign recommendations in your answer to question D.

F Suppose that Morgan considers changing the primary key of PURCHASE to (StoreSK, Date). Write correlated subqueries to display any data that indicate that this change is not justifiable.

G Suppose that (StoreSK, Date) can be made the primary key of PURCHASE. Make appropriate changes to the table design.

H Code all SQL statements necessary to implement the changes described in question G.

Multiuser Database Processing

The three chapters in Part 4 introduce and discuss the major problems of multiuser database processing and describe the features
and functions for solving those problems offered by two important
DBMS products. We begin in Chapter 9 with a description of database administration and the major tasks and techniques for multiuser database management. The next two chapters illustrate the
implementation of these concepts using Oracle (Chapter 10) and
SQL Server (Chapter 11).

Managing Multiuser Databases

Although multiuser databases offer great value to the organizations that create and use them, they also pose difficult problems for those same organizations. For one, multiuser databases are complicated to design and develop because they support many overlapping user views. Additionally, as discussed in the last chapter, requirements change over time, and those changes necessitate other changes to the database structure. Such structural changes must be carefully planned and controlled so that a change made for one group does not cause problems for another. In addition, when users process a database concurrently, special controls are needed to ensure that the actions of one user do not inappropriately influence the results for another. This topic is both important and complicated, as you will see.

In large organizations, processing rights and responsibilities need to be defined and enforced. What happens, for example, when an employee leaves the firm? When can the employee's records be deleted? For the purposes of payroll processing, records can be deleted after the last pay period. For the purposes of quarterly reporting, they can be deleted at the end of the quarter. For the purposes of end-of-year tax record processing, they can be deleted at the end of the year. Clearly, no department can unilaterally decide when to delete that data. Similar comments pertain to the insertion and changing of data values. For these and other reasons, security systems need to be developed that enable only authorized users to take authorized actions at authorized times.

Databases have become key components of organizational operations and even key components of an organization's value. Unfortunately, database failures and disasters do occur. Accordingly, effective backup and recovery plans, techniques, and procedures are essential.

Finally, over time, the DBMS itself will need to be changed to improve performance by incorporating new features and releases and to conform with changes made in the underlying operating system. All of this requires attentive management.

To ensure that these problems are addressed and solved, most organizations have a database administration office. We begin with a description of the tasks of that office. We then describe the combination of software and manual practices and procedures that are used to perform those tasks. In the next two chapters, we will discuss and illustrate features and functions of Oracle and of SQL Server, respectively, for dealing with these issues.

 # Database Administration

The terms **data administration** and **database administration** are both used in practice. In some cases, the terms are considered to be synonymous; in other cases, they have different meanings. Most commonly, the term *data administration* refers to a function that applies to an entire organization; it is a management-oriented function that concerns corporate data privacy and security issues. In contrast, the term *database administration* refers to a more technical function that is specific to a particular database, including the applications that process that database. This chapter addresses database administration.

Databases vary considerably in size and scope, from single-user personal databases to large interorganizational databases, such as airline reservation systems. All of these databases have a need for database administration, although the tasks to be accomplished vary in complexity. For personal databases, individuals follow simple procedures for backing up their data, and they keep minimal records for documentation. In this case, the person who uses the database also performs the database administration functions, even though he or she is probably unaware of it.

For multiuser database applications, database administration becomes both more important and more difficult. Consequently, it generally has formal recognition. For some applications, one or two people are given this function on a part-time basis. For large Internet or intranet databases, database administration responsibilities are often too time consuming and too varied to be handled even by a single full-time person. Supporting a database with dozens or hundreds of users requires considerable time as well as both technical knowledge and diplomatic skills. Such support usually is handled by an office of database administration. The manager of the office is often known as the **database administrator;** in this case, the acronym **DBA** refers to either the office or the manager.

The overall responsibility of the DBA is to facilitate the development and use of the database. Usually, this means balancing the conflicting goals of protecting the database and maximizing its availability and benefit to users. Specific tasks are shown in Figure 9-1. We consider each of these tasks in the following sections.

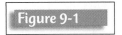

**Summary of Database
Administration Tasks**

> Managing database structure

> Controlling concurrent processing

> Managing processing rights and responsibilities

> Developing database security

> Providing for database recovery

> Managing the DBMS

> Maintaining the data repository

Managing the Database Structure

Managing the database structure includes participating in the initial database design and implementation as well as controlling and managing changes to the database. Ideally, the DBA is involved early in the development of the database and its applications; participates in the requirements study; helps evaluate alternatives, including the DBMS to be used; and helps design the database structure. For large organizational applications, the DBA usually is a manager who supervises the work of technically oriented database design personnel.

Creating the database involves several different tasks. First, the database is created and disk space is allocated for database files and logs. Then tables are generated, indexes are created, and stored procedures and triggers are written. We will discuss examples of all of these tasks in the next two chapters. Once the database structures are created, the database is filled with data.

Configuration Control

After a database and its applications have been implemented, changes in requirements are inevitable, as described in Chapter 8. Such changes can arise from new needs, from changes in the business environment, from changes in policy, and from changes in business processes that evolve with system use. When changes to requirements necessitate changes to the database structure, great care must be used, because changes to the database structure seldom involve just one application.

Hence, effective database administration includes procedures and policies by which users can register their needs for changes, the entire database community can discuss the impacts of the changes, and a global decision can be made whether to implement proposed changes. Because of the size and complexity of a database and its applications, changes sometimes have unexpected results. Thus, the DBA must be prepared to repair the database and to gather sufficient information to diagnose and correct the problem that caused the damage. The database is most vulnerable to failure after its structure has been changed.

Documentation

The DBA's final responsibility in managing the database structure is documentation. It is extremely important to know what changes have been made, how they were made, and when they were made. A change in the database structure may cause an error that is not revealed for six months; without proper documentation of the change, diagnosing the problem is next to impossible. Considerable work may be required to identify the point at which certain symptoms first appeared. For this reason, it also is important to maintain a record of the test procedures and test runs made to verify a change. If standardized test procedures, test forms, and recordkeeping methods are used, recording the test results does not have to be time consuming.

Figure 9-2

Summary of DBA's
Responsibilities for
Managing Database
Structure

**Participate in Database
and Application Development**
• Assist in requirements stage and data model
  creation
• Play an active role in database design and
  creation
Facilitate Changes to Database Structure
• Seek communitywide solutions
• Assess impact on all users
• Provide configuration control forum
• Be prepared for problems after changes are
  made
• Maintain documentation

Although maintaining documentation is tedious and unfulfilling, the effort pays off when disaster strikes and the documentation is the difference between a quick problem solution and a confused muddle of activity. Today, several products are emerging that ease the burden of documentation. Many CASE tools, for example, can be used to document logical database designs. Version-control software can be used to track changes. Data dictionaries provide reports and other outputs that present database data structures.

Another reason for carefully documenting changes in the database structure is so that historical data are used properly. If, for example, marketing wants to analyze three-year-old sales data that have been in the archives for two years, it will be necessary to know what structure was current at the time the data were last active. Records that show the changes in the structure can be used to answer that question. A similar situation arises when a six-month-old backup copy of data must be used to repair a damaged database (although this should not happen, it sometimes does). The backup copy can be used to reconstruct the database to the state it was in at the time of the backup. Then, transactions and structural changes can be made in chronological order to restore the database to its current state. Figure 9-2 summarizes the DBA's responsibilities for managing the database structure.

 ## Concurrency Control

Concurrency control measures are taken to ensure that one user's work does not inappropriately influence another user's work. In some cases, these measures ensure that a user gets the same result when processing with other users that he or she would have received if processing alone. In other cases, it means that the user's work is influenced by other users, but in an anticipated way. For example, in an order-entry system, a user should be able to enter an order and get the same result, regardless of whether there are no other users or hundreds of other users. On the other hand, a user who is printing a report of the most current inventory status may want to obtain in-process data changes from other users, even if there is a danger that those changes may later be cancelled.

Unfortunately, no concurrency control technique or mechanism is ideal for every circumstance. All involve trade-offs. For example, a program can obtain very strict concurrency control by locking the entire database, but no other programs will be able to do anything while it runs. This is strict protection, but at a high cost. As you will see, other measures are available that are more difficult to program or enforce but that allow more throughput. Still other measures are available that maximize throughput but have a low level of concurrency control. When designing multiuser database applications, you will need to choose among these trade-offs.

The Need for Atomic Transactions

In most database applications, users submit work in the form of **transactions,** which are also known as **logical units of work (LUWs).** A transaction (or LUW) is a series of actions to be taken on the database so that either all of them are performed successfully or none of them are performed at all, in which case the database remains unchanged. Such a transaction is sometimes called **atomic** because it is performed as a unit.

Consider the following sequence of database actions that could occur when recording a new order:

1 Change a customer's row, increasing AmtDue.
2 Change a salesperson's row, increasing CommissionDue.
3 Insert a new order row into the database.

Suppose that the last step failed, perhaps because of insufficient file space. Imagine the confusion if the first two changes were made but the third one was not. The customer would be billed for an order never received, and a salesperson would receive a commission on an order that was never sent to the customer. Clearly, these three actions need to be taken as a unit—either all of them should be done or none of them should be done.

Figure 9-3 compares the results of performing these activities as a series of independent steps (Figure 9-3(a)) and as an atomic transaction (Figure 9-3(b)). Notice that when the steps are carried out atomically and one fails, no changes are made in the database. Also note that the commands Start Transaction, Commit Transaction, and Rollback Transaction are issued by the application program to mark the boundaries of the transaction logic. You will learn more about these commands later in this chapter and in Chapters 10 and 11.

Concurrent Transaction Processing

When two transactions are being processed against a database at the same time, they are termed **concurrent transactions**. Although it may appear to the users that concurrent transactions are being processed simultaneously, this cannot be true because the CPU of the machine processing the database can execute only one instruction at a time. Usually, transactions are interleaved, which means that the operating system switches CPU services among tasks so that some portion of each transaction is carried out in a given interval. This switching among tasks is done so quickly that two people seated at browsers side by side, processing the same database, may believe that their two transactions are completed simultaneously; in reality, however, the two transactions are interleaved.

Figure 9-4 shows two concurrent transactions. User A's transaction reads Item 100, changes it, and rewrites it in the database. User B's transaction takes the same actions, but on Item 200. The CPU processes User A's transactions until it encounters an I/O interrupt or some other delay for User A. The operating system shifts control to User B. The CPU now processes User B's transactions until an interrupt, at which point the operating system passes control back to User A. To the users, the processing appears to be simultaneous, but it is interleaved, or concurrent.

The Lost Update Problem

The concurrent processing illustrated in Figure 9-4 poses no problems because the users are processing different data. But suppose that both users want to process Item 100. For example, User A wants to order five units of Item 100, and User B wants to order three units of the same item.

Figure 9-3

Need for Transaction Processing

(a) Errors Introduced without Transaction (b) Atomic Transaction Prevents Errors

Before

Action

After

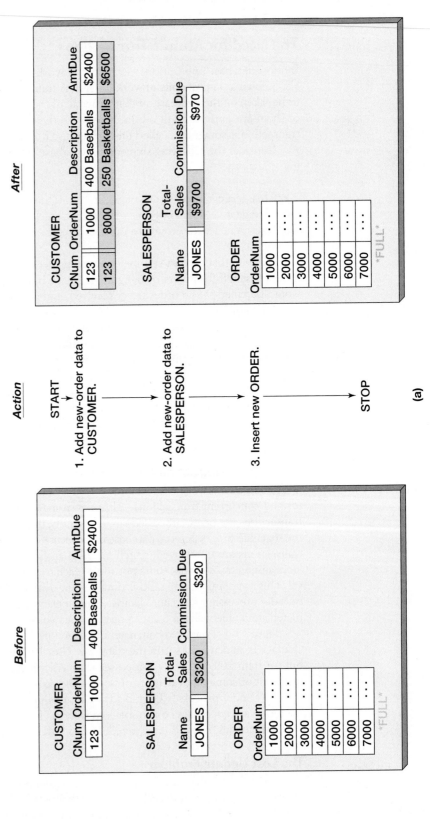

START

1. Add new-order data to CUSTOMER.

2. Add new-order data to SALESPERSON.

3. Insert new ORDER.

STOP

(a)

Before

CUSTOMER

CNum	OrderNum	Description	AmtDue
123	1000	400 Baseballs	$2400

SALESPERSON

Name	Total-Sales	Commission Due
JONES	$3200	$320

ORDER

OrderNum	
1000	...
2000	...
3000	...
4000	...
5000	...
6000	...
7000	...

FULL

Transaction

Start Transaction
  Change CUSTOMER data
  Change SALESPERSON data
  Insert ORDER data
If no errors then
  Commit Transactions
Else
  Rollback Transaction
End If

After

CUSTOMER

CNum	OrderNum	Description	AmtDue
123	1000	400 Baseballs	$2400

SALESPERSON

Name	Total-Sales	Commission Due
JONES	$3200	$320

ORDER

OrderNum	
1000	...
2000	...
3000	...
4000	...
5000	...
6000	...
7000	...

FULL

(b)

Figure 9-4

Concurrent-Processing
Example

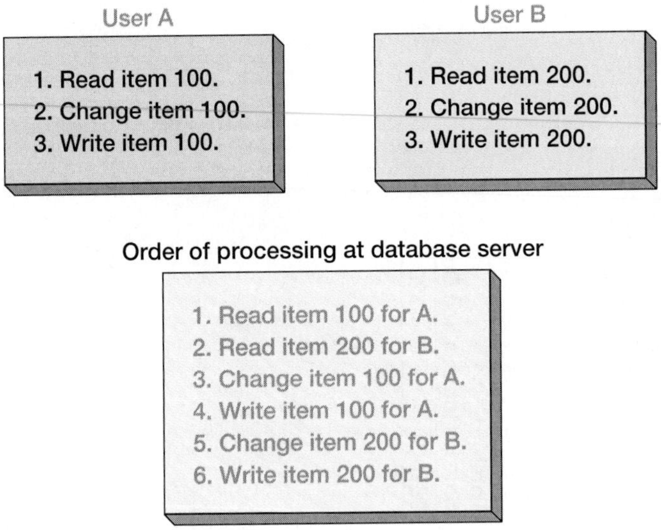

User A

1. Read item 100.
2. Change item 100.
3. Write item 100.

User B

1. Read item 200.
2. Change item 200.
3. Write item 200.

Order of processing at database server

1. Read item 100 for A.
2. Read item 200 for B.
3. Change item 100 for A.
4. Write item 100 for A.
5. Change item 200 for B.
6. Write item 200 for B.

Figure 9-5 illustrates the problem. User A reads a copy of Item 100's record into memory. According to the record, there are 10 items in inventory. Then User B reads another copy of Item 100's record into a different section of memory. Again, according to the record, there are 10 items in inventory. Now User A takes five, decrements the count of items in its copy of the data to five, and rewrites the record for Item 100. Then User B takes three, decrements the count in its copy of the data to seven, and rewrites the record for Item 100. The database now shows, incorrectly, that there are seven Item 100s in inventory. To review: We started with 10 in inventory, User A took five, User B took three, and the database shows that seven are in inventory. Clearly, this is a problem.

Both users obtained data that were correct at the time they obtained them. But when User B read the record, User A already had a copy that it was about to update. This situation is called the **lost update problem,** or the **concurrent update problem.** A similar problem is the **inconsistent read problem.** With this problem, User A reads data that have been processed by a portion of a transaction from User B. As a result, User A reads incorrect data.

Figure 9-5

Lost-Update Problem

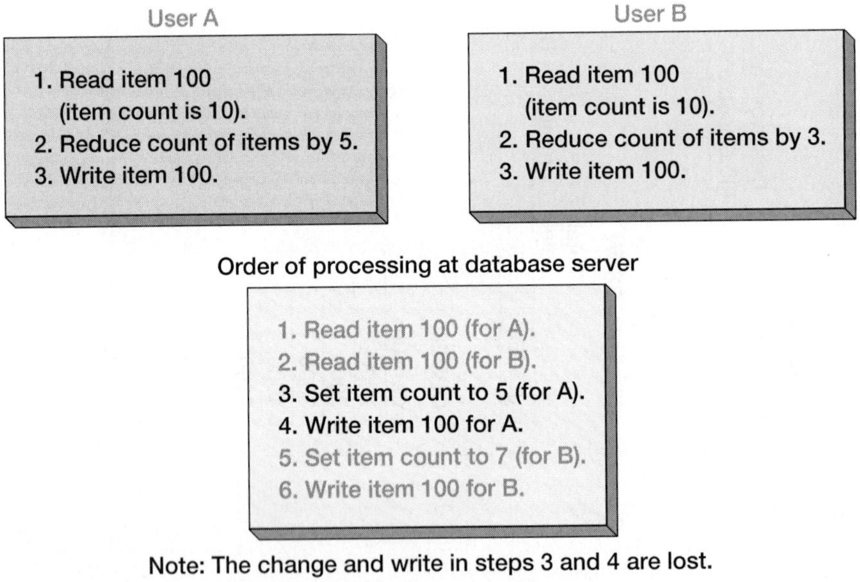

User A

1. Read item 100
   (item count is 10).
2. Reduce count of items by 5.
3. Write item 100.

User B

1. Read item 100
   (item count is 10).
2. Reduce count of items by 3.
3. Write item 100.

Order of processing at database server

1. Read item 100 (for A).
2. Read item 100 (for B).
3. Set item count to 5 (for A).
4. Write item 100 for A.
5. Set item count to 7 (for B).
6. Write item 100 for B.

Note: The change and write in steps 3 and 4 are lost.

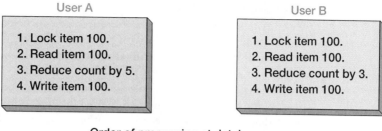

Figure 9-6

Concurrent Processing with Explicit Locks

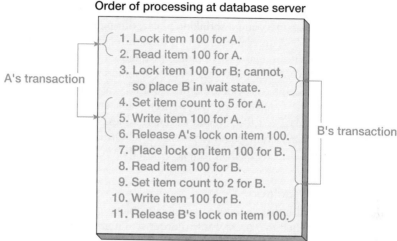

One remedy for the inconsistencies caused by concurrent processing is to prevent multiple applications from obtaining copies of the same record when the record is about to be changed. This remedy is called **resource locking**.

Resource Locking

One way to prevent concurrent processing problems is to disallow sharing by locking data that are retrieved for update. Figure 9-6 shows the order of processing using a **lock** command. Because of the lock, User B's transaction must wait until User A is finished with the Item 100 data. Using this strategy, User B can read Item 100's record only after User A has completed the modification. In this case, the final item count stored in the database is two, as it should be. (We started with 10, User A took five, and User B took three, leaving two.)

Lock Terminology

Locks can be placed either automatically by the DBMS or by a command issued to the DBMS from the application program. Locks placed by the DBMS are called **implicit locks;** those placed by command are called **explicit locks.** Today, almost all locking is implicit. The program declares the behavior it wants, and the DBMS places locks accordingly. You will learn how to do that later in this chapter.

In the preceding example, the locks were applied to rows of data. Not all locks are applied at this level, however. Some DBMS products lock groups of rows within a table, some lock entire tables, and some lock the entire database. The size of a lock is referred to as **lock granularity.** Locks with large granularity are easy for the DBMS to administer, but frequently cause conflicts. Locks with small granularity are difficult to administer (the DBMS has to track and check many more details), but conflicts are less common.

Locks also vary by type. An **exclusive lock** locks the item from any other access. No other transaction can read or change the data. A **shared lock** locks the item from change but not from read. That is, other transactions can read the item as long as they do not attempt to alter it.

Serializable Transactions

When two or more transactions are processed concurrently, the results in the database should be logically consistent with the results that would have been achieved had the transactions been processed in an arbitrary, serial fashion. A scheme for processing concurrent transactions in this way is said to be **serializable.**

Serializability can be achieved by a number of different means. One way is to process the transaction using **two-phased locking.** With this strategy, transactions are allowed to obtain locks as necessary, but once the first lock is released, no other lock can be obtained. Transactions thus have a **growing phase,** during which the locks are obtained, and a **shrinking phase,** during which the locks are released.

A special case of two-phased locking is used with a number of DBMS products. With it, locks are obtained throughout the transaction, but no lock is released until the COMMIT or ROLLBACK command is issued. This strategy is more restrictive than two-phase locking requires, but it is easier to implement.

Consider an order-entry transaction that processes data in the CUSTOMER, SALESPERSON, and ORDER tables. To avoid concurrency problems, the order-entry transaction issues locks on CUSTOMER, SALESPERSON, and ORDER, as needed; makes all database changes; and then releases all locks.

Deadlock

Although locking solves one problem, it introduces another. Consider what can happen when two users want to order two items from inventory. Suppose that User A wants to order some paper, and if she can get the paper, she wants to order some pencils. Then suppose that User B wants to order some pencils, and if he can get the pencils, he wants to order some paper. The order of processing is shown in Figure 9-7.

In this figure, Users A and B are locked in a condition known as **deadlock,** or sometimes as the **deadly embrace.** Each user is waiting for a resource that the other has locked. This problem can be solved either by preventing the deadlock from occurring or by allowing the deadlock to occur and then breaking it.

Deadlock can be prevented in several ways. One way is to require users to issue all lock requests at one time. In the illustration, if User A had locked both the paper and the pencil records at the beginning, deadlock would not occur. A second way to prevent deadlock is to require all application programs to lock resources in the same order.

Figure 9-7

Deadlock

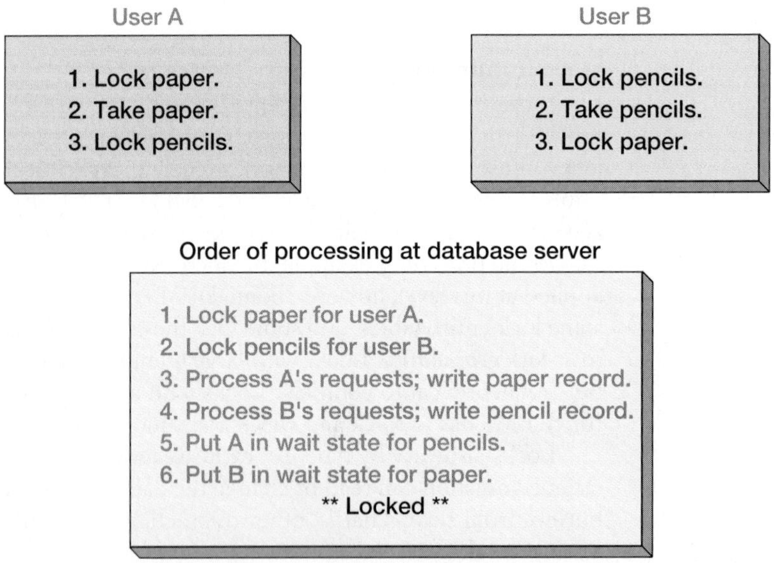

User A

1. Lock paper.
2. Take paper.
3. Lock pencils.

User B

1. Lock pencils.
2. Take pencils.
3. Lock paper.

Order of processing at database server

1. Lock paper for user A.
2. Lock pencils for user B.
3. Process A's requests; write paper record.
4. Process B's requests; write pencil record.
5. Put A in wait state for pencils.
6. Put B in wait state for paper.
   ** Locked **

> ## B T W
>
> Even if all the applications do not lock resources in the same order, deadlock will be prevented for those that do. Sometimes this policy is implemented with an organizational programming standard such as "Whenever processing rows from tables in a parent-child relationship, lock the parent row before the child rows." This policy will at least reduce the likelihood of deadlock and thus save the DBMS from having to recover from some deadlocked transactions.

Almost every DBMS has algorithms for breaking deadlock, when it does occur. First the DBMS must detect that it has occurred. Then, the typical solution is to cancel one of the transactions and remove its changes from the database. You will see variants of this with Oracle and SQL Server in the next two chapters.

Optimistic versus Pessimistic Locking

Locks can be invoked in two basic styles. With **optimistic locking,** the assumption is made that no conflict will occur. Data are read, the transaction is processed, updates are issued, and then a check is made to see if conflict occurred. If not, the transaction is finished. If conflict did occur, the transaction is repeated until it processes with no conflict. With **pessimistic locking,** the assumption is made that conflict will occur. Locks are issued, the transaction is processed, and then the locks are freed.

Figure 9-8 shows an example of each style for a transaction that is reducing the quantity of the pencil row in PRODUCT by five. Figure 9-8(a) shows optimistic locking. First, the data are read and the current value of Quantity of pencils is saved in the variable OldQuantity. The transaction is then processed, and assuming that all is OK, a lock is obtained on PRODUCT. (In fact, the lock might be only for the pencil row or it might be at a larger level of granularity, but the principle is the same.) After obtaining the lock, a SQL statement is issued to update the pencil row with a WHERE condition that the current value of Quantity equals OldQuantity. If no other transaction has changed the Quantity of the pencil row, then this UPDATE will be successful. If another transaction has changed the Quantity of the pencil row, the UPDATE will fail. In either case, the lock is released. If the transaction failed, the process is repeated until the transaction finishes with no conflict.

Figure 9-8(b) shows the logic for the same transaction using pessimistic locking. Here, a lock is obtained on PRODUCT before any work is begun. Then, values are read, the transaction is processed, the UPDATE occurs, and PRODUCT is unlocked.

The advantage of optimistic locking is that locks are held for much less time than with pessimistic locking, because locks are obtained only after the transaction has finished. If the transaction is complicated or if the client is slow (due to transmission delays, the client doing other work, or the user getting a cup of coffee or shutting down without exiting the browser), optimistic locking can dramatically improve throughput. This advantage will be especially true if the lock granularity is large—say, the entire PRODUCT table.

The disadvantage of optimistic locking is that if there is a lot of activity on the pencil row, the transaction may have to be repeated many times. Thus, transactions that involve a lot of activity on a given row (purchasing a popular stock, for example) are poorly suited for optimistic locking.

In general, the Internet is a wild and woolly place, and users are likely to take unexpected actions, such as abandoning transactions in the middle. So, unless Internet users have been prequalified (by enrolling in an online brokerage stock purchase plan, for example), optimistic locking is the better choice in that environment. On intranets, however, the decision is more difficult. Optimistic locking is probably still preferred unless some characteristic of the application causes substantial activity

SELECT   PRODUCT.Name, PRODUCT.Quantity
FROM   PRODUCT
WHERE   PRODUCT.Name = 'Pencil'

Set NewQuantity = PRODUCT.Quantity – 5

{process transaction – take exception action if NewQuantity < 0, etc.

Assuming all is OK: }

LOCK PRODUCT

UPDATE   PRODUCT
SET   PRODUCT.Quantity = NewQuantity
WHERE   PRODUCT.Name = 'Pencil'
       AND PRODUCT.Quantity = OldQuantity

UNLOCK   PRODUCT

{check to see if update was successful;
if not, repeat transaction}

(a)

LOCK   PRODUCT

SELECT   PRODUCT.Name, PRODUCT.Quantity
FROM   PRODUCT
WHERE   PRODUCT.Name = 'Pencil'

Set NewQuantity = PRODUCT.Quantity – 5

{process transaction – take exception action if NewQuantity < 0, etc.

Assuming all is OK: }

UPDATE   PRODUCT
SET   PRODUCT.Quantity = NewQuantity
WHERE   PRODUCT.Name = 'Pencil'

UNLOCK   PRODUCT

{no need to check if update was successful}

(b)

on particular rows or if application requirements make reprocessing transactions particularly undesirable.

Declaring Lock Characteristics

As you can see, concurrency control is a complicated subject; determining the level, type, and placement of the lock is difficult. Sometimes, too, the optimum locking strategy depends on which transactions are active and what they are doing. For these and other reasons, database application programs do not generally explicitly issue locks as shown in Figure 9-8. Instead, they mark transaction boundaries and then declare the type of locking behavior they want the DBMS to use. In this way, the DBMS can place and remove locks and even change the level and type of locks dynamically.

Figure 9-9

Marking Transaction Boundaries

BEGIN TRANSACTION:

SELECT   PRODUCT.Name, PRODUCT.Quantity
FROM   PRODUCT
WHERE   PRODUCT.Name = 'Pencil'

Set NewQuantity = PRODUCT.Quantity – 5

{process transaction – take exception action if NewQuantity < 0, etc.}

UPDATE   PRODUCT
SET   PRODUCT.Quantity = NewQuantity
WHERE   PRODUCT.Name = 'Pencil'

{continue processing transaction} . . .

IF transaction has completed normally   THEN

        COMMIT TRANSACTION

ELSE

        ROLLBACK TRANSACTION

END IF

Continue processing other actions not part of this transaction . . .

Figure 9-9 shows the pencil transaction with transaction boundaries marked with BEGIN TRANSACTION, COMMIT TRANSACTION, and ROLLBACK TRANSACTION statements. These boundaries are the essential information that the DBMS needs to enforce the different locking strategies. If the developer now declares via a system parameter that he or she wants optimistic locking, the DBMS will implicitly set locks for that locking style. If, on the other hand, the developer declares pessimistic locking, the DBMS will set the locks differently.

Consistent Transactions

Sometimes, you will see the acronym ACID applied to transactions. An **ACID transaction** is one that is *a*tomic, *c*onsistent, *i*solated, and *d*urable. Atomic and durable are easy to define. As you just learned, an atomic transaction is one in which either all of the database actions occur or none of them do. A durable transaction is one in which all committed changes are permanent. Once a durable change is committed, the DBMS takes responsibility for ensuring that the change will survive system failures.

The terms **consistent** and **isolated** are not as definitive as the terms **atomic** and **durable**. Consider the following SQL UPDATE command:

UPDATE   CUSTOMER

SET   AreaCode = '425'

WHERE   ZipCode = '98050';

Suppose that there are 500,000 rows in the CUSTOMER table, and that 500 of them have ZipCode equal to '98050'. It will take some time for the DBMS to find those

500 rows. During that time, other transactions may attempt to update the AreaCode or ZipCode fields of CUSTOMER. If the SQL statement is consistent, such update requests will be disallowed. Hence, the update will apply to the set of rows as they existed at the time the SQL statement started. Such consistency is called **statement-level consistency.**

Now, consider a transaction that contains two SQL UPDATE statements:

BEGIN TRANSACTION

> **UPDATE**   **CUSTOMER**
>
> **SET**   **AreaCode = '425'**
>
> **WHERE**   **ZipCode = '98050';**
>
> **{other transaction work}**
>
> **UPDATE**   **CUSTOMER**
>
> **SET**   **Discount = 0.05**
>
> **WHERE**   **AreaCode = '425';**
>
> **{other transaction work}**

COMMIT TRANSACTION

In this context, what does *consistent* mean? Statement-level consistency means that each statement independently processes rows consistently, but that changes from other users to these rows might be allowed during the interval between the two SQL statements. **Transaction-level consistency** means that all rows impacted by either of the SQL statements are protected from changes during the entire transaction.

Observe that transaction-level consistency is so strong that, for some implementations of it, a transaction will not see its own changes. In this example, the second SQL statement may not see rows changed by the first SQL statement.

Thus, when you hear the term *consistent,* look further to determine which type of consistency is meant. Be aware as well of the potential trap of transaction-level consistency.

Transaction Isolation Level

The term *isolated* has several different meanings. To understand those meanings, we need first to define several new terms.

A **dirty read** occurs when a transaction reads a row that has been changed but for which the change has not yet been committed to the database. The danger of a dirty read is that the uncommitted change can be rolled back. If so, the transaction that made the dirty read will be processing incorrect data.

Nonrepeatable reads occur when a transaction rereads data it has previously read and finds modifications or deletions caused by a committed transaction. Finally, **phantom reads** occur when a transaction rereads data and finds new rows that were inserted by a committed transaction since the prior read.

The 1992 SQL standard defines four **isolation levels** which specify which of these problems are allowed to occur. Using these levels, the application programmer can declare the type of isolation level he or she wants and the DBMS will create and manage locks to achieve that level of isolation.

As shown in Figure 9-10, the read uncommitted isolation level allows dirty reads, nonrepeatable reads, and phantom reads to occur. With read committed isolation, dirty reads are disallowed. The repeatable read isolation level disallows both dirty reads and nonrepeatable reads. The serializable isolation level will not allow any of these three problems to occur.

| Figure 9-10 | Summary of Transaction Isolation Levels |

		Isolation Level			
		Read Uncommitted	Read Committed	Repeatable Read	Serializable
Problem Type	Dirty Read	Possible	Not Possible	Not Possible	Not Possible
	Nonrepeatable Read	Possible	Possible	Not Possible	Not Possible
	Phantom Read	Possible	Possible	Possible	Not Possible

Generally, the more restrictive the level, the less the throughput, though much depends on the workload and how the application programs are written. Moreover, not all DBMS products support all of these levels. You will learn how Oracle and SQL Server support isolation levels in the next two chapters.

Cursor Type

A cursor is a pointer into a set of rows. Cursors are usually defined using SELECT statements. For example, the following statement defines a cursor named TransCursor that operates over the set of rows indicated by the following SELECT statement:

DECLARE CURSOR TransCursor AS

> **SELECT**   *
>
> **FROM**   [TRANSACTION]
>
> **WHERE**   PurchasePrice > '10000';

As explained in Chapter 7, after an application program opens a cursor, it can place the cursor somewhere in the result set. Most commonly, the cursor is placed on the first or last row, but other possibilities exist.

A transaction can open several cursors—either sequentially or simultaneously. Additionally, two or more cursors may be open on the same table; either directly on the table or through a SQL view on that table. Because cursors require considerable memory, having many cursors open at the same time for, say, a thousand concurrent transactions, will consume considerable memory. One way to reduce cursor burden is to define reduced-capability cursors and use them when a full-capability cursor is not needed.

Figure 9-11 lists four cursor types used in the Windows environment (cursor types for other systems are similar). The simplest cursor is forward only. With it, the application can only move forward through the records. Changes made by other cursors in this transaction and by other transactions will be visible only if they occur to rows ahead of the cursor.

The next three types of cursors are called **scrollable cursors** because the application can scroll forward and backward through the records. A **static cursor** takes a snapshot of a relation and processes that snapshot. Changes made using this cursor are visible; changes from other sources are not visible.

Keyset cursors combine some of the features of static cursors with some of the features of dynamic cursors. When the cursor is opened, a primary key value is saved for each row. When the application positions the cursor on a row, the DBMS uses the key value to read the current value of the row. Inserts of new rows by other cursors (in this transaction or in other transactions) are not visible. If the application issues an update on a row that has been deleted by a different cursor, the DBMS creates a new row with the old key value and places the updated values in the new row (assuming that all required

Figure 9-11

Summary of Cursor Types

CursorType	Description	Comments
Forward only	Application can only move forward through the recordset.	Changes made by other cursors in this transaction or in other transactions will be visible only if they occur on rows ahead of the cursor.
Static	Application sees the data as they were at the time the cursor was opened.	Changes made by this cursor are visible. Changes from other sources are not visible. Backward and forward scrolling allowed.
Keyset	When the cursor is opened, a primary key value is saved for each row in the recordset. When the application accesses a row, the key is used to fetch the current values for the row.	Updates from any source are visible. Inserts from sources outside this cursor are not visible (there is no key for them in the keyset). Inserts from this cursor appear at the bottom of the recordset. Deletions from any source are visible. Changes in row order are not visible. If the isolation level is dirty read, then committed updates and deletions are visible; otherwise only committed updates and deletions are visible.
Dynamic	Changes of any type and from any source are visible.	All inserts, updates, deletions, and changes in recordset order are visible. If the isolation level is dirty read, then uncommitted changes are visible. Otherwise, only committed changes are visible.

fields are present). Unless the isolation level of the transaction is a dirty read, only committed updates and deletions are visible to the cursor.

A **dynamic cursor** is a fully featured cursor. All inserts, updates, deletions, and changes in row order are visible to a dynamic cursor. As with keyset cursors, unless the isolation level of the transaction is a dirty read, only committed changes are visible.

The amount of overhead and processing required to support a cursor is different for each type of cursor. In general, the cost goes up as we move down the cursor types shown in Figure 9-11. To improve DBMS performance, the application developer should create cursors that are just powerful enough to do the job. It is also very important to understand how a particular DBMS implements cursors and whether cursors are located on the server or on the client. In some cases, it might be better to place a dynamic cursor on the client than to have a static cursor on the server. No general rule can be stated because performance depends on the implementation used by the DBMS product and the application requirements.

A word of caution: If you do not specify the isolation level of a transaction or do not specify the type of cursors you open, the DBMS will use a default level and default types. These defaults may be perfect for your application, but they also may be terrible. Thus, even though these issues can be ignored, their consequences cannot be avoided. You must learn the capabilities of your DBMS product.

Database Security

The goal of database security is to ensure that only authorized users can perform authorized activities at authorized times. This goal is difficult to achieve, and to make any progress at all the database development team must determine the processing rights and responsibilities of all users during the project's requirements specification phase. These security requirements can then be enforced using the security features of the DBMS and additions to those features written into the application programs.

Processing Rights and Responsibilities

Consider, for example, the needs of View Ridge Gallery. The View Ridge database has three types of users: sales personnel, management personnel, and system administrators. View Ridge designed processing rights for each as follows: Sales personnel are allowed to enter new customer and transaction data, to change customer data, and to query any of the data. They are not allowed to enter new artist or work data. They are never allowed to delete data.

Management personnel are allowed all of the permissions of sales personnel, plus they are allowed to enter new artist and work data and to modify transaction data. Even though management personnel have the authority to delete data, they are not given that permission in this application. This restriction is made to prevent the possibility of accidental data loss.

The system administrator can grant processing rights to other users; and he or she can change the structure of the database elements such as tables, indexes, stored procedures, and the like. The system administrator is not given rights to process the data. Figure 9-12 summarizes these requirements.

B T W

You may be wondering what good it does to say that the system administrator cannot process the data when that person has the ability to grant processing rights. He or she can just grant the right to change data to him- or herself. While this is true, the granting of those rights will leave an audit trail in the database log. Clearly, this limitation is not foolproof, but it is better than just allowing the system administrator (or DBA) full access to all rights in the database.

Figure 9-12   Processing Rights at View Ridge Gallery

	CUSTOMER	TRANSACTION	WORK	ARTIST
Sales personnel	Insert, change, query	Insert, query	Query	Query
Management personnel	Insert, change, query	Insert, change, query	Insert, change, query	Insert, change, query
System administrator	Grant rights, modify structure	Grant rights, modify structure	Grant rights, modify structure	Grant rights, modify structure

The permissions in this table are not given to particular people, but rather are given to groups of people. Sometimes these groups are termed **roles,** because they describe people acting in a particular capacity. The term **user groups** also is used. Assigning permission to roles (or user groups) is typical, but not required. It would be possible to say, for example, that the user identified as "Benjamin Franklin" has certain processing rights. Note, too, that when roles are used, it is necessary to have a way to allocate users to roles. When "Mary Smith" signs on to the computer, there must be some way to determine which role or roles she has. We will discuss this further in the next section.

In this discussion, we have used the phrase **processing rights and responsibilities.** As this phrase implies, responsibilities go with processing rights. If, for example, the manager modifies transaction data, the manager has the responsibility to ensure that these modifications do not adversely impact the gallery's operation, accounting, and so forth.

Processing responsibilities cannot be enforced by the DBMS or by the database applications. Instead, they are encoded in manual procedures and explained to users during systems training. These are topics for a systems development text, and we will not consider them further here—except to reiterate that *responsibilities* go with *rights.* Such responsibilities must be documented and enforced.

According to Figure 9-1, the DBA has the task of managing processing rights and responsibilities. As this implies, these rights and responsibilities will change over time. As the database is used and as changes are made to the applications and to the structure of the DBMS, the need for new or different rights and responsibilities will arise. The DBA is a focal point for the discussion of such changes and for their implementation.

Once processing rights have been defined, they can be implemented at many levels: operating system, network, Web server, DBMS, and application. In the next two sections, we will consider DBMS and application implementation. The other levels are beyond the scope of this text.

DBMS Security

The terminology, features, and functions of DBMS security depend on the DBMS product in use. Basically, all such products provide facilities that limit certain actions on certain objects to certain users. A general model of DBMS security is shown in Figure 9-13. A USER can be assigned to one or more ROLEs (or USER GROUPs), and a ROLE can have one or more USERs. An OBJECT is an element of a database, such as a table, view, or stored procedure. PERMISSION is an association entity among USER, ROLE, and OBJECT. Hence, the relationships from USER to PERMISSION, ROLE to PERMIS-SION, and OBJECT to PERMISSION are all 1:N, M-O.

Figure 9-13

A Model of DBMS Security

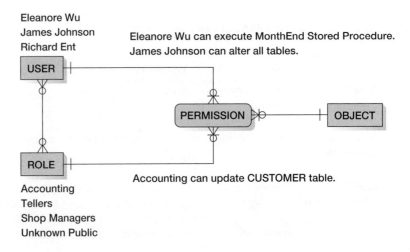

Eleanore Wu
James Johnson
Richard Ent

Eleanore Wu can execute MonthEnd Stored Procedure.
James Johnson can alter all tables.

USER

PERMISSION   OBJECT

ROLE

Accounting
Tellers
Shop Managers
Unknown Public

Accounting can update CUSTOMER table.

When a user signs on to the database, the DBMS limits the user's actions to the permissions defined for that user and to the permissions for roles to which that user has been assigned. Determining whether someone actually is who they claim to be is a difficult task in general. All commercial DBMS products use some version of user name and password verification, even though such security is readily circumvented if users are careless with their identities.

Users can enter their name and password, or, in some applications, the name and password is entered on behalf of the user. For example, the Windows user name and password can be directly passed to the DBMS. In other cases, an application program provides the name and password. Internet applications usually define a group such as "Unknown Public" and assign anonymous users to that group when they sign on. In this way, companies, such as Dell, need not enter every potential customer into their security system by name and password.

Oracle and SQL Server security systems are variations of the model in Figure 9-13. You will learn about them in Chapters 10 and 11, respectively.

DBMS Security Guidelines

Guidelines for improving security in database systems are listed in Figure 9-14. First, the DBMS must always be run behind a firewall. However, the DBA should plan security with the assumption that the firewall has been breached. The DBMS, the database, and all applications should be secure even if the firewall fails.

DBMS vendors, including IBM, Oracle, and Microsoft, are constantly adding product features to improve security and reduce vulnerability. Consequently, organizations using DBMS products should continually check the vendors' Web sites for service packs and fixes; any service packs or fixes that involve security features, functions, and processing should be installed as soon as possible.

The installation of new service packs and fixes is not quite as simple as described here. The installation of a service pack or fix can break some applications, particularly

Figure 9-14

Summary of DBMS
Security Guidelines

- Run DBMS behind a firewall, but plan as though the firewall has been breached
- Apply the latest operating system and DBMS service packs and fixes
- Use the least functionality possible
  - Support the fewest network protocols possible
  - Delete unnecessary or unused system stored procedures
  - Disable default logins and guest users, if possible
  - Unless required, never allow users to log on to the DBMS interactively
- Protect the computer that runs the DBMS
  - No user allowed to work at the computer that runs the DBMS
  - DBMS computer physically secured behind locked doors
  - Visits to the room containing the DBMS computer should be recorded in a log
- Manage accounts and passwords
  - Use a low privilege user account for the DBMS service
  - Protect database accounts with strong passwords
  - Monitor failed login attempts
  - Frequently check group and role memberships
  - Audit accounts with null passwords
  - Assign accounts the lowest privileges possible
  - Limit DBA account privileges
- Planning
  - Develop a security plan for preventing and detecting security problems
  - Create procedures for security emergencies and practice them

some licensed software that requires specific service packs and fixes to be installed (or not installed). It may be necessary to delay installation of DBMS service packs until vendors of licensed software have upgraded their products to work with the new versions. Sometimes just the possibility that a licensed application *might* fail after a DBMS service pack or fix is applied is sufficient reason to delay the fix. But, the DBMS is still vulnerable during this period. Pick your regret!

Additionally, database features and functions that are not required by the applications should be removed or disabled from the DBMS. For example, if TCP/IP is used to connect to the DBMS, other communications protocols should be removed. This action reduces the pathways by which unauthorized activity can reach the DBMS. Further, all DBMS products are installed with system-stored procedures that provide services such as starting a command file, modifying the system registry, initiating e-mail, and the like. Any of these stored procedures that are not needed should be removed. If all users are known to the DBMS, default logins and guest user accounts should be removed as well. Finally, unless otherwise required, users should never be allowed to log on to the DBMS in interactive mode. They should always access the database via an application.

In addition, the computer(s) that runs the DBMS must be protected. No one other than authorized DBA personnel should be allowed to work at the keyboard of the computer that runs the DBMS. The computer running the DBMS should be physically secured behind locked doors, and access to the facility housing the computer should be controlled. Visits to the DBMS computer room should be recorded in a log.

Accounts and passwords should be assigned carefully and continually managed. The DBMS itself should run on an account that has the lowest possible operating system privileges. In that way, if an intruder were to gain control of the DBMS, the intruder would have limited authority on that local computer or network. Additionally, all accounts within the DBMS should be protected by **strong passwords.** Such passwords have at least eight characters and contain upper- and lowercase letters; numbers; special characters, such as +, @, #, ***; and unprintable key combinations (certain Alt + key combinations).

The DBA should frequently check the accounts that have been assigned to groups and roles to ensure that all accounts and roles are known, authorized, and have the correct permissions. Further, the DBA should audit accounts with null passwords. The users of such accounts should be required to protect those accounts with strong passwords. Also, as a general rule, accounts should be granted the lowest privileges possible.

As stated, the privileges for the DBA should normally not include the right to process the users data. If the DBA grants him- or herself that privilege, the unauthorized grant operation will be visible in the database log.

In the Spring of 2003, the Slammer worm invaded thousands of sites running SQL Server. Microsoft had previously released a patch to SQL Server that prevented this attack. Sites that had installed the patch had no problems. The moral: Install security patches to your DBMS as promptly as possible. Create a procedure for regularly checking for such patches.

Finally, the DBA should participate in security planning. Procedures both for preventing and detecting security problems should be developed. Furthermore, procedures should be developed for actions to be taken in case of a security breach. Such procedures should be practiced. The importance of security in information systems has increased dramatically in recent years. DBA personnel should regularly search for security information on the Web in general and at the DBMS vendor's Web site.

Application Security

Although DBMS products such as Oracle and SQL Server do provide substantial database security capabilities, those capabilities are generic. If the application requires specific security measures such as "No user can view a row of a table or of a join of a table that has an employee name other than his or her own," the DBMS facilities will not be adequate. In these cases, the security system must be augmented by features in database applications.

For example, as you will learn in Chapter 12, application security in Internet applications is often provided on the Web server. Executing application security on this server means that sensitive security data need not be transmitted over the network.

To understand this better, suppose that an application is written so that when users click a particular button on a browser page, the following query is sent to the Web server and then to the DBMS:

SELECT   *

FROM   EMPLOYEE;

This statement will, of course, return all EMPLOYEE rows. If the application security policy only permits employees to access their own data, then a Web server could add the following WHERE clause to this query:

SELECT   *

FROM   EMPLOYEE

WHERE   EMPLOYEE.Name = '<% = SESSION(("EmployeeName)")%>';

As you will learn in Chapter 12, an expression like this one will cause the Web server to fill the employee's name into the WHERE clause. For a user signed in under the name 'Benjamin Franklin', the statement that results from this expression is:

SELECT   *

FROM   EMPLOYEE

WHERE   EMPLOYEE.Name = 'Benjamin Franklin';

Because the name is inserted by a program on the Web server, the browser user does not know that it is occurring, and cannot interfere with it even if he or she did.

Such security processing can be done as shown here on a Web server, but it also can be done within the application programs themselves or written as stored procedures or triggers to be executed by the DBMS at the appropriate times.

This idea can be extended by storing additional data in a security database that is accessed by the Web server or by stored procedures and triggers. That security database could contain, for example, the identities of users paired with additional values of WHERE clauses. For example, suppose that the users in the personnel department can access more than just their own data. The predicates for appropriate WHERE clauses could be stored in the security database, read by the application program, and appended to SQL SELECT statements as necessary.

Many other possibilities exist for extending DBMS security with application processing. In general, however, you should use the DBMS security features first. Only if they are inadequate for the requirements should you add to them with application code. The closer the security enforcement is to the data, the less chance there is for infiltration. Also, using the DBMS security features is faster, cheaper, and probably results in higher-quality results than developing your own.

SQL Injection Attack

Whenever data from the user are used to modify a SQL statement, a **SQL injection attack** is possible. For example, in the prior section, if the value of EmployeeName used in the

SELECT statement is not obtained via a secure means such as from the operating system, but rather from a Web form, there is the chance that the user can inject SQL into the statement.

For example, suppose that users are asked to enter their names into a Web form textbox. Suppose that a user enters the value *'Benjamin Franklin' OR TRUE* for his or her name. The SQL statement generated by the application will then be the following:

SELECT   *

FROM   **EMPLOYEE**

WHERE   **EMPLOYEE.Name = 'Benjamin Franklin' OR TRUE;**

Of course, the value TRUE is true for every row, so every row of the EMPLOYEE table will be returned!

Thus, any time user input is used to modify a SQL statement, that input must be carefully edited to ensure that only valid input has been received and that no additional SQL syntax has been entered.

Database Recovery

Computer systems fail. Hardware breaks. Programs have bugs. Human procedures contain errors, and people make mistakes. All of these failures can and do occur in database applications. Because a database is shared by many people and because it often is a key element of an organization's operations, it is important to recover it as soon as possible.

Several problems must be addressed. First, from a business standpoint, business functions must continue. During the failure, customer orders, financial transactions, and packing lists must be completed somehow, even manually. Later, when the database application is operational again, the data from those activities must be entered into the database. Second, computer operations personnel must restore the system to a usable state as quickly as possible and as close as possible to what it was when the system crashed. Third, users must know what to do when the system becomes available again. Some work may need to be reentered, and users must know how far back they need to go.

When failures occur, it is impossible simply to fix the problem and resume processing. Even if no data are lost during a failure (which assumes that all types of memory are nonvolatile—an unrealistic assumption), the timing and scheduling of computer processing are too complex to be accurately re-created. Enormous amounts of overhead data and processing would be required for the operating system to be able to restart processing precisely where it was interrupted. It is simply not possible to roll back the clock and put all of the electrons in the same configuration they were in at the time of the failure. Two other approaches are possible: **recovery via reprocessing** and **recovery via rollback/rollforward.**

Recovery via Reprocessing

Because processing cannot be resumed at a precise point, the next best alternative is to go back to a known point and reprocess the workload from there. The simplest form of this type of recovery is to periodically make a copy of the database (called a **database save**) and to keep a record of all transactions that have been processed since the save. Then, when there is a failure, the operations staff can restore the database from the save and then reprocess all the transactions. Unfortunately, this simple strategy is normally not feasible. First, reprocessing transactions takes the same amount of time as processing them in the first place did. If the computer is heavily scheduled, the system may never catch up.

Second, when transactions are processed concurrently, events are asynchronous. Slight variations in human activity, such as a user reading an e-mail before responding to an application prompt, can change the order of the execution of concurrent transactions. Therefore, whereas Customer A got the last seat on a flight during the original processing, Customer B may get the last seat during reprocessing. For these reasons, reprocessing is normally not a viable form of recovery from failure in concurrent processing systems.

Recovery via Rollback/Rollforward

A second approach is to periodically make a copy of the database (the database save) and to keep a log of the changes made by transactions against the database since the save. Then, when there is a failure, one of two methods can be used. Using the first method, called **rollforward,** the database is restored using the saved data, and all valid transactions since the save are reapplied. (We are not reprocessing the transactions because the application programs are not involved in the rollforward. Instead, the processed changes, as recorded in the log, are reapplied.)

The second method is **rollback.** With this method, we undo changes made by erroneous or partially processed transactions by undoing the changes they have made in the database. Then, the valid transactions that were in process at the time of the failure are restarted. Both of these methods require that a **log** of the transaction results be kept. This log contains records of the data changes in chronological order. Transactions must be written to the log before they are applied to the database. That way, if the system crashes between the time a transaction is logged and the time it is applied, at worst there is a record of an unapplied transaction. If, on the other hand, the transactions were to be applied before they were logged, it would be possible (as well as undesirable) to change the database but have no record of the change. If this happened, an unwary user might reenter an already completed transaction. In the event of a failure, the log is used both to undo and to redo transactions, as shown in Figure 9-15.

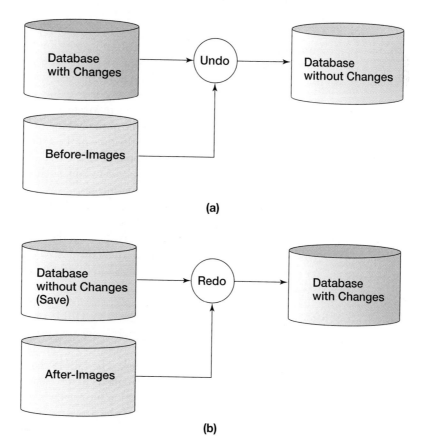

Figure 9-15

Undo and Redo Transactions
(a) Rollback and
(b) Rollforward

Figure 9-16

Example Transaction Log

Relative Record Number	Transaction ID	Reverse Pointer	Forward Pointer	Time	Type of Operation	Object	Before-Image	After-Image
1	OT1	0	2	11:42	START			
2	OT1	1	4	11:43	MODIFY	CUST 100	(old value)	(new value)
3	OT2	0	8	11:46	START			
4	OT1	2	5	11:47	MODIFY	SP AA	(old value)	(new value)
5	OT1	4	7	11:47	INSERT	ORDER 11		(value)
6	CT1	0	9	11:48	START			
7	OT1	5	0	11:49	COMMIT			
8	OT2	3	0	11:50	COMMIT			
9	CT1	6	10	11:51	MODIFY	SP BB	(old value)	(new value)
10	CT1	9	0	11:51	COMMIT			

To undo a transaction, the log must contain a copy of every database record (or page) before it was changed. Such records are called **before images.** A transaction is undone by applying before images of all of its changes to the database.

To redo a transaction, the log must contain a copy of every database record (or page) after it was changed. These records are called **after images.** A transaction is redone by applying after images of all of its changes to the database. Possible data items in a transaction log are shown in Figure 9-16.

In this example log, each transaction has a unique name for identification purposes. Furthermore, all of the images for a given transaction are linked together with pointers. One pointer points to the previous change made by this transaction (the reverse pointer), and the other points to the next change made by this transaction (the forward pointer). A zero in the pointer field means that this is the end of the list. The DBMS recovery subsystem uses these pointers to locate all of the records for a particular transaction. Figure 9-16 shows an example of the linking of log records.

Other data items in the log are the time of the action; the type of operation (START marks the beginning of a transaction and COMMIT terminates a transaction, releasing all locks that were in place); the object acted on, such as record type and identifier; and finally, the before images and the after images.

Given a log with before images and after images, the undo and redo actions are straightforward. To undo the transaction in Figure 9-17, the recovery processor simply replaces each changed record with its before image. When all of the before images have been restored, the transaction is undone. To redo a transaction, the recovery processor starts with the version of the database at the time the transaction started and applies all of the after images. As stated, this action assumes that an earlier version of the database is available from a database save.

Restoring a database to its most recent save and reapplying all transactions may require considerable processing. To reduce the delay, DBMS products sometimes use checkpoints. A **checkpoint** is a point of synchronization between the database and the transaction log. To perform a checkpoint, the DBMS refuses new requests, finishes processing outstanding requests, and writes its buffers to disk. The DBMS then waits until the operating system notifies it that all outstanding write requests to the database and to the log have been successfully completed. At this point, the log and the database are synchronized. A checkpoint record is then written to the log. Later, the database can be recovered from the checkpoint and only after images for transactions that started after the checkpoint need be applied.

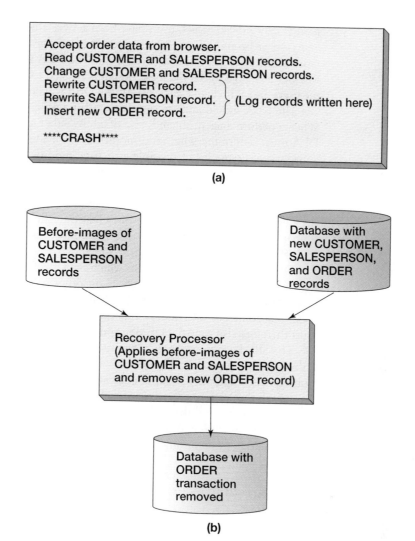

Figure 9-17

Recovery Example
(a) Processing
with Problem and
(b) Recovery Processing

Accept order data from browser.
Read CUSTOMER and SALESPERSON records.
Change CUSTOMER and SALESPERSON records.
Rewrite CUSTOMER record.
Rewrite SALESPERSON record. } (Log records written here)
Insert new ORDER record.

****CRASH****

(a)

Before-images of
CUSTOMER and
SALESPERSON
records

Database with
new CUSTOMER,
SALESPERSON,
and ORDER
records

Recovery Processor
(Applies before-images of
CUSTOMER and SALESPERSON
and removes new ORDER record)

Database with
ORDER
transaction
removed

(b)

Checkpoints are inexpensive operations, and it is feasible to take three or four (or more) per hour. In this way, no more than 15 or 20 minutes of processing need to be recovered. Most DBMS products perform automatic checkpoints, making human intervention unnecessary.

You will see specific examples of backup and recovery techniques for Oracle and SQL Server in the next two chapters. For now, you only need to understand the basic ideas and to realize that it is the responsibility of the DBA to ensure that adequate backup and recovery plans have been developed and that database saves and logs are generated as required.

Managing the DBMS

In addition to managing data activity and the database structure, the DBA must manage the DBMS itself. The DBA should compile and analyze statistics concerning the system's performance and identify potential problem areas. Keep in mind that the database is serving many user groups. The DBA needs to investigate all complaints about the system's response time, accuracy, ease of use, and so forth. If changes are needed, the DBA must plan and implement them.

The DBA must periodically monitor the users' activity on the database. DBMS products include features that collect and report statistics. For example, some of these reports may indicate which users have been active, which files—and perhaps which data items—have been used, and which access methods have been employed. Error rates and types also can be captured and reported. The DBA analyzes these data to determine whether a change to the database design is needed to improve performance or to ease the users' tasks. If change is necessary, the DBA will ensure that it is accomplished.

The DBA should analyze run-time statistics on database activity and performance. When a performance problem is identified (by either a report or a user's complaint), the DBA must determine whether a modification of the database structure or system is appropriate. Examples of possible structural modifications are establishing new keys, purging data, deleting keys, and establishing new relationships among objects.

When the vendor of the DBMS being used announces new product features, the DBA must consider them in light of the overall needs of the user community. If the DBA decides to incorporate the new DBMS features, the developers must be notified and trained in their use. Accordingly, the DBA must manage and control changes in the DBMS as well as in the database structure.

Other changes in the system for which the DBA is responsible vary widely, depending on the DBMS product as well as on other software and hardware in use. For example, changes in other software (such as the operating system or the Web server) may mean that some DBMS features, functions, or parameters must be changed. The DBA must therefore also tune the DBMS product with other software in use.

The DBMS options (such as transaction isolation levels) are initially chosen when little is known about how the system will perform in the particular user environment. Consequently, operational experience and performance analysis over a period of time may reveal that changes are necessary. Even if the performance seems acceptable, the DBA may want to alter the options and observe the effect on performance. This process is referred to as *tuning,* or *optimizing,* the system. Figure 9-18 summarizes the DBA's responsibilities for managing the DBMS product.

Maintaining the Data Repository

Consider a large and active Internet database application, such as those used by e-commerce companies—for instance, an application that is used by a company that sells clothing over the Internet. Such a system may involve data from several different databases, dozens of different Web pages, and hundreds, or even thousands, of users.

Suppose that the company using this application decides to expand its product line to include the sale of sporting goods. Senior management of this company might ask the DBA to develop an estimate of the time and other resources required to modify the database application to support this new product line.

To respond to this request, the DBA needs accurate metadata about the database, about the database applications and application components, about the users and their rights and privileges, and about other system elements. The database does carry some of this metadata in system tables, but this metadata is inadequate to answer the questions senior

---

Figure 9-18

Summary of the DBA's
Responsibilities for
Managing the DBMS

- Generate database application performance reports
- Investigate user performance complaints
- Assess need for changes in database structure or application design
- Modify database structure
- Evaluate and implement new DBMS features
- Tune the DBMS

management poses. The DBA needs additional metadata about COM and ActiveX objects, script procedures and functions, active server pages, stylesheets, document type definitions, and the like. Furthermore, although DBMS security mechanisms do document users, groups, and privileges, they do so in a highly structured and often inconvenient form.

For all of these reasons, many organizations develop and maintain **data repositories**, which are collections of metadata about databases, database applications, Web pages, users, and other application components. The repository may be virtual in that it is composed of metadata from many different sources: the DBMS, version control software, code libraries, Web page generation and editing tools, and so forth. Or, the data repository may be an integrated product from a CASE tool vendor or from a company such as Microsoft or Oracle.

Either way, the time for the DBA to think about constructing such a facility is long before senior management asks questions. In fact, the repository should be constructed as the system is developed and should be considered an important part of the system deliverables. If such a facility is not constructed, the DBA will always be playing catch-up—trying to maintain the existing applications, adapting them to new needs, and somehow gathering together the metadata to form a repository.

The best repositories are **active;** they are part of the systems development process in that metadata is created automatically as the system components are created. Less desirable, but still effective, are **passive repositories,** which are filled only when someone takes the time to generate the needed metadata and place it in the repository.

The Internet has created enormous opportunities for businesses to expand their customer bases and increase their sales and profitability. The databases and database applications that support these companies are an essential element of that success. Unfortunately, the growth of some organizations will be stymied by their inability to grow their applications or adapt them to changing needs. Often, building a new system is easier than adapting an existing one. Building a new system that integrates with an old one while it replaces that old one can be very difficult.

⊚ SUMMARY

Multiuser databases pose difficult problems for the organizations that create and use them, and most organizations have created an office of database administration to ensure that such problems are solved. In this text, the term *database administrator* refers to the person or office that is concerned with a single database. The term *data administrator* is used to describe a management function that is concerned with the organization's data policy and security. Major functions of the database administrator are listed in Figure 9-1.

The database administrator (DBA) participates in the initial development of database structures and in providing configuration control when requests for changes arise. Keeping accurate documentation of the structure and changes to it is an important DBA function.

The goal of concurrency control is to ensure that one user's work does not inappropriately influence another user's work. No single concurrency control technique is ideal for all circumstances. Trade-offs need to be made between the level of protection and throughput. A transaction, or logical unit of work (LUW), is a series of actions taken against the database that occurs as an atomic unit; either all of them occur or none of them do. The activity of concurrent transactions is interleaved on the database server. In some cases, updates can be lost if concurrent transactions are not controlled. Another concurrency problem concerns inconsistent reads.

To avoid concurrency problems, database elements are locked. Implicit locks are placed by the DBMS; explicit locks are issued by the application program. The size of the locked resource is called lock granularity. An exclusive lock prohibits other users from reading the locked resource; a shared lock allows other users to read the locked resource, but they cannot update it. Two transactions that run concurrently and generate results that are consistent with the results that would have occurred if they had run separately are referred to as serializable transactions. Two-phased locking, in which locks are acquired in a growing phase and released in a shrinking phase, is one scheme for serializability. A special case of two-phase locking is to acquire locks throughout the transaction, but not to free any lock until the transaction is finished.

Deadlock, or the deadly embrace, occurs when two transactions are each waiting on a resource that the other transaction holds. Deadlock can be prevented by requiring transactions to acquire all locks at the same time. Once deadlock occurs, the only way to cure it is to abort one of the transactions (and back out of partially completed work). Optimistic locking assumes that no transaction conflict will occur and deals with the consequences if it does. Pessimistic locking assumes that conflict will occur and so prevents it ahead of time with locks. In general, optimistic locking is preferred for the Internet and for many intranet applications.

Most application programs do not explicitly declare locks. Instead, they mark transaction boundaries with BEGIN, COMMIT, and ROLLBACK transaction statements and declare the concurrent behavior they want. The DBMS then places locks for the application that will result in the desired behavior.

An ACID transaction is one that is atomic, consistent, isolated, and durable. Durable means that database changes are permanent. Consistency can mean either statement-level or transaction-level consistency. With transaction-level consistency, a transaction may not see its own changes. The 1992 SQL standard defines four transaction isolation levels: read uncommitted, read committed, repeatable read, and serializable. The characteristics of each are summarized in Figure 9-10.

A cursor is a pointer into a set of records. Four cursor types are prevalent: forward only, static, keyset, and dynamic. Developers should select isolation levels and cursor types that are appropriate for their application workload and for the DBMS product in use.

The goal of database security is to ensure that only authorized users can perform authorized activities at authorized times. To develop effective database security, the processing rights and responsibilities of all users must be determined.

DBMS products provide security facilities. Most involve the declaration of users, groups, objects to be protected, and permissions or privileges on those objects. Almost all DBMS products use some form of user name and password security. Security guidelines are listed in Figure 9-14. DBMS security can be augmented by application security.

In the event of system failure, the database must be restored to a usable state as soon as possible. Transactions in process at the time of the failure must be reapplied or restarted. Although in some cases recovery can be done by reprocessing, the use of logs and rollback and rollforward is almost always preferred. Checkpoints can be taken to reduce the amount of work that needs to be done after a failure.

In addition to these tasks, the DBA manages the DBMS product itself, measuring database application performance and assessing the need for changes in database structure or DBMS performance tuning. The DBA also ensures that new DBMS features are evaluated and used as appropriate. Finally, the DBA is responsible for maintaining the data repository.

◎ REVIEW QUESTIONS

9.1   Briefly describe five difficult problems for organizations that create and use multiuser databases.

9.2   Explain the difference between a database administrator and a data administrator.

9.3   List seven important DBA tasks.

9.4   Summarize the DBA's responsibilities for managing database structure.

9.5   What is configuration control? Why is it necessary?

9.6   Explain the meaning of the word inappropriately in the phrase "one user's work does not inappropriately influence another user's work."

9.7   Explain the trade-off that exists in concurrency control.

9.8   Define an atomic transaction and explain why atomicity is important.

9.9   Explain the difference between concurrent transactions and simultaneous transactions. How many CPUs are required for simultaneous transactions?

9.10   Give an example, other than the one in this text, of the lost update problem.

9.11   Explain the difference between an explicit and an implicit lock.

9.12   What is lock granularity?

9.13   Explain the difference between an exclusive lock and a shared lock.

9.14   Explain two-phased locking.

9.15   How does releasing all locks at the end of the transaction relate to two-phase locking?

9.16   In general, how should the boundaries of a transaction be defined?

9.17   What is deadlock? How can it be avoided? How can it be resolved once it occurs?

9.18   Explain the difference between optimistic and pessimistic locking.

9.19   Explain the benefits of marking transaction boundaries, declaring lock characteristics, and letting the DBMS place locks.

9.20   Explain the use of BEGIN, COMMIT, and ROLLBACK TRANSACTION statements.

9.21   Explain the meaning of the expression ACID transaction.

9.22   Describe statement-level consistency.

9.23   Describe transaction-level consistency. What disadvantage can exist with it?

9.24   What is the purpose of transaction isolation levels?

9.25   Explain the read uncommitted isolation level. Give an example of its use.

9.26   Explain the read committed isolation level. Give an example of its use.

9.27   Explain the repeatable read isolation level. Give an example of its use.

9.28   Explain the serializable isolation level. Give an example of its use.

9.29   Explain the term cursor.

9.30   Explain why a transaction may have many cursors. Also, how is it possible that a transaction may have more than one cursor on a given table?

9.31   What is the advantage of using different types of cursors?

9.32   Explain forward only cursors. Give an example of their use.

9.33   Explain static cursors. Give an example of their use.

9.34   Explain keyset cursors. Give an example of their use.

9.35   Explain dynamic cursors. Give an example of their use.

9.36   What happens if you do not declare the transaction isolation level and the cursor type to the DBMS? Is this good or bad?

9.37   Explain the necessity of defining processing rights and responsibilities. How are such responsibilities enforced?

9.38   Explain the relationships among USER, GROUP, PERMISSION, and OBJECT for a generic database security system.

9.39   Should the DBA assume a firewall when planning security?

9.40   What should be done with unused DBMS features and functions?

9.41   Explain how to protect the computer that runs the DBMS.

9.42   With regard to security, what actions should the DBA take on user accounts and passwords?

9.43   List two elements of a database security plan.

9.44   Describe the advantages and disadvantages of DBMS-provided and application-provided security.

9.45   What is a SQL injection attack and how can it be prevented?

9.46   Explain how a database could be recovered via reprocessing. Why is this generally not feasible?

9.47 Define rollback and rollforward.

9.48 Why is it important to write to the log before changing the database values?

9.49 Describe the rollback process. Under what conditions should it be used?

9.50 Describe the rollforward process. Under what conditions should it be used?

9.51 What is the advantage of taking frequent checkpoints of a database?

9.52 Summarize the DBA's responsibilities for managing the DBMS.

9.53 What is a data repository? A passive data repository? An active data repository?

9.54 Explain why a data repository is important. What is likely to happen if one is not available?

PROJECT QUESTIONS

9.55 Visit **www.msdn.microsoft.com** and search for "SQL Server Security Guidelines." Read articles at three of the links that you find and summarize them. How does the information you find compare with that in Figure 9-14?

9.56 Visit **www.oracle.com** and search for "Oracle Security Guidelines." Read articles at three of the links that you find and summarize them. How does the information you find compare with that in Figure 9-14?

9.57 Use Google (**www.google.com**) or another search engine and search the Web for "Database Security Guidelines." Read articles at three of the links that you find and summarize them. How does the information you find compare with that in Figure 9-14?

9.58 Answer the following questions for the View Ridge database discussed in Chapter 7 with the tables shown in Figure 7-12.

a. Suppose that you are developing a stored procedure to record an artist who has never been in the gallery before, a work for that artist, and a row in the TRANSACTION table to record the date acquired and acquisition price. How will you declare the boundaries of the transaction? What transaction isolation level will you use?

b. Suppose that you are writing a stored procedure to change values in the CUSTOMER table. What transaction isolation level will you use?

c. Suppose that you are writing a stored procedure to record a customer's purchase. Assume that the customer's data are new. How will you declare the boundaries of the transaction? What isolation level will you use?

d. Suppose that you are writing a stored procedure to check the validity of the intersection table. Specifically, for each customer, your procedure should read the customer's transaction and determine the artist of that work. Given the artist, your procedure should then check to ensure that an interest has been declared for that artist in the intersection table. If there is no such intersection row, your procedure should create one. How will you set the boundaries of your transaction? What isolation level will you use? What cursor types (if any) will you use?

MARCIA'S DRY CLEANING

A Assume that Marcia has hired you as a database consultant to develop an operational database having the following four tables (the same tables described at the end of Chapter 7):

CUSTOMER (<u>CustomerSK</u>, Phone, Email, FirstName, LastName)

ORDER (<u>InvoiceNumber</u>, Date, *CustomerSK*, Subtotal, Tax, Total)

ORDER_ITEM (*<u>InvoiceNumber</u>*, <u>ItemNumber</u>, Qty, *Service,* UnitPrice, ExtendedPrice)

SERVICE (<u>Service</u>, Description, UnitPrice)

Assume that Marcia's has the following personnel: two owners, a shift manager, a part-time seamstress, and two salesclerks. Prepare a two-to-three-page memo that addresses the following points:

    1 The need for database administration.

    2 Your recommendation as to who should serve as database administrator. Assume that Marcia's is not sufficiently large to need or afford a full-time database administrator.

    3 Using Figure 9-1 as a guide, describe the nature of database administration activities at Marcia's. As an aggressive consultant, keep in mind that you can recommend yourself for performing some of the DBA functions.

B For the employees described in question A, define users, groups, and permissions on data in these four tables. Use the security scheme shown in Figure 9-13 as an example. Create a table like that in Figure 9-12. Don't forget to include yourself.

C Suppose that you are writing a stored procedure to create new records in SERVICE for new services that Marcia's will perform. Suppose that you know that while your procedure is running, another stored procedure that records new or modifies existing customer orders and order line items can also be running. Additionally, suppose that a third stored procedure that records new customer data also can be running.

    1 Give an example of a dirty read, a nonrepeatable read, and a phantom read among this group of stored procedures.

    2 What concurrency control measures are appropriate for the stored procedure that you are creating?

    3 What concurrency control measures are appropriate for the two other stored procedures?

MORGAN IMPORTING

A Assume that Morgan has hired you as a database consultant to develop an operational database having the following five tables (the same tables described at the end of Chapter 7):

STORE (<u>StoreSK</u>, StoreName, City, Country, Phone, Fax, Email, Contact)

PURCHASE (<u>PurchaseSK</u>, *StoreSK*, Date, Description, Category, PriceUSD)

SHIPMENT (<u>ShipmentSK</u>, ShipDate, *ShipperName*, ShipperInvoiceNumber, Origin, Destination)

SHIPMENT_ITEM (*<u>ShipmentSK</u>*, *<u>PurchaseSK</u>*, InsuredValue)

SHIPPER (<u>ShipperName</u>, Phone, Fax, Email, Contact)

Assume that Morgan personnel are the owner (Morgan), an office administrator, one full-time salesperson, and two part-time salespeople. Morgan and the office administrator want to process data in all tables. Additionally, the full-time salesperson can enter purchase and shipment data. The part-time employees can only read shipment data; they are not allowed to see InsuredValue, however. Prepare a three-to-five-page memo for the owner that addresses the following issues:

1 The need for database administration at Morgan.
2 Your recommendation as to who should serve as database administrator. Assume that Morgan is not sufficiently large that it needs or can afford a full-time database administrator.
3 Using Figure 9-1 as a guide, describe the nature of database administration activities at Morgan. As an aggressive consultant, keep in mind that you can recommend yourself for performing some of the DBA functions.

B For the employees described in question A, define users, groups, and permissions on data in these five tables. Use the security scheme shown in Figure 9-13 as an example. Create a table like that in Figure 9-12. Don't forget to include yourself.
C Suppose that you are writing a stored procedure to record new purchases. Suppose that you know that while your procedure is running, another stored procedure that records shipment data can be running, and a third stored procedure that updates shipper data can also be running.

1 Give an example of a dirty read, a nonrepeatable read, and a phantom read among this group of stored procedures.
2 What concurrency control measures are appropriate for the stored procedure that you are creating?
3 What concurrency control measures are appropriate for the two other stored procedures?

Managing Databases with Oracle

Oracle is a powerful and robust DBMS that runs on many different operating systems, including Windows 2000, Windows XP, several variations of UNIX, several mainframe operating systems, and Linux. It is the world's most popular DBMS and has a long history of development and use. Oracle exposes much of its technology to the developer, and consequently can be tuned and tailored in many ways.

All of this means, however, that Oracle can be difficult to install and that there is a lot to learn. A gauge of Oracle's breadth is that one of the most popular references, *Oracle 9i, The Complete Reference* by Loney and Koch, is more than 1,300 pages long, but it does not contain everything about Oracle. Moreover, techniques that work with a version of Oracle on one operating system may need to be altered when working with a version on a different operating system. You will need to be patient with Oracle and with yourself and not expect to master this subject overnight. The Oracle program suite has many configurations. To start, there are two different versions of the Oracle

DBMS engine: Personal Oracle and Enterprise Oracle. It addition, there are Forms and Reports, Oracle Designer, and a host of tools for publishing Oracle databases on the Web. Add to this the need for Oracle's products to operate on many different operating systems and over networks using several different communication protocols, and you can see why it is so difficult to learn.

Oracle SQL*Plus is a utility for processing SQL and for creating components such as stored procedures and triggers. It is also the one component that is constant through all of the various product configurations. Consequently, we will begin by discussing it.

SQL*Plus can be used to submit both SQL and PL/SQL statements to Oracle. The latter, PL/SQL, is a programming language that adds programming constructs to the SQL language. We will use PL/SQL to create tables, constraints, relationships, views, stored procedures, and triggers.

This chapter uses the View Ridge example from Chapter 6, and the discussion will roughly parallel the discussion of database administration in Chapter 9.

Installing Oracle

The version of Oracle that you install depends on whether you will access databases created by someone else or whether you will create databases on your own computer. If you will use a database created by someone else, you need only install Oracle Client. You should obtain instructions on how to install and connect to the database from the person who created the database you will use.

If you will create your own databases, you should install Oracle Personal Edition. See the Oracle Installation Guide link on the text's Web site at *www.prenhall.com/kroenke.*

Creating an Oracle Database

An Oracle database can be created in one of three ways: via the Oracle Database Configuration Assistant, via the Oracle-supplied database creation procedures, or via the SQL CREATE DATABASE command. The Oracle Database Configuration Assistant is by far the easiest, and you should use it.

You can find the Database Configuration Assistant in one of the directories created when Oracle was installed. You will find it by clicking Start, Programs, Oracle-Oracle9i Home/Configuration and Migration Tools or something similar, depending on your operating system. Your directories may not be named exactly as these; search through the directories under Start, Programs to find the Database Configuration Assistant.

Figure 10-1 will appear when you start the Configuration Assistant. Select Next, Create a database, General Purpose, and then type the name of your database for Global Database Name. This chapter uses the database named *VRG*. Next, select Dedicated Server Mode and Typical. At this point, you can click Finish and then OK, and Oracle will create your database with default file sizes and file locations. This process will take several minutes.

Once the database has been created, you will be asked to enter new passwords for the SYS and SYSTEM accounts. Select appropriate strong passwords. You can also select Password Management to lock or unlock accounts. At this point, you need only enter the new passwords. Click Exit in Password Management and your database will have been created.

Figure 10-1

Starting the Oracle
Database
Configuration Assistant

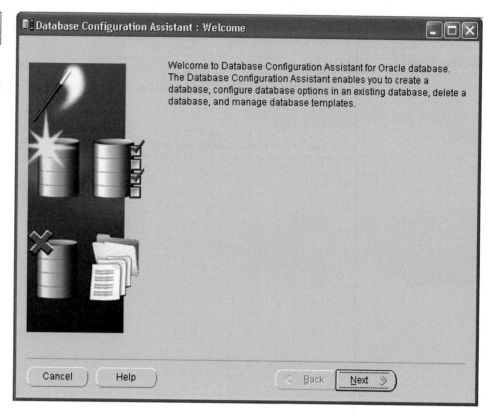

You can manage an Oracle database using either the Oracle SQL*Plus command utility program or the Oracle Enterprise Manager Console. We will begin by using SQL*Plus because it is the classic way of creating and managing Oracle databases. It is also available with all installations of Oracle on all operating systems, so if you know how to use it, you will know how to process an Oracle database on any operating system. After you have learned how to use SQL*Plus, we will discuss the Oracle Enterprise Manager.

Using SQL*Plus

To use SQL*Plus, find its icon under the Start/Programs/Oracle-Oracle 9i Home/ Application Development menu and click it. Sign on to your database using the SYS-TEM account and enter the name of your database under Host String, as shown in Figure 10-2. (This procedure might be different if you are using a version of Oracle

Figure 10-2

Logging on Using
SQL*Plus

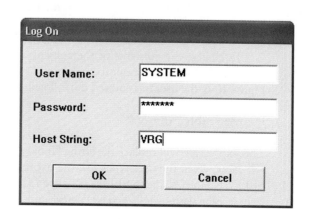

SQL*Plus Prompt

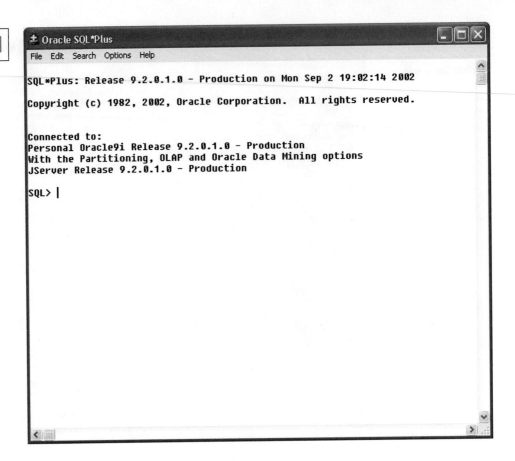

set up by someone else. If this is the case, check with your database administrator.) Click OK and you should see a window similar to the one shown in Figure 10-3.

Among its many functions, SQL*Plus is a text editor. Working with Oracle will be easier if you learn a bit about this editor. First, as you type into SQL*Plus, your keystrokes are placed into a buffer. When you press Enter, SQL*Plus will save what you just typed into a line in the buffer and go to a new line, but it will neither finish the statement nor execute it.

The SQL*Plus Buffer

For example, in Figure 10-4, the user has entered two lines of a SQL statement. The user can enter as many more lines as necessary. When the user types a semicolon and presses Enter, SQL*Plus will finish the statement and then execute it. Try this, but ignore the results—we'll worry about them later.

To see the contents of the buffer, type LIST, as shown in Figure 10-5. The line shown with an asterisk (line 3, in this case) is the current line. You can change the current line by entering LIST followed by a line number, such as LIST 1. At that point, line 1 is the current line.

To change the contents of the current line, enter change/*astring/bstring/*, where *astring* is the string you want to change and *bstring* is what you want to change it to. In Figure 10-6, the user has entered the following:

change/Table_Name/*/

This expression will replace the string 'Table_Name' with the string '*'.

Now, when the user types *list*, the expression in line 1 of the buffer changes from SELECT Table_Name to SELECT*. Type *LIST* to see the complete statement. Enter the right-leaning slash (/) followed by {Enter}, and the command in the buffer will be executed.

Figure 10-4

SQL*Plus Multiline
Buffer

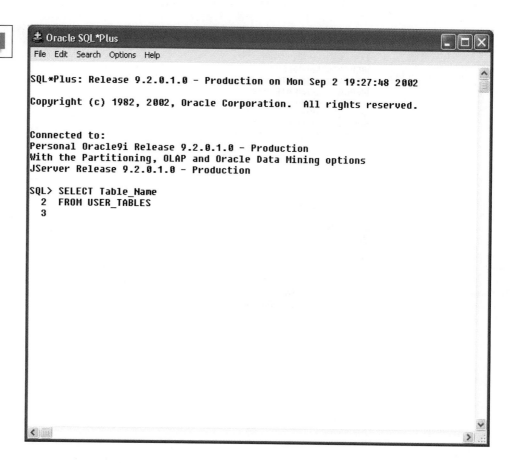

```
± Oracle SQL*Plus                                                    _ □ ×
 File  Edit  Search  Options  Help

SQL*Plus: Release 9.2.0.1.0 - Production on Mon Sep 2 19:27:48 2002

Copyright (c) 1982, 2002, Oracle Corporation.  All rights reserved.


Connected to:
Personal Oracle9i Release 9.2.0.1.0 - Production
With the Partitioning, OLAP and Oracle Data Mining options
JServer Release 9.2.0.1.0 - Production

SQL> SELECT Table_Name
  2   FROM USER_TABLES
  3
```

Figure 10-5

Using the LIST
Command

```
± Oracle SQL*Plus                                                    _ □ ×
 File  Edit  Search  Options  Help
REPCAT$_RESOLUTION_STATISTICS
REPCAT$_RESOL_STATS_CONTROL
REPCAT$_RUNTIME_PARMS

TABLE_NAME
------------------------------
REPCAT$_SITES_NEW
REPCAT$_SITE_OBJECTS
REPCAT$_SNAPGROUP
REPCAT$_TEMPLATE_OBJECTS
REPCAT$_TEMPLATE_PARMS
REPCAT$_TEMPLATE_REFGROUPS
REPCAT$_TEMPLATE_SITES
REPCAT$_TEMPLATE_STATUS
REPCAT$_TEMPLATE_TARGETS
REPCAT$_TEMPLATE_TYPES
REPCAT$_USER_AUTHORIZATIONS

TABLE_NAME
------------------------------
REPCAT$_USER_PARM_VALUES
SQLPLUS_PRODUCT_PROFILE
TRANSACTION
WORK

136 rows selected.

SQL> LIST
  1   SELECT Table_Name
  2   FROM USER_TABLES
  3*
SQL> |
```

Figure 10-6

Changing a Line in the
Buffer

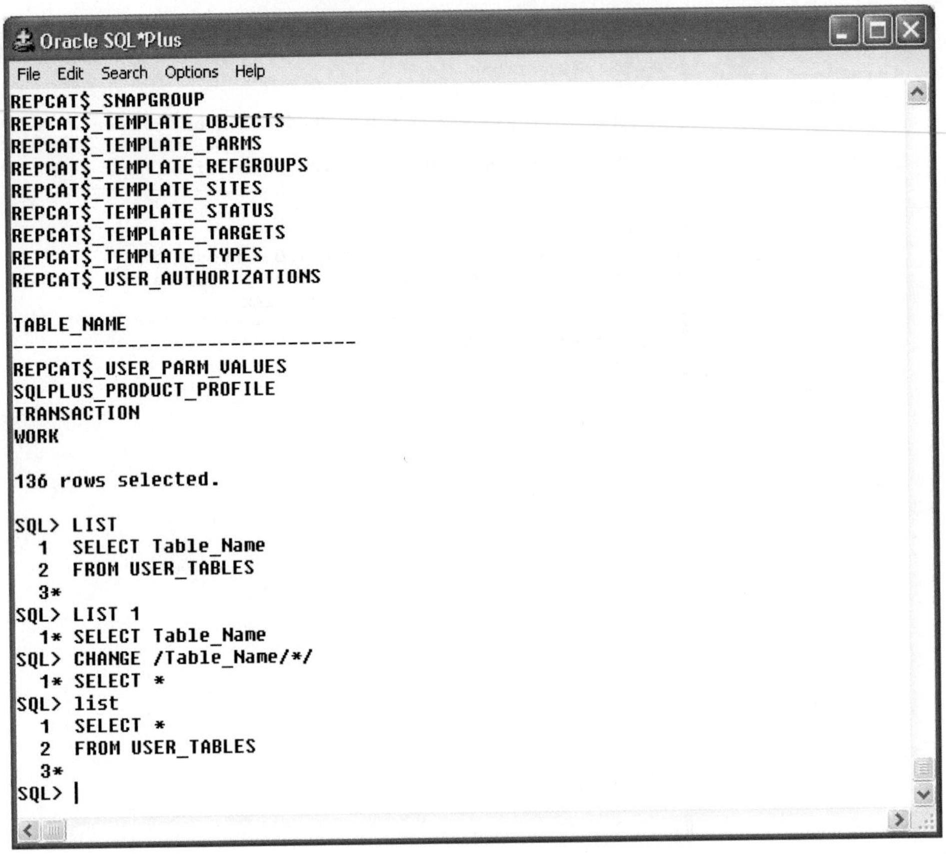

```
Oracle SQL*Plus
File  Edit  Search  Options  Help
REPCAT$_SNAPGROUP
REPCAT$_TEMPLATE_OBJECTS
REPCAT$_TEMPLATE_PARMS
REPCAT$_TEMPLATE_REFGROUPS
REPCAT$_TEMPLATE_SITES
REPCAT$_TEMPLATE_STATUS
REPCAT$_TEMPLATE_TARGETS
REPCAT$_TEMPLATE_TYPES
REPCAT$_USER_AUTHORIZATIONS

TABLE_NAME
---------------------------
REPCAT$_USER_PARM_VALUES
SQLPLUS_PRODUCT_PROFILE
TRANSACTION
WORK

136 rows selected.

SQL> LIST
  1   SELECT Table_Name
  2   FROM USER_TABLES
  3*
SQL> LIST 1
  1* SELECT Table_Name
SQL> CHANGE /Table_Name/*/
  1* SELECT *
SQL> list
  1   SELECT *
  2   FROM USER_TABLES
  3*
SQL> |
```

Before going on, you should know that Oracle commands, column names, table names, view names, and all other database elements are case insensitive. *LIST* is the same as *list,* as demonstrated in Figure 10-6. The only time that case matters is inside quotation marks of strings. Thus,

SELECT * from ARTIST;

and

select * FROM artist;

are identical. But

SELECT * FROM ARTIST WHERE Name = 'Miro';

and

SELECT * FROM ARTIST WHERE Name = 'MIRO';

are different. Case matters inside quotation marks.

There is also a difference between the semicolon and the right-leaning slash (/). The semicolon terminates a SQL statement; the right-leaning slash tells Oracle to execute whatever statement is in the buffer. If there is only one statement and no ambiguity about what is wanted, Oracle will treat the semicolon and slash as being the same. Thus, in the following line, the semicolon both terminates the statement and causes Oracle to execute the statement:

Select * from USER_TABLES;

Type / at this point, and the statement will be executed again.

Using a Text Editor

The Change command is fine for making small changes, but it becomes unworkable for editing longer expressions, such as stored procedures. For that purpose, you can set up SQL*Plus to connect to your text editor. Before doing this, however, you should create a directory for your code and point SQL*Plus to that directory.

First, exit SQL*Plus by typing *exit* at the SQL> prompt. Now, create a directory for your Oracle code: say, c:\MyDirectory\OracleCode. Find the SQL*Plus icon on your computer, right-click it to reveal properties, and enter the name of your new directory in the Start In text box. Click OK. Restart SQL*Plus.

Click the Edit item in the SQL*Plus window menu and then select Editor/Define Editor. You can enter the name of your editor here. Notepad is offered as the default and will be fine for our purposes, so click OK.

At this point, you've defined Notepad as your default editor to SQL*Plus and set it to point to your directory. Now, whenever you type *Edit,* SQL*Plus will invoke Notepad (or your editor, if you selected a different one). You can now create, save, and edit files of code in that directory. For example, reenter the following statements:

SELECT Table_Name

FROM USER_TABLES;

After the results appear, type *Edit*. SQL*Plus will bring up Notepad with the contents of the buffer. Use Save As to give this file a new name, say EX1.txt. Close Notepad and you will return to SQL*Plus. To edit the file you just created, type *Edit EX1.txt,* and you will enter your editor with that file. When you exit your editor and return to SQL*Plus, EX1.txt will be stored in the SQL*Plus buffer. To cause the buffer contents to execute, enter the right-leaning slash (/).

B T W

The default file extension for SQL*Plus is .sql. If you name a file EX1.sql, you can simply enter *Edit EX1* and SQL*Plus will add the extension for you.

Armed with this knowledge of SQL*Plus, we can now investigate some of the characteristics of Oracle. In the next section, we will use the View Ridge Gallery example introduced in Chapter 6 and create the surrogate key database schema shown in Figure 10-7.

Creating Tables

Oracle CREATE TABLE statements for the View Ridge Gallery database shown in Figure 7-9 are shown in Figure 10-7. These statements were keyed into a text file named create_tables.sql and then executed from the SQL*Plus utility via the command start create_tables.

Several alterations to the SQL-92 statements shown in Figure 7-9 had to be made for Oracle. For one, Oracle does not support a CASCADE UPDATE constraint, and that constraint had to be removed. Additionally, the constraint on Birthdate and DeceasedDate was modified because Oracle does not interpret the constraint (Birthdate LIKE '([1-2], [0–9], [0-9], [0-9])') correctly. Instead, a range constraint was created as shown in the figure. Other than these changes, the SQL in Figure 10-7 should be very familiar to you by now. Once you have executed these statements, you can check on the status of the tables via the DESCRIBE command. Figure 10-8 shows the use of DESCRIBE for the tables just defined. Notice that either DESCRIBE or DESC can be used. Also, notice that the SQL-92 data type int is interpreted by Oracle as Number (38) and that the data type varchar is interpreted as the Oracle

Figure 10-7   Oracle CREATE TABLE Statements for the View Ridge Schema

```
CREATE TABLE CUSTOMER(
        CustomerID          int             NOT NULL,
        Name                char(25)        NOT NULL,
        Street              char(30)        NULL,
        City                char(35)        NULL,
        State               char(2)         NULL,
        ZipPostalCode       char(9)         NULL,
        Country             varchar(50)     NULL,
        AreaCode            char(3)         NULL,
        PhoneNumber         char(8)         NULL,
        Email               varchar(100)    Null,
        CONSTRAINT          CustomerPK PRIMARY KEY (CustomerID)
);

CREATE TABLE ARTIST(
        ArtistID            int             NOT NULL,
        Name                char(25)        NOT NULL,
        Nationality         varchar(30)     NULL,
        Birthdate           number (4,0)    NULL,
        DeceasedDate        number (4,0)    NULL,
        CONSTRAINT          ArtistPK PRIMARY KEY (ArtistID),
        CONSTRAINT          ArtistAK1 UNIQUE (Name),
        CONSTRAINT          NationalityValues  CHECK (Nationality IN ('Canadian', 'English', 'French', 'German',
                            'Mexican', 'Russian', 'Spanish', 'US')),
        CONSTRAINT          BirthValuesCheck  CHECK (Birthdate < DeceasedDate),
        CONSTRAINT          ValidBirthYear    CHECK ((Birthdate > 1000) and (Birthdate < 2100)),
        CONSTRAINT          ValidDeathYear    CHECK ((DeceasedDate > 1000) and (DeceasedDate < 2100))
);

CREATE TABLE CUSTOMER_ARTIST_INT(
        ArtistID            int             NOT NULL,
        CustomerID          int             NOT NULL,
        CONSTRAINT          CustomerArtistPK PRIMARY KEY (ArtistID, CustomerID),
        CONSTRAINT          Customer_Artist_Int_ArtistFK    FOREIGN KEY (ArtistID) REFERENCES ARTIST (ArtistID)
                            ON DELETE CASCADE,
        CONSTRAINT          Customer_Artist_Int_CustomerFK FOREIGN KEY (CustomerID) REFERENCES CUSTOMER
                            (CustomerID) ON DELETE CASCADE
);

CREATE TABLE WORK (
        WorkID              int             NOT NULL,
        Title               varchar(25)     NOT NULL,
        Description         varchar(1000)   NULL,
        Copy                varchar(8)      NOT NULL,
        ArtistID            int             NOT NULL,
        CONSTRAINT          WorkPK PRIMARY KEY (WorkID),
        CONSTRAINT          WorkAK1 UNIQUE (Title, Copy),
        CONSTRAINT          ArtistFK FOREIGN KEY(ArtistID) REFERENCES ARTIST (ArtistID)
);

CREATE TABLE TRANSACTION (
        TransactionID       int             NOT NULL,
        DateAcquired        date            NOT NULL,
        AcquisitionPrice    number (8,2)    NULL,
        PurchaseDate        date            NULL,
        SalesPrice          number (8,2)    NULL,
        AskingPrice         number (8,2)    NULL,
        CustomerID          int             NULL,
        WorkID              int             NOT NULL,
        CONSTRAINT          TransactionPK PRIMARY KEY (TransactionID),
        CONSTRAINT          SalesPriceRange CHECK ((SalesPrice > 1000) AND (SalesPrice <=200000)),
        CONSTRAINT          ValidTransDate CHECK (DateAcquired <= PurchaseDate),
        CONSTRAINT          TransactionWorkFK FOREIGN KEY(WorkID) REFERENCES WORK (WorkID),
        CONSTRAINT          TransactionCustomerFK FOREIGN KEY(CustomerID) REFERENCES CUSTOMER
                            (CustomerID)
);
```

Figure 10-8

Using the
DESCRIBE
Command

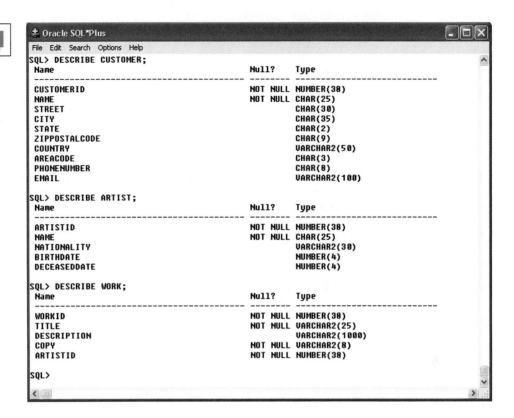

```
± Oracle SQL*Plus                                                         _ □ X
File  Edit  Search  Options  Help
SQL> DESCRIBE CUSTOMER;
 Name                                          Null?     Type
 -------------------------------------------   --------  -------------------------
 CUSTOMERID                                    NOT NULL  NUMBER(38)
 NAME                                          NOT NULL  CHAR(25)
 STREET                                                  CHAR(30)
 CITY                                                    CHAR(35)
 STATE                                                   CHAR(2)
 ZIPPOSTALCODE                                           CHAR(9)
 COUNTRY                                                 VARCHAR2(50)
 AREACODE                                                CHAR(3)
 PHONENUMBER                                             CHAR(8)
 EMAIL                                                   VARCHAR2(100)

SQL> DESCRIBE ARTIST;
 Name                                          Null?     Type
 -------------------------------------------   --------  -------------------------
 ARTISTID                                      NOT NULL  NUMBER(38)
 NAME                                          NOT NULL  CHAR(25)
 NATIONALITY                                             VARCHAR2(30)
 BIRTHDATE                                               NUMBER(4)
 DECEASEDDATE                                            NUMBER(4)

SQL> DESCRIBE WORK;
 Name                                          Null?     Type
 -------------------------------------------   --------  -------------------------
 WORKID                                        NOT NULL  NUMBER(38)
 TITLE                                         NOT NULL  VARCHAR2(25)
 DESCRIPTION                                             VARCHAR2(1000)
 COPY                                          NOT NULL  VARCHAR2(8)
 ARTISTID                                      NOT NULL  NUMBER(38)

SQL>
```

Figure 10-9

Common Oracle Data
Types

Data Type	Description
BLOB	Binary large object. Up to 4 gigabytes in length
CHAR (n)	Fixed-length character field of length n. Maximum 2,000 characters
DATE	7-byte field containing both date and time
INT	Whole number of length 38
NUMBER(n,d)	Numeric field of length n, d places to the right of the decimal
VARCHAR(n) or VARCHAR2(n)	Variable-length character field up to n characters long. Maximum value of n = 4,000

data type VarChar2. Figure 10-9 summarizes the basic Oracle data types. Observe that Oracle has a Date data type, but does not have a money or currency data type. In Oracle, money or currency is stored using the numeric data type.

All of the View Ridge tables except CUSTOMER_ARTIST_WORK have surrogate keys. Unfortunately, Oracle does not directly support the definition of such keys. Instead, Oracle sequences must be used.

Surrogate Keys Using Sequences

A **sequence** is an Oracle-supplied object that generates a sequential series of unique numbers. The following statement defines a sequence called CustID that starts at 1,000 and is incremented by one each time it is used.

Create Sequence CustID Increment by 1 start with 1000;

Two sequence methods are important to us. The method NextVal provides the next value in a sequence, and the method CurrVal provides the current value in a sequence.

Thus, CustID.NextVal provides the next value of the CustID sequence. You can insert a row into CUSTOMER using a sequence as follows:

INSERT INTO CUSTOMER

(CustomerID, Name, AreaCode, PhoneNumber)

VALUES

(CustID.NextVal, 'Mary Jones','350', '555–1234');

A CUSTOMER row will be created with the next value in the sequence as the value for CustomerID. Once this statement has been executed, you can retrieve the row just created with the CurrVal method, as follows:

SELECT   *

FROM   CUSTOMER

WHERE   CustomerID = CustID.CurrVal;

Here, CustID.CurrVal returns the current value of the sequence, which is the value just used.
  Unfortunately, using sequences for surrogate keys has three problems. First, sequences can be used for purposes other than surrogate keys. Every time NextVal is called, a number is used up. If the value returned from NextVal is not used for an insert into a surrogate key column, but is used for something else, then that value will be missing from the surrogate key range. A second, more serious, problem is that there is nothing in the schema that prevents someone from issuing an INSERT statement that does not use the sequence. Thus, Oracle accepts the following:

INSERT INTO CUSTOMER

(CustomerID, Name, Area_Code, Phone_Number)

VALUES

(350, 'Mary Jones', '350', '555–1234');

If this were done, duplicate values of a surrogate could occur. Third, it is possible that someone could accidentally use the wrong sequence when inserting into the table. If that were done, odd, erroneous, or duplicate surrogate key values will result.
  In spite of these possible problems, sequences are the recommended way for obtaining surrogate key values in Oracle. We will use the following sequences in the View Ridge database. If you are following this discussion with SQL*Plus, create them now as follows:

Create Sequence CustID Increment by 1 start with 1000;

Create Sequence ArtistID Increment by 1 start with 1;

Create Sequence WorkID Increment by 1 start with 500;

Create Sequence TransID Increment by 1 start with 100;

Entering Data

We can now use these sequences to add data. Figure 10-10 shows a file of insert statements created in Notepad. Type these into your editor, place a slash at the end of the file, and save the file using the name *ACIns.sql.* Enter the following to execute the statements in the file:

Start ACIns;

Your data should appear as shown in Figure 10-11.

| Figure 10-10 | Oracle INSERT Statements |

```
INSERT INTO ARTIST VALUES (
ArtistID.Nextval, 'Miro', 'Spanish', 1870, 1950);
INSERT INTO ARTIST VALUES (
ArtistID.Nextval,'Kandinsky', 'Russian', 1854, 1900);
INSERT INTO ARTIST (
ArtistID.Nextval,'Frings', 'US', 1950);
INSERT INTO ARTIST (ArtistID, Name, Nationality, Birthdate) VALUES (
ArtistID.Nextval,'Klee', 'German', 1900);
INSERT INTO ARTIST (ArtistID, Name, Nationality) VALUES (
ArtistID.Nextval,'Moos', 'US');
INSERT INTO ARTIST (ArtistID, Name, Nationality) VALUES (
ArtistID.Nextval,'Tobey', 'US');
INSERT INTO ARTIST (ArtistID, Name, Nationality) VALUES (
ArtistID.Nextval,'Matisse, 'French');
INSERT INTO ARTIST (ArtistID, Name, Nationality) VALUES (
ArtistID.Nextval,'Chagall', 'French');

INSERT INTO CUSTOMER VALUES (
CustID.Nextval, 'Jeffrey Janes', '123 W. Elm St', 'Renton' , 'WA', '98123', 'USA', '206', '555-1345',
'Customer1000@somewhere.com');
INSERT INTO CUSTOMER VALUES (
CustID.Nextval, 'David Smith', '813 Tumbleweed Lane', 'Loveland', 'CO', '80345', 'USA', '303', '555-5434',
'Customer1001@somewhere.com');
INSERT INTO CUSTOMER VALUES (
CustID.Nextval, 'Tiffany Twilight', '88 - First Avenue', 'Langley', 'WA', '98114', 'USA', '206', '555-1000',
'Customer1015@somewhere.com');
INSERT INTO CUSTOMER VALUES (
CustID.Nextval, 'Fred Smathers', '10899 - 88th Ave', 'Bainbridge Island', 'WA', '98108', 'USA', '206', '555-1234',
'Customer1033@somewhere.com');
INSERT INTO CUSTOMER VALUES (
CustID.Nextval, 'Mary Beth Frederickson', '25 South Lafayette', 'Denver', 'CO', '80210', 'USA', '303', '555-1000',
'Customer1034@somewhere.com');
INSERT INTO CUSTOMER VALUES (
CustID.Nextval, 'Selma Warning', '205 Burnaby', 'Vancouver', 'BC', 'V0N 1B4', 'Canada', '253', '555-1234',
'Customer1036@somewhere.com');
INSERT INTO CUSTOMER VALUES (
CustID.Nextval, 'Susan Wu', '105 Locust Ave', 'Atlanta', 'GA', '23224', 'USA', '721', '555-1234',
'Customer1037@somewhere.com');
INSERT INTO CUSTOMER VALUES (
CustID.Nextval, 'Donald G. Gray', '55 Bodega Ave', 'Bodega Bay', 'CA', '92114', 'USA', '705', '555-1234',
'Customer1040@somewhere.com');
INSERT INTO CUSTOMER VALUES (
CustID.Nextval, 'Lynda Johnson', '117 C Street', 'Washington', 'DC', '11345', 'USA', '703', '555-1000','');
INSERT INTO CUSTOMER VALUES (
CustID.Nextval, 'Chris Wilkens' , '87 Highland Drive', 'Olympia', 'WA', '98008', 'USA', '206', '555-1234','');
```

DROP and ALTER Statements

You can use the DROP statement to remove structures from the database. For example, the following statements will drop the table MYTABLE and the sequence MySequence, respectively:

DROP TABLE MYTABLE;

DROP SEQUENCE MySequence;

Any data in the MYTABLE table will be lost.
You can drop a column with the ALTER statement as follows:

ALTER TABLE MYTABLE DROP COLUMN MyColumn;

Entering Sample Data

We will assume that the VRG database contains the data shown in Figure 7-12. We will also assume that the surrogate key values in that illustration resulted from the

Figure 10-11

Data After Inserts in
Figure 10-10

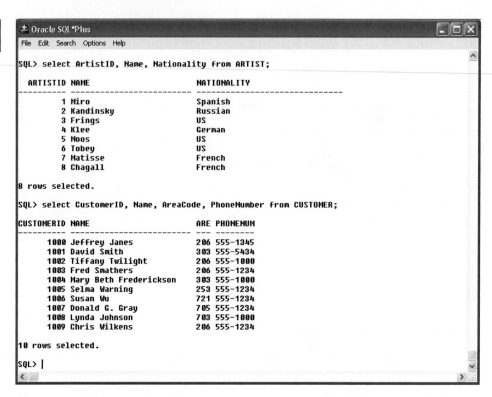

use of sequences and that the gaps in the sequence numbers resulted from inserts
and deletions over time. INSERT statements for creating the data are available at
www.prenhall.com/kroenke.

B T W

Entering values for Date data types can be problematical when using Oracle.
Oracle wants dates in a particular format, but it is sometimes difficult to determine which format it wants. The TO_DATE function can be advantageous in
such circumstances. TO_DATE takes two parameters, as shown here:

TO_DATE('11/12/2002','MM/DD/YYYY')

The first parameter is the date value, and the second is the pattern to be used
when interpreting the date. In this example, the 11 is considered to be a month;
12 is considered to be the day of the month.

   You can use the TO_DATE function with the INSERT statement to provide
date values for new rows. For example, suppose that table T1 has two
columns—A and B—where A is integer and B is date; the following insert statement can be used:

INSERT INTO T1 VALUES (100, TO_DATE ('01/05/02', 'DD/MM/YY');

The result will be a new row with the values 100 and the Oracle internal format
for May 1, 2002. TO_DATE can also be used with UPDATE statements.

Creating Indexes

Indexes are created to enforce uniqueness on columns, to facilitate sorting, and to enable fast retrieval by column values. Columns that are frequently used with equal conditions in WHERE clauses are good candidates for indexes. The equal clause can be either a simple condition in a WHERE clause or it can occur in a join. Both are shown in the following two statements:

```
SELECT      *

FROM        MYTABLE

WHERE       Column1 = 100;
```

and

```
SELECT      *

FROM        MYTABLE1, MYTABLE2

WHERE       MYTABLE1.Column1 = MYTABLE2.Column2;
```

If statements like these are frequently executed, Column1 and Column2 are good candidates for indexes.

The following statement creates an index on the Name column of the CUSTOMER table:

CREATE INDEX CustNameIdx ON CUSTOMER(Name);

The index will be called CustNameIdx. Again, the name is provided by the developer and has no significance to Oracle. To create a unique index, add the keyword UNIQUE before the keyword INDEX. For example, to ensure that no work is added twice to the WORK table, we can create a unique index on (Title, Copy, ArtistID) as follows:

CREATE UNIQUE INDEX WorkUniqueIndex ON WORK(Title, Copy, ArtistID);

Changing Table Structure

After a table has been created, its structure can be modified using the ALTER TABLE command. Be careful when you do this, however, because it is possible to lose data.

Adding or dropping a column is straightforward SQL, as shown by the following:

ALTER TABLE MYTABLE ADD C1 NUMBER(4);

ALTER TABLE MYTABLE DROP COLUMN C1;

The first statement adds a new column named C1 and gives it a numeric data type with a length of four characters. The second statement drops the column just added. Note that the keyword *column* is omitted when adding a new column.

When you issue these commands, you will receive the brief message "Table altered" in response. To ensure that the desired changes were made, use the DESCRIBE command to see the table's structure.

Restrictions on Table Column Modifications

You can drop a nonkey column at any time. All data will be lost when doing so, however. You can add a column at any time, as long as it is a NULL column.

To add a NOT NULL column, add it to the table as NULL, fill the new column in every row with data, and then change its structure to NOT NULL using the ALTER TABLE . . . MODIFY statement. For example, suppose that you have just added column C1 to table T1. After you have filled C1 in every row of T1, you can issue the following:

ALTER TABLE T1 MODIFY C1 NOT NULL;

Values will now be required for column C1.

When modifying a column, you can increase the number of characters in character columns or the number of digits in numeric columns. You can also increase or decrease the number of decimal places at any time. If the values of all rows of a given column are NULL, you can decrease the width of character and numeric data, and you can change the column's data type.

Creating Views

SQL views are created using the standard SQL-92 CREATE VIEW command. Oracle accepts all of the CREATE VIEW syntax described in Chapter 7. For example, the following statement creates the view named CustomerInterests:

CREATE VIEW CustomerInterests AS

    SELECT C.Name as Customer, A.Name as Artist

    FROM CUSTOMER C JOIN CUSTOMER_ARTIST_INT I

        ON C.CustomerID = I.CustomerID JOIN ARTIST A

        ON I.ArtistID = A.ArtistID;

The results of a query on this view for the data shown in Figure 7-12 are shown in Figure 10-12.[1] Also, unlike the SQL-92 standard, Oracle allows the ORDER BY clause in view definitions.

Figure 10-12

Using the Customer Interests View

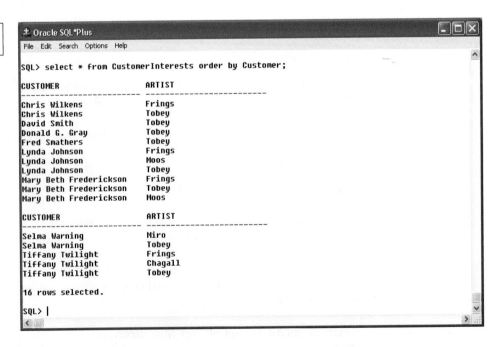

_____

[1]Oracle 9i and later versions of Oracle support the JOIN . . . ON syntax. If you are using Oracle 8i or earlier versions of Oracle, you will need to write this view using traditional join syntax.

Figure 10-13

Opening the VRG Database Using the Enterprise Manager Console

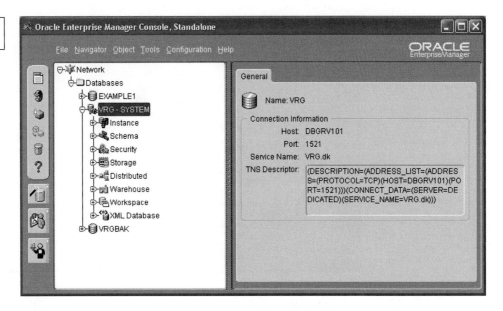

Using the Oracle Enterprise Manager Console

In addition to SQL*Plus, Oracle databases can be managed using the Oracle Enterprise Manager Console. This tool provides graphical facilities for managing the database. To start it, click Programs/Oracle-Oracle9iHome/Enterprise Manager Console. Choose Launch standalone when the console application opens.

The left side of the console has a hierarchical list. Open the Network Node to display the databases on your computer. Figure 10-13 shows the results of clicking Network and then VRG. When VRG was clicked, Oracle required the user to log on. In this case, the user logged on using the SYSTEM account. Hence, Figure 10-13 shows the database as VRG–SYSTEM.

To view the tables that have been created in this database, click Schema and then the account whose tables you want to view. In this case, the tables were created under the SYSTEM account, so the user clicked SYSTEM, as shown in Figure 10-14.

Figure 10-14

Resources in the VRG SYSTEM Account

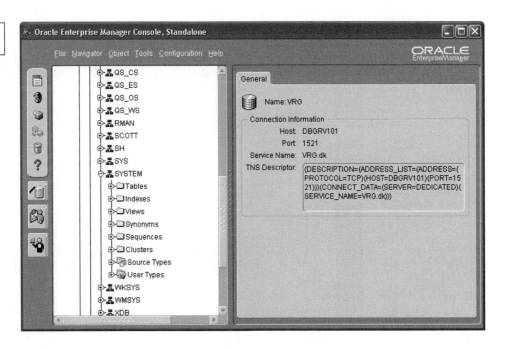

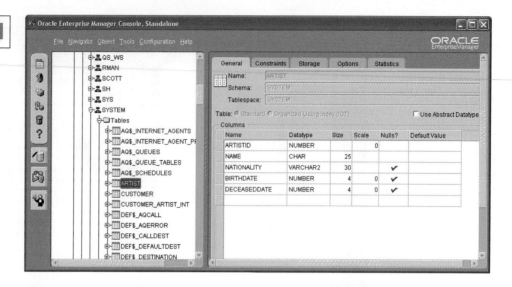

Figure 10-15

ARTIST Columns and
Properties

To see the structure of a table, click its name. The list of columns, their data types, whether they can be null, and their default values will be shown in the right panel, as depicted in Figure 10-15. This display can be used to add and remove columns and to change column properties. For example, in Figure 10-16, the user has changed the length of the Name column to 35 characters and then clicked the Show SQL button. Oracle displays the SQL statement that will be executed when the user clicks Apply. This display is useful in more complicated cases in which the developer may need to know how Oracle is interpreting a change to the database structure. In this case, the change was cancelled by clicking Revert, thus leaving the length of Name at 25.

The Enterprise Manager Console can also be used to view constraints on the table by clicking the Constraint tab. Constraints for the ARTIST table are shown in Figure 10-17. This display can also be used to manage space allocations for the table and for other purposes. These topics are beyond the scope of this chapter, however.

You can use the Enterprise Manager Console to create and drop tables as well as to view and edit them. In addition, you can use it to see, edit, add, and drop views.

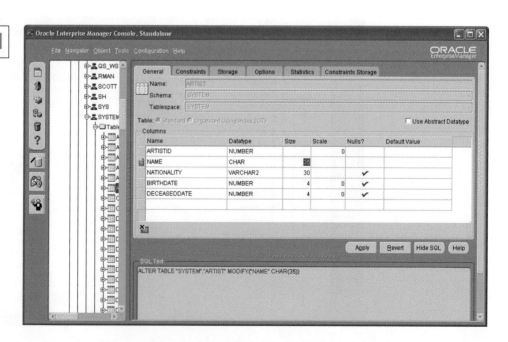

Figure 10-16

Changing a Column
Property

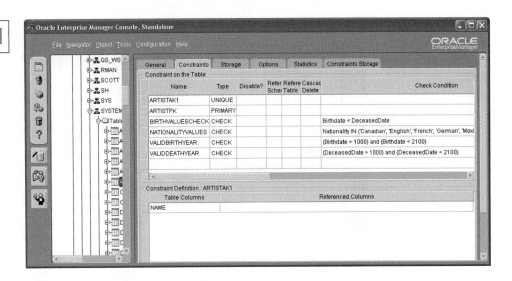

Figure 10-17

Constraints on the ARTIST Table

Figure 10-18 shows the CustomerInterests view created earlier using SQL*Plus. The view can be modified by changing the SQL statements in this view.

The Enterprise Manager Console includes a SQL scratchpad for executing SQL statements. This scratchpad is especially useful during development and testing. To access it, click the center tool in the left margin; when the tool expands, click the last element in the horizontal list, as shown in Figure 10-19(a). The scratchpad opens, as shown in Figure 10-19(b). You can key a SQL statement into the top area of the form and then click the lightning-bolt button to execute the statement.

Application Logic

There are many ways of processing an Oracle database from an application. One is to create application code using a language such as Java, C#, C++, Visual Basic, or some other programming language and then invoke Oracle DBMS commands from those programs. The modern way to do that is to use a library of object classes, create objects that accomplish database work, and process those objects by setting object properties and invoking object methods. You will see examples of such processing when we discuss ADO in Chapter 12, ADO.NET in Chapter 13, and Java Server Pages in Chapter 14.

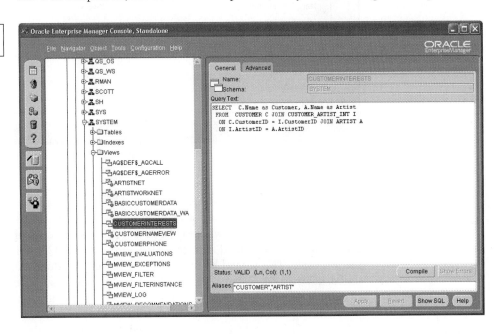

Figure 10-18

Displaying the CustomerInterests View

Figure 10-19

Using the SQL Scratchpad

(a) Starting the SQL Scratchpad and

(b) Processing a SELECT Statement in the SQL Scratchpad

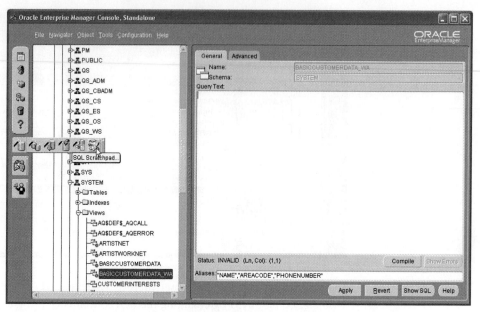

(a)

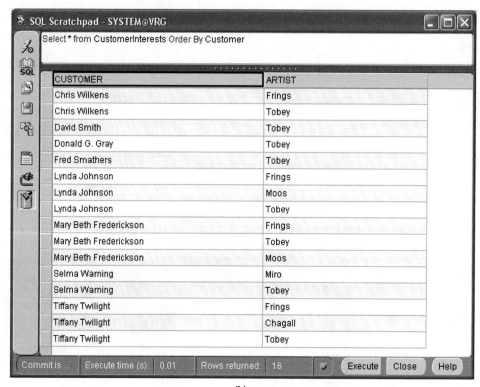

(b)

Another way of processing an Oracle database is to create stored procedures, as described in Chapter 7. These stored procedures can then be invoked from application programs or from Web pages using languages such as VBScript or JScript. Stored procedures can also be executed from SQL*Plus or from the SQL scratchpad in the management console. This should be done only when the procedures are being developed and tested, however. As described in Chapter 9, for security reasons, no one other than authorized members of the database administration staff should be allowed to interactively process an operational database.

A third means of processing an Oracle database is to save groups of database commands in .sql files. Such files are then processed using the Start command, just as we did in creating the View Ridge database in the prior section. For security, such files should be used only during application development and testing, never on an operational database.

Finally, application logic can be embedded in triggers. As you learned in Chapter 7, triggers can be used for validity checking, to set default values, to update views, and to implement referential integrity constraints.

In this chapter, we will describe and illustrate two stored procedures. We will test those procedures by invoking them from SQL*Plus. Again, this should be done only during development and testing. You will learn how to invoke those stored procedures from application code in Chapters 12 through 15. We will describe four triggers, one for each of the four trigger uses. These triggers are invoked by Oracle when the specified actions occur.

Stored Procedures

A stored procedure is a PL/SQL or Java program that is stored within the database. Stored procedures are programs; they can have parameters, they can invoke other procedures and functions, they can return values, and they can raise exceptions. Stored procedures can be invoked remotely. Here, we will consider two stored procedure examples.

Customer_Insert STORED PROCEDURE

Suppose that the View Ridge Gallery wants to be able to add a new customer to its database and record the customer's artist interests. In particular, the gallery wants to record the customer's name and phone data and then connect the customer to all artists of a specified nationality. Figure 10-20 shows a stored procedure that accomplishes this task. The procedure, named Customer_Insert, receives four parameters: newname, newareacode, newphone, and artistnationality. The keyword *IN* signifies that these are input parameters. *OUT* signifies an output parameter; *IN OUT* signifies a parameter used for both input and output. Notice that the data type is given for the parameter, but not its length. Oracle will determine the length from the context.

Variables are declared after the keyword *AS*. A **cursor variable** named *artistcursor* is defined on the SELECT statement shown. This cursor will be used to process all of the rows for an artist of the input nationality.

The first section of the procedure checks to determine whether the customer data already exist. If so, nothing is done, and an output message is printed using the Oracle package DBMS_OUTPUT. Note that the syntax for printing a string and a variable value is DBMS_OUTPUT.PUT_LINE ('String' || variable).

Before continuing with this procedure, note that this message can be seen only if the procedure is invoked from SQL*Plus or from the SQL Plus Worksheet in Oracle Enterprise Manager. If the procedure were invoked differently—say, over the Internet using a browser—this message would not be seen. The developer would need to use an output parameter or raise an error exception. These topics are beyond the scope of the present discussion, however.

To see such messages, you must execute the following prior to running the stored procedure:

Set serveroutput on;

If you are not receiving output from your procedures when using SQL*Plus, it is likely that you have not executed this statement.

The remainder of the procedure in Figure 10-20 inserts the new customer data and then loops through all artists of the given nationality. Observe the use of the special PL/SQL construct *FOR artist IN artistcursor*. This construct does several tasks. It opens the cursor and fetches the first row. Then, it iterates through all of the rows in the cursor;

| **Figure 10-20** | **Customer_Insert Stored Procedure** |

```
CREATE OR REPLACE PROCEDURE Customer_Insert
        (
        newname             IN         char ,
        newareacode         IN         char ,
        newphone            IN         char ,
        artistnationality   IN         char
        )

AS

        rowcount  int(2);

        CURSOR  artistcursor  IS
                SELECT  ArtistID
                FROM    ARTIST
                WHERE   Nationality=artistnationality;

BEGIN

        SELECT  Count (*)  INTO  rowcount
        FROM    CUSTOMER
        WHERE   Name=newname AND AreaCode=newareacode AND PhoneNumber = newphone;

        IF rowcount > 0 THEN
            BEGIN
                    DBMS_OUTPUT.PUT_LINE ('Customer Already Exists -- No Action Taken. Rowcount = '|| rowcount );
                    RETURN ;
            END;
        END IF;

        INSERT INTO CUSTOMER
                ( CustomerID, Name, AreaCode, PhoneNumber, )
                VALUES (CustID.NextVal, newname, newareacode, newphone );

        FOR artist IN artistcursor
                LOOP
                        INSERT INTO CUSTOMER_ARTIST_INT
                        (CustomerID , ArtistID )
                        VALUES (CustID.Currval, artist.ArtistID );

                END LOOP;

        DBMS_OUTPUT.PUT_LINE ('New Customer Successfully Added ');

END;
/
```

when there are no more rows, it transfers control to the next statement after the FOR. Also notice that the ArtistID value of the current cursor row can be accessed with the syntax artist.ArtistID, where *artist* is the name of the variable in the FOR statement and *not* the name of the cursor.

Once you have written this procedure, you must first compile and store it in the database. Code the procedure using your editor and save it under a name, say, SP_CI.sql. If you include a slash as your last line, the procedure will be compiled and stored when you enter the following command:

Start SP_CI

If you have made a mistake, you may have compile errors. Unfortunately, SQL*Plus does not automatically show the errors to you. Instead, it gives you the message "Warning: Procedure created with compilation errors." To see the errors, enter the following:

Show errors;

If there are no syntax errors, you receive the message "Procedure created." Now, you can invoke the procedure from SQL*Plus with the Execute or Exec command, as follows:

Exec Customer_Insert ('Michael Bench' '203' '555–2014' 'US');

After you execute this statement, you should query the CUSTOMER, ARTIST, and CUSTOMER_ARTIST_INT tables to ensure that the changes were made correctly.

If you have execution-time errors, the line numbers reported differ from the line numbers you see in your text editor. You can adjust these line numbers to conform to yours, but the process is too complicated to describe here. For the simple procedures we will do here, just work around the issue. Do not assume that the line numbers match, however.

NewCustomerWithTransaction STORED PROCEDURE

Figure 10-21 shows a second stored procedure for recording a new customer and the sale of a work to that customer. The logic of this procedure, named NewCustomerWithTransaction, is as follows. First, create new customer data and then search for TRANSACTION rows for the purchased work that have null values for CustomerID. That search involves the join of the ARTIST, WORK, and TRANS-ACTION tables because the Name of the artist is stored in ARTIST, and the Title and Copy of the work are stored in WORK. If one, and only one, such row is found, update CustomerID, SalesPrice, and PurchaseDate in that row. Then, insert a row in the intersection table to record the customer's interest in this artist. Otherwise, make no changes to the database.

NewCustomerWithTransaction accepts parameters having customer and purchase data, as shown. Next, several variables and a cursor are declared. The cursor defines the join of the ARTIST, WORK, and TRANSACTION tables. It selects TransactionID and ARTIST.ArtistID of rows that match the input artist and work data and that have a null value for CustomerID.

The procedure first checks to see whether the input customer data already exist in the database. If not, it inserts the new customer data. In PL/SQL, there is no BEGIN TRANSACTION [2] statement; the first database action automatically starts a transaction. Here, inserting the customer data starts a new transaction.

Like SQL, PL/SQL comments are enclosed between /* and */. Such comments can extend over multiple lines, and if you begin a comment with /* and fail to terminate it with */, your entire program will be treated as a comment.

After the customer data are inserted, the TransCursor is processed. The variable rowcount is used to count the rows, the value of TransactionID is stored in *tid*, and the value of ArtistID is stored in *aid*. Observe that the assignment operator in Oracle is : = . Thus, tid : = trans.TransactionID means to assign the value of trans.TransactionID to the variable *tid*.

According to this logic, if only one qualifying row is found, then *tid* and *aid* will have the values we need to continue. If zero or more than one qualifying rows are found, the transaction will be aborted, but neither *tid* nor *aid* will be used.

We could use Count(*) to count the qualifying rows, and if Count(*) equals one, execute another SQL statement to obtain the values of *tid* and *aid* we need. The logic in Figure 10-21 saves this second SQL statement.

If rowcount is greater than one or equal to zero, an error message is generated and the transaction is rolled back to remove the prior insert to CUSTOMER. If rowcount equals one, the appropriate TRANSACTION row is updated. Note the use of the function SysDate to store the current date. Finally, an intersection row is inserted for this customer and the artist of the purchased work (*aid*).

---

[2] Watch out here! We are using the word *TRANSACTION* in two ways in this section: as the name of one of the View Ridge tables and as the name of a group of statements to be executed atomically. The context will make the usage clear, but be aware of the possible confusion.

Figure 10-21	NewCustomerWithTransaction Stored Procedure

```
CREATE OR REPLACE PROCEDURE NewCustomerWithTransaction
        (
        newname IN char,
        newareacode IN char,
        newphone IN char,
        artistname IN char,
        worktitle IN char,
        workcopy IN char,
        price IN number
        )

AS

        rowcount    int;
        tid         int;
        aid         int;

        CURSOR    transcursor IS
                SELECT         TransactionID, ARTIST.ArtistID
                FROM           ARTIST, WORK, TRANSACTION
                WHERE          Name=artistname AND Title=worktitle AND Copy=workcopy AND
                               TRANSACTION.CustomerID IS NULL AND
                               ARTIST.ArtistID = WORK.ArtistID AND
                               WORK.WorkID = TRANSACTION.WorkID;

BEGIN

        /* Does Customer Already exist? */

        SELECT    Count(*) INTO rowcount
        FROM      CUSTOMER
        WHERE     Name=newname AND AreaCode=newareacode AND PhoneNumber = newphone;

        IF rowcount > 0 THEN
            BEGIN
                    DBMS_OUTPUT.PUT_LINE ('Customer Already Exists -- No Action Taken');
                    RETURN;
            END;

        END IF;


        /* Customer not exist, add new customer data */
        INSERT INTO CUSTOMER
                (CustomerID, Name, AreaCode, PhoneNumber)
                VALUES (CustID.NextVal, newname, newareacode, newphone);


        /* Look for one and only one available TRANSACTION row. */
        rowcount := 0;
        FOR trans In transcursor
                LOOP
                        tid := trans.TransactionID;
                        aid := trans.ArtistID;
                        rowcount := rowcount + 1;
                END LOOP;

        IF rowcount > 1 Then
            BEGIN
                    /* Too many available rows -- undo with message and return */
                    ROLLBACK;
                    DBMS_OUTPUT.PUT_LINE ('Invalid Artist/Work/Transaction data -- No Action Taken.  Rowcount = ' ||
                    rowcount);
                    RETURN;
            END;
        END IF;
```

```
    IF rowcount = 0 Then

        BEGIN
                /* No available row exists -- undo with message and return */
                ROLLBACK;
                DBMS_OUTPUT.PUT_LINE ('No available transaction row -- No Action Taken');
                RETURN;

        END;

    END IF;

    /* Exactly one exists -- use it (tid obtained from transcursor above) */


    UPDATE TRANSACTION
            SET    CustomerID = CustID.Currval, Salesprice = price, PurchaseDate = SysDate
            WHERE  TransactionID = tid;
    DBMS_OUTPUT.PUT_LINE ('Customer created and transaction data updated');

    /* Now create interest in this artist for this customer */
    /* Use currval of sequence and aid from transcursor above */

    INSERT INTO CUSTOMER_ARTIST_INT (ArtistID, CustomerID)
                VALUES (aid, CustID.CurrVal);

END;
/
```

This stored procedure can be invoked with a command like the following:

Exec NewCustomerWithTransaction ('Malinda Gliddens', '303', '555–6687', 'Chagall', 'Northwest by Night', '37/50', 27000);

To test this procedure, it is convenient to first define a view that shows customer purchases. Assume that the following view has been created:

CREATE VIEW WorkPurchase AS

    SELECT   **C.Name as Customer, A.Name as Artist,**
                  W.Title, W.Copy, T.PurchaseDate, T.SalesPrice

    FROM   **CUSTOMER C JOIN TRANSACTION T**

        ON   **C.CustomerID = T.CustomerID**

    JOIN WORK W

        ON   **T.WorkID = W.WorkID**

    JOIN ARTIST A

        ON   **W.ArtistID = A.ArtistID;**

Figure 10-22 shows SQL statements with queries of WorkPurchase, the CustomerInterests view, and the CUSTOMER table. If you examine this figure, you will see that the changes were made as required. Of course, to complete the testing of this stored procedure, it is necessary to test the error conditions as well. We will omit that step here, however.

Triggers

Oracle triggers are PL/SQL or Java procedures that are invoked when a specified database activity occurs. Oracle supports a variety of different types of triggers. Some triggers are invoked on SQL commands that create new tables, views, or other database triggers. Other triggers are invoked once per SQL command, and still others are invoked for each row that is involved in the processing of a SQL command.

Figure 10-22

Testing Results of the Stored Procedure in Figure 10-21

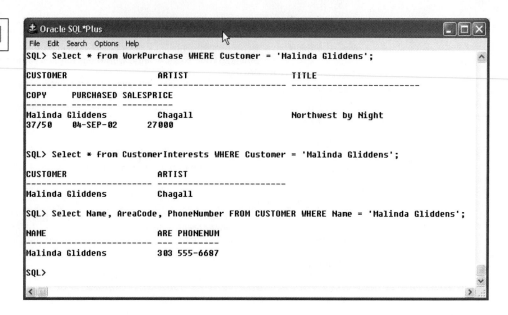

To understand the difference between the latter two trigger types, consider the following SQL update statement:

UPDATE   **CUSTOMER**

SET   **AreaCode = '425'**

WHERE   **ZipPostalCode = '98119';**

A command trigger will be fired once when the statement is processed. A row trigger will be fired once for every row that is updated during the processing of this statement. Row triggers are the most common, and we will consider only them in this chapter.

Oracle recognizes three types of row triggers: BEFORE, AFTER, and INSTEAD OF. BEFORE and AFTER triggers are placed on tables. INSTEAD OF triggers are placed on views. Each trigger type can be fired on INSERT, UPDATE, or DELETE commands.

Because of the way that Oracle manages concurrency, AFTER triggers that update the table that caused the trigger to be fired can be problematic. For example, if table T1 has an AFTER UPDATE trigger, any code in the trigger that also attempts to process table T1 may not work correctly. When this occurs, Oracle issues a message like "Table T1 is mutating, trigger/function may not see it." For this reason, any actions that require processing the table that is firing the trigger are best done with BEFORE triggers.

AFTER triggers can be useful, however, when the action of the trigger applies to a table other than the one that fired the trigger. For example, if table T1 requires a child row in table T2, an AFTER trigger on T1 insert can be used to create the required T2 child. You will see an example of that use in Figure 10-28(a).

The values of columns of the table or view upon which the trigger is based are available to the trigger. For insert and update triggers, the new values of the table or view columns can be accessed with the prefix :new. Thus, if table T1 has two columns, C1 and C2, when an insert or update trigger is fired on T1, the expression :new.C1 has the new value for the column C1 and the expression :new.C2 has the new value for the column C2.

For update and delete triggers, the old values of the table or view columns can be accessed with the prefix :old. Thus, :old.C1 will have the value of column C1 before the update or delete is processed.

In the next sections, we will discuss a trigger that computes a default value, one that enforces a data constraint, one that updates a view, and finally, one that enforces a required child constraint.

A Trigger for Setting Default Values

Triggers can be used to set default values that are more complex than those that can be set with the Default constraint on a column definition. For example, View Ridge has a pricing policy that says that the default AskingPrice of a work of art depends on whether the art has been in the gallery before. If not, the default AskingPrice is twice the AcquisitionPrice. If the work has been in the gallery before, the default price is the larger of twice the AcquisitionPrice or the AcquisitionPrice plus the average net gain of the work in the past.

The BEFORE trigger in Figure 10-23 implements this pricing policy. It is named SetAskingPrice and uses the view ArtistWorkNet, which was defined in Chapter 7 as follows:

CREATE VIEW ArtistWorkNet AS

  SELECT **W.WorkID, Name, Title, Copy, AcquisitionPrice, SalesPrice,**
       (SalesPrice – AcquisitionPrice) AS NetPrice

  FROM   **TRANSACTION T**

  JOIN   **WORK W ON T.WorkID = W .WorkID JOIN ARTIST A**

    ON **W.ArtistID = A.ArtistID;**

Figure 10-23

SetAskingPrice Trigger

```
CREATE OR REPLACE TRIGGER SetAskingPrice
            BEFORE INSERT ON TRANSACTION

FOR EACH ROW

DECLARE

        avgNetPrice number (8,2);
        newPrice number (8,2);
        rowcount int;

BEGIN
        /* First find if work has been here before */


        SELECT  Count(*) INTO rowcount
        FROM    TRANSACTION
        WHERE   WorkID = :new.WorkID;

        IF rowcount = 0 Then
                /* This is first time work has been in gallery */

                :new.AskingPrice := 2*(:new.AcquisitionPrice);
        ELSE

                /* Work has been here before */
                SELECT          Avg(NetPrice) INTO avgNetPrice
                FROM            ArtistWorkNet AW
                WHERE           AW.WorkID = :new.WorkID
                GROUP BY        AW.WorkID;

                newPrice := avgNetPrice + :new.AcquisitionPrice;

                /*   */
                IF newPrice > 2 * :new.AcquisitionPrice Then
                        :new.AskingPrice := newPrice;
                ELSE
                        :new.Askingprice := 2 * :new.AcquisitionPrice;
                END IF;

        END IF;

END;
/
```

The trigger first counts the number of rows in TRANSACTION having the :new value of WorkID. Because this is a BEFORE trigger, the work has not yet been added to the database, and the count will be zero if the work has not been to the gallery before. If this is the case, :new.AskingPrice is set to twice the AcquisitionPrice.

If the work has been to the gallery before, the average of NetPrice for this work is computed using ArtistWorkNet view. Then, the variable newPrice is computed as the sum of the average plus the acquisition price. Finally, :new.AskingPrice is set to the larger of newPrice or twice the AcqusitionPrice. Because this is a BEFORE trigger, the Avg built-in function can be used because the new row of WORK has not yet been added to the database and will not count in the average computation.

The computations in this trigger may be a problem, however, if either SalesPrice or AcquisitionPrice is null in any of the rows in the ArtistWorkView. The discussion of that problem, however, is beyond the scope of this chapter.

This trigger provides useful functionality for the gallery. It saves the gallery personnel considerable manual work in implementing their pricing policy and likely improves the accuracy of the results as well.

To create a trigger like this, write the code using a text editor and save it in a text file with a name having the suffix .sql—say, Trigger1.sql. Then, to create the trigger, open SQL*Plus and type *start Trigger1*. In response, Oracle will compile your trigger. If you have syntax errors, type *show errors*, as described for stored procedures.

A Trigger for Enforcing a Data Constraint

View Ridge Gallery keeps a list of problem-customer accounts; these are customers who have either not paid promptly or who have presented other problems to the gallery. When a customer who is on the problem list is entered into the database, the gallery manager wants to know that this insert has occurred.

The AFTER trigger in Figure 10-24 provides such notification. The phrase "AFTER INSERT OR UPDATE OF Name ON CUSTOMER" is correct, but it contains an ambiguity. It means that the trigger should fire after *any* insert on CUSTOMER or after an update of Name in CUSTOMER. Thus, any insert fires the trigger, and an update of Name fires the trigger.

The statement FOR EACH ROW causes this trigger to be a row trigger that is fired once for every row that is inserted or for which Name is updated.

To test this trigger, first create a PROBLEM_ACCOUNT table with Name, AreaCode, and PhoneNumber columns that match those in CUSTOMER. Then, place rows into that table. Next, insert a new customer with values that match one of those in the PROBLEM_ACCOUNT trigger. Figure 10-25 shows the result for the customer 'Nichole Not Pay'. Notice that this trigger writes the notification message back to the SQL*Plus utility. More realistically, such a trigger would send an email to the gallery manager or take some other more useful action.

Using a table of valid (or invalid) values is more flexible and dynamic than placing such values in a CHECK constraint. For example, consider the CHECK constraint on Nationality values in the ARTIST table. If the gallery manager wants to expand the nationality of allowed artists, the manger will have to change the CHECK constraint using the ALTER TABLE statement. In reality, the gallery manager will have to hire a consultant to change that constraint.

A better approach is to place the allowed values of Nationality in a table, say ALLOWED_NATIONALITY. Then, write a trigger like that shown in Figure 10-24 to enforce the constraint that new values of Nationality exist in ALLOWED_NATIONAL-ITY. When the gallery owner wants to change the allowed artists, the owner would simply add or remove values in the ALLOWED_NATIONALITY table.

A Trigger for Updating a View

Chapter 7 discussed the problem of updating views. One such problem concerns updating views created via joins; it is normally not possible for the DBMS to know how to update

Figure 10-24   **ValidateCustomer Trigger**

```
CREATE OR REPLACE TRIGGER ValidateCustomer
AFTER INSERT OR UPDATE OF Name ON CUSTOMER

FOR EACH ROW

DECLARE

        rowcount int;

BEGIN


/*  Look for the new customer in the Problem_Account Table.     */
        SELECT Count(*) INTO rowcount
        FROM PROBLEM_ACCOUNT PA
        WHERE :new.Name = PA.NAME
                AND :new.AreaCode = PA.AreaCode
                AND :new.PhoneNumber = PA.PhoneNumber;


/* If the customer exists in the problem table, then send warning message.  */

        If rowcount > 0 Then

                DBMS_OUTPUT.PUT_LINE ('A Customer with name 'll :new.Name ll ' and phone of ('ll
                :new.AreaCode ll ') ' ll:new.PhoneNumber ll ' has been a problem in the past.');

        End If;


END;
/
```

Figure 10-25

Execution of the ValidateCustomer Trigger

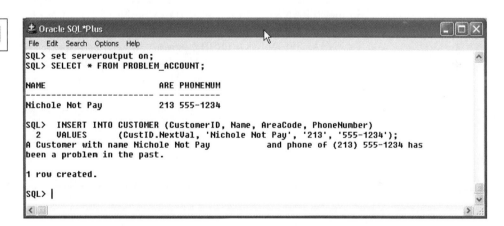

the tables that underlie the join. However, there may be application-specific knowledge that can be used to determine how to interpret a request to update a joined view.

Consider the CustomerInterests view defined earlier in this chapter. It contains rows of CUSTOMER and ARTIST joined over their intersection table. CUSTOMER.Name is given the alias Customer, and ARTIST.Name is given the alias Artist.

A request to change the name of a customer in CustomerInterests can be interpreted as a request to change the name of the underlying CUSTOMER table. Such a request, however, can be processed only if the value of Name is unique in Customer. If not, the request cannot be processed.

Figure 10-26 shows an INSTEAD OF trigger that will update CUSTOMER.Name only if the name is unique in the database. It conditions the update on the NOT EXISTS

Figure 10-26

**CustomerInterests
Update Trigger**

```
CREATE OR REPLACE TRIGGER CustomerInterests_Update
        INSTEAD OF UPDATE ON CustomerInterests

FOR EACH ROW

/* Update the name only if it is unique in the customer table   */

BEGIN
        UPDATE          CUSTOMER C1
        SET             C1.Name = :new.Customer
        WHERE           C1.Name = :old.Customer
                AND     NOT EXISTS
                        (Select *
                        FROM    CUSTOMER C2
                        WHERE   C2.Name = C1.Name
                        AND     c2.CustomerID <> C1.CustomerID);

END;
/
```

keyword rather than counting the number of rows with the given customer name and making the change only if there is one such row. Constructing the trigger with NOT EXISTS allows Oracle to optimize the SQL statement and will result in better performance.

A Trigger for Enforcing a Required Child Constraint

The View Ridge design includes a mandatory to mandatory relationship between WORK and TRANSACTION. Every WORK must have a TRANSACTION to store the price and date the work was acquired, and every TRANSACTION must relate to a WORK parent. Figure 10-27 shows the tasks that must be accomplished to enforce this constraint; it is a boilerplate of Figure 6-27(b).

Because the CREATE TABLE statement for TRANSACTION (Figure 10-7) defines TRANSACTION.WorkID to be NOT NULL and defines the FOREIGN KEY constraint without cascading deletions, the DBMS will ensure that every TRANSACTION has a WORK parent. So, we need not be concerned with enforcing the insert on TRANSACTION or the deletion on WORK. As stated in Figure 10-27, the DBMS will do that for us. Also, we need not be concerned with updates to WORK.WorkID because it is a surrogate key.

Three constraints remain that must be enforced by triggers: (1) ensuring that a TRANSACTION row is created when a new WORK is created; (2) ensuring that TRANS-

Figure 10-27

Enforcing the M-M Relationship between WORK and TRANSACTION

	WORK	**TRANSACTION**
Insert	Create a TRANSACTION row.	New TRANSACTION must have a valid work ID (enforced by DBMS).
Modify key or foreign key	Not a concern because workID is a surrogate key.	Never allowed because a TRANSACTION cannot change to a different WORK.
Delete	Cannot delete a WORK with any TRANSACTION children (enforced by DBMS by lack of CASCADE DELETE).	Cannot delete the last child. (Actually, by gallery policy, can delete NO TRANSACTION data.)

ACTION.WorkID never changes; and (3) ensuring that the last TRANSACTION child for a WORK is never deleted.

We can enforce the second constraint by writing a BEFORE trigger on update of TRANSACTION that checks for a change in WorkID. If there is such a change, the trigger can set the value of WorkID to the old value before the update occurs.

Concerning the third constraint, the gallery has a business policy that no TRANS-ACTION data ever be deleted. Thus, we need not only to disallow the deletion of the last child, we need to disallow the deletion of any child. We can do this by writing an AFTER trigger on deletion of TRANSACTION that rolls back any attempted dele-tion. (If the gallery allowed TRANSACTION deletions, we could enforce the deletion constraint using views as shown in Chapter 7, Figures 7-29 and 7-30.) The triggers for enforcing the second and third constraints are simple, and we leave them as exercises 10.58 and 10.59.

However, the first constraint is a problem. We can write an AFTER trigger on a WORK INSERT to create a default TRANSACTION row, but this trigger will be called before the application has a chance to create the TRANSACTION row. The trigger will create a TRANSACTION row and then the application may create a sec-ond one. To guard against the duplicate, we can write an AFTER trigger on TRANS-ACTION to remove the row the WORK trigger created in those cases when the application creates its own trigger.

Figures 10-28(a) and 10-28(b) show this pair of triggers. The trigger in Figure 10-28(a) creates the default TRANSACTION row. It first checks to determine whether an appropriate TRANSACTION row exists; if not, it inserts a new row into TRANSAC-TION. The trigger in Figure 10-28(b) then removes this same row if the application creates its own TRANSACTION row.

This solution is awkward, at best.

A better design is to require the applications to create the WORK/TRANSACTION combination via a view. For example, consider the view Work_Trans:

CREATE VIEW Work_Trans AS

> **SELECT   Title, Description, Copy, ArtistID, DateAcquired,
>   AcquisitionPrice**
>
> **FROM   WORK W JOIN TRANSACTION T**
>
> **ON   W.WorkID = T.WorkID;**

The DBMS will not be able to process an insert on this view. We can, however, define an INSTEAD OF trigger to process the insert. Our trigger will create both a new row in WORK and the new, required child in TRANSACTION. The code for this trigger is shown in Figure 10-29.

The solution in Figure 10-29 is more satisfying than the one in Figure 10-28. Note, however, that with this solution, applications must be prohibited from inserting WORK rows directly. They must always insert them via the Work_Trans view.

Exception Handling

This discussion has omitted a discussion of PL/SQL exception handling. This is unfor-tunate, because exception handling is both important and useful. There's just too much to do. If you program in PL/SQL in the future, however, be sure to learn about this important topic. It can be used in all types of PL/SQL programming, but it is especially useful in BEFORE and INSTEAD OF triggers for canceling pending updates. Exceptions are necessary because transactions in Oracle cannot be rolled back in triggers. Exceptions can be used instead to generate error and warning messages. They also keep users better informed about what the trigger has done.

Figure 10-28

**Triggers for Enforcing
a Required Child
Constraint**
(a) EnforceTransChild
Trigger and
(b) RemoveDupTrans
Trigger

```
CREATE OR REPLACE TRIGGER EnforceTransChild
          AFTER INSERT ON WORK

FOR EACH ROW

DECLARE

        rowCount int;
        newID int;

BEGIN

        newID := :new.WorkID;
        SELECT  Count(*) INTO rowCount
        FROM    TRANSACTION
        WHERE   WorkID = newID
            AND   CustomerID IS Null;

        If rowCount = 0 then

        /* Insert new transaction row since none available */

                INSERT  INTO TRANSACTION
                (TransactionID, DateAcquired, WorkID) VALUES
                (TransID.NextVal, SysDate, newID);
        End If;

END;
/
```

(a)

```
CREATE OR REPLACE TRIGGER RemoveDupTrans
          BEFORE INSERT ON TRANSACTION

FOR EACH ROW


/* Clean up duplicate child if necessary */

BEGIN

        DELETE    FROM TRANSACTION
        WHERE     WorkID = :new.WorkID
            AND     CustomerID is Null
            AND     TransactionID <> :new.TransactionID;


END;
/
```

(b)

Data Dictionary

Oracle maintains an extensive data dictionary of metadata. This dictionary describes the structures of tables, sequences, views, indexes, constraints, columns, and stored procedures. It also contains the source code of procedures, functions, and triggers. And it contains much more. The dictionary contains metadata about itself in the table DICT. You can query this table to learn more about the contents of the data dictionary, but be warned that it is a big table. For example, more than 800 rows will be returned if you query for the names of all tables in the data dictionary.

Suppose you want to know what tables the data dictionary contains about user or system tables. The following query obtains that result:

Figure 10-29   Enforcing a Required Child with an INSTEAD OF Trigger

```
CREATE OR REPLACE TRIGGER Insert_Work_Trans
            INSTEAD OF INSERT ON Work_Trans

FOR EACH ROW

BEGIN

/* Use the inputs from the application INSERT on the view
            to create the new rows in WORK and TRANSACTION */

            INSERT INTO WORK (WorkID, Title, Description, Copy, ArtistID) VALUES
            (WorkID.NextVal, :new.Title, :new.Description, :new.Copy, :new.ArtistID);

            INSERT INTO TRANSACTION (TransactionID, DateAquired, AcquisitionPrice, WorkID) VALUES
            (TransID.NextVAl, :new.DateAquired, :new.Acquisition, WorkID.CurrVal);
END;
```

SELECT Table_Name, Comments

FROM DICT

WHERE   Table_Name LIKE ('%TABLES%');

Forty or so rows will be returned. One of those tables is named USER_TABLES. To display the columns of that table, enter the following:

DESC USER_TABLES;

You can use this strategy of query and describe to obtain the dictionary's metadata for objects and structures you want. Figure 10-30 lists several of the tables and their purposes.

Figure 10-30

Example Oracle
Metadata

Table Name	Comments
DICT	Data dictionary metadata.
USER_CATALOG	List of tables, views, sequences, and other structures owned by the user.
USER_TABLES	User table structures.
USER_TAB_COLUMNS	A child of USER_TABLES. Has data about table columns. Synonym is COLS.
USER_VIEWS	User views.
USER_CONSTRAINTS	User constraints.
USER_CONS_COLUMNS	A child of USER_CONSTRAINTS. Has columns in constraints.
USER_TRIGGERS	Has trigger metadata. Query Trigger_Name, Trigger_Type, and Trigger_Event. Warning: Trigger_Body does not provide a useful listing.
USER_SOURCE	To obtain the text of procedure MY TRIGGER, SELECT Text FROM USER_SOURCE WHERE Name='MYTRIGGER' AND Type='PROCEDURE'

The tables USER_SOURCE and USER_TRIGGERS are useful when you want to know what source code is currently stored in the database for procedures and triggers.

By now, you should know enough SQL to navigate your way around the dictionary. Be aware that Oracle stores all names in uppercase. If you're looking for a trigger named On_Customer_Insert, search for ON_CUSTOMER_INSERT.

Concurrency Control

Oracle supports three different transaction isolation levels and also allows applications to place locks explicitly. Explicit locking is not recommended, however, because such locking can interfere with Oracle's default locking behavior and because it increases the likelihood of transaction deadlock.

The Oracle change management and locking design is ingenious and sophisticated. With it, Oracle never makes dirty reads; it only reads committed changes. Oracle supports read committed, serializable, and read only transaction isolation levels. The first two are defined in the 1992 ANSI standard; read only is unique to Oracle. Figure 10-31 summarizes these isolation levels.

Before discussing the implementation of transaction isolation levels, you need to understand how Oracle processes database changes. Oracle maintains a **System Change Number (SCN),** which is a database-wide value that is incremented by Oracle whenever database changes are made. When a row is changed, the before image of the row is placed in a **rollback segment,** which is a section of memory maintained by Oracle. The before image includes the SCN that was in the row prior to the change. Then, the row is changed, Oracle increments the SCN, and places the new SCN value in the changed row. When an application issues a SQL statement like:

UPDATE   MYTABLE

SET   MyColumn1 = 'NewValue'

WHERE   MyColumn2 = 'Something';

Figure 10-31

Oracle Transaction Isolation

Read Committed Transaction Isolation	The default Oracle isolation level. Dirty reads are not possible, but repeated reads may yield different data. Phantoms are possible.
	Each statement reads consistent data. When blocked for updates, statements are rolled back and restarted when necessary. Deadlock is detected and one of the blocking statements is rolled back.
Serializable Transaction Isolation	Dirty reads are not possible, repeated reads yield the same results, and phantoms are not possible.
	All statements in the transaction read consistent data. "Cannot serialize" error occurs when a transaction attempts to update or delete a row with a committed data change that occurred after the transaction started. Also occurs when blocking transactions or statements commit their changes or when the transaction is rolled back due to deadlock. Application programs need to be written to handle the "Cannot serialize" exception.
Read Only Transaction Isolation	All statements read consistent data. No inserts, updates, or deletions are possible.
Explicit Locks	Not recommended.

the value of SCN that was current at the time the statement started is recorded. Call this value the Statement SCN. While processing the query, in this case while looking for rows with MyColumn2 = 'Something', Oracle selects only rows that have committed changes with an SCN value less than or equal to the Statement SCN. When it finds a row with a committed change and SCN value greater than the Statement SCN, it looks in the rollback segment to find an earlier version of the row. It searches the rollback segments until it finds a version of the row with a committed change having an SCN less than the Statement SCN.

In this way, SQL statements always read a consistent set of values—those that were committed at or before the time the statement was started. As you will see, this strategy is sometimes extended to apply to transactions. In that case, all of the statements in a transaction read rows having an SCN value less than the SCN that was current when the transaction started.

Again, this design means that Oracle reads committed changes, only. Dirty reads are not possible.

Read Committed Transaction Isolation Level

Recall from Chapter 9 that dirty reads are not allowed with read committed isolation, but reads may not be repeatable and phantoms are possible. Because Oracle's design prohibits reading dirty data, read committed is Oracle's default transaction isolation level.

Because of the way Oracle implements read committed isolation, each SQL statement is consistent, but two different SQL statements in the same transaction may read inconsistent data. If transaction-level consistency is required, serializable isolation must be used. Do not confuse statement consistency with the lost update problem, however. Oracle prohibits lost updates because it never reads dirty data.

Because of the way it uses the SCN, Oracle never needs to place read locks. When a row is to be changed or deleted, however, Oracle places an exclusive lock on the row before making the change or deletion. If another transaction has an exclusive lock on the row, the statement waits. If the blocking transaction rolls back, the change or deletion proceeds.

If the blocking transaction commits, the new SCN value is given to the statement, and the statement (not the transaction) rolls back and starts over. When a statement is rolled back, changes already made by the statement are removed using the rollback segments.

Because exclusive locks are used, deadlock can occur. When that happens, Oracle detects the deadlock using a wait-for graph and rolls back one of the conflicting statements.

Serializable Transaction Isolation Level

As you learned in Chapter 9, with serializable transaction isolation, dirty reads are not possible, reads are always repeatable, and phantoms cannot occur. Oracle supports serializable transaction isolation, but the application program must play a role for it to work. Use the SET command to change the transaction isolation level. The following statement establishes serializable isolation for the duration of a transaction:

SET TRANSACTION ISOLATION LEVEL SERIALIZABLE;

To change the isolation level for all transactions, use the ALTER command:

ALTER SESSION SET ISOLATION_LEVEL SERIALIZABLE;

When the isolation level is serializable, Oracle saves the SCN at the time the transaction started. Call this value the Transaction SCN. As the transaction proceeds, Oracle only reads committed changes that have an SCN value less than or equal to the Transaction SCN. Hence, reads are always repeatable and phantoms are not possible.

As long as the transaction does not attempt to update or delete any row having a committed change with an SCN greater than the Transaction SCN, the transaction proceeds normally. If, however, the transaction does attempt to update or delete such a row, Oracle issues a "Cannot serialize" error when the update or delete occurs. At that point, the application program must play a role. It can commit changes made to that point, roll back the entire transaction, or take some other action. Any program that executes under serializable isolation must include such exception-handling code.

Also, when a transaction running under serializable isolation attempts to update or delete a row that has been locked exclusively by a different transaction or statement, the transaction waits. If the blocking transaction or statement later rolls back, the transaction can continue. If, however, the blocking transaction commits, Oracle generates the "Cannot serialize" error and the application needs to process that exception.

Similarly, if a serializable transaction is rolled back due to deadlock, the "Cannot serialize" error is also generated.

Read Only Transaction Isolation

With this isolation level, the transaction reads only rows having committed changes with an SCN value less than or equal to the Transaction SCN. If the transaction encounters rows with committed changes having an SCN value greater than the Transaction SCN, Oracle searches the rollback segments and reconstructs the row as it was prior to the Transaction SCN. With this level of transaction isolation, no inserts, updates, or deletions are allowed.

Additional Locking Comments

The application can invoke locks explicitly using the SELECT FOR UPDATE form of the SELECT statement. This is not recommended, and you should not use it until you have learned much more about Oracle locking than we have described here.

Behind the scenes, Oracle uses quite a wide variety of locks to provide isolation levels. Oracle has a row share lock as well as several different types of table locks. Other locks are used internally within Oracle. You can learn more about these locks in the Oracle documentation.

To reduce the likelihood of lock conflict, Oracle does not promote locks from one level to another. Row locks remain row locks, even if there are hundreds of them on hundreds of rows of a table. This strategy is different from SQL Server, as you will learn in the next chapter. Oracle Corporation claims that not promoting locks is an advantage, and it probably is—especially given the rest of the Oracle lock architecture.

 Oracle Security

Oracle provides robust and comprehensive security facilities. The relationships among the basic components of the Oracle security system are shown in Figure 10-32. The components are ACCOUNT, PROFILE, SYSTEM PRIVILEGE, and ROLE. An ACCOUNT is a user account such as SYSTEM, MaryJane, Fred, or some other user account.[3] A PROFILE is a set of system resource maximums that are assigned to an account. Figure 10-33 shows the definition of a typical PROFILE. Notice that the PROFILE limits both computer and database resources; it is also used for password management, as described in the next section. As shown in Figure 10-32, an ACCOUNT has exactly one PROFILE, but a PROFILE may be assigned to many accounts.

---

[3]Unfortunately, Oracle uses the word *SYSTEM* in two different ways here. There is an account named SYSTEM, and there are SYSTEM PRIVILEGEs. Figure 10-34 shows SYSTEM PRIVILEGEs for the SYSTEM account.

Figure 10-32

Relationship of Oracle
Security Components

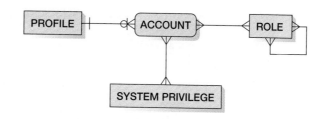

Figure 10-33

Oracle Profile
Definition

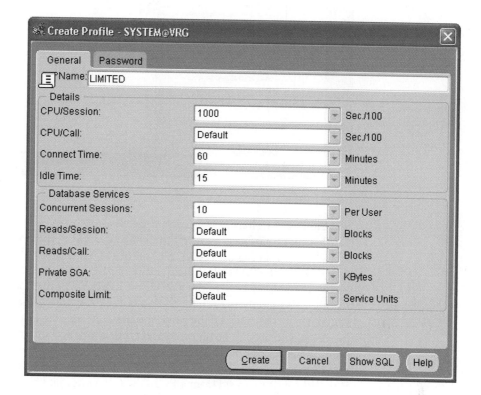

Account System Privileges

Each ACCOUNT can be allocated many SYSTEM PRIVILEGEs and many ROLEs. A SYSTEM PRIVILEGE is the right to perform some action on the database data; on a database structure, such as a table, a view, or an index; or on one of the Oracle system resources, such as a tablespace. Figure 10-34 shows the SYSTEM PRIVILEGEs for the SYSTEM account. Only one privilege is shown: UNLIMITED TABLESPACE. Other privileges that can be assigned to the SYSTEM account are shown in the panel in the upper-right portion of this figure.

A ROLE can have many SYSTEM PRIVILEGEs, and it may also have a relationship to other ROLEs. As shown in Figure 10-35(a), three roles have been assigned to the SYSTEM account. The SYSTEM account inherits the ROLEs and PRIVILEGEs of each of the three ROLEs it has been granted. For example, SYSTEM has been granted the role SALES_HISTORY_ROLE. The SYSTEM PRIVILEGEs of that ROLE are shown in Figure 10-35(b). Because the SYSTEM account has the ROLE SALES_HISTORY_ROLE, it obtains the four privileges shown in Figure 10-35(b).

As shown in Figure 10-32, a ROLE may itself have other ROLEs assigned to it. If so, it inherits the ROLEs and PRIVILEGEs of those other ROLEs as well.

To summarize, the SYSTEM PRIVILEGEs of an account consist of all of the SYSTEM PRIVILEGEs that it has been granted directly, plus the SYSTEM PRIVILEGEs of all of the ROLEs that it has, plus the privileges of all of the ROLEs

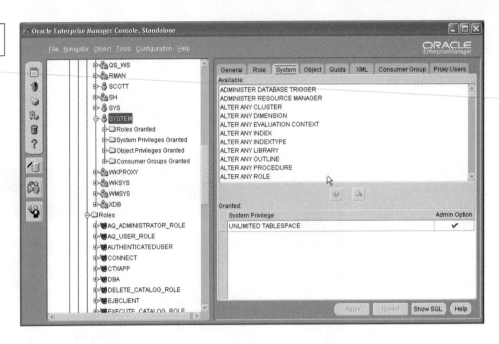

Figure 10-34

Privileges Granted to the SYSTEM Account

that those ROLEs have, and so forth through all of the ROLEs. In our example, the SYS-TEM account has been assigned the UNLIMITED TABLESPACE SYSTEM PRIVI-LEGE (shown in Figure 10-34), plus all of the SYSTEM PRIVILEGEs of the ROLEs AQ_ADMINISTRATOR_ROLE, DBA, and SALES_HISTORY_ROLE (shown in Figure 10-35(a)), plus all of the SYSTEM PRIVILEGEs that those ROLEs inherit.

ROLEs simplify the administration of the database. Without ROLEs, each account would need to be assigned the privileges that it needs, one by one. This time-consuming process would need to be repeated every time a new account is created. Using ROLEs, a set of privileges can be assigned to a ROLE just once; and when a new account is given that ROLE, all PRIVILEGEs of the ROLE are given to the new account. Also, when a PRIVILEGE is removed from a ROLE, all accounts that have that ROLE automatically have that PRIVILEGE removed as well.

Account Authentication

Figure 10-36 shows the Oracle Enterprise Manager Console form that is used to create a new user account. The DBA enters the name of the account and specifies the profile to be used, the method used to authenticate that account, and other data. In Figure 10-36(a), a password is used to authenticate the account. A new password has been placed on the account, but the Expire Password Now option has also been checked. This means that the first time the user signs on using this account, he or she is told that the password has expired and he or she needs to create a new one. This action will force the user to define his or her own password for the account before the user can use the account.

Figure 10-36(b) shows an account that is to be authenticated externally to Oracle. This type of authentication means that the host operating system authenticates that a user is who he or she says he or she is and passes the necessary credentials to Oracle. By the way, if the operating system is authenticating the account, the Oracle account for that user must begin with the characters OPS$. In Figure 10-36(b), the operating system authenticates a user named MARY_JANE in the domain MYDOMAIN1. The OPS$ is not part of the operating system user name; it is a prefix that is required by Oracle for such accounts. We will use operating system authentication in Chapters 12 and 13 when we show how to process an Oracle database using Integrated Security from ASP and ASP.NET.

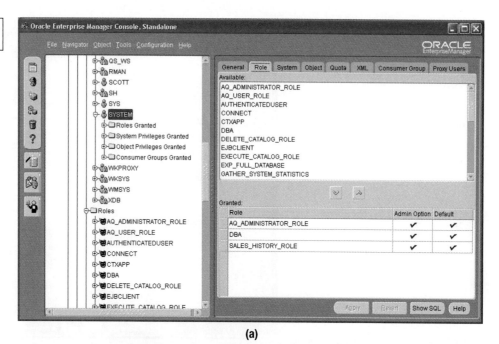

Figure 10-35

Account Role Example
(a) Roles Granted to the SYSTEM Account and
(b) Privileges Granted to the SALES_HISTORY_ROLE

Oracle provides a number of useful functions and utilities for managing passwords. Figure 10-37 shows the Password tab for the PROFILE named USERPROFILE (a PROFILE that was previously created by the DBA).

The passwords for all user accounts that are based on this PROFILE are managed according to the choices in this form. Specifically, passwords expire every 60 days, and if the user does not change the password for 30 days after that, the account is locked (made unusable). The second section of the form indicates that Oracle will store two

Figure 10-36

Account Authentication

(a) Password
Authentication and

(b) External
Authentication

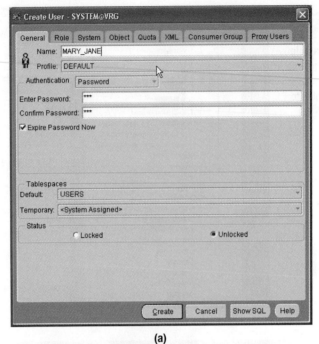

(a)

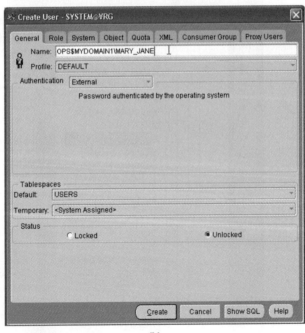

(b)

generations of the user's passwords. This means that a user cannot reuse a password until he or she has used at least two other different passwords.

Password complexity concerns how strong a password must be in terms of the number of characters required and the use of upper- and lowercase letters, numbers, and special characters. Default means that the default policy of the database is used. See the Oracle documentation for more information on this topic. Finally, if six or more attempts are made to enter a correct password, Oracle locks the account, and it will remain locked for 10 days.

This section has presented a quick summary of the security tools provided by Oracle. Of course, the tools by themselves do not make a secure database. Organizations

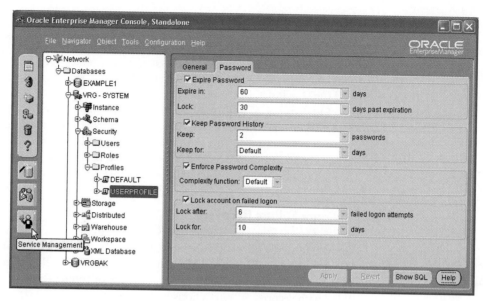

Figure 10-37

Password Management via a Profile

that use databases need to develop security plans and policies that stipulate how these tools will be used. A discussion of such plans is beyond the scope of this text, but you should learn about them in your systems development class.

 ## Oracle Backup and Recovery

Oracle provides a sophisticated set of facilities and utilities for backup and recovery processing. They can be used in many different ways to provide appropriate backup and recovery for databases, ranging from a small workgroup database that can be backed up when it is unused at night to large interorganizational databases that must be operational 24 hours per day, 7 days per week (24/7) and can never be shut down.

Oracle Recovery Facilities

Oracle maintains three types of files that are important for backup and recovery. **Datafiles** contain user and system data. Because of the way that Oracle writes data to disk, the datafiles may contain both committed and uncommitted changes at any moment in time. Of course, Oracle processes transactions so that these uncommitted changes are eventually either committed or removed, but a snapshot of the datafiles at any arbitrary moment includes uncommitted changes. Thus, when Oracle shuts down or when certain types of backups are made, the datafiles must be cleaned up so that only committed changes remain in them.

ReDo files contain logs of database changes; they are backups of the rollback segments used for concurrent processing. **Control files** are small files that describe the name, contents, and locations of various files used by Oracle. Control files are frequently updated by Oracle, and they must be available for a database to be operational.

There are two types of ReDo files. **OnLine ReDo** files are maintained on disk and contain the rollback segments from recent database changes. **Offline,** or **Archive ReDo,** files are backups of the OnLine ReDo files. They are stored separately from the OnLine ReDo files, and need not necessarily reside on disk media. Oracle can operate in either ARCHIVELOG or NOARCHIVELOG mode. If it is running in ARCHIVE mode, when the OnLine ReDo files fill up, they are copied to the Archive ReDo files.

Control files and OnLine ReDo files are so important that Oracle recommends that two active copies of them be kept, a process called **multiplexing** in Oracle terminology.

Types of Failure

Oracle recovery techniques depend on the type of failure. When an **application failure** occurs—because of application logic errors, for instance—Oracle simply rolls back uncommitted changes made by that application using the in-memory rollback segments and OnLine ReDo files as necessary.

Other types of failure recovery are more complicated and depend on the failure type. An **instance failure** occurs when Oracle itself fails due to an operating system or computer hardware failure. A **media failure** occurs when Oracle is unable to write to a physical file. This may occur because of a disk head crash or other disk failure, because needed devices are not powered on, or because a file is corrupt.

Instance Failure Recovery

When Oracle is restarted after an instance failure, it looks first to the control file to find out where all the other files are located. Then, it processes the OnLine ReDo logs against the datafiles. It rolls forward all changes in the ReDo log that were not yet written to the datafiles at the time of failure. In the process of rolling forward, rollback segments are filled with records of transactions in the ReDo log.

After rollforward, the datafiles may contain uncommitted changes. These uncommitted changes could have been in the datafiles at the time of the instance failure or they could have been introduced by rollforward. Either way, Oracle eliminates them by rolling back such uncommitted changes using the rollback segments that were created during rollforward. So that transactions do not need to wait for the rollback to complete, all uncommitted transactions are marked as DEAD. If a new transaction is blocked by a change made by a DEAD transaction, the locking manager destroys the locks held by the DEAD transaction.

The Archive ReDo logs are not used for instance recovery. Accordingly, instance recovery can be done in either ARCHIVELOG or NOARCHIVELOG mode.

Media Failure Recovery

To recover from a media failure, the database is restored from a backup. If the database was running in NOARCHIVELOG, nothing else can be done. The OnLine ReDo log is not useful because it concerns changes made long after the backup was made. The organization must find another way to recover changes to the database. (This would be the wrong time to start thinking about this, by the way.)

If Oracle was operating in ARCHIVELOG mode, the OnLine ReDo logs will have been copied to the archive. To recover, the database is restored from a backup, and the database is rolled forward by applying Archive ReDo log files. After this rollforward finishes, changes made by uncommitted transactions are removed by rolling them back, as described previously.

Two kinds of backups are possible. A **consistent backup** is one in which all uncommitted changes have been removed from the datafiles. Database activity must be stopped, all buffers must be flushed to disk, and changes made by any uncommitted transactions removed. Clearly, this type of backup cannot be done if the database supports 24/7 operations.

An **inconsistent backup** may contain uncommitted changes. It is a sort of flying backup that is made while Oracle is processing the database. For recovery, such backups can be made consistent by applying the archive log records to commit or roll back all transactions that were in process when the backup was made. Inconsistent backups can be made on portions of the database. For example, in a 24/7 application, one-seventh of the database can be backed up every night. Over a week's time, a copy of the entire database will have been made.

The Oracle Recovery Manager (RMAN) is a utility program used to create backups and to perform recovery. RMAN can be instructed to create a special recovery database that contains data about recovery files and operations. The specifics of this program are beyond the scope of this discussion.

Topics Not Discussed in This Chapter

Several important Oracle features were not discussed in this chapter. For one, Oracle supports object-oriented structures, and developers can use them to define their own abstract data types. Oracle can also be used to create and process databases that are hybrids of traditional databases and object databases. Such hybrids, called object-relational databases, have not received strong market endorsement, and we will not consider them in this text.

Also, Enterprise Oracle supports distributed database processing, whereby the database is stored on more than one computer. Additionally, there are many Oracle utilities that we have not discussed. The Oracle Loader is a utility program for inputting bulk data into an Oracle database. Other utilities can be used to measure and tune Oracle performance.

We have, however, discussed the most important Oracle features and topics here. If you have understood these concepts, you are well on your way to becoming a successful Oracle developer.

 SUMMARY

Oracle is a powerful and robust DBMS that runs on many different operating systems and has many different products. This chapter addresses the use of the Oracle utility SQL*Plus, which can be used to create and process SQL and PL/SQL with all versions of Oracle. PL/SQL is a language that adds programming facilities to the SQL language.

You can create a database using the Database Configuration Assistant, the Oracle-supplied database creation procedures, or the SQL CREATE DATABASE command. The Database Configuration Assistant creates default database and log files. SQL*Plus has a limited text editor that keeps the current statement in a multiline buffer. SQL*Plus can be configured to invoke text editors such as Notepad.

You can enter SQL statements directly into SQL*Plus or you can create files of SQL and submit the files to Oracle via SQL*Plus. Any SQL statement can be submitted to Oracle in this way.

The Oracle Enterprise Manager Console is a utility that provides graphical means for managing an Oracle database. The utility can be used to manage structures, such as tables and views, and to manage user accounts, passwords, roles, and privileges.

PL/SQL statements and Java programs can be placed in the database as stored procedures and invoked from other PL/SQL programs or from application programs. Examples of stored procedures are shown in Figures 10-20 and 10-21. Oracle triggers are PL/SQL or Java programs that are invoked when a specified database activity occurs. Examples of BEFORE, AFTER, and INSTEAD OF triggers are shown in Figures 10-23 through 10-28, respectively.

Oracle maintains a data dictionary of metadata. The metadata of the dictionary itself is stored in the table DICT. You can query this table to determine the dictionary's contents.

Oracle supports read committed, serializable, and read only transaction isolation levels. Because of the way SCN values are processed, Oracle never reads dirty data. Serializable isolation is possible, but the application program must be written to process the "Cannot serialize" exception. Applications can place locks explicitly using SELECT FOR UPDATE commands, but this is not recommended.

Oracle security components include ACCOUNTs, PROFILEs, PRIVILEGEs, and ROLEs. An ACCOUNT has a PROFILE that specifies resource limits on the ACCOUNT as well as password management. A PRIVILEGE is the right to perform a task on an Oracle resource. ROLEs can be assigned to ACCOUNTs and consist of groups of PRIVILEGEs and other ROLEs. An ACCOUNT has all of the PRIVILEGEs that have been assigned directly, plus all of the PRIVILEGEs of all of its ROLEs and all ROLEs that are inherited through ROLE connections. Passwords can be authenticated by password or by the host operating system. Password management can be specified via PROFILEs.

Three types of files are used in Oracle recovery: Datafiles, OnLine and Offline ReDo log files, and Control files. If running in ARCHIVELOG mode, Oracle logs all changes to the database. Oracle can recover from application failure and instance failure without using the archived log file. Archive logs are required, however, to recover from media failure. Backups can be consistent or inconsistent. An inconsistent backup can be made consistent by processing an archive log file.

REVIEW QUESTIONS

10.1   Describe the general characteristics of Oracle and the Oracle product suite. Explain why these characteristics mean there is considerable complexity to master.

10.2   What is SQL*Plus and what is its purpose?

10.3   Name three ways of creating an Oracle database. Which is the easiest?

10.4   Explain how to change a row in the SQL*Plus buffer. Assume that there are three statements in the buffer, the focus is on the third statement, and you want to change the second statement from CustID51000 to CustomerID51000.

10.5   How do you set the default directory for SQL*Plus?

10.6   Show the SQL statement necessary to create a table named T1 with columns C1, C2, and C3. Assume that C1 is a surrogate key. Assume that C2 has character data of maximum length 50 and that C3 contains a date.

10.7   Show the statement necessary to create a sequence starting at 50 and incremented by 2. Name your sequence T1Seq.

10.8   Show how to insert a row into table T1 (question 10.6) using the sequence created in question 10.7.

10.9   Show a SQL statement for querying the row created in question 10.8.

10.10   Explain the problems inherent in using sequences for surrogate key columns.

10.11   Show SQL statements for dropping table T1 and for dropping SeqT1.

10.12   Show SQL statements for dropping column C3 of table T1.

10.13   Show SQL statements for creating a relationship between table T2 and table T3. Assume that T3 has a foreign key column named FK1 that relates to T2 and that deletions in T2 should force deletions in T3.

10.14   Answer question 10.13, but do not force deletions.

10.15   Explain how to use the To-Date function.

10.16   Show SQL statements to create a unique index on columns C2 and C3 of table T1.

10.17   Under what circumstances should indexes be used?

10.18   Show SQL statements to add a new column C4 to table T1. Assume that table T1 will have currency values up to $1 million.

10.19   Under what conditions can you drop a column in an existing table?

10.20   Under what conditions can you add a column to an existing table?

10.21   Explain how to add a NOT NULL column to an existing table.

10.22   Under what conditions can you change the width of a character or numeric column?

10.23   Under what conditions can you change a column's data type?

10.24 Show how to add a constraint to specify that column C4 of table T1 cannot be less than 1,000.

10.25 Show how to add a constraint to specify that column C4 of table T1 cannot be less than column C5 of table T1.

10.26 For the View Ridge database discussed in this chapter, construct a view that contains Name, City, and State of a customer. Name your view CustView.

10.27 For the View Ridge database, construct a view that has the customer name and artist name for all art that the customer has purchased.

10.28 For the View Ridge database, construct a view that has customer name and artist name for all artists in which the customer is interested. Explain the difference between this view and the view in question 10.27.

10.29 Can you combine the views in questions 10.27 and 10.28 into one view? Why or why not?

10.30 How can you update a join view using Oracle?

10.31 Create a file of PL/SQL statements that describes the structure of the CUSTOMER, ARTIST, WORK, TRANSACTION, and CUSTOMER_ARTIST_INT tables. Store the file with the name VRTabs.sql and show how to invoke the PL/SQL procedure using SQL*Plus.

10.32 In a PL/SQL procedure, what do the keywords IN, OUT, and IN OUT signify?

10.33 What must be done to be able to see the output generated by the Oracle DBMS_OUTPUT package? What limits exist on such output?

10.34 Explain how the PL/SQL statement FOR variable IN cursorname works.

10.35 What statement is used to obtain errors when compiling stored procedures and triggers?

10.36 What is the syntax of the BEGIN TRANSACTION statement in PL/SQL? How is a transaction started?

10.37 In the stored procedure in Figure 10-20, how are the values of the variables tid and aid used if there are no suitable TRANSACTION rows in the database? How are they used if there is just one suitable TRANSACTION row in the database?

10.38 Explain the purpose of BEFORE, AFTER, and INSTEAD OF triggers.

10.39 When an update is in progress, how can the trigger code obtain the value of a column, say, C1, before the update began? How can the trigger code obtain the value that the column is being set to?

10.40 Explain why INSTEAD OF triggers are needed for join views.

10.41 Explain a limitation on the use of AFTER triggers.

10.42 Show a SQL statement to obtain the names of tables the data dictionary contains about triggers.

10.43 What three levels of transaction isolation are supported by Oracle?

10.44 Explain how Oracle uses the system change number to read data that are current at a particular point in time.

10.45 Under what circumstances does Oracle read dirty data?

10.46 Explain how conflicting locks are handled by Oracle when a transaction is operating in read committed isolation mode.

10.47 Show the SQL statement necessary to set the transaction isolation level to serializable for an entire session.

10.48 What happens when a transaction in serializable mode tries to update data that have been updated by a different transaction? Assume that the SCN is less than the transaction's SCN. Assume the SCN is greater than the transaction's SCN.

10.49 Describe three circumstances under which a transaction could receive the "Cannot serialize" exception.

10.50 Explain how Oracle processes the read only transaction isolation level.

10.51 Explain the use of ACCOUNT, PRIVILEGE, and ROLE in Oracle security.

10.52 What three types of files are important for Oracle backup and recovery processing?

10.53 What is the difference between the OnLine ReDo logs and the OffLine or Archive ReDo logs? How is each type used?

10.54 What does multiplexing mean in the context of Oracle recovery?

10.55 Explain how Oracle recovers from application failure.

10.56 What is instance failure and how does Oracle recover from it?

10.57 What is media failure and how does Oracle recover from it?

PROJECT QUESTIONS

Use the following tables in your answer to questions 10.58 through 10.61:

EMPLOYEE (EmpNumber, Name, Email, *DeptName*)

DEPARTMENT (DeptName, BudgetCode)

Assume the relationship is M-M.

10.58 Code an Oracle trigger to enforce the constraint that an employee can never change his or her department.

10.59 Code an Oracle trigger to allow the deletion of a department if it only has one employee. Assign the last employee to the Human Resources department.

10.60 Design a system of triggers to enforce the M-M relationship. Use Figure 10-27 as an example, but assume that departments with only one employee can be deleted. Assign the last employee in a department to Human Resources.

10.61 Write SQL to accomplish the following tasks and submit your SQL statements to Oracle using SQL*Plus.

  A Install Oracle and create the View Ridge database.

  B Create the tables in Figure 10-7, but do not create the NationalityValues constraint.

  C Fill your database with sample data. Ensure that you have at least three customers, three artists, five works, and five transactions. Set the Nationality of ARTIST to one of 'German', 'French', or 'English'.

  D Write a stored procedure to read the ARTIST table and display the artist data using the DBMS_OUTPUT.PUT_LINE command.

  E Write a stored procedure to read the ARTIST and WORK tables. Your procedure should display an artist, then display all the works for that artist, then display the next artist, and so forth. Accept the name of the artist to display as an input parameter.

  F Write a stored procedure to update customer phone data. Assume that your stored procedure receives Name, priorAreaCode, newAreaCode, priorPhoneNumber, and newPhoneNumber. Your procedure should first ensure that there is only one customer with the values of (Name, priorAreaCode, priorPhoneNumber). If not, produce an error message and quit. Otherwise, update the customer data with the new phone number data.

  G Create a table named ALLOWED_NATIONALITY with one column called Nation. Place the values 'German', 'French', and 'English' into the table. Write a trigger that will check to determine whether a new or updated value of Nationality resides in this table. If not, write an error message using DBMS_OUTPUT.PUT_LINE. Use SQL*Plus to demonstrate that your trigger works.

  H Create a view having all data from the WORK and TRANSACTION tables. Write an insert INSTEAD OF trigger on this view that will create a new row in WORK and TRANSACTION. Use SQL*Plus to demonstrate that your trigger works.

MARCIA'S DRY CLEANING

Answer questions A through M for Marcia's Dry Cleaning at the end of Chapter 7, page 262, if you have not already done so. Use the Oracle data types in your answer.

A   Using Oracle, execute all of the SQL statements that you created in your answers to A through M for Marcia's Dry Cleaning at the end of Chapter 7.

B   Assume that the relationship between ORDER and ORDER_ITEM is M-M. Design triggers to enforce this relationship. Use Figure 10-27 and the discussion of that figure as an example, but assume that Marcia does allow ORDERs and their related ORDER_ITEM rows to be deleted. Use the deletion strategy shown in Figures 7-29 and 7-30 for this case.

C   Write and test the triggers you designed in question B, above.

MORGAN IMPORTING

Answer questions A through N for Morgan Importing at the end of Chapter 7, page 263 if you have not already done so. Use the Oracle data types in your answer.

A   Using Oracle, execute all of the SQL statements that you created in your answers to A through N for Morgan Importing at the end of Chapter 7.

B   Assume that the relationship between SHIPMENT and SHIPMENT_ITEM is M-M. Design triggers to enforce this relationship. Use Figure 10-27 and the discussion of that figure as an example, but assume that Morgan does allow SHIPMENTs and their related SHIPMENT_ITEM rows to be deleted. Use the deletion strategy shown in Figures 7-29 and 7-30 for this case.

C   Write and test the triggers you designed in question B, above.

Managing Databases with SQL Server 2000

This chapter describes the basic features and functions of Microsoft SQL Server 2000. The discussion uses the View Ridge Gallery example from Chapter 7, and it parallels the discussion of the database administration tasks in Chapter 9. The presentation is similar in scope and orientation to that for Oracle in the prior chapter.

SQL Server is a large and complicated product. In this one chapter, we will be able to only scratch the surface. Your goal should be to learn sufficient basics so that you can continue learning on your own or in other classes.

By the time you read this, Microsoft may have shipped SQL Server 2005. The material you learn in this chapter will be applicable to that new version. The language Transact-SQL is still supported, and stored procedures and triggers continue to operate as described here. SQL Server 2005 extends these features and functions, but, other than a different Enterprise Manager interface, there is nothing in the discussion here that you will need to unlearn.

Installing SQL Server 2000

If you purchased the version of this book that has SQL Server, you should install it now. The SQL Server CD that comes with this text contains an evaluation copy that has a license valid for 120 days. It requires Windows NT with Service Pack 5 or later, Windows 2000 Professional, or Windows XP Professional.

To install this software, log in to your computer with Administrator privileges and insert the CD-ROM. The install program should start automatically. If not, double-click the autorun executable at the top level of the CD. Click on SQL Server Components and then click on Install Database Server. The rest of the installation process is a typical Windows program installation. As recommended in Chapter 9, you should apply the latest service pack to this product. Go to ***www.prenhall/kroenke*** for information.

After you install the software, you can start to work with SQL Server by clicking Start, Programs, Microsoft SQL Server, Enterprise Manager. After you have done this, find the icon labeled Microsoft SQL Server in the left pane. Click the plus sign to open it and then open SQL Server Group the same way. You'll next see the name of your server followed by (Windows NT). Open this and you should see the display shown in Figure 11-1. In this figure, you see the name of the server used to make this figure, which is DBGRV101\QA1.

 Creating a SQL Server 2000 Database

To create a new database, right-click Databases and select New Database. Type the name of your database (here, *VRG*) into the Name text box, as shown in Figure 11-2. By default, SQL Server creates one data file and one log file for each database. You can create multiple files for both data and logs and assign particular tables and logs to particular files and file groups. All of this is beyond the scope of this discussion, however. To learn more about it on your own, right-click Databases and select Help. In the left pane of the Help menu, search for "File Groups" in the Search text box to get started.

Figure 11-1   **Using Enterprise Manager to Display Databases on a Server**

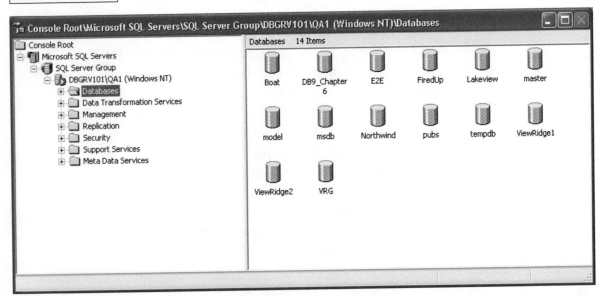

Figure 11-2

Creating the VRG
Database

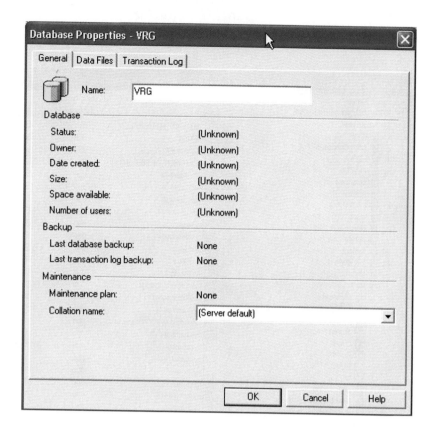

For now, accept the default sizes and files that SQL Server offers. You can see what they are by clicking the Data Files and Transaction Log tabs.

After you create your database, open the Databases folder and then open the folder with the name of your database. Then, open Tables. Your screen should look like the one shown in Figure 11-3, but you will not yet have any user tables in it. All the tables listed in your display are system tables used by SQL Server 2000 to manage your database. By the way, *dbo* stands for database owner. That will be you if you installed SQL Server and created this database.

Creating the View Ridge Database

Tables and other SQL Server structures can be created and modified in two ways. The first is to write SQL code using either the CREATE or ALTER SQL statements. The second is to use the graphical facilities of SQL Server Enterprise Manager. Although either method will work, CREATE statements are preferred for the reasons described in Chapter 7. Some professionals choose to create structures via SQL but then modify them with the graphical tools.

Use the Query Analyzer to Process CREATE TABLE Statements

SQL statements can be submitted to SQL Server in one of two ways. The oldest and most common is to open a SQL Server utility called the Query Analyzer. This utility is misnamed; although you can use it to analyze SQL statements, it is most commonly used to submit SQL to SQL Server. You can key SQL into this tool or open a file of SQL statements prepared using a text editor. Either way, Query Analyzer will check the syntax of your statements and also submit them to SQL Server. Another way of submitting SQL statements to SQL Server is to use Visual Studio.NET. We will not illustrate that technique here, however.

Figure 11-3   Tables in the VRG Database

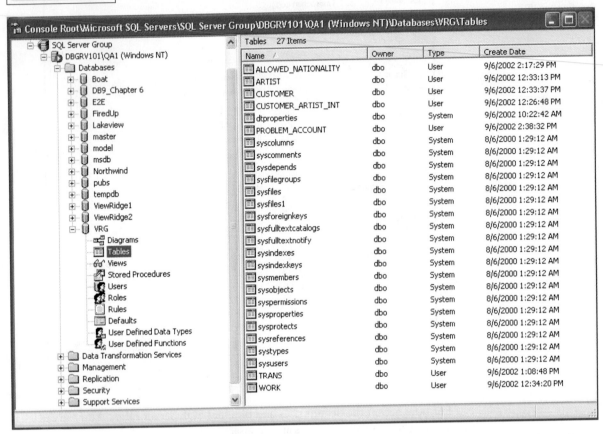

As shown in Figure 11-4, start Query Analyzer by selecting Tools/SQL Query Analyzer from the Enterprise Manager window. A new, two-part window will open. You can key SQL into the top part and see the results in the bottom part. Figure 11-5 shows the result of processing a CREATE TABLE statement. Notice the blue checkmark and

Figure 11-4

Starting the Query Analyzer

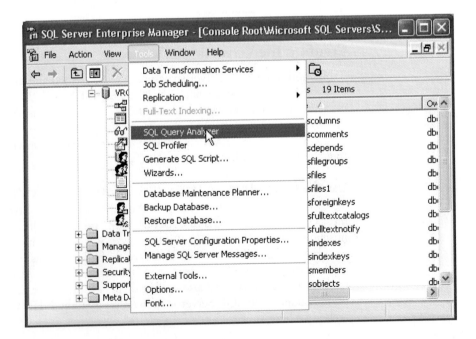

Figure 11-5

Running a CREATE TABLE Statement in the Query Analyzer

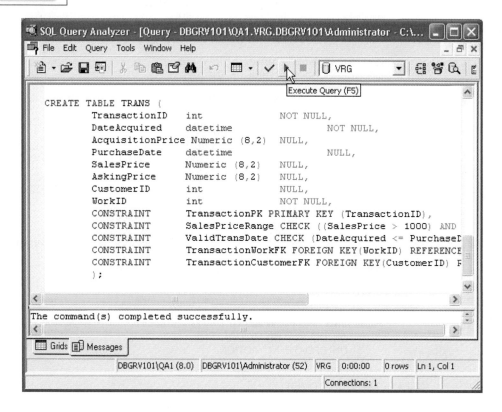

the green right-facing arrow. Click the checkmark to verify the syntax of your statements; click the green arrow to execute the statements. The green arrow has been
clicked in the display in Figure 11-5.

Creating the View Ridge Database

CREATE TABLE statements for the View Ridge database in Chapter 7 are shown in
Figure 11-6. Unlike Oracle, SQL Server supports surrogate keys, and the surrogate key
columns are created using the IDENTITY data type.

   The table name TRANSACTION was changed to TRANS in Figure 11-6. This was
done because TRANSACTION is such a special word to SQL Server. Even if you place
the name in square brackets, as in [TRANSACTION], SQL Server still becomes confused when executing the logic of stored procedures and triggers. Life became much
simpler for applications using this database when the table TRANSACTION was
renamed to TRANS. WORK is also a keyword, but SQL Server is less sensitive to it. It
can be used if enclosed in square brackets, as in [WORK], and many SQL Server statements run correctly without even doing that. However, just to be safe, use [WORK].

Review Database Structures in SQL Server Graphical Displays

Figure 11-7 shows the structure of the ARTIST table after the CREATE TABLE statements have been processed. You can open this window by right-clicking the name
ARTIST in the table list in Enterprise Manager and then selecting Design Table. Notice
that ArtistID is an Identity column, as you would expect.

   To see the constraints on the table, right-click anywhere in the white space in the table
design window and select Check Constraints. Figure 11-8 shows the NationalityValues
check constraint. Clearly, it is easier to key the constraint into SQL statements than it
would be to type it as shown in this window!

Figure 11-6

CREATE TABLE
Statements for the
View Ridge Gallery
Database from
Figure 11-5

```
CREATE TABLE ARTIST(
    ArtistID            int                 NOT NULL IDENTITY (1, 1) ,
    Name                char (25)           NOT NULL,
    Nationality         char (30)           NULL,
    Birthdate           numeric (4, 0)      NULL,
    DeceasedDate        numeric (4, 0)      NULL,

    CONSTRAINT ArtistPK PRIMARY KEY (ArtistID) ,
    CONSTRAINT ArtistAK1 UNIQUE (Name) ,

    CONSTRAINT NationalityValues CHECK
            (Nationality IN ( 'Canadian' , 'English' , 'French' , 'German',
            'Mexican' , 'Russian' , 'Spanish' , 'US' ) ) ,
    CONSTRAINT BirthValuesCheck CHECK (Birthdate < DeceasedDate) ,
    CONSTRAINT ValidBirthYear CHECK (Birthdate LIKE ' [1 - 2] [0 - 9] [0 - 9] [0 - 9] ' ) ,
    CONSTRAINT ValidDeathYear CHECK (DeceasedDate LIKE ' [1 - 2] [0 - 9] [0 - 9] [0 - 9] ' )

);

CREATE TABLE [WORK]  (
    WorkID              int                 NOT NULL IDENTITY (500, 1),
    Title               char (25)           NOT NULL,
    Copy                varchar (1000)      NULL DEFAULT 'Unknown  provenance ',
    Description         char (8)            NOT NULL,
    ArtistID            int                 NOT NULL,

    CONSTRAINT WorkPK PRIMARY KEY (WorkID) ,
    CONSTRAINT WorkAK1 UNIQUE (Title, Copy) ,

    CONSTRAINT ArtistFK FOREIGN KEY (ArtistID) REFERENCES ARTIST (ArtistID)
            ON DELETE NO ACTION
            ON UPDATE NO ACTION
);

CREATE TABLE CUSTOMER (

    CustomerID          int                 NOT NULL IDENTITY (1000, 1) ,
    Name                char (25)           NOT NULL,
    Street              char (30)           NULL,
    City                char (35)           NULL,
    State               char (2)            NULL,
    ZipPostalCode       char (9)            NULL,
    Country             varchar (50)        NULL,
    AreaCode            char (3)            NULL,
    PhoneNumber         char (8)            NULL,
    Email               char (100)          NULL,



    CONSTRAINT CustomerPK PRIMARY KEY (CustomerID) ,
    CONSTRAINT EmailAK1 UNIQUE (Email)

);

CREATE TABLE [TRANS]  (

    TransactionID       int                 NOT NULL IDENTITY (100, 1) ,
    DateAcquired        datetime            NOT NULL,
    AcquisitionPrice    numeric (8 , 2)     NOT NULL,
    PurchaseDate        datetime  NULL,
    SalesPrice          numeric (8 , 2)     NULL,
    AskingPrice         numeric (8 , 2)     NULL,
    CustomerID          int                 NULL,
    WorkID              int                 NOT NULL,
```

Figure 11-6

Continued

```
CONSTRAINT       TransactionPK  PRIMARY  KEY  (TransactionID) ,

CONSTRAINT  TransactionWorkFK  FOREIGN KEY  (WorkID)  REFERENCES  WORK  (WorkID)
                 ON  UPDATE  NO  ACTION
                 ON  DELETE  NO  ACTION,

CONSTRAINT  TransactionCustomerFK
                 FOREIGN  KEY  (CustomerID)  REFERENCES  CUSTOMER  (CustomerID)
                 ON  UPDATE  NO  ACTION
                 ON  DELETE  NO  ACTION,

CONSTRAINT       SalsePriceRange  CHECK
                 ( (SalesPrice > 1000)  AND  (SalesPrice  <= 200000) ) ,
CONSTRAINT       ValidTransDate  CHECK  (DateAcquired  <= PurchaseDate)

);

CREATE TABLE CUSTOMER_ARTIST_INT (
        ArtistID                int                     NOT NULL,
        CustomerID              int                     NOT NULL,

CONSTRAINT       CustomerArtistPK  PRIMARY  KEY  (AritistID ,  CustomerID) ,

CONSTRAINT  Customer_Artist_Int_ArtistFK
          FOREIGN  KEY  (ArtistID)  REFERENCES  ARTIST  (ArtistID)
                     ON  UPDATE  NO ACTION
                     ON  DELETE  CASCADE,
CONSTRAINT  Customer_Artist_Int_CustomerFK
FOREIGN  KEY  (CustomerID)  REFERENCES  CUSTOMER  (CustomerID)
                     ON  UPDATE  NO  ACTION
                     ON  DELETE  CASCADE

);
```

Figure 11-7

**Columns and
Properties of the
ARTIST Table**

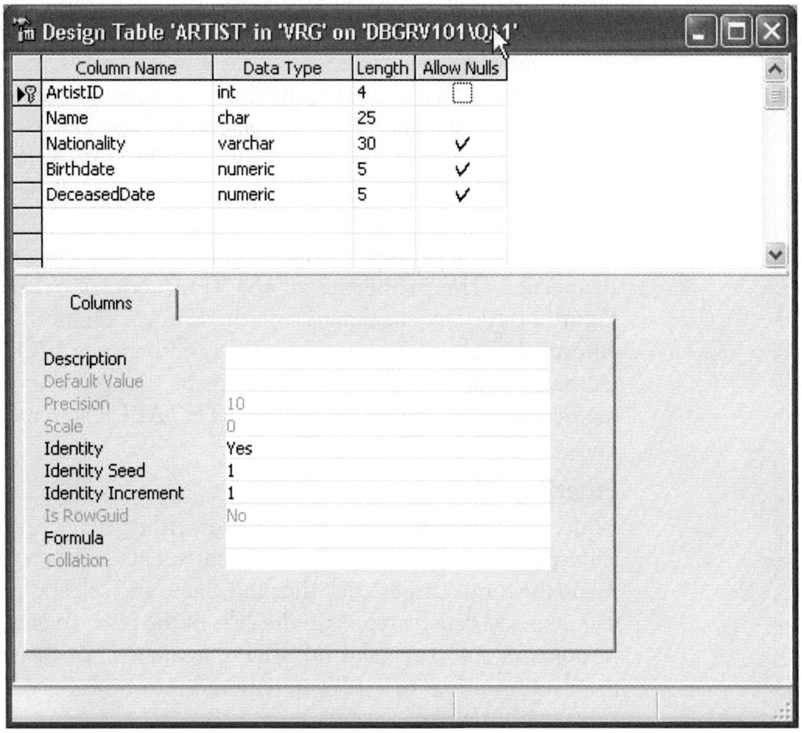

**Constraints in the
ARTIST Table**

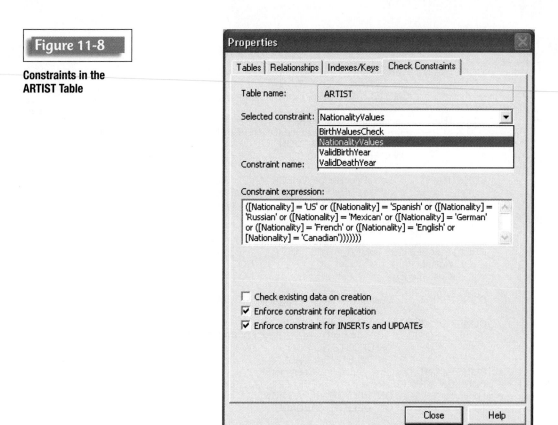

Throughout this chapter, you will see dialog boxes similar to the one shown in Figure 11-8 that have checkboxes that reference something about replication. All such references refer to distributed SQL Server databases in which data are placed in two or more databases and updates to them are coordinated in some fashion. We will not consider that topic here, so ignore checkboxes that refer to replication. You can learn more by searching for the replication topic in the SQL Server documentation.

To ensure that the relationships were created correctly, with your database open in Enterprise Manager, click on Diagrams, New Database Diagram. A wizard appears to create a new diagram. Select the ARTIST, WORK, TRANS, CUSTOMER, and CUSTOMER_ARTIST_INT tables. The result will be a diagram like that shown in Figure 11-9.

To view the properties of a relationship, right-click the relationship line and select Properties. The properties of the TransactionWorkFK relationship are shown in Figure 11-10. The checkmarks on the Enforce relationship mean that SQL Server will enforce the referential integrity constraint between WORK and TRANS. The fact that neither Cascade option is checked means that SQL Server recognizes that no cascading behavior was coded in the CREATE TABLE statement.

Entering Data

You can enter data into SQL Server either by entering data into a table grid in Enterprise Manager or via INSERT statements submitted through the Query Analyzer. To do the former, right-click the table name and select Open Table, Return all rows. You can then add data by typing in the cells of the grid. To enter data via the Query Analyzer, just open it and type valid INSERT statements. For the examples in this chapter, all of the data from Figure 7-12 were entered into SQL Server using INSERT statements in the Query Analyzer.

Figure 11-9

Table Relationships

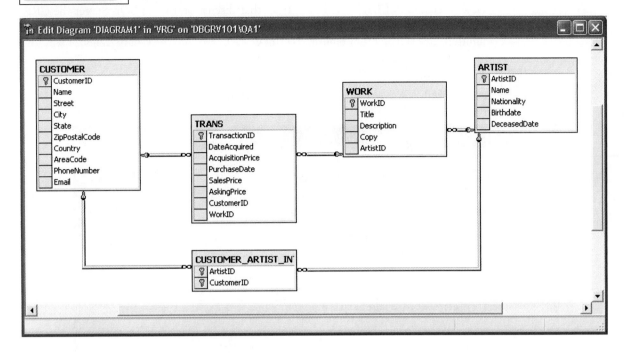

Figure 11-10

Properties of the Relationship between WORK and TRANS

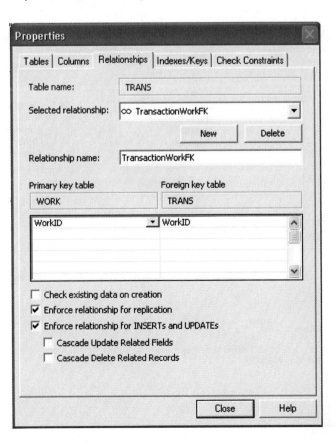

Creating Views

Figure 11-11(a) shows a CREATE VIEW statement for creating the CustomerInterests view discussed in Chapter 7. Recall from that discussion that in SQL Server the CRE-ATE VIEW statement cannot be terminated with a semicolon; the semicolon must be omitted. The statement in Figure 11-11(a) was entered into the Query Analyzer window,

Figure 11-11

Creating a View

(a) The CREATE VIEW Statement for CustomerInterests and (b) Graphical
Display of CustomerInterests

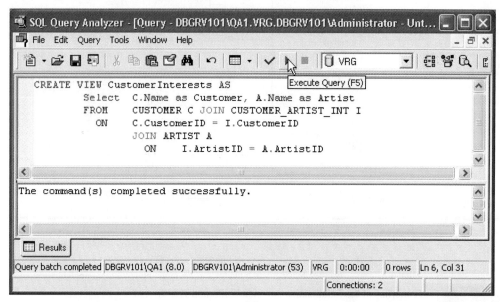

(a)

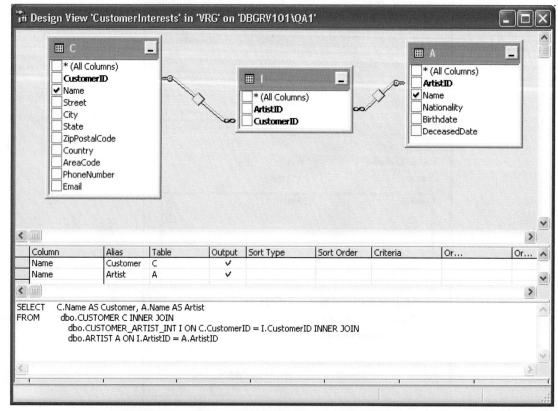

(b)

and the view was created by clicking the green arrow. The view can be opened in Enterprise Manager by clicking views and right-clicking CustomerInterests, and selecting Design View. The graphical display shown in Figure 11-11(b) will appear. Observe that the aliases for the table names appear in the table design (top) pane. Also note that the aliases for the column names appear in the second column of the view definition rows in the middle pane of the form.

Views can be created using SQL syntax or they can be created using this form by right-clicking Views and selecting New View. Again, a common strategy is to create the views using SQL, but to modify them, if necessary, by using the graphical tools.

Indexes

As stated elsewhere in this text, indexes are special data structures that are created to improve database performance (see Appendix D). SQL Server automatically creates an index on all primary and foreign keys. The developer can also direct SQL Server to create an index on other columns that are frequently used in WHERE clauses or on columns that are used for sorting data when sequentially processing a table for queries and reports.

To create an index, right-click the table that has the column you want to index, click All Tasks, and then click Manage Indexes. You will see the dialog box shown in the left portion of Figure 11-12. Click New and you will be shown the dialog box in the right portion of this figure. The developer is creating an index on the ZipPostalCode column of the CUSTOMER table. The index, named ZipPostalIndex, is to be padded, filled to 80 percent, and assigned to the PRIMARY File Group. Padding causes space to be left open for inserts in all levels of the index except the bottom one. Filling refers to the amount of empty space left in the bottom level of the index. See Appendix D and the SQL Server documentation for more information about these choices.

Click Edit SQL in this dialog box and you will see the dialog box shown in Figure 11-13. This shows the SQL statement that could be entered via the SQL Analyzer to create the index.

Figure 11-12   **Creating an Index**

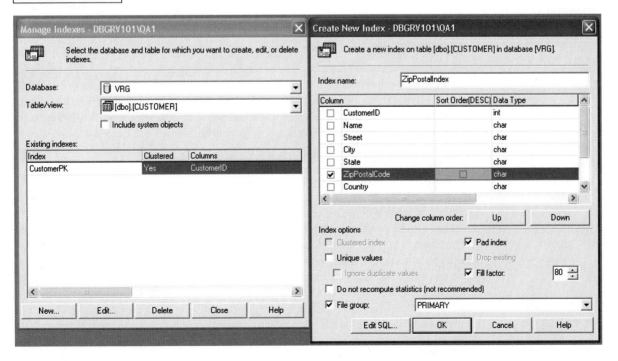

Figure 11-13

SQL for Creating an Index

SQL Server supports two kinds of indexes: **clustered** and **nonclustered.** With a clustered index, the data are stored in the bottom level of the index and in the same order as that index. With a nonclustered index, the bottom level of an index does not contain data; it contains pointers to the data. Because rows can be sorted only in one physical order at a time, only one clustered index is allowed per table.

Clustered indexes are faster than nonclustered indexes for retrieval. They are normally faster for updating as well, but not if there are many updates in the same spot in the middle of the relation. See the SQL Server documentation for more information.

 ## Application Logic

A SQL Server database can be processed from an application in a number of different ways. One is to create application code using a language such as C#, C++, Visual Basic, Java, or some other programming language and then invoke SQL Server DBMS commands from those programs. The modern way to do this is to use a library of object classes, create objects that accomplish database work, and then process those objects by setting object properties and invoking object methods. You will see examples of such processing when we discuss ADO in Chapter 12, ADO.NET in Chapter 13, and Java Server Pages in Chapter 14.

Another way of processing a SQL Server database is to create stored procedures, as described in Chapter 7. These stored procedures can then be invoked from application programs or from Web pages using languages such as VBScript or JScript. Stored procedures can also be executed from the SQL Query Analyzer. This should be done only when the procedures are being developed and tested, however. As described in Chapter 9, for security reasons, no one other than authorized members of the DBA staff should be allowed to interactively process an operational database.

A third means of processing a SQL Server database is to save groups of database commands in .sql files. Such files are then processed from the SQL Query Analyzer. For security, such files should only be used during application development and testing and never on an operational database.

Finally, application logic can be embedded in triggers. As you learned in Chapter 7, triggers can be used to set default values, to enforce data constraints, to update views, and to enforce referential integrity constraints.

In this chapter, we will describe and illustrate two stored procedures. Here, we will test those procedures by invoking them from the Query Analyzer. Again, this should be done only during development and testing. You will learn how to invoke those stored procedures from application code in Chapters 13 through 15. We also describe four triggers, one for each of the four trigger uses. These triggers will be invoked by SQL Server when the specified actions occur.

Stored Procedures

With SQL Server 2000, stored procedures must be written in Transact-SQL, or T-SQL as it is sometimes called. With the release of SQL Server 2005, stored procedures and triggers can be written in any of the .Net or Common Language Runtime languages such as VB.Net and C#. T-SQL will continue to be supported and will have improved features and functions for error handling as well as other language upgrades. The T-SQL shown here will operate in SQL Server 2005, but features will exist to improve it dramatically. In the long run, however, VB.Net or C# will become better choices for stored procedures and triggers.

As with other database structures, you can write a stored procedure in a text file and process the commands using the Query Analyzer. However, there is one little gotcha. The first time you create a stored procedure in a text file, start the procedure with the words "CREATE PROCEDURE . . . " Subsequently, if you change the procedure, substitute the words "ALTER PROCEDURE . . ." Otherwise, you will get an error message saying that the procedure already exists when you execute the modified procedure code.

You can also create a stored procedure within the Enterprise Manager by right-clicking Stored Procedures and selecting New Stored Procedure. If you do this, SQL Server takes care of the CREATE/ALTER problem just described. However, you cannot save your stored procedure until you have removed all of the syntax errors. Because this can be frustrating, using a text file with the Query Analyzer is generally preferred.

The Customer_Insert STORED PROCEDURE

Figure 11-14 illustrates a stored procedure that stores data for a new customer and connects that customer to all artists having a particular nationality. Four parameters are input to the procedure: @NewName, @NewAreaCode, @NewPhone, and @Nationality. As you can see, parameters and variables in Transact-SQL are preceded by @ signs. The first three parameters are the new customer data, and the fourth one is the nationality of the artists for which the new customer has an interest.

The first task performed by this stored procedure is to determine whether the customer already exists. If the count of the first SELECT statement is greater than zero, a row for that customer already exists. In this case, nothing is done, and the stored procedure prints an error message and exits (using the RETURN command). The error message, by the way, is visible in the Query Analyzer, but it generally would not be visible to application programs that invoked this procedure. Instead, a parameter or other facility needs to be used to return the error message back to the user via the application program. Discussion of that topic is beyond the scope of the present discussion.

If the customer does not already exist, the procedure inserts the new data into dbo.CUSTOMER and then a new value of CustomerID is read into the variable @Cid. Internally, SQL Server prefixes table names with the name of the user who created them. Here, the prefix dbo is used to ensure that the CUSTOMER table created by the database owner (dbo) is processed. Without the dbo prefix, if the user invoking the stored procedure had created a table named CUSTOMER, then the user's table and not the dbo's table would be used.

Figure 11-14

**Customer_Insert
Stored Procedure**

```
CREATE PROCEDURE Customer_Insert
                @NewName            char(50),
                @NewAreaCode        char (5),
                @NewPhone           char (8),
                @Nationality        char(25)
AS

DECLARE @Count      as smallint
DECLARE @Aid        as int
DECLARE @Cid        as int

/* Check to see if customer already exists */
SELECT      @Count = Count (*)
FROM        dbo.CUSTOMER
WHERE       [Name]=@NewName AND AreaCode=@NewAreaCode AND PhoneNumber=@NewPhone

IF @Count > 0
        BEGIN
                PRINT 'Customer Already Exists -- No Action Taken'
                RETURN
        END
/* Add new Customer data */
INSERT INTO dbo.CUSTOMER
            ([Name], AreaCode, PhoneNumber)
            VALUES
            (@NewName, @NewAreaCode, @NewPhone)

/* Get new surrogate key value */
SELECT      @Cid = CustomerID
FROM        dbo.CUSTOMER
WHERE       [Name]=@NewName AND AreaCode=@NewAreaCode
AND PhoneNumber=@NewPhone

/* Now create intersection record for each appropriate artist */
DECLARE Artist_Cursor CURSOR FOR
        SELECT      ArtistID
        FROM        dbo.ARTIST
        WHERE       Nationality = @Nationality

/* process each Artist of specified nationality */
OPEN Artist_Cursor
FETCH NEXT FROM Artist_Cursor INTO @Aid
        WHILE @@FETCH_STATUS = 0
        BEGIN
                INSERT INTO dbo.[CUSTOMER_ARTIST_INT]
                            (ArtistID,CustomerID)
                        VALUES (@Aid, @Cid)
                FETCH NEXT FROM Artist_Cursor INTO @Aid
        END

CLOSE Artist_Cursor
DEALLOCATE Artist_Cursor
```

The purpose of the second SELECT in Figure 11-14 is to obtain the value of the surrogate key CustomerID that was created by the INSERT statement. Another option is to use @@Identity, which is a built-in SQL Server function that provides the value of the most recently created surrogate key value. Using this function, you can replace the second SELECT statement with the expression: Set @Cid = @@Identity.

To create the appropriate intersection table rows, a cursor is created on a SQL statement that obtains all ARTIST rows where Nationality equals the parameter @Nationality. The cursor is opened and positioned on the first row by calling FETCH NEXT. Next, the cursor is processed in aWHILE loop. In this loop, statements between BEGIN and END are iterated until SQL Server signals end of data by setting @@FETCH_STATUS to zero.

At each iteration, a new row is inserted into the intersection table CUSTOMER_ARTIST_INT. The FETCH NEXT statement at the end of the block moves the cursor to the next row.

Figure 11-15 shows how to invoke this stored procedure using the SQL Query Analyzer to add a new customer having an interest in U.S. artists. Parameters are passed with the values shown. Figure 11-16 shows database data after the stored procedure has run. Customer Michael Bench has been added to the CUSTOMER table and assigned

Figure 11-15

Running the Customer_Insert Stored Procedure from the Query Analyzer

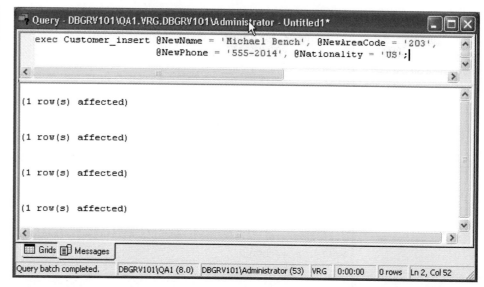

Figure 11-16

Results from Figure 11-15

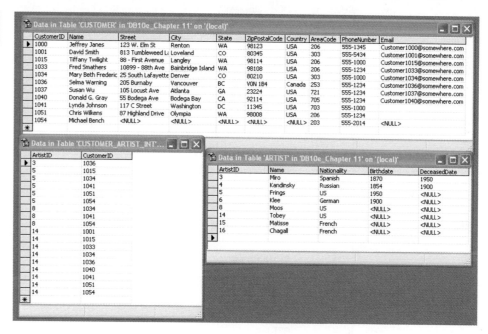

CustomerID 1054. Note that there are three U.S. artists and that a row for each of them has been inserted into the CUSTOMER_ARTIST_INT table for CustomerID of 1054.

The NewCustomerWithTransaction STORED PROCEDURE

A stored procedure that inserts data for a new customer and records a purchase is shown in Figure 11-17. This procedure receives seven parameters having data about the new customer and about the customer's purchase.

The first action is to see whether the customer already exists; if so, the procedure exits with an error message. If the customer does not exist, this procedure then starts a transaction. Recall from Chapter 9 that transactions ensure that all of the database activity is committed atomically; either all of the updates occur or none of them do. The transaction begins, and the new customer row is inserted. The new value of CustomerID is obtained, as shown previously. Next, the procedure checks to determine whether ArtistID, WorkID, and TransactionID are valid. If any are invalid, the transaction is rolled back.

If they are all valid, an UPDATE statement updates PurchaseDate, Price, and CustomerID in the appropriate TRANS row. PurchaseDate is set to system date (via the

Figure 11-17

**NewCustomerWith-
Transaction Stored
Procedure**

```
CREATE PROCEDURE dbo.NewCustomerWithTransaction
                @NewName char(50), @NewAreaCode char (3), @NewPhone char (8),
                @ArtistName char(50), @WorkTitle char(50), @WorkCopy char (10),
                @Price smallmoney
AS

DECLARE         @Count as smallint,
                @Aid as int,
                @Cid as int,
                @Wid as int,
                @Tid as int

SELECT          @Count = Count (*)
FROM            dbo.CUSTOMER
WHERE           [Name]=@NewName AND AreaCode=@NewAreaCode AND PhoneNumber=@NewPhone

IF @Count > 0
        BEGIN   PRINT 'Customer Already Exists -- No Action Taken'
                RETURN
        END

BEGIN TRANSACTION   /* Start transaction rollback everything if cannot complete it. */

INSERT INTO     dbo.CUSTOMER
                ([Name], AreaCode, PhoneNumber)
                VALUES (@NewName, @NewAreaCode, @NewPhone)

Select          @Cid = CustomerID
FROM            dbo.CUSTOMER
WHERE           [Name]=@NewName AND AreaCode=@NewAreaCode AND PhoneNumber=@NewPhone

SELECT          @Aid = ArtistID
FROM            dbo.ARTIST
WHERE           Name=@ArtistName
If @Aid IS NULL   /* Invalid Artist ID */
        BEGIN
                Print 'Artist ID not valid'
                ROLLBACK
                RETURN
        END

SELECT          @Wid = WorkID
FROM            dbo.[WORK]
WHERE           ArtistID = @Aid AND Title = @WorkTitle AND Copy = @WorkCopy
If @Wid IS NULL   /* Invalid Work ID */
        BEGIN
                Print 'Work ID not valid'
                ROLLBACK
                RETURN
        END

SELECT          @Tid = TransactionID
FROM            dbo.[TRANS]
WHERE           WorkID=@Wid AND SalesPrice IS NULL
If @Tid IS NULL   /*Invalid Transaction ID */
        BEGIN
                Print 'No valid transaction record'
                ROLLBACK
                RETURN
        END

UPDATE          dbo.[TRANS] /* ALL is OK, update TRANS row */
SET             PurchaseDate = GETDATE(), SalesPrice = @Price, CustomerID = @Cid
WHERE           TransactionID=@Tid

INSERT INTO dbo.[CUSTOMER_ARTIST_INT] /* Create interest for this artist */
        (CustomerID, ArtistID)
        Values (@Cid, @Aid)
COMMIT
```

system-supplied GETDATE() function). SalesPrice is set to the value of @Price. CustomerID is set to the value of @Cid. Finally, a row is added to CUSTOMER_ARTIST_INT to record the customer's interest in this artist. If everything proceeds normally to this point, the transaction is committed.

Figure 11-18 shows the invocation of this procedure using sample data, and Figure 11-19 shows the results in the database. The new customer was assigned CustomerID 1055, and this ID was stored in the CustomerID foreign key column of TRANS, as required. PurchaseDate

Figure 11-18

Running the NewCustomerWithTransaction Stored Procedure from the Query Analyzer

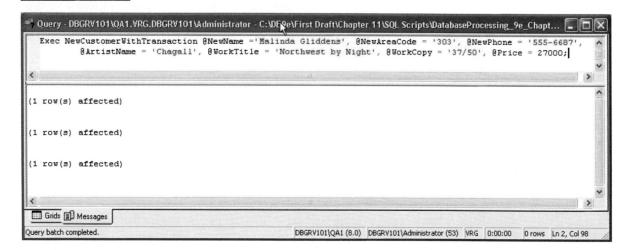

Figure 11-19

**Results from Exec in
Figure 11-18**

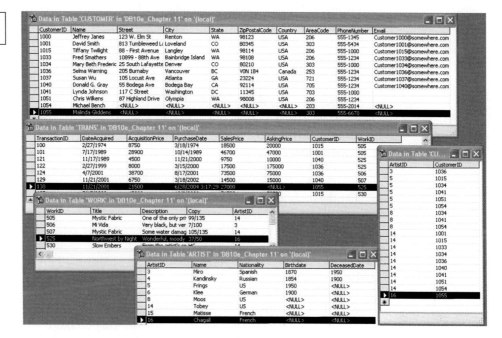

and SalesPrice were also set appropriately. Note the new row in the intersection table that records customer 1055's interest in artist 16, as required.

Triggers

SQL Server supports INSTEAD OF and AFTER triggers only. SQL Server does not support BEFORE triggers. A table may have one or more AFTER triggers for insert, update, and delete actions; AFTER triggers may not be assigned to views. A view or table may have at most one INSTEAD OF trigger for each triggering action of an insert, an update, or a delete.

In SQL Server, triggers can roll back the transactions that caused them to be fired. When a trigger executes a ROLLBACK command, all work done by the transaction that caused the trigger to be fired will be rolled back. If the trigger contains instructions after the ROLLBACK command, those instructions will be executed. However, any instructions in the transaction after the statement that caused the trigger to be fired will not be executed.

For insert and update triggers, the new values for every column of the table being processed will be stored in a pseudotable named *inserted.* If, for example, a new row is being added to the ARTIST table, the pseudotable *inserted* will have four columns: Name, Nationality, Birthdate, and DeceasedDate. Similarly, for update and delete commands, the old values for every column of the table being updated or deleted will be stored in the pseudotable named *deleted.* You will see how to use these pseudotables in the examples that follow.

The next four sections illustrate four triggers for each of the trigger functions described in Chapter 7. You can create these triggers by keying them into a text file (using CREATE TRIGGER or ALTER TRIGGER as the first statement) or by right-clicking the table name and selecting All Tasks/Manage Triggers. In the latter case, a window will appear into which you can key the trigger code. You cannot save your code in this window, however, until you have removed all syntax errors.

A Trigger for Setting Default Values

Triggers can be used to set default values that are more complex than those that can be set with the Default constraint on a column definition. For example, View Ridge has a pricing policy that says that the default AskingPrice of a work of art depends on whether the art has been in the gallery before. If not, the default AskingPrice is twice the AcquisitionPrice. If the work has been in the gallery before, the default price is the larger of twice the AcquisitionPrice or the AcquisitionPrice plus the average net gain of the work in the past.

The trigger shown in Figure 11-20 implements this pricing policy. The term *AFTER* does not appear in this trigger code, but we know that it is an AFTER trigger because SQL Server does not support BEFORE triggers.

In the trigger, after the variables are declared, the new values of WorkID and AcquisitionPrice are obtained from *inserted.* Then, a SELECT FROM dbo.TRANS is executed to count the number of rows with the given WorkID.

This trigger uses the system function @@rowCount, which contains the number of rows processed in the preceding T/SQL statement. Its value must be checked immediately after the statement is executed or saved in a variable to be checked later. Here, the trigger immediately uses the value of @@rowCount.

The variable @countPriorRows is set to @@rowCount minus one because this is an AFTER trigger, and the new row will already be in the database. The expression (@@rowCount-1) is the correct number of qualifying TRANS rows that were in the database prior to the insert.

@newPrice is then set to twice the AcquisitionPrice; it will be adjusted below, if necessary. If @countPriorRows is greater than zero, there were TRANS rows for this work in the database, and the ArtistWorkNet view (see page 244) is used to obtain the sum of the NetPrice. The AVG built-in function cannot be used because it will compute the average using @@rowCount rather than @countPriorRows. Next, the current value of @newPrice is compared with the average net gain plus the acquisition price. If less, @newPrice is recomputed to be the average net gain plus the acquisition price. Finally, an update is made to the just inserted row using the computed value of @newPrice for AskingPrice.

This trigger provides useful functionality for the gallery. It saves the gallery personnel considerable manual work in implementing their pricing policy and likely improves the accuracy of the results as well.

A Trigger for Enforcing a Data Constraint

View Ridge Gallery keeps a list of problem-customer accounts; these are customers who have either not paid promptly or who have presented other problems to the gallery. When a customer who is on the problem list is entered into the database, the gallery wants the insert or update of the customer data to be rolled back and a message displayed.

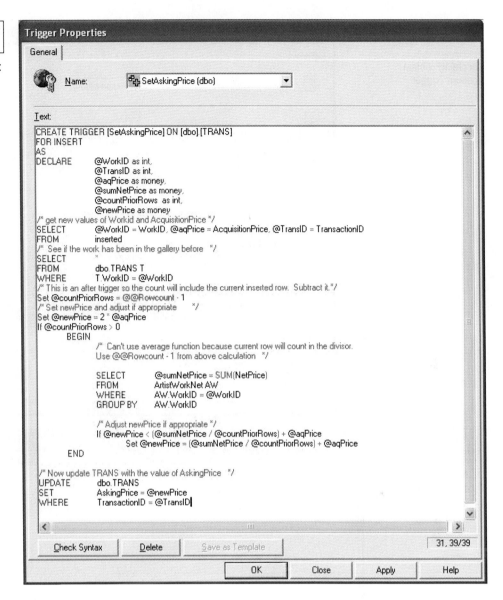

Figure 11-20

Trigger to Set a Default Value

To enforce this policy, the gallery keeps the Name, AreaCode, and PhoneNumber of problem customers in a table named PROBLEM_ACCOUNT. When customer data are inserted or updated, a trigger determines whether the new or changed customer data reside in the PROBLEM_ACCOUNT table. If so, the insert or update is rolled back and a message is displayed.

The CheckForProblemAccount trigger in Figure 11-21 enforces this policy. The code first joins the new values in the inserted table to any row in PROBLEM_ACCOUNT. If any results are returned from the join, then @@rowCount will be greater than zero. In this case, the new or updated customer does exist in the PROBLEM_ACCOUNT table, and the transaction is rolled back and the warning message printed.

B T W

In the prior two stored procedures, the @@rowCount function could have been used instead of counting rows into the variable @rowCount. Just remember to check it or store it immediately after the SQL statement is executed.

Figure 11-21

CheckForProblem-Account Trigger

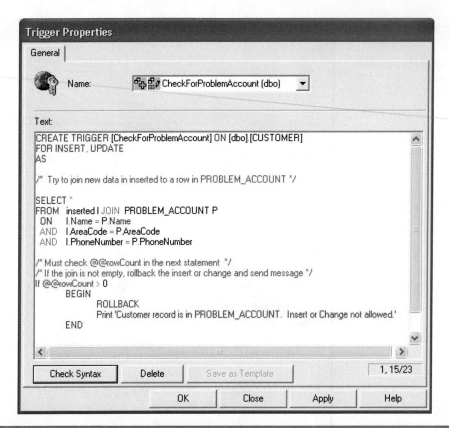

Figure 11-22

Testing for CheckForProblem-Account Trigger

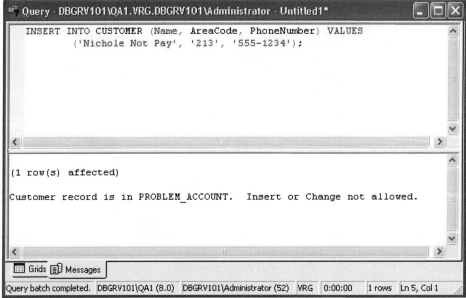

To verify that this trigger works, the row 'Nichole Not Pay', '213', '555-1234' was inserted into the PROBLEM_ACCOUNT table. Then, the INSERT statement shown in Figure 11-22 was executed. As you can see, the proper message was printed. The CUSTOMER table was also checked to ensure that the insert was not made (not shown here).

Using a table of valid or invalid values is more flexible and dynamic than placing such values in a CHECK constraint. For example, consider the CHECK constraint on Nationality values in the ARTIST table. If the gallery manager wants to expand the nationality of allowed artists, the manager will have to change the CHECK constraint using the ALTER TABLE statement. In reality, the gallery manager will have to hire a consultant to change this constraint.

A better approach is to place the allowed values of Nationality in a table, say ALLOWED_NATIONALITY. Then, write a trigger like that shown in Figure 11-21 to enforce the constraint that new values of Nationality exist in ALLOWED_NATIONALITY. When the gallery owner wants to change the allowed artists, the manager would simply add or remove values in the ALLOWED_NATIONALITY table.

A Trigger for Updating a View

Chapter 7 discussed the problem of updating views. One such problem concerns updating views created via joins; it is normally not possible for the DBMS to know how to update tables that underlie the join. However, sometimes application-specific knowledge can be used to determine how to interpret a request to update a joined view.

Consider the CustomerInterests view shown in Figure 11-11. It contains rows of CUSTOMER and ARTIST joined over their intersection table. CUSTOMER.Name is given the alias Customer, and ARTIST.Name is given the alias Artist.

A request to change the name of a customer in CustomerInterests can be interpreted as a request to change the name of the underlying CUSTOMER table. Such a request, however, can be processed only if the value of CUSTOMER.Name is unique. If not, the request cannot be processed.

The INSTEAD OF trigger shown in Figure 11-23 implements this logic. First, the new and old values of the Customer column in CustomerInterests are obtained. Then,

Figure 11-23

CustomerNameUpdate
Trigger

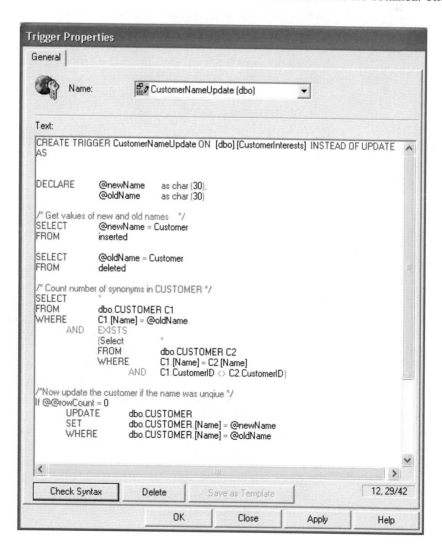

```
CREATE TRIGGER CustomerNameUpdate ON [dbo].[CustomerInterests]  INSTEAD OF UPDATE
AS


DECLARE        @newName    as char (30),
               @oldName    as char (30)

/* Get values of new and old names   */
SELECT         @newName = Customer
FROM           inserted

SELECT         @oldName = Customer
FROM           deleted

/* Count number of synonyms in CUSTOMER */
SELECT         *
FROM           dbo.CUSTOMER C1
WHERE          C1.[Name] = @oldName
      AND      EXISTS
               (Select         *
                FROM           dbo.CUSTOMER C2
                WHERE          C1.[Name] = C2.[Name]
                      AND      C1.CustomerID <> C2.CustomerID)

/*Now update the customer if the name was unqiue */
If @@rowCount = 0
         UPDATE        dbo.CUSTOMER
         SET           dbo.CUSTOMER.[Name] = @newName
         WHERE         dbo.CUSTOMER.[Name] = @oldName
```

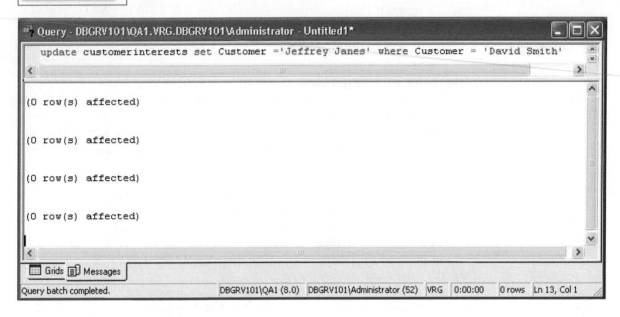

Figure 11-24   **Testing the CustomerNameUpdate Trigger**

a correlated subquery is used to determine whether the old value of CUSTOMER.Name is unique. If so, the name can be changed; otherwise, no update is made.

This trigger needs to be tested against cases in which the name is unique and cases in which the name is not unique. Figure 11-24 shows the case in which the name was not unique. First, two David Smith customers were created in the database. Then, the UPDATE command was issued against the view. As indicated in the Query Messages pane, no rows were updated.

A Trigger for Enforcing a Required Child Constraint

The View Ridge design includes an M-M relationship between WORK and TRANS. Every WORK must have a TRANS to store the price of the work and the date the work was acquired, and every TRANS must relate to a WORK parent. Figure 11-25 shows the tasks that must be accomplished to enforce this constraint; it is based on the boilerplate shown in Figure 6-27(b).

Because the CREATE TABLE statement for TRANS (Figure 11-6) defines TRANS.WorkID as NOT NULL and defines the FOREIGN KEY constraint without cascading deletions, the DBMS will ensure that every TRANS has a WORK parent. So, we need not be concerned with enforcing the insert on TRANS or the deletion on WORK. As stated in Figure 11-25, the DBMS will do that for us. Also, we need not be concerned with updates to WORK.WorkID because it is a surrogate key.

Three constraints remain that must be enforced by triggers: (1) ensuring that a TRANS row is created when a new WORK is created; (2) ensuring that TRANS.WorkID never changes; and (3) ensuring that the last TRANS child for a WORK is never deleted.

We can enforce the second constraint by writing a trigger on the update of TRANS that checks for a change in WorkID. If there is such a change, the trigger can roll back the change. Concerning the third constraint, the gallery has a business policy that no TRANS data ever be deleted. Thus, we need not only to disallow the deletion of the last child, we need to disallow the deletion of any child. We can do this by writing a trigger on the deletion of TRANS that rolls back any attempted deletion. (If the gallery allowed TRANS deletions, we could enforce the deletion constraint using views as shown in Chapter 7, Figures 7-29 and 7-30.) The triggers for enforcing the second and third constraints are simple, and we leave them as exercises 11.28 and 11.29.

Figure 11-25   Enforcing the M-M Relationship between WORK and TRANS

	WORK	TRANS
Insert	Create a TRANS row.	New TRANS must have a valid WorkID (enforced by DBMS).
Modify key or foreign key	Not a concern because workID is a surrogate key.	Never allowed because a TRANS cannot change to a different WORK.
Delete	Cannot delete a WORK with any TRANS children (enforced by DBMS by lack of CASCADE DELETE).	Cannot delete the last child. (Actually, by gallery policy, can delete NO TRANS data).

However, the first constraint is a problem. We can write a trigger on the WORK INSERT to create a default TRANS row, but this trigger will be called before the application has a chance to create the TRANS row itself. The trigger will create a TRANS row and then the application may create a second one. To guard against the duplicate, we can write a trigger on TRANS to remove the row the WORK trigger created in those cases when the application creates its own trigger.

Figures 11-26(a) and 11-26(b) show this pair of triggers. The trigger in Figure 11-26(a) creates the default TRANS row. It first checks to determine whether an appropriate TRANS row exists; if not, it inserts a new row into TRANS. The trigger in Figure 11-26(b) then removes this same row if the application creates its own TRANS row.

This solution is awkward, at best.

A better design is to require the applications to create the WORK/TRANS combination via a view. For example, consider the view Work_Trans:

CREATE VIEW Work_Trans AS

> **SELECT**   **Title, Description, Copy, ArtistID, DateAcquired, AcquisitionPrice**
>
> **FROM**   **WORK W JOIN TRANS T**
>
> **ON**   **W.WorkID = T.WorkID;**

The DBMS will not be able to process an insert on this view. We can, however, define an INSTEAD OF trigger to process the insert. Our trigger will create both a new row in WORK and the new, required child in TRANS. The code for this trigger is shown in Figure 11-27.

The solution in Figure 11-27 is more satisfying than the one in Figure 11-26. Note, however, that with this solution, applications must not be allowed to insert WORK rows directly. They must always insert them via the Work_Trans view.

Concurrency Control

SQL Server 2000 provides a comprehensive set of capabilities to control concurrent processing. Many choices and options are available, and the resulting behavior is determined by the interaction of three factors: the transaction isolation level, the cursor concurrency setting, and locking hints provided in the SELECT clause. Locking behavior is also dependent on whether the cursor is processed as part of a transaction, whether the

Figure 11-26

**Triggers for Enforcing
a Required Child**

(a) EnforceTransChild
Trigger and (b)
RemoveDupTrans Trigger

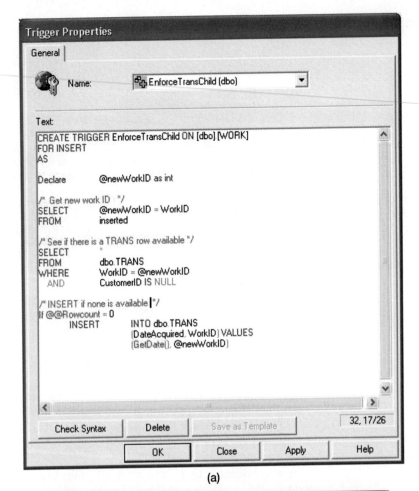

(a)

(b)

Figure 11-27

INSTEAD OF Trigger
on Work_Trans View

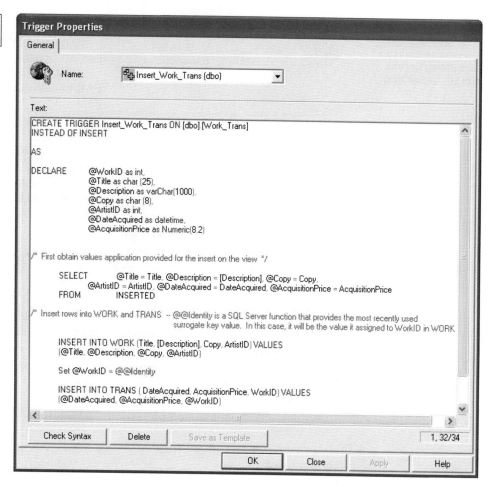

SELECT statement is part of a cursor, and whether INSERT, UPDATE, or DELETE commands occur inside of transactions or independently.

In this section, we will just describe the basics. See the SQL Server documentation for more information.

With SQL Server, developers do not place explicit locks. Instead, developers declare the concurrency control behavior they want, and SQL Server determines where to place the locks. Locks are applied on rows, pages, keys, indexes, tables, and even on the entire database. SQL Server determines what level of lock to use and may promote or demote a lock level while processing. It also determines when to place the lock and when to release it, depending on the declarations made by the developer.

Transaction Isolation Level

Figure 11-28 summarizes the concurrency control options. The broadest level of settings is the **transaction isolation level.** The four transaction isolation level options are listed in ascending level of restriction in the first row of Figure 11-28. These four options are the four you studied in Chapter 9; they are the SQL-92 standard levels. Note that with SQL Server, it is possible to make dirty reads by setting the isolation level to READ UNCOMMITTED. However, READ COMMITTED is the default isolation level.

The next most restrictive level is REPEATABLE READ, which means that SQL Server places and holds locks on all rows that are read. This means that no other user can change or delete a row that has been read until the transaction commits or aborts. Rereading the cursor may, however, result in phantom reads.

Figure 11-28

**Concurrency Options
with SQL Server 2000**

Type	Scope	Options
Transaction Isolation Level	Connection—all transactions	READ UNCOMMITTED READ COMMITTED (default) REPEATABLE READ SERIALIZABLE
Cursor Concurrency	Cursor	READ_ONLY OPTIMISTIC SCROLL_LOCK
Locking Hints	SELECT	READCOMMITTED READUNCOMMITTED REPEATABLEREAD SERIALIZABLE NOLOCK HOLDLOCK and others ...

Figure 11-28

Concurrency Options with SQL Server 2000

The strictest isolation level is SERIALIZABLE. With it, SQL Server places a range lock on the rows that have been read. This ensures that no read data can be changed or deleted, and that no new rows can be inserted in the range to cause phantom reads. This level is the most expensive to enforce and should only be used when absolutely required.

An example Transact-SQL statement to set the isolation level to, say, REPEATABLE READ is the following:

SET TRANSACTION ISOLATION LEVEL REPEATABLE READ;

This statement could be issued anyplace Transact-SQL is allowed, prior to any other database activity.

Cursor Concurrency

The second way in which the developer can declare locking characteristics is with cursor concurrency. Possibilities are read only, optimistic, and pessimistic, here called **SCROLL_LOCK.** As described in Chapter 9, with optimistic locking, no lock is obtained until the user updates the data. At that point, if the data have been changed since they were read, the update is refused. Of course, the application program must specify what to do when such a refusal occurs.

SCROLL_LOCK is a version of pessimistic locking. With it, an update lock is placed on a row when the row is read. If the cursor is opened within a transaction, the lock is held until the transaction commits or rolls back. If the cursor is outside of a transaction, the lock is dropped when the next row is read. Recall from Chapter 9 that an update lock blocks another update lock, but it does not block a shared lock. Thus, other connections can read the row with shared locks.

The default cursor concurrency setting depends on the cursor type (see Chapter 9). It is read only for static and forward only cursors, and it is optimistic for dynamic and keyset cursors.

Cursor concurrency is set with the DECLARE CURSOR statement. An example to declare a dynamic SCROLL_LOCK cursor on all rows of the TRANS table is as follows:

DECLARE MY_CURSOR CURSOR DYNAMIC SCROLL_LOCKS

FOR

SELECT *

FROM dbo.TRANS;

Locking Hints

Locking behavior can be further modified by providing locking hints in the WITH parameter of the FROM clause in SELECT statements. Figure 11-28 lists several of the locking hints available with SQL Server. The first four hints override the transaction isolation level; the next two influence the type of lock issued.

Consider the following statements:

SET TRANSACTION ISOLATION LEVEL REPEATABLE READ;

DECLARE MY_CURSOR CURSOR DYNAMIC SCROLL_LOCKS

FOR

    SELECT *

    FROM dbo.TRANS WITH READUNCOMMITTED NOLOCK;

Without the locking hints, the cursor MY_CURSOR would have REPEATABLE READ isolation and would issue update locks on all rows read. The locks would be held until the transaction committed. With the locking hints, the isolation level for this cursor becomes READ UNCOMMITTED. Furthermore, the specification of NOLOCK changes this cursor from DYNAMIC to READ_ONLY.

Consider another example:

SET TRANSACTION ISOLATION LEVEL REPEATABLE READ;

DECLARE MY_CURSOR CURSOR DYNAMIC SCROLL_LOCKS

FOR

    SELECT *

    FROM dbo.TRANS WITH HOLDLOCK;

Here, the locking hint will cause SQL Server to hold update locks on all rows read until the transaction commits. The effect is to change the transaction isolation level for this cursor from REPEATABLE READ to SERIALIZABLE.

In general, the beginner is advised not to provide locking hints. Rather, until you have become an expert, set the isolation level and cursor concurrency to appropriate values for your transactions and cursors and leave it at that.

SQL Server Security

We discussed security in general terms in Chapter 9. Here, we will summarize how those general ideas pertain to SQL Server security. You can find more information about securing SQL Server by searching for the "SQL Server Security" at *msdn.microsoft.com*.

SQL Server Security Settings

Figure 11-29 shows the form that is used to define general SQL Server policies. You can access this form by right-clicking the name of your server in the Enterprise Manager. Select the Security tab, as has been done in Figure 11-29.

As shown, SQL Server provides two modes of authentication. With Windows-only security, the authentication is provided by the Windows operating system. The user credentials used during sign on to Windows will be passed to SQL Server as the SQL Server user credentials. If both SQL Server and Windows security are selected, SQL Server will accept either the Windows-authenticated credentials or it will perform its

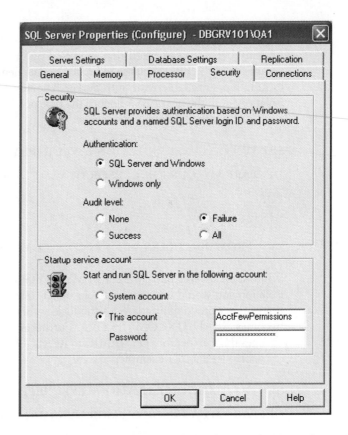

Figure 11-29

**SQL Server Security
Properties**

own authentication by presenting a sign-on dialog box to the user. This authentication mode is sometimes called *mixed security.*

Better security occurs if Windows-only authentication is selected. However, some older programs, such as ERwin, require SQL Server authentication. If SQL Server is to work with such programs, mixed security must be selected, as shown here.

In Figure 11-29, the selection of Failure (for Audit level) means that failed log in attempts will be recorded in a log. As stated in Chapter 9, DBA personnel should examine this log regularly for suspicious activity. Finally, according to Figure 11-29, SQL Server is to be started in the Windows account AcctFewPermissions. As the name of this account indicates, this account has the fewest operating system permissions needed to run SQL Server. By running SQL Server on such an account, if an intruder were to obtain control of SQL Server, he or she would have the least possible operating system authority. Never run an operational SQL Server on an account in the Windows Administrator group.

Security on Database Accounts

Figure 11-30 shows the forms used to set up security permissions for a SQL Server user account. You can access this form by right-clicking Security/Logins and selecting New Login. As shown in Figure 11-30(a), the account name is VRSalesperson in the Windows domain DBGRV101. The account is to be authenticated by Windows, and the default database is VRG.

Figure 11-30(b) shows the same form when the Database Access tab has been clicked. Here, the user is granted the authority to access the VRG database and will be given the role Public. A role is a group of predefined authorities, as discussed in the following section. By default, the Public role can only connect to the database; it has no other permissions.

To enable the user of this account to do more than connect, additional authorities must be assigned. Figure 11-31 shows the forms used to do this. Access the User Properties form by clicking Users in the database to be processed; here, that database is named VRG. Right-click and select Properties to display the properties form. Click the Permissions

Figure 11-30

Creating a New Login
(a) Setting Login
Properties and
(b) Allocating Databases
to the Login

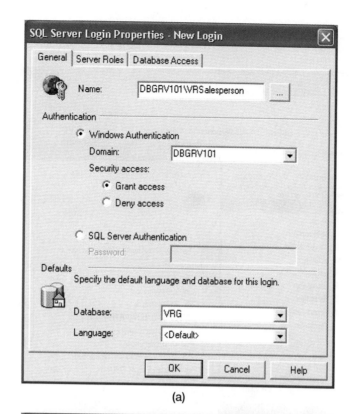

(a)

(b)

button in that form, and the Permissions form shown on the right side of Figure 11-31 will display. In this example, the VRSalesperson has been granted the capability to SELECT, INSERT, and UPDATE the ARTIST and CUSTOMER tables. This user also has the authority to SELECT the view ArtistWorkNet and to execute the Customer_Insert stored procedure.

| Figure 11-31 | Setting Login Permissions |

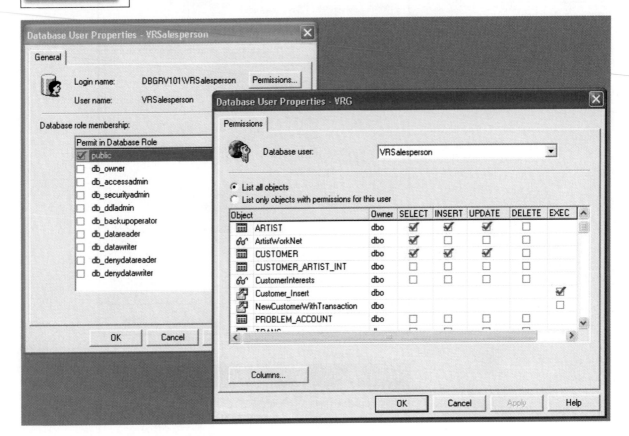

Security on Roles

In the last example, we granted authorities to a particular user login. The DBA can save some effort, however, by defining roles and granting authorities to those roles. Then, when a user login is given the defined role, it inherits all of the authorities granted to the role. Also, when an authority is removed from a role, all accounts that have that role automatically lose that authority as well.

Figure 11-32 shows the form used to define a role and allocate user accounts to that role. This form can be accessed by right-clicking Roles under the VRG (or other) database and selecting New Database Role. Permissions for the role are assigned by clicking the Permissions button, just as was done for an account in Figure 11-31.

SQL Server Backup and Recovery

When you create a SQL Server database, both data and log files are created. As explained in Chapter 9, these files should be backed up periodically. When this is done, it is possible to recover a failed database by restoring it from a prior database save and applying changes in the log.

To recover a database with SQL Server, the database is restored from a prior database backup, and log after images are applied to the restored database. When the end of the log is reached, changes from any transaction that failed to commit are then rolled back.

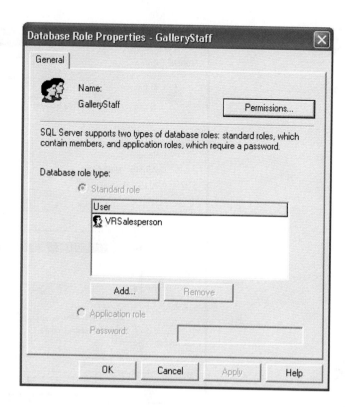

Figure 11-32

Allocating Users to Roles

It is also possible to process the log to a particular point in time or to a transaction mark. For example, the following statement causes a mark labeled NewCust to be placed into the log every time this transaction is run:

BEGIN TRANSACTION NewCust WITH MARK;

If this is done, the log can be restored to a point either just before or just after the first NewCust mark or the first NewCust mark after a particular point in time. The restored log can then be used to restore the database. Such marks consume log space, however, so they should not be used without good reason.

Types of Backup

SQL Server supports several types of backup. To see them, open the Enterprise Manager, open Databases, and right-click a database name. Select All Tasks and then select Backup Database. The dialog box shown in Figure 11-33 appears. At this point, you can create a complete or differential backup of the database, a transaction log backup, and a backup of particular files and file groups.

As the name implies, a complete backup makes a copy of the entire database. A **differential backup** makes a copy of the changes that have been made to the database since the last complete backup. This means that a complete backup must be made before the first differential backup. Because differential backups are faster, they can be taken more frequently, and the chance of data loss is reduced. On the other hand, complete backups take longer, but they are slightly simpler to use for recovery, as you will see.

The transaction log also needs to be periodically backed up to ensure that its contents are preserved. Further, the transaction log must be backed up before it can be used to recover a database.

Backups can be made either to disk or to tape. When possible, the backups should be made to devices other than those that store the operational database and log. Backing up to removable devices allows the backups to be stored in a location physically

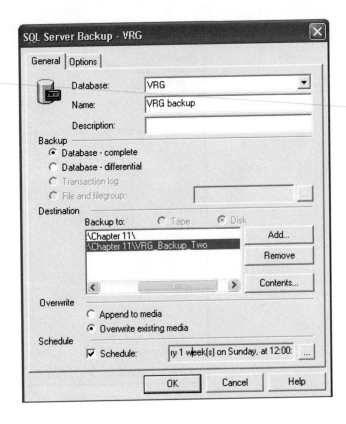

Figure 11-33

**Backing Up a SQL
Server Database**

removed from the database data center. This is important for recovery in the event of disasters caused by flood, hurricanes, and the like.

SQL Server Recovery Models

SQL Server supports three recovery models: simple, full, and bulk logged. You can set the recovery model by right-clicking a database name in the Enterprise Manager and selecting Properties. The recovery model is specified under the Options tab. Figure 11-34 shows an example.

With the simple recovery model, no logging is done. The only way to recover a database is to restore the database to the last backup. Changes made since that last backup are lost. The simple recovery model can be used for a database that is never changed—one having the names and locations of the occupants of a full graveyard, for example. Or for one that is used for read-only analysis of data that are copied from some other transactional database.

With full recovery, all database changes are logged. With bulk-logged database recovery, all changes are logged except those that cause large log entries. With bulk-logged recovery, changes to large text and graphic data items are not recorded to the log, actions such as CREATE INDEX are not logged, and some other bulk-oriented actions are not logged. An organization uses bulk-logged recovery if conserving log space is important and if the data used in the bulk operations are saved in some other way.

Restoring a Database

If the database and log files have been properly backed up, restoring the database is straightforward. First, back up the current log so that changes in the most recent log will be available. Then, right-click the database name in the Enterprise Manager, select All Tasks, and then select Restore Database. The dialog box shown in Figure 11-35 appears.

Figure 11-34

Setting the Recovery
Model

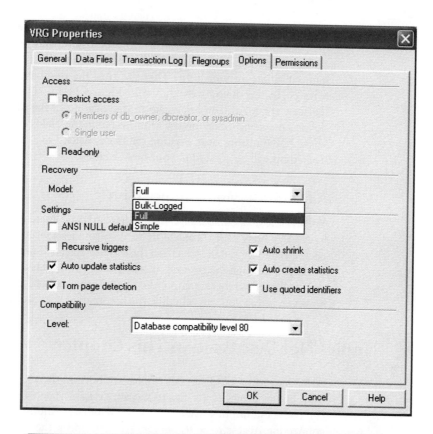

Figure 11-35

Restoring a Database
with SQL Server

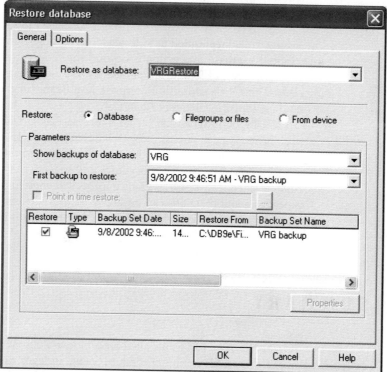

In this example, database VRG is being restored as database VRG Restore. It is not necessary to change the name of the database. Here, the plan is to restore it under a different name, test the restored database, delete what's left of the old database, and then rename the recovered database as VRG.

You can use backup and restore to transfer a database to another computer or user (for example, your professor!). Just do a full backup of the database you want to share to a file, say the file *MyBackup*. Then, create a new database on another computer and name it whatever you want. Then, restore the database using the file MyBackup as follows: In the dialog box shown in Figure 11-35, select From Device, click Select Devices, select Add, and navigate to the location of the MyBackup file. Once you have defined the device, click on the Options tab in the dialog box shown in Figure 11-35 and select Force restore over existing database. Click OK, and a copy of the database you backed up will be created in your new database.

A Database Maintenance Plan

You can create a database maintenance plan to facilitate the making of database and log backups, among other tasks. SQL Server provides a wizard for this task. To use it, right-click a database name, select All Tasks, and select Maintenance Plan. The wizard will guide you through the process of scheduling various tasks. Some of these tasks maintain the database by reorganizing indexes and other related activities. Of importance here, however, is that you can schedule the automatic backup of both database data and logs.

Topics Not Discussed in This Chapter

Several important SQL Server topics are beyond the scope of this discussion. For one, SQL Server provides utilities to measure database activity and performance. The DBA can use these utilities when tuning the database. Another facility not described here is connecting Access to SQL Server. You can check the Access documentation for more information about this topic.

As stated, SQL Server 2000 provides facilities to support distributed database processing (called **replication** in SQL Server). Although very important in its own right, distributed database processing is beyond the scope of this text. Microsoft provides an OLE DB server called the Distributed Transaction Manager that coordinates distributed transactions. Java supports Enterprise Java Beans for the same purpose. We will touch on these topics in Chapters 12 and 14.

Finally, SQL Server has facilities for processing database views in the form of XML documents. We will discuss those facilities in Chapter 13. SQL Server 2005 is supposed to ship in late 2005. It has many features in addition to those described here. The security model is enhanced; stored procedures and triggers can be written in common language runtime languages; T-SQL is vastly improved; there is integrated support for XML; stored procedures and functions can be shared as web services; as well as many other new features. As stated, the knowledge you have learned in this chapter will prepare you to work with this new version.

SUMMARY

SQL Server 2000 can be installed on Windows 2000, Windows NT with Service Pack 5, and Windows XP computers. Tables, views, indexes, and other database structures can be created in two ways. One is to use the graphical design tools, which are similar to those in Microsoft Access. The other is to write SQL statements to create the structures and submit them to SQL Server via the SQL Query Analyzer utility. SQL Server supports all of the SQL DDL that you have learned in this text, including the IDENTITY keyword for defining surrogate keys. The only change required for the View Ridge schema was to change the name of the TRANSACTION table to TRANS.

Indexes are special data structures used to improve performance. SQL Server automatically creates an index on all primary and foreign keys. Additional views can be created using CREATE INDEX or the Manage Index graphical tool. SQL Server supports clustered and nonclustered indexes.

SQL Server supports a language called TRANSACT-SQL, which surrounds basic SQL statements with programming constructs such as parameters, variables, and logic structures such as IF, WHILE, and so forth.

SQL Server databases can be processed from application programs coded in standard programming languages, such as Visual Basic or C#, or application logic can be placed in stored procedures and triggers. Stored procedures can be invoked from standard languages or from VBScript and JScript in Web pages. In this chapter, stored procedures were invoked from the SQL Server Query Manager. This technique should be used only during development and testing. For security reasons, no one should process a SQL Server operational database in interactive mode. This chapter demonstrated SQL Server triggers for computing default values, for enforcing a data constraint, for updating a view, and for enforcing a mandatory child referential integrity constraint.

Three factors determine the concurrency control behavior of SQL Server: the transaction isolation level, the cursor concurrency setting, and locking hints provided in the SELECT clause. These factors are summarized in Figure 11-28. Behavior also changes depending on whether actions occur in the context of transactions or cursors or independently. Given these behavior declarations, SQL Server places locks on behalf of the developer. Locks may be placed at many levels of granularity and may be promoted or demoted as work progresses.

SQL Server supports log backups and both complete and differential database backups. Three recovery models are available: simple, full, and bulk logged. With simple recovery, no logging is done nor are log records applied. Full recovery logs all database operations and applies them for restoration. Bulk-logged recovery omits certain transactions that would otherwise consume large amounts of space in the log.

◎ REVIEW QUESTIONS

11.1 Install SQL Server 2000 and create a database named MEDIA. Use the default settings for file sizes, names, and locations.

11.2 Write a SQL statement to create a table named PICTURE with columns Name, Description, DateTaken, and FileName. Assume that Name is char(20), Description is varchar(200), DateTaken is smalldate, and FileName is char(45). Also assume that Name and DateTaken are required. Use Name as the primary key. Set the default value of Description to '(None)'.

11.3 Use the SQL Query Analyzer to submit the SQL statement in question 11.2 to create the PICTURE table in the MEDIA database.

11.4 Write a CREATE TABLE statement to create the table SLIDE_SHOW (ShowID, Name, Description, Purpose). Assume that ShowID is a surrogate key. Set the data type of Name and Description however you deem appropriate. Set the data type of Purpose to char (15) and limit it to the set of values ('Home', 'Office', 'Family', 'Recreation', 'Sports', 'Pets'). Execute your CREATE TABLE statement using Query Analyzer.

11.5 Use SQL and the Query Analyzer to create the table SHOW_PICTURE_INT as an intersection table between PICTURE and SLIDE_SHOW. Create appropriate relationships between PICTURE and SHOW_PICTURE_INT and between SLIDE_SHOW and SHOW_PICTURE_INT. Set the referential integrity properties to disallow any deletion of a SLIDE_SHOW row that has any SHOW_PICTURE_INT rows related to it. Set the referential integrity properties to cascade deletions when a PICTURE is deleted. Cascade updates to PICTURE.Name.

11.6   Write a SQL statement to create a view name PopularShows that has SLIDE_SHOW.Name and PICTURE.Name for all slide shows that have a Purpose of either 'Home' or 'Pets'. Execute this statement using the SQL Query Analyzer.

11.7   Open the view design tool and determine that PopularShows was constructed correctly. Modify this view to include PICTURE.Description and FileName.

11.8   Can the SQL DELETE statement be used with the PopularShows view? Why or why not?

11.9   Under what circumstances can PopularShows be used for inserts and modifications?

11.10 In Figure 11-14, what is the purpose of the @Count variable?

11.11 Why is the SELECT statement that begins SELECT @Cid necessary?

11.12 Explain how you would change the stored procedure in Figure 11-14 to connect the customer to all artists who either (a) were born before 1900 or (b) had a null value for Birthdate.

11.13 Explain the purpose of the transaction shown in Figure 11-17.

11.14 What happens if an incorrect value of Copy is input to the stored procedure in Figure 11-17?

11.15 In Figure 11-17, what happens if the ROLLBACK statement is executed?

11.16 Explain the use of the join statement in Figure 11-21.

11.17 In Figure 11-20, why is SUM used instead of AVG?

11.18 What are the three primary factors that influence SQL Server locking behavior?

11.19 Explain how the strategy used to prevent the entry of problem accounts in Figure 11-21 can be used to implement the constraint on ARTIST.Nationality. Why is this strategy better?

11.20 Explain why the CustomerInterests view in Figure 11-11 is not updatable. Describe the logic of the INSTEAD OF UPDATE trigger in Figure 11-23.

11.21 Explain the purpose of the two triggers in Figure 11-26.

11.22 Explain why the trigger in Figure 11-27 is preferred to those in Figure 11-26. What limitation must be enforced for the trigger in Figure 11-27 to be effective?

11.23 Explain the meaning of each of the transaction isolation levels under Options shown in Figure 11-28.

11.24 Explain the meaning of each of the cursor concurrency settings listed in Figure 11-28.

11.25 What is the purpose of locking hints?

11.26 What is the difference between complete and differential backups? Under what conditions are complete backups preferred? Under what conditions are differential backups preferred?

11.27 Explain the differences between simple, full, and bulk-logged recovery models. Under what conditions would you choose each one?

PROJECT QUESTIONS

Use the following tables in your answers to questions 11.28 through 11.30:

EMPLOYEE (<u>EmpNumber</u>, Name, Email, *DeptName*)

DEPARTMENT (<u>DeptName</u>, BudgetCode)

Assume the relationship is M-M.

11.28 Code a SQL Server trigger to enforce the constraint that an employee can never change his or her department.

11.29 Code a SQL Server trigger to allow the deletion of a department if it only has one employee. Assign the last employee to the Human Resources department.

11.30 Design a system of triggers to enforce the M-M relationship. Use Figure 11-25 as an example, but assume that departments with only one employee can be deleted. Assign the last employee in a department to Human Resources.

11.31 Write SQL to accomplish the following tasks and submit them to SQL Server via the Query Analyzer.

    a. If you have not already done so, install SQL Server and create the View Ridge database.

    b. Create the tables shown in Figure 11-6, except do not create the NationalityValues constraint.

    c. Fill your database with sample data. Ensure that you have at least three customers, three artists, five works, and five transactions. Set the Nationality of ARTIST to one of 'German', 'French', or 'English'.

    d. Write a stored procedure to read the ARTIST table and display the artist data using Print.

    e. Write a stored procedure to read the ARTIST and WORK tables. Your procedure should display an artist, then display all of the works for that artist, then display the next artist, and so forth. Accept the name of the artist to display as an input parameter.

    f. Write a stored procedure to update customer phone data. Assume that your stored procedure receives Name, priorAreaCode, newAreaCode, priorPhoneNumber, and newPhoneNumber. Your procedure should first ensure that there is only one customer with the values of (Name, priorAreaCode, priorPhoneNumber). If not, produce an error message and quit. Otherwise, update the customer data with the new phone number data.

    g. Create a table named ALLOWED_NATIONALITY with one column, called Nation. Place the values 'German', 'French', and 'English' into the table. Write a trigger that will check to determine whether a new or updated value of Nationality resides in this table. If not, write an error message and roll back the insert or change. Use the Query Analyzer to demonstrate that your trigger works.

    h. Create a view having all of the data from the WORK and TRANS tables except for the surrogate keys. Write an insert INSTEAD OF trigger on this view that will create a new row in both WORK and TRANS. Use the Query Analyzer to demonstrate that your trigger works. Hint: Recall that you can issue an INSERT command on WORK and TRANS without specifying a value for the surrogate key. SQL Server will provide it.

M MARCIA'S DRY CLEANING

Answer questions A through M for Marcia's Dry Cleaning at the end of Chapter 7, page 262, if you have not already done so. Use the SQL Server data types in your answer.

A Using SQL Server, execute all of the SQL statements that you created in your answers to A through M for Marcia's Dry Cleaning at the end of Chapter 7.

B Assume that the relationship between ORDER and ORDER_ITEM is M-M. Design triggers to enforce this relationship. Use Figure 11-25 and the discussion of that figure as an example, but assume that Marcia does allow ORDERs and their related ORDER_ITEM rows to be deleted. Use the deletion strategy shown in Figures 7-29 and 7-30 for this case.

C Write and test the triggers you designed in question B, above.

MORGAN IMPORTING

Answer questions A through N for Morgan Importing at the end of Chapter 7, page 263, if you have not already done so. Use the SQL Server data types in your answer.

A Using SQL Server, execute all of the SQL statements that you created in your answers to A through N for Morgan Importing at the end of Chapter 7.

B Assume that the relationship between SHIPMENT and SHIPMENT_ITEM is M-M. Design triggers to enforce this relationship. Use Figure 11-25 and the discussion of that figure as an example, but assume that Morgan does allow SHIPMENTs and their related SHIPMENT_ITEM rows to be deleted. Use the deletion strategy shown in Figures 7-29 and 7-30 for this case.

C Write and test the triggers you designed in question B, above.

Database Access Standards

The three chapters in this section examine standards for database application processing. We begin in Chapter 12 by discussing older standards, including ODBC, OLE DB, and ADO. Even though these standards are no longer on the leading edge of database processing, many applications still use them, and you will likely encounter them in your career. Chapter 13 discusses one of the most important developments in information technology today, the confluence of database processing and document processing. This chapter introduces you to XML and XML Schema and describes important features and functions of ADO.NET, especially those that concern ADO.NET datasets. Finally, Chapter 14 describes the use of the Java technologies JDBC and Java Server Pages. It also introduces MySQL, an open source DBMS product. In fact, all of the examples in Chapter 14 were developed using open source software.

ODBC, OLE DB, ADO, and ASP

This chapter discusses traditional standard interfaces for accessing database servers. ODBC, or the Open Database Connectivity standard, was developed in the early 1990s to provide a product-independent interface to relational and other tabular data. In the mid-1990s, Microsoft announced OLE DB, which is an object-oriented interface that encapsulates data-server functionality. As you will learn, OLE DB was designed not just for relational databases, but for many other types of data as well. As a COM interface, OLE DB is readily accessible to C++, C#, and Java programmers, but is not as accessible to scripting developers. Therefore, Microsoft developed Active Data Objects (ADO), which is a set of objects for utilizing OLE DB that is designed for use by any language, including VBScript, and JScript.

Before considering these standards, we need to gain some perspective on the data environment that surrounds the Web server in Internet technology database applications.

The Web Server Data Environment

The environment in which today's database applications reside is rich and complicated. As shown in Figure 12-1, a typical Web server needs to publish applications that involve data of dozens of different data types. So far in this text, we have considered only relational databases, but as you can see from this figure, there are many other data types as well.

Consider the problems that the developer of Web server applications has when integrating these data. The developer may need to connect to an Oracle database; a DB2 mainframe database; a nonrelational database, such as IMS, IBM's older DBMS product; file-processing data, such as VSAM and ISAM; email directories; and so forth. Each one of these products has a different programming interface that the developer must learn. Further, these products evolve, thus new features and functions will be added over time that will increase the developer's challenge.

ODBC was created to address the part of this problem that concerns relational databases and data sources that are table-like, such as spreadsheets. As shown in Figure 12-2, ODBC is an interface between the Web server (or other database application) and the DBMS. It consists of a set of standards by which SQL statements can be issued and results and error messages can be returned. As shown in Figure 12-2, developers can call the DBMS using native DBMS interfaces if they want to (sometimes they do this to improve performance), but the developer who does not have the time or desire to learn many different DBMS native libraries can use the ODBC instead.

ODBC has been a tremendous success and has greatly simplified some database development tasks. As you will learn, it has a substantial disadvantage that was addressed by OLE DB. Figure 12-3 shows the relationship among OLE DB, ODBC, and other data types. OLE DB provides an object-oriented interface to data of almost any type. DBMS vendors can wrap portions of their native libraries in OLE DB objects to expose their product's functionality through this interface. OLE DB can also be used as an interface to ODBC data sources. Finally, OLE DB was developed to support the processing of nonrelational data as well.

Because OLE DB is an object-oriented interface, it is particularly suited to object-oriented languages such as C++. Many database application developers, however,

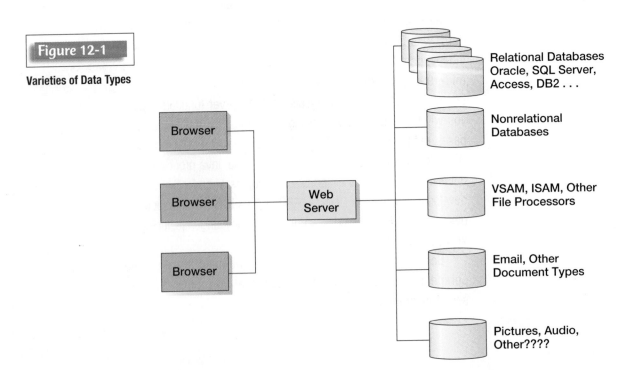

Figure 12-1

Varieties of Data Types

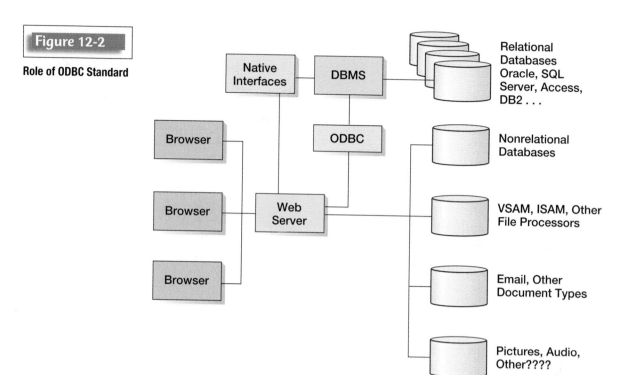

Figure 12-2

Role of ODBC Standard

program in scripting languages such as VBScript or JScript. To meet the needs of these programmers, Microsoft defined ADO as a cover over OLE DB objects (see Figure 12-4). ADO enables programmers to use almost any language to access OLE DB functionality.

You may feel uncomfortable with the strong Microsoft presence in this discussion. Both OLE DB and ADO were developed and promulgated by Microsoft, and even ODBC received prominence in large measure because of support from Microsoft. In fact, other vendors and standards committees did propose alternatives to OLE DB and ADO, but because Microsoft Windows resides on nearly 90 percent of the world's

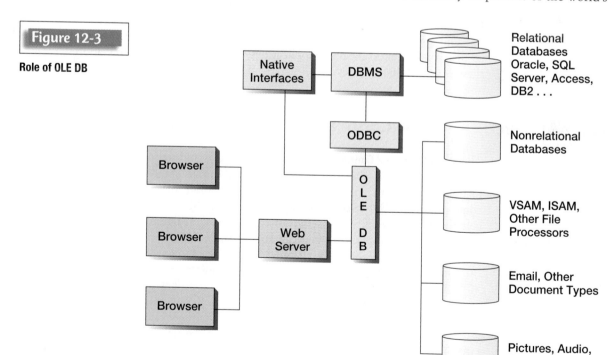

Figure 12-3

Role of OLE DB

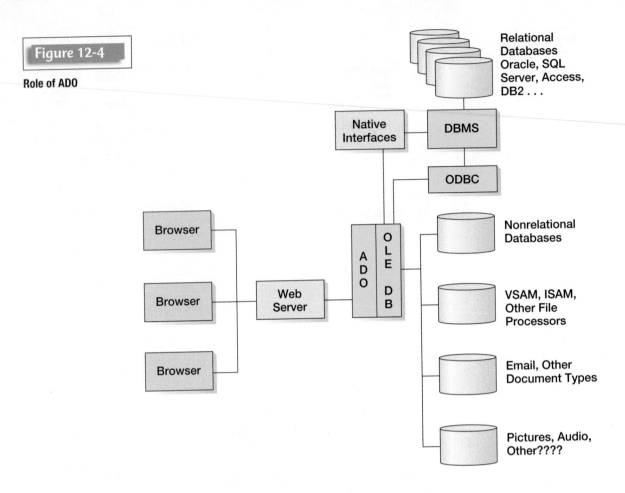

Figure 12-4

Role of ADO

desktops, it is difficult for others to establish opposing standards. Furthermore, in defense of Microsoft, both OLE DB and ADO are excellent. They simplify the job of the database developer, and they probably would have won out anyway—even on a level playing field.

Our aims, here, however, are more pedestrian. You need to learn ODBC and ADO so that you can build database applications. To that end, we will now address each of these standards in more detail.

 ## Open Database Connectivity (ODBC) Standard

The **Open Database Connectivity (ODBC)** standard is an interface by which application programs can access and process databases and tabular data in a DBMS-independent manner. This means, for example, that an application that uses the ODBC interface could process an Oracle database, a DB2 database, a spreadsheet, or any other ODBC-compliant database without making any coding changes. The goal is to allow a developer to create a single application that can access databases supported by different DBMS products without needing to be changed, or even recompiled.

ODBC was developed by a committee of industry experts from the X/Open and SQL Access Group committees. Several such standards were proposed, but ODBC emerged as the winner, primarily because it had been implemented by Microsoft and is an important part of Windows. Microsoft's initial interest in support of such a standard was to allow products such as Microsoft Excel to access database data from a variety of DBMS products without having to be recompiled. Of course, Microsoft's interests have changed since the introduction of OLE DB and ADO.NET (see Chapter 13).

ODBC Architecture

Figure 12-5 shows the components of the ODBC standard. The application program, driver manager, and DBMS drivers all reside on the application server computer. The drivers send requests to data sources, which reside on the database server. According to the standard, a **data source** is the database and its associated DBMS, operating system, and network platform. An ODBC data source can be a relational database; it can also be a file server such as BTrieve or even a spreadsheet.

The application issues requests to create a connection with a data source; to issue SQL statements and receive results; to process errors; and to start, commit, and roll back transactions. ODBC provides a standard means for each of these requests, and it defines a standard set of error codes and messages.

The **driver manager** serves as an intermediary between the application and the DBMS drivers. When the application requests a connection, the driver manager determines the type of DBMS that processes a given ODBC data source and loads that driver into memory (if it is not already loaded). The driver manager also processes certain initialization requests and validates the format and order of ODBC requests that it receives from the application. For Windows, the driver manager is provided by Microsoft.

A **driver** processes ODBC requests and submits specific SQL statements to a given type of data source. Each data source type has a different driver. For example, there are drivers for DB2, for Oracle, for Access, and for all of the other products whose vendors have chosen to participate in the ODBC standard. Drivers are supplied by DBMS vendors and by independent software companies.

It is the responsibility of the driver to ensure that standard ODBC commands execute correctly. In some cases, if the data source is itself not SQL compliant, the driver may need to perform considerable processing to fill in for a lack of capability at the data source. In other cases, when the data source supports full SQL, the driver need only pass the request through for processing by the data source. The driver also converts data source error codes and messages into the ODBC standard codes and messages.

ODBC identifies two types of drivers: single tier and multiple tier. A **single-tier** driver processes both ODBC calls and SQL statements. An example of a single-tier driver is shown in Figure 12-6(a). In this example, the data are stored in Xbase files (the format used by FoxPro, dBase, and others). Because Xbase file managers do not process SQL, it is the job of the driver to translate the SQL request into Xbase file-manipulation commands and to transform the results back into SQL form.

A **multiple-tier** driver processes ODBC calls, but passes the SQL requests directly to the database server. Although it may reformat a SQL request to conform to the dialect of a particular data source, it does not process the SQL. An example of the use of a multiple-tier driver is shown in Figure 12-6(b).

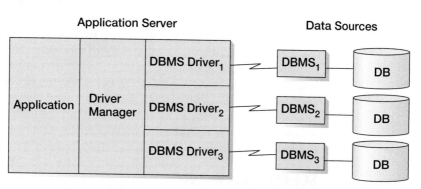

Figure 12-5

ODBC Architecture

Application can process a database using any of the three DBMS products.

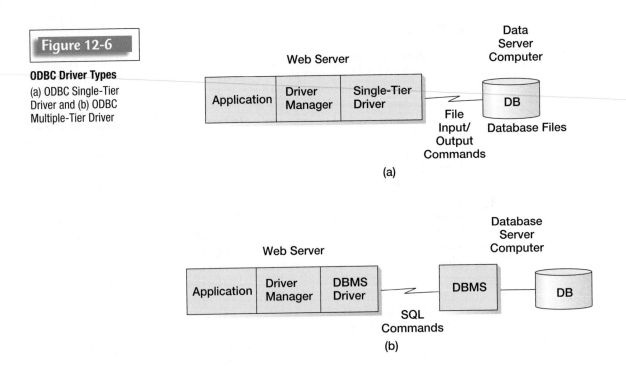

Figure 12-6

ODBC Driver Types
(a) ODBC Single-Tier
Driver and (b) ODBC
Multiple-Tier Driver

Conformance Levels

The creators of the ODBC standard faced a dilemma. If they chose to describe a standard for a minimal level of capability, many vendors would be able to comply. But if they did so, the standard would represent only a small portion of the complete power and expressiveness of ODBC and SQL. On the other hand, if the standard addressed a very high level of capability, only a few vendors would be able to comply with the standard, and it would become unimportant. To deal with this dilemma, the committee wisely chose to define levels of conformance to the standard. The committee defined two types of conformance: ODBC conformance and SQL conformance.

ODBC Conformance Level

ODBC conformance levels are concerned with the features and functions that are made available through the driver's **application program interface (API).** A driver API is a set of functions that the application can call to receive services. Figure 12-7 summarizes the three levels of ODBC conformance that are addressed in the standard. In practice, almost all drivers provide at least Level 1 API conformance, so the core API level is not too important.

An application can call a driver to determine which level of ODBC conformance it provides. If the application requires a level of conformance that is not present, it can terminate the session in an orderly fashion and generate appropriate messages to the user. Or, the application can be written to use higher-level conformance features if they are available and to work around the missing functions if a higher level is not available.

For example, drivers at the Level 2 API must provide a scrollable cursor. Using conformance levels, an application could be written to use cursors if they are available; but if they are not, to work around the missing feature, it would select needed data using very restrictive WHERE clauses. Doing this would ensure that only a few rows were returned at a time to the application, and it would process those rows using a cursor that it maintained itself. Performance would likely be slower in the second case, but at least the application would be able to successfully execute.

SQL Conformance Level

SQL conformance levels specify which SQL statements, expressions, and data types a driver can process. Three SQL conformance levels are defined, as summarized in Figure 12-8.

Figure 12-7

Summary of ODBC
Conformance Levels

Core API
- Connect to data sources
- Prepare and execute SQL statements
- Retrieve data from a result set
- Commit or roll back transactions
- Retrieve error information

Level 1 API
- Core API
- Connect to data sources with driver-specific information
- Send and receive partial results
- Retrieve catalog information
- Retrieve information about driver options, capabilities, and functions

Level 2 API
- Core and Level 1 API
- Browse possible connections and data sources
- Retrieve native form of SQL
- Call a translation library
- Process a scrollable cursor

Figure 12-8

Summary of SQL
Conformance Levels

Minimum SQL Grammar
- CREATE TABLE, DROP TABLE
- Simple SELECT (does not include subqueries)
- INSERT, UPDATE, DELETE
- Simple expressions (A > B + C)
- CHAR, VARCHAR, LONGVARCHAR data types

Core SQL Grammar
- Minimum SQL Grammar
- ALTER TABLE, CREATE INDEX, DROP INDEX
- CREATE VIEW, DROP VIEW
- GRANT, REVOKE
- Full SELECT (includes subqueries)
- Aggregate functions such as SUM, COUNT, MAX, MIN, AVG
- DECIMAL, NUMERIC, SMALLINT, INTEGER, REAL, FLOAT,
  DOUBLE PRECISION data types

Extended SQL Grammar
- Core SQL Grammar
- Outer joins
- UPDATE and DELETE using cursor positions
- Scalar functions such as SUBSTRING, ABS
- Literals for date, time, and timestamp
- Batch SQL statements
- Stored procedures

The capability of the minimum SQL grammar is very limited, and most drivers support at least the core SQL grammar.

As with ODBC conformance levels, an application can call the driver to determine what level of SQL conformance it supports. With that information, the application can then determine which SQL statements can be issued. If necessary, the application can then terminate the session or use alternative, less-powerful means of obtaining the data.

Establishing an ODBC Data Source Name

A **data source** is an ODBC data structure that identifies a database and the DBMS that processes it. Data sources identify other types of data, such as spreadsheets and other nondatabase tabular data stores, but we are not concerned with that use here.

The three types of data sources are file, system, and user. A **file data source** is a file that can be shared among database users. The only requirement is that the users have the same DBMS driver and privilege to access the database. The data source file can be emailed or otherwise distributed to possible users. A **system data source** is one that is local to a single computer. The operating system and any user on that system (with proper privileges) can use a system data source. A **user data source** is available only to the user who created it.

In general, the best choice for Internet applications is to create a system data source on the Web server. Browser users then access the Web server, which in turn uses a system data source to set up a connection with the DBMS and the database.

Figure 12-9 shows the process of creating a system data source using the ODBC Data Source Administrator Service that can be found via the Windows Control Panel. In Figure 12-9(a), the user is selecting a driver for an Oracle database. Notice that there are two such drivers: one is provided by Microsoft and the other is provided by Oracle. The drivers may have different capabilities, and the user should check the documentation for each to determine which is most appropriate for his or her application. Other drivers shown in this figure are for Paradox, text files, and Visual FoxPro.

The form shown in Figure 12-9(b) is generated by the Oracle ODBC Driver. With it, the user assigns a value for the Data Source Name (DSN), an optional Description, and the name of the database to access in the box labeled TNS Service Name. (The meaning of this term is unimportant for our purposes.) Here, the DSN is named ViewRidgeOracle2 and it is assigned to the Oracle VRG database created in Chapter 10.

We will use the ViewRidgeOracle2 DSN later in this chapter. We will also use a second DSN, named ViewRidge SS, to process the SQL Server database created in Chapter 11. ViewRidgeSS is created just like the DSN in Figure 12-9 except that it uses a SQL Server driver.

OLE DB

OLE DB is one of the foundations of data access in the Microsoft world. As such, it is important to understand the fundamental ideas of OLE DB, even if you will only work with the ADO interfaces that lie on top of it. In this section, we present essential OLE DB concepts.

OLE DB is an implementation of the Microsoft OLE object standard. OLE DB objects are COM objects and support all required interfaces for such objects. Fundamentally, OLE DB breaks the features and functions of a DBMS up into COM objects. Some objects support query operations; others perform updates; others support the creation of database schema constructs, such as tables, indexes, and views; and still others perform transaction management, such as optimistic locking.

This characteristic overcomes a major disadvantage of ODBC. With ODBC, a vendor must create an ODBC driver for almost all DBMS features and functions in order to participate in ODBC at all. This is a large task that requires a substantial investment. With OLE DB, however, a DBMS vendor can implement portions of a product. One

Figure 12-9

Creating a System Data Source

(a) Selecting the Oracle Driver and (b) Setting Data Source Properties

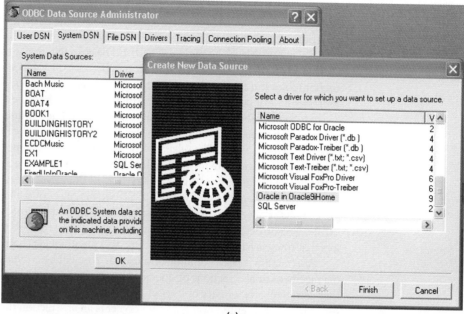

(a)

(b)

could, for example, implement only the query processor, participate in OLE DB, and hence be accessible to customers using ADO. Later, the vendor could add more objects and interfaces to increase OLE DB functionality.

This text does not assume that you are an object-oriented programmer, so we need to develop a few concepts. In particular, you need to understand abstractions, methods, properties, and collections. An **abstraction** is a generalization of something. ODBC interfaces are abstractions of native DBMS access methods. When we abstract something, we lose detail, but we gain the ability to work with a broader range of types.

For example, a **recordset** is an abstraction of a relation. In this abstraction, a recordset is defined to have certain characteristics that will be common to all recordsets. Every recordset, for instance, has a set of columns, which in this abstraction is called Fields. Now, the goal of abstraction is to capture everything important but to omit details that are not needed by users of the abstraction. Thus, Oracle relations may have some characteristics that are not represented in a recordset; the same might be true for relations in SQL Server, DB2, and in other DBMS products. These unique characteristics will be lost in the abstraction, but if the abstraction is a good one, no one will care.

Moving up a level, a **rowset** is the OLE DB abstraction of a recordset. Now, why does OLE DB need to define another abstraction? Because OLE DB addresses data sources that are not tables but that have *some of* the characteristics of tables. Consider all of the email addresses in your personal email file. Are those addresses the same as a relation? No, but they do share some of the characteristics that relations have. Each address is a semantically related group of data items. Like rows of a table, it is sensible to go to the first one, move to the next one, and so forth. But, unlike relations, they are not all of the same type. Some addresses are for individuals, others are for mailing lists. Thus, any action on a recordset that depends on everything in the recordset being the same kind of thing cannot be used on a rowset.

Working from the top down, OLE DB defines a set of data properties and behaviors for rowsets. Every rowset has those properties and behaviors. Furthermore, OLE DB defines a recordset as a subtype of a rowset. Recordsets have all of the properties and behaviors that rowsets have, plus they have some that are uniquely characteristic of recordsets.

Abstraction is both common and useful. You will hear of abstractions of transaction management or abstractions of querying or abstractions of interfaces. This simply means that certain characteristics of a set of things are formally defined as a type.

An object-oriented programming object is an abstraction that is defined by its properties and methods. For example, a recordset object has an AllowEdits property and a RecordsetType property and an EOF property. These **properties** represent characteristics of the recordset abstraction. An object also has actions that it can perform that are called **methods.** A recordset has methods such as Open, MoveFirst, MoveNext, and Close. Strictly speaking, the definition of an object abstraction is called an **object class,** or just *class.* An instance of an object class, such as a particular recordset, is called an object. All objects of a class have the same methods and the same properties, but the values of the properties vary from object to object.

The last term we need to address is *collection.* A **collection** is an object that contains a group of other objects. A recordset has a collection of other objects called Fields. The collection has properties and methods. One of the properties of all collections is Count, which is the number of objects in the collection. Thus, recordset.Fields.Count is the number of fields in the collection. In ADO and OLE DB, collections are named as the plural of the objects they collect. Thus, there is a Fields collection of Field objects, an Errors collection of Error objects, a Parameters collection of Parameters, and so forth. An important method of a collection is an iterator, which is a method that can be used to pass through or otherwise identify the items in the collection.

If you're getting frustrated with all these definitions, don't give up. You will see a practical use of these concepts before the end of this chapter!

Goals of OLE DB

The major goals for OLE DB are listed in Figure 12-10. First, as mentioned, OLE DB breaks DBMS functionality and services into object pieces. This partitioning means great flexibility for both **data consumers** (users of OLE DB functionality) and **data providers** (vendors of products that deliver OLE DB functionality). Data consumers take only the objects and functionality they need; a wireless device for reading a database can have a very slim footprint. Unlike with ODBC, data providers need only implement a portion of DBMS functionality. This partitioning also means that data providers can deliver capabilities in multiple interfaces.

This last point needs expansion. An object interface is a packaging of objects. An **interface** is specified by a set of objects and the properties and methods that they expose. An object need not expose all of its properties and methods in a given interface. Thus, a recordset object would expose only read methods in a query interface, but would expose create, update, and delete methods in a modification interface.

- Create object interfaces for DBMS functionality pieces
  - Query
  - Update
  - Transaction management
  - Etc.
- Increase flexibility
  - Allow data consumers to use only the objects they need
  - Allow data providers to expose pieces of DBMS functionality
  - Providers can deliver functionality in multiple interfaces
  - Interfaces are standardized and extensible
- Object interface over any type of data
  - Relational database
  - ODBC or native
  - Nonrelational database
  - VSAM and other files
  - Email
  - Other
- Do not force data to be converted or moved from where they are

How the object supports the interface, or the **implementation,** is completely hidden from the user. In fact, the developers of an object are free to change the implementation whenever they want. Who will know? But they may not ever change the interface without incurring the justifiable disdain of their users!

OLE DB defines standardized interfaces. Data providers, however, are free to add interfaces on top of the basic standards. Such extensibility is essential for the next goal, which is to provide an object interface to any data type. Relational databases can be processed through OLE DB objects that use ODBC or that use the native DBMS drivers. OLE DB includes support for the other types as indicated.

The net result of these design goals is that data need not be converted from one form to another, nor need they be moved from one data source to another. The Web server shown in Figure 12-1 can utilize OLE DB to process data in any of the formats, right where the data reside. This means that transactions may span multiple data sources and may be distributed on different computers. The OLE DB provision for this is the **Microsoft Transaction Manager (MTS);** however, discussion of the MTS is beyond the scope of this text.

OLE DB Terminology

As shown in Figure 12-11, OLE DB has two types of data providers. **Tabular data providers** present their data via rowsets. Examples are DBMS products, spreadsheets, and ISAM file processors such as dBase and FoxPro. Additionally, other types of data,

- Tabular data provider
  - Exposes data via rowsets
  - Examples: DBMS, spreadsheets, ISAMs, email
- Service provider
  - Transforms data through OLE DB interfaces
  - Both a consumer and a provider of data
  - Examples: query processors, XML document creator

Figure 12-12

Rowset Interfaces

- **IRowSet**
    Methods for sequential iteration through a rowset
- **IAccessor**
    Methods for setting and determining bindings between rowset
    and client program variables
- **IColumnsInfo**
    Methods for determining information about the columns in the rowset
- **Other interfaces**
    Scrollable cursors
    Create, update, delete rows
    Directly access particular rows (bookmarks)
    Explicitly set locks
    And so on

such as email, can also be presented in rowsets. Tabular data providers bring data of some type into the OLE DB world.

A **service provider,** on the other hand, is a transformer of data. Service providers accept OLE DB data from an OLE DB tabular data provider and transform it in some way. Service providers are both consumers and providers of transformed data. An example of a service provider is one that obtains data from a relational DBMS and transforms them into XML documents. Both data and service providers process rowset objects. A rowset is equivalent to what we called **cursors** in Chapter 9, and in fact the two terms are frequently used synonymously.

For database applications, rowsets are created by processing SQL statements. The results of a query, for example, are stored in a rowset. OLE DB rowsets have dozens of different methods, which are exposed via the interfaces listed in Figure 12-12. IRowSet provides object methods for forward-only sequential movement through a rowset. When you declare a forward-only cursor in OLE DB, you are invoking the IRowSet interface. The IAccessor interface is used to bind program variables to rowset fields. When using ADO (next section), this interface is hidden but it is used behind the scenes by ADO. If you work with type libraries in Visual Basic, however, you may use methods from this interface.

The IColumnsInfo interface has methods for obtaining information about the columns in a rowset. We will use this interface to advantage in two of the ADO examples at the end of this chapter. IRowSet, IAccessor, and IColumnsInfo are the basic rowset interfaces. Other interfaces are defined for more advanced operations such as scrollable cursors, update operations, direct access to particular rows, explicit locks, and so forth.

Active Data Objects (ADO)

Active Data Objects (ADO) is a simple object model that overlies the more complex OLE DB object model. ADO can be called from scripting languages, such as JScript and VBScript, and it can also be called from more powerful languages such as Visual Basic .NET, Java, C#, and C++ . Because ADO is easier to understand and use than OLE DB, ADO is more frequently used for database applications (see Figure 12-13).

Figure 12-13

Characteristics of ADO

- Simple object model for OLE DB data consumers
- Can be used from VBScript, JScript, Visual Basic, Java, C#, C++
- Single Microsoft data access standard
- Data access objects are the same for all types of OLE DB data

Invoking ADO from Active Server Pages

In this chapter, we will invoke ADO on a Web server using Active Server Pages (ASP). Such pages contain a mixture of HTML and program language statements expressed in either VBScript or JavaScript. In this chapter, we will use VBScript. ASPs can be written with any text editor, but they are easier to write with FrontPage or some similar Web-page-authoring product.

Internet Information Services (IIS) is a Web server built into Windows XP and Windows 2000 Professional. Whenever IIS receives a file with the extension .asp, it sends the file to the ASP program for processing.

In an ASP, any statements enclosed within the characters <% . . . %> will be processed on the Web server computer. Other statements will be sent to the user's browser for processing. In this chapter, all of our code will be processed on the Web server.

To invoke ASPs, place them in some directory, say, C:\MyDirectory. Then, open IIS and create a new virtual directory that points to the directory in which you have placed your ASPs. You can do this by opening Internet Information Services and right-clicking Default Web Site. Choose New/Virtual Directory, and a wizard will start that asks you to name your virtual directory and the real directory (here, C:\MyDirectory) in which your ASP files will reside. Select Read and Run Scripts on the third panel of the wizard. For the examples in this text, we will use the virtual directory name *ADOExamples.*

The DBMS and the Web server do not have to be located on the same machine. When you create the ODBC DSN, you can point to a database on a different computer that is accessible from the Web server computer. This will be easier if that other computer runs a Windows operating system, but it can be done with other operating systems as well. Of course, the Web server and the DBMS can be on the same machine.

The ADO Object Model

The ADO object model is shown in Figure 12-14. The Connection object is the first ADO object to be created and is the basis for the others. From a Connection object, a developer can create one or more RecordSet objects and one or more Command objects. In the process of creating or working with any of these objects, ADO will place any errors that are generated in the Errors collection.

Each RecordSet object has a Fields collection; each Field element corresponds to a column in the recordset. In addition, each Command object has a Parameters Collection that contains objects for the parameters of the command.

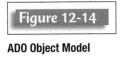

Figure 12-14

ADO Object Model

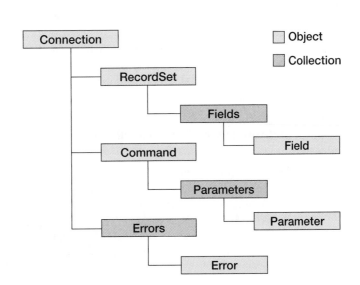

Connection Object

The following VBScript code can be embedded in an ASP to create a connection object. After it runs, the variable objConn will point to an object that is connected to the ODBC data source ViewRidgeSS.

```
<%

    Dim objConn

    Set objConn = Server.CreateObject  ("ADODB.connection")

    objConn.IsolationLevel = adXactReadCommitted ' use ADOVBS

    objConn.Open "ViewRidgeSS",

%>
```

In this code, the statement Server.CreateObject is invoking the CreateObject method of the ASP Server object, an object that is automatically created by the ASP processor. CreateObject receives one parameter, which is the type of object to be created. Here, an ADODB.connection object is to be created. After this statement executes, the variable objConn points to the new Connection object. Next, the isolation level of this connection is set using a constant from the file ADOVBS. That file can be made available to this script with the following include statement:

```
<!—#include virtual = "ADOExamples/ADOVBS.inc"—>
```

This statement must be part of the ASP file, but *outside* of the <% . . . %>. For this to work, you must copy the Windows file ADOVBS.inc into your directory (find it using Search). Also, substitute the name of your virtual directory if it is other than ADOExamples.

The names and values of some important ADOVBS constants are listed in Figure 12-15. Using the names of the constants rather than their values makes your code more readable. It also makes it easier to adapt your code should Microsoft change the meanings of these values (doubtful, but it could happen).

In the last statement, the Open method of the connection is used to open the ViewRidgeSS ODBC data source. Here, neither user ID nor password is being passed to the DBMS. Instead, the database will be opened using an authenticated name provided by the operating system. By default, ASP will use the name IUSR_*machine-name*, or in this case, IUSR_DBGRV101. To run the examples in this chapter, this account must be created in SQL Server with privileges to read and update the VRG user tables.

The Oracle ODBC driver that will be used in the figures that follow does not support machine authenticated passwords. For this driver, we will need to provide a user ID and a password. Here we will use the user ID of DK1 and the password of 'Sesame' as follows:

```
objConn.Open "DSN = ViewRidgeOracle2;UID = DK1;PWD = Sesame"
```

The account DK1 and its password must be created in Oracle with privileges to read and update the VRG tables.

At this point, a connection has been established to the DBMS via the ODBC data source and the database is open. The objConn pointer can be used to refer to any other methods for a connection (see Figure 12-14), including the creation and use of RecordSet and Command objects. The Errors collection can be processed as well.

Figure 12-15

ADO Constants

Isolation Level	Const Name	Value
Dirty reads	adXactReadUncommitted	256
Read committed	adXactReadCommitted	4096
Repeatable read	adXactRepeatableRead	65536
Serializable	adXactSerializable	1048576

(a) Isolation Levels

Cursor Type	Const Name	Value
Forward only	adOpenForwardOnly	0
Keyset	adOpenKeyset	1
Dynamic	adOpenDynamic	2
Static	adOpenStatic	3

(b) Cursor Types

Lock Type	Const Name	Value
Read only	adLockReadOnly	1
Pessimistic locking	adLockPessimistic	2
Optimistic locking	adLockOptimistic	3
Optimistic with batch updates	adBatchOptimistic	4

(c) Lock Types

RecordSet Object

Given the connection with an open database, the following statements will create a RecordSet object (we omit the <% and %> from now on, but all of these code examples must be inserted between them or they will not be executed on the Web server):

```
Dim objRecordSet, varSql

varSQL = "SELECT * FROM ARTIST"

Set objRecordSet = Server.CreateObject ("ADODB.Recordset")

objRecordSet.CursorTye = adOpenStatic

objRecordSet.LockType = adLockReadOnly

objRecordSet.Open varSQL, objConn
```

CursorType and LockType could also be passed as parameters to the RecordSet Open method, as follows:

Dim objRecordSet, varSql

    varSQL = "SELECT * FROM ARTIST"

    Set objRecordSet = Server.CreateObject ("ADODB.Recordset")

    objRecordSet.Open varSQL, objConn, adOpenStatic, adLockReadOnly

Either way, these statements cause the SQL statement in varSQL to be executed using a static, read-only cursor. All of the columns of the ARTIST table will be included as fields in the recordset. If the SELECT statement named only two columns—say, "SELECT ArtistID, Nationality FROM ARTIST"—only those two columns would be included as fields in the recordset.

By the way, there is a "gotcha" lurking here. With the SQL Server ODBC driver, if a table name has spaces or odd characters or is a SQL Server reserved word, you enclose the name in brackets [ ]. To the Oracle ODBC driver, however, a table name enclosed in brackets is illegal. For oddly named tables using the Oracle driver, you must enclose such names in quotes.

Fields Collection

After the recordset has been created, its Fields collection is instantiated. We can process that collection with the following:

Dim varI, varNumCols, objField

varNumCols = objRecordSet.Fields.Count

For varI = 0 to varNumCols - 1

    Set objField = objRecordSet.Fields(varI)

    ' objField.Name now has the name of the field

    ' objField.Value now has the value of the field

    ' can do something with them here

Next

In the second statement, varNumCols is set to the number of columns in the recordset by accessing the Count property of the Fields collection. Then a loop is executed to iterate over this collection. The property Fields(0) refers to the first column of the recordset, so the loop needs to run from 0 to varNumCols – 1.

Nothing is done with the Fields objects in this example, but in an actual application, the developer could reference objField.Name to get the name of a column and objField.Value to obtain its value. (Note in VBScript, an apostrophe starts a comment line.)

Errors Collection

Whenever an error occurs, ADO instantiates an Errors collection. It must be a collection because more than one error can be generated by a single ADO statement. This collection can be processed in a manner similar to that for the Fields collection:

```
Dim varI, varErrorCount, objError

On Error Resume Next

varErrorCount = objConn.Errors.Count

If varErrorCount > 0 Then

    For varI = 0 to varErrorCount – 1

        Set objError = objConn.Errors(varI)

        ' objError.Description contains

        ' a description of the error

    Next

End If
```

In the loop, objError is set to objConn.Errors(varI). Note that this collection belongs to objConn, not to objRecordSet. Also, the Description property of objError can be used to display the error to the user.

Unfortunately, VBScript has quite limited error processing. The code for checking errors (starting with On Error Resume Next) must be placed after every ADO object statement that might cause an error. Because this can bulk up the code, it would be better to write an error-handling function and call it after every ADO object invocation.

Command Object

The ADO Command object is used to execute queries and stored procedures that are stored with the database. The parameters collection of Command is used to pass parameters. For example, suppose that the database opened by objConn has a stored procedure called FindArtist that accepts one parameter, which is the nationality of artists to be retrieved. The following code invokes this stored procedure with the parameter value "Spanish" and creates a recordset named objRs that has the results of the stored procedure:

```
Dim objCommand, objParam, objRs

    'Create the Command object, connect it to objConn and set its format

    Set objCommand = Server.CreateObject("ADODB.command")

    Set objCommand.ActiveConnection = objConn

    objCommand.CommandText = "{call FindArtist (?)}"

    'Set up the parameter with the necessary value

    Set objParam = objCommand.CreateParameter ("Nationality",
    adChar, adParamInput, 25)

    objCommand.Parameters.Append objParam

    objParam.Value = "Spanish"

    'Fire the Stored Proc

    Set objRs = objCommand.Execute
```

This example first creates an object of type ADODB.command and then sets the connection of that object to objConn. It then declares the format of the call to the stored procedure by setting the CommandText property. This property is used to pass the name of the stored procedure and the number of parameters it has. The question mark denotes a parameter. If there were three parameters, command text would be set to "{call FindArtist (?, ?, ?)}".

Next, an object is created for the parameter. The values adChar and adParamInput are from ADOVBS and indicate that the parameter is of type char and is used as input to the stored procedure. The maximum length of the parameter value is 25. After the parameter has been created, it must be added to the command with the Append method. Finally, the stored procedure is invoked using the Execute method. At this point, a recordset named objRs has been created with the results from the stored procedure.

ADO Examples

The following five examples show how to invoke ADO from VBScript using Active Server Pages. These examples focus on the use of ADO and not on the graphics, presentation, or workflow. If you want a flashy, better-behaving application, you should be able to modify these examples to obtain that result. Here, just learn how ADO is used.

All of these examples process the View Ridge database. In some of them, we connect to ViewRidgeSS, the SQL Server database. In others, we connect to the Oracle database ViewRidgeOracle2. In fact, in the last example, only one statement needs to be changed to switch from SQL Server to Oracle! That is amazing, and exactly what the originators of ODBC hoped for when they created the ODBC specification.

The ASP processor maintains the transaction state. For each transaction, it keeps a set of session variables. In these examples, we will use session variables to preserve connection objects. The following statement creates a session variable named "abc" and gives it the string value "Wowzers":

Set Session("abc") = "Wowzers"

More useful examples follow.

To run any of these pages, open your browser and enter the following URL if you are running on the same computer as is IIS: ***http://localhost/ADOExamples/artist.asp***. Otherwise, type the name or address of your server instead of "localhost."

Example 1—Reading a Table

Figure 12-16 shows an ASP that displays the contents of the ARTIST table. In this and the next several figures, statements included within <% . . . %> are shown in red ink. Any code that will be passed to the browser—here, primarily HTML—is shown in blue ink. Any other statements are shown in gray.

The top of the page is standard HTML. The first section of the server code creates a Connection object and then a RecordSet object that has the results of the SQL statement:

SELECT   **Name, Nationality**

FROM   **ARTIST**

Because Connection objects are expensive—both in terms of time to create them and memory used—this code preserves the connection object in the session variable _conn. The first time a user invokes this page, the connection object will not exist. In this case, the function call IsObject(Session("_conn")) will return false because _conn has not been set. The code after the Else will be executed to create the connection object. Next, the variable varSQL is set to a string that has the SELECT statement, and then the recordset is opened using that SELECT statement.

The next section of the ASP contains HTML for the browser. It is followed by several snippets of server script code intermixed with HTML. The statement On Error Resume Next overrides the ASP script engine's error processing to continue the script. A better page would process the errors instead.

Figure 12-16	Artist.asp

```
<HTML>
<HEAD>
<META HTTP-EQUIV="Content-Type" CONTENT="text/html;charset=windows-1252">
<TITLE>Artist</TITLE>
</HEAD>
<!--#include virtual="ADOExamples/adovbs.inc"-->
<BODY>
<%
Dim objConn, objRecordSet, varSql

        If IsObject(Session("_conn")) Then ' if already have a connection, use it
            Set objConn = Session("_conn")
        Else
            Set objConn = Server.CreateObject("ADODB.connection") ' get connection
            objConn.open "ViewRidgeSS"  ' open VRG database using operating system authentication
            objConn.IsolationLevel = adXactReadCommitted ' avoid dirty reads
            Set Session("_conn") = objConn
        End If

        Set objRecordSet = Server.CreateObject("ADODB.Recordset") ' create the record set object

        varSql = "SELECT Name, Nationality FROM ARTIST" ' set up SQL command
        objRecordSet.Open varSql, objConn, adOpenStatic, adLockReadOnly ' static with no need to update
%>

<TABLE BORDER=1 BGCOLOR=#ffffff CELLSPACING=5><FONT FACE="Arial" COLOR=#000000><CAPTION><B>ARTIST
</B></CAPTION></FONT>
<THEAD>
<TR>
<TH BGCOLOR=#c0c0c0 BORDERCOLOR=#000000 ><FONT SIZE=2 FACE="Arial" COLOR=#000000>Name</FONT></TH>
<TH BGCOLOR=#c0c0c0 BORDERCOLOR=#000000 ><FONT SIZE=2 FACE="Arial" COLOR=#000000>Nationality</FONT>
</TH>

</TR>
</THEAD>
<TBODY>
<%
On Error Resume Next
objRecordSet.MoveFirst
do while Not objRecordSet.eof
 %>
<TR VALIGN=TOP>
<TD BORDERCOLOR=#c0c0c0 ><FONT SIZE=2 FACE="Arial" COLOR=#000000><%=Server.HTMLEncode(objRecordSet
("Name"))%><BR></FONT></TD>
<TD BORDERCOLOR=#c0c0c0 ><FONT SIZE=2 FACE="Arial" COLOR=#000000><%=Server.HTMLEncode(objRecordSet
("Nationality"))%><BR></FONT></TD>

</TR>
<%
objRecordSet.MoveNext
loop%>
</TBODY>
<TFOOT></TFOOT>
</TABLE>
</BODY>
</HTML>
```

The last part of the page simply produces the HTML and fills in read values. The objRecordSet.MoveFirst . . . MoveNext loop is the logic for standard sequential processing of a file.

The result of this ASP is shown in Figure 12-17. There is nothing spectacular about this page or about this ASP file, except the following: If this were on the Internet, any of more than 250 million people worldwide would be able to view it! They would require no other software than what is already on their computer.

Figure 12-17

Result of Artist.asp from Figure 12-16

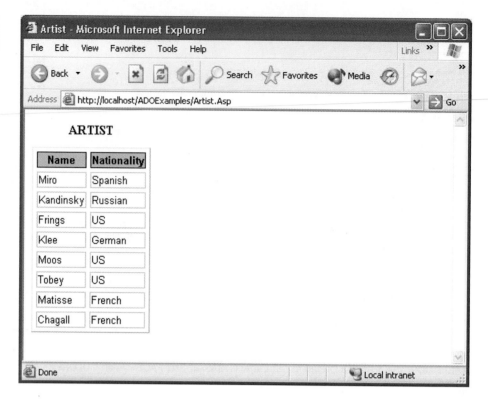

Example 2—Reading a Table in a Generalized Fashion

The first example made minimal use of the ADO objects in the object model. We can extend this example by using the Fields collection. Suppose that we want to take the name of a table as input and display all of the columns in it except the surrogate key.

The ASP shown in Figure 12-18 accomplishes this task, except that the name of the table is set in the variable varTableName. We will expand this in the next example, which shows how to obtain the table name from an HTML form.

The first part of the server script has the same function as that shown in Figure 12-16. The only difference is that it opens the Oracle data source with name ViewRidgeOracle2.

The varSql variable is set using the varTableName variable. The & operator concatenates two strings together. The result of this expression is the following string:

SELECT * FROM CUSTOMER

Note, too, that the table name is included in the HTML table caption with the code <CAPTION><B><%=varTableName%><B></CAPTION>. The code inside the % will cause the value of varTableName to be placed in HTML for the caption.

The next set of server script statements processes the Fields collection. The variable varNumCols is set to the count property of the Fields collection and then the collection is iterated in the loop. Observe that HTML is interspersed in the server code (or server code is interspersed in the HTML, depending on your point of view). Previously, varKeyName has been set to the name of the surrogate key, so this loop checks to determine that the name of the current field object is not the name of the surrogate key. If not, HTML is generated to create the table header. A similar loop is used on the next page to populate the table with values from the recordset.

The advantage of this page is that it can process any table, not just a particular one. In fact, using terminology developed earlier, we can say the page in Figure 12-18 is an abstraction of that in Figure 12-16. The results of this page are shown in Figure 12-19. The CUSTOMERID column is not displayed, as we expected.

| Figure 12-18 | CustomerOracle.asp |

```
<HTML>
<HEAD>
<META HTTP-EQUIV="Content-Type" CONTENT="text/html;charset=windows-1252">
<TITLE>Table Display Page</TITLE></HEAD>
<BODY>
<!--#include virtual="ADOExamples/adovbs.inc"-->
<%
          Dim objConn, objRecordSet, objField
          Dim varNumCols, varI, varSql
          Dim varTableName, varKeyName

          varTablename = "CUSTOMER"
          varKeyName = "CUSTOMERID"

          If IsObject(Session("_conn")) Then ' if already have a connection, use it
                    Set objConn = Session("_conn")
          Else
                    Set objConn = Server.CreateObject("ADODB.connection") ' get connection

                    ' open Oracle ODBC file using account DK1 with password
                    objConn.open "DSN=ViewRidgeOracle2;UID=DK1;PWD=Sesame"
                    objConn.IsolationLevel = adXactReadCommitted ' avoid dirty reads
                    Set Session("_conn") = objConn
          End If

          Set objRecordSet = Server.CreateObject("ADODB.Recordset")

          varSQL = "SELECT * FROM " & varTableName
          objRecordSet.Open varSql, objConn     ' cursor type and lock type not supported by Oracle
%>
<TABLE BORDER=1 BGCOLOR=#ffffff CELLSPACING=5><FONT FACE="Arial" COLOR=#000000>
<CAPTION><B><%=varTableName%> (in Oracle database)</B></CAPTION></FONT>
<THEAD><TR>
<%
varNumCols = objRecordSet.Fields.Count
For varI = 0 to varNumCols - 1
Set objField = objRecordSet.Fields(varI)
If objField.Name <> varKeyName Then   ' omit surrogate key %>
<TH BGCOLOR=#c0c0c0 BORDERCOLOR=#000000 ><FONT SIZE=2 FACE="Arial" COLOR=#000000><%=objField.Name%>
</FONT> </TH>
<%
End If
Next%>
</TR></THEAD>
<TBODY>
<%
On Error Resume Next
objRecordSet.MoveFirst
do while Not objRecordSet.eof
%>
<TR VALIGN=TOP>
<%
varNumCols = objRecordSet.Fields.Count
For varI = 0 to varNumCols - 1
Set objField = objRecordSet.Fields(varI)
If objField.Name <> varKeyName Then   ' omit surrogate key%>
<TD BORDERCOLOR=#c0c0c0 ><FONT SIZE=2 FACE="Arial" COLOR=#000000><%=Server.HTMLEncode
(objField.Value)%><BR></FONT></TD>
<%
End If
Next%>
</TR>
<%
</FONT></TD>
<%
End If
Next %>
</TR>
<%
objRecordSet.MoveNext
loop%>
</TBODY>
</TABLE>
</BODY>
</HTML>
```

**Result of
CustomerOracle.asp**

Table Display Page - Microsoft Internet Explorer

File   Edit   View   Favorites   Tools   Help

Back · · Search Favorites Media

Address http://localhost/ADOExamples/CustomerOracle.asp

CUSTOMER (in Oracle database)

NAME	STREET	CITY	STATE	ZIPPOSTALCODE	COUNTRY	AREACODE	PHONENUMBER	EMAIL
Jeffrey Janes	123 W. Elm St	Renton	WA	98123	USA	206	555-1345	Customer1000@somewhere.com
David Smith	813 Tumbleweed Lane	Loveland	CO	80345	USA	303	555-5434	Customer1001@somewhere.com
Tiffany Twilight	88 - First Avenue	Langley	WA	98114	USA	206	555-1000	Customer1015@somewhere.com
Fred Smathers	10899 - 88th Ave	Bainbridge Island	WA	98108	USA	206	555-1234	Customer1033@somewhere.com
Mary Beth Frederickson	25 South Lafayette	Denver	CO	80210	USA	303	555-1000	Customer1034@somewhere.com
Selma Warning	205 Burnaby	Vancouver	BC	V0N 1B4	Canada	253	555-1234	Customer1036@somewhere.com
Susan Wu	105 Locust Ave	Atlanta	GA	23224	USA	721	555-1234	Customer1037@somewhere.com
Donald G. Gray	55 Bodega Ave	Bodega Bay	CA	92114	USA	705	555-1234	Customer1040@somewhere.com
Lynda Johnson	117 C Street	Washington	DC	11345	USA	703	555-1000	
Chris Wilkens	87 Highland Drive	Olympia	WA	98008	USA	206	555-1234	
Malinda Gliddens						303	555-6687	

Done   Local intranet

Example 3—Reading Any Table

Figure 12-20(a) shows a data entry form in which a customer can type the name of the table to be displayed. (A better design would be to use a drop-down list to display valid choices, but that discussion would take us away from the discussion of ADO.) The user of this form has typed *artist*. Assume now that when the user clicks the Show Table button, the form is to cause a script to be executed on the server that will display the ARTIST table in this same browser session. Also, assume that the surrogate key is not to be displayed. The desired results are shown in Figure 12-20(b).

This processing necessitates two ASP pages. The first, shown in Figure 12-21(a), is an HTML page that contains the FORM tag:

<FORM METHOD = "post" ACTION = "GeneralTable.asp">

This tag defines a form section on the page; the section will be set up to contain data entry values. This form has only one: the table name. The post METHOD refers to an HTML process that causes the data in the form (here, the table name *artist*) to be delivered to the ASP server in an object called Form. An alternative method is *get,* which would cause the data values to be delivered via parameters. This distinction is not too important to us here. The second parameter of the FORM tag is ACTION, which is set to GeneralTable.asp. This parameter tells IIS that when it receives the response from this form, it should pass the ASP file GeneralTable.asp to the ASP processor. The values from the form will be passed in an object called Form.

The rest of the page is standard HTML. Note that the name of the text input box is text1. Figure 12-21(b) shows GeneralTable.asp, the page that will be invoked when the response is received from the form page in Figure 12-21(a). The first executable script statement is:

varTableName = Request.Form("text1")

Figure 12-20

Displaying Any Table
(a) Entering the Name of
the Table to Display and
(b) Display of the Artist
Table

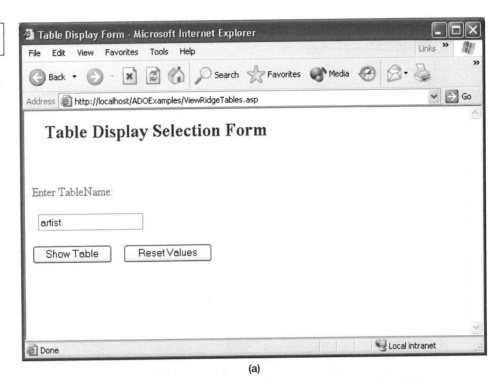

(a)

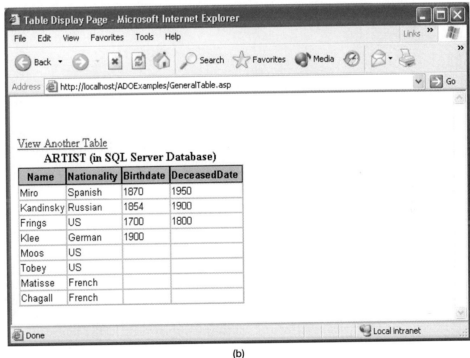

(b)

Request.Form is the name of the object that contains the values sent back from the browser. In this case, text1 will be set to *artist.*

This version of GeneralTable processes the SQL Server View Ridge database. The surrogate key names in SQL Server are in the form ArtistID, not ARTISTID. Because VBScript comparisons are case sensitive, we need to ensure that varKeyName has the surrogate key name in the required format. The user might enter *ARTIST, artist, Artist,* or *aRtIsT,* for that matter; so we cannot just append *ID* to the input table name.

Figure 12-21   **Pages to Display Any Table**
(a) ViewRidge Tables.asp and (b) GeneralTable.asp

```
<HTML>
<HEAD>
<META HTTP-EQUIV="Content-Type" CONTENT="text/html;charset=windows-1252">
<TITLE>Table Display Form</TITLE>
</HEAD>
<BODY>

<FORM METHOD="post" ACTION="GeneralTable.asp">

 <P><STRONG><FONT color=purple face="" size=5>   Table Display Selection Form</FONT>
</STRONG>
<P></P>
<P> </P>

<P><FONT style="BACKGROUND-COLOR: #ffffff"><FONT color=forestgreen face=""
style="BACKGROUND-COLOR: #ffffff">Enter
TableName:</FONT>     </FONT></P>

<P></P>

<P><FONT style="BACKGROUND-COLOR: #ffffff"></FONT> 
<INPUT id=text1 name=text1 size="20"></P>

<P><FONT style="BACKGROUND-COLOR: #ffffff">
<INPUT id=submit1 name=submit1 type=submit value="Show Table" >   
<INPUT id=reset1 name=reset1 type=reset value="Reset Values"></FONT></P>
</FORM>
</BODY>
</HTML>
```

(a)

The three statements starting with varKeyNameFirst employ the UCase and LCase functions to set varKeyName correctly.

The remainder of this page is the same as the CustomerOracle.asp page shown in Figure 12-18. Note again that varKeyName will be set to ArtistID, which is the name of the surrogate key column that we do not wish to display.

Example 4—Updating a Table

The three previous examples just read data. This next example shows how to update table data by adding a row with ADO. Figure 12-22(a) shows a data entry form that will capture artist name and nationality and create a new row. This form is similar to ViewRidgeTables.asp; it has two data entry fields rather than one. When the user clicks Save New Artist, the artist is added to the database; and if the results are successful, the form in Figure 12-22(b) is produced. The See New List reference will invoke Artist.asp, which will display the ARTIST table with the new row, as shown in Figure 12-22(c).

The two ASPs are shown in Figure 12-23. The first page is a data entry form with two fields, one for artist name (named *Name*) and a second for artist nationality (named *Nation*). When the user clicks the Submit button, these data are to be sent back to IIS, which in turn sends it along with the page AddArtist.asp to the ASP processor.

AddArtist.asp, which is shown in Figure 12-23(b), obtains Connection and RecordSet objects. No attempt here is made to save Connection and RecordSet object pointers in session variables. (The assumption is that only one artist will be added per session and saving them would be unnecessary.) If desired, code to save them could certainly be added as shown in the previous examples.

Figure 12-21   **Continued**

```
<HTML>
<HEAD>
<META HTTP-EQUIV="Content-Type" CONTENT="text/html;charset=windows-1252">
<TITLE>Table Display Page</TITLE>
</HEAD>
<BODY>
<!--#include virtual="ADOExamples/adovbs.inc"-->
<%

Dim objConn, objRecordSet, objField
Dim varNumCols, varI, varSql
Dim varTableName, varRecordSetName, varKeyName
Dim varTableNameFirst, varTableNameRest

varTablename = Request.Form("text1")

' set key name to upper first initial and lower remainder with ID, e.g., CustomerID
varTableNameFirst = UCase(Left(varTableName, 1))
varTableNameRest = LCase(Right(varTableName, Len(varTableName)-1))
varKeyName = varTableNameFirst & varTableNameRest &"ID"

varRecordSetName = "_rs_" & varTableName ' use for saving recordset object pointer

If IsObject(Session("_conn")) Then
          Set objConn = Session("_conn")
Else
          Set objConn = Server.CreateObject("ADODB.connection")
          objConn.IsolationLevel = adXactReadCommitted ' avoid dirty reads
          objConn.open "ViewRidgeSS" ' use operating system security
          Set Session("_conn") = objConn
End If

If IsObject(Session(varRecordSetName)) Then
          Set objRecordSet = Session(varRecordSetName) ' used saved recordset object if possible
          objRecordSet.Requery
Else
          varSql = "SELECT * FROM " & "[" & varTableName & "]" ' put brackets in case table name has spaces, etc.
          Set objRecordSet = Server.CreateObject("ADODB.Recordset")
          ' in the next statement, note use of cursor and lock types
          objRecordSet.Open varSql, objConn ', adOpenDynamic ',   adLockOptimistic ' allow for updates
          Set Session(varRecordSetName) = objRecordSet
End If
%>
<TABLE BORDER=1 BGCOLOR=#ffffff CELLSPACING=0><FONT FACE="Arial" COLOR=#000000>
<CAPTION><B><%=UCase(varTableName)%> (in SQL Server Database)</B></CAPTION></FONT>
<THEAD><TR>
<%
varNumCols = objRecordSet.Fields.Count
For varI = 0 to varNumCols - 1
Set objField = objRecordSet.Fields(varI)
If objField.Name <> varKeyName Then %>
<TH BGCOLOR=#c0c0c0 BORDERCOLOR=#000000 ><FONT SIZE=2 FACE="Arial" COLOR=#000000><%=objField.Name%>
</FONT> </TH>
<%
End If
Next%>
</TR></THEAD>
<TBODY>
<%
On Error Resume Next
objRecordSet.MoveFirst
do while Not objRecordSet.eof
%>
<TR VALIGN=TOP>
<%
varNumCols = objRecordSet.Fields.Count
For varI = 0 to varNumCols - 1
Set objField = objRecordSet.Fields(varI)
If objField.Name <> varKeyName Then %>
<TD BORDERCOLOR=#c0c0c0 ><FONT SIZE=2 FACE="Arial" COLOR=#000000><%=Server.HTMLEncode(objField.Value)%><BR></FONT></TD>
<%
End If
Next%>
</TR>

<%
objRecordSet.MoveNext
loop%>
<BR><BR><A HREF="ViewRidgeTables.asp">View Another Table</A>
</TBODY></TABLE>
</BODY>
</HTML>
```

(b)

Figure 12-22

Entering a New Artist
(a) Form to Enter Artist
Data; (b) Results of
Add Operation; and
(c) Display of New
Artist Table

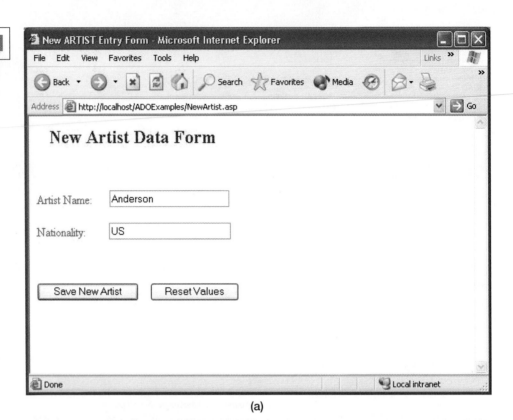

(a)

(b)

Figure 12-22

Continued

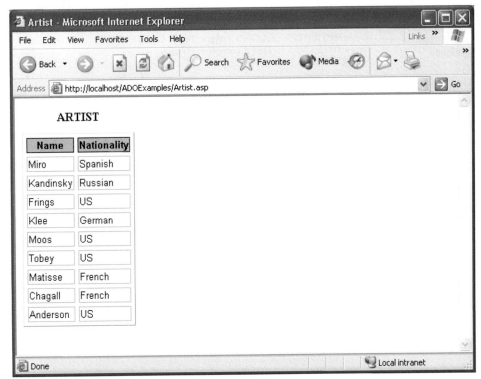

(c)

Figure 12-23

Pages to Enter New Artist Data

(a) NewArtist.asp and (b) AddArtist.asp

```html
<HTML>
<HEAD>
<META HTTP-EQUIV="Content-Type" CONTENT="text/html;charset=windows-1252">
<TITLE>New ARTIST Entry Form</TITLE>
</HEAD>
<BODY>

<FORM METHOD="post" ACTION="AddArtist.ASP">

 <P><STRONG><FONT color=purple face="" size=5>   New Artist Data Form</FONT></STRONG>
<P></P>
<P> </P>

<P><FONT style="BACKGROUND-COLOR: #ffffff"><FONT color=forestgreen face=""
style="BACKGROUND-COLOR: #ffffff">Artist Name:</FONT>     
<INPUT id=text1 name=Name style="HEIGHT: 22px; WIDTH: 164px" size="20"></FONT></P>

<P><FONT color=forestgreen face=""
style="BACKGROUND-COLOR: #ffffff">Nationality:       
<INPUT id=text2 name=Nation style="HEIGHT: 22px; WIDTH: 167px" size="20"></FONT></P>

<P> </P>

<P><FONT style="BACKGROUND-COLOR: #ffffff">
<INPUT id=submit1 name=submit1 type=submit value="Save New Artist">   
<INPUT id=reset1 name=reset1 type=reset value="Reset Values"></FONT></P>
</FORM>
</BODY>
</HTML>
```

(a)

(continued)

Figure 12-23

Continued

```
<HTML>
<HEAD>
<META HTTP-EQUIV="Content-Type" CONTENT="text/html;charset=windows-1252">
<TITLE>Add ARTIST Example</TITLE>
</HEAD>
<BODY>
<!--#include virtual="ADOExamples/adovbs.inc"-->
<%

Dim objConn, objRecordSet, objField
Dim varNumCols, varl, varSql

Set objConn = Server.CreateObject("ADODB.connection")
objConn.open "ViewRidgeSS" ' open with operating system security
objConn.IsolationLevel = adXactReadCommitted ' avoid dirty reads

varSql = "SELECT * FROM [ARTIST]"
Set objRecordSet = Server.CreateObject("ADODB.Recordset")
' in the next statement, note use of cursor and lock types
objRecordSet.Open varSql, objConn, adOpenDynamic, adLockOptimistic

objRecordSet.AddNew
objRecordSet("Name")= Request.Form("Name")
objRecordSet("Nationality")= Request.Form("Nation")
objRecordSet.Update

On Error Resume Next
varErrorCount = objConn.Errors.Count
If varErrorCount > 0 Then
        For varl = 0 to varErrorCount - 1
                Response.Write "<BR><I>" & objConn.Errors(varl).Description & "</I><BR>"
        Next
End If

objRecordSet.Close
objConn.Close

Response.Write "<BR>Data has been added.  Thank you!<BR>"
Response.Write "<A HREF="& """" &"artist.asp" & """"& ">See New List</A>"

%>
<BR><BR>
</BODY>
</HTML>
```

(b)

The key difference of this page is shown in the following statements:

objRecordSet.AddNew

objRecordSet("Name") = Request.Form("Name")

objRecordSet("Nationality") = Request.Form("Nation")

objRecordSet.Update

The first statement obtains a new row in the objRecordSet object and then values are obtained for the Name and Nationality columns from the Request.Form object. Note that the column names and the Request.Form names do not have to be the same. Here, the second column name is Nationality, but the second value from the form is Nation. The objRecordSet.Update call causes the database update. Note the error-processing code that will cause error messages to be displayed via the Response.Write statement (this is a method available in the Response object of ASP). The page ends with two calls to send a confirmation message back to the user and to create a URL to Artist.asp if the user wants to see the table with the new values.

Example 5—Invoking a Stored Procedure

We created a stored procedure named Customer_Insert in both the Oracle and SQL Server databases (in Chapters 10 and 11, respectively). In both cases, the stored procedure accepts a new customer name, area code, local number, and nationality of all artists in whom the customer is interested. It then creates a new row in CUSTOMER and adds appropriate rows to the intersection table.

To invoke the stored procedure using an ASP page, we create a Web page to collect the necessary data, as shown in Figure 12-24(a). Now, when the user clicks Add Customer, we want to invoke an ASP that calls the stored procedure with the form data. So the user can verify that the new data have been entered correctly, the ASP then queries a view that joins customer names with artist names and nationalities. The result is shown in Figure 12-24(b).

Figure 12-25(a) shows the code to generate the data-gathering form. The parameter fields are named *text1* through *text4*. The form invokes the ASPCustomerInsertOracle in the FORM METHOD statement, so when the user clicks Add Customer, the data will be sent to CustomerInsertOracle, the page shown in Figure 12-25(b).

This page looks for a saved connection, and if one is not found, it obtains a new one, as shown earlier. Then, it creates a command object, *objCommand,* and associates it with objConn. It then sets up the call to the Customer_Insert stored procedure with CommandText = "{call Customer_Insert(?, ?, ?, ?)}". This pattern indicates that four parameters will be passed. The next sections of code create the parameters and append them to the Command object. Finally, the command is executed, which causes the stored procedure to be invoked. No transaction isolation level or cursor properties are set because the stored procedure will set them for itself.

After the command is executed, a RecordSet is created on a select of all columns of the view CUSTOMERINTERESTS, and finally the columns are displayed in the browser using the techniques shown in earlier examples.

Figure 12-24

Adding a New Customer via a Stored Procedure

(a) Customer Data Entry Form and (b) Display of Customer Interests View

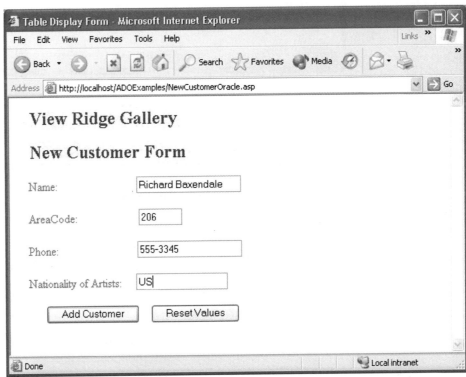

(a)

Continued

Customer Update Display Page - Microsoft Internet Explorer

File   Edit   View   Favorites   Tools   Help   Links »

Back   •   ⊗ ⊠ ☆   Search   Favorites   Media   ⊗ ⊗ • ⊜

Address http://localhost/ADOExamples/CustomerInsertOracle.ASP   Go

Customers and Interests After Update

Customer	Artist
Chris Wilkens	Frings
Chris Wilkens	Tobey
Donald G. Gray	Tobey
Fred Smathers	Tobey
Jeffrey Janes	Tobey
Lynda Johnson	Frings
Lynda Johnson	Moos
Lynda Johnson	Tobey
Malinda Gliddens	Chagall
Mary Beth Frederickson	Frings
Mary Beth Frederickson	Tobey
Mary Beth Frederickson	Moos
Michael Bench	Tobey
Michael Bench	Moos
Michael Bench	Frings
Richard Baxendale	Frings
Richard Baxendale	Anderson
Richard Baxendale	Moos
Richard Baxendale	Tobey
Selma Warning	Tobey
Selma Warning	Miro

Done   Local intranet

(b)

In both the Oracle and SQL Server databases, this view was defined as the join of CUSTOMER and ARTIST over the intersection table. The syntax used for Oracle was

CREATE VIEW CUSTOMERINTERESTS AS

   SELECT CUSTOMER.NAME CUSTNAME, ARTIST.NAME

      ARTISTNAME, ARTIST.NATIONALITY

   FROM CUSTOMER, CUSTOMER_ARTIST_INT, ARTIST

   WHERE CUSTOMER.CUSTOMERID = CUSTOMER_ARTIST_

      INT.CUSTOMERID AND

      ARTIST.ARTISTID = CUSTOMER_ARTIST_INT.ARTISTID

Figure 12-25(b) shows the advantage of working with abstractions. The only difference between the Oracle version shown here and the SQL Server version is the name of the

Figure 12-25

Pages to Invoke Stored Procedure

(a) NewCustomerOracle.asp and (b) CustomerInsertOracle.asp

```
<HTML>
<HEAD>
<META HTTP-EQUIV="Content-Type" CONTENT="text/html;charset=windows-1252">
<TITLE>Table Display Form</TITLE>
</HEAD>
<BODY>

<FORM METHOD="post" ACTION="CustomerInsertOracle.ASP">

 <P><STRONG><FONT color=purple face="" size=5>   View Ridge Gallery</FONT></STRONG>

 <P>   <strong><font color="purple" face size="5"> New Customer Form</font></strong>
<P><font style="background-color: #ffffff" color="forestgreen" face>   
 Name:   </font><FONT style="BACKGROUND-COLOR: #ffffff">     
               
  
 </FONT><INPUT id=text1 name=text1 size="20"></P>

 <P> <font style="background-color: #ffffff" color="forestgreen" face>   AreaCode
<font style="background-color: #ffffff">:   </font>     
           
 </font><INPUT id=text2 name=text2 size="6"></P>

 <P><font style="background-color: #ffffff" color="forestgreen" face>   
 Phone:              
          
 </font><INPUT id=text3 name=text3 size="20">       </P>

 <P>    <font style="background-color: #ffffff" color="forestgreen" face>Nationality
 of Artists:  </font>   <INPUT id=text4 name=text4 size="17"></P>

 <P> <FONT style="BACKGROUND-COLOR: #ffffff">
   </FONT>     <FONT style="BACKGROUND-COLOR: #ffffff">
<INPUT id=submit1 name=submit1 type=submit value="Add Customer" >   
<INPUT id=reset1 name=reset1 type=reset value="Reset Values"></FONT></P>

</FORM>
</BODY>
</HTML>
```

(a)

ODBC data source and the account name and password used. Note the comment line under the objConn.open statement. We can switch from the Oracle database to the SQL Server database by commenting out the Oracle DSN line and uncommenting the SQL Server DSN line. All of the idiosyncrasies of the DBMS products are hidden from the creator of this ASP, and he or she need know nothing about them.

These examples give you an idea of the use of ADO. The best way to learn more is to write some pages yourself. This chapter has shown all the basic techniques that you will need. You've worked hard to get to this point, and if you are able to understand enough to create some of your own pages, you have come very far indeed since Chapter 1!

☺ SUMMARY

Today, database applications reside in rich and complicated environments. In addition to relational databases, there are nonrelational databases, VSAM and other file-processing data, email, and other types of data. To ease the job of the application programmer, various standards have been developed. The ODBC standard is for

Figure 12-25   Continued

```
<HTML>
<HEAD>
<META HTTP-EQUIV="Content-Type" CONTENT="text/html;charset=windows-1252">
<TITLE>Customer Update Display Page</TITLE>
</HEAD>
<BODY>

<P><STRONG><FONT color=purple face="" size=5>   Customers and Interests After Update</FONT></STRONG>
<!--#include virtual="ADOExamples/adovbs.inc"-->
<%

        Dim objConn, objCommand, objParam, oRs
        Dim objRecordSet, objField
        Dim varI, varSql, varNumCols, varValue

        If IsObject(Session("_conn")) Then
                Set objConn = Session("_conn") ' use current session if available
        Else
                Set objConn = Server.CreateObject("ADODB.connection")
                ' stored procedure will set its own isolation level
                objConn.open "DSN=ViewRidgeOracle2;UID=DK1;PWD=Sesame"
                'objConn.open "ViewRidgeSS",  could use this to update via SQL Server
                Set Session("_conn") = objConn
        End If

        Set objCommand = Server.CreateObject("ADODB.Command") ' create a command object
        Set objCommand.ActiveConnection = objConn ' set the command objects connection

        objCommand.CommandText="{call Customer_Insert (?, ?, ?, ?)}" ' setup call to stored procedure

        ' Set up four parameters with necessary values
        Set objParam = objCommand.CreateParameter("NewName", adChar, adParamInput, 50)
        objCommand.Parameters.Append objParam
        objParam.Value = Request.Form("text1")

        Set objParam = objCommand.CreateParameter("AreaCode", adChar, adParamInput, 5)
        objCommand.Parameters.Append objParam
        objParam.Value = Request.Form("text2")

        Set objParam = objCommand.CreateParameter("PhoneNumber", adChar, adParamInput, 8)
        objCommand.Parameters.Append objParam
        objParam.Value = Request.Form("text3")

        Set objParam = objCommand.CreateParameter("Nationality", adChar, adParamInput, 25)
        objCommand.Parameters.Append objParam
        objParam.Value = Request.Form("text4")

' Fire the Stored Proc

        Set oRs = objCommand.Execute

        ' now read the data from a view having both CUSTOMER and ARTIST
        varSql = "SELECT * FROM CUSTOMERINTERESTS ORDER BY CUSTOMER" ' use that joins via the intersection table
        Set objRecordSet = Server.CreateObject("ADODB.Recordset")
        objRecordSet.Open varSql, objConn

%>
<TABLE BORDER=1 BGCOLOR=#ffffff CELLSPACING=5><FONT FACE="Arial" COLOR=#000000><CAPTION><B>
<CUSTOMERS AND INTERESTS</B></CAPTION></FONT>
<THEAD>
<TR>
<%
varNumCols = objRecordSet.Fields.Count
For varI = 0 to varNumCols - 1
Set objField = objRecordSet.Fields(varI)
%>
<TH BGCOLOR=#c0c0c0 BORDERCOLOR=#000000 ><FONT SIZE=2 FACE="Arial" COLOR=#000000><%=objField.Name%>
</FONT> </TH>
```

(b)

| Figure 12-25 | **Continued** |

```
<%
Next%>
</TR>
</THEAD>
<TBODY>
<%
On Error Resume Next
objRecordSet.MoveFirst
do while Not objRecordSet.eof
%>
<TR VALIGN=TOP>
<%
varNumCols = objRecordSet.Fields.Count
For varl = 0 to varNumCols - 1
Set objField = objRecordSet.Fields(varl)
If objRecordSet.Fields(varl).Type = adNumeric then
        varValue=CDbl(objField.Value)
        varValue = convert(char, varValue)
else
        varValue=Server.HTMLEncode(objField.Value)
End If
%>
<TD BORDERCOLOR=#c0c0c0 ><FONT SIZE=2 FACE="Arial" COLOR=#000000><%=(varValue)%><BR></FONT></TD>
<%
varValue=""
Next%>
</TR>

<%
objRecordSet.MoveNext
loop%>
</TBODY>
<TFOOT></TFOOT>
</TABLE>
</BODY>
</HTML>
```

(b) *continued*

relational databases; the OLE DB standard is for relational databases and other data sources. ADO was developed to provide easier access to OLE DB data for the non-object-oriented programmer.

ODBC, or the Open Database Connectivity standard, provides an interface by which database applications can access and process relational data sources in a DBMS-independent manner. ODBC was developed by an industry committee and has been implemented by Microsoft and many other vendors. ODBC consists of an applications program, a driver manager, DBMS drivers, and data source components. Single-tier and multiple-tier drivers are defined. The three data source names are file, system, and user. System data sources are recommended for Web servers. The process of defining a system data source name involves specifying the type of driver and the identity of the database to be processed.

OLE DB is one of the foundations of the Microsoft data access world. It implements the Microsoft OLE and COM standards, and is accessible to object-oriented programs through those interfaces. OLE DB breaks the features and functions of a DBMS into objects, thus making it easier for vendors to implement portions of functionality. Key object terms are *abstraction, methods, properties,* and *collections.* A rowset is an abstraction of a recordset, which in turn is an abstraction of a relation. Objects are defined by properties that specify their characteristics and by methods, which are the actions they can perform. A collection is an object that contains a group of other objects. The goals of OLE DB are listed in Figure 12-10. An interface is a set of objects and the properties and methods they expose in that interface. Objects may expose different properties and methods in different interfaces. An implementation is how an object accomplishes its tasks. Implementations are hidden from the outside world and may be changed without impacting the users of the objects. An interface ought not to be changed, ever.

Tabular data providers present data in the form of rowsets. Service providers transform data into another form; such providers are both consumers and providers of data. A rowset is equivalent to a cursor. Basic rowset interfaces are IRowSet, IAccessor, and IColumnsInfo. Other interfaces are defined for more advanced capabilities.

ADO is a simple object model used by OLE DB data consumers. It can be used from any language supported by Microsoft. The ADO object model has Connection, RecordSet, Command, and Errors collection objects. RecordSets have a Fields collection, and Commands have a Parameters collection.

A Connection object establishes a connection to a data provider and a data source. Connections have an isolation level. Once a connection is created, it can be used to create RecordSet and Command objects. RecordSet objects represent cursors; they have both CursorType and LockType properties. RecordSets can be created with SQL statements. The Fields collection of a RecordSet can be processed to individually manipulate fields.

The Errors collection contains one or more error messages that result from an ADO operation. The Command object is used to execute stored parameterized queries or stored procedures. Input data can be sent to the correct ASP using the HTML FORM tag. Table updates are made using the RecordSet Update method.

REVIEW QUESTIONS

12.1   Describe why the data environment is complicated.
12.2   Explain how ODBC, OLE DB, and ADO are related.
12.3   Explain the author's justification for describing Microsoft standards. Do you agree?
12.4   Name the components of the ODBC standard.
12.5   What role does the driver manager serve? Who supplies it?
12.6   What role does the DBMS driver serve? Who supplies it?
12.7   What is a single-tier driver?
12.8   What is a multiple-tier driver?
12.9   Do the uses of the term tier in the three-tier architecture and its use in ODBC have anything to do with each other?
12.10   Why are conformance levels important?
12.11   Summarize the three ODBC API conformance levels.
12.12   Summarize the three SQL grammar conformance levels.
12.13   Explain how the three types of data sources differ.
12.14   Which data source type is recommended for Web servers?
12.15   What are the two tasks to be accomplished when setting up an ODBC data source name?
12.16   Why is OLE DB important?
12.17   What disadvantage of ODBC does OLE DB overcome?
12.18   Define abstraction and explain how it relates to OLE DB.
12.19   Give an example of abstraction involving rowset.
12.20   Define object properties and methods.
12.21   What is the difference between an object class and an object?

12.22   Explain the role of data consumers and data providers.

12.23   What is an interface?

12.24   What is the difference between an interface and an implementation?

12.25   Explain why an implementation can be changed but an interface should not be changed.

12.26   Summarize the goals of OLE DB.

12.27   What is MTS? What does it do?

12.28   Explain the difference between a tabular data provider and a service provider. Which transforms OLE DB data into XML documents?

12.29   In the context of OLE DB, what is the difference between a rowset and a cursor?

12.30   What languages can use ADO?

12.31   List the objects in the ADO object model and explain their relationships.

12.32   What is the function of the Connection object?

12.33   Show a snippet of VBScript for creating a Connection object.

12.34   What is the function of the RecordSet object?

12.35   Show a snippet of VBScript for creating a RecordSet object.

12.36   What does the Fields collection contain? Explain a situation in which you would use it.

12.37   Show a snippet of VBScript for processing the Fields collection.

12.38   What does the Errors collection contain? Explain a situation in which you would use it.

12.39   Show a snippet of VBScript for processing the Errors collection.

12.40   What is the purpose of the Command object?

12.41   Show a snippet of VBScript for executing a stored parameterized query that has two parameters: A and B.

12.42   Explain the purpose of the <% and %> tags in ASP.

12.43   Explain the purpose of the _conn variable in Figure 12-16.

12.44   What is the reason for the code that creates varKeyName in Figure 12-21(b).

12.45   Explain the purpose of the ACTION parameter of the FORM tag in Figure 12-21(a).

12.46   Explain what happens when the following statement is executed in the ASP in Figure 12-21(b):

   varTableName = Request.Form("text1")

12.47   Show a VBScript snippet for adding a new record to a recordset named objMyRecordSet. Assume that the fields are A and B and that their values are to be "Avalue" and "Bvalue", respectively.

12.48   What purpose is served by the Response.Write statement?

⊚ PROJECT QUESTIONS

12.49   Microsoft expends much effort to promote the OLE DB and ADO standards. It does not directly receive revenue from these standards. IIS is free with Windows XP and 2000. Microsoft's Web sites have numerous articles to help developers learn more about these standards, and all of the information is free. Why do you think Microsoft does this? What goal is served?

12.50   In the code in Figure 12-23(b), the cursor type is set to dynamic. What effect does this have on the processing of this and the Customer.asp and Artist.asp pages? Explain how you think the isolation level, cursor type, and lock type parameters should be set for an application that involves all three of these pages.

12.51   Explain how to change the example ASP in Figure 12-16 to run with the DSN ViewRidgeOracle2. Explain how to change the ASP in Figure 12-18 to run with

ViewRidgeSS. Although the ease of making these changes is interesting from a technology standpoint, does this capability have any importance in the world of commerce?

12.52 If you have installed Oracle, use your browser to execute the page shown in Figure 12-18. Now, open SQL*Plus and delete two rows of CUSTOMER data using the SQL DELETE command. Go back to your browser and execute the page shown in Figure 12-18 again. Explain the results.

12.53 If you have installed SQL Server, use your browser to execute the page in Figure 12-18. Now, open SQL Query Analyzer and delete two rows of CUSTOMER data using the SQL DELETE command. Go back to your browser and execute the page in Figure 12-18 again. Explain the results. If you answered question 12.52, explain the difference in results you received, if any.

MARCIA'S DRY CLEANING

If you have not already done so, answer questions A through G for Marcia's Dry Cleaning at the end of Chapter 7 (page 262). Use either Oracle or SQL Server to implement your database.

A Add a new column Status to ORDER. Assume that Status can have the values ['Waiting', 'In-process', 'Finished', 'Pending'].

B Create a view called CustomerOrder that has the columns LastName, FirstName, Phone, InvoiceNumber, Date, Total, and Status.

C Create an appropriate ODBC data source for your database.

D Code an ASP to display CustomerOrder. Using your sample database, demonstrate that your page works.

E Code two ASP pages to receive a date value AsOfDate and to display rows of CustomerOrder for orders having Date greater than or equal to AsOfDate. Use the scheme in the ASPs in Figures 12-20 as a pattern. Using your sample database, demonstrate that your pages work.

F Code two ASP pages to receive customer Phone, LastName, and FirstName and to display rows for customers having that Phone, LastName, and FirstName. Using your sample database, demonstrate that your pages work.

G Write a stored procedure that receives values for InvoiceNumber and NewStatus and that sets the value of Status to NewStatus for the row having the given value of InvoiceNumber. Generate an error message if no row has the given value of InvoiceNumber. Using your sample database, demonstrate that your stored procedure works.

H Code an ASP to invoke the stored procedure created in task G. Use Figure 12-25 as an example. Using your sample database, demonstrate that your page works.

MORGAN IMPORTING

If you have not already done so, answer questions A through H for Morgan Importing at the end of Chapter 7 (page 263). Use either Oracle or SQL Server.

A Create a view called StorePurchases that has the columns StoreName, City, Country, Email, Contact, Date, Description, Category, and PriceUSD.

B Create an appropriate ODBC data source for your database.

C Code an ASP to display StorePurchases. Using your sample database, demonstrate that your page works.

D Code two ASP pages to receive a date value AsOfDate and display rows of StorePurchases for purchases having Date greater than or equal to AsOfDate. Use the scheme in the ASPs in Figures 12-20 as a pattern. Using your sample database, demonstrate that your pages work.

E Code two ASP pages to receive values of Country and Category and display rows of StorePurchases having values for input Country and Category values. Using your sample database, demonstrate that your pages work.

F Write a stored procedure that receives values for PurchaseSK and NewPriceUSD and sets the value of PriceUSD to NewPriceUSD for the row having the given value of PurchaseSK. Generate an error message if no row has the given value of PurchaseSK. Using your sample database, demonstrate that your stored procedure works.

G Code an ASP to invoke the stored procedure created in task F. Use Figure 12-25 as an example. Using your sample database, demonstrate that your page works.

XML and ADO.NET

This chapter considers one of the most important, if not *the* most important, developments in information systems technology today. It discusses the confluence of two information technology subject areas: database processing and document processing. For more than 20 years, these two subject areas developed independently of one another. With the advent of the Internet, however, they crashed together in what some industry pundits called a technology train wreck. The result is still being sorted out, with new products, product features, technology standards, and development practices emerging every month.

The Importance of XML

Database processing and document processing need each other. Database processing needs document processing for transmitting database views; document processing needs database processing for storing and manipulating data. However, even though these technologies need each other, it took the popularity of the Internet to make that need obvious. As Web sites evolved, organizations wanted to use Internet technology to display and update data from organizational databases. Web developers began to take a serious interest in SQL, database performance, database security, and other aspects of database processing.

As the Web developers invaded the database community, database practitioners wondered, "Who are these people and what do they want?" Database practitioners began to learn about HTML, the language used to mark up documents for display by Web browsers. At first, the database community scoffed at HTML because of its limitations, but they soon learned that HTML was the output of a more robust document markup language called **SGML, or Standard Generalized Markup Language.** SGML was clearly important, just as important to document processing as the relational model was to database processing. Obviously, this powerful language had some role to play in the display of database data, but what role?

In the early 1990s, the two communities began to meet, and the result of their work is a series of standards that concerns a language called **XML, or Extensible Markup Language.** XML is a subset of SGML, but additional standards and capabilities have been added to XML, and today XML technology is a hybrid of document processing and database processing. In fact, as XML standards evolved, it became clear that the communities had been working on different aspects of the same problem for many years. They even used the same terms, but with different meanings. You will see later in this chapter how the term *schema* is used in XML for a concept that is completely different from the use of *schema* in the database world.

XML provides a standardized yet customizable way to describe the content of documents. As such, it can be used to describe any database view, but in a standardized way. As you will learn, unlike SQL views, XML views are not limited to one multivalued path.

In addition, when used with the XML Schema standard, XML documents can automatically be generated from database data. Further, database data can automatically be extracted from XML documents. Even more, there are standardized ways of defining how document components are mapped to database schema components and vice versa.

Meanwhile, the rest of the computing community began to take notice of XML. **SOAP,** which originally meant **Simple Object Access Protocol,** was defined as an XML-based standard for providing remote procedure calls over the Internet. Initially, SOAP assumed the use of HTTP as a transport mechanism. When Microsoft, IBM, Oracle, and other large companies joined forces in support of the SOAP standard, this assumption was removed, and SOAP was generalized to become a standard protocol for sending messages of any type, using any protocol. With this change, SOAP no longer meant Simple Object Access Protocol, so now SOAP is just a name, and not an acronym.

Today, XML is used for many purposes. One of the most important is its use as a standardized means to define and communicate documents for processing over the Internet. XML plays a key role in Microsoft's .NET initiative; and in 2001 Bill Gates called XML the "*lingua franca* of the Internet age."

We will begin the discussion of XML by describing its use for displaying Web pages. As you will learn, however, XML uses go far beyond Web page display. In fact, Web page display is one of the least important applications of XML. We begin with page display only because it is an easy way to introduce XML documents. After that, we will explain the XML Schema standard and discuss its use for database processing. Finally, we will show examples of the integrated processing of database data and XML using Microsoft ADO.NET.

As you read this chapter, keep in mind that this area is at the leading edge of database processing. Standards, products, and product capabilities are changing frequently. You can keep abreast of these changes by checking the following Web sites: ***www.w3c.org, www.xml.org, msdn.microsoft.com, www.oracle.com, www.ibm.com,*** and other vendor sites. Learning as much as you can about XML and database processing is one of the best ways you can prepare yourself for a successful career in database processing.

XML as a Markup Language

As a markup language, XML is significantly better than HTML in several ways. For one, XML provides a clean separation between document structure, content, and materialization. XML has facilities for dealing with each, and they cannot be confounded, as they are with HTML.

Additionally, XML is standardized, but as its name implies, the standards allow for extension by developers. With XML, you are not limited to a fixed set of elements such as <TITLE>, <h1>, and <P>; you can create your own.

Third, XML eliminates the inconsistent tag use that is possible (and popular) with HTML. For example, consider the following HTML:

<h2>Hello World </h2>

Although the <h2> tag can be used to mark a level two heading in an outline, it can be used for other purposes, too, such as causing "Hello World" to be displayed in a particular font size, weight, and color. Because a tag has potentially many uses, we cannot rely on tags to discern the structure of an HTML page. Tag use is too arbitrary; <h2> may mean a heading or it may mean nothing at all.

As you will see, the structure of an XML document can be formally defined. Tags are defined in relationship to one another. In XML, if we find the tag <street>, we know exactly what data we have, where that data belongs in the document, and how that tag relates to other tags.

XML Document Type Declarations

Figure 13-1 shows a sample XML document. Notice that the document has two sections. The first section defines the structure of the document; it is referred to as the document type declaration, or **DTD.** The second part is the document data.

The DTD begins with the word DOCTYPE and specifies the name of this type of document, which is customer. Then, it specifies the content of the customer document. The customer document consists of two groups: name and address. The name group consists of two elements: firstname and lastname. Firstname and lastname are defined as #PCDATA, which means that they are strings of character data. Next, the address element is defined to have four elements: street, city, state, and zip. Each of these is also defined as character data. The plus sign after street indicates that one value is required and that multiple values are possible.

The data instance of customer shown in Figure 13-1 conforms to the DTD; hence, this document is said to be a **type-valid** XML document. If it did not conform to the DTD, it would be a **not-type-valid** document. Documents that are not-type-valid can still be perfectly good XML; they just do not conform to their type description. For example, if the document in Figure 13-1 had two city elements, it would be valid XML, but it would be not-type-valid.

Although DTDs are almost always desirable, they are not required in XML documents. Documents that have no DTD are by definition not-type-valid, because there is no type to validate them against.

Figure 13-1

**XML Document
with Internal DTD**

```
<?xml version="1.0" encoding="UTF-8"?>
<!-- edited with XML Spy v3.5 NT (http://www.xmlspy.com) by David Kroenke (private) -->
<!DOCTYPE customer [
    <!ELEMENT customer (name, address)>
    <!ELEMENT name (firstname, lastname)>
    <!ELEMENT firstname (#PCDATA)>
    <!ELEMENT lastname (#PCDATA)>
    <!ELEMENT address (street+, city, state, zip)>
    <!ELEMENT street (#PCDATA)>
    <!ELEMENT city (#PCDATA)>
    <!ELEMENT state (#PCDATA)>
    <!ELEMENT zip (#PCDATA)>
]>
<customer>
    <name>
        <firstname>Michelle</firstname>
        <lastname>Correlli</lastname>
    </name>
    <address>
        <street>1824 East 7th Avenue</street>
        <street>Suite 700</street>
        <city>Memphis</city>
        <state>TN</state>
        <zip>32123-7788</zip>
    </address>
</customer>
```

The DTD does not need to be contained inside the document. Figure 13-2 shows a customer document in which the DTD is obtained from the file D:\DBBooks\DB10e\First Draft\Chapter 13\XML Docs\Customer.dtd. In this case, the DTD is located on the computer that stores this document. DTDs can also be referenced by URL Web addresses. The advantage of storing the DTD externally is that many documents can be validated against the same DTD.

The creator of a DTD is free to choose any elements he or she wants. Hence, XML documents can be extended, but in a standardized and controlled way.

Materializing XML Documents with XSLT

The XML document shown in Figure 13-1 shows both the document's structure and content. Nothing in the document, however, indicates how it is to be materialized. The designers of XML created a clean separation among structure, content, and format.

Figure 13-2

**XML Document
with External DTD**

```
<?xml version="1.0" encoding="UTF-8"?>
<!DOCTYPE customer SYSTEM "D:\DB Books\DB 10e\FirstDraft\Chapter 13\XML Docs\customer.dtd">
<customer>
    <name>
        <firstname>Michelle</firstname>
        <lastname>Correlli</lastname>
    </name>
    <address>
        <street>1824 East 7th Avenue</street>
        <street>Suite 700</street>
        <city>Memphis</city>
        <state>TN</state>
        <zip>32123-7788</zip>
    </address>
</customer>
```

The most popular way to materialize XML documents is to use XSLT, or Extensible Style Language: Transformations. XSLT is a powerful and robust transformation language. It can be used to materialize XML documents into HTML, and it can be used for many other purposes as well. One common application of XSLT is to transform an XML document in one format into a second XML document in another format. A company can, for example, use XSLT to transform an XML order document in its own format into an equivalent XML order document in its customer's format. We will be unable to discuss many of the features and functions of XSLT here. See *www.w3.org* for more information.

XSLT is a declarative transformation language. It is declarative because you create a set of rules that govern how the document is to be materialized instead of specifying a procedure for materializing document elements. It is transformational because it transforms the input document into another document.

Figure 13-3(a) shows a DTD for a document that has a list of customers, and Figure 13-3(b) shows an XML document that is type-valid on that DTD. The DOCTYPE statement in Figure 13-3(b) points to a file that contains the DTD shown in Figure 13-3(a).

Figure 13-3

CustomerList DTD and Example Document
(a) CustomerList DTD and (b) Example with Two Customers

```
<?xml version="1.0" encoding="UTF-8"?>
<!-- edited with XML Spy v3.5 NT (http://www.xmlspy.com) by David Kroenke (private) -->
<!ELEMENT customerlist (customer+)>
<!ELEMENT customer (name, address)>
<!ELEMENT name (firstname, lastname)>
<!ELEMENT firstname (#PCDATA)>
<!ELEMENT lastname (#PCDATA)>
<!ELEMENT address (street+, city, state, zip)>
<!ELEMENT street (#PCDATA)>
<!ELEMENT city (#PCDATA)>
<!ELEMENT state (#PCDATA)>
<!ELEMENT zip (#PCDATA)>
```

(a)

```
<?xml version="1.0" encoding="UTF-8"?>
<!-- edited with XML Spy v3.5 NT (http://www.xmlspy.com) by David Kroenke (private) -->
<!DOCTYPE customerlist SYSTEM "D:\DB Books\DB 10e\FirstDraft\Chapter 13\XML Docs\customerlist.dtd">
<?xml-stylesheet type="text/xsl" href="D:\DB Books\DB 10e\FirstDraft\Chapter 13\XML Docs\customerList.xsl"?>
<customerlist>
    <customer>
        <name>
            <firstname>Michelle</firstname>
            <lastname>Correlli</lastname>
        </name>
        <address>
            <street>1824 East 7th Avenue</street>
            <street>Suite 700</street>
            <city>Memphis</city>
            <state>TN</state>
            <zip>32123-7788</zip>
        </address>
    </customer>
    <customer>
        <name>
            <firstname>Lynda</firstname>
            <lastname>Jaynes</lastname>
        </name>
        <address>
            <street>2 Elm Street</street>
            <city>New York City</city>
            <state>NY</state>
            <zip>02123-7445</zip>
        </address>
    </customer>
</customerlist>
```

(b)

The next statement in the XML document indicates the location of another document called a **stylesheet** (shown in Figure 13-4). Stylesheets are used by XSLT to indicate how to transform the elements of the XML document into another format; here, those elements will transform it into an HTML document that will be acceptable to a browser.

The XSLT processor copies the elements of the stylesheet until it finds a command in the format {*item, action*}. When it finds such a command, it searches for an instance of the indicated item; when it finds one, it takes the indicated action. For example, when the XSLT processor encounters

<xsl:for-each select = "customerlist/customer">

it starts a search in the document for an element named customerlist. When it finds such an element, it looks further within the customerlist element for an element named customer. If a match is found, it takes the actions indicated in the loop that ends with </xsl:for-each> (third from the bottom of the stylesheet).

Within the loop, styles are set for each element in the customerlist document. The results of applying the stylesheet in Figure 13-4 to the document in Figure 13-3(b) are shown in Figure 13-5(a). Read through the document and the stylesheet and see how the results are generated.

XSLT processors are context oriented; each statement is evaluated in the context of matches that have already been made. Thus, the following statement:

<xsl:value-of select = "name/lastname">

operates in the context of the customerlist/customer match that was made above. There is no need to code

<xsl:select = "customerlist/customer/name/lastname">/

because the context has already been set to customerlist/customer. In fact, if the select were coded in this second way, nothing would be found. Similarly, <xsl:select "lastname"/>

Figure 13-4

Example XSL Stylesheet

```
<?xml version="1.0"?>
<HTML xmlns:xsl="http://www.w3.org/TR/WD-xsl">
 <BODY STYLE="font-family:Arial, helvetica, sans-serif; font-size:14pt;
    background-color:teal">
 <xsl:for-each select="customerlist/customer">
   <DIV STYLE="background-color:brown; color:white; padding:4px">
    <SPAN STYLE="font-weight:bold; color:white"><xsl:value-of select="name/lastname"/></SPAN>
    - <xsl:value-of select="name/firstname"/>
   </DIV>
   <xsl:for-each select="address/street">
     <DIV STYLE="margin-left:20px; margin-bottom:1em; font-size:10pt; font-style:bold; color:yellow">
       <xsl:value-of select="node()"/>
     </DIV>
   </xsl:for-each>
   <DIV STYLE="margin-left:20px; margin-bottom:1em; font-size:12pt; font-style:bold">
     <xsl:value-of select="address/city"/>, <xsl:value-of select="address/state"/>
   </DIV>

   <DIV STYLE="margin-left:20px; margin-bottom:1em; font-size:14pt; color:blue">
     <xsl:value-of select="address/zip"/>
   </DIV>

 </xsl:for-each>
 </BODY>
</HTML>
```

Figure 13-5

**HTML Result
from Application
of Stylesheet**

(a) Generated HTML and
(b) HTML in Browser

```
<HTML xmlns:xsl="http://www.w3.org/TR/WD-xsl">
<BODY STYLE="font-family:Arial, helvetica, sans-serif; font-size:14pt;
      background-color:teal">
<DIV STYLE="background-color:brown; color:white; padding:4px">
<SPAN STYLE="font-weight:bold; color:white">Correlli</SPAN>
      - Michelle
</DIV>
<DIV STYLE="margin-left:20px; margin-bottom:1em; font-size:10pt; font-style:bold; color:yellow">
1824 East 7th Avenue
</DIV>
<DIV STYLE="margin-left:20px; margin-bottom:1em; font-size:10pt; font-style:bold; color:yellow">
Suite 700
</DIV>
<DIV STYLE="margin-left:20px; margin-bottom:1em; font-size:12pt; font-style:bold">
Memphis, TN
</DIV>
<DIV STYLE="margin-left:20px; margin-bottom:1em; font-size:14pt; color:blue">
32123-7788
</DIV>
<DIV STYLE="background-color:brown; color:white; padding:4px">
<SPAN STYLE="font-weight:bold; color:white">Jaynes</SPAN>
      - Lynda
</DIV>
<DIV STYLE="margin-left:20px; margin-bottom:1em; font-size:10pt; font-style:bold; color:yellow">
2 Elm Street
</DIV>
<DIV STYLE="margin-left:20px; margin-bottom:1em; font-size:12pt; font-style:bold">
New York City, NY
</DIV>
<DIV STYLE="margin-left:20px; margin-bottom:1em; font-size:14pt; color:blue">
02123-7445
</DIV>
</BODY>
</HTML>
```

(a)

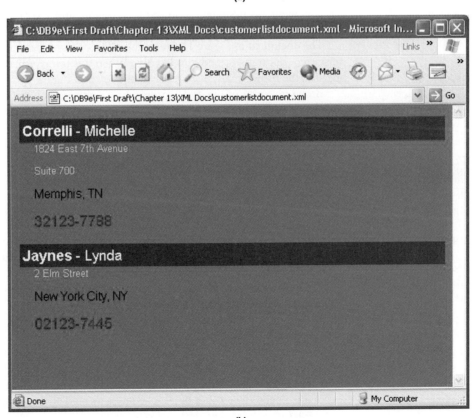

(b)

results in no match, because lastname occurs only in the context customerlist/customer/name, and not in the context customerlist/customer.

B T W

The nature of XSLT processing is: "When you find one of these, do this." Thus, the document in Figure 13-4 says, for each customer that you find under the tag customerlist, do the following: output an HTML DIV section and then some HTML with the value that you find in the document for name/lastname. Then, output more HTML and the value that you find for name/firstname. Then, for each address/street you find, output some HTML along with the value of the address/street you just found, and so forth.

XSL can output anything. Instead of outputting HTML, it could be writing Russian or Chinese or algebraic equations. XSL is simply a transformation facility for structured documents such as XML documents.

This context orientation explains the need for the following statement (in the center of the style sheet):

`<xsl:value-of select = "node()"/>`

The context at the location of this statement has been set to customerlist/customer/address/street. Hence, the current node is a street element, and this expression indicates that the value of that node is to be produced.

Observe, too, that a small transformation has been made by the stylesheet. The original document has firstname followed by lastname, but the output stream has lastname followed by firstname.

The document in Figure 13-5(a) is the XML document in Figure 13-3(b) with which we started, but transformed into HTML. When this transformed document is input to a browser, the browser will materialize it, as shown in Figure 13-5(b).

Browsers have built-in XSLT processors. You need only supply the document to the browser; it will locate the stylesheet and apply it to the document for you. The results will be like those shown in Figure 13-5(b).

XML Schema

DTDs were the XML community's first attempt at developing a document structure specification language. DTDs work, but they have some limitations, and embarrassingly, DTD documents are not XML documents. To correct these problems, the W3C committee defined another specification language called **XML Schema**. Today, XML Schema is the preferred method for defining document structure.

XML Schemas are XML documents. This means that you use the same language to define an XML Schema as you would use to define any other XML document. It also means that you can validate an XML Schema document against its schema, just as you would any other XML document.

If you are following this discussion, then you realize that there is a chicken-and-the-egg problem here. If XML Schema documents are themselves XML documents, what document is used to validate them? What is the schema of all of the schemas? There is such a document; the mother of all schemas is located at ***www.w3.org***. All XML Schema documents are validated against that document.

B   T   W

XML Schema validation requires thinking at two meta levels. To understand why, recall that metadata is data about data. The statement *CUSTOMER contains column CustomerName Char(25)* is metadata. Extending this idea, the statement *SQL has a data type Char(n) for defining character data of length n* is data about metadata, or meta-metadata.

XML has the same meta levels. An XML document has a structure that is defined by an XML Schema document. The XML Schema document contains metadata, because it is data about the structure of other XML documents. But an XML Schema document has its own structure that is defined by another XML Schema. That XML Schema document is data about metadata, or meta-metadata.

The XML case is elegant. You can write a program to validate an XML document (but don't; use one of the hundreds that already exist). Once you have such a program, you can validate any XML document against its XML Schema document. The process is exactly the same, regardless of whether you are validating an XML document, an XML Schema document, or a document at any other level.

XML Schema is a broad and complex topic. Dozens of sizable books have been written just on XML Schema alone. Clearly, we will not be able to discuss even the major topics of XML Schema in this chapter. Instead, we will focus on a few basic terms and concepts and show how those terms and concepts are used with database processing. Given this introduction, you will then be able to learn more on your own.

XML Schema Validation

Figure 13-6(a) shows a simple XML Schema document that can be used to represent a single row from the ARTIST table at View Ridge Gallery. The second line indicates what schema is to be used to validate this document. Because this is an XML Schema document, it is to be validated against the mother of all schemas, the one at **www.w3.org**. This same reference will be used in all XML Schemas, in every company, worldwide. (By the way, this reference address is used only for identification purposes. Because this schema is so widely used, most schema validation programs have their own built-in copy of it.)

This first statement not only specifies the document that is to be used for validation, it also establishes a labeled namespace. Namespaces are a complicated topic in their own right, and we will not discuss them in this chapter other than to explain the use of labels. In this first statement, the label *xsd* is defined by the expression: xmlns:xsd. The first part of that expression stands for *xml n*amespace, and the second part defines the label *xsd*. Notice that all of the other lines in the document use the label xsd. The expression *xsd:complexType* simply tells the validating program to look into the namespace called xsd (here, the one specified as **www.w3.org/2001/XMLSchema**) to find the definition of the term *complexType*.

The name of the label is up to the designer of the document. You could change xmlns:xsd to xmlns:mylabel, and you would set mylabel to point to the w3 document. Documents can have multiple namespaces, but that topic is beyond the scope of this discussion.

Elements and Attributes

As shown in Figure 13-6(a), schemas consist of elements and attributes. Elements are either simple or complex. Simple elements have a single data item. In Figure 13-6(a), the elements Name, Nationality, Birthdate, and DeceasedDate are all simple elements.

Figure 13-6

Use of an XML Schema
(a) Schema Document and (b) Schema-Valid XML Document

```xml
<?xml version="1.0" encoding="UTF-8"?>
<xsd:schema xmlns:xsd="http://www.w3.org/2001/XMLSchema" elementFormDefault="qualified">
    <xsd:element name="Artist">
        <xsd:complexType>
            <xsd:sequence>
                <xsd:element name="Name"/>
                <xsd:element name="Nationality"/>
                <xsd:element name="Birthdate" minOccurs="0"/>
                <xsd:element name="DeceasedDate" minOccurs="0"/>
            </xsd:sequence>
            <xsd:attribute name="ArtStyle"/>
        </xsd:complexType>
    </xsd:element>
</xsd:schema>
```

(a)

```xml
<?xml version="1.0" encoding="UTF-8"?>
<Artist xmlns:xsi="http://www.w3.org/2000/10/XMLSchema-instance"
    xsi:noNamespaceSchemaLocation="D:\DB Books\DB 10e\FirstDraft\Chapter 13\XML Docs\Artist1.xsd" ArtStyle="Modern">
    <Name>Miro</Name>
    <Nationality>Spanish</Nationality>
    <Birthdate>1893</Birthdate>
    <DeceasedDate>1983</DeceasedDate>
</Artist>
```

(b)

Complex elements contain other elements that can be either simple or complex. In Figure 13-6(a), the Artist element is complexType. It contains a sequence of four simple elements: Name, Nationality, Birthdate, and DeceasedDate. Later you will see examples of complex types that contain other complex types.

Complex types can have attributes. Figure 13-6(a) defines the attribute ArtStyle. The creator of an XML document uses this attribute to specify a characteristic about an artist; in this case, his or her style. The example document in Figure 13-6(b) specifies the ArtStyle for this artist (Miro) as Modern.

B T W

Elements and attributes both carry data, and you may be wondering when to use one or the other. As a general rule, for database/XML applications, use elements to store data and attributes to store metadata. For example, define an ItemPrice element to store the value of a price, and define a Currency attribute to store the currency type of that price, such as USD, Aus$, or Euros.

The XML standards do not require that elements and attributes be used in this way. It is a matter of style, and in subsequent sections we will show how it is possible to cause SQL Server to place all of the column values in attributes, to place all of them in elements, or to mix them up so that some columns are placed in attributes and others are placed in elements. Thus, these decisions are a matter of design choice rather than XML standard.

By default, the cardinality of both simple and complex elements is 1.1, meaning that a single value is required and no more than a single value can be specified. For the schema in Figure 13-6(a), the minOccurs = "0" expressions indicate that the defaults are being overridden for Birthdate and DeceasedDate so that they need not have a value. This is similar to the NULL constraint in SQL schema definitions.

Figure 13-6(b) shows an XML document that is valid on the schema shown in Figure 13-6(a). Observe that the value of the ArtStyle attribute is given with the heading of the Artist element. Also note that a namespace of *xsi* is defined. This namespace is used just once—for the noNamespaceSchemaLocation attribute. Do not be concerned about the name of this attribute; it is simply a means of telling the XML parser where to find the XML Schema for this document. Focus your attention on the relationship of the structure of the document and the description in the XML Schema.

Flat versus Structured Schemas

Figure 13-7 shows an XML Schema and an XML document that represent the columns of the CUSTOMER table in the View Ridge database. As shown in Figure 13-7(a), Country and EmailAddress are optional, but all of the other elements are required. The document in Figure 13-7(b) contains one of the rows of the CUSTOMER table.

XML Schemas like the one shown in Figure 13-7 are sometimes called *flat,* because all of the elements reside at the same level. Figure 13-7(c) is a diagram drawn by an XML editing tool called XML Spy. Figure 13-7(c) graphically depicts why this schema is called flat. Also note that optional elements are shown in boxes drawn with dashed lines.

> **B T W**
>
> **You can find out more about this excellent product from a small company, which is not yet owned by Microsoft or some other behemoth corporation, from the Web site *www.xmlspy.com*. The Home Edition is free; you should download it from *www.xmlspy.com/support_freexmlspyhome.asp*. You can process all of the XML code in this chapter using the Home Edition. The XML code for this chapter is available on this text's Web site at *www.prenhall.com/kroenke*.**

If you think about these elements for a moment, you will realize that something about the semantics of them has been left out. In particular, the group {Street, City, State, ZipPostalCode, Country} is part of the Address theme. Also, the group {AreaCode, PhoneNumber} is part of the Phone theme. As you know, in the relational model, all columns are considered equal, and there is no way to represent these themes.

With XML, however, such groups can be modeled. The schema shown in Figure 13-8(a) structures the appropriate columns into an Address complexType and other columns into a Phone complexType. An XML document for one of the rows of CUSTOMER expressed in this format is shown in Figure 13-8(b). A graphical display of this schema is shown in Figure 13-8(c).

Such schemas are sometimes called **structured schemas** because they add structure to table columns. Such a model captures additional user meaning, so it is superior to the relational model from a descriptive standpoint.

Global Elements

Suppose that we want to use XML Schema to represent a document that extends the customer data in Figure 13-8 to include the salesperson assigned to that customer. Further, suppose that both customers and salespeople have address and phone data. We can use the techniques shown so far to represent this new customer structure, but if we do so, we will duplicate the definition of Phone and Address.

Figure 13-7

Example of a Flat Schema Structure
(a) XML Schema with Flat Structure; (b) Schema-Valid Document; and
(c) Graphical Representation of Schema

```xml
<?xml version="1.0" encoding="UTF-8"?>
<!-- edited with XML Spy v3.5 NT (http://www.xmlspy.com) by David Kroenke (private) -->
<xsd:schema xmlns:xsd="http://www.w3.org/2001/XMLSchema" elementFormDefault="qualified">
    <xsd:element name="Customer">
        <xsd:complexType>
            <xsd:sequence>
                <xsd:element name="CustomerID" type="xsd:int"/>
                <xsd:element name="Name" type="xsd:string"/>
                <xsd:element name="Street" type="xsd:string"/>
                <xsd:element name="City" type="xsd:string"/>
                <xsd:element name="State" type="xsd:string"/>
                <xsd:element name="ZipPostalCode" type="xsd:string"/>
                <xsd:element name="Country" type="xsd:string" minOccurs="0"/>
                <xsd:element name="AreaCode" type="xsd:string"/>
                <xsd:element name="PhoneNumber" type="xsd:string"/>
                <xsd:element name="EmailAddress" type="xsd:string" minOccurs="0"/>
            </xsd:sequence>
        </xsd:complexType>
    </xsd:element>
</xsd:schema>
```

(a)

```xml
<?xml version="1.0" encoding="UTF-8"?>
<Customer xmlns:xsi="http://www.w3.org/2000/10/XMLSchema-instance" xsi:noNamespaceSchemaLocation="D:\DB Books\DB
10e\FirstDraft\Chapter 13\XML Docs\FlatCustomer.xsd">
    <CustomerID>1000</CustomerID>
    <Name>Jeffrey Janes</Name>
    <Street>123 W. Elm St</Street>
    <City>Renton</City>
    <State>WA</State>
    <ZipPostalCode>98123</ZipPostalCode>
    <AreaCode>206</AreaCode>
    <PhoneNumber>555-1234</PhoneNumber>
    <EmailAddress>Customer1000@somewhere.com</EmailAddress>
</Customer>
```

(b)

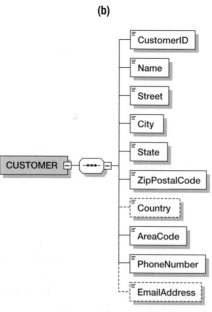

(c)

Figure 13-8

Example of a Structured Schema

(a) Structured XML Schema; (b) Schema-Valid Document; and (c) Graphical
Representation of Schema

```xml
<?xml version="1.0" encoding="UTF-8"?>
<!-- edited with XMLSPY v5 U (http://www.xmlspy.com) by David Kroenke (private) -->
<!-- edited with XML Spy v3.5 NT (http://www.xmlspy.com) by David Kroenke (private) -->
<xsd:schema xmlns:xsd="http://www.w3.org/2001/XMLSchema" elementFormDefault="qualified">
    <xsd:complexType name="AddressType">
        <xsd:sequence>
            <xsd:element name="Street" maxOccurs="3"/>
            <xsd:element name="City"/>
            <xsd:element name="State"/>
            <xsd:element name="ZipPostalCode"/>
            <xsd:element name="Country" minOccurs="0"/>
        </xsd:sequence>
    </xsd:complexType>
    <xsd:complexType name="PhoneType">
        <xsd:sequence>
            <xsd:element name="AreaCode"/>
            <xsd:element name="PhoneNumber"/>
        </xsd:sequence>
    </xsd:complexType>
    <xsd:element name="Customer">
        <xsd:complexType>
            <xsd:sequence>
                <xsd:element name="CusotmerID" type="xsd:integer"/>
                <xsd:element name="Name"/>
                <xsd:element name="Address" type="AddressType"/>
                <xsd:element name="Phone" type="PhoneType" maxOccurs="3"/>
                <xsd:element name="EmailAddress" minOccurs="0"/>
            </xsd:sequence>
        </xsd:complexType>
    </xsd:element>
</xsd:schema>
```

(a)

```xml
<?xml version="1.0" encoding="UTF-8"?>
<!-- edited with XML Spy v3.5 NT (http://www.xmlspy.com) by David Kroenke (private) -->
<Customer xmlns:xsi="http://www.w3.org/2000/10/XMLSchema-instance" xsi:noNamespaceSchemaLocation="D:\DB Books\DB
10e\FirstDraft\Chapter 13\XML Docs\CustomerWithGroups.xsd">
    <CustomerID>1000</CustomerID>
    <Name>Jeffrey Janes</Name>
    <Address>
        <Street>123 W. Elm St.</Street>
        <City>Renton</City>
        <State>WA</State>
        <ZipPostalCode>98123</ZipPostalCode>
    </Address>
    <Phone>
        <AreaCode>206</AreaCode>
        <PhoneNumber>555-1234</PhoneNumber>
    </Phone>
    <EmailAddress>Customer1000@somewhere.com</EmailAddress>
</Customer>
```

(b)

In the relational world, we worry about duplication of data, not so much because of
wasted file space, but more because there is always the chance of inconsistent data when
one copy of the data is changed and the other copy is not changed. Similarly, in the
document-processing world, people worry about duplicate definition of elements
because there is always the chance that they will become inconsistent when one is
changed and the other is not.

Figure 13-8   **Continued**

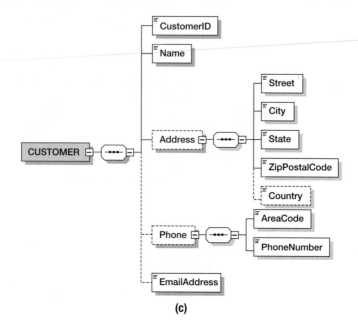

(c)

To eliminate the definition duplication, elements can be declared globally and then reused. In Figure 13-9(a), for example, the Address group is defined as the global element AddressType, and the Phone group is defined as the global element PhoneType. According to the XML Schema standard, these are global elements because they reside at the top level of the schema.

If you examine Figure 13-9(a) further, you will see that both Customer and Salesperson within Customer use the AddressType and PhoneType global definitions. They are referenced by notations such as *type = "AddressType."* By using these global definitions, if either PhoneType or AddressType is changed, the definition of Customer and Salesperson will inherit the change.

One other change in this figure is that the cardinality of the Phone group of Customer has been set to 1..3. This notation means that at least one Phone group is required and as many as three are allowed. As you learned in Chapter 5, representing such multivalued attributes in the entity-relationship model requires the definition of an ID-dependent entity. That entity will later be transformed into a table in the relational model. We will ignore this issue here. This notation is shown only so that you can see how multivalued elements are documented in an XML Schema.

Figure 13-9(b) shows how XML Spy graphically represents the PhoneType global element, and Figure 13-9(c) illustrates the way that the PhoneType reference is shown for Customer and Salesperson.

Creating XML Documents from Database Data

Both Oracle and SQL Server have facilities for generating XML documents from database data. The Oracle XML features require the use of Java. Because we do not assume that you are a Java programmer, we will not discuss those features further in this chapter. If you are a Java programmer, you can learn more about Oracle's XML features at **www.oracle.com.** (Later in this chapter, we will illustrate how to generate XML documents from Oracle data using ADO.NET. In that case, however, Oracle is providing the data in non-XML format, and ADO.NET programs are formatting that data in XML.)

The facilities in both Oracle and SQL Server are undergoing rapid development. In the case of SQL Server, version 7.0 added the expression FOR XML to SQL SELECT

Figure 13-9

Example of a Schema with Global Elements

(a) Schema with Global PhoneType; (b) PhoneType Global Element; and (c) Graphical Representation of Schema

```xml
<xsd:schema xmlns:xsd="http://www.w3.org/2001/XMLSchema" elementFormDefault="qualified">
    <xsd:complexType name="AddressType">
        <xsd:sequence>
            <xsd:element name="Street"/>
            <xsd:element name="City"/>
            <xsd:element name="State"/>
            <xsd:element name="ZipPostalCode"/>
            <xsd:element name="Country" minOccurs="0"/>
        </xsd:sequence>
    </xsd:complexType>
    <xsd:complexType name="PhoneType">
        <xsd:sequence>
            <xsd:element name="AreaCode"/>
            <xsd:element name="PhoneNumber"/>
        </xsd:sequence>
    </xsd:complexType>
    <xsd:element name="Customer">
        <xsd:complexType>
            <xsd:sequence>
                <xsd:element name="CustomerID" type="xsd:integer"/>
                <xsd:element name="Name"/>
                <xsd:element name="Address" type="AddressType"/>
                <xsd:element name="Phone" type="PhoneType" maxOccurs="3"/>
                <xsd:element name="EmailAddress" minOccurs="0"/>
                <xsd:element name="Salesperson">
                    <xsd:complexType>
                        <xsd:sequence>
                            <xsd:element name="Name"/>
                            <xsd:element name="Address" type="AddressType"/>
                            <xsd:element name="Phone" type="PhoneType"/>
                        </xsd:sequence>
                        <xsd:attribute name="SalespersonID" type="xsd:string"/>
                    </xsd:complexType>
                </xsd:element>
            </xsd:sequence>
        </xsd:complexType>
    </xsd:element>
</xsd:schema>
```

(a)

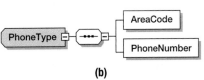

(b)

syntax. That expression was carried forward to SQL Server 2000. In 2002, the SQL Server group extended the SQL Server capabilities with SQLXML, a class library that can be downloaded from *msdn.microsoft.com*. SQLXML, which was produced by the SQL Server group, is different from ADO.NET. All of these features and functions are merged together in SQL Server 2005.

SELECT . . . FOR XML

Consider the following SQL statement:

```
SELECT        *
FROM          ARTIST
    FOR    XML RAW;
```

Figure 13-9   **Continued**

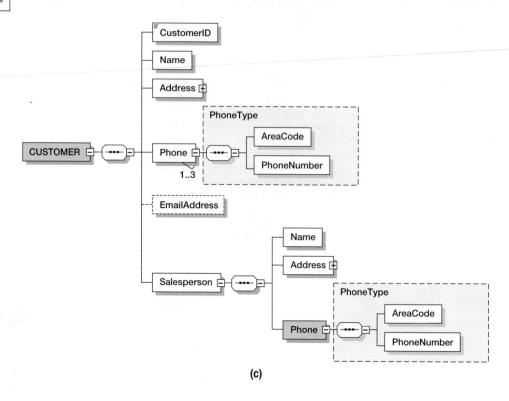

(c)

The expression FOR XML RAW tells SQL Server to place the values of the columns as attributes in the resulting XML document. Figure 13-10(a) shows an example of the results of this statement. As expected, each column is placed as an attribute of the element named ARTIST.[1]

It is also possible to cause SQL Server to place the values of the columns into elements rather than attributes. The following statement produces a document like the one shown in Figure 13-10(b):

```
SELECT        *
FROM          ARTIST
    FOR       XML AUTO, ELEMENTS;
```

Using another option, FOR XML EXPLICIT, you can cause SQL Server to place some columns into elements and others into attributes. For example, you might decide to place all column values except surrogate key values into elements and all surrogate key values into attributes. The justification for this design is that surrogate key values have no meaning to the users, so they are more like metadata than data. The means by which this is done is beyond the scope of this discussion. See FOR XML EXPLICIT in the SQL Server documentation for more information.

---

[1]In the interest of full disclosure, the figures in this section were produced by a Visual Basic .NET application that invoked the SQL . . . FOR XML statements via the SQLXML class SqlXMLCommand and saved them to a file using the ExecuteToStream method of that class. The application added the root element MyData. None of this is important for understanding the essential ideas in this section. Strive instead to understand how SQL statements can be mapped to XML documents. But if you want to produce them yourself, download SQLXML and read the tutorial documentation.

Figure 13-10

FOR XML Examples

(a) FOR XML RAW
Example and (b) FOR
XML AUTO, ELEMENTS
Example

```
<MyData>
    <ARTIST ArtistID="3" Name="Miro            " Nationality="Spanish      " Birthdate="1870" DeceasedDate="1950"/>
    <ARTIST ArtistID="4" Name="Kandinsky       " Nationality="Russian       " Birthdate="1854" DeceasedDate="1900"/>
    <ARTIST ArtistID="5" Name="Frings          " Nationality="US           " Birthdate="1700" DeceasedDate="1800"/>
    <ARTIST ArtistID="6" Name="Klee            " Nationality="German       " Birthdate="1900"/>
    <ARTIST ArtistID="8" Name="Moos            " Nationality="US           "/>
    <ARTIST ArtistID="14" Name="Tobey          " Nationality="US           "/>
    <ARTIST ArtistID="15" Name="Matisse        " Nationality="French        "/>
    <ARTIST ArtistID="16" Name="Chagall        " Nationality="French        "/>
</MyData>
```

(a)

```
<MyData>
    <ARTIST>
        <ArtistID>3</ArtistID>
        <Name>Miro            </Name>
        <Nationality>Spanish      </Nationality>
        <Birthdate>1870</Birthdate>
        <DeceasedDate>1950</DeceasedDate>
    </ARTIST>
    <ARTIST>
        <ArtistID>4</ArtistID>
        <Name>Kandinsky       </Name>
        <Nationality>Russian      </Nationality>
        <Birthdate>1854</Birthdate>
        <DeceasedDate>1900</DeceasedDate>
    </ARTIST>
    <ARTIST>
        <ArtistID>5</ArtistID>
        <Name>Frings          </Name>
        <Nationality>US           </Nationality>
        <Birthdate>1700</Birthdate>
        <DeceasedDate>1800</DeceasedDate>
    </ARTIST>
    <ARTIST>
        <ArtistID>6</ArtistID>
        <Name>Klee            </Name>
        <Nationality>German       </Nationality>
        <Birthdate>1900</Birthdate>
    </ARTIST>
    <ARTIST>
        <ArtistID>8</ArtistID>
        <Name>Moos            </Name>
        <Nationality>US           </Nationality>
    </ARTIST>
    <ARTIST>
        <ArtistID>14</ArtistID>
        <Name>Tobey           </Name>
        <Nationality>US           </Nationality>
    </ARTIST>
    <ARTIST>
        <ArtistID>15</ArtistID>
        <Name>Matisse         </Name>
        <Nationality>French       </Nationality>
    </ARTIST>
    <ARTIST>
        <ArtistID>16</ArtistID>
        <Name>Chagall         </Name>
        <Nationality>French       </Nationality>
    </ARTIST>
</MyData>
```

(b)

Multitable SELECT with FOR XML

FOR XML SELECT statements are not limited to single-table SELECTs; they can be applied to joins as well. For example, the following join produced the XML document shown in Figure 13-11:

Figure 13-11

FOR XML AUTO ELEMENTS Displaying Customer and Artist Interests

```
yData xmlns:xsi="http://www.w3.org/2000/10/XMLSchema-instance"
    xsi:noNamespaceSchemaLocation="D:\DB Books\DB 10e\FirstDraft\Chapter 13\XML Docs\CustomerArtistInt.xsd">
    <CUSTOMER>
        <Name>Chris Wilkens        </Name>
        <ARTIST>
            <Name>Frings        </Name>
        </ARTIST>
        <ARTIST>
            <Name>Tobey        </Name>
        </ARTIST>
    </CUSTOMER>
    <CUSTOMER>
        <Name>Donald G. Gray        </Name>
        <ARTIST>
            <Name>Tobey        </Name>
        </ARTIST>
    </CUSTOMER>
    <CUSTOMER>
        <Name>Fred Smathers        </Name>
        <ARTIST>
            <Name>Tobey        </Name>
        </ARTIST>
    </CUSTOMER>
    <CUSTOMER>
        <Name>Jeffrey Janes        </Name>
        <ARTIST>
            <Name>Tobey        </Name>
        </ARTIST>
    </CUSTOMER>
```

```
SELECT      CUSTOMER.Name, ARTIST.Name

FROM        CUSTOMER, CUSTOMER_ARTIST_INT, ARTIST

WHERE       CUSTOMER.CustomerID =
            CUSTOMER_ARTIST_INT.CustomerID

    AND     CUSTOMER_ARTIST_INT.ArtistID = ARTIST.ArtistID

ORDER BY    CUSTOMER.Name

FOR XML AUTO, ELEMENTS;
```

SQL Server uses the order of the tables in the FROM clause to determine the hierarchical placement of the elements in the generated XML document. Here, the top-level element is CUSTOMER, and the next element is ARTIST. The CUSTOMER_ARTIST_INT table does not appear in the generated document because no column from that table appeared in the SELECT.

You can write the expression FOR XML AUTO, XMLDATA to cause SQL Server to produce an XML Schema statement in front of the XML document that it writes. The schema produced, however, involves topics that we will not cover in this chapter, so we will not do that. Another way to produce an XML Schema for an XML document is to have XML Spy generate one, using the document as an example. The schema in Figure 13-12(a) was produced in just this way. Observe that the MyData element can have an unbounded number of CUSTOMER elements, and each CUSTOMER can have an unbounded number of ARTIST elements, one for each artist interest. Figure 13-12(b) shows a graphical display of this same schema. In this figure, the notation $1..\infty$ means that at least one CUSTOMER is required and an unlimited number will be allowed.

An XML Schema for All CUSTOMER Purchases

Suppose now that we want to produce a document that has all of the customer purchase data. To do that, we need to join CUSTOMER to TRANS to WORK to

Figure 13-11

Continued

```
                        <CUSTOMER>
                            <Name>Lynda Johnson        </Name>
                            <ARTIST>
                                <Name>Moos             </Name>
                            </ARTIST>
                            <ARTIST>
                                <Name>Tobey            </Name>
                            </ARTIST>
                            <ARTIST>
                                <Name>Frings           </Name>
                            </ARTIST>
                        </CUSTOMER>
                        <CUSTOMER>
                            <Name>Malinda Gliddens     </Name>
                            <ARTIST>
                                <Name>Chagall          </Name>
                            </ARTIST>
                        </CUSTOMER>
                        <CUSTOMER>
                            <Name>Mary Beth Frederickson   </Name>
                            <ARTIST>
                                <Name>Frings           </Name>
                            </ARTIST>
                            <ARTIST>
                                <Name>Moos             </Name>
                            </ARTIST>
                            <ARTIST>
                                <Name>Tobey            </Name>
                            </ARTIST>
                        </CUSTOMER>
                        <CUSTOMER>
                            <Name>Michael Bench        </Name>
                            <ARTIST>
                                <Name>Moos             </Name>
                            </ARTIST>
                            <ARTIST>
                                <Name>Frings           </Name>
                            </ARTIST>
                            <ARTIST>
                                <Name>Tobey            </Name>
                            </ARTIST>
                        </CUSTOMER>
                        <CUSTOMER>
                            <Name>Selma Warning        </Name>
                            <ARTIST>
                                <Name>Miro             </Name>
                            </ARTIST>
                            <ARTIST>
                                <Name>Tobey            </Name>
                            </ARTIST>
                        </CUSTOMER>
                        <CUSTOMER>
                            <Name>Tiffany Twilight     </Name>
                            <ARTIST>
                                <Name>Tobey            </Name>
                            </ARTIST>
                            <ARTIST>
                                <Name>Chagall          </Name>
                            </ARTIST>
                            <ARTIST>
                                <Name>Frings           </Name>
                            </ARTIST>
                        </CUSTOMER>
                    </MyData>
```

Figure 13-12

**XML Schema for
Document in
Figure 13-11**
(a) XML Schema Inferred
by XML Spy and (b)
Graphical Display of
Schema

```
<xsd:schema xmlns:xsd="http://www.w3.org/2001/XMLSchema"
            elementFormDefault="qualified">
   <xsd:element name="MyData">
      <xsd:complexType>
         <xsd:sequence>
            <xsd:element name="CUSTOMER" maxOccurs="unbounded">
               <xsd:complexType>
                  <xsd:sequence>
                     <xsd:element ref="Name"/>
                     <xsd:element name="ARTIST" maxOccurs="unbounded">
                        <xsd:complexType>
                           <xsd:sequence>
                              <xsd:element ref="Name"/>
                           </xsd:sequence>
                        </xsd:complexType>
                     </xsd:element>
                  </xsd:sequence>
               </xsd:complexType>
            </xsd:element>
         </xsd:sequence>
      </xsd:complexType>
   </xsd:element>
   <xsd:element name="Name" type="xsd:string"/>
</xsd:schema>
```

(a)

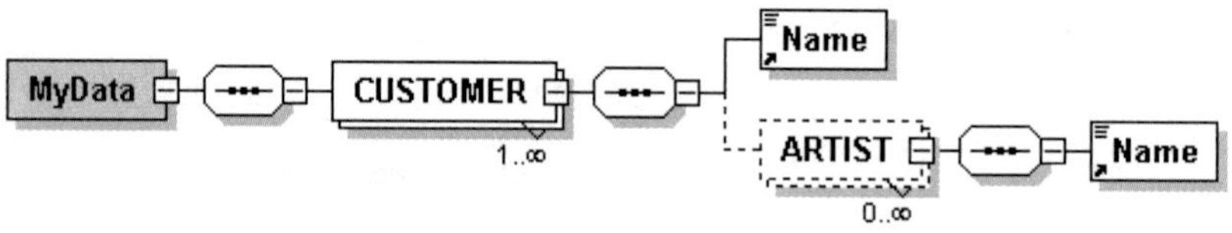

ARTIST and select the appropriate data. The following SQL statement produces the
required data:

SELECT	**CUSTOMER.CustomerID, CUSTOMER.Name, TRANS.TransactionID, SalesPrice, [WORK].WorkID, Title, Copy, ARTIST.ArtistID, ARTIST.Name**
FROM	**CUSTOMER, TRANS, [WORK], ARTIST**
WHERE	**CUSTOMER.CustomerID = TRANS.CustomerID**
AND	**TRANS.WorkID = [WORK].WorkID**
AND	**[WORK].ArtistID = ARTIST.ArtistID**
ORDER BY	**CUSTOMER.Name**

FOR XML AUTO, ELEMENTS;

Figure 13-13(a) shows an XML Schema document for this SQL statement. It was
produced by having SQL Server create an XML document having all of the VRG data
and then using XML Spy to generate this schema. A graphical view of it is shown in
Figure 13-13(b).

This schema is close, but not quite correct. According to the schema, the MyData schema has at least one and an unlimited number of CUSTOMER elements, and CUSTOMER has at least one and an unlimited number of TRANS elements. That latter statement is not correct. According to our data model, each CUSTOMER should have from zero to many TRANS elements.

This error occurred because we constructed the schema from an existing XML document that was produced from an inner join between CUSTOMER and TRANS. Because it was an inner join, only customers having a TRANS row appeared in the XML document. Thus, every CUSTOMER in the document had at least one TRANS row. Had we produced the XML document from an outer join that allowed customers to appear who have no transaction data, then there would have been instances of CUSTOMER without TRANS, and XML Spy would have created the correct cardinality

Figure 13-13

Customer Purchase View

(a) XML Schema Generated by XML Spy; (b) Graphical Display of Schema; and (c) Schema with Correct Minimum Cardinalities

```xml
<!--W3C Schema generated by XML Spy v3.5 NT (http://www.xmlspy.com)-->
<xsd:schema xmlns:xsd="http://www.w3.org/2001/XMLSchema" elementFormDefault="qualified">
    <xsd:element name="MyData">
        <xsd:complexType>
            <xsd:sequence>
                <xsd:element name="CUSTOMER" maxOccurs="unbounded">
                    <xsd:complexType>
                        <xsd:sequence>
                            <xsd:element ref="Name"/>
                            <xsd:element name="TRANS" minOccurs="0" maxOccurs="unbounded"
                                <xsd:complexType>
                                    <xsd:sequence>
                                        <xsd:element name="SalesPrice"/>
                                        <xsd:element name="WORK">
                                            <xsd:complexType>
                                                <xsd:sequence>
                                                    <xsd:element name="Title" type="xsd:string"/>
                                                    <xsd:element name="Copy" type="xsd:string"/>
                                                    <xsd:element name="ARTIST">
                                                        <xsd:complexType>
                                                            <xsd:sequence>
                                                                <xsd:element ref="Name"/>
                                                            </xsd:sequence>
                                                        </xsd:complexType>
                                                    </xsd:element>
                                                </xsd:sequence>
                                            </xsd:complexType>
                                        </xsd:element>
                                    </xsd:sequence>
                                </xsd:complexType>
                            </xsd:element>
                        </xsd:sequence>
                    </xsd:complexType>
                </xsd:element>
            </xsd:sequence>
        </xsd:complexType>
    </xsd:element>
    <xsd:element name="Name" type="xsd:string"/>
</xsd:schema>
```

(a)

Figure 13-13

Continued

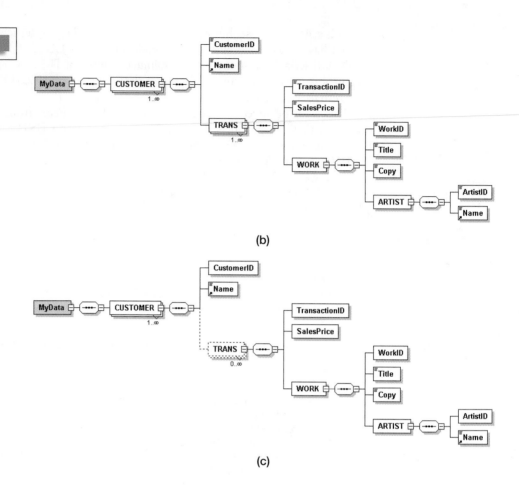

(b)

(c)

on TRANS. Rather than do all that at this point, we can instead just use XML Spy to make the correction.[2]

According to the corrected XML Schema in Figure 13-13(c), a CUSTOMER has from zero to unlimited TRANS elements. The cardinalities in the rest of the schema were correctly produced from our XML document. A TRANS element has exactly one WORK element, and a WORK element has exactly one ARTIST element.

A Schema with Two Multivalue Paths

Suppose now that we want to construct an XML document that has all of the View Ridge customer data. We cannot construct such a view from a single SQL statement because it has two multivalued paths. We need one SQL statement to obtain all of the customer purchase data and a second SQL statement to obtain all of the customer/artist interests.

XML Schema does not have this limitation, however. An XML document may have as many multivalued paths as the application requires. In our case, all we need to do is to combine the schemas in Figure 13-12(a) and Figure 13-13(a). While we're at it, we can also add the surrogate keys for each of the underlying tables.

The result of combining these results (using cut and paste in XML Spy!) is shown in Figure 13-14. Observe in Figure 13-14(b) that MyData may have from one to an unlimited

---

[2]Actually, the same error occurred in the construction of the CUSTOMER/ARTIST schema shown in Figure 13-12(b). It, too, was corrected in XML Spy; only the corrected version is shown there.

Figure 13-14

View Ridge Customer with Two Multivalue Paths

(a) XML Schema and (b) Graphical Display of Schema

```xml
<xsd:schema xmlns:xsd="http://www.w3.org/2000/10/XMLSchema" elementFormDefault="qualified">
    <xsd:element name="MyData">
        <xsd:complexType>
            <xsd:sequence>
                <xsd:element name="CUSTOMER" maxOccurs="unbounded">
                    <xsd:complexType>
                        <xsd:sequence>
                            <xsd:element name="CustomerID" type="xsd:integer"/>
                            <xsd:element ref="Name"/>
                            <xsd:element name="TRANS" minOccurs="0" maxOccurs="unbounded">
                                <xsd:complexType>
                                    <xsd:sequence>
                                        <xsd:element name="TransactionID" type="xsd:integer"/>
                                        <xsd:element name="SalesPrice"/>
                                        <xsd:element name="WORK">
                                            <xsd:complexType>
                                                <xsd:sequence>
                                                    <xsd:element name="WorkID" type="xsd:integer"/>
                                                    <xsd:element name="Title" type="xsd:string"/>
                                                    <xsd:element name="Copy" type="xsd:string"/>
                                                    <xsd:element name="ARTIST">
                                                        <xsd:complexType>
                                                            <xsd:sequence>
                                                                <xsd:element name="ArtistID" type="xsd:integer"/>
                                                                <xsd:element ref="Name"/>
                                                            </xsd:sequence>
                                                        </xsd:complexType>
                                                    </xsd:element>
                                                </xsd:sequence>
                                            </xsd:complexType>
                                        </xsd:element>
                                    </xsd:sequence>
                                </xsd:complexType>
                            </xsd:element>
                            <xsd:element name="ArtistInterests" minOccurs="0" maxOccurs="unbounded">
                                <xsd:complexType>
                                    <xsd:sequence>
                                        <xsd:element name="ArtistID" type="xsd:integer"/>
                                        <xsd:element ref="Name"/>
                                        <xsd:element name="Nationality"/>
                                    </xsd:sequence>
                                </xsd:complexType>
                            </xsd:element>
                        </xsd:sequence>
                    </xsd:complexType>
                </xsd:element>
            </xsd:sequence>
        </xsd:complexType>
    </xsd:element>
    <xsd:element name="Name" type="xsd:string"/>
</xsd:schema>
```

(a)

number of CUSTOMER elements, and that each such element may have from zero to many TRANS and from zero to many ArtistInterests elements. All of the simple elements in this schema are required.

Why Is XML Important?

At this point, you should have some idea of the nature of XML and the XML standards. You know that XML makes a clear separation between structure, content, and materialization. Structure is defined by either a DTD or an XML Schema document. Content is expressed in an XML document, and the materializations of a document are expressed in an XSL document. You also understand that SQL statements can be used to create

Figure 13-14

Continued

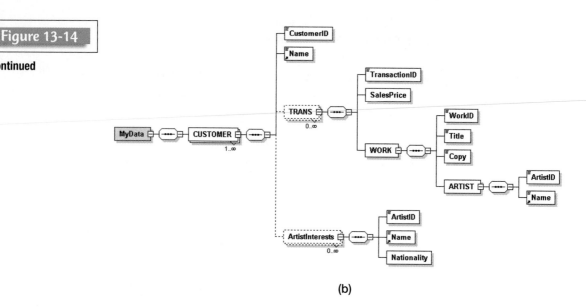

(b)

XML documents, but only as long as those documents involve at most one multivalue path. If more than one such path exists in the document, multiple SQL statements need to be issued to fill the document in some fashion.

You may be asking, "These are interesting ideas, but why do they matter? What's so important about all of this?" The answer to these questions is that XML processing provides a standardized facility to describe, validate, and materialize any database view.

Consider the View Ridge Gallery. Suppose that the gallery wants to share all of its customer data with another gallery, maybe because of a joint sales program. If both galleries agree on an XML Schema like the one shown in Figure 13-14, they can prepare customer data documents in accordance with that schema. Before sending a document, they can run an automated process to validate the document against the schema. In this way, only correct data are transmitted. Of course, this process works in both directions. Not only can View Ridge ensure that it is sending only valid documents; by validating the documents it receives, it can ensure that it is receiving only valid documents.

Best of all, the programs for document validation are publicly available and free to the galleries. The galleries do not need to write program code for validation.

Additionally, each gallery can develop its own set of XSL documents to materialize the customer data documents in whatever ways they want. View Ridge can develop one XSL document to display the data on a customer's computer, another to display it on salespersons' computers, another to display it on mobile devices when art buyers are on the road, and so forth. Given these XSLs, customer data can be displayed regardless of whether it came from one gallery or the other.

Now, broaden this idea from two small businesses to an industry. Suppose, for example, that the real estate industry agrees on an XML Schema document for property listings. Every real estate company that can produce data in the format of the schema can then exchange listings with every other real estate company. Given the schema, each company can ensure that it is transmitting valid documents, and it can also ensure that it is receiving valid documents. Further, each company can develop its own set of XSL documents to materialize property listings in whatever way it wants. Once the XSL documents have been prepared, any listing from any participating agent can be displayed in the local agency's materializations. Figure 13-15 lists some XML standards work that is under way in various industries.

For another example, consider business-to-business e-commerce. Suppose that Wal-Mart wants to send orders to its vendors in a particular standardized format and that it wants to receive Shipment responses to those orders in another particular standardized format. To do this, Wal-Mart can develop an XML Schema for Order documents and another for Shipment documents. It can then publish those XML Schemas on a Web site accessible to its vendors. In this way, all vendors can determine how they will receive orders from Wal-Mart and how they should send their Shipment notifications back.

The schemas can be used by Wal-Mart and all of its vendors to ensure that they are sending and receiving only valid XML documents. Further, Wal-Mart can develop XSL documents to cause the Order and Shipment documents to be transformed into the specific formats needed by its accounting, operations, marketing, and general management departments. These XSL documents work for any Order or Shipment from any of its vendors.

Figure 13-15	**Example XML Industry Standards**

Industry Type	Example Standards
Accounting	• American Institute of Certified Public Accountants (AICPA): Extensible Financial Reporting Markup Language (XFRML)[OASIS Cover page] • Open Applications Group, Inc (OAG)
Architecture and Construction	• Architecture, Engineering, and Construction XML Working Group (aecXML Working Group) • ConSource.com: Construction Manufacturing and Distribution Extensible Markup Language (cmdXML)
Automotive	• Automotive Industry Action Group (AIAG) • Global Automedia • MSR: Standards for Information Exchange in the Engineering Process (MEDOC) • The Society of Automotive Engineers (SAE): XML for the Automotive Industry–SAE J2008[OASIS Cover page] • Open Applications Group, Inc (OAG)
Banking	• Banking Industry Technology Secretariat (BITS): [OASIS Cover page] • Financial Services Technology Consortium (FSTC): Bank Internet Payment System (BIPS)[OASIS Cover page] • Open Applications Group, Inc (OAG)
Electronic Data Interchange	• Data Interchange Standards Association (DISA): [OASIS Cover page] • EEMA EDI/EC Work Group[OASIS Cover page] • European Committee for Standardization/Information Society Standardization System (CEN/ISSS; The European XML/EDI Pilot Project)[OASIS Cover page] • XML/EDI Group[OASIS Cover page]
Human Resources	• DataMain: Human Resources Markup Language (hrml) • HR-XML Consortium[OASIS Cover page]: JobPosting, CandidateProfile, Resume • Open Applications Group (OAG): Open Applications Group Interface Specification (OASIS)[OASIS Cover page] • Tapestry.Net: JOB Markup Language (JOB) • Open Applications Group, Inc (OAG)
Insurance	• ACORD: Property and Casualty[OASIS Cover page], Life (XMLife)[OASIS Cover page] • Lexica: iLingo

Figure 13-15   Continued

Industry Type	Example Standards
Real Estate	• OpenMLS: Real Estate Listing Management System (OpenMLS)[OASIS Cover page]
	• Real Estate Transaction Standard working group (RETS): Real Estate Transaction Standard (RETS)[OASIS Cover page]
Software	• IBM: [OASIS Cover page]
	• Flashline.com: Software Component Documentation DTD
	• Flashline.com:
	• INRIA: Koala Bean Markup Language (KBML)[OASIS Cover page]
	• Marimba and Microsoft: Open Software Description Format (OSD)[OASIS Cover page]
	• Object Management Group (OMG): [OASIS Cover page]
Workflow	• Internet Engineering Task Force (IETF): Simple Workflow Access Protocol (SWAP)[OASIS Cover page]
	• Workflow Management Coalition (MfMC): Wf-XML[OASIS Cover page]

In all of these cases, once the XML Schema documents have been prepared and the XSL documents have been written, all validation and materialization is done via automated processes. Thus, there is no need for any human to touch the Order document between its origination at Wal-Mart and the picking of the inventory at the supplier.

So, the only challenge that remains is to populate the XML documents with database data in accordance with the relevant XML Schema. SQL can be used to populate schemas that have only one multivalue path, but this is too restrictive. A new technology is needed to ease the transformation of database data into XML documents and to ease the transformation of XML documents into database data. That need brings us to ADO.NET.

ADO.NET

ADO.NET is a new, improved, and greatly expanded version of ADO that was developed as part of Microsoft's .NET initiative. It incorporates the functionality of ADO and OLE DB, which were discussed in Chapter 12, but adds much more. In particular, ADO.NET facilitates the transformation of XML documents to and from relational database constructs. ADO.NET also provides the ability to create and process in-memory databases called *datasets*.

Figure 13-16 shows the general role of ADO. As shown, it serves as an intermediary between all types of .NET applications and the DBMS and database. ADO.NET can work with any OLE DB–compliant DBMS, and there are special high-performance drivers for both SQL Server and Oracle.

An ADO.NET **data provider** is a class library that provides ADO.NET services. As shown in Figure 13-17, there are currently three Microsoft-supplied data providers. The OLE DB data provider can be used for ADO.NET processing of any OLE DB–compliant data source. The SQLClient data provider processes SQL Server databases, and the OracleClient data provider processes Oracle databases.

All of these data providers were written by Microsoft. The information necessary for organizations to create data providers is publicly available, however. By the time you

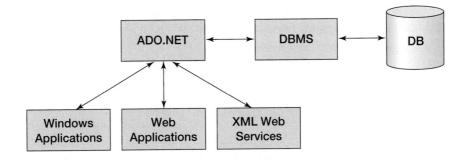

Figure 13-16

Role of ADO.NET

read this chapter, there will likely be data providers from the Oracle Corporation, from IBM, and from other companies.

Figure 13-17 depicts the major components of a .NET data provider. The Connection object is similar to the Connection object discussed in Chapter 12, except that ODBC is not used as a data source. Instead, the name of the data provider and the database are provided, as you will see.

Once a connection is established, a Command object is created on that connection. Three options are then available. First, the application can use Data Reader to obtain read-only, forward-only, fast access to database data. Second, an application can get and put data to and from the database using Command objects in a way similar to that shown in Chapter 12. This facility is represented by the double-headed arrow in the middle of the Command object. Stored procedures can be executed in this way as well. Third, the application can use a **Data Adaptor** to create and process datasets.

The first two options are important, but they are just extensions and improvements on existing ADO features and functions. It is the Data Adaptor and dataset that distinguish ADO.NET and that provide the capabilities we need to process XML documents against database data.

The ADO.NET Dataset

A **dataset** is an in-memory database. Datasets have all the characteristics, features, and functions of a regular database. They can have multiple tables, and those tables can have relationships. The tables in a dataset can have foreign keys and referential integrity, and

Figure 13-17

Components of an
ADO.NET Data Provider

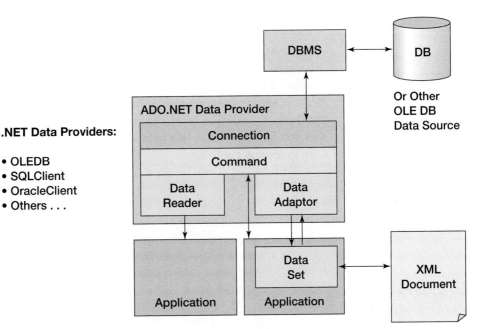

referential integrity actions can be defined on them as well. Tables in a dataset can have surrogate keys, meaning that new rows are given a value by ADO.NET rather than by the DBMS. Columns of dataset tables can be defined to be unique.

Relationships among dataset tables can be processed just as relationships in a database can be processed. Later in this chapter, you will see an example of how a relationship can be used to compute the values of a column. Dataset tables can also have views.

The data in a dataset are disconnected from any regular database. Data can be created in a dataset without first being added to a database. Further, if the dataset's data were read from a database, no connection is maintained back to the source database for that data. A dataset is an independent, fully functioned, in-memory database. Dataset data can be constructed from data in multiple databases, and they can be managed by different DBMS products.

Once a dataset is constructed, its contents can be formatted as an XML document with a single command. Similarly, an XML Schema document for the dataset can also be produced with a single command. This process works in reverse as well. An XML Schema document can be used to create the structure of a dataset, and the dataset data can then be filled by reading an XML document.

B T W

You may be wondering, "Why is all of this necessary? Why do we need an in-memory database?" The answer lies in database views like that shown in Figure 13-14. There is no standardized way to describe and process such data structures. Because it involves two multivalue paths through the data, SQL cannot be used to describe the data. Instead, we must execute two SQL statements and somehow patch the results to obtain the view.

Views like that shown in Figure 13-14 have been processed for many years, but only by private, proprietary means. Every time such a structure needs to be processed, a developer designs programs for creating and manipulating the data in memory and for saving them to the database. Object-oriented programmers define a class for this data structure and create methods to serialize objects of this class into the database. Other programmers use other means. The problem is that every time a different view is designed, a different scheme must be designed and developed to process the new view.

As Microsoft developed .NET technology, it became clear that a generalized means was needed to define and process database views and related structures. Microsoft could have defined a new proprietary technology for this purpose, but thankfully it did not. Instead, it recognized that the concepts, techniques, and facilities used to manage regular databases can be used to manage in-memory databases as well. The benefit to you is that all of the concepts and techniques that you have learned to this point for processing regular databases can also be used to process datasets.

Datasets do have a downside, and a serious one for some applications. Because dataset data are disconnected from the regular database, only optimistic locking can be used. The data are read from the database, placed into the dataset, and processed there. No attempt is made to propagate changes in the dataset back to the database. If, after processing, the application later wants to save all of the dataset data into a regular database, it needs to use optimistic locking. If some other application has changed the data, either the dataset will need to be reprocessed or the data change will be forced onto the database, causing the lost update problem.

Thus, datasets cannot be used for applications in which optimistic locking is problematic. For such applications, the ADO.NET Command object should be used instead. But for applications in which conflict is rare or for those in which reprocessing after conflict can be accommodated, datasets provide significant value.

Using ADO.NET to Process View Ridge Customer Data

The remainder of this section discusses a Visual Basic .NET application that creates a dataset for the view shown in Figure 13-14. Visual Basic .NET is an object-oriented programming language, and if you are not yet an object-oriented programmer, you will have to cope as best you can. Most of the examples can be understood intuitively, even if you do not understand the syntax.

B T W

The only way to use Oracle's XML facilities is to write in Java, an object-oriented programming language. Further, the only way to process ADO.NET is from one of the .NET languages, all of which, like Visual Basic .NET, are object-oriented languages. Thus, if you do not yet know object-oriented design and programming, and if you want to work in the emerging world of database processing, you should run, not walk, to your nearest object-oriented design and programming class!

Purpose of the Application

The purpose of this application is to demonstrate the creation and processing of a dataset. This application, which is an ASP.NET application, creates a Web page and, in the code behind file, constructs a dataset from the five View Ridge tables. The application reads all of the data for one customer (here, hard coded as the customer with CustomerID = 1015).

Once the dataset is populated, the user of this application can display the contents of the tables (called datatables) in the dataset, display the dataset as an XML document, or display the structure of the dataset as an XML Schema document.

Additionally, the user can cause the application to examine all transactions for this customer. If any have a SalesPrice less than the AskingPrice, the user can set the SalesPrice equal to the AskingPrice. Finally, the changed dataset data are written back to the database. A log of the data activity is produced; we will examine it to see how the dataset tracks changes.

In the next sections, we will examine important portions of this code. The point, however, is not for you to understand this particular application; rather you should strive to understand the ideas behind datasets and the relationship between datasets and the database.

Getting a Connection and Filling the Dataset

Figure 13-18 shows a code snippet that imports the necessary class libraries, defines the variables used throughout the application, and initiates processing. This code was placed in a Visual Basic module named DataSetElements; this module contains subroutines used by the code that processes the Web page. Only the first subroutine of this module is shown in Figure 13-18. Other subroutines will be shown as we proceed.

The action starts in the subroutine ConstructDataSet. This routine is called when the Web page is loaded (not shown). It instantiates a new dataset in the dataset object variable

```
Imports System.Data
Imports System.Data.OracleClient ' use the Oracle client Data Provider

Module DataSetElements


    Public drcTransRows As DataRow()
    Public drTransRow As DataRow
    Public dtUpdatedRows As DataTable

    Public intCustomerID As Integer

    Public dsCustomerView As DataSet
    Public conViewRidge As OracleConnection
    Public daViewRidge As OracleDataAdapter

    Public Sub ConstructDataSet()

        ' Create data set and get connection to Oracle database
        dsCustomerView = New DataSet()
        conViewRidge = New OracleConnection("Data Source=VRG;Integrated Security = SSPI")
        ' instantiate the data adapter; set select command below
        daViewRidge = New OracleDataAdapter("", conViewRidge)

    End Sub
```

dsCustomerView, and it obtains a Connection object in the variable conViewRidge. The connection is to the Oracle database VRG using Integrated Security. The connection format shown here can be used when Oracle is running on the same machine as the Web server and when the database is also located on that same machine. Additionally, the use of Integrated Security means that the operating system (in this case, Windows XP Professional) provides the user's credentials. The last statement in this subroutine instantiates a new data adapter object named daViewRidge. Note that the data adapter uses the connection, but not the dataset object. Thus, the same data adapter can be used for different datasets, if necessary. In this application, we will process only one dataset: dsCustomerView.

B T W

ASP.NET connects to the DBMS using the default user name ASPNET. As stated in Chapter 10, Oracle requires any user name that has operating system authentication to begin with the letters OPS$. Thus, for this application to run, there must be an account named OPS$ASPNET in the Oracle VRG database, and that account must have privileges necessary to read and update the View Ridge tables in VRG. If you do not want to use the default name ASPNET, you can cause ASP.NET to pass the user's credentials through to Oracle. That technique, however, is beyond the scope of this discussion.

The Web page next calls the subroutine FillDataSet, shown in Figure 13-19. This routine uses the data adapter to fill the dataset tables. First, a string variable is set to the syntax of the appropriate SQL command. Then, the SelectCommand property of the data adapter is set to the SQL text. After that, the data adapter method FillSchema is invoked to obtain the schema metadata for the SelectCommand into a new table called CustomerAlias. Then, the data adapter Fill method is called to place the data results of the SelectCommand into the dataset.

The SELECT statement uses the value of the public integer variable intCustomerID to qualify the rows to be read. In this application, the form load routine sets intCustomerID to 1015 prior to calling this routine. Thus, only data for the customer with CustomerID = 1015 will be read into the dataset. Obviously, this variable can be changed to read data for other customers.

Figure 13-19

**Using the Data Adapter
to Fill the Dataset
Tables**

```
Public Sub FillDataSet()
    Dim strSQLCommand As String

    'Fill the CustomerAlias table in the data set with qualifying CUSTOMER data from the database
    'First get schema info and then get data
    strSQLCommand = "Select * from SYSTEM.CUSTOMER where CustomerID = " & Str(intCustomerID)
    daViewRidge.SelectCommand.CommandText = strSQLCommand
    daViewRidge.FillSchema(dsCustomerView, SchemaType.Mapped, "CustomerAlias")
    daViewRidge.Fill(dsCustomerView, "CustomerAlias")

    'Fill the intersection table in the data set with CUSTOMER_ARTIST_INT data from the database
    strSQLCommand = "Select * from SYSTEM.CUSTOMER_ARTIST_INT where CustomerID = " & Str(intCustomerID)
    daViewRidge.SelectCommand.CommandText = strSQLCommand
    daViewRidge.FillSchema(dsCustomerView, SchemaType.Mapped, "IntersectionAlias")
    daViewRidge.Fill(dsCustomerView, "IntersectionAlias")

    'Fill the TransactionAlias table in the data set with TRANSACTION data from the database
    strSQLCommand = "Select * from SYSTEM.TRANSACTION where CustomerID = " & Str(intCustomerID)
    daViewRidge.SelectCommand.CommandText = strSQLCommand
    daViewRidge.FillSchema(dsCustomerView, SchemaType.Mapped, "TransactionAlias")
    daViewRidge.Fill(dsCustomerView, "TransactionAlias")

    ' Read Qualifying WORK table rows into the data set
    strSQLCommand = "Select * from SYSTEM.WORK where WorkID IN " _
        & "(Select WorkID from SYSTEM.TRANSACTION WHERE CustomerID = " & Str(intCustomerID) & ")"
    daViewRidge.SelectCommand.CommandText = strSQLCommand
    daViewRidge.FillSchema(dsCustomerView, SchemaType.Mapped, "WorkAlias")
    daViewRidge.Fill(dsCustomerView, "WorkAlias")

    ' Read qualifying ARTIST table rows into the data set via the interesection table
    strSQLCommand = "Select * from SYSTEM.ARTIST where ArtistID IN " _
        & "(Select ArtistID from SYSTEM.CUSTOMER_ARTIST_INT WHERE CustomerID = " & Str(intCustomerID) & "
    daViewRidge.SelectCommand.CommandText = strSQLCommand
    daViewRidge.FillSchema(dsCustomerView, SchemaType.Mapped, "ArtistAlias")
    daViewRidge.Fill(dsCustomerView, "ArtistAlias")

    ' Read any ARTIST table rows that weren't picked up from the intersection
    ' table
    strSQLCommand = "Select * from SYSTEM.ARTIST A where A.ArtistID IN " _
        & "(Select W.ArtistID from SYSTEM.WORK W Join SYSTEM.TRANSACTION T " _
        & "ON T.WorkID = W.WorkID Join SYSTEM.CUSTOMER C ON T.CustomerID = C.CustomerID " _
        & "AND C.CustomerID = " & Str(intCustomerID) & ") " _
        & "AND NOT EXISTS (Select * from SYSTEM.CUSTOMER_ARTIST_INT I " _
        & "WHERE I.ArtistID = A.ArtistID " _
        & "AND I.CustomerID = " & Str(intCustomerID) & ")"

    daViewRidge.SelectCommand.CommandText = strSQLCommand
    daViewRidge.FillSchema(dsCustomerView, SchemaType.Mapped, "ArtistAlias")
    daViewRidge.Fill(dsCustomerView, "ArtistAlias")

End Sub
```

In this application, all SQL statements for Oracle must be preceded by the word SYS-TEM. Thus, to query all rows from CUSTOMER, we would code SELECT * from SYS-TEM.CUSTOMER. This is necessary because the tables were created under the SYSTEM account and they will be processed by the OPS$ASPNET account as explained.

To ease readability, the code was written so that all names of tables in the dataset terminate in the word *Alias*. Thus, application in the dataset, table names are CustomerAlias, WorkAlias, ArtistAlias, and so on. The application uses the name IntersectionAlias for the intersection table; Customer_Artist_IntAlias was just too cumbersome a name!

The only notable characteristic of this routine is the SQL statements used to obtain the ARTIST data. First, all of the ARTIST data needed by the intersection table rows are selected. Then, any ARTIST data referenced by WORK that was not obtained from the intersection table are read. At this point, all data for the customer having a CustomerID equal to the value of intCustomerID have been read into the dataset. All of the metadata that the OracleClient data provider obtained from Oracle about these tables has also been placed into the dataset.

Adding Structures to the Dataset

The next series of subroutines adds structure to the dataset. Figure 13-20 shows the BuildRelationships subroutine, which defines the relationships among the tables. The Add method of the Relations class of the dataset is used to do this. In each case, the Add method is passed the name of the relationship, the name of the key in the parent, and the

Figure 13-20

Building Relationships

```
Public Sub BuildRelationships()

    'Create the relationships

    dsCustomerView.Relations.Add("CustomerTransactionRel", _
        dsCustomerView.Tables("CustomerAlias").Columns("CustomerID"), _
        dsCustomerView.Tables("TransactionAlias").Columns("CustomerID"))

    dsCustomerView.Relations.Add("WorkTransRel", _
        dsCustomerView.Tables("WorkAlias").Columns("WorkID"), _
        dsCustomerView.Tables("TransactionAlias").Columns("WorkID"))

    dsCustomerView.Relations.Add("ArtistWorkRel", _
        dsCustomerView.Tables("ArtistAlias").Columns("ArtistID"), _
        dsCustomerView.Tables("WorkAlias").Columns("ArtistID"))

    dsCustomerView.Relations.Add("CustomerIntRel", _
        dsCustomerView.Tables("CustomerAlias").Columns("CustomerID"), _
        dsCustomerView.Tables("IntersectionAlias").Columns("CustomerID"))

    dsCustomerView.Relations.Add("ArtistIntRel", _
        dsCustomerView.Tables("ArtistAlias").Columns("ArtistID"), _
        dsCustomerView.Tables("IntersectionAlias").Columns("ArtistID"))

End Sub
```

name of the foreign key in the child. The relationships created here can be used to process tables in the dataset. Given a WorkAlias row, for example, it is possible to use the relationship to obtain the parent of the WORK. Similarly, given an ArtistAlias row, it is possible to use the relationship to obtain all related rows in WorkAlias.

The referential integrity constraints for the relationships are created in the subroutine shown in Figure 13-21. In each case, the parent and child tables are identified and then a ForeignKeyConstraint object is created for each constraint. ForeignKeyConstraint objects have properties DeleteRule and UpdateRule. These properties can be set to specify foreign key behavior when the parents' keys are updated or deleted. Allowed values are {None, Cascade, Set Null, and Set Default}. Here, we set the values to be consistent with the referential integrity constraints in the Oracle database.

Finally, the AddDataColumn subroutine in Figure 13-22 is called to create a new column in the CustomerAlias datatable. The new column will contain the sum of the SalesPrice columns in all TransactionAlias tables that are related to the CustomerAlias row. Notice how the CustomerTransactionRel relationship object is used to provide the TRANSACTION rows.

B T W

Keep in mind that the dataset and all of the structures created here are in-memory. We have created a mini-database, but one that is in memory, not on disk. Furthermore, dataset data are disconnected from the database. We can close the Connection object if we want and process the dataset independently without problem.

Processing the Dataset

Datasets have built-in capabilities that make them very easy to process. Figure 13-23(a) shows the Visual Basic .NET code necessary to fill a data grid for display on the Web page. All that is required is to set the DataSource property of the grid to the dataset and the

Figure 13-21

Creating Referential Integrity Constraints

```
Sub CreateRefIntegrityConstraints()

    'Create the constraints
    Dim dtParent As DataTable
    Dim dtChild As DataTable
    Dim fkConstraint As ForeignKeyConstraint

    dtParent = dsCustomerView.Tables("ArtistAlias")
    dtChild = dsCustomerView.Tables("WorkAlias")
    fkConstraint = New ForeignKeyConstraint _
        ("WorkFK", dtParent.Columns("ArtistID"), dtChild.Columns("ArtistID"))
    fkConstraint.DeleteRule = Rule.None
    fkConstraint.UpdateRule = Rule.None

    dtParent = dsCustomerView.Tables("WorkAlias")
    dtChild = dsCustomerView.Tables("TransactionAlias")
    fkConstraint = New ForeignKeyConstraint _
        ("WorkTransFK", dtParent.Columns("WorkID"), dtChild.Columns("WorkID"))
    fkConstraint.DeleteRule = Rule.None
    fkConstraint.UpdateRule = Rule.None

    dtParent = dsCustomerView.Tables("CustomerAlias")
    dtChild = dsCustomerView.Tables("TransactionAlias")
    fkConstraint = New ForeignKeyConstraint _
        ("CustomerTransFK", dtParent.Columns("CustomerID"), dtChild.Columns("CustomerID"))
    fkConstraint.DeleteRule = Rule.None
    fkConstraint.UpdateRule = Rule.None

    dtParent = dsCustomerView.Tables("CustomerAlias")
    dtChild = dsCustomerView.Tables("IntersectionAlias")
    fkConstraint = New ForeignKeyConstraint _
        ("CustomerArtistFK", dtParent.Columns("CustomerID"), dtChild.Columns("CustomerID"))
    fkConstraint.DeleteRule = Rule.Cascade
    fkConstraint.UpdateRule = Rule.Cascade

    dtParent = dsCustomerView.Tables("ArtistAlias")
    dtChild = dsCustomerView.Tables("IntersectionAlias")
    fkConstraint = New ForeignKeyConstraint _
        ("ArtistCustomerFK", dtParent.Columns("ArtistID"), dtChild.Columns("ArtistID"))
    fkConstraint.DeleteRule = Rule.Cascade
    fkConstraint.UpdateRule = Rule.Cascade

End Sub
```

Figure 13-22

Adding a Computed Column to a Data Table

```
Sub AddDataColumn()
    Dim tCol As DataColumn

    ' Create new column Total Purchases and set to sum of child SalesPrice

    tCol = New DataColumn("Total Purchases", GetType(Int32))
    tCol.Expression = "Sum (Child(CustomerTransactionRel).SalesPrice)"
    dsCustomerView.Tables("CustomerAlias").Columns.Add(tCol)

End Sub
```

DataMember property to the name of the datatable that the grid is to contain. The grid's DataBind method can then be used to fill the grid with the datatable's data. Figure 13-23(b) shows the results of this binding.

The data grids in this figure have a number of interesting characteristics. First, observe that the column names were obtained from Oracle. At no point did we code these names into the application. They were obtained when the data adapter FillSchema method read the metadata from the database. All of these names are shown in uppercase letters because Oracle stores them that way.

Also note that the TotalPurchases column has been added to the CustomerAlias datatable. Its value has been set correctly to 91000, which is the sum of SalesPrice for this customer's purchases. This means the relationship between CustomerAlias and TransactionAlias was correctly processed. All of the rest of the data for customer 1015 appear, as you would expect.

Using Data Grids
(a) Filling the Grids with
Dataset Tables and (b)
Grid Display in Browser

```
Private Sub FillGrids()

    ' bind data to grids
    grdCustomer.DataSource = dsCustomerView
    grdCustomer.DataMember = "CustomerAlias"
    grdCustomer.DataBind()

    grdTransaction.DataSource = dsCustomerView
    grdTransaction.DataMember = "TransactionAlias"
    grdTransaction.DataBind()

    grdWork.DataSource = dsCustomerView
    grdWork.DataMember = "WorkAlias"
    grdWork.DataBind()

    grdArtist.DataSource = dsCustomerView
    grdArtist.DataMember = "ArtistAlias"
    grdArtist.DataBind()

    grdIntersection.DataSource = dsCustomerView
    grdIntersection.DataMember = "IntersectionAlias"
    grdIntersection.DataBind()

End Sub
```

(a)

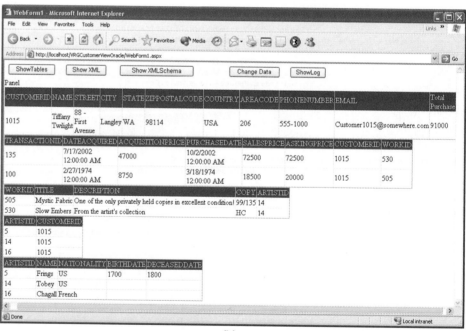

(b)

Although datasets can be accessed from a table perspective like that shown in Figure 13-23, they can also be processed from an XML perspective. The code in Figure 13-24(a) shows the use of the dataset method GetXml. Here, that method is used to place the XML version of this dataset into a string variable. The string variable is then displayed in a text box. The result is shown in Figure 13-24(b).

Additionally, we can cause the dataset to produce the XML Schema for this dataset. To do this, we just call the dataset method GetXmlSchema and place the resulting string into our text box, as shown in Figure 13-25(a). The result is the XML Schema document for the XML document shown in Figure 13-24(b).

Figure 13-24

Generating an XML Document from the Dataset
(a) Code to Generate the XML Document and
(b) Portion of Resulting XML Document

```
Private Sub btnShowXML_Click _
    (ByVal sender As System.Object, ByVal e As System.EventArgs) _
    Handles btnShowXML.Click

    'get the xml document for the dataset and place in the textbox
    strXml = dsCustomerView.GetXml()
    txtXMLShow.Text = strXml
    pnlTables.Visible = False
    txtXMLShow.Visible = True

End Sub
```

(a)

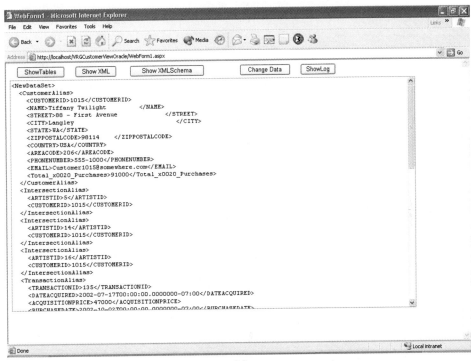

(b)

B T W

Without intending to shill for Microsoft, this is an amazing capability for very little work on our part. We can create a dataset and fill it with data for a database view of any level of complexity. After we have done so, we can readily process that dataset data either as tables or as XML. Furthermore, if we change the XML document, the changes will be updated in the dataset and hence in the tables. Similarly, if we change the dataset tables, those changes will automatically be reflected in the XML document produced. Thus, we can process the same data from either perspective.

If we save the XML Schema document in a file, we can later use that file to re-create the dataset. All of the dataset tables, columns, and relationships will be restored correctly from the XML Schema document. Note, however, that some characteristics of the dataset are not placed in the XML Schema. For example, although relationships are shown in the XML Schema, referential integrity is not. Referential

Figure 13-25

Generating an XML Schema from the Dataset
(a) Code to Generate the XML Schema (b) Portion of Resulting XML Schema

```
Private Sub btnShowXMLSchema_Click _
    (ByVal sender As System.Object, ByVal e As System.EventArgs) _
    Handles btnShowXMLSchema.Click

    ' Get the xmlschema for the dataset and place in the textbox
    strXml = dsCustomerView.GetXmlSchema()
    txtXMLShow.Text = strXml
    pnlTables.Visible = False
    txtXMLShow.Visible = True

End Sub
```

(a)

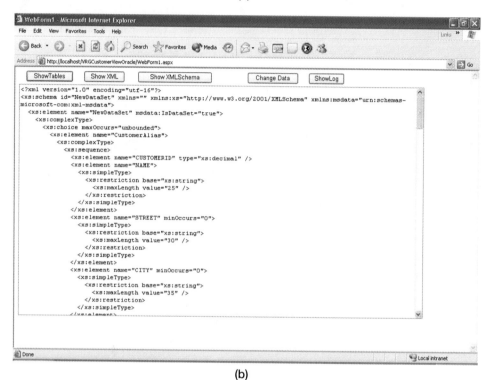

(b)

integrity constraints have to be added to the dataset after it is constructed from the XML Schema.

Updating the Dataset Data and Updating the Database

Data in the dataset can be updated just like regular database data. The difference is that changes to the dataset are not necessarily propagated to the database. To illustrate how the dataset update process works, we will change some dataset data, examine the status of the dataset rows, make database changes from the dataset, and then reexamine the status of the dataset rows. All of the action will be recorded in a text box log for illustration.

Figure 13-26(a) shows the code used. As you read this code, reference Figure 13-18, in which the important object variables are declared. In particular, the variable drcTransRow (drc for *DataRow Collection*) is defined as an array of DataRow objects, and drTransRow is declared as a single DataRow object. dtUpdatedRows is a DataTable object that contains the updated rows. Finally, dtTrans is defined as a DataTable object. For reasons unimportant to us here, that object is declared elsewhere in the code, but it is defined as a DataTable object.

Figure 13-26

Updating a Dataset and Database

(a) Update Code;
(b) Trigger-like Event;
(c) Display RowVersion Code; and (d) Creating the UpdateCommand

```
Private Sub btnChangeData_Click(ByVal sender As System.Object, ByVal e As System.EventArgs) _
        Handles btnChangeData.Click
    txtBoxMessage.Visible = True ' make log visible
    txtBoxMessage.Text = "****   Start column change in TransactionAlias Table. ****" ' start log

    dtTrans = dsCustomerView.Tables("TransactionAlias") ' point dtTrans to proper dataset table
    drcTransRows = dtTrans.Select("(SalesPrice < AskingPrice) ") ' find qualifying rows
    For Each drTransRow In drcTransRows ' for each qualifying row
        drTransRow("SalesPrice") = drTransRow("AskingPrice") ' set salesprice to askingprice
    Next
    DisplayRowState() ' write to log

    dtUpdatedRows = dsCustomerView.Tables("TransactionAlias") ' make data table of updated rows
    dtUpdatedRows = dsCustomerView.Tables("TransactionAlias").GetChanges(DataRowState.Modified)

    BuildOracleUpdateCommand() ' Create updateCommand property for the Oracle Data Adapter
    daViewRidge.Update(dtUpdatedRows) ' Update database

    txtBoxMessage.Text = txtBoxMessage.Text & _
        "****         Oracle Updated From Data Set           **** "
    DisplayRowState() ' write to log

    dsCustomerView.AcceptChanges() ' accept changes into dataset
    txtBoxMessage.Text = txtBoxMessage.Text & _
        "****          Data Set Accept Changes Issued        **** "
    DisplayRowState() ' write to log last time
    FillGrids() 'fill grids with latest dataset data
End Sub
```

(a)

```
Private Sub dtTrans_ColumnChanging(ByVal sender As Object, _
            ByVal e As System.Data.DataColumnChangeEventArgs) _
            Handles dtTrans.ColumnChanging

    ' this is the dataset equivalent of a before trigger
    ' place before logic here; for example, could alter e.ProposedValue
    txtBoxMessage.Text = txtBoxMessage.Text & _
        "****   Column is changing.  Proposed value is:  " & _
        e.ProposedValue & "       ****"

End Sub
```

(b)

```
Sub DisplayRowState()

    For Each drTransRow In dtTrans.Rows
        'show current version of SalesPrice in this row
        txtBoxMessage.Text = txtBoxMessage.Text & _
        " Transaction with TransactionID" & Str(drTransRow("TransactionID")) _
        & " Current Value Is " & drTransRow("SalesPrice", DataRowVersion.Current)

        'show original version of SalePrice in this row
        txtBoxMessage.Text = txtBoxMessage.Text & _
        " Transaction with TransactionID" & Str(drTransRow("TransactionID")) _
        & " Original Value Is " & drTransRow("SalesPrice", DataRowVersion.Original) & " "
    Next

End Sub
```

(c)

```
Sub BuildOracleUpdateCommand()
    Dim cmdUpdate As OracleCommand

    ' Create the UpdateCommand.
    cmdUpdate = New OracleCommand("UPDATE SYSTEM.Transaction SET SalesPrice = :pSalesPrice " & _
            "WHERE TransactionID = :pTransactionID", conViewRidge)
    cmdUpdate.Parameters.Add("pSalesPrice", OracleType.Number, 8, "SalesPrice")
    cmdUpdate.Parameters.Add("pTransactionID", OracleType.Int32, 0, "TransactionID")

    daViewRidge.UpdateCommand = cmdUpdate

End Sub
```

(d)

As changes are made, the dataset keeps three versions of each column in each data-table. These versions are the *original* value, the *current* value, and the *proposed* value. The original value is the value of the column when first read from the database or the value of the column after changes have been committed in the dataset via the AcceptChanges method. The current value is the value after changes have been made, but before those changes have been committed to the dataset. If no changes have been made to a column value, the original and current values are the same. Finally, the proposed value is a value that exists during a modification. We will trap that value in the ADO.NET equivalent of a trigger.

Updating the Dataset

When the user clicks the button Change Data, the procedure in Figure 13-26(a) is executed. First, it writes a start message to the text box control txtBoxMessage. Then, dtTrans is set to the TransactionAlias table. Next, the drcTransRows is set equal to all of the rows in TransAlias for which SalesPrice is less than AskingPrice. After that, the SalesPrice of all the rows in the drcTransRow collection is set to AskingPrice. For the data in our dataset (see Figure 13-23(b)), there is one such row that will be updated.

When the change is made, the ColumnChanging event of dtTrans is invoked and the code in Figure 13-26(b) is executed. In this example, the code simply displays the proposed value in the text box log. Of course, the application can place before trigger logic here, if appropriate. Note, too, that the proposed value can be changed here, prior to the dataset update.

After updating the SalesPrice column, the subroutine calls DisplayRowState. As shown in Figure 13-26(c), this routine adds a message to the text box that shows the current and original values of SalesPrice for all rows in the TransactionAlias datatable.

As you can tell from the log shown in Figure 13-27, the change was trapped by the ColumnChanging event, and the proposed value of 20000 was displayed. Next, the DisplayRowState routine printed the current and original values for all the rows in dtTrans (there are two, as shown in Figure 13-23). Observe that the current and original values of the first row are the same, but the current and original values for the second row differ because of the change to SalesPrice.

Figure 13-27

Log Showing Dataset Updates

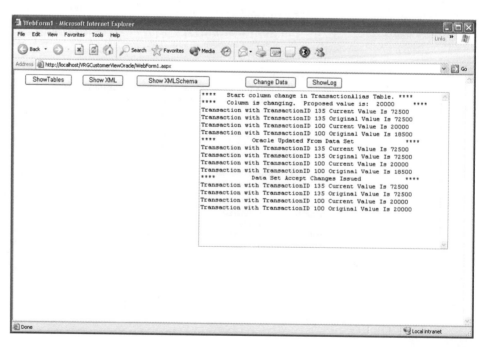

Updating the Oracle Database

At this point, the dataset values have been altered in the dataset, but nothing has been changed in the database. The next statements, shown in Figure 13-26(a), propagate the dataset changes to the database. To do this, a datatable called dtUpdatedRows is created and the GetChanges method of a datatable is called to fill that datatable. GetChanges places all rows for which the current value is different from the original value into the dtUpdatedRows datatable.

The next statement calls a subroutine to build an Oracle UPDATE command. The code is shown in Figure 13-26(d). The purpose of this subroutine is to provide a value for the UpdateCommand property of the Oracle data adapter. Every data adapter has four such properties: SelectCommand, InsertCommand, UpdateCommand, and DeleteCommand. These commands are used to perform the indicated action. If, for example, a row needs to be updated, the data adapter calls the UpdateCommand to make the update in the database. Similarly, if a row needs to be deleted, the data adapter calls the DeleteCommand property to make the deletion. We used the SelectCommand of the data adapter in Figure 13-19 when we filled the dataset.

Any valid SQL command can be entered for these properties. Alternatively, these commands can invoke stored procedures to make the appropriate data changes. It is also possible to have Visual Studio .NET write these commands for you, but that option is beyond the scope of our present discussion. Instead, here we will create our own update command, as shown.

Before continuing, note that the ability to tailor how the data adapter makes insert, update, and delete commands gives tremendous flexibility to the developer. With ADO, the developer was stuck with ADO's particular implementation of these actions. By allowing the developer to specify his or her own commands, much more flexibility exists to build particular logic and functionality into the process of propagating dataset changes into the database.

Note one small point in Figure 13-26(d). As you know from Chapter 10, in PL/SQL stored procedures, variables are preceded by a colon. This means that the parameters provided to the UPDATE command must also be preceded by a colon, as shown in Figure 13-26(d). The Microsoft OracleClient data provider documentation is unclear as to this need.

After the UpdateCommand property has been set, the updates can be made. In Figure 13-26(a), this is done by invoking the Update method on the data adapter and passing it the datatable with the updated rows as a parameter. At this point, the Oracle database has been updated.

As the log in Figure 13-27 indicates, however, the changes have not yet been committed to the dataset. You can tell this from the log because after the Oracle update is issued, the Original and Current values of SalesPrice in the second dtTrans row are different.

The changes are committed in the dataset by invoking the dataset's AcceptChanges method. After that is done, the original and current values of all columns in all rows of tables in the dataset will be the same. This is demonstrated by the last four lines of the log shown in Figure 13-27.

The final values of all datatables in the dataset are shown in Figure 13-28. Observe that the computed value of TotalPurchases has been correctly updated as well.

We showed only a few of the features and functions of ADO.NET in this section. Although this discussion does not prepare you to write your own ADO.NET applications, you should now be familiar with the overall concept of datasets and how they can be processed. You also should be able to understand how relational databases and document processing have been integrated into the idea of a dataset. This technology will be important for many, many years to come, and learning more about it would be an excellent investment of your time.

Figure 13-28

Dataset Tables after Update

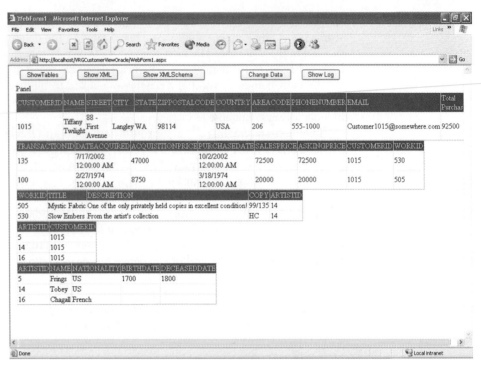

Additional XML Standards

As you know, XML was developed as a series of standards. So far, we have mentioned XML, XSL, XSLT, and XML Schema. There are a number of other XML standards that you will hear about. Figure 13-29 shows some that you may encounter. You can find the standards, their documentation, and some tutorials on the **www.w3.org** and **www.xml.org** Web sites.

In addition to the four standards discussed in this chapter, XPath is a standard for addressing elements within documents. In Figure 13-4, expressions like <xsl: value-of-select = "name/lastname"/> use XPath to locate a particular element in the document. XPath includes concepts from another standard, XPointer, which was developed to provide a sophisticated means for documents to reference elements in other documents.

SAX and *DOM* refer to different methods of parsing XML documents. The process of parsing consists of reading a document, breaking it into components, and responding to those components in some way—perhaps storing them into a database. XML parsers also validate documents against the DTDs and XML Schemas.

To use the SAX API, a program that is working on an XML document—an XSLT processor, for example—invokes the SAX-compliant parser and passes it the name of the document to parse. The SAX parser processes the document and calls back objects within the XSLT processor whenever particular structures are encountered. A SAX parser, for example, calls the XSLT parser when it encounters a new element, passing the name of the element, its content, and other relevant items.

The DOM API works from a different paradigm. A DOM-compliant parser processes the entire XML document and then creates a tree representation of it. Each element of the document is a node on the tree. The XSLT processor can then call the DOM parser to obtain particular elements using XPath or a similar addressing scheme. DOM requires the entire document to be processed at one time and may require an unreasonable amount of storage for very large documents. If the document is large, SAX is the better choice. On the other hand, if all of the document contents need to be available for use at once, DOM is the only choice.

Figure 13-29

Important XML Standards

Standard	Description
XML	Extensible Markup Language. A document markup language that started the following:
XSL	XSLT Stylesheet. The document that provides the {match, action} pairs and other data for XSLT to use when transforming an XML document.
XSLT	A program (or process) that applies XSLT Stylesheets to an XML document to produce a transformed XML document.
XML Schema	An XML-compliant language for constraining the structure of an XML document. Extends and replaces DTDs. Under development and *very* important to database processing.
XPath	A sublanguage within XSLT that is used to identify parts of an XML document to be transformed. Can also be used for calculations and string manipulation. Comingled with XSLT.
XPointer	A standard for linking one document to another. XPath has many elements from XPointer.
SAX	Simple API (application program interface) for XML. An event-based parser that notifies a program when the elements of an XML document have been encountered during document parsing.
DOM	Document Object Model. An API that represents an XML document as a tree. Each node of the tree represents a piece of the XML document. A program can directly access and manipulate a node of the DOM representation.
XQuery	A standard for expressing database queries as XML documents. The structure of the query uses XPath facilities, and the result of the query is represented in an XML format. Under development and likely to be important in the future.
XML Namespaces	A standard for allocating terminology to defined collections. X:Name is interpreted as the element Name as defined in namespace X. Y:Name is interpreted as the element Name as defined in namespace Y. Useful for disambiguating terms.

XQuery is an emerging standard for expressing generalized queries on XML documents. You can think of XQuery as SQL for XML documents. When it becomes available, this standard will be very important to the database/XML world. Check **www.w3.org** for more on XQuery; it will likely be finalized by the time you read this.

The last XML standard we will mention, XML Namespaces, is very important because it is used to combine different vocabularies into the same XML Schema. It can be used to define and support domains and to disambiguate terms. The need for the latter occurs when a document contains synonyms. For example, consider a document that has two different uses for the term *Instrument*. Suppose that one use of this term refers to musical instruments and has subelements {Manufacturer, Model, Material}, as in {Horner, Bflat Clarinet, Wood}, and a second use of this term refers to electronic instruments and has subelements {Manufacturer, Model, Voltage}, as in {RadioShack, Ohm-meter, 12-volt}. The author of the XML Schema for such a document can define two different namespaces that each contain one of these definition. Then, the complexType definition for each of these definitions of Instrument can be prefixed by the label of the namespace, as was done in our schema documents when we used the label xsd. There is more to XML Namespaces, and you will undoubtedly learn more as you work with XML.

The XML standards committee continues its important work, and more standards will be developed as the needs arise. At present, work is underway for developing security standards. Keep checking ***www.w3.org*** for more information.

◎ SUMMARY

The confluence of database processing and document processing is one of the most important developments in information systems technology today. Database processing and document processing need each other. Database processing needs document processing for the representation and materialization of database views. Document processing needs database processing for the permanent storage of data.

SGML is as important to document processing as the relational model is to database processing. XML is a series of standards that were developed jointly by the database processing and document processing communities. XML provides a standardized yet customizable way to describe the contents of documents. XML documents can automatically be generated from database data, and database data can be automatically extracted from XML documents.

Although XML can be used to materialize Web pages, this is one of its least important uses. More important is its use for describing, representing, and materializing database views. XML is on the leading edge of database processing; check ***www.w3.org*** and ***www.xml.org*** for latest developments.

XML is a better markup language than HTML primarily because XML provides a clear separation between document structure, content, and materialization. Also, XML tags are not ambiguous.

The content of XML documents can be described by Document Type Declarations (DTDs) and by XML Schemas. An XML document that conforms to its DTD is called type-valid. A document can be well formed and not be type-valid, either because it violates the structure of its DTD or because it has no DTD.

XML documents are transformed when an XSLT processor applies an XSL document to the XML document. A common transformation is to convert the XML document into HTML format. In the future, other transformations will be more important. For example, XSL documents can be written to transform the same Order document into different formats needed by different departments, say for sales, accounting, or production. XSLT processing is context oriented; given a particular context, an action is taken when a particular item is located. Today, most browsers have built-in XSLT processors.

XML Schema is a standard for describing the content of an XML document. XML Schema can be used to define custom vocabularies. Documents that conform to an XML Schema are called schema-valid. Unlike DTDs, XML Schema documents are themselves XML documents and can be validated against their schema, which is maintained by W3C.

Schemas consist of elements and attributes. There are two types of elements: simple and complex. Simple elements have one data value. ComplexType elements can have multiple elements nested within them. ComplexTypes may also have attributes. The elements contained in a ComplexType may be simple or other ComplexTypes. ComplexTypes may also define element sequences. A good rule of thumb is that elements represent data and attributes represent metadata, although this rule of thumb is not part of any XML standard.

XML Schemas (and documents) may have more structure than the columns of a table. Groups, such as Phone and Address, can be defined. An XML Schema that has all elements at the same level is a flat schema. Structured schemas are those that have defined subgroups, such as Phone and Address. To avoid definition duplication, elements can be defined globally. Duplication is undesirable because there is the risk that definitions will become inconsistent if a change is made to one definition and not the other.

Both Oracle and SQL Server can produce XML documents from database data. The Oracle facilities require the use of Java; see *www.oracle.com* for more information. SQL Server supports an add-on expression to the SQL SELECT statement, the FOR XML expression. FOR XML can be used to produce XML documents in which all data are expressed as attributes or as elements. FOR XML can also write an XML Schema description as well as the XML document. Using FOR XML EXPLICIT, the developer can place some columns into elements and others into attributes.

When interpreting multitable selects, the FOR XML processor uses the order of the tables to determine the hierarchical order of elements in the document. FOR XML can be used to produce XML documents with one multivalue path. Documents with more than one multivalue path must be patched together in the application by some means.

XML is important because it facilitates the sharing of XML documents (and hence database data) among organizations. After an XML Schema has been defined, organizations can ensure that they are receiving and sending only schema-valid documents. Additionally, XSL documents can be coded to transform any schema-valid XML document, from any source, into other standardized formats. These advantages become even more important as industry groups standardize their own XML Schemas. XML also facilitates business-to-business processing.

ADO.NET is a new, improved, and greatly expanded version of ADO that was developed for the Microsoft .NET initiative. ADO.NET incorporates all of the functionality of ADO, but adds much more. In particular, ADO.NET facilitates the transformation of XML documents to and from database data. Most importantly, ADO.NET introduces the concept of datasets, which are in-memory, fully functioned, independent databases.

A .NET data provider is a library of classes that provides ADO.NET services. Microsoft provides three data providers. The OLE DB data provider can be used to process any OLE DB–compliant data source. The SQLClient data provider is purpose-built for use with SQL Server, and the OracleClient data provider is purpose-built for use with Oracle. Data providers from companies other than Microsoft are likely in the near future.

A data provider data reader provides fast, forward-only access to data. A Command object can be processed to execute SQL and also to invoke stored procedures in a manner similar to but improved from that in ADO. The major new concept of ADO.NET is the dataset.

A dataset in an in-memory database that is disconnected from any regular database, but has all the important characteristics of a regular database. Datasets can have multiple tables, relationships, referential integrity rules, referential integrity actions, views, and the equivalent of triggers. Dataset tables may have surrogate key columns (called auto increment columns) and primary keys and may be declared unique.

Datasets are disconnected from the database(s) from which they are constructed, and they may be constructed from several different databases, possibly managed by different DBMS products. After a dataset is constructed, an XML document of its contents and an XML Schema of its structure are easily produced. Further, that process works in reverse as well. XML Schema documents can be read to create the structure of the dataset, and XML documents can be read to fill the dataset.

Datasets are needed to provide a standardized, nonproprietary means to process database views. They are especially important for the processing of views with multiple multivalue paths.

The potential downside of datasets is that because they are disconnected, any updates against the databases they access must be performed using optimistic locking. In the case of conflict, either the dataset must be reprocessed or the data change must be forced onto the database, causing the lost update problem.

Dataset concepts are illustrated by an ASP.NET application developed in Visual Basic .NET. The example processes a View Ridge Gallery view that has all of the customer data. A connection is established to an Oracle database, and a data adapter is defined that is used to read all five tables into the dataset. Then, relationships and referential integrity are defined, and a new data column that uses a relationship is created.

The dataset is then processed to show all tables, to produce an equivalent XML document, and to produce the XML Schema document for the dataset. Finally, a row of the dataset is updated and written back to the Oracle database by appropriately setting the UpdateCommand property of the data adapter.

This chapter concludes with a brief description of additional XML standards: XPath, SAX, DOM, XQuery, and XML Namespaces.

REVIEW QUESTIONS

13.1   Why do database processing and document processing need each other?
13.2   How are HTML, SGML, and XML related?
13.3   Explain the phrase standardized but customizable.
13.4   What is SOAP? What did it stand for originally? What does it stand for today?
13.5   What are the problems in interpreting a tag such as <h2> in HTML?
13.6   What is a DTD and what purpose does it serve?
13.7   What is the difference between a well-formed XML document and a type-valid XML document?
13.8   Why is it too limiting to say that XML is just the next version of HTML?
13.9   How are XML, XSL, and XSLT related?
13.10 Explain the use of the pattern {item, action} in the processing of an XSL document.
13.11 What is the purpose of XML Schema?
13.12 How does XML Schema differ from DTD?
13.13 What is a schema-valid document?
13.14 Explain the chicken-and-egg problem concerning the validation of XML Schema documents.
13.15 Explain the difference between simple and complex elements.
13.16 Explain the difference between elements and attributes.
13.17 What is a good rule of thumb for using elements and attributes to represent database data?
13.18 Give an example, other than one in this text, of a flat XML Schema.
13.19 Give an example, other than one in this text, of a structured XML Schema.
13.20 What is the purpose of global elements?
13.21 What requirement is necessary for processing XML documents with Oracle?

13.22   Explain the difference between FOR XML RAW and FOR XML AUTO, ELEMENTS.

13.23   When would you use FOR XML EXPLICIT?

13.24   What is the importance of the order of tables in a SQL statement that uses FOR XML?

13.25   Explain why the schema in Figure 13-13(b) is incorrect. How did this come about?

13.26   Why would an outer join fix the problem in Figure 13-25? Under what circumstances would that not fix that problem?

13.27   Explain, in your own words, why SQL with FOR XML cannot be used to construct an XML document having two multivalue paths.

13.28   Why is the limitation in question 13.27 important?

13.29   Explain, in your own words, why XML is important to database processing.

13.30   Why is XML Schema important for interorganizational document sharing?

13.31   What is ADO.NET?

13.32   What is a data provider?

13.33   What data providers are mentioned in the text?

13.34   What is a data reader?

13.35   How can ADO.NET be used to process a database without using data readers or datasets?

13.36   What is a dataset?

13.37   How do datasets differ conceptually from databases?

13.38   List the primary structures of a dataset, as described in this chapter.

13.39   How do datasets solve the problem of views with multivalue paths?

13.40   What is the chief disadvantage of datasets? When is this likely to be a problem?

13.41   Why, in database processing, is it important to become an object-oriented programmer?

13.42   What is an ADO.NET connection?

13.43   By default, what user account needs to exist in Oracle in order to use integrated security in an ASP.NET application?

13.44   What is a data adapter?

13.45   What is the purpose of the SelectCommand property of a data adapter?

13.46   Explain the difference between a data adapter's Fill and FillSchema methods.

13.47   How is a datatable relationship constructed in ADO.NET?

13.48   How is referential integrity defined in ADO.NET? What referential integrity actions are possible?

13.49   Explain how the TotalPurchases column of the CustomerAlias datatable gets its value.

13.50   Show the commands necessary to create an XML document from a dataset.

13.51   Show the commands necessary to create an XML Schema document from a dataset.

13.52   Explain how original, current, and proposed values differ.

13.53   How does a dataset allow for trigger processing?

13.54   What is the purpose of the UpdateCommand property of a data adapter?

13.55   Describe the means by which parameters are created for the UPDATE command in Figure 13-26(d).

13.56   What are the purposes of the InsertCommand and DeleteCommand of a data adapter?

13.57   Explain the flexibility inherent in the use of the InsertCommand, UpdateCommand, and DeleteCommand properties.

13.58   What is XPath?

13.59   How does DOM differ from SAX?

13.60   What is XQuery? What is it used for?

13.61   What is XML Namespaces? What is its purpose?

PROJECT QUESTIONS

13.62   Create a DTD and XML document like that shown in Figure 13-1 to represent the first row in the ARTIST table (see Figure 7-12).

13.63   Using Figure 13-4 as an example, create an XSL document to materialize the document in your answer to question 13.62. Materialize your document using a browser.

13.64   Create an XML Schema document for a row of TRANSACTION. Place TransactionID as an attribute. Group acquisition data into a complexType, and group sales data into a second complexType. Use Figure 13-7 as an example.

13.65   Create an XML Schema for artists and the customers who are interested in them. Use Figure 13-12 as an example.

13.66   Create an XML Schema for artist, work, transaction, and customer data. Use Figure 13-13 as an example and include your answer to question 13.64 in the schema.

13.67   Create an XML Schema for all artist data. Use Figure 13-14 and your answer from question 13.64.

 MARCIA'S DRY CLEANING

If you have not already done so, answer questions A through G for Marcia's Dry Cleaning at the end of Chapter 7 (page 262). Use either SQL Server or Oracle.

A   Using Figure 13-1 as an example, create an XML document with a DTD for a row of the CUSTOMER table.

B   Using Figure 13-4 as an example, create an XSL document to materialize the document you created in question A. Show your document in a browser.

C   Create an XML Schema document for a join of CUSTOMER and ORDER data. Assume that the document has one customer and from zero to many orders for that customer. Use Figure 13-12 as an example.

D   Code a SQL statement with FOR XML that will produce the document you created in question C.

E   Create an XML Schema document that has all of the data for a given customer. How many multivalue paths does this schema have?

F   Explain how the XML Schema document you created in question E can be used to advantage by Marcia's Dry Cleaning.

G   Explain how a dataset can be used to create documents like that defined in your answer to question E.

 MORGAN IMPORTING

If you have not already done so, answer questions A through H for Morgan Importing at the end of Chapter 7 (page 263). Use either SQL Server or Oracle.

A   Using Figure 13-1 as an example, create an XML document with a DTD for a row of the PURCHASE table.

B   Using Figure 13-4 as an example, create an XSL document to materialize the document you created in question A. Show your document in a browser.

C   Create an XML Schema document for a join of STORE and PURCHASE data. Assume that the document has one store and from zero to many purchases for that store. Use Figure 13-12 as an example.

D   Code a SQL statement with FOR XML that will produce the document you created in question C.

E   Create an XML Schema document that has all of the data for a given purchase. How many multivalue paths does this schema have?

F   Explain how the XML Schema document you created in question E can be used to advantage by Morgan Importing.

G   Explain how a dataset can be used to create documents like that defined in your answer to question E.

JDBC, Java Server Pages, and MySQL

This chapter discusses alternatives to Microsoft's OLE DB, ADO, and .NET technology and products. In particular, we will discuss JDBC, Java Server Pages (JSP) using Apache/Tomcat, and the DBMS product MySQL. The open source movement has played a large role in the development of these technologies, and all of these are open source products. In fact, only open source software was used to develop all of the examples in this chapter.

Open source is not a requirement for use of JDBC, however. You can employ JDBC on Windows XP, Windows 2000, and other operating systems to access SQL Server, Oracle, or other prominent DBMS products. You can run JSP and Apache/Tomcat on Windows XP or Windows 2000 as well. In this chapter, however, all of the examples were developed and run on Linux.

As you might guess, the one requirement for using JDBC is that programs be written in Java. Because this text does not assume that you are a Java programmer, we will explain examples at a high level. It will not be important to understand every line of code. Your goal should be to understand the nature and capability of the technologies presented here. If you already know how to program in Java, these examples should stimulate your thinking for more complex and realistic examples. In any case, after reading this chapter, you will be able to compare the capabilities of ODBC, ADO, and ASP to JDBC and JSP.

 JDBC

To begin, contrary to many sources, JDBC does *not* stand for Java Database Connectivity. According to Sun—the inventor of Java and the source of many Java-oriented products—JDBC is not an acronym; it just stands for JDBC. One can only imagine what legal or ego wrangles lie behind that assertion, but JDBC it is.

A JDBC driver is available for almost every conceivable DBMS product. Sun maintains a directory of them at *java.sun.com/products/jdbc.* Some of the drivers are free, and almost all of them have an evaluation edition that can be used for free for a limited period of time. The JDBC drivers used for the preparation of this chapter are the MySQL open source drivers named MySQL Connector/J; they can be downloaded from *www.mysql.com/products.*

So that you do not develop unfortunate habits, we will correct one other possible mistake before we continue. The DBMS product MySQL is pronounced "my ess-queue-lll," not "my see-quel." This is not very important, but if you want to be cool, always say "my ess-queue-lll."

Driver Types

Sun defines four driver types. Type 1 drivers are JDBC-ODBC bridge drivers, which provide an interface between Java and regular ODBC drivers. Most ODBC drivers are written in C or C++. For reasons unimportant to us here, there are incompatibilities between Java and C/C++. Bridge drivers resolve these incompatibilities and allow access to ODBC data sources from Java. Because we described the use of ODBC in Chapter 12, we will not consider bridge drivers any further here. If you want to use MySQL with ODBC, download the driver MySQL Connector/ODBC from *www.mysql.com/products.*

Drivers of Types 2 through 4 are written entirely in Java; they differ only in how they connect to the DBMS. Type 2 drivers connect to the native API of the DBMS; they call Oracle, for example, using the standard (non-ODBC) programming interface to Oracle. Drivers of Types 3 and 4 are intended for use over communications networks. A Type 3 driver translates JDBC calls into a DBMS-independent network protocol. This protocol is then translated into the network protocol used by a particular DBMS. Finally, Type 4 drivers translate JDBC calls into DBMS-specific network protocols.

To understand how drivers Types 2 through 4 differ, you must first understand the difference between a *servlet* and an *applet*. As you probably know, Java was designed to be portable. To accomplish portability, Java programs are not compiled into a particular machine language, but instead are compiled into machine-independent bytecode. Sun, Microsoft, and others have written **bytecode interpreters** for each machine environment (Intel 386, Alpha, and so on). These interpreters are referred to as **Java virtual machines.**

To run a compiled Java program, the machine-independent bytecode is interpreted by the virtual machine at run time. The cost of this, of course, is that bytecode interpretation constitutes an extra step, so such programs can never be as fast as programs that are compiled directly into machine code. This may or may not be a problem, depending on the application's workload.

An **applet** is a Java bytecode program that runs on the application user's computer. Applet bytecode is sent to the user via HTTP and is invoked using the HTTP protocol on the user's computer. The bytecode is interpreted by a virtual machine, which is

Figure 14-1

Summary of JDBC
Driver Types

Driver Type	Characteristics
1	JDBC-ODBC bridge. Provides a Java API that interfaces to an ODBC driver. Enables processing of ODBC data sources from Java.
2	A Java API that connects to the native-library of a DBMS product. The Java program and the DBMS must reside on the same machine, or the DBMS must handle the intermachine communication, if not.
3	A Java API that connects to a DBMS-independent network protocol. Can be used for servlets and applets.
4	A Java API that connects to a DBMS-dependent network protocol. Can be used for servlets and applets.

usually part of the browser. Because of portability, the same bytecode can be sent to a Windows, a UNIX, or an Apple computer.

A **servlet** is a Java program that is invoked via HTTP on the Web server computer. It responds to requests from browsers. Servlets are interpreted and executed by a Java virtual machine running on the server.

Because they have a connection to a communications protocol, Type 3 and Type 4 drivers can be used in either applet or servlet code. Type 2 drivers can be used only in situations where the Java program and the DBMS reside on the same machine or where the Type 2 driver connects to a DBMS program that handles the communications between the computer running the Java program and the computer running the DBMS.

Thus, if you write code that connects to a database from an applet (two-tier architecture), only a Type 3 or Type 4 driver can be used. In these situations, if your DBMS product has a Type 4 driver, use it; it will be faster than a Type 3 driver.

In three-tier or *n*-tier architecture, if the Web server and the DBMS are running on the same machine, you can use any of the four types of drivers. If the Web server and the DBMS are running on different machines, Type 3 and Type 4 drivers can be used without a problem. Type 2 drivers can also be used if the DBMS vendor handles the communications between the Web server and the DBMS. Characteristics of JDBC driver types are summarized in Figure 14-1. MySQL Connector/J, the Java connector that you can download from *www.mysql.com/products,* is a Type 4 driver.

Using JDBC

Unlike ODBC, JDBC does not have a separate utility for creating a JDBC data source. Instead, all of the work to define a connection is done in Java code via the JDBC driver. The coding pattern for using a JDBC driver is as follows:

1. Load the driver.
2. Establish a connection to the database.
3. Create a statement.
4. Do something with the statement.

As you will see, the name of the DBMS product to be used and the name of the database are provided at step 2.

Loading the Driver

To load the driver, you must first obtain the driver library and install it in a directory. You need to ensure that the directory is named in the CLASSPATH for both the Java compiler and for the Java virtual machine. There are several ways to load the driver into the program; the most reliable is

Class.forName(string).newInstance( );

The value of the string parameter depends on the driver you use. For the Connector/J drivers, use the following method:

Class.forName("org.gjt.com.mysql.jdbc.Driver").newInstance( );

This method will throw an exception, so you should write this code in a try:catch block. (If you're not a Java programmer, don't despair, just understand that these statements are making the JDBC classes available to the program.)

Establishing a Connection to the Database

After you have loaded the driver, the next step is to create an object that has a connection to your database. The format is as follows:

Connection conn = DriverManager.getConnection (string);

The DriverManager class is part of the JDBC library you loaded in step 1. It plays the same role as the ODBC driver manager. JDBC drivers register themselves with this class. On a given machine, several drivers may be registered. When you call DriverManager.getConnection, it looks through its list of JDBC drivers for a suitable driver and uses it. It will pick the first suitable driver it finds, so if more than one driver can process your connection, you may not get the driver you expect.

The string parameter passed to getConnection has three parts, separated by colons. The first part is always "jdbc," the second is a keyword that identifies the DBMS you are using, and the third is a URL to the database you want to process, along with optional parameters such as user and password.

The following statement connects to a MySQL database named vr1 with user *dk1* and password *sesame*:

Connection conn = DriverManager.getConnection

("jdbc:mysql://localhost/vr1?user=dk1&password=sesame")

The content of the second and third part of this string depends on your JDBC driver. In fact, with some drivers, you specify the user name and password as separate parameters. Consult your driver's documentation to find out what to code.

By the way, most of this technology arose in the UNIX world. UNIX is case sensitive, and almost everything you enter here also is case sensitive. Thus, *jdbc* and *JDBC* are *not* the same. Enter everything in the case that is shown here. There are a few case-insensitive exceptions, but they're not worth remembering. Just type the case as shown.

The getConnection method also throws an exception, so it, too, should appear in a try:catch block.

Creating a Statement

The next step is to create a new Statement object. This is similar to what we did in Chapter 12 when we created a Command object with ADO. The syntax is as follows:

Statement stmt = conn.createStatement( );

There are no parameters to pass to this method.

At this point, you can process the statement in various ways, as discussed next.

Processing the Statement

The Statement methods are standardized in the JDBC specification. Your driver will process any of the statements shown here (and many more as well). See your driver's API documentation for details. In our examples, we will use the executeQuery and executeUpdate methods, as follows:

ResultSet rs = stmt.executeQuery (querystring);

and

int result = stmt.executeUpdate (updatestring);

The first statement returns a result set that can be used in the same way we have used cursors in earlier chapters. The second statement returns an integer that indicates the number of rows updated. Specific examples include the following:

ResultSet rs = stmt.executeQuery ("SELECT * FROM CUSTOMER");

and

int result = stmt.executeUpdate ("UPDATE ARTIST SET Nationality='English'
**   WHERE Name= 'Foster' ");**

Note the use of single quotes to avoid problems with quoting inside quotation marks.

After the executeQuery method has run, the resultset object can be iterated to obtain all rows. The number of columns and the column names in the resultset can be obtained from the getMetaData method. Its syntax is as follows:

ResultSetMetaData rsMeta = rs.getMetaData();

At this point, the getColumnCount and getColumnName methods can be invoked on rsMeta, as you will see in the examples that follow.

Prepared Statements and Callable Statements

Prepared Statement objects and Callable Statement objects can be used to invoke compiled queries and stored procedures in the database. Their use is similar to the use of the Command object discussed in Chapter 12.

To illustrate a callable statement, suppose that we are processing the View Ridge database created with Oracle in Chapter 10 and that we want to invoke the CustomerInsert stored procedure. Assume in the following that *conn* has been set to a connection to the Oracle View Ridge database:

CallableStatement cs = conn.prepareCall ("{call CustomerInsert(?, ?, ?, ?)}");

cs.setString (1, "Mary Johnson");

cs.setString (2, "212");

cs.setString (3, "555–1234");

cs.setString (4, "US");

cs.execute();

This sequence, which invokes the CustomerInsert stored procedure with the data shown, is very similar to that shown for ODBC in Chapter 12. It is possible to receive values back from procedures as well, but that is beyond the scope of our discussion. See

Figure 14-2   JDBC Components

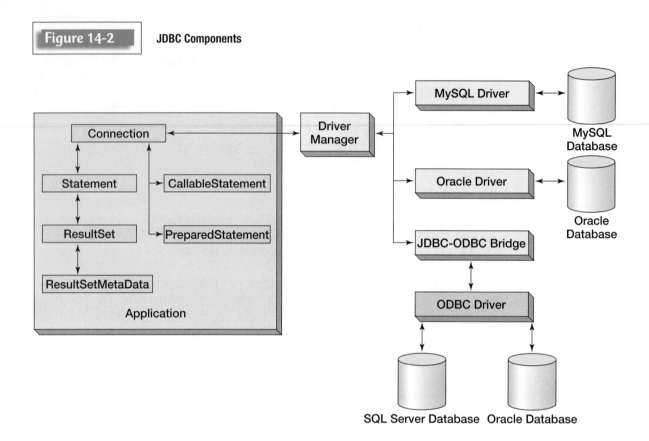

java.sun.com/products/jdk/1.1/docs/guide/jdbc for more information. Figure 14-2 summarizes the JDBC components. The application creates Connection, Statement, ResultSet, and ResultSetMetaData objects. Calls from these objects are routed via the DriverManager to the proper driver. Drivers then process their databases. Notice that the Oracle database in this figure could be processed via either a JDBC-ODBC bridge or via a pure JDBC driver.

JDBC Examples

Figures 14-3 and 14-4 present two examples using the MySQL Connector/J JDBC drivers and MySQL. Note that both of these programs import various java sql libraries. Also, note that the JDBC drivers are not imported; they are loaded instead. If you try to import them, the result is a mess.

    The database used in all of these examples is the View Ridge database shown in Figure 7-12. Tables in the database are:

CUSTOMER (<u>CustomerID</u>, Name, AreaCode, PhoneNumber, Street,
        City, State, Zip)

ARTIST (<u>ArtistID</u>, Name, Nationality, Birthdate, DeceasedDate)

CUSTOMER_ARTIST_INT (*CustomerID*, *ArtistID*)

WORK (<u>WorkID</u>, Description, Title, Copy, *ArtistID*)

TRANSACTION (<u>TransactionID</u>, DateAcquired, PurchasePrice, SalesPrice,
        ***CustomerID*, *WorkID*)**

Relationships and referential integrity are as described in Chapter 6.

The GeneralTable Class

Figure 14-3 shows the Java class GeneralTable. It accepts a single parameter, the name of a table in the MySQL database vr1. MySQL is case sensitive, and all table names in the database were created in uppercase letters. Thus, the code must convert the input table name from lowercase to uppercase.

This example is a straightforward application of the concepts we just described. The GeneralTable class has a publicly accessible method that returns no parameters. (That's the meaning of "public static void main.") The program checks for at least one input parameter, sets the variable varTableName to the input table name, and converts that name to uppercase. It then processes the database using the JDBC drivers in a try block. A try block is used because many of the methods throw exceptions; these exceptions will be caught in the catch block.

In these examples, all exception handling is generic. If you program in Java, you will see many ways to improve exception handling from that shown here. Our focus in on database concepts. If you do not program in Java, just assume that all of the state-

---

Figure 14-3   **GeneralTable Class**

```java
import java.sql.Connection ;
import java.sql.DriverManager ;
import java.sql.ResultSetMetaData ;
import java.sql.Statement ;

public class GeneralTable {

    /**
     * A Java program to present the contents of any table Call with one
     *   parameter which is table name - - table name parameter will be converted
     *   to uppercase
     */

    private static String dbHost   = "localhost" ;
    private static String dbName = " vr1 " ;
    private static String dbUser   = " dk1 " ;


    public static void main ( String [ ] args ) {
        if ( args.length < 1 ) {
            System.out.println ( " Insufficient data provided. " ) ;
            return ;
        }
        String varTableName = args [ 0 ] ;
        varTableName = varTableName.toUpperCase ( ) ;
        System.out.println ( " Showing Table " + varTableName ) ;
        try {

            // Load the MySQL Connector / J classes

            Class.forName ( " com.mysql.jdbc.Driver " ).newInstance ( ) ;

            // Set connect string to local MySQL database , user is dk1
            String connString = " jdbc : mysql : // " + dbhost + " / " + dbName + " ?user= " + dbUser ;

            System.out.println ( " Trying connection with " + connString ) ;
            Connection conn = DriverManager.getConnection ( connString ) ;

            // Get result set
            Statement stmt = conn.createStatement ( ) ;
            String varSQL = " SELECT * FROM " + varTableName ;
            ResultSet rs = stmt.executeQuery ( varSQL ) ;

            // Get meta data on just opened result set
            ResultSetMetaData rsMeta = rs.getMetaData ( ) ;
```

(continued)

Figure 14-3   **Continued**

```
                    // Display  column  names  as  string
                    String  varColNames  =  " " ;
                    int  varColCount  =  rsMeta.getColumnCount ( ) ;
                    for  ( int  col  =  1 ;  col  <=  varColCount ;  col + + ) {
                            varColNames  =  varColNames  +  rsMeta.getColumnName  ( col )  +  "   " ) ;
                    }
                    System.out.println ( varColNames )  ;

                    // Display  column  values
                    while  ( rs.next ( )  )  {
                            for  ( int  col  =  1 ;  col  <=  varColCount ;  col + +  ) {
                                    System.out.print ( rs.getString ( col )  +  "   " )  ;
                            }
                            System.out.println ( )  ;
                    }

                    // Clean  up
                    rs.close ( )  ;
                    stmt.close ( )  ;
                    conn.close ( )  ;

            } catch  ( Exception  e ) {
                    e.printStackTrace ( )  ;
            }
        }
}
```

ments that appear in the try block, denoted by "try { . . . . . }," are what happen under normal circumstances. All statements that appear in the catch block, denoted "catch { . . . }," are what happen when an error occurs. Also, like SQL, in Java a multiline comment is started with "/*" and terminated with "*/." A single line comment is started with "//."

The MySQL Connector/J drivers are loaded as described previously and then a Connection object conn and a Statement object stmt are created. The database is vr1, and the user is dk1. There is no password. (For this to work, user dk1 must have been defined in MySQL and granted permission to use database vr1 without a password. We will discuss these actions in the last section.)

A ResultSetMetaData named rsMeta is then created for the result set rs. After this has been done, the column names are obtained and printed in one long string (varColumnNames). Then rs is iterated, and each column in each row is displayed. The output is not pretty, but it works and gets us started.

The following is a typical display:

Showing Table ARTIST

Trying connection with jdbc:mysql://localhost/vr1?user=dk1

Name Nationality Birthdate DeceasedDate ArtistID

Miro Spanish null null 1

Tobey US null null 2

Van Vronken US null null 3

Matisse French null null 4

Like I said, it's not pretty!

The CustomerInsert Class

Figure 14-4 shows a second Java program that updates the vr1 database. This program implements the logic for the View Ridge CustomerInsert procedure, as described in Chapters 7, 10, 11, and 12. (Are you tired of it yet? At least the logic is familiar!)

Figure 14-4

CustomerInsert Class

```java
import java.sql.Connection ;
import java.sql.DriverManager ;
import java.sql.Statement ;
import java.sql.ResultSet ;

public class CustomerInsert {

        private static String dbHost = " localhost " ;
        private static String dbName = " vr1 " ;
        private static String dbUser = " dk1 " ;

        /** A Java implementation of the View Ridge Gallery's CustomerInsert procedure.
         *   Receives values Customer Name, AreaCode, LocalNumber and Nationality
         *   Inserts the new customer if not already in the database and then
         *   connects that customer to Artists of the given nationality by
         *   adding appropriate rows to the intersection table.
         * /

        public static void main ( String [ ] args ) {

                if ( args.length < 4 ) {
                        System.out.println ( " Insufficient data provided " ) ;
                        return ;
                }

                String varName = args [ 0 ] ;
                String varAreaCode = args [ 1 ] ;
                String varLocalNumber = args [ 2 ] ;
                String varNationality = args [ 3 ] ;

                insertData ( varName, varAreaCode, varLocalNumber, varNationality ) ;

        }

        public static void insertData ( String varName, String varAreaCode,
                        String varLocalNumber, String varNationality ) {

                System.out.println ( " Adding row for " + varName ) ;

                try {

                        // Load the MySQL Connector / J classes

                        Class.forName ( " com.mysql.jdbc.Driver " ).newInstance ( ) ;

                        // Set up connection to the db with no password
                        String connString = " jdbc : mysql : // " + dbHost + " / " + dbName
                                + " ?user= " + dbUser ;
                        System.out.println ( " Trying connection with " + connString ) ;
                        Connection conn = DriverManager.getConnection ( connString ) ;


                        // If we get here, we have a connection. Now check for duplicated data
                        Statement stmt = conn.createStatement ( ) ;
                        String varSQL = " SELECT Name " ;
                        String varWhere = " FROM CUSTOMER WHERE Name= ' " ;
                        varWhere = varWhere + varName + " ' AND AreaCode = ' " ;
                        varWhere = varWhere + varAreaCode + " ' AND PhoneNumber = ' " ;
                        varWhere = varWhere + varLocalNumber + " ' " ;
                        varSQL = varSQL + varWhere ;
```

Figure 14-4   Continued

```java
        ResultSet rs = stmt.executeQuery ( varSQL ) ;
        while ( rs.next ( ) )   {
                // if get here, there is duplicate data
                System.out.println ( " Data duplicates an existing customer. No changes made. " ) ;
                rs.close ( ) ;
                stmt.close ( ) ;
                conn.close ( ) ;
                return ;
    }

    // OK to insert new data
    varSQL = " INSERT INTO CUSTOMER ( Name, AreaCode, PhoneNumber ) " ;
    varSQL = varSQL + " VALUES ( ' " + varName " ' , ' " ;
    varSQL = varSQL + varAreaCode + " ' , ' " ;
    varSQL = varSQL + varLocalNumber + " ' ) " ;
    int result = stmt.executeUpdate ( varSQL ) ;
    if ( result = = 0 ) {
        System.out.println ( " Problem with insert " ) ;
        rs.close ( ) ;
        stmt.close ( ) ;
        conn.close ( ) ;
        return ;
    }

    // Update OK , add intersection rows - first get new ID
    varSQL = " SELECT CustomerID " = varWhere ;
    rs = stmt.executeQuery ( varSQL ) ;
    String varCid = " " ;
    while ( rs.next ( ) ) {
        varCid = rs.getString ( 1 ) ;
        if ( varCid = = " 0 " ) {
                System.out.println ( " Can't find new CustomerID " ) ;
                rs.close ( ) ;
                stmt.close ( ) ;
                conn.close ( ) ;
                return ;
        }
    }

    // Now add to intersection table
    varSQL = " SELECT ArtistID FROM ARTIST WHERE Nationality = ' "
                + varNationality + " ' " ;
    String varInsertStart = " INSERT INTO CUSTOMER_ARTIST_INT ( CustomerID , ArtistID ) VALUES ( "
                + varCid + " , " ;
    String varInsertEnd = " ) " ;
    rs = stmt.executeQuery ( varSQL ) ;
    System.out.println ( " Adding intersection values for customer "
                + varCid ) ;
    while ( rs.next ( ) ) {
        result = stmt.executeUpdate ( varInsertStart + rs.getString ( 1 )
                + varInsertEnd ) ;
    }

        // Clean up
        rs.close ( ) ;
        stmt.close ( ) ;
        conn.close ( ) ;
    }

    catch ( Exception e ) {
        e.printStackTrace ( ) ;
    }
  }
}
```

Recall that this procedure accepts four parameters: a new customer's Name, AreaCode, LocalNumber, and the Nationality of all artists in whom the customer maintains an interest. These parameters are received by the main procedure and passed to the method InsertData. The InsertData method is not necessary here; we could have a single method class, as shown in Figure 14-3. The logic is isolated in a separate method here because we will transform this method into a Java bean in the next section. That transformation will be easier if we isolate the code here.

The InsertData method first loads the drivers and then sets up a connection string to vr1 for user dk1. Next, it checks for duplicate data by querying vr1 for the input Name, AreaCode, and LocalNumber. If one is found, a message is printed and the resultset, statement, and connection are closed. Otherwise, a new row is inserted in CUSTOMER.

CustomerID, which is the surrogate key column for CUSTOMER, has been defined as an AUTO_INCREMENT column in the database. Thus, no value need be provided for it. MySQL will set it.

If the insert is successful, the variable *result* should not equal zero; if it does, an error occurred during the update. In that case, a message is printed and the objects are cleaned up. Assuming that no error occurred, the value of CustomerID is read back from the database and then rows are inserted into the intersection table CUSTOMER_ARTIST_INT. This is very similar to the logic shown for the CustomerInsert stored procedures in Oracle and SQL Server.

In this code section, the variable *result* is not checked for zero; a better version of this program would do so. In fact, if you are a Java programmer, you know that all of these error messages and cleanup activities should be done using exceptions. We're stepping around those issues to focus on the database-only matters.

Given this quick introduction to JDBC, we will now discuss its use in Java Server Pages.

Java Server Pages

Java Server Pages (JSP) technology provides a means to create dynamic Web pages using HTML (and XML) and the Java programming language. JSP looks very much like ASP, but this is deceptive because the underlying technology is quite different. JSP and ASP look similar because they both blend HTML with program code. The difference is that ASP is restricted to using scripting languages such as VBScript or JScript. With JSP, however, the coding is done in Java, and only in Java—VBScript and JScript are not allowed. With Java, the capabilities of a complete object-oriented language are directly available to the Web page developer.

Because Java is machine independent, JSP is also machine independent. With JSP, you are not locked into using Windows and IIS. You can run the same JSP page on a Linux server, on a Windows server, and on others as well.

The official specification for JSP can be found at *java.sun.com/products/jsp.*

JSP Pages and Servlets

JSP pages are transformed into standard Java language and then compiled just like a regular program. In particular, they are transformed into Java servlets, which means that JSP pages are transformed into subclasses of the HttpServlet class behind the scenes. JSP code thus has access to the HTTP request and response objects and also to their methods and to other HTTP functionality.

Because JSP pages are converted into servlet subclasses, you do not need to code complete Java classes or methods. You can insert snippets of Java code wherever you like, and they will be placed correctly into a servlet subclass when the page is parsed.

Thus, you can plop the following statements into a JSP page without any other Java code and they execute just fine:

```
<% String partyName ="fiesta";

partyName = partyName.toUpperCase();

out.println ("Come to our " + partyName); %>
```

In this case, the string "Come to our FIESTA" would be displayed in the browser when this section of the JSP code is processed. By the way, note that the Java code is isolated between <% and %>, just as VBScript and JScript are in ASP.

To use JSP, your Web server must implement the Java Servlet 2.1+ and the JSP 1.0 + specifications. You can check *java.sun.com/products/servlet/industry.html* for a list of servers that support these specifications. At least half a dozen or so possibilities are available. For the rest of this chapter, we will use Apache Tomcat for this purpose.

Apache Tomcat

The Apache Web server does not support servlets. However, the Apache Foundation and Sun cosponsored the Jakarta Project that developed a servlet processor named Apache Tomcat. You can obtain the source and binary code of Tomcat from the Jakarta Project Web site at *jakarta.apache.org.*

Tomcat is a servlet processor that can work in conjunction with Apache or as a standalone Web server. Tomcat has limited Web server facilities, however; so it is normally used in standalone mode only for testing servlets and JSP pages. For commercial production applications, Tomcat should be used in conjunction with Apache.

If you are running Tomcat and Apache separately on the same Web server, they need to use different ports. The default port for a Web server is 80, and Apache normally uses it. When used in standalone mode, Tomcat is usually configured to listen to port 8080, though this, of course, can be changed.

In the examples that follow, Tomcat is using port 8080. These examples were run on a private intranet in which the Tomcat server machine was assigned the IP address 10.0.0.3. Thus, to invoke the page *somepage.jsp*, we will use the string *http://10.0.0.3:8080/somepage.jsp* in the browser address field.

Setting Up Tomcat for JSP Processing

When you install Tomcat, it creates a directory structure into which you must place class libraries and Web pages. As of the Tomcat 3.1 release, place class libraries in the *install-dir*/lib directory. Place JSP pages in the *install-dir*/webapps/ROOT/WEB-INF/classes directory. On Linux, the RPM utility installs Tomcat in the directory/usr/local/jakarta-tomcat/ by default. Hence, in this case, place the class libraries into /usr/local/jakarta-tomcat/lib and the JSP pages into /usr/local/jakarta-tomcat/webapps/ROOT/WEB-INF/classes. If you are installing with other operating systems or installing a different servlet processor altogether, consult your documentation.

When installing new class files in the lib subdirectory, there is a small "gotcha." Tomcat creates its CLASSPATH when it is started. Therefore, after you have installed a new class file into the lib directory, you must stop and restart Tomcat before it will see your new file. If you just copy the new file into the lib subdirectory without restarting Tomcat, you will receive class not found exceptions. (Trust me, I know.)

The following JSP pages all use the MySQL Connector/J drivers. In order to work, the appropriate driver class library must be placed into the lib subdirectory.

Figure 14-5 shows the process by which JSP pages are compiled. When a request for a JSP page is received, a Tomcat (or other) servlet processor finds the compiled version of the page and checks to determine whether it is current. It does this by looking for an

Figure 14-5

**JSP Compilation
Process**

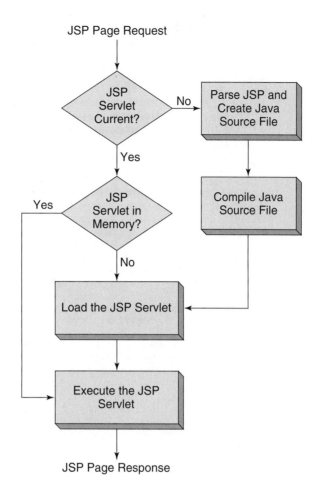

uncompiled version of the page having a creation date and time later than the compiled page's creation date and time. If the page is not current, the new page is parsed and transformed into a Java source file and that source file is then compiled. The servlet is then loaded and executed. If the compiled JSP page is current, then it is loaded into memory, if not already there, and then executed. If it is in memory, it is simply executed.

By the way, the downside of such automatic compilation is that if you make syntax errors and forget to test your pages, the first user to access your page will receive the compiler errors!

Unlike CGI files and some other Web server programs, only one copy of a JSP page can be in memory at a time. Further, pages are executed by one of Tomcat's threads, not by an independent process. This means that much less memory and processor time are required to execute a JSP page than to execute a comparable CGI script.

JSP Examples

This section discusses two simple examples of JSP. The first is a JSP version of the GeneralTable class shown in Figure 14-3. The second encapsulates the logic in Figure 14-4 in a Java bean and then invokes that bean from a JSP page.

GeneralTable.JSP

Figure 14-6 shows a JSP page that displays the contents of any table in the MySQL database named vr1. The format and logic of this page are very similar to that in GeneralTable.asp, shown in Figure 12-21(b). Here, we assume that the user passes the name of the table to be displayed as a parameter to the page.

Figure 14-7 shows the results of invoking this page using Internet Explorer on a Windows computer. The page itself was processed by Tomcat on a Linux computer.

Figure 14-6

GeneralTable JSP

```
<!DOCTYPE HTML PUBLIC "-//W3C//DTD HTML 4.0 Transitional//EN">
<!--Example of Database  Access from a JSP Page -->
<%@page import="java.sql.Connection" %>
<%@page import="java.sql.DriverManager" %>
<%@page import="java.sql.SQLException" %>
<HTML>
<HEAD>
<TITLE>Table Display Using JDBC and MySQL</TITLE>
<META NAME="author" CONTENT="David Kroenke">
<META NAME="keywords"
    CONTENT="JSP,JDBC,Database Access">
<META NAME="description"
    CONTENT="An example of displaying a table using JSP.">
<LINK REL=STYLESHEET HREF="JSP-Styles.css" TYPE="text/css">
</HEAD>
<BODY>
<H2>Database Access Example</H2>
<% String varTableName= request.getParameter("Table");
  varTableName = varTableName.toUpperCase( ); %>
<H3>Showing Data from MySQL Database vr1</H3>
<%
try {
     // Load the MySQL Connector / J drivers
     Class.forName ("com.mysql.jdbc.Driver").newInstance( );

     // Connect to vr1 with user dk1
     String connString = "jbdc:mysql//localhost/" + "vr1" + "?user=dk1";
     Connection conn = DriverManager.getConnection(connString);

     // Get rs and rsMeta for the SELECT statement
     Statement stmt = conn.createStatement( );
     String varSQL = "SELECT * FROM" + varTableName:
     ResultSet rs = stmt.executeQuery(varSQL);
     ResultSetMetaData rsMeta = rs.getMetaData( );
%>
<TABLE BORDER=1 BGCOLOR=#ffffff CELLSPACING=5><FONT FACE="Arial" COLOR=#000000
><CAPTION><B><%=varTableName%></B></CAPTION></FONT>
<THEAD>
<TR><%
     String varColNames ="";
     int varColCount = rsMeta.getColumnCount( );
     for (int col =1, col <= varColCount; col++) {
        %><TH BGCOLOR=#c0c0c0 BORDERCOLOR=#000000 ><FONT SIZE=2 FACE ="Arial"
COLOR=#000000
        ><%=rsMETA.getColumnName(col)%></FONT> </TH>
<%}%>
</TR>
</THEAD>
<TBODY><%
     while (rs next( )) {
        %><TR VALIGN=TOP><%
           for (int col = 1; col <= varColCount; col++) {
           %><TD BORDERCOLOR=#C0C0C0 ><FONT SIZE=2 FACE="Arial" COLOR=#000000
           ><%=rs.getString(col)%><BR></FONT></TD>
<%    }
     }
     // Clean up
     rs.close ( ) ;
     stmt.close ( ) ;
     conn.close ( ) ;
}
catch (ClassNotFoundException e) {
     out.println("Driver Exception " + e);
}%>
</TR>
</TBODY>
</TFOOT></TFOOT>
>/TABLE>
</BODY>
</HTML>
```

Figure 14-7

GeneralTable
ARTISTDisplay

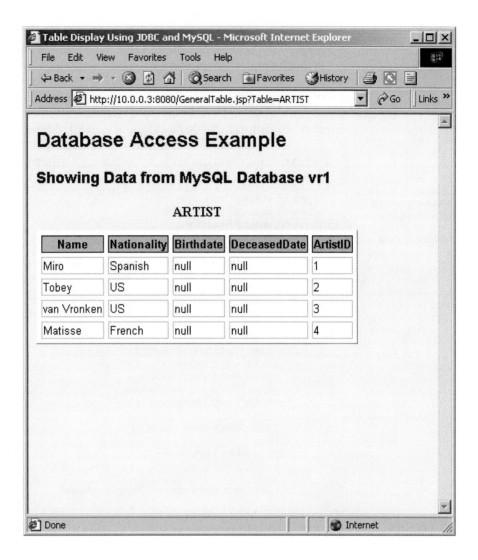

Note the call to port 8080; in production, Tomcat would be running with Apache on default port 80, and this port specification would not be needed.

In Figure 14-6, all of the Java code is shown in red ink. The first line invokes a page directory, which imports the java.sql library. Then, the parameter having the table name is obtained using the HTTP request object method getParameter. The value is set to uppercase. Next, the JDBC classes are loaded, as was done in Figure 14-3, and a connection is created to the vr1 database for user dk1. The rest of the code is the same as that shown in Figure 14-4—it is just spread among the HTML statements used for displaying results.

Again, this page appears deceptively similar to the ASP version of this page, GeneralTable.asp, shown in Chapter 12. The difference is not just that JDBC is used instead of ADO and ODBC. An even greater difference is that this page will be compiled into a Java program, and hence is portable and will be faster.

CustomerInsertUsingBean.JSP

Because Java is used with JSP, the full capabilities of an object-oriented program are available. This means that JSP pages can invoke precompiled objects. Doing this is important and useful for a number of reasons. For one, it separates the tasks of writing program logic from generating HTML. Organizations can have different groups and people working on these two very different tasks. It also enables logic to be encapsulated into independent modules for reuse and the other benefits of encapsulation. Finally, it reduces the complexity of managing a Web site.

(If you are not a Java programmer, ignore the following paragraph. Think of a bean as a properly mannered Java class. One you could take home to meet Mother.)

In simple terms, a Java bean is a Java class that has three properties. First, there are no public instance variables. Second, all persistent values are accessed using methods named get*xxx* and set*xxx*. For example, a persistent value named myValue is obtained via a method named getmyValue() and is set by a method named setmyValue(). Finally, the bean class must either have no constructors or it must have one explicitly defined zero-argument constructor.

Figure 14-8 shows a Java bean named CustomerInsertUsingBean. This class has a method that implements the View Ridge Gallery CustomerInsert procedure (yes, it's

Figure 14-8

CustomerInsertBean Class

```java
import java.sql.Connection ;
import java.sql.DriverManager ;
import java.sql.ResultSet ;
import java.sql.Statement ;

/** A Java bean for the View Ridge Galleries CustomerInsert procedure .
 *   Persistent values obtained by accessors getxxx and setxxx
 *
 *   Inserts the new customer if not already in the database and then
 *   connects that customer to Artists of the given nationality by
 *   adding appropriate row to the intersection table.
 */
public class CustomerInsertBean {
        private String newName = "unknown" ;
        private String newAreaCode = " " ;
        private String newLocalNumber = " " ;
        private String newNationality = " " ;

        public String getnewName ()
        {
             return ( newName ) ;
        }

        public void setNewName (String newName)
        {
             if ( newName ! = null )
             {
                  this.newName = newName ;
             }
             else
             {
                  this.newName = "unknown" ;
             }
        }

        public String getNewAreaCode ()
        {
             return ( newAreaCode ) ;
        }

        public void setNewAreaCode ( String newAreaCode )
        {
             if ( newAreaCode ! = null )
             {
                  this.newAreaCode = newAreaCode ;
             }
             else
             {
                  this.newAreaCode = "unknown" ;
             }
        }

        public String getNewLocalNumber ()
        {
             return ( newLocalNumber ) ;
        }
```

Figure 14-8

Continued

```
public void setNewLocalNumber ( String newLocalNumber )
{
    if ( newLocalNumber ! = null )
    {
        this.newLocalNumber = newLocalNumber ;
    }
    else
    {
        this.newLocalNumber = "unknown" ;
    }
}

public String getNewNationality ()
{
    return ( newNationality ) ;
}

public void setNewNationality ( String newNationality )
{
    if (newNationality ! = null )
    {
        this.newNationality = newNationality ;
    }
    else
    {
        this.newNationality = "unknown" ;
    }
}

public String InsertData ()
{

    try
    {

        // Load the MySQL Connector / J classes

        Class.forName ( "com.mysql.jdbc.Driver" ).newInstance () ;


        // Set up connnection to db vr1 with user dk1 , no password
        String connString = " jdbc : mysql : / / localhost / " + " vrl " + " ?user=dk1 " ;
        Connection conn = DriverManager.getConnection ( connString ) ;

        // If we get here , we have a connection.  Now check for duplicated data
        Statement stmt = conn.createStatement () ;
        String varSQL = " SELECT Name " ;
        String varWhere = " FROM CUSTOMER WHERE Name= ' " ;
        varWhere = varWhere + newName + " ' AND AreaCode = ' " ;
        varWhere = varWhere + newAreaCode + " ' AND PhoneNumber = ' " ;
        varWhere = varWhere + newLocalNumber + " ' " ;
        varSQL = varSQL + varWhere ;
        ResultSet rs = stmt.executeQuery ( varSQL ) ;
        while ( rs.next () )
        {
```

(continued)

BAAAACK!!! But this is the last time). This class has four persistent values: newName, newAreaCode, newLocalNumber, and newNationality. For each of these persistent values, get*xxx* and set*xxx* accessor methods are defined. It does not have public persistent values or a constructor method. Hence, CustomerInsertUsingBean meets the requirements for a bean.

The actual update procedure is coded in a method named InsertData. This method is identical to the InsertData method shown in Figure 14-4.

Figure 14-9(a) shows a data entry form to gather the new customer data. The HTML page for this form is shown in Figure 14-9(b). Note that the FORM

Figure 14-8   **Continued**

```java
                          // if get here, there is duplicate data
                          rs.close () ;
                          stmt.close () ;
                          conn.close () ;
                          return ( " Duplicate data - no action taken " ) ;
              }

              // OK to insert new data
              varSQL = " INSERT INTO CUSTOMER ( Name , AreaCode , PhoneNumber ) " ;
              varSQL = varSQL + " VALUES ( ' " + NewName " ', ' " ;
              varSQL = varSQL + newAreaCode + " ', ' " ;
              varSQL = varSQL + newLocalNumber + " ' ) ' " ;
              int result = stmt.executeUpdate ( varSQL ) ;
              if ( result = = 0 )
              {
                          // if get here , there is a problem with insert
                          rs.close () ;
                          stmt.close () ;
                          conn.close () ;
                          return ( " Problem with insert " ) ;
              }

              // Update OK , add intersection rows - first get new ID
              varSQL = " SELECT CustomerID " + varWhere ;
              rs = stmt.executeQuery ( varSQL ) ;
              String varCid = " " ;
              while ( rs.next () )
              {
                          varCid = rs.getString ( 1 ) ;
                          if ( varCid = = " 0 " )
                          {
                            // if get here , can't find new CustomerID
                            rs.close () ;
                            stmt.close () ;
                            conn.close () ;
                            return ( " Can't find new customer after insert " ) ;
                          }
              }
              // Now add to intersection table
              varSQL = " SELECT ArtistID FROM ARTIST WHERE Nationality = ' " + newNationality + " ' " ;
              String varInsertStart =
                          " INSERT INTO CUSTOMER_ARTIST_INT ( CustomerID, ArtistID ) VALUES ( " + varCid + " , " ;
              String varInsertEnd = " ) " ;
              rs = stmt.executeQuery ( varSQL ) ;
              while ( rs.next () )
              {
                          result = stmt.executeUpdate ( varInsertStart + rs.getString ( 1 ) + varInsertEnd ) ;
              }
              // Clean up
              rs.close () ;
              stmt.close () ;
              conn.close () ;
              return ( " Success " ) ;
      }

      catch ( Exception e )
      {
              return ( " Exception :  " + e ) ;
      }
  }
}
```

ACTION value is CustomerInsertUsingBean.jsp. Also observe that the text boxes are named newName, NewAreaCode, NewLocalNumber, and newNationality. These names matter because when the Add Customer button is clicked, CustomerInsertUsingBean.jsp will be passed parameters with those names. JSP can match the input parameters with same-named object properties when told to do so, as you will see.

The JSP page CustomerInsertUsingBean.jsp is listed in Figure 14-10. The important statements in this page are the following two jsp: statements:

<jsp:useBean id="insert" class="CustomerInsertBean" />

and

<jsp:setProperty name="insert" property="*" />

The first statement tells the JSP compiler to load the class CustomerInsertBean and to affiliate it with the name *insert*. For this to work with Tomcat 3.1, a compiled version of the bean, named CustomerInsertBean.class, must reside in the directory *install-dir*/webapps/ROOT/WEB-INF/classes. For the standard RPM install, this would be /usr/local/jakarta-tomcat/webapps/ROOT/WEB-INF/classes.

Figure 14-9

**Obtaining
Customer Data**

(a) NewCustomer.htm
Form (b) HTML Code

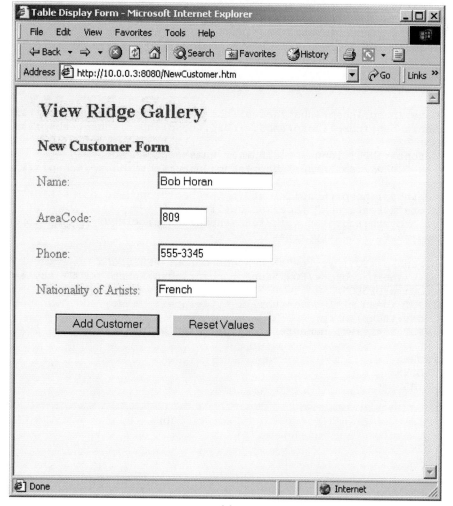

(a)

Figure 14-9   Continued

```
<HTML>
<HEAD>
<META HTTP-EQUIV="Content-Type" CONTENT="text/html">
<TITLE>Table Display Form</TITLE>
<LINK REL=STYLESHEET HREF="JSP-Styles.css" TYPE="text/css">
</HEAD>
<BODY>

<FORM METHOD="post" ACTION="CustomerInsertUsingBean.jsp">

 <P><STRONG><FONT color=purple face="" size=5>   View Ridge
Gallery</FONT></STRONG>

 <P>   <strong><font color="purple" face size="4"> New Customer
Form</font></strong><P><font style="background-color: #FDF5EC"
color="forestgreen" face>   
 Name:   </font><FONT style="BACKGROUND-COLOR:
#FDF5EC">           &nbs
p;          
 </FONT><INPUT id=newName name=newName></P>

 <P> <font style="background-color: #FDF5EC" color="forestgreen"
face>   AreaCode<font style="background-color:
#FDF5E6">:   </font>       &n
bsp;         
 </font><INPUT id=newAreaCode name=newAreaCode size="6"></P>

 <P><font style="background-color: #FDF5EC" color="forestgreen"
face>   

Phone:            &
nbsp;           &n
bsp;
 </font><INPUT id=newLocalNumber name=newLocalNumber
size="20">        </P>

 <P>    <font style="background-color: #FDF5EC"
color="forestgreen" face>Nationality
 of Artists:  </font>   <INPUT id=newNationality
name=newNationality size="17"></P>

 <P> <FONT style="BACKGROUND-COLOR: #FDF5EC">
   </FONT>     <FONT style="BACKGROUND-
COLOR: #FDF5EC">
<INPUT id=submit1 name=submit1 type=submit value="Add Customer"
>   
<INPUT id=reset1 name=reset1 type=reset value="Reset Values"></FONT></P>

</FORM>
</BODY>
</HTML>
```

(b)

The second jsp: statement tells the JSP parser to set the class properties using form input parameters. The "*" signals that all properties should be matched with same-named parameters. This statement is a shorthand substitute for the following:

<jsp:setProperty name="insert"

property="newName"

value='<%= request.getParameter("newName") %>' />

<jsp:setProperty name="insert"

property="newAreaCode"

value='<%= request.getParameter("newAreaCode") %>' />

<jsp:setProperty name="insert"

property="newLocalNumber"

value='<%= request.getParameter ("newLocalNumber") %>' />

<jsp:setProperty name="insert"

property="newName"

value='<%= request.getParameter ("newNationality") %>' />

<table>
<tr><td>

Figure 14-10

CustomerInsertUsing Bean.jsp

</td><td>

```
<!DOCTYPE HTML PUBLIC "-//W3C//DTD HTML 4.0 Transitional//EN">
<!--Example of Database  Access from a JSP Page-->
<%@page import="java.sql.Connection" %>
<%@page import="java.sql.DriverManager" %>
<%@page import="java.sql.SQLException" %>
<%@page import="java.sql.Statement" %>
<%@page import="java.sql.ResultSet" %>
<HTML>
<HEAD>
<TITLE>Updating Using a Java Bean</TITLE>
<META NAME="author" CONTENT="David Kroenke">
<META NAME="keywords"
      CONTENT="JSP,JDBC,Database Access">
<META NAME="description"
      CONTENT="An example of invoking a bean and displaying results.">
<LINK REL=STYLESHEET HREF="JSP-Styles.css" TYPE="text/css">
</HEAD>
<BODY>
<H2>Database Update Using JDBC from a Java Bean</H2>
<H3>Processing the View Ridge Customer Insert for MySQL Database vr1</H3>
<jsp:useBean id="insert" class="CustomerInsertBean" />
<jsp:setProperty name="insert" property="*" />
<%
// Bean properties were set in statement above, now call the
// bean for insert
String result=insert.InsertData( );

if (result != "Success") {
    // print problem and return
    out.println("Problem" + result);
    return;
}
// Data was inserted successfully; now display the intersection table
try {
    // Load the MySQL Connector / J drivers
    Class.forName("com.mysql.jdbc.Driver").newInstance( );

    String connString = "jdbc:mysql://localhost/" + "vr1" + "?user=dk1";

    Connection conn = DriverManager.getConnection(connString);
```

</td></tr>
</table>

Figure 14-10   **Continued**

```
// Join Customer to Artist via intersection table
// Note synonyms for CUSTOMER.Name and ARTIST.Name
Statement stmt = conn.createStatement( );
String varSQL = "SELECT CUSTOMER.Name Customer, ARTIST.Name Artist, Nationality ";
varSQL = varSQL + "FROM CUSTOMER, CUSTOMER_ARTIST_INT, ARTIST ";
varSQL = varSQL + "WHERE CUSTOMER.CustomerID = CUSTOMER_ARTIST_INT.CustomerID AND ";
varSQL = varSQL + "ARTIST.ArtistID = CUSTOMER_ARTIST_INT.ArtistID ";
ResultSet rs = stmt.executeQuery(varSQL);
ResultSetMetaData rsMeta = rs.getMetaData( );
%>
<TABLE BORDER=1 BGCOLOR=#ffffff CELLSPACING=5><FONT FACE="Arial" COLOR=#000000>
<CAPTION><B>Customers and Interests</B></CAPTION></FONT>
<THEAD>
<TR><%
    String varColNames ="";
    int varColCount = rsMeta.getColumnCount( );
    for (int col =1; col <= varColCount; col++) {
        %><TH BGCOLOR=#c0c0c0 BORDERCOLOR=#000000 ><FONT SIZE=2 FACE ="Arial"
COLOR=#000000
        ><%=rsMeta.getColumnName(col)%></FONT> </TH>
<%}%>
</TR>
</THEAD>
<TBODY><%
    while (rs next( ) ) {
        %><TR VALIGN=TOP><%
    for (int col = 1; col <= varColCount; col++) { %>
                <TD BORDERCOLOR=#C0C0C0 ><FONT SIZE=2 FACE="Arial" COLOR=#000000
                ><%=rs.getString(col)%><BR></FONT></TD><%
        }

    }
    // Clean up
    rs.close( );
    stmt.close( );
    conn.close( );
}
catch (ClassNotFoundException e) {
    out.println("Driver Exception " + e);
}%>
</TR>
</TBODY>
</TFOOT></TFOOT>
>/TABLE>
</BODY>
</HTML>
```

Of course, either version can be used. In fact, the longer version is required if the names of the form parameters are different from the names of the object properties.

In Figure 14-10, the InsertData method is invoked by the following statement:

String result=insert.InsertData();

If the result is not "Success," the result message is printed. Otherwise, the join of the CUSTOMER, CUSTOMER_ARTIST_INT, ARTIST tables is displayed using code very similar to that shown in Figure 14-3. The result appears as shown in Figure 14-11.

This is a very short introduction to JSP development. There is much more to use and understand, but a longer discussion is beyond the scope of this text. An excellent reference on this topic is *Core Servlets and Java Server Pages* by Marty Hall.[1]

---

[1]Marty Hall, *Core Servlets and Java Server Pages*. Upper Saddle River, NJ: Prentice Hall, 2000.

Figure 14-11

**Result from
Figure 14-10**

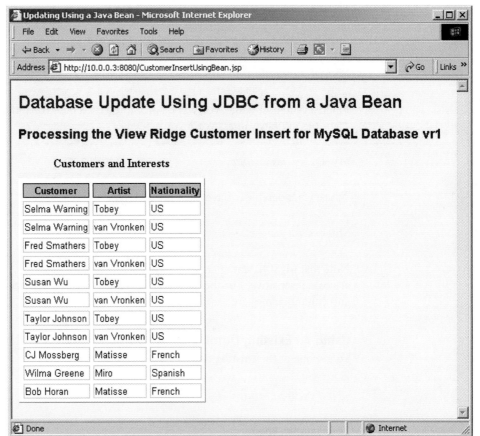

MySQL

MySQL is an open source DBMS product that runs on UNIX, Linux, and Windows. You can download MySQL source and binary code from the MySQL Web site (**www.mysql.com**). The examples in this text were run on MySQL on Linux, but they will work on MySQL on other operating systems as well. Currently, MySQL does not require a license fee unless you build MySQL into a commercial application, and even then it is free if you're willing to distribute your source code. See the license agreement on the MySQL Web site for more information.

MySQL lacks some of the capabilities of commercial DBMS products such as Oracle and SQL Server. If you have access to one of those products, you probably should use it. If, however, you're working with a low budget or if you want to participate in the open source movement, MySQL can be a good choice. In the Linux/UNIX environment, MySQL is not only cheaper than Oracle and other commercial products, it is also easier to install. A good reference for MySQL is *MySQL* by Paul DuBois.[2]

Ironically, because of its limited transaction management and logging capabilities, MySQL is very fast for pure query applications. Some Web-oriented data publishing companies maintain their databases using Oracle but download them to MySQL for query publishing on their Web servers.

---

[2]Paul DuBois, *MySQL*. Indianapolis, IN: New Riders, 2000.

Using MySQL

To start MySQL from the command prompt, type

MySQL -u *username* -p

Fill in a valid user name; you will be prompted for a password. If you're using an account that does not have a password, you can enter

MySQL -u *username*

To see what databases have been created, type

Show databases;

Note that MySQL statements are terminated with a semicolon. Also, MySQL commands are case insensitive, but the names of developer-defined constructs such as table names and column names are case sensitive.

Using an Existing Database

To use one of the existing databases, enter

Use *databasename*;

For example, enter

Use vr1;

To determine the tables in this database, enter

Show tables;

You can display the table metadata with the Describe command:

Describe CUSTOMER;

At this point, any standard SQL statement can be used. SELECT, UPDATE, INSERT, and DELETE work, as you would expect.

Creating a New Database

To create a new database, sign on to MySQL with the account that you want to own the new database. Then enter

Create Database *newdatabasename*;

For example, enter

Create Database vr2;

The database is created at this point. You can now enter SQL create statements, as we have done before. Figure 14-12 shows the statements that you can use to create the

Figure 14-12	View Ridge Database CREATE TABLE Statements for MySQL

```
CREATE TABLE CUSTOMER (
       CustomerID        int             AUTO_INCREMENT,
       Name              char (25)       NOT NULL,
       Street            char (30)       NULL,
       City              char (35        NULL,
       State             char (2)        NULL,
       ZipPostalCode     char (9)        NULL,
       Country           varchar (50)    NULL,
       AreaCode          char (3)        NULL,
       PhoneNumber       char (8)        NULL,
       Email             varchar (100)   NULL,
       CONSTRAINT  CustomerPK  PRIMARY  KEY  (CustomerID)
);


CREATE TABLE ARTIST(
       ArtistID          int             AUTO_INCREMENT,
       Name              char (25)       NOT NULL,
       Nationality       varchar (30)    NULL,
       Birthdate         year            NULL,
       DeceasedDate      year            NULL,
       CONSTRAINT  ArtistPK  PRIMARY  KEY  (ArtistID) ,
       CONSTRAINT  ArtistAK1  UNIQUE  (Name)
);


CREATE TABLE CUSTOMER_ARTIST_INT (
       ArtistID          int                NOT NULL,
       CustomerID        int                NOT NULL,
       CONSTRAINT  CustomerArtistPK  PRIMARY  KEY  (ArtistID,  CustomerID) ,
       CONSTRAINT  Customer_Artist_Int_ArtistFK
                   FOREIGN  KEY  (ArtistID)  REFERENCES  ARTIST  (ArtistID)  ON  DELETE  CASCADE ,
       CONSTRAINT  Customer_Artist_Int_CustomerFK
                   FOREIGN  KEY  (CustomerID)  REFERENCES  CUSTOMER  (CustomerID)  ON  DELETE  CASCADE
);


CREATE TABLE WORK (
       WorkID            int             AUTO_INCREMENT,
       Title             varchar(25)     NOT NULL,
       Description       text            NULL,
       Copy              varchar(8)      NOT NULL,
       ArtistID          int             NOT NULL,
       CONSTRAINT  WorkPK  PRIMARY  KEY  (WorkID),
       CONSTRAINT  WorkAK1  UNIQUE  (Title, Copy),
       CONSTRAINT  ArtistFK  FOREIGN  KEY(ArtistID)  REFERENCES  ARTIST  (ArtistID)
);



CREATE TABLE TRANSACTION (
       TransactionID     int             AUTO_INCREMENT
       DateAcquired      Date            NOT NULL,
       AcquisitionPrice  Decimal (8,2)   NULL,
       PurchaseDate      Date            NULL,
       SalesPrice        Decimal (8,2)   NULL,
       AskingPrice       Decimal (8,2)   NULL,
       CustomerID        int             NULL,
       WorkID            int             NOT NULL,

       CONSTRAINT  TransactionPK  PRIMARY  KEY  (TransactionID),
       CONSTRAINT  TransactionWorkFK  FOREIGN KEY(WorkID)  REFERENCES  WORK  (WorkID),
       CONSTRAINT  TransactionCustomerFK  FOREIGN KEY(CustomerID)  REFERENCES  CUSTOMER  (CustomerID)
);
```

View Ridge database. All surrogate keys are given the property AUTO_INCRE-MENT. This data type is a sequence maintained by MySQL that starts at one and increases by increments of one. Note that MySQL supports a data type of Year. This data type, which is a four-digit integer, is used for the Birthdate and DeceasedDate columns in ARTIST.

The schema shown in Figure 14-12 creates a unique index on (Title, Copy, ArtistID) in WORK. This unique index prevents duplicate work rows from being inserted in the database. This means the logic in the Java programs shown earlier to prevent duplicate rows is unnecessary. It doesn't hurt anything, except perhaps performance just a bit. Still, as stated in Chapter 6, it is always better to enforce integrity rules via the DBMS, if possible.

You can type all of these statements into MySQL. If you have them in a file, however, you can import them into MySQL. To illustrate, suppose that the statements in Figure 14-12 are in a file named VRSQL.txt. To process them using Linux, enter the following command at a shell prompt (not in MySQL!):

command prompt$ mysql --user=dk1 --password=sesame < VRSQL.txt

This command starts MySQL for user *dk1* and password *sesame* and processes the statements in the text file.

Setting Access Permissions for JDBC Use

After you understand the limitations of MySQL, it is quite easy to use. SQL statements are processed exactly as you would expect. However, you need to know about one small idiosyncrasy. Connections from JDBC are treated differently from other user connections. To understand how to deal with this, first consider the MySQL data dictionary.

MySQL maintains metadata in the database *mysql*. Two tables of special interest are *user* and *db*. To see their metadata, open the *mysql* database and use the DESCRIBE command on *user* and *db*. To see a list of users and their hosts, enter the following at the mysql prompt:

Use mysql;

SELECT Host, User FROM user;

To see users, hosts, and their allowed databases, enter

SELECT Host, User, Db FROM db;

Values of Host are typically *localhost* or names of the MySQL and other computers. They can also be IP addresses. A value of host of "%" means that the user can connect from anywhere.

Now, you might assume that JDBC programs running on the same machine as MySQL are considered to arise from host localhost. This is not true. The problem is that to MySQL, localhost means connect via a socket, and JDBC connections are via TCP/IP. Thus, if you want to connect using JDBC, the simplest (but least-secure) method of doing so is to grant access to a database for the account you want from anywhere. The following GRANT does this:

GRANT ALL ON vr1.* TO dk1@"%" IDENTIFIED BY "sesame";

This statement grants all privileges to all tables in the database vr1 to the user account named *dk1* with password *sesame*. The wildcard % indicates that dk1 can connect from any location. For better security, you can replace the wildcard with a specific IP address.

After you have executed this statement, query the db table for User, Host, Db to ensure that there is an entry for your user with host value of %. If so, you should be able to connect via JDBC to that database.

Concurrency Control

Recent releases of MySQL have added important new concurrency control mechanisms. MySQL now has support for transactions, and you can use BEGIN TRANSACTION/ COMMIT/ROLLBACK with MySQL just as you can with Oracle and SQL Server currency control.

As of the 5.0 release, all locking is performed at the table level. When executing a SELECT statement, MySQL obtains read locks on all of the tables in the SELECT statement. Such a lock blocks other sessions from writing to any of those tables, but it does not block other reads. When executing an INSERT, UPDATE, or DELETE statement, MySQL obtains write looks on all of the tables involved. Such a lock blocks other sessions from either reading or writing. The result of this locking strategy is that consistent data is read or updated on a SQL statement-by-statement basis. By default, SELECT statements run at a lower priority than INSERT, UPDATE, and DELETE statements. Thus, a large modification command may inhibit query activity.

MySQL can be used with several different database engines. Some of these engines have different locking features, functions, and characteristics from those described here. See the documentation at *dev.MySQL.com* for more information.

Backup and Recovery

MySQL provides limited backup and recovery facilities. It provides a utility for saving the database and for saving individual tables within the database. In some cases, however, it is faster and just as easy to use the operating system copy commands to save the MySQL database files to backup media.

MySQL maintains a log file of actions that it has processed. This log is one of commands and work, however, and not one of before and after images. To restore a database, an older version of the database is copied back, and the commands in the log are reapplied. Bulk changes are logged as commands; only the name of the file used as a source of data changes appears in the log. The individual changes do not appear.

By the way, if you're recovering a database because of a mistake such as an erroneous command like

DROP TABLE CUSTOMER;

be sure to remove this DROP statement from the log before you reprocess the log. Otherwise, the DROP TABLE will be processed by the log manager, and you will have recovered exactly to where you were when you started—without the CUSTOMER table.

Comments on Using MySQL

MySQL lacks some features and functions of a modern DBMS product. In particular, it does not support views or triggers, and it has rather limited backup and recovery capabilities. You might be wondering why you should use it at all. As mentioned, it is free and open source; if you want to participate in an open source project in the DBMS domain, this is a good one. Also, MySQL is easy and even fun to use. The features and functions that it does have work well. It appears that the community that is developing MySQL chooses to do only a few things, but to do them well. It is a pleasure to work with such a product.

SUMMARY

JDBC is an alternative to ODBC and ADO that provides database access to programs written in Java. A JDBC driver is available for almost every conceivable DBMS product. Sun defines four driver types. Type 1 drivers provide a bridge between Java and ODBC. Types 2, 3, and 4 are written entirely in Java. Type 2 drivers rely on the DBMS product for intermachine communication, if any. Type 3 drivers translate JDBC calls into a DBMS-independent network protocol. Type 4 drivers translate JDBC calls into a DBMS-dependent network protocol.

An applet is a compiled Java bytecode program that is transmitted to a browser via HTTP and is invoked using the HTTP protocol. A servlet is a Java program that is invoked on the server to respond to HTTP requests. Type 3 and Type 4 drivers can be used for both applets and servlets. Type 2 drivers can be used only in servlets, and only then if the DBMS and Web server are on the same machine or if the DBMS vendor handles the intermachine communication between the Web server and the database server.

There are four steps when using JDBC: (1) Load the driver; (2) establish a connection to the database; (3) create a statement; (4) execute the statement. The driver class libraries need to be in the CLASSPATH for the Java compiler and for the Java virtual machine. They are loaded into a Java program with the forName method of Class. A connection is established using the getConnection method of DriverManager. A connection string includes the literal jdbc: followed by the name of the driver and a URL to the database.

Statement objects are created using the createStatement method of a Connection object. Statements can be processed with the executeQuery and executeUpdate methods of a Statement object. ResultSetMetaData objects are created using the getMetaData method of a ResultSet object. Both compiled queries and stored procedures can be processed via JDBC using PreparedStatement and CallableStatement objects.

Java Server Pages (JSP) technology provides a means to create dynamic Web pages using HTML (and XML) and Java. JSP pages provide the capabilities of a full object-oriented language to the page developer. Neither VBScript nor JavaScript can be used in a JSP page. JSP pages are compiled into machine-independent bytecode.

JSP pages are compiled as subclasses of the HTTPServlet class. Consequently, small snippets of code can be placed in a JSP page, as well as complete Java programs. To use JSP, the Web server must implement the Java Servlet 2.1+ and JSP 1.0+ specifications. Apache Tomcat, an open source product from the Jakarta Project, implements these specifications. Tomcat can work in conjunction with Apache or as a standalone Web server for testing purposes.

When using Tomcat (or any other JSP processor), the JDBC drivers and JSP pages must be located in specified directories. Any Java beans used by the JSP page must also be stored in particular directories. When a JSP page is requested, Tomcat ensures that the most recent page is used. If an uncompiled newer version is available, Tomcat will automatically cause it to be parsed and compiled. Only one JSP page can be in memory at a time, and JSP requests are executed as a thread of the servlet processor, not as a separate process. The Java code in a JSP page can invoke a compiled Java bean, if desired.

MySQL is an open source DBMS that runs on UNIX, Linux, and Windows. It does not require a license fee. MySQL maintains a data dictionary in a database named *mysql*.

The user and db tables can be queried to determine user permissions. To access MySQL from JDBC, the user account must be granted access to the database, either from any location or from a TCP/IP address that represents the local computer.

MySQL provides limited support for transactions and provides locking at the table level. Shared read locks are obtained when processing SELECT statements, and exclusive locks are obtained when writing. MySQL can be used with several different database engines, and the locking and concurrency control options vary among them. See the documentation for the engine you are using for particulars on concurrency control.

MySQL provides limited backup and recovery facilities. It has a backup utility that augments the operating system copy utilities. MySQL maintains a log of commands processed. The log does not include before and after images, nor does it include data values from bulk updates or deletions. Even though it has some limitations, MySQL is easy to use and its features and functions are well implemented.

⊚ REVIEW QUESTIONS

14.1   What is the one major requirement for using JDBC?

14.2   What does JDBC stand for?

14.3   What are the four JDBC driver types?

14.4   Explain the purpose of Type 1 JDBC drivers.

14.5   Explain the purpose of Types 2, 3, and 4 JDBC drivers.

14.6   Define applet and servlet.

14.7   Explain how Java accomplishes portability.

14.8   List the four steps of using a JDBC driver.

14.9   Show the Java statement for loading the MySQL Connector/J drivers used in this chapter.

14.10   Show the Java statement for connecting to a database using the MySQL Connector/J drivers. Assume that the database is named CustData, the user is Lew, and the password is Secret.

14.11   Show the Java statement for creating a Statement object.

14.12   Show the Java statement for creating a ResultSet object that will display the Name and Nationality of the ARTIST table using an already created Statement object named s.

14.13   Show Java statements for iterating the resultset created in question 14.12.

14.14   Show the Java statement for executing an update to change the Nationality of an artist named "Jones" to "French." Use an already created Statement object named s.

14.15   In question 14.14, how can you determine if the update was successful?

14.16   Show a Java statement for creating an object referencing metadata for the result-set created in question 14.12.

14.17   Show the Java statements necessary to invoke a stored procedure named Customer_Delete. Assume that the procedure has three text parameters with values of customer name, area code, and phone number. Pass the values 'Mary Orange', '206', and '555–1234' to this procedure.

14.18   What is the purpose of Java Server Pages?

14.19   Describe the differences between ASP and JSP.

14.20   Explain how JSP pages are portable.

14.21   How is it possible that small segments of Java can be coded in JSP? Why are incomplete Java programs required?

14.22   What is the purpose of Tomcat?

14.23   With the standard installation of Tomcat, what actions must be taken before using JSP pages that load JDBC classes?

14.24   When adding new class libraries for Tomcat to use, what must you do to place the library in Tomcat's CLASSPATH?

14.25   Describe the process by which JSP pages are compiled and executed. Can a user ever access an obsolete page? Why or why not?

14.26   Why are JSP programs preferable to CGI programs?

14.27   What conditions are necessary for a Java class to be a bean?

14.28   Show the jsp directive to access a bean named CustomerDeleteBean. Give this bean the identity custdel.

14.29   Show the jsp directives to set a bean property named Prop1 to the value of a form parameter named Param1.

14.30   Why is it advantageous to give object properties and form parameters the same names? Show a jsp directive to associate properties and parameters when this is the case.

14.31   What is the difference between invoking a bean from a pure Java program and invoking a bean from Java code in a JSP page?

14.32   Under what conditions would you choose to use MySQL?

14.33   For what type of workload does MySQL excel?

14.34   What statement do you use for creating a new table using MySQL?

14.35   What issue must be addressed when connecting to MySQL using JDBC?

14.36   Show the MySQL command for giving the user Lew permission to access any table in the database in the CustData database. Assume that the password is Secret.

14.37   Describe transaction-management facilities in MySQL as described in this chapter.

14.38   How does MySQL use read locks?

14.39   How does MySQL use write locks?

14.40   At what level does MySQL invoke locks? What are the advantages and disadvantages of this?

14.41   Describe the MySQL facilities for backup.

14.42   What are the limits on MySQL logging?

14.43   According to the author, why would one choose to use MySQL?

◉ PROJECT QUESTIONS

14.44   Compare and contrast ASP and JSP. Describe the relative strengths and weaknesses of each. Under what circumstances would you recommend one over the other? How important is portability for Web servers? How much of a disadvantage is it to be Microsoft dependent? Some people say that preferring one over the other is more a matter of personal preference and values than anything else. Do you agree or disagree?

14.45   Rewrite the Java bean shown in Figure 14-8 to use exceptions rather than the *result* return parameter. Modify the JSP to correctly process this bean. In what ways is your bean better than the one in Figure 14-8?

14.46   Write a Java program to use MySQL and the MySQL Connector/J drivers used in this chapter. Your program should implement the logic of the CustomerInsertWithTransaction stored procedure described for Oracle in Chapter 10 and for SQL Server in Chapter 11. Add logic to your program to display the same results as are displayed in the CustomerPurchasesView. Run your program as a standalone program.

14.47   Convert the program you wrote in question 14.46 to a Java bean. Write a JSP to invoke your bean.

14.48   Obtain a JDBC Oracle driver and write a Java program to connect to the Oracle version of the View Ridge database and display the contents of any table in the database. Write a Java program to invoke the CustomerInsert stored procedure. Use a JDBC CallableStatement object to invoke that procedure.

14.49   Convert the program you wrote in question 14.47 to a Java bean. Write a JSP to invoke your bean.

14.50   Obtain a JDBC SQL Server driver and write a Java program to connect to the SQL Server version of the View Ridge database and display the contents of any table in the database. Write a Java program to invoke the CustomerInsert stored procedure. Use a JDBC CallableStatement object to invoke that procedure.

14.51   Convert the program you wrote in question 14.50 to a Java bean. Write a JSP to invoke your bean.

MARCIA'S DRY CLEANING

Answer questions A through M for Marcia's Dry Cleaning at the end of Chapter 7, page 262, if you have not already done so. Use MySQL data types.

A   Use MySQL to execute all of the SQL statements that you created in your answers to A through M at the end of Chapter 7.

B   Assume that the relationship between ORDER and ORDER_ITEM is M-M. Triggers are not supported by MySQL. Describe how minimum cardinality can be enforced without them. What limitations and potential problems exist in your design?

MORGAN IMPORTING

Answer questions A through N for Morgan Importing at the end of Chapter 7, page 263, if you have not already done so. Use MySQL data types.

A   Use MySQL to execute all of the SQL statements that you created in your answers to A through N at the end of Chapter 7.

B   Assume that the relationship between SHIPMENT and SHIPMENT_ITEM is M-M. Triggers are not supported by MySQL. Describe how minimum cardinality can be enforced without them. What limitations and potential problems exist in your design?

Conclusion

Database data are valuable organizational assets, and, unlike many assets, the more they are used, the more valuable they become. Data that are created and processed to support transaction processing and other operational activities can be used again to assist in planning, organization, and control.

We conclude this text with discussion of business intelligence systems, which are systems designed to increase the utility of existing database data. As you will learn in Chapter 15, such systems consist of reporting and data mining applications.

Database Processing for Business Intelligence Systems

Business intelligence (BI) systems are information systems that assist managers and other professionals in the analysis of current and past activities and in the prediction of future events. Unlike transaction processing systems, they do not support operational activities, such as the recording and processing of orders. Instead, BI systems are used to support management by producing information for assessment, analysis, planning, and control.

BI systems fall into two broad categories: reporting and data mining. As you will learn in this chapter, reporting systems sort, filter, group, and make elementary calculations on operational data. Data mining applications conduct sophisticated analyses on data by performing complex statistical and mathematical processing.

We begin this chapter with a summary of the characteristics of each type of BI system. We then survey the problems of using operational data for BI applications and describe how some organizations solve those problems with data warehouses and data marts. We then describe two common reporting systems in detail: RFM analysis and OnLine Analytical Processing (OLAP). Finally, we conclude this chapter with a survey of data mining applications and show the use of SQL for market basket analysis, a common data mining application.

Reporting and Data Mining Applications

Figure 15-1 summarizes how operational and business intelligence systems are related. Operational systems such as order entry, purchasing, manufacturing, and inventory support primary business activities. They use the DBMS to both read data from and store data in the operational database.

BI systems obtain data in three different ways. For one, they read and process data from the operational database. Note they use the operational DBMS to obtain data, but they do not insert, modify, or delete operational data. Second, BI systems process operational database extracts. In this situation, they manage the extracted database using a BI DBMS, which may be the same or different from the operational DBMS. Finally, BI systems read data that are purchased from data vendors.

Reporting Applications

The characteristics of BI applications are summarized in Figure 15-2. **Reporting systems** filter, sort, group, and make simple calculations. All reporting analyses can be performed using standard SQL, although extensions to SQL, such as those used for **OnLine Analytical Processing (OLAP)** are sometimes employed to ease the task of report production.

Reporting systems summarize the current status of business activities and compare that status with past or predicted future activities. Reporting systems are also used to classify entities such as customers, prospects, employees, and products. One popular classification technique is called **RFM analysis.** With RFM analysis, customers are classified according to how recently (R) a customer has ordered, how frequently (F) a customer orders, and how much money (M) a customer spends on an order. We will consider RFM further later in the chapter.

Figure 15-1   **Relationship of Operational and BI Applications**

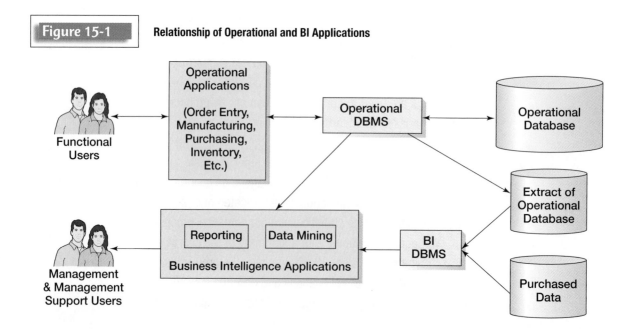

Figure 15-2

**Characteristics of
Business Intelligence
Applications**

- Reporting
    - Filter, sort, group, and make simple calculations
    - Summarize current status
    - Compare current status to past or predicted status
    - Classify entities (customers, products, employees, etc.)
    - Report delivery crucial
- Data Mining
    - Often employ sophisticated statistical and mathematical
      techniques
    - Used for:
        - What-if analyses
        - Predictions
        - Decisions
    - Results often incorporated into some other report
      or system

Report delivery is crucial. Reports must be delivered to the proper users in the appropriate format and on a timely basis. Reports may be delivered on paper, via a browser, over the telephone, via a digital dashboard, or in some other format. In many cases, it is more difficult to develop the report delivery system than it is to produce the report in the first place.

Data Mining Applications

Data mining applications use sophisticated statistical and mathematical techniques to perform what-if analyses, to make predictions, and to facilitate decision making. For example, data mining techniques can analyze past cell phone usage and predict which customers are likely to switch to a competing phone company. Or, data mining can be used to analyze past loan behavior to determine which customers are most (or least) likely to default on a loan.

Report delivery is not as difficult for data mining systems as it is for reporting systems. For one, most data mining applications only have a few users, and those users have sophisticated computer skills. Also, the results of data mining analyses are usually incorporated into some other report, analysis, or information system. In the case of cell phone usage, the characteristics of customers who are in danger of switching to another company are given to the sales department for action. Or, the parameters of an equation for determining the likelihood of a loan default are incorporated into a loan approval application.

Data Warehouses and Data Marts

According to Figure 15-1, some BI systems read and process operational data directly from the operational database. Although this is possible for simple reporting systems and small databases, such direct reading of operational data is not feasible for more complex applications or larger databases. Those larger applications usually process a separate database constructed from an extract of the operational database.

Operational data are difficult to read for several reasons. For one, querying data for BI applications can place a substantial burden on the DBMS and unacceptably slow the performance of operational applications. Additionally, operational data have problems that limit their use for BI applications. Further, the creation and maintenance of BI systems require programs, facilities, and expertise that are not normally available from operations.

Because of these problems, many organizations have chosen to develop **data warehouses** and **data marts** to support BI applications. Before we consider the components of data warehouses and data marts, let's first consider some of the problems of using operational data for BI processing.

Problems with Operational Data

Most operational databases have problems that limit their usefulness to all but the simplest BI applications. Figure 15-3 lists the major problem categories. First, although data that are critical for successful operations must be complete and accurate, data that are only marginally necessary need not be. For example, some operational systems gather customer demographic data during the ordering process. But, because such data are not needed to fill, ship, or bill orders, the quality of the demographic data suffers.

Problematic data are termed **dirty data.** Examples are a value of "G" for customer sex and a value of "213" for customer age. Other examples are a value of "999-999-9999" for a U.S. phone number, a part color of "gren," and an email address of "WhyMe@somewhereelseintheuniverse.who." All of these values pose problems for reporting and data mining purposes.

Purchased data often contain missing elements. In fact, most data vendors state the percentage of missing values for each attribute in the data they sell. An organization buys such data because, for some uses, some data are better than no data at all. This is especially true for data items whose values are difficult to obtain, such as the number of adults in a household, household income, dwelling type, and the education of primary income earner. Some missing data are not too much of a problem for reporting applications. For data mining applications, however, a few missing or erroneous data points can actually be worse than no data at all, because they bias the analysis.

Inconsistent data, the third problem in Figure 15-3, is particularly common for data that have been gathered over time. When an area code changes, for example, the phone number for a given customer before the change will differ from the customer's phone number after the change. Part codes can change, as can sales territories. Before such data can be used, it must be recoded for consistency over the period of the study.

Some data inconsistencies occur because of the nature of the business activity. Consider a Web-based order entry system used by customers around the world. When the Web server records the time of order, which time zone does it use? The server's system clock time is irrelevant to an analysis of customer behavior. Any standard time such as Universal Time Coordinate (UTC) time is also meaningless. Somehow, Web server time must be adjusted to the time zone of the customer.

Figure 15-3

Problems of Using Transaction Data for Business Intelligence

- Dirty data
- Missing values
- Inconsistent data
- Data not integrated
- Wrong format
    - Too fine
    - Not fine enough
- Too much data
    - Too many attributes
    - Too much volume

Another problem is **nonintegrated data.** Suppose, for example, that an organization wants to report on customer order and payment behavior. Unfortunately, order data are stored in a CRM system developed by Siebel, whereas payment data are recorded in a PeopleSoft financial management database. To perform the analysis, the data must somehow be integrated.

Data can also be too fine or too coarse. With regards to the former, suppose that we want to analyze the placement of graphics and controls on an order entry Web page. It is possible to capture the customers' clicking behavior in what is termed **click-stream data.** However, click-stream data include *everything* the customer does. In the middle of the order stream there may be data for clicks on the news, email, instant chat, and the weather. Although all of this data might be useful for a study of consumer computer behavior, it will be overwhelming if all we want to know is how customers respond to an ad located on the screen. Because the data are too fine, the data analysts must throw millions and millions of clicks away before they can proceed.

Data can also be too coarse. A file of order totals cannot be used for a **market basket analysis,** which identifies items that are commonly purchased together. Market basket analyses require item-level data; we need to know which items were purchased with which others. This doesn't mean the order total data are useless; it can be adequate for other analyses, it just won't do for a market basket analysis.

If the data are too fine, they can be made coarser by summing and combining. An analyst and a computer can sum and combine such data. If the data are too coarse, however, they cannot be separated into their constituent parts.

The final problem listed in Figure 15-3 concerns data volume. We can have an excess of columns, rows, or both. Suppose that we want to know the attributes that influence customers' responses to a promotion. Between customer data stored within the organization and customer data that can be purchased, we might have a hundred or more different attributes, or columns, to consider. How do we select among them? Because of a phenomenon called the **curse of dimensionality,** the more attributes there are, the easier it is to build a model that fits the sample data but that is worthless as a predictor. For this and other reasons, the number of attributes should be reduced and one of the major activities in data mining concerns the efficient and effective selection of variables.

Finally, we may have too many instances, or rows, of data. Suppose that we want to analyze click-stream data on CNN.com. How many clicks does this site receive per month? Millions upon millions! To meaningfully analyze such data, we need to reduce the number of instances. A good solution to this problem is statistical sampling. However, developing a reliable sample requires specialized expertise and information system tools.

Components of a Data Warehouse

To overcome the problems just described, many organizations have created data warehouses, which are database systems that have data, programs, and personnel that specialize in the preparation of data for BI processing. Data warehouse databases differ from operational databases because the data warehouse data are frequently denormalized. Data warehouses vary in scale and scope. They can be as simple as a sole employee processing a data extract on a part time basis or as complex as a department with dozens of employees maintaining libraries of data and programs.

Figure 15-4 shows the components of a data warehouse. Extraction programs read data from operational databases and clean and prepare it for BI processing. The extracted data are stored in a data warehouse database using a data warehouse DBMS, which can be different from the organization's operational DBMS. For example, an organization might use Oracle for its operational processing, but use SQL Server for its data warehouse. Other organizations use SQL Server for operational processing and data management programs from statistical package vendors such as SAS or SPSS in the data warehouse.

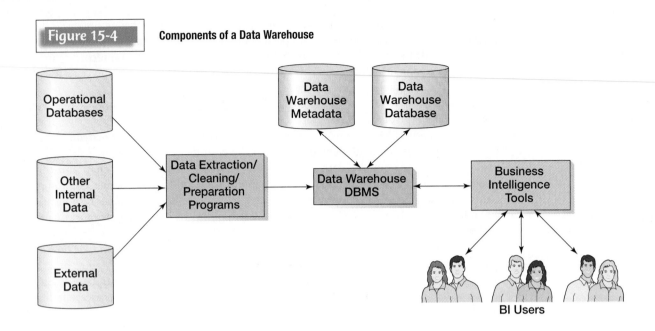

Figure 15-4   Components of a Data Warehouse

BI Users

Data warehouses often include data that are purchased from outside sources. A typical example is customer credit data. Figure 15-5 lists some of the consumer data than can be purchased from a vendor called AmeriLINK. An amazing, and from a privacy standpoint frightening, amount of data is available just from this one vendor.

Metadata concerning the data's source, format, assumptions and constraints, and other facts are kept in a **data warehouse metadata database.** The data warehouse DBMS extracts and provides data to BI tools, such as data mining programs.

Data Warehouses versus Data Marts

You can think of a data warehouse as a distributor in a supply chain. The data warehouse takes data from the data manufacturers (operational systems and purchased data), cleans and processes them, and locates the data on the shelves, so to speak, of the data

Figure 15-5

AmeriLink Sells Data on 230+ Million Americans

Source: www.kbm1.com/ AmeriLink.

- Name, Address, Phone
- Age, Gender
- Ethnicity, Religion
- Income
- Education
- Marital Status, Life Stage
- Height, Weight, Hair and Eye Color
- Spouse Name, Birth Date, etc.
- Kids' Names and Birth Dates
- Voter Registration
- Home Ownership
- Vehicles
- Magazine Subscriptions
- Catalog Orders
- Hobbies
- Attitudes

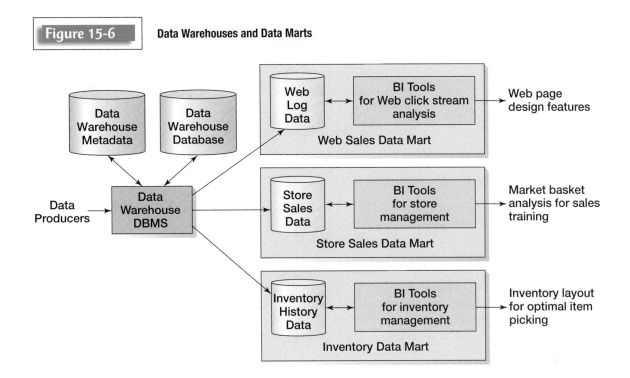

Figure 15-6   Data Warehouses and Data Marts

warehouse. The people who work in a data warehouse are experts at data management, data cleaning, data transformation, and the like. However, they are not usually experts in a given business function.

A **data mart** is a collection of data that is smaller than that in the data warehouse and that addresses a particular component or functional area of the business. A data mart is like a retail store in a supply chain. Users in the data mart obtain data that pertain to a particular business function from the data warehouse. Such users do not have the data management expertise that data warehouse employees have, but they are knowledgeable analysts for a given business function.

Figure 15-6 illustrates these relationships. The data warehouse takes data from the data producers and distributes the data to three data marts. One data mart analyzes click-stream data for the purpose of designing Web pages. The second analyzes store sales data and determines which products tend to be purchased together. This information is used to train salespeople on the best way to up-sell customers. The third data mart analyzes customer order data for the purpose of reducing labor for item picking from the warehouse. A company such as Amazon.com, for example, goes to great lengths to organize its warehouses to reduce picking expenses.

As you can imagine, it is expensive to create, staff, and operate data warehouses and data marts. Only large organizations with deep pockets can afford to operate a system such as that shown in Figure 15-6. Smaller organizations operate subsets of this system; for example, they may just have a simple data mart for analyzing promotion data.

 # Reporting Systems

The purpose of a reporting system is to create meaningful information from disparate data sources and to deliver that information to the proper users on a timely basis. As stated earlier, reporting systems differ from data mining because they create information using the simple operations of sorting, filtering, grouping, and making simple calculations. We begin this section with a description of a typical reporting problem: RFM analysis.

Figure 15-7

RFM Analysis

- Simple report-based customer classification scheme
- Score customers on recentness, frequency, and monetary size of orders
- Typically, divide each criterion into 5 groups and score from 1 to 5

RFM Analysis

As discussed earlier, *RFM analysis* is a way of analyzing and ranking customers according to their purchasing patterns. It is a simple technique that considers how recently (R) a customer ordered, how frequently (F) a customer orders, and how much money (M) the customer spends per order. RFM is summarized in Figure 15-7.

To produce an RFM score, customer purchase records are first sorted by the date of their most recent (R) purchase. In a common form of this analysis, the customers are divided into five groups, and a score of 1 to 5 is given to customers in each group. Thus, the 20 percent of the customers having the most recent orders are given an R score of 1, the 20 percent of the customers having the next most recent orders are given an R score of 2, and so forth, down to the last 20 percent, who are given an R score of 5.

The customers are then resorted on the basis of how frequently they order. The 20 percent of the customers who order most frequently are given an F score of 1, the next 20 percent most frequently ordering customers are given a score of 2, and so forth, down to the least frequently ordering customers, who are given an F score of 5.

Finally, the customers are sorted again according to the amount of their orders. The 20 percent who have ordered the most expensive items are given an M score of 1, the next 20 percent are given an M score of 2, and so forth, down to the 20 percent who spend the least, who are given an M score of 5.

Figure 15-8 shows sample RFM data. The first customer, Ajax, has ordered recently, and it orders frequently. Its M score of 3 indicates, however, that it does not order the most expensive goods. From these scores, the sales team can surmise that Ajax is a good customer, and that they should attempt to up-sell Ajax to more expensive goods.

The second customer in Figure 15-8 could be a problem. Bloominghams has not ordered in some time, but in the past, when it did order, it ordered frequently, and its orders were of the highest monetary value. These data suggest that Bloominghams may be about to take its business to another vendor. Someone from the sales team should contact it immediately. On the other hand, no one on the sales team should be talking to the third customer, Caruthers. It hasn't ordered for some time, it doesn't order frequently, and when it does order, it only buys cheap items, and not many of them.

Figure 15-8

Example RFM Score Data

Customer	RFM Score
Ajax	1 1 3
Bloominghams	5 1 1
Caruthers	5 4 5
Davidson	3 3 3

Caruthers can go to the competition. The last customer, Davidson, is right in the middle. Davidson is an OK customer, but no one in sales should spend much time with it.

Producing the RFM Report

Like most reports, an RFM report can be created using a series of SQL expressions. This section presents two SQL Server stored procedures that produce RFM scores. The four tables in Figure 15-9 are used. CUSTOMER_RFM contains CustomerID and the final R, F, and M scores. The remaining three tables, CUSTOMER_R, CUSTOMER_F, and CUSTOMER_M are used to store intermediate results. Note that all CustomerID columns are NOT NULL.

The procedure in Figure 15-10 begins by deleting the results from any prior analysis from the CUSTOMER_R, CUSTOMER_F, and CUSTOMER_M tables. It then calls three procedures for computing the R, F, and M scores. Finally, it stores the R, F, and M scores in the CUSTOMER_RFM table. Only this table is needed for reporting purposes.

The Calculate_R procedure is shown in Figure 15-11. This procedure first places the date of each customer's most recent order into the MostRecentOrderDate column. Then, it uses the Top . . . Percent option of SQL SELECT statements to set the R_Score values. The first UPDATE statement sets the value of R_Score to 1 for the top 20 percent of customers (after they have been sorted in descending order according to MostRecentOrderDate). Then, it sets the R_Score to 2 for the top 25 percent of customers who have a null value for R_Score in descending order of MostRecentOrderDate. The procedure continues to set the R values for all customers. The Calculate_F and Calculate_M procedures are similar and will be left to you as exercise 15.53.

The CUSTOMER_RFM table is used for reporting purposes. Figure 15-12 shows a SELECT on CUSTOMER_RFM that was prepared using a database of more than 5,000 customers and over 1 million transactions. The preparation of the CUSTOMER_RFM table required less than 30 seconds on a moderately powered personal computer.

Figure 15-9

SQL Server Tables for RFM Analysis

```
CREATE TABLE CUSTOMER_RFM (
        CustomerID      Int       NOT NULL,
        R               Smallint,
        F               Smallint,
        M               Smallint
);

CREATE TABLE CUSTOMER_R (
        CustomerID              Int      NOT NULL,
        MostRecentOrderDate     Char (10),
        R_Score                 SmallInt
);

CREATE TABLE CUSTOMER_F (
        CustomerID              Int      NOT NULL,
        OrderCount              Int,
        F_Score                 SmallInt
);

CREATE TABLE CUSTOMER_M (
        CustomerID              Int      NOT NULL,
        AverageOrderAmount      Money,
        M_Score                 SmallInt
);
```

Figure 15-10

RFM_Analysis Stored Procedure

```
CREATE PROCEDURE RFM_Analysis

AS

/* Delete any existing RFM data */

DELETE FROM CUSTOMER_R;
DELETE FROM CUSTOMER_F;
DELETE FROM CUSTOMER_M;

/* Compute R, F, M Scores */
Exec Calculate_R;
Exec Calculate_F;
Exec Calculate_M;

/* Show Results */
SELECT       R_Score, Count(*)AS R_Count
FROM         CUSTOMER_R
GROUP BY     R_Score;

SELECT       F_Score, Count(*)AS F_Count
FROM         CUSTOMER_F
GROUP BY     F_Score;

SELECT       M_Score, Count(*) AS M_Count
FROM         CUSTOMER_M
GROUP BY     M_Score;

/* Store Results */
INSERT INTO CUSTOMER_RFM (CustomerID)
        (SELECT       CustomerID
         FROM  CUSTOMER_SALES);

UPDATE CUSTOMER_RFM
SET    R =
        (SELECT R_Score
         FROM CUSTOMER_R
         WHERE CUSTOMER_RFM.CustomerID = CUSTOMER_R.CustomerID);

UPDATE CUSTOMER_RFM
SET    F =
        (SELECT F_Score
         FROM CUSTOMER_F
         WHERE CUSTOMER_RFM.CustomerID = CUSTOMER_F.CustomerID);

UPDATE CUSTOMER_RFM
SET    M =
        (SELECT M_Score
         FROM CUSTOMER_M
         WHERE CUSTOMER_RFM.CustomerID = CUSTOMER_M.CustomerID);
```

The results in Figure 15-12 are interesting, but unless this information is delivered to the correct users, it will be of no ultimate value to the organization. For example, the twelfth row in this figure shows that 202 customers have an RFM score of 5 1 1. These customers order frequently, they order items of high monetary value, but they have not ordered recently. The company may be in danger of losing them. Somehow this report and the customers who have these scores (see exercise 15.23) need to be made available to the appropriate sales personnel. To understand the modern means for accomplishing this, we will consider the components of a reporting system.

Reporting System Components

Figure 15-13 shows the major components of a reporting system. Data from disparate data sources are read and processed. As shown, reporting systems can obtain data from operational databases, from data warehouses, and from data marts. Some data are generated within the organization, other data are obtained from public sources, and still other data may be purchased from data utilities.

A reporting system maintains a database of reporting metadata. The metadata describes reports, users, groups, roles, events, and other entities involved in the reporting activity. The reporting system uses the metadata to prepare and deliver appropriate reports to the proper users in the correct format on a timely basis.

Calculate_R Stored Procedure

```
CREATE PROCEDURE Calculate_R

AS

/* Compute R_Score */

INSERT INTO CUSTOMER_R (CustomerID, MostRecentOrderDate)
        (SELECT       CustomerID, Max (TransactionDate)
         FROM  CUSTOMER_SALES
         GROUP BY CustomerID);

UPDATE         CUSTOMER_R
SET     R_Score = 1
WHERE CustomerID IN
        (Select Top 20 Percent CustomerID
         FROM CUSTOMER_R
         ORDER BY MostRecentOrderDate DESC);

UPDATE         CUSTOMER_R
SET     R_Score = 2
WHERE CustomerID IN
        (Select Top 25 PERCENT CustomerID
         FROM CUSTOMER_R
         WHERE R_Score IS NULL
         ORDER BY MostRecentOrderDate DESC);

UPDATE         CUSTOMER_R
SET     R_Score = 3
WHERE CustomerID IN
        (Select Top 33 PERCENT CustomerID
         FROM CUSTOMER_R
         WHERE R_Score IS NULL
         ORDER BY MostRecentOrderDate DESC);

UPDATE         CUSTOMER_R
SET     R_Score = 4
WHERE CustomerID IN
        (Select Top 50 PERCENT CustomerID
         FROM CUSTOMER_R
         WHERE R_Score IS NULL
         ORDER BY MostRecentOrderDate DESC);

UPDATE         CUSTOMER_R
SET     R_Score = 5
WHERE CustomerID IN
        (Select CustomerID
         FROM CUSTOMER_R
         WHERE R_Score IS NULL);
```

As shown in Figure 15-13, reports can be prepared in a variety of formats. Figure 15-14 lists report characteristics.

Report Types

Some reports are **static.** They are prepared once from the underlying data, and they do not change. A report of last year's sales, for example, is a static report. Other reports are **dynamic;** at the time of their creation, the reporting system reads the latest, most current data and generates the report using those fresh data. Reports on today's sales or on current stock prices are dynamic reports.

Query reports are prepared in response to information entered by users. Google is an example of a query report. You enter the keywords you want to search for, and the reporting system within Google searches its database and generates a response

Figure 15-12

Example RFM Results

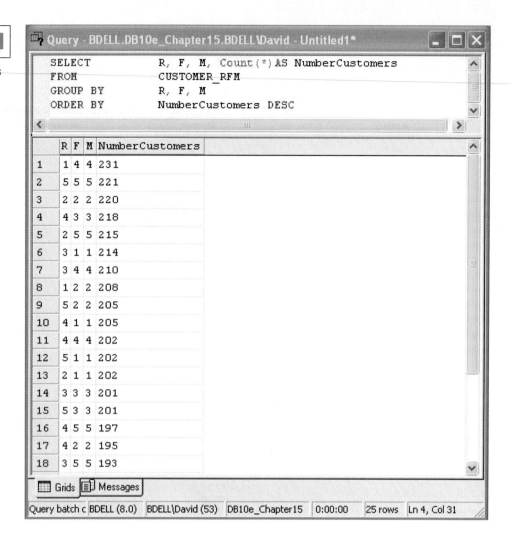

Figure 15-13   Components of a Reporting System

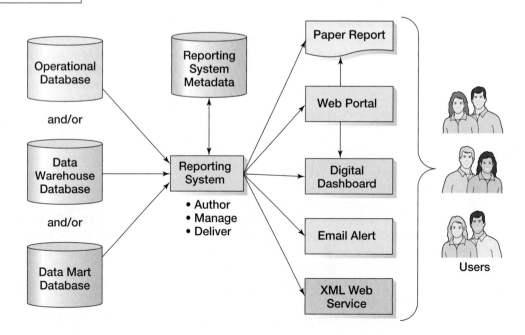

Figure 15-14

Report Characteristics

Type	Media	Mode
Static	Paper	Push
Dynamic	Web portal	Pull
Query	Digital dashboard	
OnLine Analytical Processing (OLAP)	Email/alert	
	XML Web service and application specific	

that is particular to your query. Within an organization, a query report could be generated to show current inventory levels. The user enters item numbers, and the reporting system responds with inventory levels of those items at various stores and warehouses.

Another type of report is an OLAP, or OnLine Analytical Processing, report. OLAP reports enable the user to dynamically change the report grouping structures. An OLAP reporting application is illustrated later in this chapter.

Report Media

Today, reports are delivered via many different channels. Some reports are printed on paper, others are created in formats such as PDF that can be printed or viewed electronically. Other reports are delivered via Web portals. An organization might place sales reports on the sales department's Web portal and a report on customers serviced on the customer service department's Web portal.

A **digital dashboard** is an electronic display that is customized for a particular user. Companies such as Yahoo! and MSN offer digital dashboard services. Users of these services can define the content they want to see—say, a local weather forecast, a list of stock prices, and a list of news sources—and the vendor constructs the customized display for each user. Such pages are called My Yahoo! or My MSN, or some similar title. Other dashboards are particular to an organization. Executives at a manufacturing organization, for example, might have a dashboard that shows up-to-the-minute production and sales activities.

Reports can also be delivered via **alerts.** Users can declare that they wish to be notified of news and events by email or on their cell phone. Of course, some cell phones are capable of displaying Web pages and can use digital dashboards as well.

Finally, reports can be delivered to other information systems. The modern way to do that is to publish reports as an XML Web service. The reporting Web service can then be consumed as discussed in Chapter 13. This style of reporting is particularly useful for interorganizational information systems, such as supply chain management.

Report Mode

The final report characteristic in Figure 15-14 is report mode. A **push report** is sent to users based on a predetermined schedule. Users receive the report without any activity on their part. A **pull report** is one that users must request. To obtain a pull report, a user goes to a Web portal or digital dashboard and clicks on a link or button to cause the reporting system to produce and deliver the report.

Report System Functions

As shown in Figure 15-13, report systems serve three functions: authoring, management, and delivery.

Report Authoring

Authoring a report involves connecting to the required data sources, creating the report structure, and formatting the report. Figures 15-15 and 15-16 show the use of Visual Studio .NET to author a report that publishes the results of an RFM analysis. In Figure 15-15, the developer has specified a database that contains the CUSTOMER_RFM table and has just entered the SQL statement shown in Figure 15-12. You can see the SQL statement in the lower-center portion of this display.

In Figure 15-16, the report author creates the format of the report by specifying the headings and selecting the format for the data items. In a more complicated report, the author would specify the sorting and grouping of data items as well as page headers and footers. The developer uses the property list in the right-hand side of the display in Figure 15-16 to set the values for item properties. The final report, as it appears in a browser window, is shown in Figure 15-17. To learn more about this application, search for "reporting services" at **www.microsoft.com**.

Report Management

The purpose of report management is to define who receives what reports, when, and by what means. Most report management systems enable the report administrator to define user accounts and user groups and to assign particular users to particular groups. For

Figure 15-15

Setting Up a Report Data Source Using Visual Studio .NET

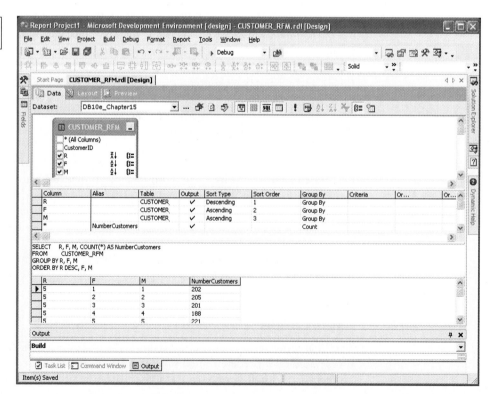

Figure 15-16

Formatting a Report
Using Visual Studio .NET

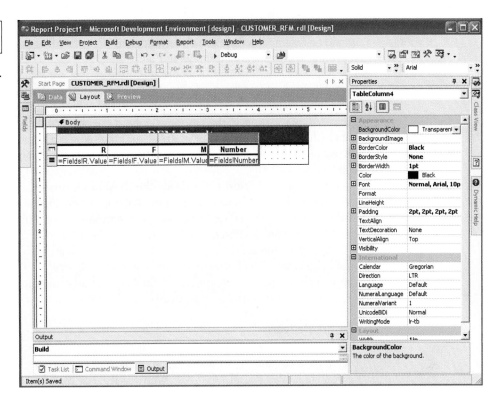

Figure 15-17

Sample Report
in Browser

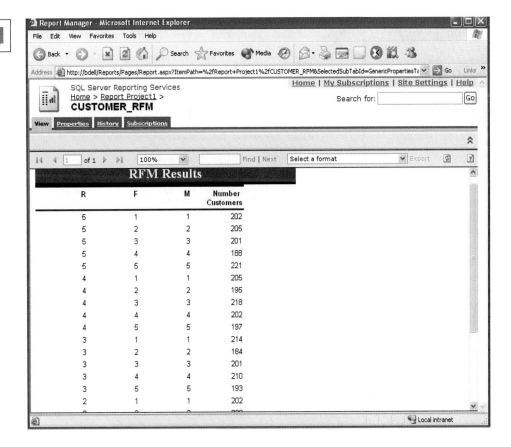

example, all of the salespeople would be assigned to the sales group, all of the executives would be assigned to the executive group, and so forth. All of these data are stored in the reporting system metadata shown in Figure 15-13.

Reports created using the report authoring system are assigned to groups and users. Assigning reports to groups saves the administrator work; when a report is created, changed, or removed, the administrator need only change the report assignments to the group. All of the users in the group will inherit the changes. The report assignment metadata includes not only the user or group and the reports assigned, but also indicates the format of the report that should be sent to that user and the channel by which the report will be delivered.

For example, Figure 15-18 shows the RFM report materialized in XML. The XML file can then be input into any program that consumes XML and manipulated via XSL, as described in Chapter 13. Note that the report authoring tool automatically generated the XML Schema document referenced at the top of this report.

As stated, the report management metadata indicates which format of the report should be sent to which user. It also indicates what channel is to be used and whether the report is to be pushed or pulled. If pushed, the administrator declares whether the report is to be generated on a regular schedule or as an alert.

Report Delivery

The report delivery function of a reporting system pushes reports or allows them to be pulled based on the report management metadata. Reports can be delivered via an email server, via a Web portal, via XML Web services, or by other program-specific means. The report delivery system uses the operating system and other program security components to ensure that only authorized users receive authorized reports. It also ensures that push reports are produced at appropriate times.

Figure 15-18

Sample Report in XML Format

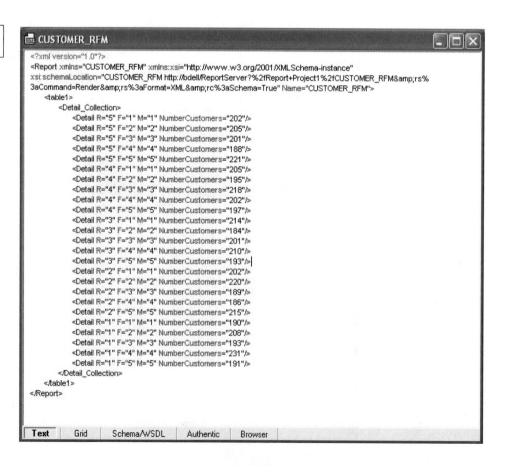

For query reports, the report delivery system serves as an intermediary between the user and the report generator. It receives user query data, such as the item numbers in an inventory query, passes the query data to the report generator, receives the resulting report, and delivers the report to the user.

OLAP

OLAP, a second type of reporting system, is a more generic category of applications than is RFM. OLAP provides the ability to sum, count, average, and perform other simple arithmetic operations on groups of data. The remarkable characteristic of OLAP reports is that they are dynamic. The format of the report can be changed by the viewer, hence the term *OnLine* in OnLine Analytical Processing.

An OLAP report has measures and dimensions. A **measure** is the data item of interest; it is the item that is to be summed or averaged or otherwise processed in the OLAP report. Total sales, average sales, or average cost are examples of measures. A **dimension** is a characteristic of a measure. Purchase date, customer type, customer location, and sales region are all examples of dimensions.

Figure 15-19 shows a typical OLAP report. Here, the measure is Store Sales Net, and the dimensions are Product Family and Store Type. This report shows how Store Sales Net varies by Product Family and Store Type. For example, stores of type Supermarket sold a net of $36,189 worth of nonconsumable goods.

A presentation of a measure with associated dimensions like that in Figure 15-19 is often called an **OLAP cube,** or sometimes just a **cube.** The reason for this term is that some products show these displays using three axes, like a geometric cube. The origin of the term is unimportant here, however. Just know that an *OLAP cube* and an *OLAP report* are the same thing.

The OLAP report in Figure 15-19 was generated by SQL Server Analysis Services and is displayed in an Excel pivot table. The data are from a sample, instructional database called Food Mart that is provided with SQL Server. It is possible to display OLAP cubes in many ways besides with Excel. Some third-party vendors provide more sophisticated graphical displays. Also, OLAP reports can be delivered just like any of the other reports described for report management systems.

As stated earlier, the distinguishing characteristic of an OLAP report is that the format of the report can be altered by the user. Figure 15-20 shows such an alteration. Here, the user added another dimension, Store Location, to the horizontal display. Product Family sales are now broken out by store location. Note that this sample data includes stores only in the western U.S. states of California, Oregon, and Washington.

With an OLAP report, it is possible to **drill down** into the data. To *drill down* means to further divide the data into more detail. In Figure 15-21, for example, the user has drilled down into the stores located in California, and the OLAP report now shows sales data for the four cities in California that have stores.

Figure 15-19 **OLAP Product Family by Store Type**

	A	B	C	D	E	F	G
1							
2							
3	Store Sales Net	Store Type					
4	Product Family	Deluxe Supermarket	Gourmet Supermarket	Mid-Size Grocery	Small Grocery	Supermarket	Grand Total
5	Drink	$8,119.05	$2,392.83	$1,409.50	$685.89	$16,751.71	$29,358.98
6	Food	$70,276.11	$20,026.18	$10,392.19	$6,109.72	$138,960.67	$245,764.87
7	Non-Consumable	$18,884.24	$5,064.79	$2,813.73	$1,534.90	$36,189.40	$64,487.05
8	Grand Total	$97,279.40	$27,483.80	$14,615.42	$8,330.51	$191,901.77	$339,610.90

Figure 15-20	OLAP Product Family and Store Location by Store Type

	A	B	C	D	E	F	G	H	I
1									
2									
3	Store Sales Net			Store Type ▼					
4	Product Family ▼	Store ▼	Store State	Deluxe Superma	Gourmet Supermar	Mid-Size Groce	Small Grocery	Supermarket	Grand Total
5	Drink	USA	CA		$2,392.83		$227.38	$5,920.76	$8,540.97
6			OR	$4,438.49				$2,862.45	$7,300.94
7			WA	$3,680.56		$1,409.50	$458.51	$7,968.50	$13,517.07
8		USA Total		$8,119.05	$2,392.83	$1,409.50	$685.89	$16,751.71	$29,358.98
9	Drink Total			$8,119.05	$2,392.83	$1,409.50	$685.89	$16,751.71	$29,358.98
10	Food	USA	CA		$20,026.18		$1,960.53	$47,226.11	$69,212.82
11			OR	$37,778.35				$23,818.87	$61,597.22
12			WA	$32,497.76		$10,392.19	$4,149.19	$67,915.69	$114,954.83
13		USA Total		$70,276.11	$20,026.18	$10,392.19	$6,109.72	$138,960.67	$245,764.87
14	Food Total			$70,276.11	$20,026.18	$10,392.19	$6,109.72	$138,960.67	$245,764.87
15	Non-Consumable	USA	CA		$5,064.79		$474.35	$12,344.49	$17,883.63
16			OR	$10,177.89				$6,428.53	$16,606.41
17			WA	$8,706.36		$2,813.73	$1,060.54	$17,416.38	$29,997.01
18		USA Total		$18,884.24	$5,064.79	$2,813.73	$1,534.90	$36,189.40	$64,487.05
19	Non-Consumable Total			$18,884.24	$5,064.79	$2,813.73	$1,534.90	$36,189.40	$64,487.05
20	Grand Total			$97,279.40	$27,483.80	$14,615.42	$8,330.51	$191,901.77	$339,610.90

Notice another difference between Figures 15-20 and 15-21. The user has not only drilled down, the user has also changed the order of the dimensions. Figure 15-20 shows Product Family and then Store Location within Product Family. Figure 15-21 shows Store Location and then Product Family within Store Location.

Both displays are valid and useful, depending on the user's perspective. A product manager might like to see product families first, and then store location data. A sales manager might like to see store locations first, and then product data. OLAP

Figure 15-21	OLAP Store Location and Product Family by Store Type

	A	B	C	D	E	F	G	H	I	J
1										
2										
3	Store Sales Net				Store Type ▼					
4	Store Country ▼	Store Sta	Store City	Product Family ▼	Deluxe Super	Gourmet Superm	Mid-Size Gro	Small Grocery	Supermarket	Grand Total
5	USA	CA	Beverly Hills	Drink		$2,392.83				$2,392.83
6				Food		$20,026.18				$20,026.18
7				Non-Consumable		$5,064.79				$5,064.79
8			Beverly Hills Total			$27,483.80				$27,483.80
9			Los Angeles	Drink					$2,870.33	$2,870.33
10				Food					$23,598.28	$23,598.28
11				Non-Consumable					$6,305.14	$6,305.14
12			Los Angeles Total						$32,773.74	$32,773.74
13			San Diego	Drink					$3,050.43	$3,050.43
14				Food					$23,627.83	$23,627.83
15				Non-Consumable					$6,039.34	$6,039.34
16			San Diego Total						$32,717.61	$32,717.61
17			San Francisco	Drink				$227.38		$227.38
18				Food				$1,960.53		$1,960.53
19				Non-Consumable				$474.35		$474.35
20			San Francisco Total					$2,662.26		$2,662.26
21		CA Total				$27,483.80		$2,662.26	$65,491.35	$95,637.41
22		OR		Drink	$4,438.49				$2,862.45	$7,300.94
23				Food	$37,778.35				$23,818.87	$61,597.22
24				Non-Consumable	$10,177.89				$6,428.53	$16,606.41
25		OR Total			$52,394.72				$33,109.85	$85,504.57
26		WA		Drink	$3,680.56		$1,409.50	$458.51	$7,968.50	$13,517.07
27				Food	$32,497.76		$10,392.19	$4,149.19	$67,915.69	$114,954.83
28				Non-Consumable	$8,706.36		$2,813.73	$1,060.54	$17,416.38	$29,997.01
29		WA Total			$44,884.68		$14,615.42	$5,668.24	$93,300.57	$158,468.91
30	USA Total				$97,279.40	$27,483.80	$14,615.42	$8,330.51	$191,901.77	$339,610.90
31	Grand Total				$97,279.40	$27,483.80	$14,615.42	$8,330.51	$191,901.77	$339,610.90

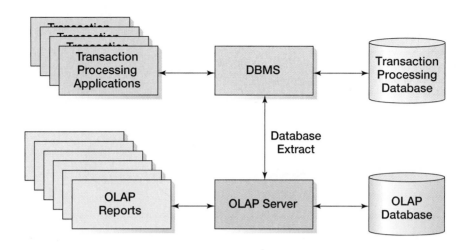

Figure 15-22

Role of OLAP Server and OLAP Database

reports provide both perspectives, and the user can switch between them while viewing the report.

Unfortunately, all of this flexibility comes at a cost. If the database is large, doing the necessary calculating, grouping, and sorting for such dynamic displays will require substantial computing power. Although standard, commercial DBMS products do have the features and functions required to create OLAP reports, they are not designed for such work. They are designed to provide rapid response to transaction processing applications such as order entry or manufacturing planning.

Accordingly, special purpose products called **OLAP servers** have been developed to perform OLAP analyses. As shown in Figure 15-22, an OLAP server reads data from an operational database, performs preliminary calculations, and stores the results of those calculations in an OLAP database. For performance and security reasons, the OLAP server and the DBMS usually run on separate computers. The OLAP server would normally be located in the data warehouse or a data mart.

Several different schemes are used for this storage, but the particulars of those schemes are beyond this discussion. If you purchased the copy of this text that has the SQL Server trial version, you can learn more by installing Analysis Services and running the tutorials. They are easy to work through and will give you a basic understanding of the preparation of OLAP reports.

Data Mining

Data mining is the application of mathematical and statistical techniques to find patterns and relationships that can be used to classify and predict. As shown in Figure 15-23, data mining represents the convergence of several phenomena. Data mining techniques have emerged from the statistical and mathematics disciplines and from the artificial intelligence and machine learning communities. In fact, data mining terminology is an odd combination of terms used by these different disciplines.

Data mining techniques take advantage of developments for processing enormous databases that have emerged in the last 10 years. Of course, all of these data would not have been generated were it not for fast and cheap computers, and, without such computers, the new techniques would be impossible to compute.

Most data mining techniques are sophisticated and difficult to use. However, such techniques are valuable to organizations, and some business professionals, especially those in finance and marketing, have developed expertise in their use. In fact, many interesting and rewarding careers are available to database professionals who have knowledge of data mining techniques.

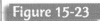

Figure 15-23

Convergence of
Disciplines for Data
Mining

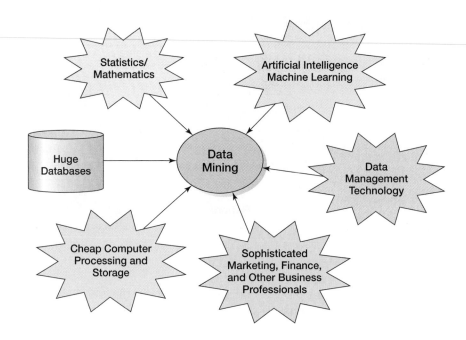

Unsupervised Data Mining

Data mining techniques fall into two broad categories: unsupervised and supervised.
With **unsupervised data mining,** analysts do not create a model or hypothesis prior to
beginning the analysis. Instead, the data mining technique is applied to the data, and
results are observed. After the analysis, explanations and hypotheses are created to
explain the patterns found.

One common unsupervised technique is **cluster analysis.** With cluster analysis, statistical techniques are used to identify groups of entities that have similar characteristics. A
common use for cluster analysis is to find customer groups in order and customer demographic data. Suppose that a cluster analysis identifies two very different customer groups:
One group has an average age of 33, owns at least one PC and at least one PDA, drives an
expensive SUV, and tends to buy expensive children's play equipment. The second group
has an average age of 64, owns vacation property, plays golf, and buys expensive wines.
Suppose that the analysis also finds that both groups buy designer children's clothing.

These findings were obtained solely by data analysis. No model was used to find
these patterns and relationships. The analysis speaks for itself. It is up to the analyst to
form hypotheses, after the fact, to explain why two such different groups are both buying designer children's clothes.

Supervised Data Mining

With **supervised data mining,** data miners develop a model prior to the analysis and then
apply statistical techniques to the data to estimate parameters of the model. For example,
suppose that marketing experts at a communications company believe that the use of cell
phone weekend minutes is determined by the age of the customer and the number of
months the customer has had the cell phone account. A data mining analyst would then
run an analysis called a **regression analysis** to determine the coefficients of the equation of
that model. A possible result is:

$$\text{CellPhoneWeekendMinutes} = 12 + 17.5 * \text{CustomerAge} + 23.7 * \qquad (15.1)$$
$$\text{NumberMonthsOfAccount}$$

As you will learn in your statistics classes, considerable skill is required to interpret the quality of such a model. The regression tool will create an equation; whether the equation is a good predictor of future cell phone usage depends on t values, confidence intervals, and related statistical techniques.

Three Popular Data Mining Techniques

Three popular data mining techniques are decision trees, logistic regression, and neural networks. **Decision tree analysis** classifies customers or other entities of interest into two or more groups according to past history. Figure 15-24 shows an example decision tree for classifying loan defaults. According to this figure, on the basis of past history, customers who have less than 50 percent of their loan past due and a credit score of less than 654.42 default on 33 percent of their loans. Other customer characteristics and loan default rates are shown on other branches of this tree. The results of this analysis can be used to create loan approval and management policies and procedures.

Logistic regression produces equations that offer probabilities that particular events will occur. Common applications of logistic regression are using donor characteristics to predict the likelihood of a donation in a given period and using customer characteristics to predict the likelihood that customers will switch to another vendor.

Neural networks are complex statistical prediction techniques. The name is a misnomer. Although there is some loose similarity between the structure of a neural network and a network of biological neurons, the similarity is only superficial. Data mining neural networks are just a technique for creating very complex mathematical functions for making predictions.

These three techniques, like almost all data mining techniques, require specialized software. Popular data mining products are Enterprise Miner from the SAS Corporation, Clementine from SPSS, and Insightful Miner from the Insightful Corporation.

All of these products have facilities for importing data from relational databases, and, as a database professional, you may be asked to prepare data for input to a data mining product. Typically, this work involves joining relations together into a large

Figure 15-24

Credit Score Decision Tree

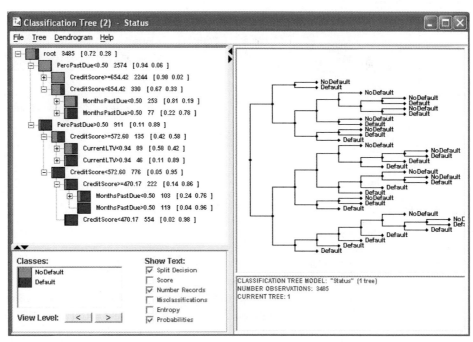

flat file and then filtering the data for particular data cases. Simple SQL is used to create such files.

However, one data mining technique, market basket analysis, can be readily implemented with pure SQL. We consider it next.

Market Basket Analysis

Suppose that you run a dive shop and one day you realize that one of your salespeople is much better at up-selling your customers. Any of your sales associates can fill a customer's order, but this one salesperson is especially able to sell customers items in addition to those for which they ask. One day you ask him how he does it.

"It's simple," he says, "I just ask myself what is the next product they'd want to buy. If someone buys a dive computer, I don't try to sell her fins. If she's buying a dive computer, she's already a diver, and she already has fins. But, look, these dive computer displays are hard to read. A better mask makes it easier to read the display and get the full benefits from the dive computer." A market basket analysis is a data mining technique for determining such patterns. A market basket analysis shows the products that customers tend to purchase at the same time. Several different statistical techniques can be used to generate a market basket analysis. Here we will discuss a technique that involves conditional probabilities.

Figure 15-25 shows hypothetical data from 1,000 transactions at a dive shop. The first row of numbers under each column is the total number of transactions that include the product in that column. For example, the 270 in the first row of Mask means that 270 of the 1,000 transactions include the purchase of a mask. The 120 under Dive Computer means that 120 of the 1,000 purchased transactions included a dive computer.

We can use the numbers in the first row to estimate the probability that a customer will purchase an item. Because 270 out of 1,000 transactions included a mask, we can estimate the likelihood that a customer will buy a mask to be 270/1,000, or .27. Similarly, the likelihood of a tank purchase is 200/1,000, or .2, and that for fins is 280/1,000, or .28.

Figure 15-25   **Market Basket Example**

1,000 Transactions	Mask	Tank	Fins	Weights	Dive Computer
	270	200	280	130	120
Mask	20	20	150	20	50
Tank	20	80	40	30	30
Fins	150	40	10	60	20
Weights	20	30	60	10	10
Dive Computer	50	30	20	10	5
No Additional Product	10	–	–	–	5

Support = P (A & B)   Example: P (Fins & Mask) = 150 / 1000 = .15

Confidence = P (A I B)   Example: P (Fins I Mask) = 150 / 270 = .55556

Lift = P (A I B)/ P (A)   Example: P (Fins I Mask) / P (Fins) = .55556 / .28 = 1.98

Note: P (Mask I Fins) / Fins) / P (Mask) = 150 / 280 / .27 = 1.98

The remaining rows in this table show the occurrences of transactions that involve two items. For example, the last column indicates that 50 transactions included both a dive computer and a mask, 30 transactions included a dive computer and a tank, 20 included a dive computer and fins, 10 included a dive computer and weights, 5 included a dive computer with another dive computer (meaning the customer bought two dive computers), and 5 transactions had a dive computer and no other product.

These data are interesting, but we can refine the analysis by computing additional factors. Marketing professionals define **support** as the probability that two items will be purchased together. From these data, the support for fins and mask is 150 out of 1,000, or .15. **Confidence** is defined as the probability of buying one product given that a customer purchased another product. The confidence of fins, given that the customer has already purchased a mask, is the number of purchases of fins and masks out of the number of purchases of masks. Thus, in this example, the confidence is 150 out of 270, or .55556. The confidence that a customer purchases a tank, given that the customer has purchased fins, is 40 out of 280, or .14286.

Lift is defined as the ratio of confidence divided by the base probability of an item purchase. The lift for fins given a mask is the probability that a customer buys fins, given the customer has purchased a mask, divided by the overall probability that the customer buys fins. If the lift is greater than one, then the probability of buying fins goes up when a customer buys a mask; if the lift is less than one, the probability of buying fins goes down when a customer buys a mask.

For the data in Figure 15-25, the lift for fins given a mask purchase is .55556/.28, or 1.98. This means that when someone purchases a mask, the likelihood he or she will also purchase fins almost doubles. The lift for fins given a dive computer purchase is 20/120 (the confidence of fins, given a dive computer) divided by .28, the probability that someone buys fins (280 of the 1,000 transaction involved fins): 20/120 is .16667, and .16667/.28 is .59524. Therefore, the lift for fins given a dive computer is just under .6, meaning that when a customer buys a dive computer, the likelihood that he or she will buy fins decreases.

Surprisingly, as shown in the last line of Figure 15-25, lift is symmetric. If the lift of fins given mask is 1.98, then the lift of mask given fins is also 1.98.

Using SQL for Market Basket Analysis

All of the major data mining products have features and functions to perform market basket analysis. These products, however, are expensive; you can perform a market basket analysis with basic SQL, if necessary.

The key SQL statement is shown in Figure 15-26. That SQL statement processes a relation named TRANS_DATA that stores line item data. Here, suppose that TRANS_DATA has a column TransactionID that stores an identifier of a transaction, and ItemID that stores the identifier of an item in that transaction. A given transaction may have multiple items, so the key of TRANS_DATA is (TransactionID, ItemID). TRANS_DATA has other data, such as ItemPrice, Qty, and ExtendedPrice, but those data are unnecessary for a market basket analysis and we ignore them here.

Figure 15-26

SQL Statement for Creating a Two-Item Basket

```
CREATE VIEW   TwoItemBasket AS
SELECT        T1.ItemID as FirstItem, T2.ItemID as SecondItem
FROM          TRANS_DATA T1 JOIN TRANS_DATA T2 ON
              T1.TransactionID = T2.TransactionID
   AND        T1.ItemID <> T2.ItemID
```

The SQL statement in Figure 15-26 creates a view of all items that have appeared together in two or more transactions. You can then compute support in a view using the following statement:

CREATE VIEW ItemSupport AS

SELECT	FirstItem, SecondItem, Count(*) as SupportCount
FROM	TwoItemBasket
GROUP BY	FirstItem, SecondItem;

This view produces the count of transactions in which each pair of items appears. You can divide the SupportCount in each row by the total number of transactions to obtain support for the two items. You can then use standard SQL to compute confidence and lift for each pair of items. See exercises 15.55–15.57.

SUMMARY

Business intelligence (BI) systems assist managers and other professionals in the analysis of current and past activities and in the prediction of future events. BI applications are of two major types: reporting applications and data mining applications. Reporting applications make elementary calculations on data; data mining applications use sophisticated mathematical and statistical techniques.

BI applications obtain data from three sources: operational databases, extracts of operational databases, and purchased data. BI systems sometimes have their own DBMS, which may or may not be the operational DBMS. Characteristics of reporting and data mining applications are listed in Figure 15-2.

Direct reading of operational databases is not feasible for all but the smallest and simplest BI applications and databases for several reasons. Querying operational data can unacceptably slow the performance of operational systems, operational data have problems that limit their usefulness for BI applications, and BI system creation and maintenance requires programs, facilities, and expertise that are normally not available for an operational database.

Problems with operational data are listed in Figure 15-3. Because of these problems with operational data, many organizations have chosen to create and staff data warehouses and data marts. Data warehouses extract and clean operational data and store the revised data in data warehouse databases. Organizations may also purchase and manage data obtained from data vendors. Data warehouses maintain metadata that describes the source, format, assumptions, and constraints about the data they contain. A data mart is a collection of data that is smaller than that held in a data warehouse and that addresses a particular component or functional area of the business. In Figure 15-6, the data warehouse distributes data to three smaller data marts. Each data mart services the needs of a different aspect of the business.

The purpose of a reporting system is to create meaningful information from disparate data sources and to deliver that information to the proper users on a timely basis. Reports are produced by sorting, filtering, grouping, and making simple calculations on the data. RFM analysis is a typical reporting application. Customers are grouped and classified according to how recently they have placed an order (R), how frequently they order (F), and how much money (M) they spend on orders. The result of an RFM analysis is three scores. In a typical analysis, the scores range from 1 to 5. An RFM score of 1 1 4 indicates that the customer has purchased recently, purchases frequently, but does not purchase large-dollar items. An RFM report can be produced using simple SQL. Figures 15-10 and 15-11 show stored procedures for computing these scores.

For the RFM data to add value to the organization, an RFM report must be prepared and delivered to the appropriate users. The components of a modern reporting system are shown in Figure 15-13. Reporting systems maintain metadata that supports the three basic report functions: authoring, managing, and delivering reports. The metadata includes information about users, user groups, and reports and data about which users are to receive which reports, in what medium, and when. As shown in Figure 15-14, reports vary by type, media, and mode.

OnLine Analytical Processing (OLAP) is a generic category of reporting applications that enable users to dynamically restructure reports. A measure is the data item of interest. A dimension is a characteristic of a measure. An OLAP cube is an arrangement of measures and dimensions. With OLAP, users can drill down and exchange the order of dimensions. Because of the high processing requirements, some organizations designate separate computers to function as OLAP servers.

Data mining is the application mathematical and statistical techniques to find patterns and relationships and to classify and predict. Data mining has arisen in recent years because of the confluence of factors shown in Figure 15-19.

With unsupervised data mining, analysts do not create models or hypotheses prior to the analysis. Results are explained after the analysis has been performed. With supervised techniques, hypotheses are formed and tested before the analysis. Three popular data mining techniques are decision trees, logistic regression, and neural networks.

Although most data mining techniques require special-purpose software, one data mining technique, market basket analysis, can be performed by using only SQL. According to market basket analysis terminology, the *support* for two products is the frequency that they appear together in a transaction. The *confidence* is the conditional probability that one item will be purchased given that another item has already been purchased. *Lift* is confidence divided by the base probability that an item will be purchased.

A SQL join statement can be written to create a view showing products that have appeared together in a transaction. That view can then be processed to compute support, and the support view can then be processed to compute confidence and lift.

REVIEW QUESTIONS

15.1   What are BI systems?

15.2   How do BI systems differ from transaction processing systems?

15.3   Name and describe the two main categories of BI systems.

15.4   What are the three sources of data for BI systems?

15.5   Explain the difference in processing between reporting and data mining applications.

15.6   Describe three reasons why direct reading of operational data is not feasible for BI applications.

15.7   Summarize the problems with operational databases that limit their usefulness for BI applications.

15.8   What are dirty data? How do dirty data arise?

15.9   Why is server time not useful for Web-based order entry BI applications?

15.10 What is click-stream data? How is it used in BI applications?

15.11 Why are data warehouses necessary?

15.12 Why does the author describe the data in Figure 15-5 as "frightening"?

15.13 Give examples of data warehouse metadata.

15.14 Explain the difference between a data warehouse and a data mart. Use the analogy of a supply chain.

15.15   State the purpose of a reporting system.

15.16   What do the letters *RFM* stand for in RFM analysis?

15.17   Describe, in general terms, how to perform an RFM analysis.

15.18   Explain the characteristics of customers having the following RFM scores: 1 1 5, 1 5 1, 5 5 5, 2 5 5, 5 1 2, 1 1 3.

15.19   In the RFM analysis in Figures 15-9 through 15-11, what role does the CUSTOMER_RFM table serve? What role does the CUSTOMER_R table serve?

15.20   Explain the purpose of the following SQL statement from Figure 15-11:

    INSERT INTO CUSTOMER_R (CustomerID, MostRecentOrderDate)

        (SELECT   CustomerID, Max (TransactionDate)

        FROM CUSTOMER_SALES

        GROUP BY CustomerID);

15.21   Explain the purpose and operation of the following SQL statement from Figure 15-11:

    UPDATE   CUSTOMER_R

    SET   R_Score = 1

    WHERE   CustomerID IN

        (Select Top 20 Percent CustomerID

        FROM CUSTOMER_R

        ORDER BY MostRecentOrderDate DESC)

           GROUP BY CustomerID);

15.22   Explain the purpose and operation of the following SQL statement from Figure 15-11:

    UPDATE   CUSTOMER_R

    SET   R_Score = 2

    WHERE   CustomerID IN

        (Select Top 25 PERCENT CustomerID

        FROM CUSTOMER_R

        WHERE R_Score IS NULL

        ORDER BY MostRecentOrderDate DESC);

15.23   Write a SQL statement to query the CUSTOMER_RFM table and display the CustomerID values for all customers having an RFM score of 5 1 1 or 4 1 1. Why are these customers important?

15.24   Name and describe the purpose of the major components of a reporting system.

15.25   What are the major functions of a reporting system?

15.26   Summarize the types of reports described in this chapter.

15.27   Describe the various media used to deliver reports.

15.28   Summarize the modes of reports described in this chapter.

15.29   Name three tasks of report authoring.

15.30   Describe the major tasks in report management. Explain the role of report metadata in report management.

15.31   Describe the major tasks in report delivery.

15.32   What does OLAP stand for?

15.33   What is the distinguishing characteristic of OLAP reports?

15.34   Define measure, dimension, and cube.

15.35   Give an example, other than one in this text, of a measure, two dimensions related to your measure, and a cube.

15.36   What is drill down?

15.37   Explain two ways that the OLAP report in Figure 15-21 differs from that in Figure 15-20.

15.38   What is the purpose of an OLAP server?

15.39   Define data mining.

15.40   Explain the difference between unsupervised and supervised data mining.

15.41   Give examples, other than one in this text, of unsupervised and supervised data mining.

15.42   For the example cluster analysis result described on page 550, give an explanation for the two groups.

15.43   Name three popular data mining techniques.

15.44   In Figure 15-24, explain the meaning of the bottom node on the tree.

15.45   What is the purpose of logistic regression?

15.46   What is the purpose of a neural network?

Use the data in Figure 15-25 to answer questions 15.47 through 15.52.

15.47   What is the probability that someone will buy a tank?

15.48   What is the support for buying a tank and fins? What is the support for buying two tanks?

15.49   What is the confidence for fins given that a tank has been purchased?

15.50   What is the confidence for a second tank given that a tank has been purchased?

15.51   What is the lift for fins given that a tank has been purchased?

15.52   What is the lift for a second tank given that a tank has been purchased?

⊚ PROJECT QUESTIONS

15.53   Using the code in Figure 15-11 as an example, write the procedures Calculate_F and Calculate_M that are called from the Calculate_RFM stored procedure in Figure 15-10.

15.54   Install the trial version of SQL Server and install Analysis Services. Check **www.microsoft.com** to determine if any service packs need to be installed. If so, install them. Work through the first three tutorials in the Analysis Services tutorial. To find them, start Analysis Services and then click Concepts and Tutorial. Use Analysis Services and Excel to reproduce Figures 15-19 through 15-21.

For questions 15.55 to 15.57, use SQL Server or Oracle.

15.55   Write a stored procedure to calculate support. Use the view shown in Figure 15-26. Place your results in a view name SupportView.

15.56   Write a stored procedure to calculate confidence. Use the TRANS_DATA described on page 553 and the SupportView. Place your results in a view named ConfidenceView.

15.57   Write a stored procedure to compute lift. Use the TRANS_DATA table described on page 553 to compute unconditional probabilities and use the ConfidenceView for Confidence.

MARCIA'S DRY CLEANING

Assume that Marcia uses a database that includes the following three tables:

CUSTOMER (<u>CustomerSK</u>, Phone, Email, FirstName, LastName)

ORDER (<u>InvoiceNumber</u>, Date, *CustomerSK*, Subtotal, Tax, Total)

ORDER_ITEM (<u>*InvoiceNumber*</u>, <u>ItemNumber</u>, Qty, Service, UnitPrice, ExtendedPrice)

(ORDER_ITEM.Service is a foreign key to the SERVICE table, but the SERVICE table is not needed for these exercises.)

A Describe how an RFM analysis could be useful in Marcia's business.
B Using the four tables in Figure 15-9, write a set of stored procedures to compute an RFM analysis on Marcia's data.
C Show SQL to process the table generated in your answer to B to display the names and email data for all customers having an RFM score of 5 1 1 or 4 1 1.
D Describe in general terms how a market basket analysis can be used on the items in a dry cleaning order.
E Using the instructions in questions 15.55 through 15.57, write stored procedures to perform a market basket analysis on the items in a dry cleaning order.

MORGAN IMPORTING

The tables we have used for Morgan Importing have no natural application for either RFM or market basket analysis, at least not to Morgan. However, consider the following three tables from the standpoint of a shipper:

SHIPMENT   (<u>ShipmentSK</u>, ShipDate, *ShipperName*, ShipperInvoiceNumber, Origin, Destination)

SHIPMENT_ITEM (<u>*ShipmentSK*</u>, <u>*PurchaseSK*</u>, InsuredValue)

SHIPPER (<u>ShipperName</u>, Phone, Fax, Email, Contact)

If we substitute CUSTOMER for SHIPPER, we can create the structure of a database that would record customers and shipments and items they've shipped with us. The modified tables are:

SHIPMENT   (<u>ShipperInvoiceNumber</u>, ShipDate, *CustomerSK*, Origin, Destination, Subtotal, Tax, Total)

SHIPMENT_ITEM (<u>*ShipperInvoiceNumber*</u>, <u>ItemNumber</u>, ShippingCost)

CUSTOMER (<u>CustomerSK</u>, CustomerName, Phone, Fax, Email, Contact)

where CustomerSK is a surrogate key for the customer data. Use these revised tables to answer the following questions.

A Describe how an RFM analysis could be useful to the shipper.
B Using the four tables in Figure 15-9, write a set of stored procedures to compute an RFM analysis for shipments.

C Show SQL to process the table generated in your answer to B to display the names and email data for all customers having an RFM score of 5 1 1 or 4 1 1.

D Describe in general terms how a market basket analysis can be used on the items in a shipment.

E Using the instructions in questions 15.55 through 15.57, write stored procedures to perform a market basket analysis on the items in a shipment.

APPENDIX A

Introduction to Microsoft Access

This appendix introduces the basics of Microsoft Access. After you read this appendix, you will be able to create tables and table relationships, fill those tables with data, and create simple forms and queries. This discussion just scratches the surface of Access' capabilities. This appendix focuses on the features and functions that will enable you to create tables so that you can use Access to practice writing SQL statements, as described in Chapter 2.

All of the instructions and screen displays in this appendix pertain to Microsoft Access 2003. If you are using a different version of Access, the commands and screen displays may vary slightly from those shown here, but you should have no difficulty following this discussion.

 ## Example Database Design

This appendix will create and process the STUDENT, CLASS, and GRADE tables shown in Figure A-1. These are the same three tables shown in Figure 1-1. The tables and their column specifications are listed in Figure A-2. Note that Access uses the term *field* rather than *column*. Because *column* is the standard term in the database discipline, we will use it here.

Tables Used in This Appendix

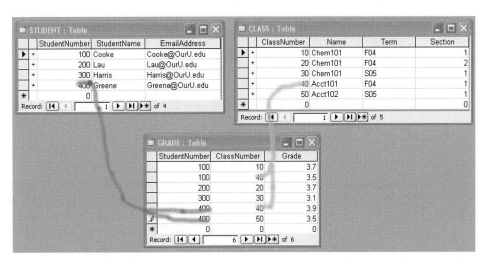

Figure A-2

Example Database Design

Table	Column (Field)	Data Type
STUDENT	StudentNumber	Number, Long Integer (Table Key)
STUDENT	StudentName	Text, 50
STUDENT	EmailAddress	Text, 50
CLASS	ClassNumber	Number, Long Integer (Table Key)
CLASS	Name	Text, 50
CLASS	Term	Text, 5
CLASS	Section	Number, Integer
GRADE	StudentNumber	Number, Long Integer Table Key is (StudentNumber, ClassNumber)
GRADE	ClassNumber	Number, Long Integer
GRADE	Grade	Number, Single, Fixed, two decimal places

Column Data Types

The data type of each column is shown in Figure A-2. StudentNumber has a Number data type. In Access, number data may be one of three lengths: Long Integer, Integer, or Byte. We will use Long Integer for StudentNumber, as shown in Figure A-2. Both StudentName and EmailAddress are Text of length 50. The columns of the other two tables have the data types shown in Figure A-2.

Note that for the Grade column in the GRADE table we chose the data type Number, Single, Fixed, two decimal places. This choice was made because grades are not integers (whole numbers), but rather numbers with decimal places. *Single* refers to the size of the numbers allowed; the Single size is more than ample for grade data. *Fixed* means that the decimal point is fixed in the same position for all values. We chose two decimal places so that we can display grades such as 3.75, and not just 3.7. See the Access documentation to learn more about data types and lengths.

Table Keys

Each table has a key, which is one or more columns that uniquely identify a row. You will learn the importance of keys, their properties, and their uses throughout this text. For now, just understand that the values of a key column identify a unique row in the table. According to Figure A-2, the key of STUDENT is StudentNumber; this means that a particular value of StudentNumber, say 400, identifies one and only one row in STUDENT. The key of CLASS is ClassNumber.

No single column can be a key for the GRADE table. A student may have several grades recorded, so StudentNumber, by itself, is not a key. Similarly, a class will have many students, so ClassNumber, by itself, cannot be the key either. However, if we assume that a student takes a class just once, then the combination (StudentNumber, ClassNumber) is a key. We make that assumption in this database.

To summarize, the key of STUDENT is StudentNumber, the key of CLASS is ClassNumber, and the key of GRADE is the combination (StudentNumber, ClassNumber).

Relationships Among Tables

As described in Chapter 1, one of the characteristics of a database is that the rows in tables can relate to one another. For the example in Figure A-1, rows in the STUDENT table are related to rows in the GRADE table by the column StudentNumber. As shown in that figure, the student with StudentNumber 400 has earned all of the grades in the GRADE table that have a matching value of 400 in the StudentNumber column. Similarly, rows in the CLASS table are related to rows in the GRADE table by the column ClassNumber. You will learn how to define these relationships for Access later in this appendix.

Creating a Database and a Table

When you start Access, a window like that shown in Figure A-3 will appear. Because we are creating a new database, select *Create a new file . . .* from the bottom of the window on the right. Navigate using the dialog box that appears to locate the directory in which you want to store your database, name the database *Appendix_A* (or some other suitable name), and click Create.

The window shown in Figure A-4 will appear. Select *Create table in Design view.* The next window to appear is a form that you fill out to define the columns (fields) in your table. Type StudentNumber as the first Field Name and tab over to the Data Type entry. Click the combo box that appears and select Number from the combo box list, as shown in Figure A-5. At this point, look down in the lower part of the form under the heading Field Properties. Access has chosen Long Integer for Field Size, which is what you want, so you need do nothing else for this column definition.

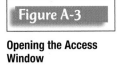

Opening the Access Window

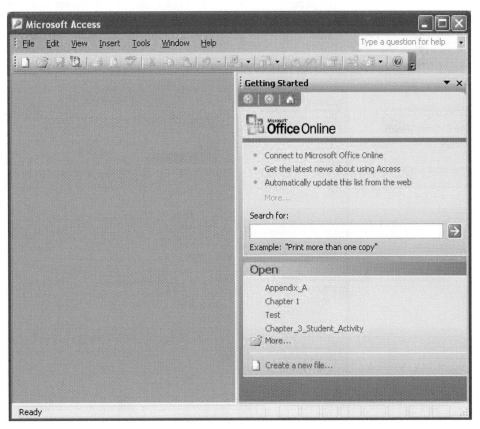

Figure A-4

Creating a New Table Using Design View

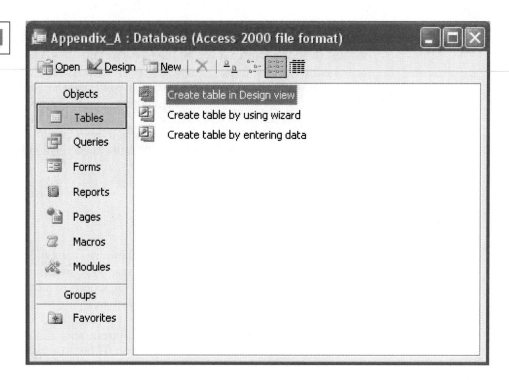

The third column in the table creation form is Description. You can use it to enter optional documentation comments about your column. Access ignores any comments you make. We will not use Description in this appendix.

Now fill out two more rows of the table design form for the StudentName and EmailAddress columns. Both of these columns are of data type Text and Length 50. Field Length 50 is the Access default, so you do not need to change the Field Properties for those columns.

To define the table key, highlight the StudentNumber row by clicking the gray square in the left-most position of that row and then click the small key icon in the menu

Figure A-5

The Column (Field) Design Form

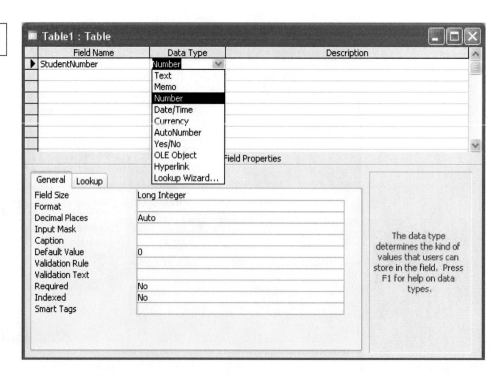

Figure A-6

**The Completed
STUDENT Table
Definition**

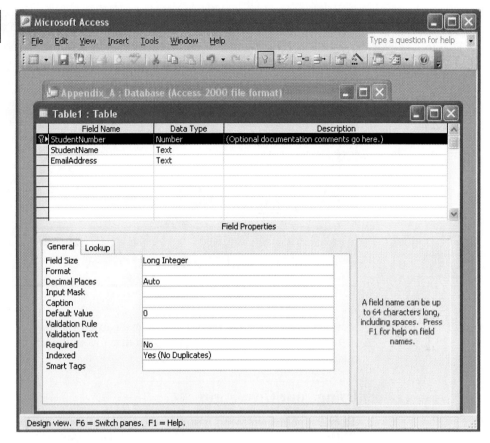

bar. This icon is highlighted in Figure A-6. Access places a small key icon next to the StudentNumber row to indicate that StudentNumber is the key.

At this point, your table definition is complete. Your form should look like the one in Figure A-6. Close the table design window and click Yes when asked if you want to save the table design. Access will ask you for a table name; type in STUDENT for the table name. Capitalize STUDENT in accordance with the conventions in this text.

You can create the other two tables at this point if you want. However, we will not do that here; instead, we will add data to the STUDENT data and process it in elementary ways. Then we will return to create the other two tables.

Adding Data to Tables

You can add data to a table by using the Datasheet View, a built-in Access data entry form, or a data entry form that you create on your own.

Using the Datasheet View

To use the Datasheet View, double-click the table name (STUDENT if you followed the instructions in the previous section) in the main database window (the window shown in Figure A-4). A form having the structure of the STUDENT table will open. You can use that form to insert data, as shown in Figure A-7. In Figure A-7, the data for student Cooke have been entered, and the data for student Lau are in the process of being entered. Click a cell to enter data for that cell or tab from cell to cell. Enter all four rows of STUDENT data shown in Figure A-1.

You can use the Datasheet View to add, modify, and delete data. To modify data, just position the cursor in the cell you want to modify and change the data. When you

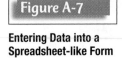

Figure A-7

**Entering Data into a
Spreadsheet-like Form**

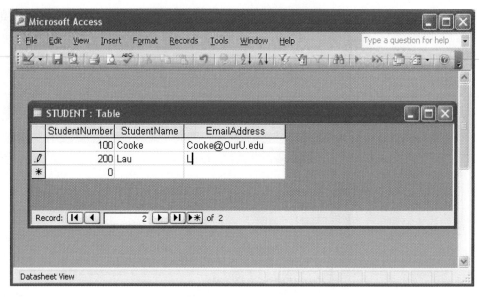

move to another cell, the change will be made in the database. To delete data, highlight the row you want to delete by clicking on that row in the left-most column. Then press the Delete key.

Using Your Own Form

To create your own form, return to the main database window and in the list under Objects click *Forms,* as shown in Figure A-8. Double-click *Create form by using wizard* and the form in Figure A-9 will appear. To include all of the columns of the STUDENT table, click the right-facing double-chevron button (>>), and all of the columns will be added to the Selected Fields list. This has been done in Figure A-9; the >> button is grayed out in this figure because all of the columns have already been entered.

Figure A-8

Creating a Form

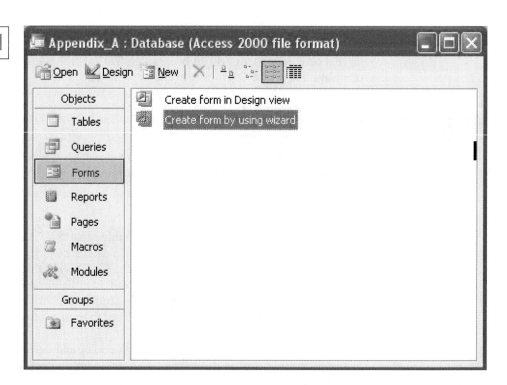

Figure A-9

Creating a Form: Selecting the Columns of the STUDENT Table

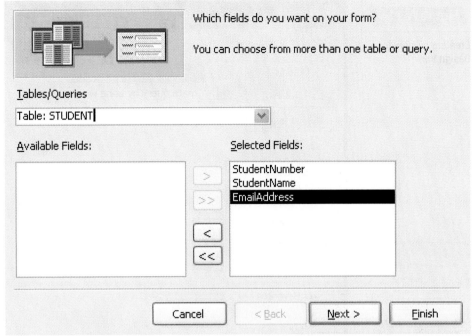

Which fields do you want on your form?

You can choose from more than one table or query.

Tables/Queries

Table: STUDENT

Available Fields:

Selected Fields:

StudentNumber
StudentName
EmailAddress

Cancel | < Back | Next > | Finish

Click Finish and the new form will open as shown in Figure A-10, but the form will be positioned to the first row in STUDENT. To move to other rows of the table, press the right-facing arrow at the bottom of the form. In Figure A-10, the user has pressed that arrow three times, and the fourth row of data is shown in the form.

You can use this form to add new data and to modify existing data. To add data, just click past the end of the data; Access will open a blank form into which you can add a new row. To modify data, just change the data in the form. To delete data, position the form to display the data from the row you want to delete and choose Edit/Delete Record from the main Access menu.

Creating Queries

To create a query, go to the main database form and click *Queries* under Objects, as shown in Figure A-11. Select *Create query in Design view.* In the dialog box labeled Show Table, double-click the STUDENT table and then Close the Show Table dialog box. A form like that in Figure A-12 will open, but the Field data will be blank. To fill in the Field data, from the top pane drag StudentName out of the STUDENT box and drop it on the first Field column in the lower pane. Repeat and drop EmailAddress on the second Field column as shown in Figure A-12.

To demonstrate one of the capabilities of an Access query, suppose that we only want to see data for students having the name 'Lau.' We can restrict, or **filter,** the query

Figure A-10

Using the Form to Insert, Modify, or Delete Data

STUDENT	
StudentNumber	400
StudentName	Greene
EmailAddress	Greene@OurU.edu

Record: 4 of 4

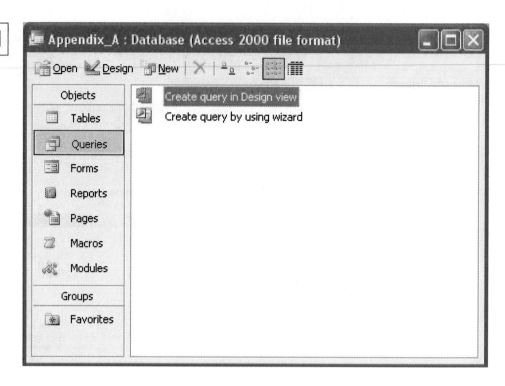

Figure A-11

Creating a Query in Design View

results by specifying 'Lau' in the Criteria row, underneath StudentName, as shown in Figure A-12.

To run the query, click the red exclamation point icon in the Access toolbar. The result is shown in Figure A-13; only the StudentName and EmailAddress for the student named 'Lau' appear.

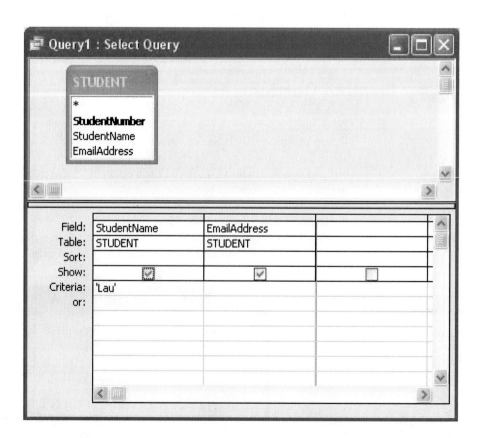

Figure A-12

Selecting the Columns of the Query and the Filter Criterion

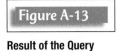

Figure A-13

Result of the Query

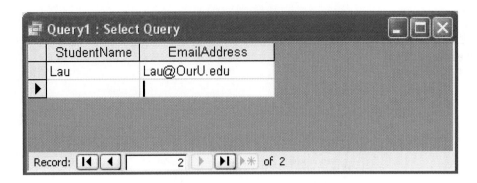

To see the SQL statement that Access used to process this query, right-click in the gray area of the form in Figure A-13 and select SQL View. Alternatively, with the form in Figure A-13 open, select View/SQL View from the main SQL menu. The SQL statement appears as shown in Figure A-14.

You can enter any SQL statement you like into this form, even one that processes a table other than STUDENT. You can use this facility to help you learn the SQL statements in Chapters 2 and 7.

Close the window that has the query; Access will ask if you want to save the query changes. Click Yes and name the query something like *Student_Lau_Info.*

Creating Relationships

To demonstrate how to create table relationships in Access, we must first create the other two tables. Use a procedure similar to that for creating the STUDENT table. Columns and data types for the CLASS and GRADE tables are shown in Figure A-2.

Creating the CLASS and GRADE Tables

The creation of the CLASS and GRADE tables differs from the creation of the STUDENT table in several ways. First, when you create the Term column in CLASS, set the Field Size to 5, as shown in Figure A-15. Second, when you create the Section column of CLASS, select Integer rather than Long Integer as the Field Size. To do this, after you have set the Data Type of Section to Number, click the Field Size property in the lower pane. A list of number-type Field Sizes will appear. Select Integer. We use Integer rather than Long Integer because section numbers are small and do not need the space that Long Integer provides.

Third, when you create the Grade column in GRADE, set the Field Size to Single. Also, set Grade's Format property to Fixed and its Decimal Places property to two, as shown in Figure A-15. Setting Format and Decimal Places this way enables you to enter grades such as 3.75 and will cause Access to show Grade data with two decimal places.

Finally, you need to use a slightly different procedure for creating the key of GRADE. According to Figure A-2, the key is the combination of the StudentNumber and ClassNumber columns. To set the key to a combination, in the GRADE table

Figure A-14

SQL Used in Query in Figure A-12

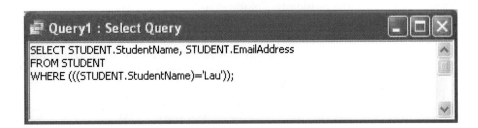

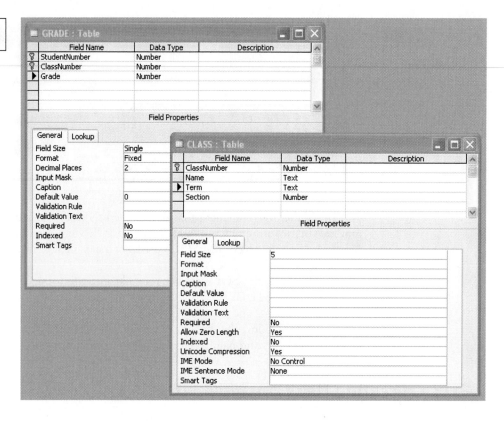

Figure A-15

**Creating the GRADE
and CLASS Tables**

definition form, click the left gray square next to StudentNumber. The entire row will be highlighted. Hold the Shift key down and click again on the left column opposite ClassNumber so that both rows are highlighted. Now, with both rows highlighted, click the key icon in the toolbar, and Access will set the key to the combination of (StudentNumber, ClassNumber). A small key will appear to the left of both rows.

Using the Relationships Window

To create relationships among tables, select Tools/Relationships from the main Access menu. The Show Table dialog box will appear. Double-click STUDENT, CLASS, and GRADE and then close the Show Table dialog. In response, Access will place the three tables into the relationships window.

Now, as shown in Figure A-1, StudentNumber in STUDENT relates to StudentNumber in GRADE. To create that relationship, drag StudentNumber from STUDENT and drop it on top of StudentNumber in GRADE. When you do this, Access opens the dialog box shown in Figure A-16. Check the box labeled Enforce Referential Integrity as shown in Figure A-16. This will create a **referential integrity constraint,** which was discussed in Chapter 3. Such a constraint ensures that any value for StudentNumber that is entered into GRADE will match an existing value of StudentNumber in STUDENT. If not, Access will generate an error message and disallow the insertion of the unmatched StudentNumber in GRADE. Click Create to store the relationship information.

You can create the relationship between CLASS and GRADE in the same way. Drag ClassNumber from CLASS and drop it on ClassNumber in GRADE. Check Enforce Referential Integrity and click Create. Now both relationships have been created. The final relationship window is shown in Figure A-17. Close this window and save the changes when asked.

Once you have created the CLASS and GRADE tables and their relationships, open the Datasheet View for CLASS and GRADE and add the data shown in Figure A-1. Just

Figure A-16

Creating a Relationship between STUDENT and GRADE

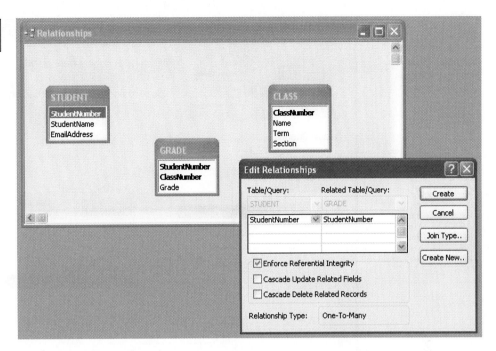

Figure A-17

The Completed Relationships

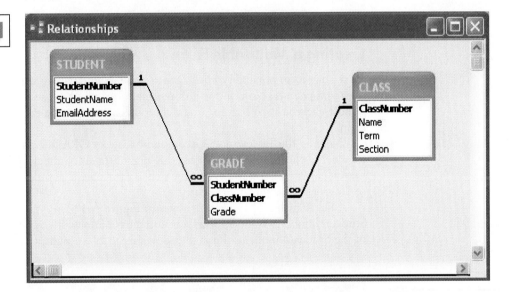

to see how the referential integrity constraint works, try to add a row to GRADE using a StudentNumber of 5. If you have checked Enforce Referential Integrity in the relationship dialog correctly, you will receive an error message. By the way, you can always review a relationship's properties by right-clicking on the relationship line and choosing Properties.

Creating Multitable Forms and Reports

Once you have defined the relationships, it is relatively easy to create multitable forms and reports. However, this subject can become quite complicated, and those complications involve more details about Access form and report processing than is appropriate in this appendix. Here, we will stick with the basics.

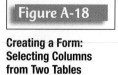

Figure A-18

Creating a Form:
Selecting Columns
from Two Tables

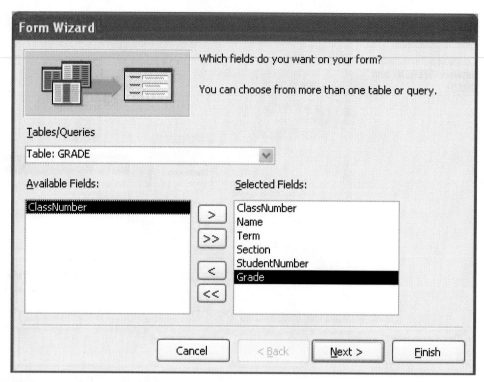

Creating a Multitable Form

To see one form possibility, click *Forms* in the main database window and select *Create form using wizard*. Now, in the Tables/Queries combo box, select CLASS and click the double-chevron (>>) button. This action will add all of the columns of CLASS to the form.

Next, in the Tables/Queries combo box, select GRADE, but this time do not click the double-chevron button. Instead, highlight StudentNumber, click the single-chevron button (>), highlight Grade, and then click the single-chevron button again. The result of these actions is shown in Figure A-18.

Click Finish and the form shown in Figure A-19 will appear. If only part of the StudentNumber column appears, expand the column width by clicking the right margin of the StudentNumber column and dragging it to the right. Click the record advance

Figure A-19

A Form Based on Two
Tables

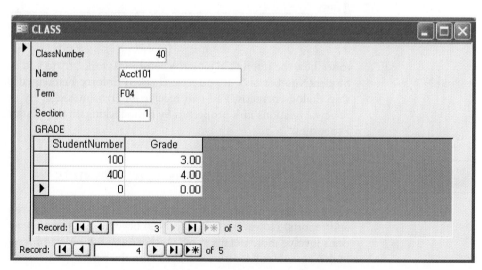

   **A Report Based on Three Tables**

CLASS

lassNumber	Name	Term	Section	udentNumber	Grade	StudentName
10	Chem 101	F04	1			
				100	4.00	Cooke
20	Chem 101	F04	2			
				200	4.00	Lau
30	Chem 101	S05	1			
				300	3.00	Harris
40	Acct 101	F04	1			
				400	4.00	Greene
				100	3.00	Cooke
50	Acct 102	S05	1			
				400	4.00	Greene

arrow to navigate to class number 40, and you will see the two rows of GRADE for this class. Notice that grades are shown with two decimal places, as desired.

Creating a Multitable Report

The process for creating a multitable report is very similar to that for creating a multitable form. In the main database window, click *Reports* under the list of Objects. Double-click *Create report by using wizard.* Select all of the columns for the CLASS table and the StudentNumber and Grade columns of the GRADE table. Also, select StudentName from the STUDENT table. Click Finish and the report shown in Figure A-20 will appear.

Notice that the ClassNumber heading is partly obscured. You can adjust its size and location in the report by selecting View/Design View from the main Access menu. Access will open the form in Design View and you can move the ClassNumber label around. To return to the data view, select View/Print Preview from the main Access menu.

Of course, you can embellish this report by adding colors and graphics. You can also add calculated fields to the report, but all of these actions are not related to database processing and we will not consider them here.

 ## Other Access Features

Access has many different features and functions—hundreds of them, in fact. Most of these features involve more sophisticated forms and reports. Because the focus of this text is on database processing, and not on database application development, we will not delve into these features.

Access provides a number of events that you can use to simulate triggers (see Chapters 6 and 7). It also provides a macro language and an interface to Visual Basic that you can use to write stored procedures (described in Chapter 7). However, these facilities are unique to Access and are not typical of database processing using enterprise-class products such as Oracle, SQL Server, DB2, and MySQL. Accordingly, we will not consider them in this text.

At this point, you have sufficient knowledge of Access to create the example tables in this book and to open the SQL View so that you can practice coding SQL statements.

REVIEW QUESTIONS

A.1   Suppose that you are creating a database for a soccer league and you have two tables: TEAM (TeamName, HomeFieldNumber, SponsorName) and PLAYER (Name, Phone, Email, TeamName), where TeamName in PLAYER relates to TeamName in TEAM. Assume that a player belongs to just one team, but that a TEAM may have many players. Create a database design similar to that shown in Figure A-2 for these two tables. Make your own assumptions about data types and lengths.

A.2   Start Access and create a new database named Soccer_Players.

A.3   Create the TEAM table described in A.1.

A.4   Using the Datasheet View, add data for three teams for the table you created in A.3.

A.5   Create a form for the TEAM data similar to the form in Figure A-10. Use your form to add a team, to delete a team, and to modify team data.

A.6   Create a query to find one of your teams. Use the query in Figure A-12 as an example. Run your query to demonstrate that it works.

A.7   Display the SQL that Access uses to process the query you created in A.6.

A.8   Create the PLAYER table described in A.1.

A.9   Create the relationship between TEAM and PLAYER. Check Enforce Referential Integrity.

A.10   Using the Datasheet View, add five players to your database. Try to add a player to a team that does not exist. Describe what happens.

A.11   Create a form that shows teams and their players. Use Figures A-18 and Figure A-19 as examples.

A.12   Create a report that shows teams and players. Use Figure A-20 as an example.

The IDEF1X Standard

IDEF1X (Integrated Definition 1, Extended) is a variation of the entity-relationship (E-R) model. IDEF1X, which was announced as a national standard in 1993, is based on earlier work done for the U.S. military in the mid-1980s. IDEF1X assumes that a relational database is to be created. IDEF1X is complex and unwieldy and is not as popular as the crow's foot model used throughout this text. However, because IDEF1X is a national standard, all vendors of entity-relationship data modeling products that wish to sell to the U.S. government must comply with it. Accordingly, most popular data modeling products have the capability to produce at least rudimentary IDEF1X diagrams. Further, if you work for a U.S. government organization or for an organization that does business with the U.S. government, you may be required to use it. Consequently, we present an overview of IDEF1X here.

IDEF1X includes entities, relationships, and attributes, but it tightens the meaning of these terms and qualifies them with more specific terminology. In addition, IDEF1X includes the definition of domains, a component not present in the extended E-R model. Finally, IDEF1X changed the E-R graphical symbols, using a dot instead of a crow's foot and adding a new structure called categories, a version of generalization hierarchies and subtypes. Differences between the extended E-R model and the IDEF1X model are summarized in Figure B-1.

IDEF1X Entities

IDEF1X entities are the same as the entities in the extended E-R model. They represent something that the users want to track—something about which users want to keep data. Like the extended E-R model, entities are shown with either square or rounded corners, although the meaning of entities with rounded corners is slightly different in IDEF1X, as you will learn when we discuss identifying relationships.

IDEF1X Relationships

Figure B-2 lists the four types of IDEF1X relationships. Although the terminology is awkward, it is very specific—just what you would expect from a national standard. We will consider each type in turn.

Figure B-1

Correspondence of
Terms between the
Extended E-R Model
and the IDEF1X Version
of the E-R Model

Extended E-R Model Term	Corresponding IDEF1X E-R Version Term	Remarks
Entity	Entity	Same.
Attribute	Attribute	Same.
Relationship	Relationship	Same.
1:1 and 1:N relationships	Nonidentifying connection relationship	Connection relationship is the same as HAS-A relationship.
N:M relationship	Nonspecific relationship	
ID-dependent relationship	Identifying connection relationship	
Weak entity, but not ID dependent	None	
Supertype entity	Generic entity	Generic entity has an IS-A relationship to a category cluster.
Subtype entity	Category entity	Category entities are mutually exclusive in their category cluster.
None	Domain	

Figure B-2

IDEF1X Relationship
Types

- Nonidentifying Connection Relationships
- Identifying Connection Relationships
- Nonspecific Relationships
- Categorization Relationships

Nonidentifying Connection Relationships

Nonidentifying connection relationships are 1:1 or 1:N relationships between two non-ID-dependent (hence, *nonidentifying*) entities. Connection relationships are the same as what are called HAS-A relationships in the extended E-R model.

Figure B-3 shows examples of nonidentifying connection relationships. According to the standard, nonidentifying relationships are represented with a dashed line. Furthermore, in IDEF1X, connection relationships are always drawn from a parent to a child entity. For 1:1 relationships, either entity can be considered the parent, but IDEF1X forces you to pick one of the entities for that role. As shown in Figure B-3, a filled-in circle is placed on the relationship line adjacent to the child entity in an IDEF1X E-R diagram.

In IDEF1X, the default cardinality of a nonidentifying connection relationship is one-to-many, with a mandatory parent and an optional child. Such relationships are shown by a dashed line with a filled-in circle by the child and no other notation. Thus, in Figure B-3, the relationship from DEPARTMENT to FURNITURE is 1:N; no DEPARTMENT is required to have any FURNITURE, and every FURNITURE entity must be assigned to a DEPARTMENT. If the relationship cardinality is different from this default, additional notation is added to the diagram. If the child is required, a *P* is placed near the circle, indicating that one or more child entities are required (the *P* stands for "positive," as in *positive number*). If the parent is optional, a diamond is added to the line, adjacent to the parent. In Figure B-3, the relationship from DEPARTMENT to EMPLOYEE is 1:N; a DEPARTMENT must have at least one EMPLOYEE, and an EMPLOYEE is not required to be related to a DEPARTMENT.

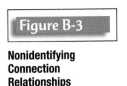

Figure B-3

Nonidentifying
Connection
Relationships

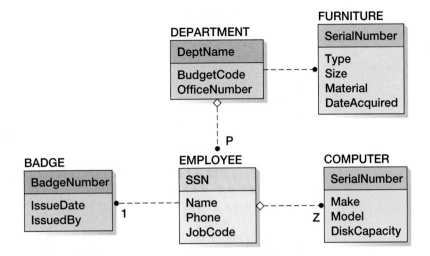

The 1:1 relationships are denoted by adding notation near the circle on the relationship line. A one indicates that exactly one child is required; a Z indicates that zero or one children are allowed. Thus, in Figure B-3, an EMPLOYEE is connected to exactly one BADGE entity and is also connected to zero or one COMPUTER entities. The diamond indicates that a COMPUTER need not be related to an EMPLOYEE. Because there is no diamond on the EMPLOYEE side of the BADGE:EMPLOYEE relationship, a BADGE must be connected to an EMPLOYEE.

Identifying Connection Relationships

Identifying connection relationships are the same as ID-dependent relationships in the extended E-R model. The identifier of the parent is always part of the identifier of the child. In Figure B-4, a BUILDING entity is the parent of an ID-dependent relationship to the OFFICE entity. Note that the identifier of BUILDING, BuildingNumber, is part of the identifier of OFFICE. The notation (FK) means that this attribute is a foreign key of another entity (here, BUILDING). Identifying relationships are portrayed with solid lines, and child entities in identifying relationships are shown with rounded corners.

In this example, there is no additional notation beside the filled-in circle, so the default cardinality is assumed. Thus, a BUILDING may be connected to zero, one, or many OFFICEs. If a *1, Z,* or *P* were placed by the circle, a BUILDING would connect to at most one, to zero or one, or to one or more OFFICE entities, respectively. There can never be a diamond on the parent side of an identifying relationship because children in identifying relationships always require a parent.

Like the crow's foot model, IDEF1X allows for weak entities that are not identifying. However, it provides no special notation for such entities. The minimum cardinality for the parent in such relationships is one, but no other means exists for documenting the fact that they are logically dependent on their parent.

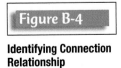

Figure B-4

Identifying Connection
Relationship

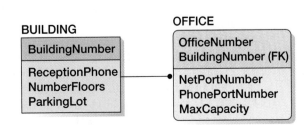

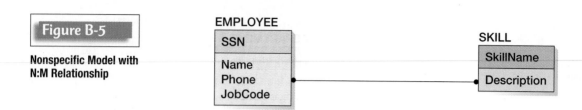

Figure B-5

Nonspecific Model with N:M Relationship

Nonspecific Relationships

A nonspecific IDEF1X relationship is simply a many-to-many relationship. Nonspecific relationships are shown with a filled-in circle on each end of the solid relationship line, as shown in Figure B-5. In IDEF1X, there is no way to set minimum cardinalities of a nonspecific relationship.

Like the crow's foot model, IDEF1X treats many-to-many relationships as poor stepchildren of nonidentifying connection relationships. This is done because such relationships have no direct expression in the relational model. As discussed in Chapter 6, such relationships must be converted to two 1:N relationships before they can be processed in a relational database.

To some people, this is a glaring fault in IDEF1X, because it confuses conceptual schema ideas with internal schema ideas. These people would say that one should be able to fully document an N:M relationship, including minimum cardinalities, in the conceptual model. What happens to that relationship later in designing the internal schema should not be a factor in conceptual design.

> ### B T W
>
> All of the comments about N:M relationships pertain equally well to ERwin's implementation of the crow's foot model. That problem, however, is just in ERwin's implementation. The model itself allows the specification of minimum cardinality on many-to-many relationships. But with both ERwin's implementation and the IDEF1X model, at least you can specify many-to-many relationships. As noted on page 129, with Visio, you cannot specify a many-to-many relationship at all!

 ## Categorization Relationships

Categorization relationships are a specialization of generalization/subtype relationships in the extended E-R model. Specifically, a categorization relationship is a relationship between a **generic entity** and another entity called a **category entity.** Category entities are grouped into **categorization clusters.** For example, in Figure B-6, EMPLOYEE is a generic entity; PROGRAMMER, PQA_ENGINEER, and TECH_WRITER are category entities; and the category cluster, represented by the filled-in circle over two horizontal lines, is the collection of PROGRAMMER, PQA_ENGINEER, and TECH_WRITER.

Categorization relationships are IS-A relationships. A programmer is an employee, for example. Because they are IS-A relationships, the primary key of the category entities is the same as the category key of the generic entity. In this case, the primary key of PROGRAMMER, PQA_ENGINEER, and TECH_WRITER is SSN. Because of this, category entities are shown without primary keys.

In IDEF1X, the entities in a category cluster are mutually exclusive. In Figure B-6, an EMPLOYEE can be a PROGRAMMER, a PQA_ENGINEER, *or* a TECH_WRITER. An employee cannot be two or more of these.

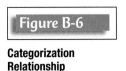

Figure B-6

Categorization
Relationship

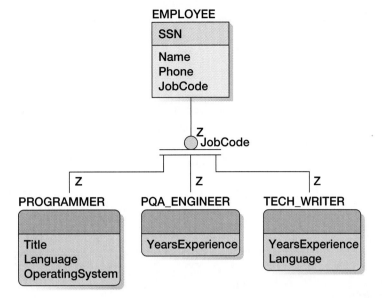

Category clusters may have a **discriminator,** which is an attribute of the generic entity that indicates the type of the EMPLOYEE. In Figure B-6, JobCode is the discriminator. This means that the value of JobCode can be used to determine whether the EMPLOYEE is a PROGRAMMER, a PQA_ENGINEER, or a TECH_WRITER. The means by which this is done is not specified in the conceptual model; we are simply stating here that it can be done. Some category clusters do not have a discriminator; the determination of the category entity is left unspecified.

Category clusters are of two types: complete and incomplete. In a **complete category cluster,** every possible type of category for the cluster is shown. Complete category clusters are denoted by two horizontal lines with a gap in between. The category cluster in Figure B-6 is complete. Because this cluster is complete, all of the categories of EMPLOYEE are shown; there is no missing category. Hence, every EMPLOYEE can be categorized as a PROGRAMMER, a PQA_ENGINEER, or a TECH_WRITER.

B T W

You may be saying, "Wait a minute. Of course, there are other types of employees. What about accountants, for example?" The point is that *according to this model,* there are no other types of employees. Maybe this model is used only in a software development group in which there are no other employee types. Or maybe this model is in error. Whatever the case, however, there are no other types of employees according to this model.

All category entities are existence dependent on the generic category, so the minimum cardinality from the category entity to the generic entity is one. Because this is always true, that cardinality is not shown in the diagram.

According to the IDEF1X standard, the cardinalities of the relationships from the generic entity to the category entities are always zero or one. The Z on the line between the generic entity and the cluster symbol indicates that an EMPLOYEE may or may not have one of the category entities. The Z on the lines to the category entities shows that the generic entity may or may not be one of those types.

Figure B-7   Incomplete and Complete Category Clusters

EMPLOYEE

SSN
Name Phone JobCode

Z   Z JobCode

Z   Z   Z   Z   Z

MANAGER	STAFF	PROGRAMMER	PQA_ENGINEER	TECH_WRITER
LevelCode LastBonus	HourlyRate VacationDays	Title Language OperatingSystem	YearsExperience	YearsExperience Language

Many people find this use of the Z notation to be puzzling, if not wrong. As stated, categories in a cluster are mutually exclusive. Thus, after an entity has a relationship to one category entity, the cardinality of the relationship to the other entities in that cluster is zero. Additionally, the Z on the line between the generic entity and the cluster symbol indicates that a generic entity may or may not have a category entity. For complete clusters, the Z should be a one, indicating that the generic entity must have a relationship to one of the entities in the cluster. There is no way to specify a one in the IDEF1X model for this case.

Figure B-7 shows a second category cluster that consists of MANAGER and STAFF category entities. This is an **incomplete** category cluster, which is indicated by placing the category cluster circle on top of a single line; there is no gap between the horizontal lines. This notation means that a least one category is missing. An employee might be a PART_TIME employee, for example. Again, all of the cardinalities are marked as Z.

We stated that within category clusters, category entities are mutually exclusive. This does not mean, however, that an entity cannot have a relationship to two or more category entities in different clusters. Thus, as shown in Figure B-7, an EMPLOYEE can be a MANAGER and also a PROGRAMMER. An EMPLOYEE cannot, however, be both a MANAGER and STAFF.

As you can see, the IDEF1X model adds structure to the generalization/subtype relationships in the extended E-R model. By further defining these concepts, the IDEF1X model makes them more meaningful, and hence more useful.

Domains

IDEF1X introduced the concept of domains to the extended E-R model. A **domain** is a named set of values that an attribute can have. A domain can consist of a specific list of values or it can be defined more generally, for example, as a set of strings of maximum length 50. As an example of the former, a university could have a domain called DEPARTMENT_NAMES that consists of the names of all official departments at that university. The domain would be defined by enumerating that list: {Accounting, Biology, Chemistry, Computer Science, Information Systems, Management, Physics, etc}. As an example of the latter, the domain STUDENT_NAMES could be defined as any character string of length less than 75.

Domains Reduce Ambiguity

Domains are both important and useful. For example, in Figure B-7, notice that both PROGRAMMER and TECH_WRITER have an attribute named Language. Without domains, these attribute names are ambiguous. Do they refer to the same thing or not? It might be that Language for PROGRAMMER is a computer language, whereas Language for TECH_WRITER is a human language. Or they may both be computer languages. This ambiguity can be eliminated by specifying the domain upon which each of these attributes is based.

We can define the domain COMPUTER_LANGUAGE to be the list {'C#', 'C++', 'Java', 'VisualBasic', 'VisualBasic.NET'} and the domain HUMAN_LANGUAGE to be {'Canadian French', 'France French', 'Spanish', 'UK English', 'US English'}. If we now say that Language of PROGRAMMER is based on the COMPUTER_LANGUAGE domain and that Language of TECH_WRITER is based on the HUMAN_LANGUAGE domain, the ambiguity between these two attributes is removed.

Furthermore, named domains eliminate ambiguity from attributes whose values look similar but are not the same. In Figure B-7, suppose that staff employees can accrue only 30 days of vacation. Further, suppose that employees are assumed to never work more than 30 years. In this case, the attributes STAFF.VacationDays, PQA_ENGINEER.YearsExperience, and TECH_WRITER.YearsExperience will all have values from 0 to 30. (In this notation, we identify attributes by appending the entity name to the attribute name with a period in between.) Without domain specification, we cannot tell whether these values refer to the same thing or not. Suppose we define a domain VACATION_DAYS as integers from 0 to 30 and a second domain EXPERIENCE as integers from 0 to 30. Now, we can state that the attribute STAFF.VacationDays is based on the VACATION_DAYS domain; the attributes PQA_ENGINEER.YearsExperience and TECH_WRITER.YearsExperience are based on the EXPERIENCE domain.

Domains Are Useful

Domains not only reduce ambiguity, they are also quite useful. Suppose that in a model of a university database we have an attribute called CampusAddress that is used in many different entities. It could be used in STUDENT, PROFESSOR, DEPARTMENT, LAB, and so forth. Further suppose that we base all of these CampusAddress attributes on the same domain, called CAMPUS_ADDRESS, and define that domain as all values of the pattern BBB-NNN, in which BBB is a list of building codes and NNN is a list of room numbers. When we define the domain in this way, all of the attributes in the model will inherit this definition.

Now, suppose that as we build our model, we discover that some room numbers have four digits. Without a domain definition, we would need to find all of the attributes in the model that use a campus address and change them to have NNNN for room number. With domains, we simply change the domain definition, and all of the attributes based on the domain will inherit the change. This not only reduces work, it eliminates errors that are difficult to find and that are hard to fix when they are found.

Another practical use for domains is to assess whether two attributes with different names refer to the same thing. For example, an entity named DEPARTMENT might have an attribute named BudgetCode and a second entity named PROJECT might have an attribute named ExpenseCategory. Using domains, we can readily check to determine whether these two attributes are based on the same domain. Without domains, it would be difficult to know. Even if attribute values look similar, they may have different meanings.

Figure B-8	Example of Domain Hierarchy

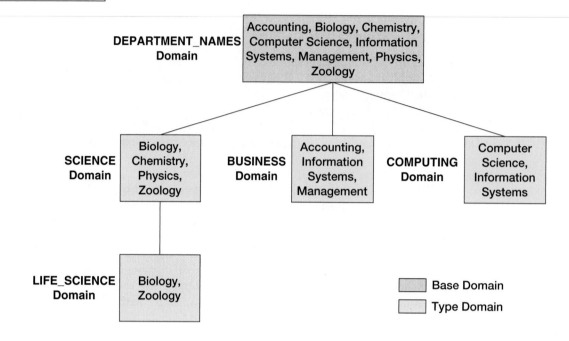

Base Domains and Typed Domains

IDEF1X defines two types of domains. A **base domain** is a domain having a data type and possibly a value list or range definition. The default data types are Character, Numeric, and Boolean. The specification enables users to define additional data types such as Date, Time, Currency, and so forth. A value list is a set of values like that described for the COMPUTER_LANGUAGE domain, and a range definition is like that described for the EXPERIENCE domain.

A **type domain** is a subset of a base domain or a subset of another type domain. Figure B-8 illustrates type domains based on the DEPARTMENT_NAMES domain. Type domains allow the definition of domain hierarchies that can be used for greater specificity.

REVIEW QUESTIONS

B.1   Why is the IDEF1X model important?

B.2   Name four types of IDEF1X relationships.

B.3   What is a nonidentifying connection relationship? How do such relationships relate to the extended E-R model described in Chapter 5?

B.4   What is an identifying connection relationship? How do such relationships relate to the extended E-R model described in Chapter 5?

B.5   What is a nonspecific relationship? How do such relationships relate to the extended E-R model described in Chapter 5?

B.6   Explain the major differences between categorization relationships and super-type/subtype relationships in the extended E-R model described in Chapter 5.

B.7   What are the major advantages of the modeling of domains?

B.8   Redraw the E-R diagram in Figure 5.54 using IDEF1X.

B.9   Answer question 5.59, but use IDEF1X instead of the crow's foot model.

B.10   Answer question 5.63, but use IDEF1X instead of the crow's foot model. Redraw Figure 5-59 in IDEF1X notation.

C

UML-Style Entity-Relationship Diagrams

The **Unified Modeling Language (UML)** is a set of structures and techniques for modeling and designing object-oriented programs (OOP) and applications. UML has come to prominence due to the Object Management Group, an organization that has been developing OOP models, technology, and standards since the 1980s. It is also beginning to see widespread use among OOP practitioners. UML is the basis of the object-oriented design tools from Rational Systems.

Because it is an application development methodology, UML is a subject for a course on systems development and is of limited concern to us. However, some UML diagrams are used to model database designs, and you may encounter them during your career. Accordingly, you should be familiar with their style.

UML Entities and Relationships

Figure C-1 shows the UML representation of a 1:1, a 1:N, and an N:M HAS-A relationship. Each entity is represented by an **entity class,** which is shown as a rectangle with three segments. The top segment shows the name of the entity and other data that we will discuss. The second segment lists the names of the attributes in the entity, and the third documents constraints and lists methods (program procedures) that belong to the entity.

Relationships are shown with a line between two entities. Cardinalities are represented in the format **x..y,** where x is the minimum required and y is the maximum allowed. Thus, 0..1 means that no entity is required and that at most one is allowed. An asterisk represents an unlimited number. Thus, 1..* means that one is required and an unlimited number is allowed.

Representation of Weak Entities

Figure C-2 shows the UML representation of weak entities. A filled-in diamond is placed on the line to the parent of the weak entity (the entity on which the weak entity depends). In Figure C-2(a), PRESCRIPTION is the weak entity and PATIENT is the parent entity. All weak entities have a parent, so the cardinality on their side of the weak relationship is always 1..1. Because of this, the cardinality on the parent entity is shown simply as 1.

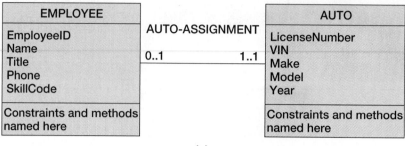

EMPLOYEE	AUTO-ASSIGNMENT	AUTO
EmployeeID Name Title Phone SkillCode	0..1 1..1	LicenseNumber VIN Make Model Year
Constraints and methods named here		Constraints and methods named here

(a)

DORMITORY	DORM-OCCUPANT	STUDENT
Name CampusAddress Capacity HousePhone	0..1 1..*	StudentNumber StudentName Phone Class AssignedRoom
Constraints and methods named here		Constraints and methods named here

(b)

STUDENT	STUDENT-CLUB	CLUB
StudentNumber StudentName Phone Class AssignedRoom	0..* 0..*	ClubNumber BudgetCode Description President PresidentPhone
Constraints and methods named here		Constraints and methods named here

(c)

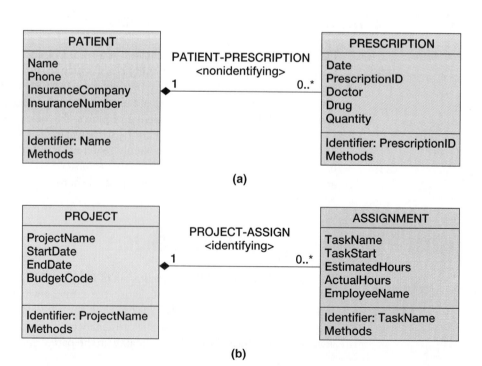

PATIENT	PATIENT-PRESCRIPTION <nonidentifying>	PRESCRIPTION
Name Phone InsuranceCompany InsuranceNumber	1 0..*	Date PrescriptionID Doctor Drug Quantity
Identifier: Name Methods		Identifier: PrescriptionID Methods

(a)

PROJECT	PROJECT-ASSIGN <identifying>	ASSIGNMENT
ProjectName StartDate EndDate BudgetCode	1 0..*	TaskName TaskStart EstimatedHours ActualHours EmployeeName
Identifier: ProjectName Methods		Identifier: TaskName Methods

(b)

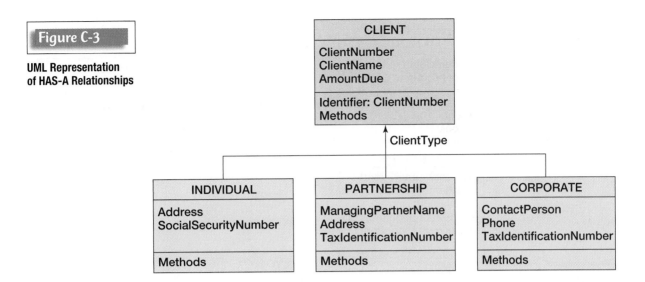

Figure C-3

**UML Representation
of HAS-A Relationships**

Figure C-2(a) shows a weak entity that is not an ID-dependent entity. It is denoted by the expression **<non-identifying>** on the PATIENT-PRESCRIPTION relationship. Figure C-2 (b) shows a weak entity that is ID-dependent. It is denoted with the label **<identifying>**.

Representation of Subtypes

UML represents subtypes, as shown in Figure C-3. In this figure, INDIVIDUAL, PARTNERSHIP, and CORPORATE subtypes of CLIENT are allowed. According to this figure, a given CLIENT could be one, two, or three of these subtypes. This does not make sense for this particular situation; a CLIENT should be one and only one of these types. The current version of UML does not provide a means to document exclusivity. Such notation can be added to a UML diagram, however.

OOP Constructs Introduced by UML

Because UML is an object-oriented technology, several OOP constructs have been added to UML entity classes. We will touch on these ideas here; you will learn more about them when you study object-oriented systems development. Consider the UML diagram in Figure C-4, which shows an E-R diagram with the full UML decoration.

First, the classes of all entities that are to be stored in the database are labeled with the keyword **<<Persistent>>.** This simply means that data should continue to exist even if the object that processes it is destroyed. In simpler terms, it means that the entity class is to be stored in the database.

Next, UML entity classes allow for **class attributes.** Such attributes differ from entity attributes because they pertain to the class of all entities of a given type. Thus, in Figure C-4, PatientCount of PATIENT is an attribute of the collection of all PATIENTs in the database. PatientSource is an attribute that documents the source of all of the PATIENTs in the database.

As you will learn, such class attributes have no place to reside when using the relational model. Instead, in some cases, attributes such as PatientCount are not stored in the database but are computed at run time. In other cases, a new entity is introduced to contain the class attributes. For the entity in Figure C-4, a new entity called PATIENT-SOURCE could be defined to hold both PatientCount and PatientSource attributes. In this case, all of the entities in PATIENT are connected to PATIENT-SOURCE.

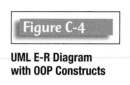

**UML E-R Diagram
with OOP Constructs**

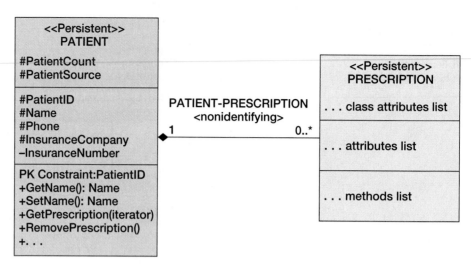

A third new feature is that UML uses object-oriented notation for the visibility of attributes and methods. Attributes preceded by a + are public, those with a # are protected, and those with a – are private. Thus, in Figure C-4, Name in PATIENT is a protected attribute. These terms arise from the discipline of object-oriented programming. A **public** attribute can be accessed and changed by any method of any object. A public method can be invoked by any method of any object. **Protected** means that the attribute or method is accessible only by methods of this class or of its subclasses, and **private** means that the attribute or method is accessible only by methods of this class.

Finally, UML entities specify constraints and methods in the third segment of the entity classes. In Figure C-4, a primary key constraint is placed on PatientID. This simply means that PatientID is a unique identifier. Additionally, Figure C-4 documents that GetName() is to be created to provide public access (note the + in front of GetName) to the Name attribute; SetName() is to be used to set its value; and the method GetPrescription() can be used to iterate over the set of Prescription entities related to this PATIENT entity.

 ## The Role of UML in Database Processing Today

The ideas illustrated in Figure C-4 lie in the murky water where database processing and object thinking merge. Such object-oriented notation doesn't fit with the practices and procedures of commercial database processing today. The notion that an entity attribute can be hidden in an object doesn't make sense unless only object-oriented programs are processing the database; even then, those programs must process the data in conformance with that policy. This is almost never done.

Instead, most commercial DBMS products have features that allow all types of programs to access the database and process any data that they have permission to access. Moreover, with facilities such as SQL, there is no way to limit access to attribute values to a single object.

So, the bottom line is that you should know how to interpret UML-style E-R diagrams. They can be used for database design just as extended E-R diagrams can. At present, however, the object-oriented notation they introduce is of limited practical value to database practitioners. The extended E-R model using the crow's foot notation is far more common and useful for database (as opposed to OO) design.

REVIEW QUESTIONS

C.1   Why is UML important? Why is it of concern to database designers?

C.2   Show a 1:1 relationship in UML format.

C.3   Show a 1:N relationship in UML format.

C.4   Show an N:M relationship in UML format.

C.5   Explain how UML documents minimum cardinality.

C.6   Show identifying and nonidentifying weak entities in UML format.

C.7   Show subtypes in UML format.

C.8   What are class attributes? How are they documented in UML?

C.9   How would class attributes be represented in the extended E-R model described in Chapter 5?

C.10   Explain the significance of the +, #, and – signs in a UML diagram.

C.11   Give an example of a constraint on an entity in a UML diagram.

C.12   Redraw the E-R diagram in Figure 5-54 using UML.

C.13   Describe the ways in which UML and commercial database processing are misfits. How do you think this situation will be resolved?

C.14   Answer question 5.59, but use UML instead of the crow's foot model.

C.15   Answer question 5.63, but use UML instead of the crow's foot model. Redraw Figure 5-59 using UML notation.

APPENDIX

D

Data Structures for Database Processing

All operating systems provide data management services. These services, however, are generally not sufficient for the specialized needs of a DBMS. Therefore, to enhance performance, DBMS products build and maintain specialized data structures, which are the topic of this appendix.

We begin by discussing flat files and some of the problems that can occur when such files need to be processed in different orders. Then, we turn to three specialized data structures: sequential lists, linked lists, and indexes (or inverted lists). Next, we illustrate how each of three special structures—trees, simple networks, and complex networks—are represented using various data structures. Finally, we explore how to represent and process multiple keys.

Although a thorough knowledge of data structures is not required to use most DBMS products, this background is essential for database administrators and systems programmers working with a DBMS. Being familiar with the data structures also helps you evaluate and compare database products.

Flat Files

A *flat file* is a file that has no repeating groups. Figure D-1(a) shows a flat file, and D-1(b) shows a file that is not flat because of the repeating field Item. A flat file can be stored in any common file organization, such as sequential, indexed sequential, or direct. Flat files have been used for many years in commercial processing. They are usually processed in some predetermined order—for example, in an ascending sequence on a key field.

Processing Flat Files in Multiple Orders

Sometimes users may want to process flat files in ways that are not readily supported by the file organization. Consider, for example, the ENROLLMENT records shown in Figure D-1(a). To produce student schedules, they must be processed in StudentNumber sequence. But to produce class rosters, the records need to be processed in ClassNumber sequence. The records, of course, can be stored in only one physical sequence. For example, they can be in order on StudentNumber or on ClassNumber, but not on both at the same time. The traditional solution to the problem of processing records in different

Examples of (a) a Flat and (b) a Nonflat File Invoice Record

Enrollment Record

StudentNumber	ClassNumber	Semester

Invoice Record

InvoiceNumber	Item(s)

Sample Data

200	70	2000S
100	30	2001F
300	20	2001F
200	30	2000S
300	70	2000S
100	20	2000S

(a)

Sample Data

1000	10	20	30	40
1010	50			
1020	10	20	30	
1030	50	90		

(b)

orders is to sort them in student order and process the student schedules and then sort the records in class order and produce class rosters.

For some applications, such as batch-mode systems, this solution is effective, although cumbersome. But suppose that both orders need to exist simultaneously because two concurrent users have different views of the ENROLLMENT records. What do we do then?

One solution is to create two copies of the ENROLLMENT file and sort them, as shown in Figure D-2. Because the data are listed in sequential order, this data structure is sometimes called a *sequential list.* Sequential lists can be readily stored as sequential files. This solution, however, is not generally done by DBMS products because sequentially reading a file is a slow process. Further, sequential files cannot be updated in the middle without rewriting the entire file. Also, maintaining several orders by keeping multiple copies of the same sequential list is usually not effective because the duplicated sequential list can create data integrity problems. Fortunately, other data structures allow us to process records in different orders and do not require the duplication of data. These data structures include *linked lists* and *indexes.*

A Note on Record Addressing

Usually, the DBMS creates large physical records, or blocks, on its direct access files. These records are used as containers for logical records. Typically, each physical record has many logical records. Here, we assume that each physical record is addressed by its relative record number (RRN). Thus, a logical record might be assigned to physical record number 7, 77, or 10,000. The relative record number is thus the logical record's physical address. If each physical record has more than one logical record, the address must also specify where the logical record is within the physical record. Thus, the complete address for a logical

ENROLLMENT Data Stored as Sequential Lists (a) Stored by StudentNumber and (b) Stored by ClassNumber

Student-Number	Class-Number	Semester
100	30	2001F
100	20	2000S
200	70	2000S
200	30	2000S
300	20	2001F
300	70	2000S

(a)

Student-Number	Class-Number	Semester
300	20	2001F
100	20	2000S
100	30	2001F
200	30	2000S
200	70	2000S
300	70	2000S

(b)

record might be relative record number 77, byte location 100. This means the record begins in byte 100 of physical record 77.

To simplify the illustrations in this text, we assume that there is only one logical record per physical record, so we need not be concerned with byte offsets within physical records. Although this is unrealistic, it limits our discussion to the essential points.

Maintaining Order with Linked Lists

Linked lists can be used to keep records in logical order that are not necessarily in physical order. To create a linked list, we add a field to each data record. The *link* field holds the address (in our illustrations, the relative record number) of the *next* record in logical sequence. For example, Figure D-3 shows the ENROLLMENT records expanded to include a linked list; this list maintains the records in StudentNumber order. Notice that the link for the numerically last student in the list is zero.

Figure D-4 shows ENROLLMENT records with two linked lists: One list maintains the StudentNumber order and the other list maintains the ClassNumber order. Two link fields have been added to the records, one for each list.

When insertions and deletions are made, linked lists have a great advantage over sequential lists. For example, to insert the ENROLLMENT record for Student 200 and Class 45, both of the lists shown in Figure D-2 would need to be rewritten. For the linked lists in Figure D-4, however, the new record could be added to the physical end of the list, and only the values of two link fields would need to be changed to place the new record in the correct sequences. These changes are shown in Figure D-5.

When a record is deleted from a sequential list, a gap is created. But in a linked list, a record can be deleted simply by changing the values of the link, or the *pointer* fields. In Figure D-6, the ENROLLMENT record for Student 200, Class 30, has been logically deleted. No other record points to its address, so it has been effectively removed from the chain, even though it still exists physically.

There are many variations of linked lists. We can make the list into a *circular list,* or *ring,* by changing the link of the last record from zero to the address of the first record in

---

Figure D-3

ENROLLMENT Data in
StudentNumber Order
Using a Linked List

Relative Record Number	Student-Number	Class-Number	Semester	Link
1	200	70	2000S	4
2	100	30	2001F	6
3	300	20	2001F	5
4	200	30	2000S	3
5	300	70	2000S	0
6	100	20	2000S	1

Start of list = 2

Figure D-4

ENROLLMENT Data in
Two Orders Using
Linked Lists

Relative Record Number	Student-Number	Class-Number	Semester	Student Link	Class Link
1	200	70	2000S	4	5
2	100	30	2001F	6	1
3	300	20	2001F	5	4
4	200	30	2000S	3	2
5	300	70	2000S	0	0
6	100	20	2000S	1	3

Start of student list = 2
Start of class list = 6

Figure D-5

ENROLLMENT Data after Inserting New Record (in Two Orders Using Linked Lists)

Relative Record Number	Student-Number	Class-Number	Semester	Student Link	Class Link
1	200	70	2000S	4	5
2	100	30	2001F	6	7
3	300	20	2001F	5	4
4	200	30	2000S	7	2
5	300	70	2000S	0	0
6	100	20	2000S	1	3
7	200	45	2000S	3	1

Start of student list = 2
Start of class list = 6

Figure D-6

ENROLLMENT Data after Deleting Student 200, Class 30 (in Two Orders Using Linked Lists)

Relative Record Number	Student-Number	Class-Number	Semester	Student Link	Class Link
1	200	70	2000S	7	5
2	100	30	2001F	6	7
3	300	20	2001F	5	2
4	200	30	2000S	7	2
5	300	70	2000S	0	0
6	100	20	2000S	1	3
7	200	45	2000S	3	1

Start of student list = 2
Start of class list = 6

the list. Now we can reach every item in the list starting at any item in the list. Figure D-7(a) shows a circular list for the StudentNumber order. A *two-way linked list* has links in both directions. In Figure D-7(b), a two-way linked list has been created for both ascending and descending student orders.

Figure D-7

ENROLLMENT Data Sorted by StudentNumber Using (a) a Circular and (b) a Two-way Linked List

Relative Record Number	Student-Number	Class-Number	Semester	Link
1	200	70	2000S	4
2	100	30	2001F	6
3	300	20	2001F	5
4	200	30	2000S	3
5	300	70	2000S	2
6	100	20	2000S	1

Start of list = 2

(a)

Relative Record Number	Student-Number	Class-Number	Semester	Ascending Link	Descending Link
1	200	70	2000S	4	6
2	100	30	2001F	6	0
3	300	20	2001F	5	4
4	200	30	2000S	3	1
5	300	70	2000S	0	3
6	100	20	2000S	1	2

Start of ascending list = 2
Start of descending list = 5

(b)

Records ordered using linked lists cannot be stored on a sequential file because some type of direct-access file organization is needed to use the link values. Thus, either indexed sequential or direct file organization is required for linked-list processing.

Maintaining Order with Indexes

A logical record order can also be maintained using *indexes*, or *inverted lists*, as they are sometimes called. An index is simply a table that cross-references record addresses with some field value. For example, Figure D-8(a) shows the ENROLLMENT records stored in no particular order, and Figure D-8(b) shows an index on StudentNumber. In this index, the StudentNumbers are arranged in sequence, with each entry in the list pointing to a corresponding record in the original data.

As you can see, the index is simply a sorted list of StudentNumbers. To process ENROLLMENT sequentially on StudentNumber, we simply process the index sequentially, obtaining ENROLLMENT data by reading the records indicated by the pointers. Figure D-8(c) shows another index for ENROLLMENT—one that maintains ClassNumber order.

To use an index, the data to be ordered (here, ENROLLMENT) must reside on an indexed sequential or direct file, although the indexes can reside on any type of file. In practice, almost all DBMS products keep both the data and the indexes on direct files.

If you compare the linked list with the index, you will notice the essential difference between them. In a linked list, the pointers are stored along with the data. Each record contains a link field containing a pointer to the address of the next related record. But in an index, the pointers are stored in indexes, separate from the data. Thus, the data records themselves contain no pointers. Both techniques are used by commercial DBMS products.

B-Trees

A special application of the concept of indexes, or inverted lists, is a *B-tree*, which is a multi-level index that allows both sequential and direct processing of data records. It also ensures a certain level of efficiency in processing because of the way that the indexes are structured.

A B-tree is an index that is made up of two parts: the sequence set and the index set. (These terms are used by IBM's VSAM file organization documentation. You may encounter other synonymous terms.) The *sequence set* is an index containing an entry for every record in the file. This index is in physical sequence, usually by primary key value. This arrangement allows sequential access to the data records, as follows: Process the sequence set in order, read the address of each record, and then read the record.

The *index set* is an index pointing to groups of entries in the sequence set index. This arrangement provides rapid direct access to records in the file, and it is the index set that makes B-trees unique.

An example of a B-tree appears in Figure D-9, and an occurrence of this structure can be seen in Figure D-10. Notice that the bottom row in Figure D-9, the sequence set, is

---

Figure D-8   **ENROLLMENT Data and Corresponding Indexes (a) ENROLLMENT Data; (b) Index on StudentNumber; and (c) Index on ClassNumber**

Relative Record Number	Student- Number	Class- Number	Semester
1	200	70	2000S
2	100	30	2001F
3	300	20	2001F
4	200	30	2000S
5	300	70	2000S
6	100	20	2000S

(a)

Student- Number	Relative Record Number
100	2
100	6
200	1
200	4
300	3
300	5

(b)

Class- Number	Relative Record Number
20	3
20	6
30	2
30	4
70	1
70	5

(c)

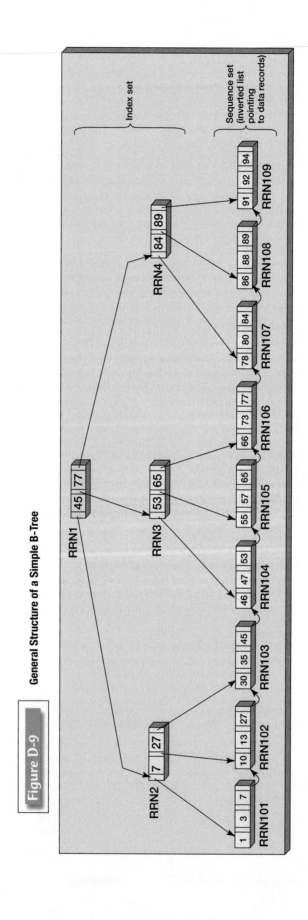

Figure D-9

General Structure of a Simple B-Tree

Figure D-10   Occurrence of the B-Tree in Figure D-9

RRN	Link1	Value1	Link2	Value2	Link3	
1	2	45	3	77	4	
2	101	7	102	27	103	Index Set
3	104	53	105	65	106	
4	107	84	108	89	109	

.
.
.

	R1	Addr1	R2	Addr2	R3	Addr3	Link	
101	1	Data or pointer	3	Data or pointer	7	Data or pointer	102	
102	10	⋯	13	⋯	27	⋯	103	
103	30	⋯	35	⋯	45	⋯	104	Sequence Set
104	46	⋯	47	⋯	53	⋯	105	(Addresses of
105	55	⋯	57	⋯	65	⋯	106	data records
106	66	⋯	73	⋯	77	⋯	107	are omitted)
107	78	⋯	80	⋯	84	⋯	108	
108	86	⋯	88	⋯	89	⋯	109	
109	91	⋯	92	⋯	94	⋯	0	

simply an index. It contains an entry for every record in the file (although for brevity, both the data records and their addresses have been omitted). Also, notice that the sequence set entries are in groups of three. The entries in each group are physically in sequence, and each group is chained to the next one by means of a linked list, as can be seen in Figure D-10.

Examine the index set in Figure D-9. The top entry contains two values: 45 and 77. By following the leftmost link (to RRN2), we can access all the records whose key field values are less than or equal to 45; by following the middle pointer (to RRN3), we can access all the records whose key field values are greater than 45 and less than or equal to 77; and by following the rightmost pointer (to RRN4), we can access all the records whose key field values are greater than 77.

Similarly, at the next level there are two values and three pointers in each index entry. Each time we drop to another level, we narrow our search for a particular record. For example, if we continue to follow the leftmost pointer from the top entry and then follow the rightmost pointer from there, we can access all the records whose key field value is greater than 27 and less than or equal to 45. We have eliminated all that were greater than 45 at the first level.

B-trees are, by definition, balanced. That is, all of the data records are exactly the same distance from the top entry in the index set. This aspect of B-trees ensures performance efficiency, although the algorithms for inserting and deleting records are more complex than those for ordinary trees (which can be unbalanced), because several index entries may need to be modified when records are added or deleted to keep all records the same distance from the top index entry.

Summary of Data Structures

Figure D-11 summarizes the techniques for maintaining ordered flat files. Three supporting data structures are possible. Sequential lists can be used, but the data must be duplicated in order to maintain several orders. Because sequential lists are not used in database processing, we will not consider them further. Both linked lists and indexes can be used without data duplication. B-trees are special applications of indexes.

As shown in Figure D-11, sequential lists can be stored using any of three file organizations. In practice, however, they are usually kept on sequential files. In addition,

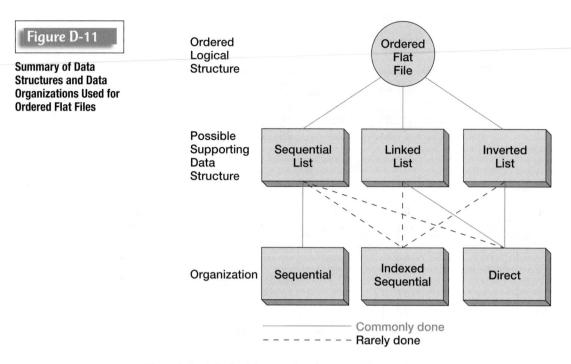

Figure D-11

Summary of Data Structures and Data Organizations Used for Ordered Flat Files

—————— Commonly done
– – – – – – Rarely done

although both linked lists and indexes can be stored using either indexed sequential or direct files, DBMS products almost always store them on direct files.

Representing Binary Relationships

In this section, we examine how each of the specialized record relationships—trees, simple networks, and complex networks—can be represented using linked lists and indexes.

Review of Record Relationships

Records can be related in three ways. A *tree* relationship has one or more one-to-many relationships, but each child record has at most one parent. The occurrence of faculty data shown in Figure D-12 illustrates a tree. There are several 1:N relationships, but any child record has only one parent, as shown in Figure D-13.

Figure D-12   Occurrence of a Faculty Member Record

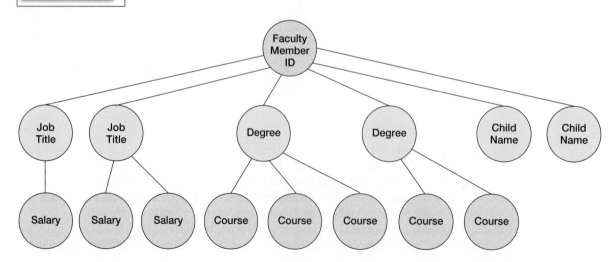

Schematic of a Faculty Member Tree Structure

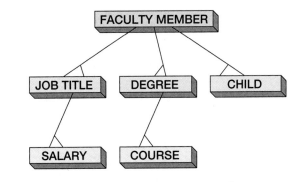

Occurrence of a Simple Network

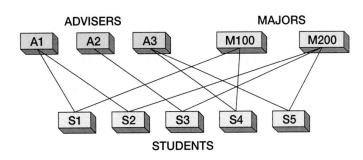

A *simple network* is a collection of records and the 1:N relationships among them. What distinguishes a simple network from a tree is the fact that in a simple network, a child can have more than one parent as long as the parents are different record types. The occurrence of a simple network of students, advisers, and major fields of study shown in Figure D-14 is represented schematically in Figure D-15.

A *complex network* is also a collection of records and relationships, but the relationships are many-to-many instead of one-to-many. The relationship between students and classes is a complex network. An occurrence of this relationship can be seen in Figure D-16, and the general schematic is in Figure D-17.

We saw earlier that we can use linked lists and indexes to process records in orders different from the one in which they are physically stored. We can also use those same data structures to store and process the relationships among records.

General Structure of a Simple Network

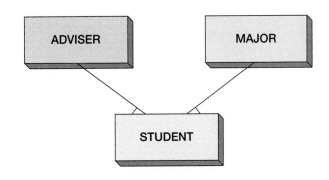

Occurrence of a Complex Network

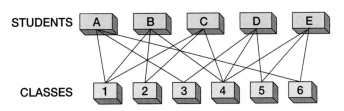

Figure D-17

**Schematic of
a Complex Network**

Representing Trees

We can use sequential lists, linked lists, and indexes to represent trees. When using sequential lists, we duplicate many data; and furthermore, sequential lists are not used by DBMS products to represent trees. Therefore, we describe only linked lists and indexes.

Linked-List Representation of Trees

Figure D-18 shows a tree structure in which the VENDOR records are parents and the INVOICE records are children. Figure D-19 shows two occurrences of this structure, and all of the VENDOR and INVOICE records have been written to a direct access file in Figure D-20. VENDOR AA is in relative record number 1 (RRN1), and VENDOR BB is in relative record number 2. The INVOICE records have been stored in subsequent records, as illustrated. Note that these records are not stored in any particular order and that they do not need to be.

Our problem is that we cannot tell which invoices belong to which vendors from this file. To solve this problem with a linked list, we add a pointer field to every record. In this field, we store the address of some other related record. For example, we place in VENDOR AA's link field the address of the first invoice belonging to it. This is RRN7, which is Invoice 110. Then, we make Invoice 110 point to the next invoice belonging to VENDOR AA, in this case RRN3. This slot holds Invoice 118. To indicate that there are no more children in the chain, we insert a 0 in the link field for RRN3.

This technique is shown in Figure D-21. If you examine the figure, you will see that a similar set of links has been used to represent the relationship between VENDOR BB and its invoices.

The structure in Figure D-21 is much easier to modify than is a sequential list of the records. For example, suppose that we add a new invoice, say number 111, to

Figure D-18

**Sample Tree Relating
VENDOR and INVOICE
Records**

Figure D-19   **Two Occurrences of VENDOR-INVOICE Tree**

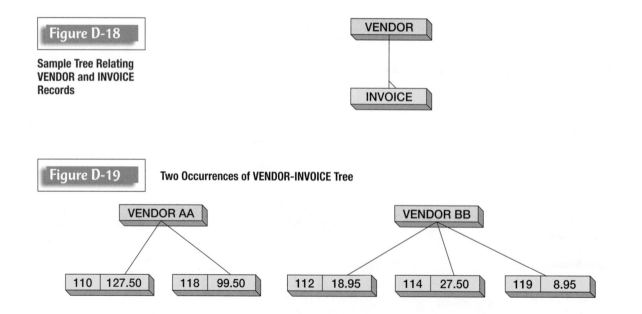

Figure D-20

File Representation
of the Trees in
Figure D-19

Record Number	Record Contents	
1	VENDOR AA	
2	VENDOR BB	
3	118	99.50
4	119	8.95
5	112	18.95
6	114	27.50
7	110	127.50

Figure D-21

Tree Occurrences
Represented by Linked
Lists

Relative Record Number	Record Contents		Link Field
1	VENDOR AA		7
2	VENDOR BB		5
3	118	99.50	0
4	119	8.95	0
5	112	18.95	6
6	114	27.50	4
7	110	127.50	3

VENDOR AA. To do this, we just add the record to the file and insert it into the linked list. Physically, the record can be placed anywhere. But where should it be placed logically? Usually, the application will have a requirement; for example, children are to be kept in ascending order on invoice number. If so, we need to make Invoice 110 point to Invoice 111 (at RRN8), and we need to make Invoice 111, the new invoice, point to Invoice 118 (at RRN3). This modification is shown in Figure D-22.

Similarly, deleting an invoice is easy. If Invoice 114 is deleted, we simply modify the pointer in the invoice that is now pointing to Invoice 114. In this case, it is Invoice 112 at RRN5. We give Invoice 112 the pointer that Invoice 114 had before deletion. In this way, Invoice 112 points to Invoice 119 (see Figure D-23). We have effectively cut one link out of the chain and welded together the ones it once connected.

Index Representation of Trees

A tree structure can readily be represented using indexes. The technique is to store each one-to-many relationship as an index. These lists are then used to match parents and children.

Using the VENDOR and INVOICE records in Figure D-19, we see that VENDOR AA (in RRN1) owns INVOICEs 110 (RRN7) and 118 (RRN3). Thus, RRN1 is the parent

Figure D-22

Inserting Invoice 111
into File in Figure D-21

Relative Record Number	Record Contents		Link Field	
1	VENDOR AA		7	
2	VENDOR BB		5	
3	118	99.50	0	
4	119	8.95	0	
5	112	18.95	6	
6	114	27.50	4	
7	110	127.50	8	
8	111	19.95	3	Inserted Record

Figure D-23

Deleting Invoice
114 from File in
Figure D-22

Relative Record Number	Record Contents		Link Field
1	VENDOR AA		7
2	VENDOR BB		5
3	118	99.50	0
4	119	8.95	0
5	112	18.95	4
6	114	27.50	4
7	110	127.50	8
8	111	19.95	3

← Deleted Record (pointing at row 6)

Figure D-24

Index Representation
of VENDOR-INVOICE
Relationship

Parent Record	Child Record
1	7
1	3
2	5
2	6
2	4

of RRN7 and RRN3. We can represent this fact with the index in Figure D-24. The list simply associates a parent's address with the addresses of each of its children.

If the tree has several 1:N relationships, several indexes will be required—one for each relationship. For the structure in Figure D-13, five indexes are needed.

Representing Simple Networks

As with trees, simple networks can also be represented using linked lists and indexes.

Linked-List Representation of Simple Networks

Consider the simple network shown in Figure D-25. It is a simple network because all of the relationships are 1:N, and the SHIPMENT records have two parents of different types. Each SHIPMENT has a CUSTOMER parent and a TRUCK parent. The relationship between CUSTOMER and SHIPMENT is 1:N because a customer can have several shipments, and the relationship from TRUCK to SHIPMENT is 1:N because one truck can hold many shipments (assuming that the shipments are small enough to fit in one truck or less). An occurrence of this network is shown in Figure D-26.

To represent this simple network with linked lists, we need to establish one set of pointers for each 1:N relationship. In this example, that means one set of pointers to connect CUSTOMERs with their SHIPMENTs and another set of pointers to connect TRUCKs with their SHIPMENTs. Thus, a CUSTOMER record will contain one pointer (to the first SHIPMENT it owns); a TRUCK record will contain one pointer (to the first SHIPMENT it owns); and a SHIPMENT record will have two pointers, one for the next SHIPMENT owned by the same CUSTOMER and one for the next SHIPMENT owned by the same TRUCK. This scheme is illustrated in Figure D-27.

Figure D-25

Simple Network
Structure

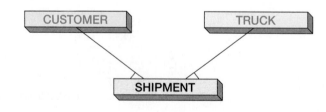

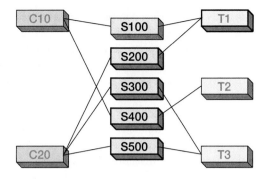

Figure D-26

Occurrence of the
Simple Network in
Figure D-25

Figure D-27

Representation of
a Simple Network
with Linked Lists

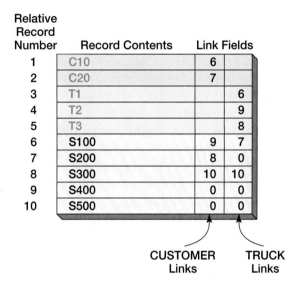

A simple network has at least two 1:N relationships, each of which can be represented using an index, as we explained in our discussion of trees. For example, consider the simple network shown in Figure D-25. It has two 1:N relationships, one between TRUCK and SHIPMENT and one between CUSTOMER and SHIPMENT. We can store each of these relationships in an index. Figure D-28 shows the two indexes needed to represent the example in Figure D-26. Assume that the records are located in the same positions as shown in Figure D-27.

Representing Complex Networks

Complex networks can be represented in a variety of ways. They can be decomposed into trees or simple networks, and these simpler structures can then be represented using one of the techniques just described. Alternatively, they can be represented directly using indexes. Linked lists are not used by any DBMS product to represent complex networks

Figure D-28

Representation of
Simple Network
with Index

Customer Record	Shipment Record
1	6
1	9
2	7
2	8
2	10

Truck Record	Shipment Record
3	6
3	7
4	9
5	8
5	10

directly. In practice, complex networks are nearly always decomposed into simpler structures, so we consider only those representations using decomposition.

A common approach to representing complex networks is to reduce them to simple networks and then to represent the simple networks with linked lists or indexes. Note, however, that a complex network involves a relationship between two records, whereas a simple network involves relationships among three records. Thus, in order to decompose a complex network into a simple one, we need to create a third record type.

The record that is created when a complex network is decomposed into a simple one is called an *intersection record.* Consider the StudentClass complex network. An intersection record contains a unique key from a STUDENT record and a unique key from a corresponding CLASS record. It will contain no other application data, although it might contain link fields. The general structure of this relationship is shown in Figure D-29. Assuming that the record names are unique (such as S1, S2, and C1), an instance of the STUDENT-CLASS relationship is illustrated in Figure D-30.

Notice that the relationship between STUDENT and the intersection record and that between CLASS and the intersection record both are 1:N. Thus, we have created a simple network that can now be represented with the linked-list or index techniques shown earlier. A file of this occurrence using the linked-list technique is shown in Figure D-31.

Summary of Relationship Representations

Figure D-32 summarizes the representations of record relationships. Trees can be represented using sequential lists (although we did not discuss this approach), linked lists, or

Figure D-29

Decomposition of Complex Network into Simple Network

Figure D-30

Instance of STUDENT-CLASS Relationship Showing Intersection Records

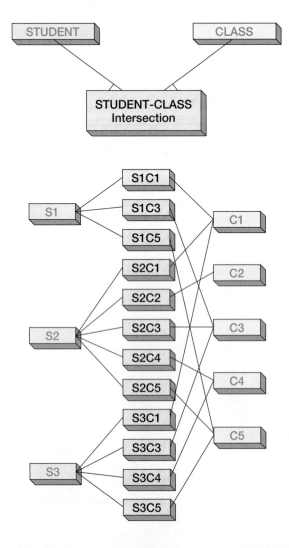

Figure D-31

Occurrence of Network in Figure D-30

Relative Record Number	Record Contents	Link Fields	
1	S1	9	
2	S2	12	
3	S3	17	
4	C1		9
5	C2		13
6	C3		10
7	C4		15
8	C5		11
9	S1C1	10	12
10	S1C3	11	14
11	S1C5	0	16
12	S2C1	13	17
13	S2C2	14	0
14	S2C3	15	18
15	S2C4	16	19
16	S2C5	0	20
17	S3C1	18	0
18	S3C3	19	0
19	S3C4	20	0
20	S3C5	0	0

STUDENT
Links

CLASS
Links

Figure D-32

Record Relationships, Data Structures, and File Organizations

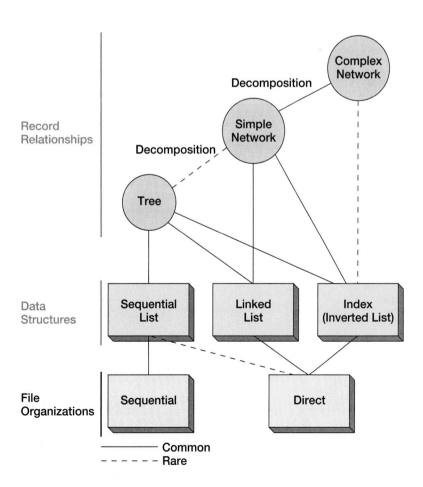

indexes. Sequential lists are not used in DBMS products. A simple network can be decomposed into trees and then represented or it can be represented directly using either linked lists or indexes. Finally, a complex network can be decomposed into a tree or a simple network (using intersection records) or it can be represented directly using indexes.

Secondary-Key Representations

In many cases, the word *key* indicates a field (or fields) whose value uniquely identifies a record. This is usually called the *primary key.* Sometimes, however, applications need to access and process records by means of a *secondary key*, one that is different from the primary key. Secondary keys may be unique (such as a professor's name) or nonunique (such as a customer's Zip code). In this section, we use the term *set* to refer to all records having the same value of a nonunique secondary key; for example, a set of records having Zip code 98040.

Both linked lists and indexes are used to represent secondary keys, but linked lists are practical only for nonunique keys. Indexes, however, can be used for both unique and nonunique key representations.

Linked-List Representation of Secondary Keys

Consider the example of CUSTOMER records shown in Figure D-33. The primary key is AccountNumber, and there is a secondary key on CreditLimit. Possible CreditLimit values are 500, 700, and 1000. Thus, there will be a set of records for the limit of 500, a set for 700, and a set for 1000.

To represent this key using linked lists, we add a link field to the CUSTOMER records. Inside this link field, we create a linked list for each set of records. Figure D-34 shows a database of 11 customers; but, for brevity, only AccountNumber and CreditLimit are shown. A link field has been attached to the records. Assume that one database record occupies one physical record on a direct file using relative record addressing.

Figure D-33

CUSTOMER Record

Account-Number	Name	Address	Credit-Limit	Account-Balance

Primary Key → (AccountNumber)

Secondary Key → (CreditLimit)

Figure D-34

Representing CreditLimit Secondary Key Using Linked list

Relative Record Number	Link	Account-Number	Credit-Limit	Other Data
1	2	101	500	
2	7	301	500	
3	5	203	700	
4	6	004	1000	
5	10	204	700	
6	8	905	1000	
7	0	705	500	
8	9	207	1000	
9	11	309	1000	
10	0	409	700	
11	0	210	1000	

HEAD-500 = 1
HEAD-700 = 3
HEAD-1000 = 4

Three pointers need to be established so that we know where to begin each linked list. These pointers, called *heads*, are stored separately from the data. The head of the $500 linked list is RRN1. Record 1 links to record 2, which in turn links to record 7. Record 7 has a zero in the link position, indicating that it is the end of the list. Consequently, the $500 credit limit set consists of records 1, 2, and 7. Similarly, the $700 set contains records 3, 5, and 10; and the $1000 set contains relative records 4, 6, 8, 9, and 11.

The 1000-set linked list can be used to answer a query such as "How many accounts in the 1000 set have a balance in excess of 900?" In this way, only those records in the 1000 set need to be read from the file and examined. Although the advantage of this approach is not readily apparent in this small example, suppose that there are 100,000 CUSTOMER records, and only 100 of them are in the 1000 set. If there is no linked list, all 100,000 records must be examined; but with the linked list, only 100 records need to be examined—namely, the ones in the 1000 set. Using the linked list, therefore, saves 99,900 reads.

Using linked lists is not an effective technique for every secondary-key application. In particular, if the records are processed nonsequentially in a set, linked lists are inefficient. For example, if it is often necessary to find the 10th or 120th or *n*th record in the 500 CreditLimit set, processing will be slow. Linked lists are inefficient for direct access.

In addition, if the application requires that secondary keys be created or destroyed dynamically, the linked-list approach is undesirable. Whenever a new key is created, a link field must be added to every record, which often requires reorganizing the database, which is a time-consuming and expensive process.

Finally, if the secondary keys are unique, each list will have a length of one, and a separate linked list will exist for every record in the database. Because this situation is unworkable, linked lists cannot be used for unique keys. For example, suppose that the CUSTOMER records contain another unique field, say, Social Security Number. If we attempt to represent this unique secondary key using a linked list, every Social Security Number will be a separate linked list. Furthermore, each linked list will have just one item in it: the single record having the indicated Social Security Number.

Index Representation of Secondary Keys

A second technique for representing secondary keys uses an index; one is established for each secondary key. The approach varies, depending on whether the key values are unique or nonunique.

Unique Secondary Keys

Suppose that the CUSTOMER records in Figure D-33 contain Social Security Numbers (SSN) as well as the fields shown. To provide key access to the CUSTOMER records using SSN, we simply build an index on the SSN field. Sample CUSTOMER data are shown in Figure D-35(a), and a corresponding index is illustrated in Figure D-35(b). This index uses relative record numbers as addresses. It is possible to use AccountNumbers instead, in which case the DBMS locates the desired SSN in the index, obtains the matching AccountNumber, and then converts the AccountNumber to a relative record address.

Figure D-35

Representing a Unique Secondary Key with Indexes (a) Sample CUSTOMER Data (with SSN) and (b) Index for SSN Secondary Key

Relative Record Number	Account-Number	Credit-Limit	Social Security Number (SSN)
1	101	500	000-01-0001
2	301	500	000-01-0005
3	203	700	000-01-0009
4	004	1000	000-01-0003

(a)

SSN	Relative Record Number
000-01-0001	1
000-01-0003	4
000-01-0005	2
000-01-0009	3

(b)

Figure D-36

Index for CreditLimit
Key in Figure D-33

CreditLimit	AccountNumber				
500	101	301	705		
700	203	204	409		
1000	004	905	207	309	210

Nonunique Secondary Keys

Indexes can also be used to represent nonunique secondary keys, but because each set of related records can contain an unknown number of members, the entries in the index are of variable length. For example, Figure D-36 shows the index for the CreditLimit sets for the CUSTOMER data. The $500 set and the $700 set both have three members, so there are three account numbers in each entry. The $1000 set has five members, so there are five account numbers in that entry.

In reality, representing and processing nonunique secondary keys are complex tasks. Several different schemes are used by commercial DBMS products. One common method uses a values table and an occurrence table. Each values table entry consists of two fields, the first of which has a key value. For the CUSTOMER CreditLimit key, the values are 500, 700, and 1000. The second field of the values table entry is a pointer into the occurrence table. The occurrence table contains record addresses, and those having a common value in the secondary-key field appear together in the table. Figure D-37 shows the values and occurrence tables for the CreditLimit key.

To locate records having a given value of the secondary key, the values table is searched for the desired value. After the given key value is located in the values table, the pointer is followed to the occurrence table to obtain the addresses of those records having that key value. These addresses are then used to obtain the desired records.

When a new record is inserted into the file, the DBMS must modify the indexes for each secondary-key field. For nonunique keys, it must make sure that the new record key value is in the values table; if it is, it adds the new record address to the appropriate entry in the occurrence table. If it is not, it must insert new entries in the values and occurrence tables. When a record is deleted, its address must be removed from the occurrence table. If no addresses remain in the occurrence table entry, the corresponding values table entry must also be deleted.

When the secondary-key field of a record is modified, the record address must be removed from one occurrence table entry and inserted into another. If the modification is a new value for the key, an entry must be added to the values table.

The index approach to representing secondary keys overcomes the objections to the linked-list approach. Direct processing of sets is possible. For example, the third record in a set can be retrieved without processing the first or second one. Also, it is possible to dynamically create and delete secondary keys. No changes are made in the records themselves; the DBMS merely creates additional values and occurrence tables. Finally, unique keys can be processed efficiently.

Figure D-37

Values and Occurrence
Tables for CreditLimit
Key in Figure D-33

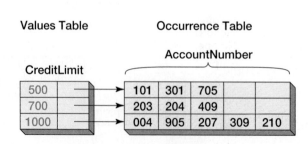

Values Table   Occurrence Table

CreditLimit		AccountNumber				
500	→	101	301	705		
700	→	203	204	409		
1000	→	004	905	207	309	210

The disadvantages of the index approach are that it requires more file space (the tables use more overhead than the pointers do) and that the DBMS programming task is more complex. Note that the *application programming* task is not necessarily any more or less difficult—but it is more complex to write DBMS software that processes indexes than it is to write software that processes linked lists. Finally, modifications are usually processed more slowly because of the reading and writing actions required to access and maintain the values in the occurrence tables.

SUMMARY

In this appendix, we surveyed data structures used for database processing. A flat file is a file that contains no repeating groups. Flat files can be ordered using sequential lists (physically placing the records in the sequence in which they will be processed), linked lists (attaching to each data record a pointer to another logically related record), and indexes (building a table, separate from the data records that contains pointers to related records). B-trees are special applications of indexes.

Sequential lists, linked lists, and indexes (or inverted lists) are fundamental data structures. (Sequential lists, however, are seldom used in database processing.) These data structures can be used to represent record relationships as well as secondary keys.

The three basic record structures—trees, simple networks, and complex networks—can be represented using linked lists and indexes. Simple networks can be decomposed into trees and then represented; complex networks can be decomposed into simple networks containing an intersection record and then represented.

Secondary keys are used to access the data on some field besides the primary key. Secondary keys can be unique or nonunique. Nonunique secondary keys can be represented with both linked lists and indexes. Unique secondary keys can be represented only with indexes.

REVIEW QUESTIONS

D.1   Define a flat file. Give an example (other than one in this text) of a flat file and an example of a file that is not flat.

D.2   Show how sequential lists can be used to maintain the file in question D.1 in two different orders simultaneously.

D.3   Show how linked lists can be used to maintain the file in question D.1 in two different orders simultaneously.

D.4   Show how inverted lists can be used to maintain the file in question D.1 in two different orders simultaneously.

D.5   Define a tree. Offer an example tree structure.

D.6   Give an occurrence of the tree in question D.5.

D.7   Represent the occurrence in question D.6 using linked lists.

D.8   Represent the occurrence in question D.6 using indexes.

D.9   Define a simple network and give an example structure.

D.10   Give an occurrence of the simple network in question D.9.

D.11   Represent the occurrence in question D.10 using linked lists.

D.12   Represent the occurrence in question D.10 using indexes.

D.13   Define complex network. Offer an example of a complex network structure.

D.14   Give an occurrence of the complex network in question D.13.

D.15   Decompose the complex network in question D.14 into a simple network and represent an occurrence of it using indexes.

D.16 Explain the difference between primary and secondary keys.

D.17 Explain the difference between unique and nonunique keys.

D.18 Define a file containing a unique secondary key. Represent an occurrence of that file using an index on the secondary key.

D.19 Define a nonunique secondary key for the file in question D.18. Represent an occurrence of that file using a linked list on the secondary key.

D.20 Perform the same task as in question D.19, but use an index to represent the secondary key.

D.21 Develop an algorithm to produce a report listing the IDs of students enrolled in each class using the linked-list structure in Figure D-4.

D.22 Develop an algorithm to insert records into the structure in Figure D-4. The resulting structure should resemble the one shown in Figure D-5.

D.23 Develop an algorithm to produce a report listing the IDs of students enrolled in each class using the index structure shown in Figures D-8(a), D-8(b), and D-8(c).

D.24 Develop an algorithm to insert a record into the structure shown in Figure D-8(a). Be sure to modify both of the associated indexes shown in Figure D-8(b) and D-8(c).

D.25 Develop an algorithm to delete a record from the structure shown in Figure D-34, which shows a secondary key represented with a linked list. If all records for one of the credit-limit categories (say, $1000) are deleted, should the associated head pointer also be deleted? Why or why not?

D.26 Develop an algorithm to insert a record into the structure shown in Figure D-34. Suppose that the new record has a credit-limit value different from those already established. Should the record be inserted and a new linked list established? Or should the record be rejected? Who should make that decision?

E

The Semantic Object Model

This appendix discusses the semantic object model, which is used to create data models like the E-R model discussed in Chapters 5 and 6. As shown in Figure E-1, the development team interviews users; analyzes the users' reports, forms, and queries; and constructs a model of the users' data from these reports. This data model is later transformed into a database design.

The particular form of the data model depends on the constructs used to build it. If an E-R model is used, the model will have entities, relationships, and the like. If a semantic model is used, the model will have semantic objects and related constructs, which are discussed here.

The E-R model and the semantic object model are like lenses through which the database developers look when studying and documenting the users' data. Both lenses work, and they both ultimately result in a database design. They use different lenses to form that design, however; and because the lenses create different images, the designs

Figure E-1   **Using Different Data Models for Database Designs**

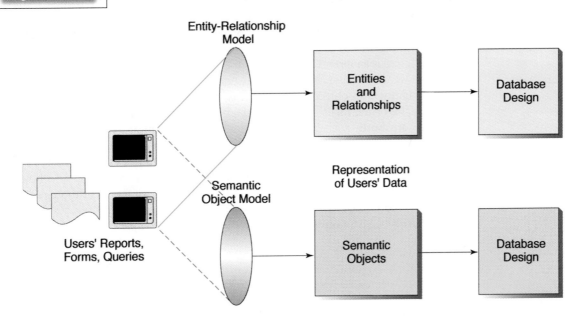

they produce may not be exactly the same. When developing a database, you must decide which approach to use, just as a photographer needs to decide which lens to use. Each approach has strengths and weaknesses, which we discuss at the end of this appendix.

The semantic object model was first presented in 1988, in the third edition of this text. It is based on concepts that were developed and published by Codd and by Hammer and McLeod.[1] The semantic object model is a data model. It differs from **object-oriented database processing,** which was discussed in Chapter 1. Whereas object-oriented databases concern the storage of OOP objects, the semantic object model is a data model and is an alternative to the E-R model.

 # Semantic Objects

The purpose of a database application is to provide forms, reports, and queries so that the users can track entities or objects important to their work. The goals of the early stages of database development are to determine the things to be represented in the database, to specify the characteristics of those things, and to establish the relationships among them.

In Chapters 2 and 3, we referred to these things as *entities*. In this appendix, we refer to them as **semantic objects,** or sometimes as just **objects.** The word *semantic* means "meaning," and a semantic object is one that models, in part, the "meaning" of the users' data. Semantic objects model the users' perceptions more closely than does the E-R model. We use the adjective *semantic* with the word *object* to distinguish the objects discussed in this appendix from the objects defined in object-oriented programming (OOP) languages.

Defining Semantic Objects

Entities and objects are similar in some ways, but they differ in others. We begin with the similarities. A semantic object is a representation of some identifiable thing in the users' work environment. More formally, a semantic object is a *named collection of attributes that sufficiently describes a distinct identity.*

Like entities, semantic objects are grouped into classes. An object class has a *name* that distinguishes it from other classes and that corresponds to the names of the things it represents. Thus, a database that supports users who work with student records has an object class called STUDENT. Note that object class names, like entity class names, are spelled with capital letters. A particular semantic object is an instance of the class. Thus, 'William Jones' is an instance of the STUDENT class, and 'Accounting' is an instance of the DEPARTMENT class.

Like entities, an object has a *collection of attributes*. Each attribute represents a characteristic of the identity being represented. For instance, the STUDENT object can have attributes such as Name, HomeAddress, CampusAddress, DateOfBirth, DateOfGraduation, and Major. This collection of attributes also is a *sufficient description,* which means that the attributes represent all of the characteristics that the users need in order to do their work. As we stated in Chapter 3, things in the world have an infinite set of characteristics; we cannot represent all of them. Instead, we represent those necessary for the users to satisfy their information needs so that they can successfully perform their jobs. Sufficient description also means that the objects are complete in and of themselves.

[1]E. F. Codd, "Extending the Relational Model to Capture More Meaning," *ACM Transactions on Database Systems,* December 1976, pp. 397–424; and Michael Hammer and Dennis McLeod, "Database Description with SDM: A Semantic Database Model," *ACM Transactions on Database Systems,* September 1981, pp. 351–386.

All of the data required about a CUSTOMER, for example, is located in the CUSTOMER object, so we need not look anywhere else to find data about CUSTOMERs.

Objects represent *distinct identities;* that is, they are something that users recognize as independent and separate and that they want to track and report. These identities are the nouns about which the information is to be produced. To understand the term *distinct identity,* recall that there is a difference between objects and object instances. CUSTOMER is the name of an object, and 'CUSTOMER 12345' is the name of an instance of an object. When we say that an object represents a distinct identity, we mean that users consider each *instance* of an object to be unique and identifiable in its own right.

Finally, note that the identities that the objects represent may or may not have a physical existence. For example, EMPLOYEEs physically exist, but ORDERs do not. Orders are models of a contractual agreement to provide certain goods or services under certain terms and conditions. They are not physical things, but rather representations of agreements. Thus, something need not be physical to be considered an object; it need only be identifiable in its own right in the minds of the users.

Attributes

Semantic objects have attributes that define their characteristics. There are three types of attributes. **Simple attributes** have a single element. Examples are DateOfHire, InvoiceNumber, and SalesTotal. **Group attributes** are composites of other attributes. One example is Address, which contains the attributes {Street, City, State, Zip}; another example is FullName, which contains the attributes {FirstName, MiddleInitial, LastName}. **Semantic object attributes** are attributes that establish a relationship between one semantic object and another.

To understand these statements better, look at Figure E-2(a), which is an example of a **semantic object diagram,** or **object diagram.** Such diagrams are used by development teams to summarize the structures of objects and to present them visually. Objects are shown in portrait-oriented rectangles. The name of the object appears at the top, and attributes are written in order after the object name.

The DEPARTMENT object contains an example of each of the three types of attributes. DepartmentName, PhoneNumber, and FaxPhoneNumber are simple attributes, each of which represents a single data element. CampusAddress is a group attribute containing the simple attributes Building and OfficeNumber. Finally, COLLEGE, PROFESSOR, and STUDENT each are semantic object attributes, which means that those objects are connected to and logically contained in DEPARTMENT.

Figure E-2

DEPARTMENT
Object Diagram
(a) DEPARTMENT
Object and
(b) DEPARTMENT
Object with
Cardinalities

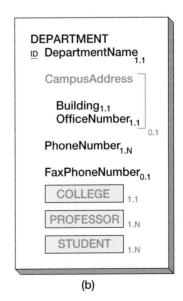

(a)   (b)

The object attributes, or **object links** as they are sometimes called, mean that when a user thinks about a DEPARTMENT, he or she thinks not only about DepartmentName, CampusAddress, PhoneNumber, and FaxPhoneNumber, but also about the COLLEGE, PROFESSORs, and STUDENTs that are related to that department. Because COLLEGE, PROFESSOR, and STUDENT also are objects, the complete data model contains object diagrams for them, too. The COLLEGE object contains attributes of the college; the PROFESSOR object contains attributes of the faculty; and the STUDENT object contains attributes of the students.

Attribute Cardinality

Each attribute in a semantic object has both a minimum cardinality and a maximum cardinality. The minimum cardinality indicates the number of instances of the attribute that must exist for the object to be valid. Usually, this number is either zero or one. If it is zero, the attribute is not required to have a value; if it is one, it must have a value. Although it is unusual, the minimum cardinality can sometimes be larger than one. For example, the attribute PLAYER in an object called BASKETBALL-TEAM might have a minimum cardinality of five because this is the smallest number of players required to make up a basketball team.

The maximum cardinality indicates the maximum number of instances of the attribute that the object may have. It is usually either one or N. If it is one, the attribute can have no more than one instance; if it is N, the attribute can have many values, and the absolute number is not specified. Sometimes, the maximum cardinality is a specific number, such as five, meaning that the object can contain no more than exactly five instances of the attribute. For example, the attribute PLAYER in BASKETBALL-TEAM might have a maximum cardinality of 15, which would indicate that no more than 15 players could be assigned to a team's roster.

Cardinalities are shown as subscripts of attributes in the format $n.m$, where n is the minimum cardinality and m is the maximum. In Figure E-2(b), the minimum cardinality of DepartmentName is one and the maximum is also one, which means that exactly one value of DepartmentName is required. The cardinality of PhoneNumber is 1.N, meaning that a DEPARTMENT is required to have at least one PhoneNumber, but may have many. The cardinality of 0.1 in FaxPhoneNumber means that a DEPARTMENT may have either zero or one FaxPhoneNumber.

The cardinalities of groups and the attributes in groups can be subtle. Consider the attribute CampusAddress. Its cardinalities are 0.1, meaning that a DEPARTMENT need not have an address and has at most one. Now, examine the attributes inside CampusAddress. Both Building and OfficeNumber have the cardinalities 1.1. You might be wondering how a group can be optional if the attributes in that group are required. The answer is that the cardinalities operate only between the attribute and the container of that attribute. The minimum cardinality of CampusAddress indicates that there need not be a value for address in DEPARTMENT, but the minimum cardinalities of Building and OfficeNumber indicate that both Building and OfficeNumber must exist in CampusAddress. Thus, a CampusAddress group need not appear; but if one does, it must have a value for both Building and OfficeNumber.

Object Instances

The object diagrams for DEPARTMENT shown in Figure E-2 are a format, or general structure, that can be used for any department. An instance of the DEPARTMENT object is shown in Figure E-3, with each attribute's value for a particular department. The DepartmentName is Information Systems, and it is located in Room 213 of the Social Science Building. Observe that there are three values for PhoneNumber—the Information Systems Department has three phone lines in its office. Other departments may have fewer or more, but every department has at least one.

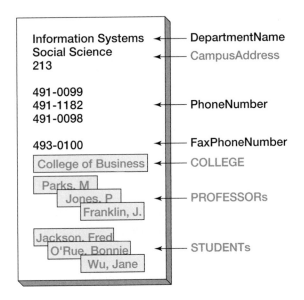

Figure E-3

An Instance of the
DEPARTMENT Object
in Figure E-2

Furthermore, there is one instance of COLLEGE—the College of Business, and there are multiple values for the PROFESSOR and STUDENT object attributes. Each of these object attributes is a complete object; each has all the attributes defined for an object of that type. To keep this diagram simple, only the identifying names are shown for each of the instances of object attribute.

An object diagram is a picture of the user's perception of an object in the work environment. Thus, in the user's mind, the DEPARTMENT object includes all of these data. A DEPARTMENT logically contains data about the COLLEGE in which it resides as well as the PROFESSORs and STUDENTs who are related to that department.

Paired Attributes

The semantic object model has no one-way object relationships. If an object contains another object, the second object will contain the first. For example, if DEPARTMENT contains the object attribute COLLEGE, then COLLEGE will contain the matching object attribute DEPARTMENT. These object attributes are called **paired attributes** because they always occur as a pair.

Why must object attributes be paired? The answer lies in the way in which human beings think about relationships. If object A has a relationship with object B, then object B will have a relationship with object A. At the very least, B is related to A in the relationship of "things that are related to B." If this argument seems obscure, try to envision a one-way relationship between two objects. It cannot be done.

Object Identifiers

An **object identifier** is one or more object attributes that the users employ to identify object instances. Such identifiers are potential names for a semantic object. In CUSTOMER, for example, possible identifiers are CustomerID and CustomerName. These are attributes that users consider to be valid names of CUSTOMER instances. Compare these identifiers with attributes such as DateOfFirstOrder, StockPrice, and NumberOfEmployees. Such attributes are not identifiers because the users do not think of them as names of CUSTOMER instances.

A **group identifier** is an identifier that has more than one attribute. Examples are {FirstName, LastName}, {FirstName, PhoneNumber}, and {State, License Number}.

Object identifiers may or may not be unique, depending on how the users view their data. For example, InvoiceNumber is a unique identifier for ORDER, but StudentName is not a unique identifier for STUDENT. For example, two students may be named

"Mary Smith." If so, the users will employ StudentName to identify a group of one or more students and then, if necessary, use values of other attributes to identify a particular member of that set.

In semantic object diagrams, object identifiers are denoted by the letters *ID* in front of the attribute. If the identifier is unique, these letters will be underlined. In Figure E-2(b), for example, the attribute DepartmentName is a unique identifier of DEPARTMENT.

Normally, if an attribute is to be used as an identifier, its value is required. Also, generally there is no more than one value of an identifier attribute for a given object. In most cases, therefore, the cardinality of an ID attribute is 1.1, so we use this value as a default.

However, in a few, rare cases the cardinality of an identifier may be other than 1.1. Consider, for example, the attribute Alias in the semantic object PERSON. A person need not have an alias, or he or she may have several aliases. Hence, the cardinality of Alias is 0.N.

Showing the subscripts of all attributes clutters the semantic object diagram. To simplify, we will assume that the cardinalities of simple-value identifier attributes are 1.1 and that the cardinalities of other simple-value attributes are 0.1. If the cardinality of the simple-value attribute is other than these assumptions, we will show it on the diagram. Otherwise, subscripts on simple-value attributes will be omitted.

Attribute Domains

The **domain** of an attribute is a description of an attribute's possible values. The characteristics of a domain depend on the type of the attribute. The domain of a simple attribute consists of both a physical and a semantic description. The physical description indicates the type of data (for example, numeric versus string), the length of the data, and other restrictions or constraints (for example, the first character must be alphabetic or the value must not exceed 9999.99). The semantic description indicates the function or purpose of the attribute—it distinguishes this attribute from other attributes that might have the same physical description.

For example, the domain of DepartmentName can be defined as "the set of strings of up to seven characters that represent names of departments at Highline University." The phrase *strings of up to seven characters* is the physical description of the domain, and the phrase *that represent names of departments at Highline University* is the semantic description. The semantic description differentiates strings of seven characters that represent names of departments from similar strings that represent names of courses, buildings, or some other attribute.

In some cases, the physical description of a simple attribute domain is an **enumerated list,** the set of an attribute's specific values. The domain of the attribute PartColor, for example, might be the enumerated list {'Blue', 'Yellow', 'Red'}.

The domain of a group attribute also has a physical and a semantic description. The physical description is a list of all of the attributes in the group and the order of those attributes. The semantic description is the function or purpose of the group. Thus, the physical domain description of CampusAddress (shown in Figure E-2) is the list {Building, OfficeNumber}; the semantic description is *the location of an office at Highline University.*

The domain of an object attribute is the set of object instances of that type. In Figure E-2, for example, the domain of the PROFESSOR object attribute is the set of all PROFESSOR object instances in the database. The domain of the COLLEGE object is the set of all COLLEGEs in the database. In a sense, the domain of an object attribute is a dynamically enumerated list; the list contains all of the object instances of a particular type.

Semantic Object Views

Users access the values of object attributes through database applications that provide data entry forms, reports, and queries. In most cases, such forms, reports, and queries do not require access to all of an object's attributes. For example, Figure E-4 shows two application

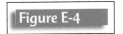

StudentListing and Staff Views of the DEPARTMENT Semantic Object

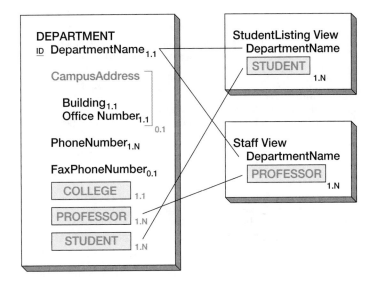

views of DEPARTMENT. Some attributes of DEPARTMENT (its DepartmentName, for example) are visible in both application views. Other attributes are visible in only one. For example, STUDENT is seen only in the StudentListing View, but PROFESSOR is visible only in the Staff View.

The portion of an object that is visible to a particular application is called the **semantic object view,** or simply the **view.** A view consists of the name of the object plus a list of all of the attributes visible from that view.

Views are used in two ways. First, when developing the data model, the database and application developers can use views to work backward. That is, they begin with the forms, reports, and queries that the users say they need and then work backward to the database design. To do this, the team selects a required form, report, or query and determines the view that must exist in order for the form, report, or query to be created. Then, the team selects the next form, report, or query and does the same. These two views are then integrated. This process is repeated until the structure of the entire database has been created.

The second way in which views are used occurs after the database structure has been created. At this point, views are constructed to support new forms, reports, and queries based on the existing database structure. Examples of this second use were shown for Oracle and SQL Server in Chapters 10 and 11, respectively.

 Types of Objects

This section describes and illustrates seven types of objects. For each type, we examine a report or form and show how to model that report or form with an object. Then, we transform each of these types of objects into database designs.

Three new terms are used in this section: A **single-value attribute** is an attribute whose maximum cardinality is one; a **multivalue attribute** is one whose maximum cardinality is greater than one; and a **nonobject attribute** is a simple or group attribute.

Simple Objects

A **simple object** is a semantic object that contains only single-value, simple, or group attributes. An example is shown in Figure E-5. Figure E-5(a) shows two instances of a report called an *Equipment Tag.* Such tags are applied to items of office equipment to help keep track of inventory. These tags can be considered a report.

Figure E-5

Example of a Simple Object
(a) Reports Based on a Simple Object; (b) EQUIPMENT Simple Object;
and (c) Relation Representing EQUIPMENT

EQUIPMENT TAG:
    EquipmentNumber: 100   Description: Desk
    AcquisitionDate: 2/27/2000 PurchaseCost: $350.00

EQUIPMENT TAG:
    EquipmentNumber: 200   Description: Lamp
    AcquisitionDate: 3/1/2000   PurchaseCost: $39.95

(a)

EQUIPMENT
 ID   EquipmentNumber
      Description
      AcquisitionDate
      PurchaseCost

(b)

EQUIPMENT (EquipmentNumber, Description, AcquisitionDate, PurchaseCost)

(c)

Figure E-5(b) shows a simple object, EQUIPMENT, that models Equipment Tag. The attributes of the object include the items shown on the tag: EquipmentNumber, Description, AcquisitionDate, and PurchaseCost. Note that none of these attributes are multivalue, and none are object attributes. Hence, EQUIPMENT is a simple object.

Figure E-5(b) is an example of a simple object, EQUIPMENT, which can be represented by a single relation, as shown in Figure E-5(c). Each attribute of the object is defined as an attribute of the relation. The identifying attribute, EquipmentNumber, becomes the key attribute of the relation, denoted by underlining EquipmentNumber in Figure E-5(c).

The general transformation of simple objects is illustrated in Figure E-6. Object OBJECT1 is transformed into relation R1. The attribute that identifies OBJECT1 instances is O1; it becomes the key of relation R1. Nonkey data are represented in this and subsequent figures with ellipses (. . .).

Because a key is an attribute that uniquely identifies a row of a table, only unique identifiers—those with the ID underlined—can be transformed into keys. If there is no unique identifier in the object, one must be created by combining the existing attributes to form a unique identifier or by defining a surrogate key.

Composite Objects

A **composite object** is a semantic object that contains one or more multivalue simple or group attributes but no object attributes. The hotel bill shown in Figure E-7(a) gives rise to the need for a composite object. The bill includes data that concern the bill as a whole: InvoiceNumber, ArrivalDate, CustomerName, and TotalDue. It also contains a group of attributes that is repeated for services provided to the guest. Each group includes ServiceDate, ServiceDescription, and Price.

Figure E-6

General Transformation of Simple Object into a Relation

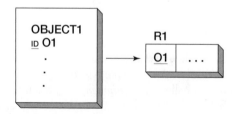

Example of a Composite Object

(a) Report Based on a Composite Object; (b) HOTEL-BILL Composite Object; and (c) Relational Representation

GRANDVIEW HOTEL
Sea Bluffs, California

Invoice Number: 1234   Arrival Date: 10/12/2001
Customer Name: Mary Jones

10/12/2001	Room	$ 99.00
10/12/2001	Food	$ 37.55
10/12/2001	Phone	$ 2.50
10/12/2001	Tax	$ 15.00
10/13/2001	Room	$ 99.00
10/13/2001	Food	$ 47.90
10/13/2001	Tax	$ 15.00
	Total Due	$ 315.95

(a)

HOTEL-BILL
ID InvoiceNumber
   ArrivalDate $_{1.1}$
ID CustomerName

   LineItem
      ServiceDate $_{1.1}$
      ServiceDescription $_{1.1}$
      Price $_{1.1}$
                                    0.N
   TotalDue $_{1.1}$

(b)

HOTEL-BILL (InvoiceNumber, ArrivalDate, CustomerName, TotalDue)

LINEITEM (*InvoiceNumber*, ServiceDate, ServiceDescription, Price)

Referential integrity constraint:

InvoiceNumber in LINEITEM must exist
in InvoiceNumber in HOTEL-BILL

(c)

Figure E-7(b) shows an object diagram for the HOTEL-BILL object. The attribute LineItem is a group attribute having a maximum cardinality of N, which means that the group ServiceDate, ServiceDescription, Price can occur many times in an instance of the HOTEL-BILL semantic object.

LineItem is not modeled as an independent semantic object; instead, it is considered to be an attribute within a HOTEL-BILL. This design is appropriate because the hotel does not view one line of a guest's charges as a separate thing, so line items on the guest's bill do not have identifiers of their own. No employee attempts to enter a LineItem except in the context of a bill. The employee enters the data for bill number 1234 and then, in the context of that bill, enters the charges. Or the employee retrieves an existing bill and enters additional charges in the context of that bill.

The minimum cardinality of LineItem is zero, which means that a HOTEL-BILL object can exist without any LineItem data. This allows a bill to be started when the customer checks in and before there are any charges. If the minimum cardinality were one, no HOTEL-BILL could be started until there was at least one charge. This design decision must be made in light of the business rules. It may be that the hotel's policy is not to start the bill until there has been a charge. If so, then the minimum cardinality of LineItem should be one.

To represent this object, one relation is created for the base object, HOTEL-BILL, and an additional relation is created for the repeating group attribute, DailyCharge. This relational design is shown in Figure E-7(c).

In the key of DAILY-CHARGE, InvoiceNumber is underlined because it is part of the key of DAILY-CHARGE, and it is italicized because it is also a foreign key. (It is a key of HOTEL-BILL.) ChargeDate is underlined because it is part of the key of DAILY-CHARGE, but it is not italicized because it is not a foreign key.

In general, composite objects are transformed by defining one relation for the object itself and another relation for each multivalue attribute. In Figure E-8(a), object OBJECT1 contains two groups of multivalue attributes, each of which is represented by a relation in the database design. The key of each of these tables is the composite of the identifier of the object plus the identifier of the group. Thus, the representation of OBJECT1 is a relation R1 with key O1, a relation R2 with key (O1, G1), and a relation R3 with key (O1, G2).

The minimum cardinality from the object to the group is specified by the minimum cardinality of group attribute. In Figure E-8(a), the minimum cardinality of Group1 is

Figure E-8

General Transformation of Composite Objects

(a) Composite Object with Separate Groups and (b) Composite Object with Nested Groups

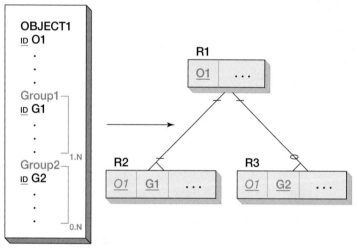

Referential integrity constraints:

O1 in R2 must exist in O1 in R1
O1 in R3 must exist in O1 in R1

(a)

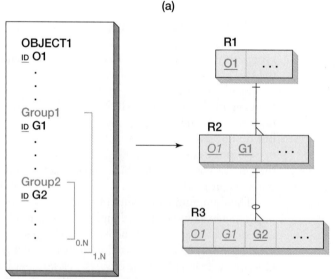

Referential integrity constraints:

O1 in R2 must exist in O1 in R1
(O1, G1) in R3 must exist in (O1, G1) in R2

(b)

one and that of Group2 is zero. These cardinalities are shown as a hash mark (on R2) and an oval (on R3) in the data structure diagram. The minimum cardinality from the group to the object is always one by default because a group cannot exist if the object that contains that group does not exist. These minimum cardinalities are shown by hash marks on the relationship lines into R1.

Groups can be nested. Figure E-8(b) shows an object in which Group2 is nested within Group1. When this occurs, the relation representing the nested group is made subordinate to the relation that represents its containing group. In Figure E-8(b), relation R3 is subordinate to relation R2. The key of R3 is the key of R2, which is (O1, G1) plus the identifier of Group2, which is G2; thus the key of R3 is (O1, G1, G2).

Make sure that you understand why the keys in Figure E-8(b) are constructed as they are. Also note that some attributes are underlined and italicized and some are simply underlined because some attributes are both local and foreign keys and some are just local keys.

Compound Objects

A **compound object** contains at least one object attribute. Figure E-9(a) shows two different data entry forms. One form, used by the company's motor pool, is used to keep track of the vehicles. The second form is used to maintain data about the employees. According to these forms, a vehicle is assigned to at most one employee, and an employee has at most one auto assigned.

We cannot tell from these forms whether an auto must be assigned to an employee or whether every employee must have an auto. To obtain that information, we have to ask the users in the motor pool or the human resources department. Assume that we find out that an EMPLOYEE need not have a VEHICLE, but that a VEHICLE must be assigned to an employee.

Figure E-9

Compound Objects with 1:1 Paired Properties

(a) Example Vehicle and Employee Data Entry Forms and (b) EMPLOYEE and VEHICLE Compound Objects

VEHICLE DATA			
License number	Serial number		
Make	Type	Year	Color
Employee assignment			

EMPLOYEE WORK DATA			
Employee name		Employee ID	
MailStop		Division	Phone
Pay code	Skill code	Hire date	Auto assigned

(a)

(b)

Figure E-9(b) shows object diagrams for EMPLOYEE and VEHICLE. An EMPLOYEE contains VEHICLE as one of its attributes, and VEHICLE in turn contains EMPLOYEE as one of its attributes. Because both EMPLOYEE and VEHICLE contain object attributes, they both are compound objects. Furthermore, because neither attribute is multivalue, the relationship from EMPLOYEE to VEHICLE is one to one, or 1:1.

In Figure E-9(a), the Employee and Vehicle forms contain each other. That is, VEHICLE DATA has a field Employee assignment, and EMPLOYEE WORK DATA has a field Auto assigned. However, this is not always the case; sometimes the relationship can appear in only one direction. Consider the report and form in Figure E-10(a),

Figure E-10

Compound Objects with 1:N Paired Properties

(a) Example Dormitory Report and Student Data Form and
(b) DORMITORY and STUDENT Compound Objects

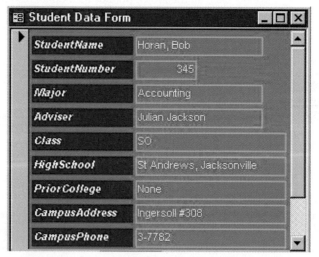

DORMITORY OCCUPANCY REPORT		
Dormitory	Resident Assistant	Phone
Ingersoll	Sarah and Allen French	3-5567

Student name	Student Number	Class
Adams, Elizabeth	710	SO
Baker, Rex	104	FR
Baker, Brydie	744	JN
Charles, Stewart	319	SO
Scott, Sally	447	SO
Taylor, Lynne	810	FR

Student Data Form

StudentName	Horan, Bob
StudentNumber	345
Major	Accounting
Adviser	Julian Jackson
Class	SO
HighSchool	St Andrews, Jacksonville
PriorCollege	None
CampusAddress	Ingersoll #308
CampusPhone	3-7782

(a)

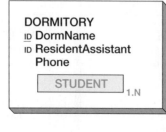

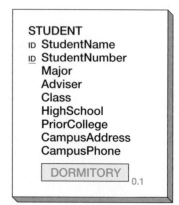

DORMITORY
ID DormName
ID ResidentAssistant
   Phone
   STUDENT   1.N

STUDENT
ID StudentName
ID StudentNumber
   Major
   Adviser
   Class
   HighSchool
   PriorCollege
   CampusAddress
   CampusPhone
   DORMITORY   0.1

(b)

which concern two objects: DORMITORY and STUDENT. From the Dormitory Occupancy Report, we can see that users think of a dorm as having attributes regarding the dorm (Dormitory, ResidentAssistant, Phone) and also attributes regarding the students (StudentName, StudentNumber, Class) who live in the dorm.

On the other hand, the Student Data Form shows only student data; it does not include any dormitory data. (The campus address might contain a dorm address, but if so, it is apparently not important enough to document on the form. In a database development project, this possibility should be checked out with the users in an interview. Here, we will assume that the Student Data Form does not include dormitory data.)

As we stated earlier, object attributes always occur in pairs. Even if the forms, reports, and queries indicate that only one side of the relationship can be seen, both sides of the relationship always exist. By analogy, a bridge that connects two islands touches both islands and can be used in both directions, even if the bridge is, by custom or law, a one-way bridge.

When no form or report can be found to document one side of a relationship, the development team must ask the users about the cardinality of that relationship. In this case, the team needs to find out how many DORMITORY(ies) a STUDENT could have and whether a STUDENT must be related to a DORMITORY. Here, let us suppose that the answers to these questions are that a STUDENT is related to just one DORMITORY and may be related to no DORMITORY. Thus, in Figure E-10(b), DORMITORY contains multiple values of STUDENT, and STUDENT contains one value of DORMITORY. The relationship from DORMITORY to STUDENT is one to many, or 1:N.

A third illustration of compound objects appears in Figure E-11(a). From these two forms, we can deduce that one book can be written by many authors (from the Book Stock Data form) and that one author can write many books (from the Books in Stock,

Figure E-11   **Compound Objects with N:M Paired Properties**
(a) Bookstore Data Entry Forms and (b) BOOK and AUTHOR Objects

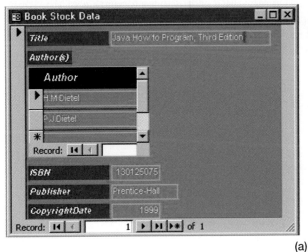
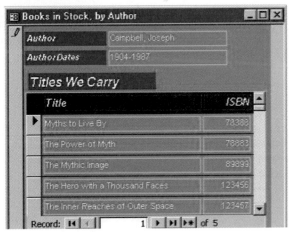

(a)

(b)

Figure E-12

Four Types of Compound Objects

	Object1 Can Contain	
Object2	One	Many
Can One	1:1	1:N
Contain Many	M:1	M:N

by Author form). Thus, in Figure E-11(b), the BOOK object contains many values of AUTHOR, and AUTHOR contains many values of BOOK. Hence, the relationship from BOOK to AUTHOR is many to many, or N:M. Furthermore, a BOOK must have an AUTHOR, and an AUTHOR (to be an author) must have written at least one BOOK. Therefore, both of these objects have a minimum cardinality of one.

Figure E-12 summarizes the four types of compound objects. In general, OBJECT-1 can contain a maximum of one or many OBJECT-2s. Similarly, OBJECT-2 can contain one or many OBJECT-1s. All of these relationships involve some variation of one-to-one, one-to-many, or many-to-many relationships. Specifically, the relationship from OBJECT1 to OBJECT2 can be 1:1, 1:N, or N:M, whereas the relationship from OBJECT2 to OBJECT1 can be 1:1, 1:M, or M:N. To represent any of these, we need only address the representation of the 1:1, 1:N, and N:M variations.

Representing One-to-One Compound Objects

Consider the assignment of a LOCKER to a health club MEMBER. A LOCKER is assigned to one MEMBER, and each MEMBER has one and only one LOCKER. Figure E-13(a) shows the object diagrams. To represent these objects with relations, we define a relation for each object; and, as with 1:1 entity relationships, we place the key of either relation in the other relation. That is, we can place the key of MEMBER in LOCKER or the key of LOCKER in MEMBER. Figure E-13(b) shows the placement of the key of LOCKER in MEMBER. Note that LockerNumber is underlined in LOCKER because it is the key of LOCKER and is italicized in MEMBER because it is a foreign key in MEMBER.

In general, for a 1:1 relationship between OBJECT1 and OBJECT2, we define one relation for each object, R1 and R2. Then, we place the key of either relation (O1 or O2) as a foreign key in the other relation, as shown in Figure E-14.

Figure E-13

Example Relational Representation of 1:1 Compound Objects

(a) Example 1:1 Compound Objects and (b) Their Representation

MEMBER
ID MemberNumber
Name
Address
City
State
Zip
LOCKER
1.1

LOCKER
ID LockerNumber
Type
Combination
Location
MEMBER
0.1

(a)

MEMBER (MemberNumber, Name, Address, City, State, Zip, *LockerNumber*)

LOCKER (LockerNumber, Type, Combination, Location)

Referential integrity constraint:

LockerNumber in MEMBER must exist in
LockerNumber in LOCKER

(b)

| Figure E-14 | General Transformation of 1:1 Compound Objects |

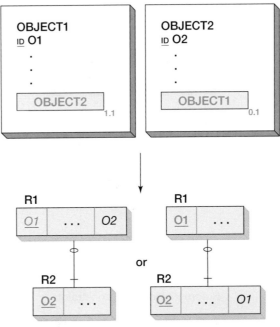

Referential integrity constraint: Referential integrity constraint:

O2 in R1 must exist in O2 in R2   O1 in R2 must exist in O1 in R1

Representing One-to-Many and Many-to-One Relationships

Now, consider 1:N relationships and N:1 relationships. Figure E-15(a) shows an example of a 1:N object relationship between EQUIPMENT and REPAIR. An item of EQUIPMENT can have many REPAIRs, but a REPAIR can be related to only one item of EQUIPMENT.

| Figure E-15 |

Example Relational Representation of 1:N Compound Objects

(a) Example 1:N Compound Objects and (b) Their Representation

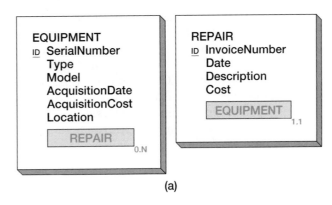

(a)

EQUIPMENT (SerialNumber, Type, Model, AcquisitionDate, AcquisitionCost, Location)

REPAIR (InvoiceNumber, Date, Description, Cost, *SerialNumber*)

Referential integrity constraint:

SerialNumber in REPAIR must exist in
SerialNumber in EQUIPMENT

(b)

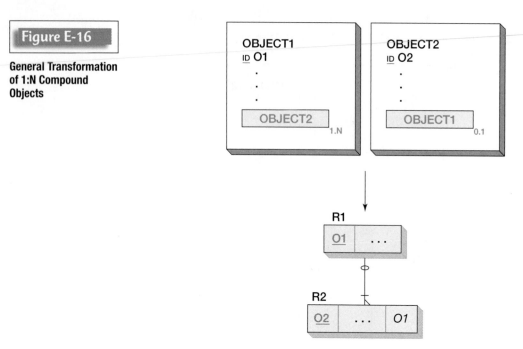

Figure E-16

General Transformation of 1:N Compound Objects

Referential integrity constraint:

O1 in R2 must exist in O1 of R1

The objects in Figure E-15(a) are represented by the relations in Figure E-15(b). Observe that the key of the parent (the object on the one side of the relationship) is placed in the child (the object on the many side of the relationship).

Figure E-16 shows the general transformation of 1:N compound objects. Object OBJECT1 contains many OBJECT2s, and object OBJECT2 contains just one OBJECT1. To represent this structure by means of relations, we represent each object with a relation and place the key of the parent in the child. Thus, in Figure E-16, the attribute O1 is placed in R2.

If OBJECT2 were to contain many OBJECT1s and OBJECT1 were to contain just one OBJECT2, we would use the same strategy, but reverse the role of R1 and R2. That is, we would place O2 in R1.

The minimum cardinalities in either case are determined by the minimum cardinalities of the object attributes. In Figure E-16, OBJECT1 requires at least one OBJECT2, but OBJECT2 does not necessarily require an OBJECT1. These cardinalities are shown in the data structure diagram as an oval on the R1 side of the relationship and as a hash mark on the R2 side of the relationship. These minimum cardinality values are simply examples; either or both objects can have a cardinality of zero, one, or some other number.

Representing Many-to-Many Relationships

Finally, consider M:N relationships. As with M:N entity relationships, we define three relations: one for each of the objects and a third intersection relation. The intersection relation represents the relationship of the two objects and consists of the keys of both of its parents. Figure E-17(a) shows the M:N relationship between BOOK and AUTHOR. Figure E-17(b) depicts the three relations that represent these objects: BOOK; AUTHOR; and BOOK-AUTHOR-INT, the intersection relation. Notice that BOOK-AUTHOR-INT has no nonkey data. Both the attributes ISBN and SocialSecurityNumber are underlined and in italics because they are both local and foreign keys.

Figure E-17

Relational Representation of Example N:M Compound Objects

(a) BOOK and AUTHOR Objects and (b) Their Relational Representation

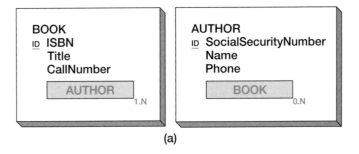

(a)

BOOK (ISBN, Title, CallNumber)

AUTHOR (SocialSecurityNumber, Name, Phone)

BOOK-AUTHOR-INT (*ISBN, SocialSecurityNumber*)

Referential integrity constraints:

> ISBN in BOOK-AUTHOR-INT must exist in
> ISBN in BOOK

> SocialSecurityNumber in BOOK-AUTHOR-INT must exist in
> SocialSecurityNumber in AUTHOR
>
> (b)

In general, for two objects that have an M:N relationship, we define a relation R1 for object OBJECT1, a relation R2 for object OBJECT2, and a relation R3 for the intersection relation. The general scheme is shown in Figure E-18. Note that the attributes of R3 are only O1 and O2. For M:N compound objects, R3 never contains nonkey data. The importance of this statement will become clear when we contrast M:N compound relationships with association relationships.

Figure E-18

General Transformation of M:N Compound Objects into Relations

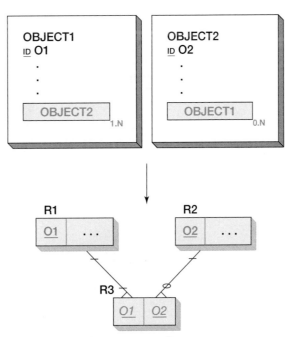

Referential integrity constraints:

> O1 in R3 must exist in O1 in R1
> O2 in R3 must exist in O2 in R2

Considering minimum cardinality, the parents of the intersection relation are always required. The minimum cardinalities of the relationships into the intersection relation are determined by the minimum cardinalities of the object links. In Figure E-18, for example, a row in R1 requires a row in R3 because the minimum cardinality of OBJECT2 in OBJECT1 is one. Similarly, a row in R2 does not require a row in R3 because the minimum cardinality of OBJECT1 in OBJECT2 is zero.

Hybrid Objects

Hybrid objects are combinations of composite and compound objects. In particular, a hybrid object is a semantic object with at least one multivalue group attribute that includes a semantic object attribute.

Figure E-19(a) is a second version of the report about dormitory occupancy shown in Figure E-10(a). The difference is that the third column of the student data contains Rent instead of Class. This is an important difference because Rent is not an attribute of STUDENT, but pertains to the combination of STUDENT and DORMITORY and is an attribute of DORMITORY.

Figure E-19

DORMITORY Hybrid Object

(a) Dormitory Report with Rent Property; (b) Correct DORMITORY and STUDENT Objects; and (c) Incorrect DORMITORY and STUDENT Objects

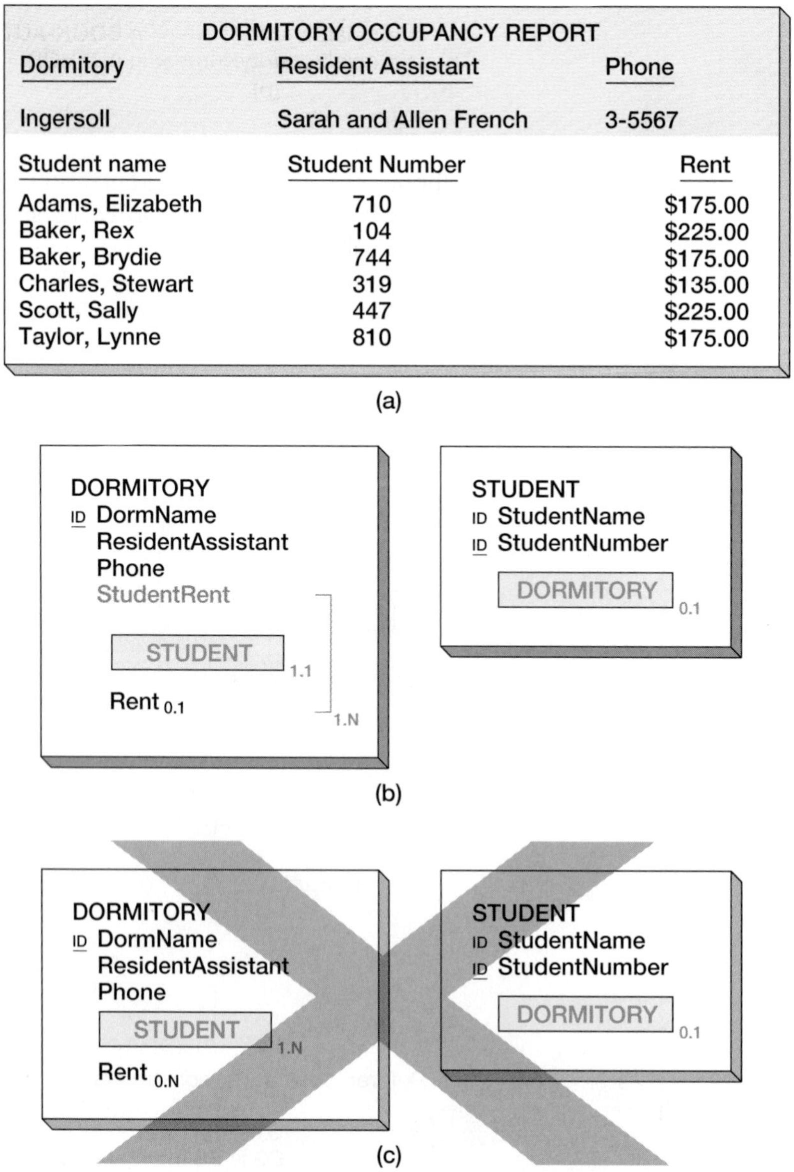
DORMITORY OCCUPANCY REPORT
Dormitory
Resident Assistant
Phone
Ingersoll
Sarah and Allen French
3-5567
Student name
Student Number
Rent
Adams, Elizabeth 710 $175.00
Baker, Rex 104 $225.00
Baker, Brydie 744 $175.00
Charles, Stewart 319 $135.00
Scott, Sally 447 $225.00
Taylor, Lynne 810 $175.00
(a)
DORMITORY
ID DormName
ResidentAssistant
Phone
StudentRent
STUDENT 1.1
Rent 0.1
1.N
STUDENT
ID StudentName
ID StudentNumber
DORMITORY 0.1
(b)
DORMITORY
ID DormName
ResidentAssistant
Phone
STUDENT 1.N
Rent 0.N
STUDENT
ID StudentName
ID StudentNumber
DORMITORY 0.1
(c)

Figure E-19(b) is an object diagram that models this form. DORMITORY contains a multivalue group having the object attribute STUDENT and the nonobject attribute Rent. This means that Rent is paired with STUDENT in the context of DORMITORY.

Now, examine the alternative DORMITORY object shown in Figure E-19(c). This is an *incorrect* model of the report in Figure E-19(a) because it shows that Rent and STUDENT are independently multivalue, which is incorrect because Rent and STUDENT are multivalue as a pair.

Figure E-20(a) shows a form based on another hybrid object. This Sales Order Form contains data about an order (Sales Order Number, Date, Subtotal, Tax, and Total), data about a CUSTOMER and a SALESPERSON, and a multivalue group that itself contains data about items on the order. Furthermore, ITEM data (Item Number, Description, and Unit Price) appear within the multivalue group.

Figure E-20(b) shows the SALES-ORDER semantic object. It contains the nonobject attributes SalesOrderNumber, Date, Subtotal, Tax, and Total. It also contains the CUSTOMER and SALESPERSON object attributes and a multivalue group that represents each line item on the sales order. The group contains nonobject attributes Quantity and ExtendedPrice, and the object attribute ITEM.

The object diagrams shown in Figure E-20(b) are ambiguous in one aspect that may or may not be important, depending on the application. According to the ITEM object diagram, an ITEM can be connected to more than one SALES-ORDER. But because the multivalue group LineItem is encapsulated (hidden within) SALES-ORDER, it is not clear from this diagram whether an ITEM can occur *once or many times* on the same SALES-ORDER.

In general, there are four interpretations of maximum cardinality for the paired attributes in the SALES-ORDER hybrid object:

1. An ITEM can appear on only one SALES-ORDER and in only one of the LineItems within that SALES-ORDER.
2. An ITEM can appear on only one SALES-ORDER, but in many different LineItems within that SALES-ORDER.
3. An ITEM can appear on many different SALES-ORDERs, but in only one LineItem within each of those SALES-ORDERs.
4. An ITEM can appear on many different SALES-ORDERs and in many different LineItems within those SALES-ORDERs.

When it is important to distinguish between these cases, the following notation should be used: If either case 1 or 2 is in force, the maximum cardinality of the hybrid object attribute should be set to one. Thus, for this example, the maximum cardinality of SALES-ORDER in ITEM is set to one. If an ITEM is to appear in only one LineItem of the SALES-ORDER (case 1), it should be marked as having a unique ID in that group. Otherwise (case 2), it need not be marked. These two cases are shown in Figures E-21(a) and E-21(b).

If either case 3 or 4 is in force, the maximum cardinality of the hybrid object attribute is set to N. Thus, for this example, the maximum cardinality of SALES-ORDER in ITEM is set to N. Furthermore, if an ITEM is to appear in only one LineItem of a SALES-ORDER (case 3), it should be marked as having a unique ID in that group. Otherwise (case 4), it need not be marked. These two cases are shown in Figures E-21(c) and E-21(d).

Representing Hybrid Relationships

A general description of these four cases is shown in Figure E-22. Cases 3 and 4 are more common than cases 1 and 2, so we consider them first. OBJECT1 in Figure E-23 shows two groups; Group1 illustrates case 3 and Group2 illustrates case 4.

Group1 has a maximum cardinality of N, which means that there can be many instances of Group1 within an OBJECT1. Furthermore, because OBJECT2 is marked as

Figure E-20

Hybrid SALES-ORDER and Related Objects
(a) Sales Order Form and (b) Objects to Model Sales Order Form

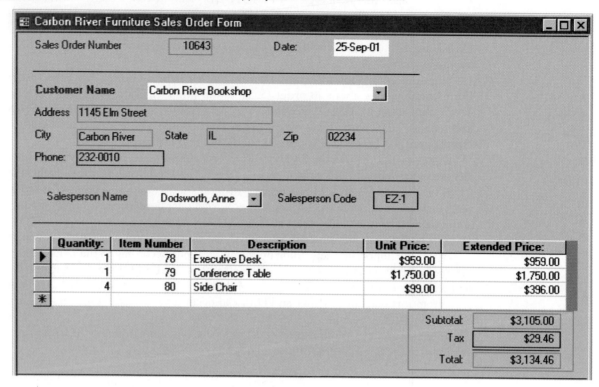

(a)

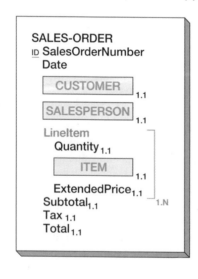
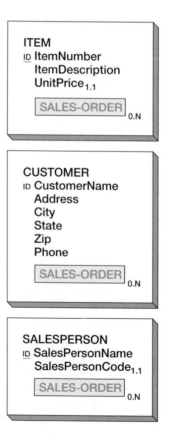

(b)

Figure E-21

Examples of the Four Cases of Maximum Cardinality in a Hybrid Object (a) ITEM in One ORDER; (b) ITEM in (Possibly) Many LineItems of One ORDER; (c) ITEM in One LineItem of (Possibly) Many ORDERS; and (d) ITEM in (Possibly) Many LineItems of (Possibly) Many ORDERs

629

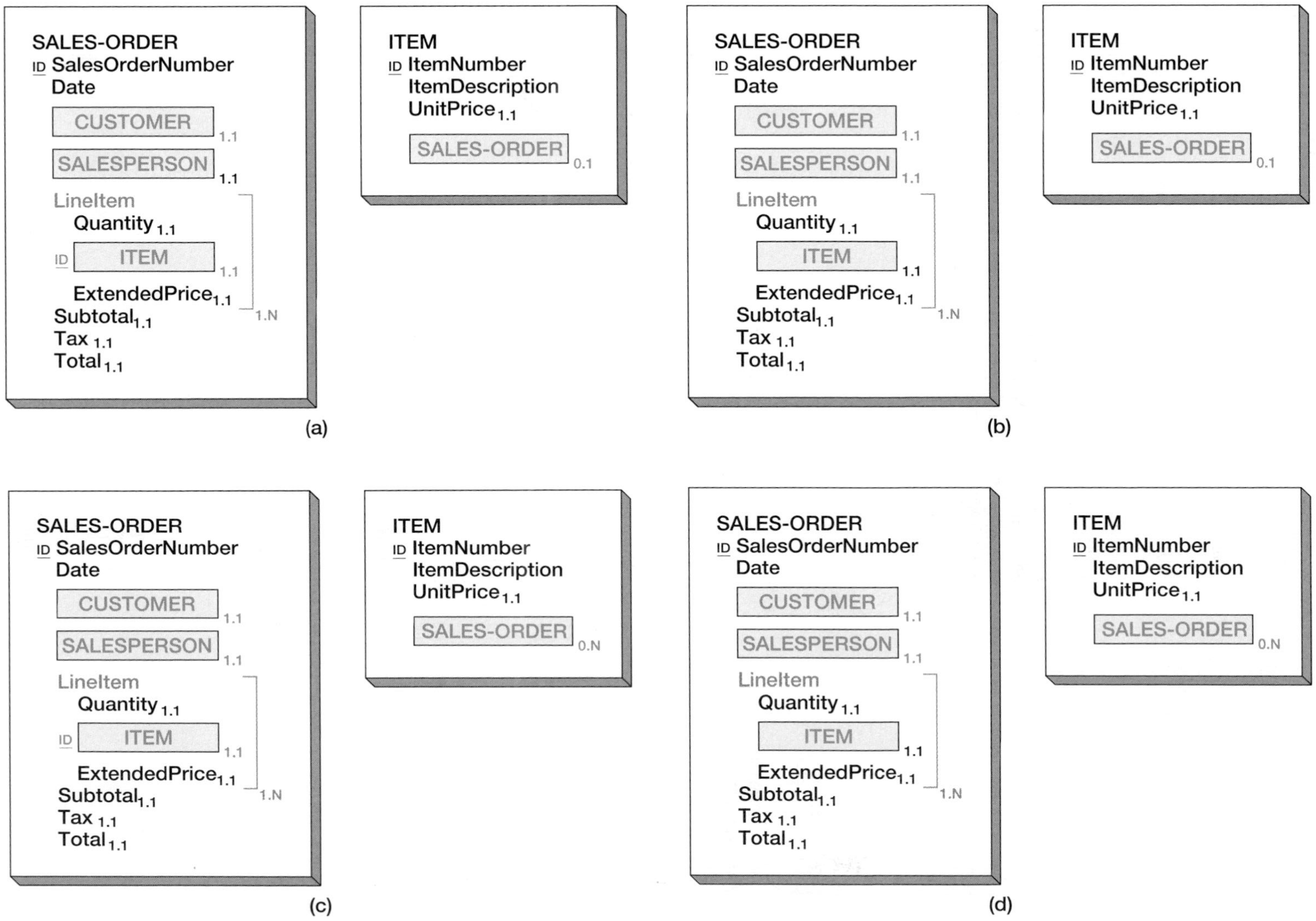

Figure E-22

Four Cases of Hybrid Object Cardinality

Case	Description	Example
1	OBJECT2 relates to one instance of OBJECT1 and appears in only one group instance within that object.	ITEM relates to one ORDER and can appear on only one LineItem of that ORDER.
2	OBJECT2 relates to one instance of OBJECT1 and appears in possibly many group instances within that object.	ITEM relates to one ORDER and can appear on many LineItems of that ORDER.
3	OBJECT2 relates to possibly many instances of OBJECT1 and appears in only one group instance within each object.	ITEM relates to many ORDERs and can appear on only one LineItem of that ORDER.
4	OBJECT2 relates to possibly many instances of OBJECT1 and appears in possibly many group instances within those objects.	ITEM relates to many ORDERs and can appear on many LineItems of that ORDER.

Figure E-23

General Transformation of Hybrid Object into Relations

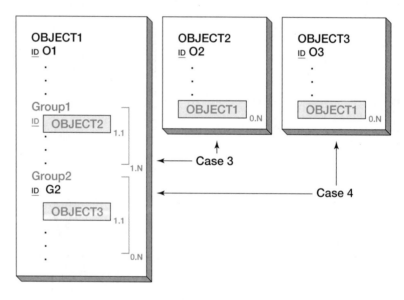

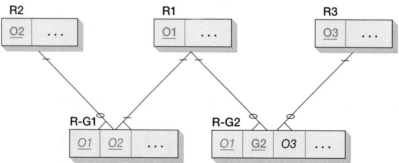

Referential integrity constraints:

O1 in R-G1 must exist in O1 in R1
O2 in R-G1 must exist in O2 in R2
O1 in R-G2 must exist in O1 in R1
O3 in R-G2 must exist in O3 of R3

ID unique, this means that a particular OBJECT2 can appear in only one of the Group1 instances within an OBJECT1. Thus, OBJECT2 acts as an identifier for Group1 within OBJECT1.

Consider the relational representation of Group1 in Figure E-23. A relation, R1, is created for OBJECT1; and a relation, R2, is created for OBJECT2. In addition, a third relation, R-G1, is created for Group1. The relationship between R1 and R-G1 is 1:N, so we place the key of R1 (which is O1) into R-G1; the relationship between R2 and R-G1 is also 1:N, so we place the key of R2 (which is O2) in R-G1. Because an OBJECT2 can appear with a particular value of OBJECT1 only once, the composite (O1, O2) is unique to R-G1 and can be made the key of that relation.

Now, consider Group2. OBJECT3 does not identify Group2, so OBJECT3 can appear in many Group2 instances in the same OBJECT1. Because OBJECT3 is not the identifier of Group2, we assume that some other attribute, G2, is the identifier.

In Figure E-23, we create a relation R3 for OBJECT3 and another relation R-G2 for Group2. The relationship between R1 and R-G2 is 1:N, so place the key of R1 (which is O1) into R-G2. The relationship between R3 and R-G2 is also 1:N, so place the key of R3 (which is O3) into R-G2.

Unlike Group1, however, (O1, O3) cannot now be the key of R-G2 because an O3 can be paired with a given O1 many times. That is, the composite (O1, O3) is not unique to R-G2, so the key of R-G2 must be (O1, G2).

Case 1 is similar to case 3, except for the restriction that an OBJECT2 can be related to only one OBJECT1. The relations in Figure E-23 still work, but we must add the key of R1 (which is O1) to R2 and establish the restriction that (O1, O2) of R-G1 must equal (O1, O2) of R2.

Case 2 is similar to case 4, except for the restriction that an OBJECT3 can be related to only one OBJECT1. Again, the relations in Figure E-23 will work, but we must add the key of R1 (which is O1) to R3 and establish the restriction that (O1, O3) of R-G2 is a subset of (O1, O3) in R3 (see questions E.21 and E.22).

Association Objects

An **association object** is an object that relates two (or more) objects and stores data that are peculiar to that relationship. Figure E-24(a) shows a report and two data entry screens that give rise to the need for an association object. The report contains data about an airline flight and data about the particular airplane and pilot assigned to that flight. The two data entry forms contain data about a pilot and an airplane.

In Figure E-24(b), the object FLIGHT is an association object that associates the two objects AIRPLANE and PILOT and stores data about their association. FLIGHT contains one each of AIRPLANE and PILOT, but both AIRPLANE and PILOT contain multiple values of FLIGHT. This particular pattern of associating two (or more) objects with data about the association occurs frequently, especially in applications that involve the assignment of two or more things. Other examples are a JOB that assigns an ARCHITECT to a CLIENT, a TASK that assigns an EMPLOYEE to a PROJECT, and a PURCHASE-ORDER that assigns a VENDOR to a SERVICE.

For the example shown in Figure E-24, the association object FLIGHT has an identifier of its own: the group {FlightNumber, Date}. Often, association objects do not have identifiers of their own, in which case the identifier is the combination of the identifiers of the objects that are associated.

To understand this better, consider Figure E-25(a), which shows a report about the assignment of architects to projects. Although the assignment has no obvious identifier, the identifier is the combination {ProjectName, ArchitectName}. These attributes, however, belong to PROJECT and ARCHITECT, not to ASSIGNMENT. The identifier of ASSIGNMENT is thus the combination of those identifiers of the things that are assigned.

Figure E-25(b) shows the object diagrams for this situation. Both PROJECT and ARCHITECT are object attributes of ASSIGNMENT, and the group {PROJECT,

Figure E-24

Examples of an Association Object
(a) Example Flight Report and Forms and (b) FLIGHT, PILOT, AIRPLANE Objects

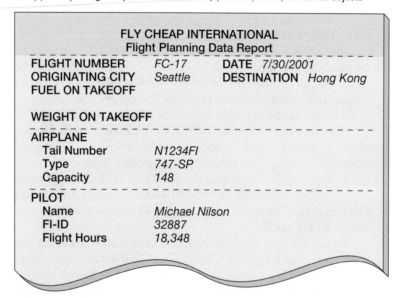

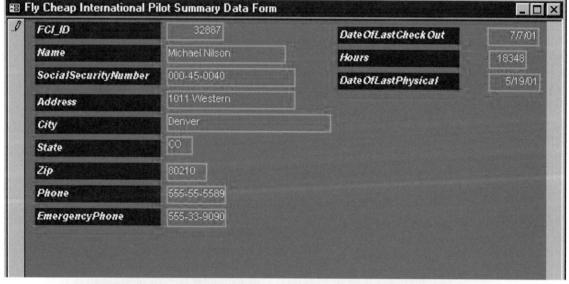

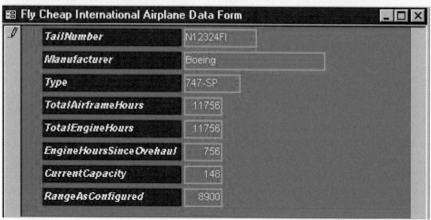

(a)

Figure E-24

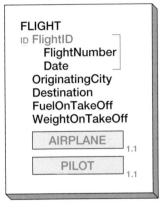

(b)

Figure E-25

**ASSIGNMENT
Association Object**

(a) Example
Assignment Report
and (b) ASSIGNMENT
Object with Semantic
Object ID

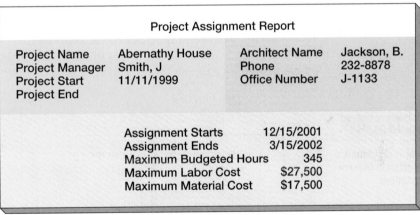

(a)

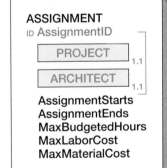

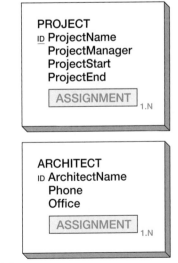

(b)

ARCHITECT} is the identifier of ASSIGNMENT. This means that the combination of an instance of PROJECT and an instance of ARCHITECT identifies a particular ASSIGNMENT.

Note that the AssignmentID identifier shown in Figure E-25(b) is not unique, thereby indicating that an architect may be assigned to a project more than once. If this is not correct, the identifier should be declared to be unique. Also, if an employee may be assigned to a project more than once, and if for some reason it is important to have a unique identifier for an ASSIGNMENT, the attribute Date or some other time-indicating attribute (Week, Quarter, and so forth) should be added to the group.

In general, when transforming association object structures into relations, we define one relation for each of the objects participating in the relationship. In Figure E-26, OBJECT3 associates OBJECT1 and OBJECT2. In this case, we define R1, R2, and R3, as shown. The key of each of the parent relations, O1 and O2, appears as foreign key attributes in R3, the relation representing the association object. If the association object has no unique identifying attribute, the combination of the attributes of R1 and R2 is used to create a unique identifier.

Note the difference between the association relation shown in Figure E-26 and the intersection relation shown in Figure E-18. The principal distinction is that the association table carries data that represent some aspect of the combination of the objects. The intersection relation carries no data; its only reason for existence is to specify which objects have a relationship with one another.

Parent/Subtype Objects

To understand parent and subtype objects, consider the object EMPLOYEE shown in Figure E-27(a). Some of the attributes in EMPLOYEE pertain to all employees, and others pertain only to employees who are managers. The object in Figure E-27(a) is

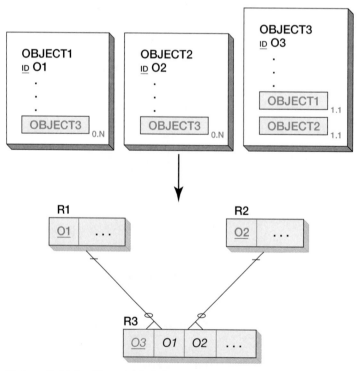

Figure E-26

General Transformation of Association Objects into Relations

Referential integrity constraints:

O1 in R3 must exist in O1 in R1
O2 in R3 must exist in O2 in R2

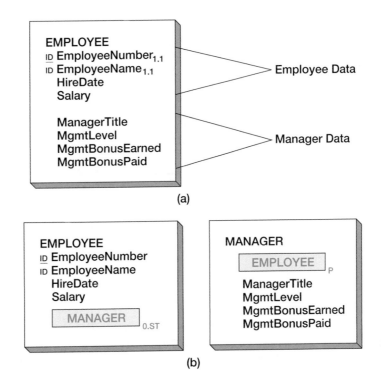

Figure E-27

Need for MANAGER Subtype

(a) EMPLOYEE without Subtype and (b) EMPLOYEE with MANAGER Subtype

not very precise because the manager-oriented attributes are not suitable for nonmanager employees.

A better model is shown in Figure E-27(b), in which the EMPLOYEE object contains a subtype object: MANAGER. All of the manager-oriented attributes have been moved to the MANAGER object. Employees who are not managers have one EMPLOYEE object instance and no MANAGER object instances. Employees who are managers have both an EMPLOYEE instance and a MANAGER instance. In this example, the EMPLOYEE object is called a **parent object,** or **supertype object;** the MANAGER object is called a **subtype object.**

The first attribute of a subtype, the parent attribute, is denoted by the subscript P. Parent attributes are always required. The identifiers of the subtype are the same as the identifiers of the parent. In Figure E-27(b), EmployeeNumber and EmployeeName are identifiers of both EMPLOYEE and MANAGER.

Subtype attributes are shown with the subscript 0.ST or 1.ST. The first digit (0 or 1) is the minimum cardinality of the subtype. If 0, the subtype is optional; if 1, the subtype is required. (A required subtype does not make sense for this example, but it will for the more complicated examples to follow.) The *ST* indicates that the attribute is a subtype, or IS-A attribute.

Parent/subtype objects have an important characteristic called inheritance. A subtype acquires, or *inherits,* all of the attributes of its parent; therefore a MANAGER inherits all of the attributes of an EMPLOYEE. In addition, the parent acquires all of the attributes of its subtypes, and an EMPLOYEE who is a MANAGER acquires all of the attributes of MANAGER.

A semantic object may contain more than one subtype attribute. Figure E-28 shows a second EMPLOYEE object that has two subtype attributes: MANAGER and PROGRAMMER. Because all of these attributes are optional, an EMPLOYEE can have neither, one, or both of these subtypes. This means that some employees are neither managers nor programmers, some are managers but not programmers, some are programmers but not managers, and some are both programmers and managers.

Subtypes sometimes exclude one another. That is, a VEHICLE can be an AUTO or a TRUCK, but not both. A CLIENT can be an INDIVIDUAL, a PARTNERSHIP, or

Figure E-28

**EMPLOYEE with Two
Subtype Properties**

a CORPORATION, but only one of these three types. When subtypes exclude one another, they are placed into a subtype group, and the group is assigned a subscript of the format $X.Y.Z$. X is the minimum cardinality and is zero or one, depending on whether or not the subtype group is required. Y and Z are counts of the number of attributes in the group that are allowed to have a value. Y is the minimum number required, and Z is the maximum number allowed.

Figure E-29(a) shows three types of CLIENT as a subtype group. The subscript of the group, 0.1.1, means that the subtype is not required; but if it exists, a minimum of one and a maximum of one (or exactly one) of the subtypes in the group must exist. Note that each of the subtypes has the subscript 0.ST, meaning that they all are optional, as they must be. If they all were required, the maximum count would have to be three, not one. This notation is robust enough to allow for situations in which three out of five or seven out of 10 of a list of subtypes must be required.

Even more complex restrictions can be modeled when subtypes are nested. The subtype group in Figure E-29(b) models a situation in which the subtype CORPORA-TION must be either a TAXABLE-CORP or a NONTAXABLE-CORP. If it is a NONTAXABLE-CORP, it must be either GOV-AGENCY or a SCHOOL. Only a few nonobject attributes are shown in this example. In reality, if such a complex structure were required, there would likely be more attributes.

A general scheme for representing subtypes is shown in Figure E-30. One relation is created for the parent and one each for the subtypes. The key of all of the relations is the identifier of the parent. All relationships between the parent and the subtype are 1:1. Note the bar across the relationship lines and the presence of the subtype group's cardinality. The value shown, 0.1.1, means that no subtype is required, but, if present, at most one of the subtypes is allowed.

Archetype/Version Objects

The final type of object is the **archetype/version object.** An archetype object is a semantic object that produces other semantic objects that represent versions, releases, or editions of the archetype. For example, in Figure E-31, the archetype object TEXTBOOK produces the version objects EDITIONs. According to this model, the attributes Title, Author, and Publisher belong to the object TEXTBOOK; the attributes EditionNumber, PublicationDate, and NumberOfPages belong to the EDITION of the TEXTBOOK.

The ID group in EDITION has two portions: TEXTBOOK and EditionNumber; this is the typical pattern for an ID of a version object. One part of the ID contains the

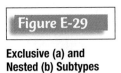

Figure E-29

Exclusive (a) and Nested (b) Subtypes

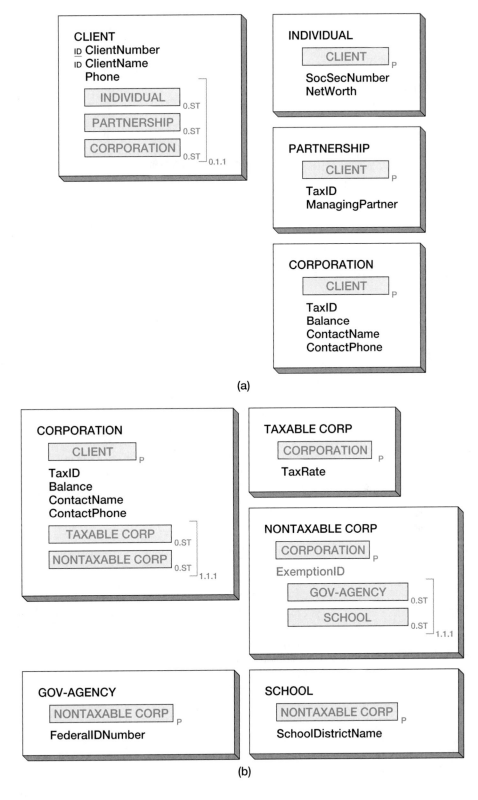

(a)

(b)

archetype object, and the second part is a simple attribute that identifies the version within the archetype. Figure E-32 shows another instance of archetype/version objects. Figure E-33 shows the general transformation of archetype/version objects. Attribute O1 of R2 is both a local and a foreign key, but O2 is only a local key.

Figure E-30

General Transformation
of Parent/Subtype
Objects into Relations

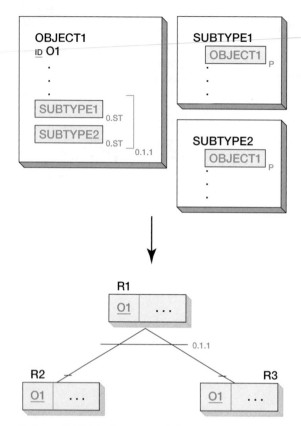

Referential integrity constraints:

O1 in R2 must exist in O1 in R1
O1 in R3 must exist in O1 in R1

Figure E-31

Example of an
Archetype/Version
Object

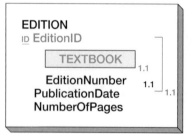

Figure E-32

Another Example of an
Archetype/Version
Object

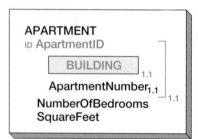

Figure E-33

General Transformation of Archetype/Version Objects and RELEASE Version Objects

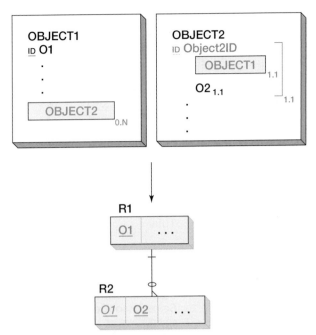

Referential integrity constraint:

O1 in R2 must exist in O1 in R1

Comparing the Semantic Object and the E-R Models

The E-R model and the semantic object model have both similarities and differences. They are similar in that both are tools for understanding and documenting the structure of the users' data. They both strive to model the structure of the things in the users' world and the relationships among them.

The principal difference between the two models is one of orientation. The E-R model sees the concept of *entity* as basic. Entities and their relationships are considered the atoms, if you will, of a data model. These atoms can be combined to form what the E-R model calls *user views,* which are combinations of entities whose structures are similar to those of semantic objects.

The semantic object model takes the concept of *semantic object* as basic. The set of semantic objects in a data model is a map of the essential structure of the things that the user considers to be important. These objects are the atoms of the users' world and are the smallest distinguishable units that the users want to process. They may be decomposed into smaller parts inside the DBMS (or application), but those smaller parts are of no interest or utility to the users.

According to the semantic object perspective, entities, as defined in the E-R model, do not exist. They are only pieces or chunks of the real entities. The only entities that have meaning to users are, in fact, semantic objects. Another way to state this is to say that semantic objects are *semantically self-contained,* or *semantically complete.* Consider an example. Figure E-34 shows four semantic objects: SALES-ORDER, CUSTOMER, SALESPERSON, and ITEM. When a user says, "Show me sales order number 2000," he or she means show SALES-ORDER, as modeled in Figure E-34. That includes, among other attributes, CUSTOMER data. Because CUSTOMER is part of SALES-ORDER, the SALES-ORDER object includes CUSTOMER.

Figure E-35 is an E-R model of this same data and contains the SALES-ORDER, CUSTOMER, SALESPERSON, LINE-ITEM, and INVENTORY entities. The SALES-ORDER entity includes the attributes OrderNumber, Date, Subtotal, Tax, and Total.

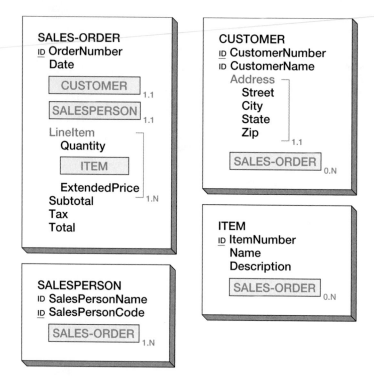

SALES-ORDER and Related Semantic Objects

Now if a user were to say, "Show me sales order number 2000" and be given only the attributes Date, Subtotal, Tax, and Total, he or she would be disappointed. Most likely, the user's response would be, "Where's the rest of the data?" That is, the entity SALES-ORDER does not represent the user's meaning of the distinct identity SALES-ORDER. The entity is only a part of SALES-ORDER.

At the same time, when a user (perhaps even the same user) says, "Show me customer 12345," he or she means to show all of the data modeled for CUSTOMER shown in Figure E-34—including CustomerName, all of the attributes of the group Address, and all of the SALES-ORDERs for that CUSTOMER. The entity CUSTOMER shown in Figure E-35 has only the attributes CustomerName, Street, City, State, Zip. If the user

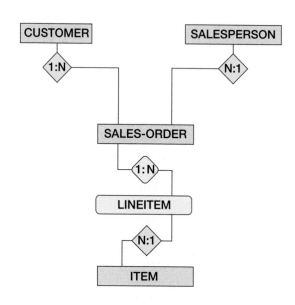

Figure E-35

Entity-Relationship Model of SALES-ORDER and CUSTOMER

were to say, "Show me customer ABC," and be given only this data, he or she again would be disappointed: "No, that's only part of what I want."

According to the semantic object view, E-R entities are unnecessary. Semantic objects can be readily transformed into database designs without ever considering E-R model entities. They are halfway houses, so to speak, constructed in the process of moving away from the paradigm of computer data structures to the paradigm of the user.

Another difference is that the semantic objects contain more metadata than do the entities. In Figure E-34, the semantic object model records the fact that CustomerNumber is a unique identifier in the users' minds. It may or may not be used as an identifier for the underlying table, but that fact is not important to the data model. In addition, CustomerName is a nonunique identifier to the users. Furthermore, the semantic objects represent the fact that there is a semantic group of attributes called *Address.* This group contains other attributes that form the address. The fact that this group exists becomes important when forms and reports are designed. Finally, the semantic objects indicate that an ITEM may relate to more than one SALES-ORDER, but that it can relate to only one LineItem within that SALES-ORDER. This fact cannot be shown on the E-R diagram.

In the final analysis, decide whether Figure E-34 or Figure E-35 gives you a better idea of what the database should contain. Many people find that the boundaries drawn around the semantic objects and the brackets around the group attributes help them get a better idea of the overall picture of the data model.

REVIEW QUESTIONS

E.1 Explain why the E-R model and the semantic object model are like lenses.

E.2 Define semantic object.

E.3 Explain the difference between an object class name and an object instance name. Give an example of each.

E.4 What is required for a set of attributes to be a sufficient description?

E.5 Explain the words distinct identity as they pertain to the definition of a semantic object.

E.6 Explain why a line item of an order is not a semantic object.

E.7 List the three types of attributes.

E.8 Give an example of each of the following:
  a. a simple, single-value attribute
  b. a group, single-value attribute
  c. a simple, multivalue attribute
  d. a group, multivalue attribute
  e. a simple object attribute
  f. a multivalue object attribute

E.9 What is minimum cardinality? How is it used? Which types of attributes have minimum cardinality?

E.10 What is maximum cardinality? How is it used? Which types of attributes have maximum cardinality?

E.11 What are paired attributes? Why are they needed?

E.12 What is an object identifier? Give an example of a simple attribute object identifier and an example of a group attribute object identifier.

E.13 Define attribute domain. What are the types of attribute domains? Why is a semantic description necessary?

E.14 What is a semantic object view? Give an example of an object and two views other than those in this text.

E.15 Give an example of a simple object, other than one in this text. Show how to represent this object by means of a relation.

E.16   Give an example of a composite object, other than one in this text. Show how to represent this object by means of relations.

E.17   Give an example of a 1:1 compound object, other than one in this text. Show two ways to represent it by means of relations.

E.18   Give an example of a 1:N compound object, other than one in this text. Show how to represent it by means of relations.

E.19   Give an example of an M:1 compound object, other than one in this text. Show how to represent it by means of relations.

E.20   Give an example of an M:N compound object, other than one in this text. Show how to represent it by means of relations.

E.21   Give an example of a case 1 (see Figure E.22) hybrid object. Show how to represent it by means of relations.

E.22   Give an example of a case 2 (see Figure E.22) hybrid object. Show how to represent it by means of relations.

E.23   Give an example of an association and related objects, other than one in this text. Show how to represent these objects by means of relations. Assume that the association object has an identifier of its own.

E.24   Do the same as for question E.23, but assume that the association object does not have an identifier of its own.

E.25   Give an example of a parent object with at least two exclusive subtypes. Show how to represent these objects by means of relations. Use a type indicator attribute.

E.26   Give an example of a parent object with at least two nonexclusive subtypes. Show how to represent these objects by means of relations. Use a type indicator attribute.

E.27   Find an example of a form on your campus that would be appropriately modeled with a simple object. Show how to represent this object by means of a relation.

E.28   Find an example of a form on your campus that would be appropriately modeled with a composite object. Show how to represent this object by means of relations.

E.29   Find an example of a form on your campus that would be appropriately modeled with one of the types of a compound object. Show how to represent these objects by means of relations.

E.30   Find an example of a form on your campus that would be appropriately modeled with a hybrid object. Classify the object according to Figure E-22. Show how to represent these objects by means of relations.

E.31   Find an example of a form on your campus that would be appropriately modeled with an association and related objects. Show how to represent these objects by means of relations.

E.32   Find an example of a form on your campus that would be appropriately modeled with parent/subtype objects. Show how to represent these objects by means of relations.

E.33   Find an example of a form on your campus that would be appropriately modeled with archetype/version objects. Show how to represent these objects by means of relations.

E.34   Explain the similarities between the E-R model and the semantic object model.

E.35   Explain the major differences between the E-R model and the semantic object model.

E.36   Explain the reasoning that entities, as defined in the E-R model, do not truly exist.

E.37   Show how both the E-R model and the semantic object model would represent the data underlying the SALES-ORDER form shown in Figure E-20(a), and explain the main differences.

BIBLIOGRAPHY

 ## Web Links

News

CNET News.com: *www.news.com*
Advisor: *www.advisor.com*
Intelligent Enterprise: *www.intelligententerprise.com*
ZDNet: *www.zdnet.com*

Data Mining

KDnuggets: *www.kdnuggets.com*
Google Dating Mining Directory: *directory.google.com/Top/Computers/*
        Software/Databases/Data_Mining
Insightful Miner 3: *www.insightful.com/products/iminer*
SAS Enterprise Miner: *www.sas.com/technologies/analytics/datamining/miner*
SPSS Clementine: *www.spss.com/Clementine*

DBMS and Other Vendors

Java: *java.sun.com*
MySQL: *www.mysql.com*
Oracle: *www.oracle.com*
SQL Server: *www.microsoft.com/sql*
Tabledesigner: *www.tabledesigner.com*

Standards

JDBC: *java.sun.com/products/jdbc* and *www.mysql.com*
ODBC: *www.liv.ac.uk/middleware/html/odbc.html* and *www.mysql.com*
Worldwide Web Consortium (W3C): *www.w3.org*
XML: *www.xml.org*

 ## Classic Articles and References

ANSI X3. *American National Standard for Information Systems—Database Language SQL.* ANSI, 1992.

Bruce, T. *Designing Quality Databases with IDEF1X Information Models.* New York: Dorset House, 1992.

Chamberlin, D. D., et al. "SEQUEL 2: A Unified Approach to Data Definition, Manipulation, and Control." *IBM Journal of Research and Development* 20 (November 1976).

Chen, P. "The Entity-Relationship Model: Toward a Unified Model of Data." *ACM Transactions on Database Systems* 1 (March 1976).

Chen, P. *Entity-Relationship Approach to Information Modeling.* E-R Institute, 1981.

Coar, K. A. L. *Apache Server for Dummies.* Foster City, CA: IDG Books, 1997.

Codd, E. F. "A Relational Model of Data for Large Shared Data Banks." *Communications of the ACM* 25 (February 1970).

Codd, E. F. "Extending the Relational Model to Capture More Meaning." *Transactions on Database Systems* 4 (December 1979).

Date, C. J. *An Introduction to Database Systems,* 8th ed. Upper Saddle River, NJ: Pearson Education, 2003.

Embley, D. W. "NFQL: The Natural Forms Query Language." *ACM Transactions on Database Systems* 14 (June 1989).

Eswaran, K. P., J. N. Gray, R. A. Lorie, and I. L. Traiger. "The Notion of Consistency and Predicate Locks in a Database System." *Communications of the ACM* 19 (November 1976).

Fagin, R. "A Normal Form for Relational Databases That Is Based on Domains and Keys." *Transactions on Database Systems* 6 (September 1981).

Fagin, R. "Multivalued Dependencies and a New Normal Form for Relational Databases." *Transactions on Database Systems* 2 (September 1977).

Hammer, M., and D. McLeod. "Database Description with SDM: A Semantic Database Model." *Transactions on Database Systems* 6 (September 1981).

Keuffel, W. "Battle of the Modeling Techniques." *DBMS Magazine* (August 1996).

Kroenke, D. "Waxing Semantic: An Interview." *DBMS Magazine* (September 1994).

Moriarty, T. "Business Rule Analysis." *Database Programming and Design* (April 1993).

Muller, R. J. *Database Design for Smarties: Using UML for Data Modeling.* San Francisco, CA: Morgan Kaufmann, 1999.

Nijssen, G., and T. Halpin. *Conceptual Schema and Relational Database Design: A Fact-Oriented Approach.* Upper Saddle River, NJ: Prentice Hall, 1989.

Nolan, R. *Managing the Data Resource Function.* St. Paul: West Publishing, 1974.

Ratliff, C. Wayne, "dStory: How I Really Developed dBASE." *Data Based Advisor* (March 1991).

Rogers, D. "Manage Data with Modeling Tools." *VB Tech Journal* (December 1996).

Ross, R. *Principles of the Business Rule Approach.* Boston, Ma: Addison-Wesley, 2003.

Zloof, M. M. "Query by Example." *Proceedings of the National Computer Conference, AFIPS* 44 (May 1975).

 ## Useful Books

Berry, M., and G. Linoff. *Data Mining Techniques for Marketing, Sales, and Customer Support.* New York: Wiley, 1997.

Celko, J. *SQL for Smarties,* 2d ed. San Francisco, CA: Morgan Kaufmann, 2000.

Celko, J. *SQL Puzzles and Answers.* San Francisco, CA: Morgan Kaufmann, 1997.

Fields, D. K., and M. A. Kolb. *Web Development with Java Server Pages.* Greenwich, CT: Manning Press, 2000.

Flanagan, D., J. Farley, W. Crawford, and K. Magnusson. *Java Enterprise in a Nutshell.* Sebastopol, CA: O'Reilly, 1999.

Hall, M. *Core Servlets and Java Server Pages.* Upper Saddle River, NJ: Sun Microsystems Press, 2000.

Harold, E. R. *XML: Extensible Markup Language.* New York: IDG Books Worldwide, 1998.

Kay, M. *XSLT: Programmer's Reference.* Birmingham, United Kingdom: WROX Press, 2000.

Loney, K. *Oracle Database 10g: The Complete Reference.* Berkeley, CA: Osborne/McGraw-Hill, 2004.

McLaughlin, B. *Java and XML.* Sebastopol, CA: O'Reilly, 2000.

Meyers, N. *Java Programming on Linux.* Indianapolis, IN: Waite Group Press, 2000.

Monson-Haefel, R. *Enterprise Java Beans,* 2d ed. Sebastopol, CA: O'Reilly, 2000.

Muench, S. *Building Oracle XML Applications.* Sebastopol, CA: O'Reilly, 2000.

Muller, R. J. *Database Design for Smarties: Using UML for Data Modeling.* San Francisco, CA: Morgan Kaufmann, 1999.

Pyle, D. *Data Preparation for Data Mining.* San Francisco, CA: Morgan Kaufmann, 1999.

Abstraction. A generalization of something that hides some unimportant details but enables work with a wider class of types. A recordset is an abstraction of a relation. A rowset is an abstraction of a recordset.

ACID transaction. ACID stands for "*atomic, consistent, isolated,* and *durable.*" An *atomic* transaction is one in which all of the database changes are committed as a unit; either all are done, or none are. A *consistent* transaction is one in which all actions are taken against rows in the same logical state. An *isolated* transaction is one that is protected from changes by other users. A *durable* transaction is one that is permanent after it is committed to the database, regardless of subsequent failures. There are different levels of consistency and isolation. *See also* transaction-level consistency, statement-level consistency, and transaction isolation level.

Active Server Page (ASP). A file containing markup language, server script, and client script that is processed by the Active Server Processor in Microsoft Internet Information Server (IIS).

ActiveX control. An ActiveX object that supports interfaces that enable the control's properties and methods to be accessed in many different development environments.

ActiveX object. A COM object that supports a slimmed-down version of the OLE object specification.

ADO. Stands for "active data objects"; an implementation of OLE DB that is accessible via object- and non-object-oriented languages. It is used primarily as a scripting-language (JScript, VBScript) interface to OLE DB.

ADO.NET. A data access technology that is part of Microsoft's .NET initiative. ADO.NET provides the capabilities of ADO, but with a different object structure. ADO.NET also includes new capabilities for the processing of datasets. *See also* dataset.

After-image. A record of a database entity (normally a row or a page) after a change. Used in recovery to perform rollforwards.

Alert. In reporting systems, a type of report that is triggered by an event.

Alternate key. In entity-relationship models, a synonym for candidate key.

Anomaly. An undesirable consequence of a data modification. The term is used in normalization discussions. With an insertion anomaly, facts about two or more different themes must be added to a single row of a relation. With a deletion anomaly, facts about two or more themes are lost when a single row is deleted.

API. *See* Application Program Interface (API).

Applet. A compiled, machine-independent Java bytecode program that is run by the Java virtual machine embedded in a browser.

Application. A business computer system that processes a portion of a database to meet a user's information needs. It consists of menus, forms, reports, queries, Web pages, and application programs.

Application design. (1) The process of creating the structure of programs and data to meet the application's requirements. (2) The structure of the users' interface.

Application failure. A failure in the processing of a DBMS statement or in a transaction that is caused by application logic errors.

Application metadata. Data dictionary data concerning the structure and contents of application menus, forms, and reports.

Application program. A custom-developed program for processing a database. It can be written in a standard procedural language, such as Java, C#, Visual Basic .NET, or C++, or in a language unique to the DBMS, such as PL/SQL or T-SQL.

Application Program Interface (API). A set of program procedures or functions that can be called to invoke a set of services. The API includes the names of the procedures and functions and a description of the name, purpose, and data type of parameters to be provided. For example, a DBMS product can provide a library of functions to call for database services. The names of procedures and their parameters constitute the API for that library.

Archetype/version entity. A two-entity structure that represents multiple versions of a standardized item; for example, a SOFTWARE-PRODUCT (the archetype) and PRODUCT-RELEASE (the version of the archetype). The identifier of the version always includes the identifier of the archetype entity.

ASP. *See* Active Server Page (ASP).

Association entity. An entity that represents the combination of at least two other entities and that contains data about that combination. It is often used in contracting and assignment applications.

Atomic. A set of actions that is completed as a unit. Either all of the actions are completed, or none of them are.

Atomic transaction. A group of logically related database operations that is performed as a unit. Either all of the operations are performed, or none of them are.

Attribute. (1) A column of a relation; also called a *column, field,* or *data item.* (2) A property in an entity.

Authorization rules. A set of processing permissions that describes which users or user groups can take particular actions against particular portions of the database.

Axis. In OLAP, a coordinate of a cube or a hypercube.

Base domain. In IDEF1X, a domain definition that stands alone. Other domains may be defined as subsets of a base domain.

Before-image. A record of a database entity (normally a row or a page) before a change. Used in recovery to perform rollback.

BI. *See* business intelligence (BI) systems.

Binary relationship. A relationship between exactly two entities or tables.

Bind. To connect a program variable or a GUI control to a column of a table or query.

Boyce-Codd normal form. A relation in which every determinant is a candidate key.

Branch. A subelement of a tree that may consist of one or many nodes.

Buffer. An area of memory used to hold data. For a read, data are read from a storage device into a buffer; for a write, data are written from the buffer to storage.

Built-in function. In SQL, the functions COUNT, SUM, AVG, MAX, or MIN.

Business intelligence (BI) systems. Information systems that assist managers and other professionals in the analysis of current and past activities and in the prediction of future events. Two major categories of BI systems are reporting systems and data mining systems.

Candidate key. An attribute or group of attributes that identifies a unique row in a relation. One of the candidate keys is chosen to be the primary key.

Cardinality. In a binary relationship, the maximum or minimum number of elements allowed on each side of the relationship. The maximum cardinality can be 1:1, 1:N, N:1, or N:M. The minimum cardinality may be optional-optional, optional-mandatory, mandatory-optional, or mandatory-mandatory.

Cartesian product. A relational operation on two relations, A and B, producing a third relation, C, with C containing the concatenation of every row in A with every row in B.

Cascading deletions. A referential integrity action specifying that when a parent row is deleted, related child rows should be deleted as well.

Cascading updates. A referential integrity action specifying that when the key of a parent row is updated, the foreign keys of matching child rows should be updated as well.

Categorization cluster. In IDEF1X, a group of mutually exclusive category entities. *See also* complete category cluster.

Categorization relationships. In IDEF1X, a structured arrangement of subtypes. *See also* categorization cluster, category entity, and generic entity.

Category entity. In IDEF1X, a subtype that belongs to a category cluster.

Checkpoint. The point of synchronization between a database and a transaction log. All buffers are force-written to external storage. The term is sometimes used in other ways by DBMS vendors.

Child. An entity or row on the many side of a one-to-many relationship.

Class attributes. In the uniform modeling language (UML), attributes that pertain to the class of all entities of a given type.

Clickstream data. Data about a customer's clicking behavior on a Web page; such data are often analyzed by e-commerce companies.

Client computer. (1) A personal computer on a local area network (LAN) with client-server architecture. In a database application, the client computer processes database application programs. Requests for actions on the database are sent to the database computer. (2) In the three-tier architecture, a computer that hosts a browser for accessing a Web server.

Client-server database architecture. The structure of a networked computing system in which one computer performs services on behalf of other computers (usually personal computers). For a database system, the server computer, which is called a database server, processes the DBMS; and client computers process the application programs. All database activities are carried out by the database server.

Client-server system. A system of two or more computers in which at least one computer provides services to one or more computers. The services may be database services, communication services, printer services, or some other function.

Cluster analysis. A form of unsupervised data mining in which statistical techniques identify groups of entities that have similar characteristics.

Collection. An object that contains a group of other objects. Examples are the ADO Names, Errors, and Parameters collections.

Column. A logical group of bytes in a row of a relation or a table. The meaning of a column is the same for every row of the relation.

COM. *See* Component Object Model (COM).

Commit. A command issued to the DBMS that makes database modifications permanent. After the command has been processed, database changes are written to the database and to a log so that they will survive system crashes and other failures. A commit is usually used at the end of an atomic transaction. Contrast this with rollback.

COM object. An object that conforms to the COM standard.

Complete category cluster. A category cluster in which all possible category entities are defined. The generic entity must also be one of the category entities.

Component Object Model (COM). A Microsoft specification for the development of object-oriented programs.

Composite key. A key with more than one attribute.

Computed value. A column of a table that is computed from other column values. Values are not stored, but are computed when they are to be displayed.

Concurrency. A condition in which two or more transactions are processed against the database at the same time. In a single CPU system, the changes are interleaved; in a multi-CPU system, the transactions may be processed simultaneously, and the changes on the database server are interleaved.

Concurrent processing. The sharing of the CPU among several transactions. The CPU is allocated to each transaction in a round robin or in some other fashion for a certain period of time. Operations are performed so quickly that they appear to users to be simultaneous. In local area networks (LANs) and other distributed applications, concurrent processing is used to refer to the (possibly simultaneous) processing of applications on multiple computers.

Concurrent update problem. An error condition in which one user's data changes are overwritten by another user's data changes. Same as lost update problem.

Confidence. In market basket analysis, the probability of a customer's buying one product, given that the customer has purchased another product.

Conflict. Two operations conflict if they operate on the same data item and at least one of the operations is a write.

Connection relationships. In IDEF1X, HAS-A relationships.

Consistency. Two or more concurrent transactions are consistent if the result of their processing is the same as it would have been if they had been processed in some serial order.

Consistent backup. A backup file from which all uncommitted changes have been removed.

Consistent schedule. An ordered list of transaction operations against a database in which the result of the processing is consistent.

Correlated subquery. A type of subquery in which an element in the subquery refers to an element in the containing query. A subquery that requires nested processing.

Cube. In OLAP, a presentation structure having axes upon which data dimensions are placed. Measures of the data are shown in the cells of the cube. Also called a hypercube.

Curse of dimensionality. In data mining applications, the phenomenon that the more attributes there are, the easier it is to build a model that fits the sample data but that is worthless as a predictor.

Cursor. An indicator of the current position in a pseudofile for a SQL SELECT that has been embedded in a program; it shows the identity of the current row.

Cursor type. A declaration on a cursor that determines how the DBMS places implicit locks. Four types of cursor discussed in this text are forward only, snapshot, keyset, and dynamic.

Data administration. The enterprisewide function that concerns the effective use and control of the organization's data assets. Data administration may be handled by an individual, but it is usually handled by a group. Specific functions include setting data standards and policies and providing a forum for conflict resolution. *See also* database administrator (DBA).

Database. A self-describing collection of integrated records.

Database administration. The function that concerns the effective use and control of a particular database and its related applications.

Database administrator (DBA). The person or group responsible for establishing policies and procedures to control and protect a database. The database administrator works within guidelines set by data administration to control the database structure, manage data changes, and maintain DBMS programs.

Database data. The portion of a database that contains data of interest and use to the application end users.

Database Management System (DBMS). A set of programs used to define, administer, and process the database and its applications.

Database redesign. The process of changing the structure of a database to adapt the database to changing requirements or to fix it so that it has the structure it should have had in the first place.

Database save. A copy of database files that can be used to restore the database to some previous consistent state.

Database server. (1) On a local area network (LAN) with a client-server database architecture, the computer that runs the DBMS and processes actions against the database on behalf of its client computers. (2) In three-tier and multitier architectures, a computer that hosts a DBMS and responds to database requests from the Web server.

Data consumer. A user of OLE DB functionality.

Data Definition Language (DDL). A language used to describe the structure of a database. SQL DDL is that portion of SQL that is used to create, modify, and drop database structures.

Data dictionary. A user-accessible catalog of database and application metadata. The contents of an *active* data dictionary are automatically updated by the DBMS whenever changes are made in the database or application structure. The contents of a *passive* data dictionary must be updated manually when changes are made.

Data integrity. The state of a database in which all constraints are fulfilled. Usually refers to interrelation constraints in which the value of a foreign key is required to be present in the table having that foreign key as its primary key.

Data item. (1) A logical group of bytes in a record, usually used with file processing. (2) In the context of the relational model, a synonym for attribute.

Data Manipulation Language (DML). A language used to describe the processing of a database. SQL DML is that portion of SQL that is used to query, insert, update, and modify data.

Data mart. A facility similar to a data warehouse, but with a restricted domain. Often, the data are restricted to particular types, business functions, or business units.

Data mining. Business intelligence systems that use sophisticated statistical and mathematical techniques to perform what-if analyses, to make predictions, and to facilitate decisions. Contrast with reporting systems.

Data model. A model of the users' data requirements usually expressed in terms of the entity-relationship model.

Data owner. Same as data proponent.

Data proponent. In data administration, a department or other organizational unit in charge of managing a particular data item.

Data provider. A provider of OLE DB functionality. Examples are tabular data providers and service data providers.

Data replication. A term that indicates whether any portion or all of a database resides on more than one computer. If so, the data are said to be replicated.

Dataset. In ADO.NET, an in-memory collection of tables that is not connected to any database. Datasets have relationships, referential integrity constraints, referential integrity actions, and other important database characteristics. They are processed by ADO.NET objects. A single dataset may be materialized as tables, as an XML document, or as an XML Schema.

Data source. In the ODBC standard, a database and its associated DBMS, operating system, and network platform.

Data structure diagram. A graphical display of tables (files) and their relationships. The tables are shown as rectangles, and the relationships are shown as lines. A many relationship is shown with a fork at the end of the line, an optional relationship is depicted by an oval, and a mandatory relationship is shown as hash marks.

Data sublanguage. A language for defining and processing a database to be embedded in programs written in another language, in most cases a procedural language such as Java, C#, Visual Basic, or C++. A data sublanguage is an incomplete programming language because it contains only constructs for data access.

Data warehouse. A store of enterprise data that is designed to facilitate management decision making. A data warehouse includes not only data, but also metadata, tools, procedures, training, personnel information, and other resources that make access to the data easier and more relevant to decision makers.

Data warehouse metadata. In a data warehouse, metadata concerning the data, its source, its format, its assumptions and constraints, and other facts about the data.

DBA. *See* Database administrator (DBA).

DBMS. *See* Database Management System (DBMS).

DBMS engine. A DBMS subsystem that processes logical input/output requests from other DBMS subsystems and submits physical input/output requests to the operating system.

DDL. *See* Data Definition Language (DDL).

Deadlock. A condition that can occur during concurrent processing in which each of two (or more) transactions is waiting to access data that the other transaction has locked. Also called a deadly embrace.

Deadlock detection. The process of determining whether two or more transactions are in a state of deadlock.

Deadlock prevention. A way of managing transactions so that a deadlock cannot occur.

Deadly embrace. *See* deadlock.

Decision tree analysis. A form of unsupervised data mining that classifies entities of interest into two or more groups according to values of attributes that measure the entities' past history.

Default namespace. In an XML Schema document, the namespace that is used for all unlabeled elements.

Definition tools subsystem. The portion of the DBMS program used to define and change the database structure.

Degree. For relationships in the entity-relationship model, the number of entities participating in the relationship. In almost all cases, such relationships are of degree two.

Deletion anomaly. In a relation, the situation in which the removal of one row of a table deletes facts about two or more themes.

Dependency graph. A network of nodes and lines that represents the logical dependencies among tables, views, triggers, stored procedures, indexes, and other database constructs.

Determinant. One or more attributes that functionally determine another attribute or attributes. In the functional dependency (A, B) → C, the attributes (A, B) are the determinant.

Differential backup. A backup file that contains only changes made since a prior backup.

Digital dashboard. In reporting systems, a display that is customized for a particular user. Typically, a digital dashboard has links to many different reports.

Dimension. In OLAP, a data characteristic that is placed on an axis.

Dirty data. In a business intelligence system, data with errors. Examples are a value of "G" for customer sex and a value of "213" for customer age. Other examples are a value of "999-999-9999" for a U.S. phone number, a part color of "gren," and an email address of "WhyMe@somewhereelseintheuniverse.who." Dirty data pose problems for reporting and data mining applications.

Dirty read. Reading data that has been changed but not yet committed to the database. Such changes may later be rolled back and removed from the database.

Discriminator. In the entity-relationship model, an attribute of a supertype entity that determines which subtype pertains to the supertype.

Distributed database. A database stored on two or more computers.

Distributed database processing. Database processing in which transaction data are retrieved and updated across two or more independent and usually geographically separated computers.

Distributed system. A system in which the application programs of a database are processed on two or more computers.

Distributed Transaction Service (DTS). An OLE service developed by Microsoft that supports distributed processing and implements two-phased commits.

DK/NF. *See* domain/key normal form.

DML. *See* Data Manipulation Language (DML).

Document Object Model (DOM). An API that represents an XML document as a tree. Each node of the tree represents a piece of the XML document. A program can directly access and manipulate a node of the DOM representation.

Document Type Declaration (DTD). A set of markup elements that defines the structure of an XML document.

DOM. *See* Document Object Model.

Domain. A named set of all possible values that an attribute can have. Domains can be defined by listing allowed values or by defining a rule for determining allowed values.

Domain/key normal form (DK/NF). A relation in which all constraints are logical consequences of domains and keys.

Download. Copying database data from one computer to another, usually from a mainframe or minicomputer to a personal computer or local area network (LAN).

Drill down. User-directed disaggregation of data used to break higher-level totals into components.

Driver. In ODBC, a program that serves as an interface between the ODBC driver manager and a particular DBMS product. Runs on the client machines in a client-server architecture.

Driver manager. In ODBC, a program that serves as an interface between an application program and an ODBC driver. It determines the required driver, loads it into memory, and coordinates activity between the application and the driver. On Windows systems, it is provided by Microsoft.

DTD. *See* Document Type Declaration.

DTS. *See* Distributed Transaction Service.

Dynamic report. In reporting systems, a report that reads the most current data at the time of the report's creation. Contrast with static report.

Encapsulated data. Properties or attributes contained in a program or object not visible or accessible to other programs or objects.

Enterprise Java Beans. A facility for managing distributed objects and distributed processing in the Java development world.

Entity. (1) In the entity-relationship model, a representation of something that users want to track. *See also* entity class and entity instance. (2) In a generic sense, something that users want to track. In the relational model, an entity is stored in one row of a table.

Entity class. In the entity-relationship model, a collection of entities of a given type; for example, EMPLOYEE and DEPARTMENT. The class is described by its attributes.

Entity instance. A particular occurrence of an entity; for example, Employee 100 and the Accounting Department. An entity instance is described by values of its attributes.

Entity-relationship (E-R) diagram. A graphic used to represent entities and their relationships. In the traditional E-R model, entities are shown as squares or rectangles, and relationships are shown as diamonds. The cardinality of the relationship is shown inside the diamond. In the crow's foot model, entities are shown in rectangles, and relationships are shown by lines between the rectangles. Attributes are generally listed within the rectangle. The many side of many relationships is represented by a crow's foot.

Entity-relationship (E-R) model. A set of constructs and conventions used to create data models. The things in the users' world are represented by entities, and the associations among those things are represented by relationships. The results are usually documented in an entity-relationship (E-R) diagram.

Enumerated list. A list of allowed values for a domain, attribute, or column.

Equijoin. The process of joining relation A containing attribute A1 with B containing attribute B1 to form relation C, so that for each row in C, A1 = B1. Both A1 and B1 are represented in C.

E-R diagram. *See* entity-relationship diagram.

Exclusive lock. A lock on a data resource such that no other transaction can either read or update that resource.

Existence-dependent entity. Same as a weak entity. An entity that cannot appear in the database unless an instance of one or more other entities also appears in the database. A subclass of existence-dependent entities is ID-dependent entities.

Explicit lock. A lock requested by command from an application program.

Export. A function of the DBMS; to write a file of data in bulk. The file is intended to be read by another DBMS or program.

Extensible Markup Language. *See* XML.

Extensible Style Language. *See* XSLT.

Extract. A portion of an operational database downloaded to a local area network (LAN) or personal computer for local processing. Extracts are created to reduce communication cost and time when querying and creating reports from data created by transaction processing.

Field. (1) A logical group of bytes in a record such as Name or PhoneNumber. (2) In the relational model, a synonym for attribute.

File data source. An ODBC data source stored in a file that can be emailed or otherwise distributed among users.

First normal form (1NF). Any table that fits the definition of a relation.

Flat file. A file that has only a single value in each field. The meaning of the columns is the same in every row.

Force-write. A write of database data in which the DBMS waits for acknowledgment from the operating system that the after-image of the write has been successfully written to the log.

Foreign key. An attribute that is a key of one or more relations other than the one in which it appears. Used to represent relationships.

Forward engineering. The automated process of using data model changes to drive changes in the database structure. Forward engineering is provided as a feature in data modeling tools such as ERwin and Visio.

Fourth normal form (4NF). A relation in Boyce-Codd normal form in which there are no multivalued dependencies or in which all attributes participate in a single multivalued dependency.

Fragment. A row in a table (or record in a file) in which a required parent or child is not present; for example, a row in a LINE-ITEM table for which no ORDER row exists.

Functional dependency. A relationship between attributes in which one attribute or group of attributes determines the value of another. The expression $X \to Y$ means that given a value of X, we can determine the value of Y. A given value of X may appear in a relation more than once, but if so, it is always paired with the same value of Y. Also, if $X \to (Y, Z)$, then $X \to Y$ and $X \to Z$. However, if $(X, Y) \to Z$, then, in general X Not $\to$ Z and Y Not $\to$ Z.

Generic entity. In IDEF1X, an entity that has one or more category clusters. The generic entity takes the role of a supertype for the category entities in the category cluster.

Granularity. The size of the database resource that is locked. Locking the entire database is large granularity; locking a column of a particular row is small granularity.

Growing phase. The first stage in two-phase locking in which locks are acquired but not released.

HAS-A relationship. A relationship between two entities or objects that are of different logical types; for example, EMPLOYEE HAS-A(n) AUTO. Contrast this with an IS-A relationship.

Hierarchical data model. A data model that represents all relationships using hierarchies or trees. Network structures must be decomposed into trees before they can be represented by a hierarchical data model. DL/I is the only surviving hierarchical data model.

HOLAP. Hybrid OLAP using a combination of ROLAP and MOLAP for supporting OLAP processing.

Horizontal security. Limiting access to certain rows of a table or join.

HTML. *See* Hypertext Markup Language.

HTTP. *See* Hypertext Transfer Protocol.

Hypercube. In OLAP, a presentation structure having axes upon which data dimensions are placed. Measures of the data are shown in the cells of the hypercube. Also called a cube.

Hypertext Markup Language (HTML). A standardized set of text tags for formatting text, locating images and other nontext files, and placing links or references to other documents.

Hypertext Transfer Protocol (HTTP). A standardized means for using TCP/IP to communicate over the Internet.

ID-dependent entity. An entity whose identifier contains the identifier of a second entity. For example, APPOINTMENT is ID-dependent on CLIENT, where the identifier of APPOINTMENT is (Date, Time, ClientNumber) and the identifier of CLIENT is ClientNumber. An ID-dependent entity is weak, meaning that it cannot logically exist without the existence of that second entity. Not all weak entities are ID-dependent, however.

IDEF1X. A version of the entity-relationship model, adopted as a national standard, but difficult to understand and use. Most organizations use a simpler E-R version like the crow's foot model.

Identifying connection relationship. In IDEF1X, a 1:1 or 1:N HAS-A relationship in which the child entity is ID-dependent on the parent.

IIS. *See* Internet Information Server.

Implementation. In object-oriented programming, a set of objects that instantiates a particular object-oriented interface.

Implicit lock. A lock that is automatically placed by the DBMS.

Import. A function of the DBMS; to read a file of data in bulk.

Inconsistent backup. A backup file that contains uncommitted changes.

Inconsistent read problem. In a transaction, a series of reads of a set of rows in which some of the rows have been updated by a second transaction and some of the rows have not been updated by that second transaction. Can be prevented by two-phase locking and other strategies.

Index. Data created by the DBMS to improve access and sorting performance. Indexes can be constructed for a single column or groups of columns. They are especially useful for columns used by WHERE clauses, for conditions in joins, and for sorting.

Inner join. Synonym for join. Contrast with outer join.

Insertion anomaly. In a relation, the condition that exists when, to add a complete row to a table, one must add facts about two or more logically different themes.

Instance failure. A failure in the operating system or hardware that causes the DBMS to fail.

Interface. (1) The means by which two or more programs call each other; the definition of the procedural calls between two or more programs. (2) In object-oriented programming, the design of a set of objects that includes the objects' names, methods, and attributes.

Internet Information Server (IIS). A Microsoft product that operates as an HTTP server.

Intersection relation. A relation used to represent a many-to-many relationship. It contains the keys of the relations in the relationship. The relationships from the parent tables to the intersection tables must have a minimum cardinality of either mandatory-optional or mandatory-mandatory.

IS-A relationship. A relationship between a supertype and a subtype. For example, EMPLOYEE and ENGINEER have an IS-A relationship.

Isolation level. *See* transaction isolation level.

IUnknown. An ActiveX interface in which one ActiveX program can call an unknown ActiveX program. After a connection has been established, the first program can use the query interface to determine which objects, methods, and properties the second program supports.

Java. An object-oriented programming language that has better memory management and bounds checking than C++. It is used primarily for Internet applications, but it also can be used as a general-purpose programming language. Java compilers generate Java bytecode that is interpreted on client computers. Many believe that Microsoft C# is a near-copy of Java.

Java bean. A properly mannered Java class, suitable for taking home to Mother. Beans have no public instance variables; all of their persistent values are accessed via accessor methods, and they have either no constructors or only one explicitly defined zero-argument constructor.

JavaScript. A proprietary scripting language owned by Netscape. The Microsoft version is called JScript; the standard version is called ECMAScript-262. These are easily learned interpreted languages that are used for both Web server and Web client application processing. Sometimes written as *Java Script*.

Java servlet. *See* servlet.

Java Server Page (JSP). A combination of HTML and Java that is compiled into a Java servlet that is a subclass of the HttpServlet class. Java code embedded in a JSP has access to HTTP objects and methods. JSPs are used similarly to ASPs, but they are compiled rather than interpreted, as ASP pages are.

Java virtual machine. A Java bytecode interpreter that runs on a particular machine environment; for example, Intel 386 or Alpha. Such interpreters are usually embedded in browsers, included with the operating system, or included as part of a Java development environment.

JDBC. A standard interface by which application programs written in Java can access and process SQL databases (or table structures such as spreadsheets and text tables) in a DBMS-independent manner. It does not stand for Java Database Connectivity; it is not an acronym.

Join. A relational algebra operation on two relations, A and B, which produces a third relation, C. A row of A is concatenated with a row of B to form a new row in C if the rows in A and B meet a restriction concerning their values. Normally, the restriction is that one or more columns of A equal one or more columns of B. For example, suppose that A1 is an attribute in A, and B1 is an attribute in B. The join of A with B in which A1 = B1 will result in a relation, C, having the concatenation of rows in A and B in which the value of A1 equals the value of B1. In theory, restrictions other than equality are allowed; a join could be made in which A1 < B1. Such nonequal joins are not used in practice, however.

JScript. A proprietary scripting language owned by Microsoft. The Netscape version is called JavaScript; the standard version is called ECMAScript-262. These are easily learned interpreted languages used for both Web server and Web client application processing.

JSP. *See* Java Server Page.

Key. (1) A group of one or more attributes identifying a unique row in a relation. Because relations may not have duplicate rows, every relation must have at least one key, which is the composite of all of the attributes in the relation. A key is sometimes called a logical key. (2) With some relational DBMS products, an index on a column used to improve access and sorting speed. It is sometimes called a physical key.

Labeled namespace. In an XML Schema document, a namespace that is given a name (label) within the document. All elements preceded by the name of the labeled namespace are assumed to be defined in that labeled namespace.

Level. In OLAP, a (possibly hierarchical) subset of a dimension.

Lift. In market basket analysis, confidence divided by the base probability of an item purchase.

Lock. The process of allocating a database resource to a particular transaction in a concurrent-processing system. The size of the resource locked is known as the lock granularity. With an exclusive lock, no other transaction may read or write the resource. With a shared lock, other transactions may read the resource, but no other transaction may write it.

Lock granularity. The size of a locked data element. The lock of a column value of a particular row is a small granularity lock, and the lock of an entire table is a large granularity lock.

Log. A file containing a record of database changes. The log contains before-images and after-images.

Logistic regression. A form of supervised data mining that estimates the parameters of an equation to calculate the odds that a given event will occur.

Lost update problem. Same as concurrent update problem.

Market basket analysis. A type of data mining that estimates the correlations of items that are purchased together. See also confidence and lift.

Maximum cardinality. (1) In a binary relationship in the entity-relationship model, the maximum number of entities on each side of the relationship. Common values are 1:1, 1:N, and N:M. (2) In a relationship in the relational model, the maximum number of rows on each side of the relationship. Common values are 1:1 and 1:N. An N:M relationship is not possible in the relational model.

Measure. In OLAP, the source data for the cube—data that are displayed in the cells. It may be raw data or it may be functions of raw data, such as SUM, AVG, or other computations.

Media failure. A failure that occurs when the DBMS is unable to write to a disk. Usually caused by a disk head crash or other disk failure.

Member. In OLAP, the value of a dimension.

Metadata. Data concerning the structure of data that are used to describe tables, columns, constraints, indexes, and so forth. Metadata is data about data.

Method. A program attached to an object-oriented programming (OOP) object. A method can be inherited by lower-level OOP objects.

Minimum cardinality. (1) In a binary relationship in the entity-relationship model, the minimum number of entities required on each side of a relationship. (2) In a binary relationship in the relational model, the minimum number of rows required on each side of a relationship. Common values of minimum cardinality for both definitions are optional to optional (O-O), mandatory to optional (M-O), optional to mandatory (O-M), and mandatory to mandatory (M-M).

Minimum cardinality enforcement actions. Activities that must be taken to preserve minimum cardinality restrictions. Summarized in Figure 6-27. *See also* referential integrity actions.

Modification anomaly. In a relation, the situation that exists when the storage of one row records facts about two or more entities or when the deletion of one row removes facts about two or more entities.

MOLAP. Multidimensional OLAP using a purpose-built processor for supporting OLAP processing.

Multiple-tier driver. In ODBC, a two-part driver, usually for a client-server database system. One part of the driver resides on the client and interfaces with the application; the second part resides on the server and interfaces with the DBMS.

Multivalue dependency. A condition in a relation with three or more attributes in which independent attributes appear to have relationships they do not have. Formally, in a relation R (A, B, C), having key (A, B, C) where A is matched with multiple values of B (or of C or both), B does not determine C, and C does not determine B. An example is the relation EMPLOYEE (EmpNumber, EmpSkill, DependentName), where an employee can have multiple values of EmpSkill and DependentName. EmpSkill and DependentName do not have any relationship, but they do appear to in the relation.

Natural join. A join of a relation A having attribute A1 with relation B having attribute B1, where A1 equals B1. The joined relation, C, contains either column A1 or B1, but not both. Contrast this with equijoin.

Network data model. A data model supporting at least simple network relationships. The CODASYL DBTG, which supports simple network relationships, but not complex ones, is the most important network data model.

Neural networks. A form of supervised data mining that estimates complex mathematical functions for making predictions. The name is a misnomer. Although there is some loose similarity between the structure of a neural network and a network of biological neurons, the similarity is only superficial.

N:M. The abbreviation for a many-to-many relationship between two entities or relations.

Nonidentifying connection relationships. In IDEF1X, 1:1 and 1:N HAS-A relationships that do not involve ID-dependent entities.

Nonintegrated data. Data that are stored in two incompatible information systems.

Nonrepeatable reads. The situation that occurs when a transaction reads data it has previously read and finds modifications or deletions caused by a committed transaction.

Nonspecific relationships. In IDEF1X, an N:M relationship.

Normal form. A rule or set of rules governing the allowed structure of relations. The rules apply to attributes, functional dependencies, multivalue dependencies, domains, and constraints. The most important normal forms are first normal form, second normal form, third normal form, Boyce-Codd normal form, fourth normal form, fifth normal form, and domain/key normal form.

Normalization. (1) The process of constructing one or more relations such that in every relation the determinant of every functional dependency is a candidate key (BCNF). (2) The process of removing multivalued dependencies (4NF). (3) In general, the process of evaluating a relation to determine whether it is in a specified normal form and of converting it to relations in that specified normal form, if necessary.

Not-type-valid document. An XML document that either does not conform to its Document Type Declaration (DTD) or does not have a DTD. *See also* type-valid document and schema-valid document.

Null value. An attribute value that has never been supplied. Such values are ambiguous and can mean that (a) the value is unknown, (b) the value is not appropriate, or (c) the value is known to be blank.

Object class. In object-oriented programming, a set of objects with a common structure.

Object class library. In object-oriented programming, a collection of object classes, usually a collection that serves a particular purpose.

Object constructor. In object-oriented programming, a function that creates an object.

Object destructor. In object-oriented programming, a function that destroys an object.

Object persistence. In object-oriented programming, the characteristic that an object can be saved to nonvolatile memory, such as a disk. Persistent objects exist between executions of a program.

Object-relational DBMS. DBMS products that support both relational and object-oriented programming data structures, such as Oracle.

ODBC. *See* Open Database Connectivity standard.

OLAP. *See* On-Line Analytical Processing.

OLE DB. The COM-based foundation of data access in the Microsoft world. OLE DB objects support the OLE object standard. ADO is based on OLE DB.

OLE object. Stands for "Object Linking and Embedding object;" COM objects that support interfaces for embedding into other objects.

1:N. The abbreviation for a one-to-many relationship between two entities or relations.

On-Line Analytical Processing (OLAP). A form of dynamic data presentation in which data are summarized, aggregated, deaggregated, and viewed in the frame of a table or a cube.

Open Database Connectivity standard (ODBC). A standard interface by which application programs can access and process relational databases, spreadsheets, text files, and other table-like structures in a DBMS or in a program-independent manner. The driver manager portion of ODBC is incorporated into Windows. ODBC drivers are supplied by DBMS vendors, Microsoft, and by third-party software developers.

Optimistic locking. A locking strategy that assumes no conflict will occur, processes a transaction, and then checks to determine whether conflict did occur. If conflict did occur, no changes are made to the database and the transaction is repeated. *See also* pessimistic locking.

Orphan. Any row (record) that is missing a required parent.

Outer join. A join in which all of the rows of a table appear in the join result, regardless of whether they have a match in the join condition. In a left outer join, all of the rows in the left-hand relation appear; in a right outer join, all of the rows in the right-hand relation appear.

Owner. In data administration, the department or other organizational unit in charge of the management of a particular data item. An owner can also be called a data proponent.

Parent. An entity or row on the one side of a one-to-many relationship.

Persistent object. In object-oriented programming, an object that has been written to persistent storage.

Pessimistic locking. A locking strategy that prevents conflict by locking data resources, processing the transaction, and then unlocking the data resources. *See also* optimistic locking and deadlock.

Phantom reads. The situation that occurs when a transaction reads data it has previously read and finds new rows that were inserted by a committed transaction.

Physical key. A column that has an index or other data structure created for it; a synonym for an index. Such structures are created to improve searching and sorting on the column values.

PL/SQL. *See* Programming Language for SQL.

Primary key. A candidate key selected to be the key of a relation; the primary key is used as a foreign key for representing relationships.

Processing rights and responsibilities. Organizational policies regarding which groups can take which actions on specified data items or other collections of data.

Program/data independence. The condition existing when the structure of the data is not defined in application programs. Rather, it is defined in the database and then the application programs obtain it from the DBMS. In this way, changes can be made in the data structures that may not necessarily be made in the application programs.

Programming Language for SQL (PL/SQL). An Oracle-supplied language that augments SQL with programming language structures such as while loops, if-then-else blocks, and other such constructs. PL/SQL is used to create stored procedures and triggers.

Property. Same as attribute.

Proponent. *See* data proponent.

Prototype. A quickly developed demonstration of an application or portion of an application.

Pull report. In reporting systems, a report that must be requested by users.

Push report. In reporting systems, a report that is sent to users according to a schedule.

QBE. *See* query by example.

Query by example (QBE). A style of query interface, first developed by IBM but now used by other vendors, that enables users to express queries by providing examples of the results they seek.

Query interface. An interface in Microsoft COM that can be used to determine the objects, methods, and properties supported by an ActiveX program.

Read committed. A level of transaction isolation that prohibits dirty reads but allows nonrepeatable reads and phantom reads.

Read uncommitted. A level of transaction isolation that allows dirty reads, nonrepeatable reads, and phantom reads.

Record. (1) In a relational model, a synonym for row and tuple. (2) A group of fields pertaining to the same entity; used in file-processing systems.

Recordset. An ADO object that encapsulates a relation; created as the result of the execution of a SQL statement or a stored procedure.

Recursive relationship. A relationship among entities or rows of the same type. For example, if CUSTOMERs refer to other CUSTOMERs, the relationship is recursive.

ReDo files. In Oracle, backups of rollback segments used for backup and recovery. ReDo files may be online or off-line.

Referential integrity actions. In general, rules that specify the activities that must take place when insert, update, or delete actions occur on either the parent or child entities in a relationship. In this text, we use referential integrity actions only to document activities needed to preserve required parents. Other actions can be defined as part of the database design. *See* minimum cardinality enforcement actions and Figure 6-27.

Referential integrity constraint. A relationship constraint on foreign key values. A referential integrity constraint specifies that the values of a foreign key must be a subset of the values of the primary key to which it refers.

Regression analysis. A form of supervised data mining in which the parameters of equations are estimated by data analysis.

Relation. A two-dimensional array containing single-value entries and no duplicate rows. Values for a given entity are shown in rows; values of attributes of that entity are shown in columns. The meaning of the columns is the same in every row. The order of the rows and columns is immaterial.

Relational database. A database consisting of relations. In practice, relational databases contain relations with duplicate rows. Most DBMS products include a feature that removes duplicate rows when necessary and appropriate. Such a removal is not done as a matter of course because it can be time-consuming to enforce.

Relational data model. A data model in which data are stored in relations and relationships between rows are represented by data values.

Relational schema. A set of relations with interrelation constraints.

Relationship. An association between two entities or rows.

Relationship cardinality constraint. A constraint on the number of rows that can participate in a relationship. Minimum cardinality constraints determine the number of rows that must participate; maximum cardinality constraints specify the largest number of rows that can participate.

Repeatable read. A level of transaction isolation that disallows both dirty reads and nonrepeatable reads. Phantom reads can occur.

Replicated data. In a distributed database, data that are stored on two or more computers.

Replication. For both Oracle and SQL Server, a term that refers to databases that are distributed on more than one computer.

Replication transparency. In a distributed database system, the condition in which application programs do not know and do not need to know whether data are replicated.

Reporting systems. Business intelligence systems that process data by filtering, sorting, and making simple calculations. OLAP is a type of reporting system. Contrast with data mining systems.

Repository. A collection of metadata about database structure, applications, Web pages, users, and other application components. Active repositories are maintained automatically by tools in the application-development environment. Passive repositories must be maintained manually.

Resource locking. *See* lock.

Resource-sharing architecture. The structure of a local area network (LAN) in which one microcomputer performs file-processing services for other microcomputers. In a database application, each user computer contains a copy of the DBMS that forwards input/output requests to the file server. Only file input/output is processed by the file server; all database activities are processed by the DBMS on the user's computer.

Reverse-engineered data model. The structure that results from reverse engineering. It is not really a data model, because it includes physical structures such as intersection tables. It is, instead, a thing unto itself; midway between a data model and a relational database design.

Reverse engineering. The process of reading the structure of an existing database and creating a reverse-engineered data model from that schema.

RFM analysis. A type of reporting system in which customers are classified according to how recently (R), how frequently (F), and how much money (M) they spend on their orders.

ROLAP. Relational OLAP using a relational DBMS to support OLAP processing.

Rollback. The process of recovering a database in which before-images are applied to the database to return to an earlier checkpoint or other point at which the database is logically consistent.

Rollback segment. In Oracle, a buffer used to store before-images for the purposes of concurrency control and transaction logging. Rollback segments can be archived and used for recovery.

Rollforward. The process of recovering a database by applying after-images to a saved copy of the database to bring it to a checkpoint or other point at which the database is logically consistent.

Root. The top record, row, or node in a tree. A root does not have a parent.

Row. A group of columns in a table. All the columns in a row pertain to the same entity. A row is the same as a tuple and a record.

Rowset. In OLE DB, an abstraction of data collections such as recordsets, email addresses, and non-relational and other data.

SAX. Simple API (Application Program Interface) for XML. An event-based parser that notifies a program when the elements of an XML document have been encountered during document parsing.

Schema. A complete logical view of the database.

Schema-valid document. An XML document that conforms to its XML Schema definition.

SCN. *See* system change number.

Scrollable cursor. A cursor type that enables forward and backward movement through a recordset. Three scrollable cursor types discussed in this text are snapshot, keyset, and dynamic.

Second normal form (2NF). A relation in first normal form in which all nonkey attributes are dependent on all of the key attributes.

Semantic object model. The constructs and conventions used to create a model of the users' data. The things in the users' world are represented by semantic objects (sometimes called objects). Relationships are modeled in the objects, and the results are usually documented in object diagrams.

Serializable. A level of transaction isolation that disallows dirty reads, nonrepeatable reads, and phantom reads.

Service provider. An OLE DB data provider that transforms data. A service provider is both a data consumer and a data provider.

Servlet. A compiled, machine-independent Java bytecode program that is run by a Java virtual machine located on a Web server.

SGML. *See* Standard Generalized Markup Language.

Shared lock. A lock against a data resource in which only one transaction may update the data, but many transactions can concurrently read that data.

Shrinking phase. In two-phase locking, the stage at which locks are released but no lock is acquired.

Sibling. A record or node that has the same parent as another record or node.

Simple Object Access Protocol. A standard used for remote procedure calls. It uses XML for definition of the data and HTTP for transport. Contrast with SOAP.

Single-tier driver. In ODBC, a database driver that accepts SQL statements from the driver manager and processes them without invoking another program or DBMS. A single-tier driver is both an ODBC driver and a DBMS. It is used in file-processing systems.

Slice. In OLAP, a dimension or measure held constant for a display.

Snowflake schema. In an OLAP database, the structure of tables such that dimension tables may be several levels away from the table storing the measure values. Such dimension tables are usually normalized. Contrast with star schema.

SOAP. Originally, Simple Object Access Protocol. Today, it is a protocol for remote procedure calls that differs from the Simple Object Access Protocol because it involves transport protocols in addition to HTTP. It is no longer an acronym.

SQL. *See* Structured Query Language.

SQL view. A relation that is constructed from a single SQL SELECT statement. SQL views have at most one multivalued path. The term *view* in most DBMS products, including Access, Oracle, and SQL Server, means SQL view.

Standard Generalized Markup Language (SGML). A standard means for tagging and marking the format, structure, and content of documents. HTML is an application of SGML. XML is a subset of SGML.

Star schema. In an OLAP database, the structure of tables such that every dimension table is adjacent to the table storing the measure values. In the star schema, the dimension tables are often not normalized. Contrast with snowflake schema.

Statement-level consistency. All rows impacted by a single SQL statement are protected from changes made by other users during the execution of the statement. Contrast with transaction-level consistency.

Static report. In reporting systems, a report that is prepared once from underlying data and does not change when the underlying data change. Contrast with dynamic report.

Stored procedure. A collection of SQL statements stored as a file that can be invoked by a single command. Usually, DBMS products provide a language for creating stored procedures that augments SQL with programming language constructs. Oracle provides PL/SQL for this purpose; SQL Server provides T-SQL. With some products, stored procedures can be written in a standard language such as Java. Usually, stored procedures are stored within the database itself.

Strong entity. In an entity-relationship model, any entity whose existence in the database does not depend on the existence of any other entity. *See also* ID-dependent entity and weak entity.

Structured Query Language (SQL): A language for defining the structure and processing of a relational database. It can be used as a stand-alone language or it may be embedded in application programs. SQL has been adopted as a national standard by the American National Standards Institute (ANSI). The most common version used today is SQL-92, the version adopted by ANSI in 1992. SQL was originally developed by IBM.

Structured schema. An XML schema that is not flat.

Subtype. In generalization hierarchies, an entity or object that is a subspecies or subcategory of a higher-level type, called a supertype. For example, ENGINEER is a subtype of EMPLOYEE.

Supertype. In generalization hierarchies, an entity or object that logically contains subtypes. For example, EMPLOYEE is a supertype of ENGINEER, ACCOUNTANT, and MANAGER.

Supervised data mining. A form of data mining in which an analyst creates a prior model or hypothesis and then uses the data to test that model or hypothesis.

Support. In market basket analysis, the probability that two items will be purchased together.

Surrogate key. A unique, system-supplied identifier used as the primary key of a relation. It is created when a row is created, it never changes, and it is destroyed when the row is deleted. The values of a surrogate key have no meaning to the users and are usually hidden within forms and reports.

System change number (SCN). In Oracle, a database-wide value that is used to order changes made to database data. The SCN is incremented whenever database changes are committed.

System data source. An ODBC data source that is local to a single computer and can be accessed by that computer's operating system and select users of that operating system.

Tabular data provider. An OLE DB data provider that presents data in the form of rowsets.

Target namespace. In an XML Schema document, the namespace that the schema is creating.

Third normal form (3NF). A relation in second normal form that has no transitive dependencies.

Three-tier architecture. A system of computers having a database server, a Web server, and one or more client computers. The database server hosts a DBMS, the Web server hosts an HTTP server, and the client computer hosts a browser. Each tier can run a different operating system.

Transaction. (1) A group of actions that is performed on the database atomically; either all actions are committed to the database, or none of them are. (2) In general, the record of an event in the business world.

Transaction boundary. A group of database commands that must be committed or aborted as a unit.

Transaction isolation level. The degree to which a database transaction is protected from actions by other transactions. The 1992 SQL standard specified four isolation levels: Read Uncommitted, Read Committed, Repeatable Reads, and Serializable.

Transaction-level consistency. All rows impacted by any of the SQL statements in a transaction are protected from changes during the entire transaction. This level of consistency is expensive to enforce and reduces throughput. It may also mean that a transaction cannot see its own changes. Contrast with statement-level consistency.

Transact-SQL. A Microsoft-supplied language that is part of SQL Server. It augments SQL with programming language structures such as while loops, if-then-else blocks, and other such constructs. Transact-SQL is used to create stored procedures and triggers.

Transitive dependency. In a relation having at least three attributes, for example, R (A, B, C), the situation in which A determines B, B determines C, but B does not determine A.

Tree. A collection of records, entities, or other data structures in which each element has at most one parent, except for the top element, which has no parent.

Trigger. A special type of stored procedure that is invoked by the DBMS when a specified condition occurs. BEFORE triggers are executed before a specified database action, AFTER triggers are executed after a specified database action, and INSTEAD OF triggers are executed in place of a specified database action. INSTEAD OF triggers are normally used to update data in SQL views.

T-SQL. *See* Transact-SQL.

Tuple. Same as row.

Two-phase commitment. In a distributed database system, a process of commitment among nodes in which the nodes first vote on whether they can commit a transaction. If all the nodes vote yes, the transaction is committed. If any node votes no, the transaction is aborted. A two-phase commitment is required to prevent inconsistent processing in distributed databases.

Two-phase locking. The procedure by which locks are obtained and released in two phases. During the growing phase, the locks are obtained; during the shrinking phase, the locks are released. After a lock is released, no other lock will be granted that transaction. Such a procedure ensures consistency in database updates in a concurrent-processing environment.

Type domain. In IDEF1X, a domain that is defined as a subset of a base domain or another type of domain.

Type-valid document. An XML document that conforms to its Document Type Declaration (DTD). Contrast with not-type-valid document.

UML. *See* Unified Modeling Language.

Unified Modeling Language (UML). A set of structures and techniques for modeling and designing object-oriented programs and applications. It is a set of tools for object-oriented development that has led to a development methodology. UML incorporates the entity-relationship model for data modeling.

Unsupervised data mining. A form of data mining in which analysts do not create a prior model or hypothesis, but rather let the data analysis reveal a model.

Updatable view. A SQL view that can be updated. Such views are usually very simple, and the rules that allow updating are normally quite restrictive. Nonupdatable views can be made updatable by writing application-specific INSTEAD OF triggers.

User data source. An ODBC data source that is available only to the user who created it.

VBScript. An easily learned, interpreted language used for both Web server and Web client applications processing. It is a subset of Microsoft Visual Basic, Release 6.

Vertical security. Limiting access to certain columns of a table or join.

Weak entity. In an entity-relationship model, an entity whose logical existence in the database depends on the existence of another entity. All ID-dependent entities are weak, but not all weak entities are ID-dependent.

XML (Extensible Markup Language). A standard markup language that provides a clear separation between structure, content, and materialization. It can represent arbitrary hierarchies and hence can be used to transmit any database view.

XML Namespaces. A standard for assigning names to defined collections. X:Name is interpreted as the element Name as defined in namespace X. Y:Name is interpreted as the element Name as defined in namespace Y. Useful for disambiguating terms.

XML Schema. An XML document that defines the structure of other XML documents. Extends and replaces Document Type Declarations (DTDs).

XPath. A sublanguage within XSLT that is used to identify parts of an XML document to be transformed. Can also be used for calculations and string manipulation. Commingled with XSLT.

XPointer. A standard for linking one document to another. XPath has many elements from XPointer.

XQuery. A standard for expressing database queries as XML documents. The structure of the query uses XPath facilities, and the result of the query is represented in an XML format. Currently under development and likely to be important in the future.

XSL (XSLT Stylesheet). The document that provides the {match, action} pairs and other data for XSLT to use when transforming an XML document.

XSLT (Extensible Style Language: Transformations). A program (or process) that applies XSLT Stylesheets to an XML document to produce a transformed XML document.

INDEX